# Teaching Adolescents with Mild Disabilities

## About the Authors

**Jennifer M. Platt** is Professor of Exceptional Education and Interim Chair of the Department of Exceptional and Physical Education at the University of Central Florida. She received her B.S. degree from Central Connecticut State University, her M.S.Ed. from the University of Kansas, and her Ed.D. from West Virginia University. Jennifer co-authored *Teaching Children and Adolescents with Special Needs* and *A Comprehensive Curriculum for Youthful Offenders in Delinquent and Corrections Facilities*. She is currently working on a preservice project with the University of Kansas that involves collaborating with university faculty in secondary education in order to address the academic diversity in middle and high school content classrooms. She is a national trainer in the Learning Strategies Model and received the 1996 Jane Langenbach Outstanding Trainer Award in Learning Strategies for the state of Florida.

**Judy L. Olson** is Professor of Exceptional Education in the Department of Exceptional and Physical Education at the University of Central Florida. She received her B.S. degree from Western Illinois University, her M.A. degree from the University of Iowa, and her Ph.D. from the University of Florida. Judy co-authored *Teaching Children and Adolescents with Special Needs* and *A Comprehensive Curriculum for Youthful Offenders in Delinquent and Corrections Facilities*. She is currently the principal investigator of The Varying Exceptionalities Training Grant funded by the U.S. Department of Education. The grant is designed to address the critical shortage in exceptional education in the state of Florida. She also co-authored, with Brian Booth and Melinda Demott, technology modules that have had a major impact on the incorporation of technology in teacher training at the University of Central Florida.

# Teaching Adolescents with Mild Disabilities

**Jennifer M. Platt** ▪ **Judy L. Olson**

*University of Central Florida*

**Brooks/Cole Publishing Company**

I(T)P® *An International Thomson Publishing Company*

Pacific Grove ▪ Albany ▪ Belmont ▪ Bonn ▪ Boston ▪ Cincinnati ▪ Detroit ▪ Johannesburg ▪ London
Madrid ▪ Melbourne ▪ Mexico City ▪ New York ▪ Paris ▪ Singapore ▪ Tokyo ▪ Toronto ▪ Washington

Sponsoring Editor: *Vicki Knight*
Marketing Team: *Margaret Parks, Jean Thompson*
Editorial Assistant: *Jana Garnett*
Production Editor: *Nancy L. Shammas*
Production Service: *Scratchgravel Publishing Services*
Manuscript Editor: *Margaret C. Tropp*
Permissions Editor: *Mary Kay Hancharick*
Interior Design: *Lisa Mirski Devenish*

Interior Illustrations: *Greg Draus, Cheryl Parke*
Cover Design: *E. Kelly Shoemaker*
Cover Photo: *Elizabeth Crews*
Photo Researcher: *Monica Suder & Associates*
Indexer: *Do Mi Stauber*
Typesetting: *Scratchgravel Publishing Services*
Printing and Binding: *Edwards Brothers, Inc.*

*The photographs in this book are reprinted with the permission of the photographers and photo agencies. Inclusion of the photographs in this book is not meant to state or imply that the individuals shown in the photographs have any disabilities.*

*For more information, contact:*

BROOKS/COLE PUBLISHING COMPANY
511 Forest Lodge Road
Pacific Grove, CA 93950
USA

International Thomson Publishing Europe
Berkshire House 168-173
High Holborn
London WC1V 7AA
England

Thomas Nelson Australia
102 Dodds Street
South Melbourne, 3205
Victoria, Australia

Nelson Canada
1120 Birchmount Road
Scarborough, Ontario
Canada M1K 5G4

International Thomson Editores
Seneca 53
Col. Polanco
México, D. F., México
C. P. 11560

International Thomson Publishing GmbH
Königswinterer Strasse 418
53227 Bonn
Germany

International Thomson Publishing Asia
221 Henderson Road
#05-10 Henderson Building
Singapore 0315

International Thomson Publishing Japan
Hirakawacho Kyowa Building, 3F
2-2-1 Hirakawacho
Chiyoda-ku, Tokyo 102
Japan

Printed in the United States of America

10  9  8  7  6  5  4  3  2  1

**Library of Congress Cataloging-in-Publication Data**
Platt, Jennifer M., [date]
   Teaching adolescents with mild disabilities / Jennifer Platt, Judy
Olson.
      p.  cm.
   Includes bibliographical references and index.
   ISBN 0-534-21006-6 (alk. paper)
   1. Learning disabled children—Education (Secondary)—United
States.   2. Problem children—Education (Secondary)—United States.
3. Adolescent psychology—United States.   I. Olson, Judy L.
II. Title.
LC4704.74.P53   1997
371.92'82—dc20                                        96-19715
                                                         CIP

*To our children,*

*Chris Platt, Brendan Olson, and Heather Olson Leonard,*

*whose journeys through adolescence taught us so much*

and

*to the memory of our friend and colleague,*

*Dr. Patricia Patton*

The secondary classrooms of today present special challenges because of increased academic diversity, pressures on adolescents, external influences such as legislative mandates and funding, and internal factors such as school restructuring and changing policies and procedures. We have written this text to address the challenges that teachers face as they motivate, instruct, give feedback, monitor, and provide support to adolescents in special and regular education situations.

*Teaching Adolescents with Mild Disabilities* is based on current research in special and regular education in secondary schools as well as on our own work with middle and high school students and teachers. We describe the practical application of research-based practices and how to implement them with adolescents with mild disabilities in both special and regular education settings in the school and community. We also include our personal experiences in teaching middle and high school students, supervising student teachers in secondary settings, training preservice and inservice secondary teachers, and conducting research in secondary settings.

The text emphasizes how to teach middle and high school students with disabilities both in school settings and in out-of-school settings and how to prepare these adolescents for the postsecondary and work environments of the twenty-first century. It describes the role of the special educator as an adapter of materials and curriculum, a facilitator of learning with adolescents with mild disabilities and youth from different cultures, and a collaborator in the inclusive, collaborative model of special education. It focuses on the organization and curriculum of the secondary school environment, on a wide variety of instructional interventions, and on functional and lifelong learning skills. Most importantly, the text focuses on the *how* of teaching and offers generic strategies that are effective for teaching all content areas. We believe that the teacher who knows generic strategies will be better prepared to teach academically diverse groups of secondary students in special and regular education settings.

## Organization of the Text

The text is organized into three parts. Part One, The Student and the Secondary School Environment, includes Chapter 1, Characteristics, Problems, and Issues of Adolescence; Chapter 2, Regular and Special Education

Programs in Middle Schools and High Schools; Chapter 3, Assessment for Instructional Planning in Secondary Schools; Chapter 4, Diverse Populations in the Secondary Schools; Chapter 5, Communication and Collaboration in the School, Home, and Community; and Chapter 6, Motivating Secondary Students.

Part Two, entitled Effective Instructional Interventions for Inclusive and Pullout Settings, includes Chapter 7, Basic Principles of Effective Teaching; Chapter 8, Academic Content; Chapter 9, Cognitive Strategies; and Chapter 10, School Survival and Study Skills.

The last section of the text, Part Three, is called Instruction in Functional and Lifelong Learning Skills. It includes Chapter 11, Career Education, Vocational Development, and Work-Related Social Skills; and Chapter 12, The Transition Planning Process.

## Features of the Text

We incorporate many recommendations for teacher effectiveness from the literature along with other helpful practices. The text includes the following features:

*Personal tone:* We use an informal, personal tone in our writing, much as we would in a class or seminar with our undergraduate and graduate students. You will note the use of the pronouns *you* and *we*.

*Chapter highlights:* At the beginning of each chapter, we have listed the key topics included in the chapter. This helps readers mentally prepare for the content.

*Advance and post organizers:* We begin each chapter by asking, "Before you read this chapter, use your prior knowledge to complete this advance organizer." The advance organizer takes the form of a list of questions that require readers to activate their schemata on the topic. We conclude each chapter by asking, "Now that you have read this chapter, reflect on your responses at the beginning of the chapter, and complete this post organizer." The post organizer includes the same or similar questions that appeared at the beginning of the chapter. This encourages readers to reflect upon the chapter content in relation to their prior knowledge. Note our emphasis on prediction and reflection.

*Comprehension monitoring:* The metacognitive literature places a high degree of importance on self-monitoring. Therefore, interspersed throughout each chapter are stop points called Comprehension Monitoring of Key Concepts. These boxes list the key points to help readers monitor their comprehension and review the concepts of the preceding section.

*Visual aids:* Throughout the text we have included numerous photos, tables, illustrations, diagrams, charts, boxes, and figures. These are provided to enhance the text and provide information in ways that the narrative alone cannot.

*Multicultural and diversity theme:* A multicultural emphasis is integrated throughout the text, and an entire chapter is devoted to diverse populations in the secondary schools (Chapter 4). We give suggestions on how to incorporate multicultural education into the secondary curriculum, how to teach language-minority special learners, and how to use alternative assessments for instructional planning.

*Use of examples:* The text includes extensive examples from our own experiences, those of our students, and also those of the teachers with whom we work. These examples help to clarify key concepts and show how specific strategies may be implemented.

*Technology applications:* There is an emphasis on technology applications throughout the text. Chapters 8, 9, and 11, in particular, contain information about software, videodiscs, CD-ROMs, and technology tools for students and teachers.

## Acknowledgements

We wish to acknowledge the contributions of everyone who assisted us in the completion of this project. To Vicki Knight, our acquisitions editor, who recognized the need for this text and who advised and guided us throughout the process, we express our heartfelt gratitude for making our dream a reality. To the rest of the Brooks/Cole staff, we offer our sincere thanks for their expertise and patience. We acknowledge and appreciate the guidance of Nancy Shammas, our production editor; the tireless efforts of our production managers, Anne and Greg Draus of Scratchgravel Publishing Services; and the work of Kelly Shoemaker, our cover designer, Mary Kay Hancharick, our permissions editor, Peggy Tropp, our copy editor, Monica Suder, our photo researcher, and all the others who contributed their time and talent to our project.

We are particularly appreciative of the work of our dear friend and colleague, Dr. Patricia Patton. Not only did she write Chapter 12, The Transition Planning Process, but she also provided insight and suggestions throughout the preparation of the other chapters and, perhaps most important, provided her support, encouragement, and enthusiasm. Her contributions to the field of special education will be greatly missed.

To our graduate assistant, Holly Sanchez, we give our thanks for her efforts on references, research, and permissions. Thanks also to Holly

Sanchez and Martha Bruno for authoring and preparing the instructor's manual that accompanies the textbook.

We recognize the sacrifices that our families made during the preparation of this text, and we wish to express our appreciation for their patience and understanding. Special thanks go to Chris Platt and Susan Wiehn for planning family activities around the textbook schedule. Special thanks also go to Larry Olson, whose patience with and support of a part-time wife during this process are deeply appreciated.

Without the input of our colleagues and students at the University of Central Florida and the support and encouragement of our families and friends, we would not have had an opportunity to make a difference in the lives of adolescents with mild disabilities as they plan for their successful transition from school to the adult community. We are deeply grateful for these many contributions.

Finally, we would like to acknowledge the efforts of our reviewers who gave us so many valuable suggestions. They are Mary Beirne-Smith, University of Alabama, Tuscaloosa; Kathy Boyle-Gast, Clarke County Public Schools, Athens, Georgia; Gary Clark, University of Kansas; Evelyn Dailey, Towson State University; Donald Doorlag, San Diego State University; Pam Hudson, Utah State University; John Schuster, University of Kentucky; Steven Smith, University of Florida; and David Test, University of North Carolina–Charlotte. We thank them for their assistance.

*Jennifer M. Platt* and *Judy L. Olson*

# Teaching Adolescents with Mild Disabilities

# PART ONE

# The Student and the Secondary School Environment

© Nita Winter/The Image Works

# Characteristics, Problems, and Issues of Adolescence

© Elizabeth Crews

**CHAPTER HIGHLIGHTS**

*Typical Adolescent Development*

*Characteristics of Adolescents with Mild Disabilities*

*Problems of Adolescence*

---

 Before you read Chapter 1, use your prior knowledge to complete this advance organizer.

1. Working with three of your peers, list several characteristics of typical adolescents.

2. Now, working with your peers again, describe characteristics specific to adolescents with mild disabilities.

3. What are the three greatest problems/challenges that a typical adolescent has to face? What are they for an adolescent with a learning or behavior problem?

---

Over the decade of the 1990s, the U.S. Bureau of the Census (1992) estimates that more than 65 million children will enter the phase of development known as adolescence—the stage of development that falls between childhood and adulthood. In U.S. society, the period of adolescence covers the age range from 11 to 21 years. Social scientists separate adolescence into three classifications—early, middle, and late—based on the grouping system found in the schools (Steinberg, 1989): 11- through 14-year-olds, in middle or junior high school, form the early group; 15- through 18-year-olds, in high school, form the middle group; and 18- through 21-year-olds, in postsecondary situations, are the late group.

The adolescent period of development is characterized by dramatic physical, cognitive, and social changes brought about by maturation, cultural influences, and societal expectations (Masters, Mori, & Mori, 1993). This stage of development is challenging for all youth preparing for transition to postsecondary education options, work, and adult living environments, but is particularly overwhelming for adolescents with mild disabilities. While most youth with mild disabilities achieve physical maturation in a manner similar to their peers, they frequently encounter problems in the areas of cognitive and social development as they struggle to meet the academic and social demands of the secondary school setting.

According to the National Longitudinal Transition Study of Special Education Students, (Wagner, 1993), almost 38% of students with disabilities who left school did so by dropping out—8% in middle school and 30% in high school. These rates were higher than the rates for the general population. Dropout rates were particularly high for youth with severe emotional disturbances and for students with learning disabilities, mental retardation, and other disabilities (Wagner, 1993). Given these statistics, parents, teachers, employers, and others who interact with youth need to be aware of the challenges involved in negotiating this challenging period of adolescence, and need to understand the special needs of young people with mild disabilities. The purpose of this chapter is to discuss the characteristics, problems, and issues of adolescence. We begin with a discussion of the challenges of normal adolescent development. Next we describe the characteristics of adolescents with mild disabilities. We conclude with a discussion of the problems currently facing adolescents.

## Typical Adolescent Development

The distinctiveness of adolescence involves changes in physical, cognitive, and social/personal development. Many adolescents experience these changes with turmoil. As Baughman (1974) describes it, "Adolescence is like a hitch in the Army. You'd hate to have missed it, and yet you'd hate to repeat it" (p. 91). Before we can look at how these changes may affect adolescents with mild disabilities, we need to look at normal adolescent development.

## Physical Development

In some cultures, the physical changes of adolescence are symbolized in rites of passage with separate ceremonies for boys and girls (Whiting & Whiting, 1991). For example, the Wadadika Paiute of Harney Valley, Oregon, isolated a girl during her first period in a menstrual hut. During this time, her mother or grandmother instructed her about menstrual taboos, hygiene, and valued physical and social traits. When the month had ended, the girl took a bath, put on a new dress, painted her face with red paint, and returned home. Now the tribe was ready for the girl to assume adult responsibilities (Whiting, 1950).

Steinberg (1989) has identified five chief physical changes that occur for both boys and girls during adolescence: (1) rapid acceleration in both height and weight; (2) development of sex glands, testes in males and ovaries in females; (3) development of secondary sex characteristics such as voice changes and the growth of facial, body, and pubic hair; (4) changes in body composition of fat and muscle; and (5) changes in the circulatory and respiratory systems. These changes occur at different times for males and females.

Females tend to experience the growth spurt and puberty much earlier than boys. The growth spurt in most girls begins at age 10½ and lasts for about two years, with a height gain of about 3½ inches per year (Santrock, 1987). Boys usually grow about 4 inches per year when they begin their growth spurt at about 12½ years of age (Santrock, 1987). This represents the most dramatic growth in height for both sexes except for the first years after birth (Furstenberg, 1991). Even though at the beginning of adolescence, girls tend to be taller, boys usually catch up by the end of the junior year of high school (Santrock, 1987). Most girls have reached 98% of their adult height at 16¼ years, while boys do not reach 98% of their adult height until 17¾ years (Rice, 1990).

For both genders, peak height is reached before peak body weight during the growth spurt (Walker & Lirgg, 1995). Body fat increases for girls during this time and hips become wider, while body fat decreases in boys as muscle cells multiply (Buchanan, 1991). Often bone growth is faster than muscle development, resulting in a lack of coordination and an increase in awkwardness (Whisler, 1990).

The onset of puberty, or the period during which a person attains sexual maturity and the capacity to bear offspring, again occurs about two years earlier in girls (Weinstein & Rosen, 1991). The average girl begins puberty between 10 and 11 years of age with breast development (Rice, 1990) and reaches menarche (time of first menstruation) between 12 and 13 (Kerr, Nelson, & Lambert, 1987; Scott-Jones, 1993; Steinberg, 1989). The average age of the onset of puberty for boys is between 12 and 13 years, with beginning growth of the testes and scrotum and the development of pubic hair (Rice, 1990). Generally, puberty has ended long before the end of adolescence, with most changes occurring during early adolescence (Santrock, 1987; Steinberg, 1989). Over the years, with better nutrition and health care, boys and girls mature at younger ages. According to Males (1990), in 1950 only 80% of 15- to 19-year-old females were able to reproduce, while in 1985, 90% were.

Within this range of development, there are many adolescents who mature early; that is, they begin their growth spurt and progress through puberty before the rest of their peer group. Much of the research (Dubas, Graber, & Petersen, 1991; Stallin & Magnusson, 1990) analyzing the effect of the timing of physical maturation shows that early-maturing boys are usually more popular with peers and show higher achievement. The data for early-maturing girls are more mixed. Early-maturing girls are often more popular with adults and older peers, while late-maturing girls generally show higher achievement (Dubas et al., 1991; Santrock, 1987).

## Cognitive Development

Cognition is the mental activity or thinking involved in understanding (Rice, 1990). When viewing the S>R paradigm in psychology, it is what happens in the black box after a stimulus is presented and before a response is made. It is all the nonobservable events that occur in the mind. For example, as you are reading this text, you see the visual stimulus of words and eventually, you may be asked to demonstrate your understanding of these words on an exam. How you make sense of the words and how you prepare for the exam are examples of cognition. As we explore the realm of adolescence, we examine how these mental processes change with age.

Piaget (1896–1980) theorized that children pass through stages of cognitive development, with the last stage, that of formal operational thought, occurring during early adolescence. Four major aspects of formal operational thought are introspection, abstract thinking, logical thinking, and hypothetical reasoning (Rice, 1990). In introspection, the adolescent thinks about thought and can regulate his or her own thinking (metacognition). For example, the adolescent may think, "I can spell words better when I write each word five times."

Unlike the child who thinks in concrete terms, the adolescent can go beyond the real to what is possible. Verbal problem solving improves dramatically (Santrock, 1987). Adolescents can solve problems such as "If B = C and C = D, then B = D" without concrete referents. An adolescent demonstrates planned logical thought as he or she develops hypotheses or hunches about correct solutions. Facility in thinking through hypotheses allows an adolescent to answer the following question correctly:

> If this is Room 154, then this is a class in adolescent development. This is not Room 154. Is this a class in adolescent development? (Steinberg, 1989, p. 61; adapted from Flavell, 1977, p. 112)

The adolescent is able to answer that the class in Room 154 may or may not be a class in adolescent development.

Information processing theorists have a different viewpoint concerning the development of cognitive processes in adolescents. According to the information processing model of cognitive development, cognition consists of attention, perception, memory, thinking, and problem solving (Santrock, 1987). For example, when an adolescent is presented with a problem such as $3x + 10 = 34$, the adolescent first *attends* to it and *perceives* that he or she must solve for $x$; uses *memory* (at least to write the problem down); *thinks* about it (a product of perception and memory), such as "Let's see, I have $x$ as the unknown to figure out"; and then *problem-solves*, beginning with "To solve, I must end up with $x$ alone on one side of the equation." Of course, this example is a simplification, as the dynamic processes often overlap.

During adolescence, the memory capacity is enlarged (Case, 1985; Linn & Songer, 1991), selective and divided attention is improved (Higgins & Turnure, 1984; Schiff & Knopf, 1985), and metamemory (knowledge of one's own memory processes) becomes more sophisticated (Santrock, 1987). In addition, adolescents demonstrate an advanced understanding of formal and pragmatic language (Santrock, 1987). For example, adolescents are better than children at understanding abstract meanings of words, better at writing, and better at understanding the key points when reading prose. They are also more adept at understanding and following the rules of conversation. For instance, depending on cultural background, they know to wait their turn to speak during discussion time and to use language that is appropriate for the situation and audience.

The cognitive development of adolescents is also affected by the social environment (Brown, Collins, & Dugrud, 1989; Foster & Sprinthall, 1992;

Linn & Songer, 1991). Students often consider the opinions of families, teachers, counselors, and peers when they make decisions concerning themselves as learners. In adolescence, males and females start to construct quite different views of their learning capability frequently based on the social environment. For example, males see math and science as male-domain subjects (Hyde, Fennema, & Lamon, 1990). Might this be one of the reasons that more adolescent boys than girls tend to select science and math as fields of study?

Often the level of cognitive development varies depending on the situation or issues (Brown et al., 1989; Foster & Sprinthall, 1992). When the situation is more personal, cognitive development is lower. For example, adolescents tend to demonstrate lower stages of cognitive development when reasoning about personal sexual activity (Gilligan, Kohlberg, Lerner, & Belenky, 1987) and personal drug usage (Mohr, Gerler, & Sprinthall, 1987) than they do when reasoning about standard moral dilemmas and issues.

## Social/Personal Development

In all societies, adolescence is a period of social redefinition (Steinberg, 1989). In our society, three major issues of social/personal development are the search for identity, the development of independence and autonomy, and a shift in allegiance from family to peers (Coleman, 1986).

### *Search for Identity*

The search for identity involves the way we see and feel about ourselves. The search is a lifelong process that begins during adolescence as this is the first time an individual has the necessary physical, cognitive, and social skills to seriously inquire and investigate into who he or she is as a person (Rice, 1990; Santrock, 1987). The adolescent begins to ask questions dealing with basic values, plans, priorities, goals, and lifestyles. Erikson (1968) describes the search for identity as the fifth stage of psychosocial development. During this stage, adolescents, responding to the reactions of significant others, select and choose the elements that will become part of their final identities. "From among all possible and imaginable relations, [the adolescent] must make a series of ever-narrowing selections of personal, occupational, sexual, and ideological commitments" (Erikson, 1968, p. 245). Most adolescents experience conflict, anxiety, and self-doubt as they try to find out who they are (Rice, 1990).

Spencer (1991) asserts that communities with clearly defined social and ideological roles frequently do not encourage individuals to explore their own identities. For example, according to Spencer, exploration is generally discouraged and cultural norms encouraged in Native American adolescents who are raised on reservations and Hispanic youth who live in predominantly Hispanic communities.

An important aspect of thinking about the self and others is egocentrism (Santrock, 1987). Egocentrism is a type of self-centering that occurs in the transition from childhood to adulthood. Two aspects of egocentrism identified by Elkind (1978) include the imaginary audience and the personal fable. The imaginary audience accounts for the self-conscious behavior of many adolescents as they are unable to distinguish between what is of interest to themselves and others. They feel that they are on stage at all times and under the scrutiny of others (Buis & Thompson, 1989). The ninth-grader who believes everyone in the restaurant is staring at her outfit is demonstrating egocentric behavior. The personal fable refers to the belief of adolescents that personal feelings are unique (Elkind, 1978). It is exemplified in the voiced comment "No one understands how I feel" from an adolescent after the breakup of a relationship. In part, this feeling of uniqueness may explain such risk-taking behaviors as engaging in sex without protection. Adolescents often feel they are indestructible and such actions will never result in their being harmed.

### Development of Autonomy

A simplified definition of autonomy is the perception that one has control over behavior. In adolescence, autonomy is often confused with rebellion (Steinberg, 1989) as teenagers strive to select clothing, music, and friends that may not be to their parents' liking. Parents and adolescents tend to argue over such autonomy-related issues as driving the car or setting curfews (Montemayor, 1986). However, studies (Hill, 1987; Offer, 1985; Offer & Church, 1991; Petersen, 1988) show that there is less family conflict and stress than once thought in the adolescents' quest for autonomy. Often adolescents desire autonomy in some areas such as clothing and music selection, but follow parents' suggestions in others such as choice of school or elective subjects (Rice, 1990).

Steinberg (1989) identifies emotional, behavioral, and ethical autonomy as central to adolescent development. Emotional autonomy occurs as teenagers become less emotionally dependent on parents and more on peers. For example, many older adolescents do not generally rush to parents when upset, nor do they see parents as all-knowing (Steinberg, 1989). Behavioral autonomy involves the capacity to make independent decisions and to follow through on them. Ethical autonomy is having a set of values or principles about right and wrong and about what is important and what is not (Steinberg, 1989). Like identity, autonomy is a lifelong process, that takes on new significance in adolescence.

### Shift in Allegiance from Family to Peers

Research does show that peers become increasingly important in adolescence (Petersen & Epstein, 1991). Peers exert explicit pressures for conformity, give social support, and promote self-worth and standards (Santrock, 1987; Steinberg, 1989; Rice, 1990). Adolescents usually select friends to share common interests, find identities, and overcome loneliness. Adolescents are most likely to select peer groups that support or complement parental values (Brown, 1990; Youniss & Smollar, 1985). Thus, even though an adolescent shifts allegiance from family to peers, family values are still influential.

Compared to peer groups of younger children, adolescent peer groups consist of more formalized structures, display greater heterogeneity of members, and are frequently cross-sexed (Santrock, 1987). The '90s version of teen dating is dating in packs, roaming malls, bowling alleys, or pizza parlors, and even congregating at each other's homes to watch videos (Shrieves, 1993). Conformity to peers increases up to middle adolescence and then declines (Foster-Clark & Blyth, 1991).

Rice (1990) notes six important needs of youth in the establishment of social relationships: (1) to establish caring, meaningful, satisfying relationships with individuals; (2) to broaden childhood friendships by getting acquainted with new people of differing backgrounds, experiences, and ideas; (3) to find acceptance, belonging, recognition, and status in social groups; (4) to pass from the homosocial interests and playmates of middle childhood to heterosocial concerns and friendships; (5) to learn about, adopt, and practice dating patterns and skills that contribute to personal and social development, intelligent mate selection, and successful marriage; and (6) to find an acceptable masculine or feminine sex role and to learn sex-appropriate behavior. Peers can help adolescents meet these needs.

---

**COMPREHENSION MONITORING OF KEY CONCEPTS**

### Typical Adolescent Development

1. Major physical changes occurring during adolescence include an increase in height and weight, the development of sex glands and characteristics, and the ability to reproduce.

2. In adolescence, verbal problem solving improves, higher-level thought develops, memory capacity enlarges, language use expands, and knowledge of individual thinking processes evolves.

3. Adolescents attempt to establish their identity, strive for control over ethical, behavioral, and emotional decisions, and move from a dependence on family to friends.

4. Social thought is egocentric, including the imaginary audience (as in "Everyone is looking at me") and the personal fable (as in "Nothing will harm me").

## Characteristics of Adolescents with Mild Disabilities

As we have just seen, the adolescent period of an individual's life includes a progression of experiences that are at times exciting, discouraging, challenging, and confusing. As most normally developing adolescents move toward adulthood, the problems and challenges of the adolescent period are eased through maturation and experience (Mercer, 1987). However, some adolescents, such as those with mild disabilities, do not find that these challenges are eased by maturation and experience. Consequently, they fail to meet some of the challenges of adolescence with respect to the various cognitive, academic, social/emotional, and motivational areas of development (Mercer & Mercer, 1993).

We define adolescents with mild disabilities as those youth between the ages of 11 and 21 who evidence mild learning and/or behavior problems and who require special education services to meet their individual needs. This includes the categories of adolescents with mild learning disabilities, mental disabilities, and emotional disabilities. For a composite picture of some general characteristics of secondary students with mild disabilities, see Table 1.1, which summarizes the findings of the National Longitudinal Transition Study of Special Education Students (Wagner, Blackorby, Cameto,

**TABLE 1.1** **Characteristics of Secondary Students with Mild Disabilities**

| Disability | Male | Minority | Poor (<$25,000) | IQ |
|---|---|---|---|---|
| Learning | 73.4% | 32.8% | 65% | 87.1 |
| Emotional | 76.4% | 32.9% | 70% | 86.4 |
| Mental | 58.0% | 39.0% | 75% | 60.2 |

*Source:* From "The Transition Experience of Young People with Disabilities: A Summary of Findings from the National Longitudinal Transition Study of Special Education Students, Postschool Outcomes" by M. Wagner, J. Blackorby, R. Cameto, K. Hebbeler, and L. Newman, 1993, Menlo Park, CA: SRI International (ERIC Document Reproduction ED365 086).

Hebbeler, & Newman 1993). Of the adolescents with mild disabilities in grades 9–12, 70% were male; 68% were poor (income less than $25,000), compared to only 39% in the general population; 37% came from single-parent homes, compared to 25.6% in the general population; and 24% were African American, compared to 14% in the general population. Other findings indicated that absenteeism for adolescents with learning disabilities ranged from 13 to 17 days; for adolescents with emotional handicaps, 15 to 20 days; and for students with mental disabilities, 12 to 16 days.

Although it is inappropriate to make general statements about the characteristics of each and every student who has a mild disability, descriptive data suggest that students with mild learning, emotional, and mental disabilities share similar characteristics (Taylor, Sternberg, & Richards, 1995) and benefit from similar educational interventions (Cegelka & Berdine, 1995). Throughout this text, we use the generic term *students with mild disabilities* to describe students in all three categories (learning, emotional, and mental disabilities). However, if we describe a study that was conducted within a specific category we use that categorical designation. We agree with the statement "The preponderance of research demonstrating the efficacy of instructional programs and approaches with one category of disability is generalizable to other categories of mild cognitive disabilities as well as to the broader group of academically at risk or low-achieving students" (Cegelka & Berdine, 1995, p. 6).

Many adolescents with mild disabilities experience academic failure and demonstrate language and cognitive deficits (Taylor et al., 1995). Many of these adolescents have problems in reading, oral and written language, arithmetic, and other school subjects (Masters et al., 1993). In addition, these youth often have social/personal problems exhibited as inadequate participation in school and extracurricular activities, and as infrequent and negative interactions with peers without disabilities (Polloway, Patton, Epstein, & Smith, 1989; Smith, Polloway, Patton, & Dowdy, 1995). Social skill deficits may be a major source of conflict with teachers, peers, the school, and the community (Schloss, Smith, & Schloss, 1995).

One of the expectations of parents, teachers, and the community is for adolescents to prepare for employment and eventual economic independence. Adequate social/personal skills are important to both school and community adjustment (Lovett & Harris, 1987; Schloss & Schloss, 1987). Deficits in this area may pose problems for adolescents with mild disabilities in the area of career preparedness. Students with mild disabilities tend to drop out before graduation, are unemployed at a higher rate than their peers without disabilities, and tend to live in a dependent situation for a longer period of time than their peers without disabilities (Edgar, 1988).

As noted previously, adolescents with learning disabilities, emotional disabilities, and mental disabilities share many similar characteristics. For purposes of discussion, we organize these characteristics into the categories of cognitive, academic, and social/personal characteristics. We do not discuss physical characteristics, because the physical development of adolescents with and without disabilities is very similar and is usually not a concern except in regard to problems that any adolescent may encounter (for example, eating disorders, drug-related physiological effects, early and late maturers). As you read, please be aware that adolescents with mild disabilities are a heterogeneous group, and do not have to possess all of the following characteristics to be considered students with mild disabilities.

## Cognitive Characteristics

Characteristics that may affect the cognitive functioning of adolescents with disabilities include poor problem-solving skills (Smith, Finn, & Dowdy, 1993). As mentioned earlier, during normal adolescent development, problem-solving abilities typically improve dramatically. However, many adolescents with disabilities will need specific, systematic instruction in problem-solving procedures (as in estimating the answers to math problems, interpreting the author's message in a reading passage, or analyzing a social situation). Students with poor problem-solving skills, as well as deficits in language functioning, may experience difficulty deciding what to do in new social situations (Smith et al., 1995), resulting in possible failures in communication and increased social rejection (Polloway & Smith, 1989).

Cronin and Gerber (1982) found that thinking and reasoning skills— such as problem solving, abstract thinking, organizational judgment, and verbal comprehension—pose difficulty for adolescents with learning disabilities. For example, an adolescent may have difficulty writing themes in English class, solving word problems in math, and putting together reports in science, all for lack of a systematic approach to these tasks.

Adolescents with behavior disorders may also experience difficulty with abstract concepts and demonstrate confusion and an inability to understand material (Masters et al., 1993). The adolescent who has difficulty with abstract thinking may experience difficulty interpreting poetry, solving math problems, and converting units of measure in home economics. Coleman, Levine, and Sandler (1987) found that students with deficits in nonverbal reasoning have difficulty with nonverbal concepts in math, such as place value, directionality, and spatial relationships. Executive functioning (creating and applying a strategy to a novel problem/situation) is another cognitive problem for adolescents with learning disabilities

(Ellis, Deshler, & Schumaker, 1989). An adolescent with this difficulty most likely does not stop to consider the requirements of a task or assignment before completing it. In fact, Deshler, Warner, Schumaker, and Alley (1983) state that adolescents with learning disabilities may have difficulty with all types of cognitive tasks because they do not spontaneously apply rehearsal, clustering, and error-monitoring strategies to tasks. Adolescents with poor metacognitive (thinking about one's own thinking) and metalinguistic (thinking about one's own language) skills may be at a disadvantage compared to adolescents with these skills intact. An adolescent with these difficulties does not know why writing a journal entry or a book report is so difficult for him/her.

Language, both oral and written, appears to be a problem for adolescents with learning disabilities (Coleman et al., 1987). Polloway and Smith (1989) state, "No other area is more frequently associated with disabilities" (p. 137). Clearly, difficulties with language impact the student's performance in (1) academic subjects (reading, math, spelling, science, history, and English); (2) activities requiring listening, following directions, and organizing information; and (3) social interactions. In a study of students with mild mental disabilities, Epstein, Patton, Polloway, and Foley (1989) found speech and language disabilities were the most frequently mentioned secondary handicapping condition for this population.

Smith et al. (1993) report attentional difficulties as one characteristic of adolescents with learning disabilities. Bender (1985) points out that adolescents with learning disabilities appear to be passive learners, exhibit attention problems, and are off task approximately 40% of the time. Others report that students with mild disabilities exhibit impulsivity, distractibility, hyperactivity, and inattention (Masters et al., 1993). Epstein et al. (1989) found distractibility and inattentiveness to be the most frequently mentioned behavioral characteristic of students with mild mental disabilities, a finding supported in previous research (Polloway, Epstein, & Cullinan, 1985). Students with learning difficulties seem to be easily distracted by irrelevant information, resulting in problems attending to relevant information (Masters et al., 1993). If attention is a prerequisite for problem solving, listening and following directions, abstract reasoning, organizing, comprehending, and monitoring one's performance, then the adolescent with attentional problems is at a severe disadvantage.

## Academic Characteristics

Academic problems, particularly in reading and math, constitute major problems for adolescents with learning disabilities, resulting in achievement levels from three to five years below grade level by the ninth grade

(Zigmond & Thornton, 1989). The findings from the National Longitudinal Transition Study of Special Education Students indicate that adolescents with learning disabilities average 3.1 years below grade level in reading and 2.7 years below grade level in math; adolescents with emotional handicaps average 2.2 years below grade level in reading and 1.8 below grade level in math; and adolescents with mental disabilities average 5.6 years below grade level in reading and 5.7 years below grade level in math (Wagner, Blackorby, Cameto, Hebbeler, & Newman, 1993).

Although a greater percentage of students failed regular education courses than special education courses, some students did fail special education courses (see Table 1.2). Notice that the grade point averages (GPAs) of students with mild disabilities were consistently lower in regular education courses than in special education courses. Further examination reveals

**TABLE 1.2** **Academic Performance of Secondary Students with Mild Disabilities in Regular and Special Education Courses**

| Disability | GPA in regular education courses | GPA in special education courses | Percentage who failed at least one regular education course |
|---|---|---|---|
| *9th grade* | | | |
| Learning | 1.9 | 2.2 | 45% |
| Emotional | 1.7 | 1.9 | 57% |
| Mental | 2.0 | 2.2 | 34% |
| *10th grade* | | | |
| Learning | 1.9 | 2.3 | 45% |
| Emotional | 1.6 | 1.8 | 57% |
| Mental | 2.1 | 2.3 | 37% |
| *11th grade* | | | |
| Learning | 2.0 | 2.3 | 39% |
| Emotional | 1.8 | 2.9 | 54% |
| Mental | 2.2 | 2.4 | 29% |
| *12th grade* | | | |
| Learning | 2.3 | 2.5 | 24% |
| Emotional | 2.1 | 2.3 | 30% |
| Mental | 2.4 | 2.6 | 18% |

that students with emotional handicaps had lower grade point averages and a higher percentage of failure than did students with mental or learning disabilities, in grades 9–12. These findings indicate that the emotional and behavior problems of adolescents appear to interfere with the academic achievement of a population that typically has good academic potential.

### Reading

Reading problems are quite evident among adolescents with mild disabilities (Masters et al., 1993). In a study of adults and high school students with learning disabilities, reading and spelling were the academic areas in which problems were reported most frequently (Minskoff, Sautter, Sheldon, Steidle, & Baker, 1988). Masters et al. (1993) report that the reading achievement of adolescents with behavior disorders appears to be from three to five years below grade level by the beginning of ninth grade, and that the reading skills of students with mild mental disabilities tends to plateau at the second- to sixth-grade level.

Typical reading difficulties of adolescents with mild disabilities include problems with vocabulary, word recognition, reading comprehension, and reading rate. Reading appears to affect performance in all other academic subjects as well as to impact vocational needs and options (Feagans, 1983; Hallahan, Kauffman, & Lloyd, 1985). Adolescents need flexible reading habits for success in content-area subjects. For example, the adolescent needs to know when to read slowly and carefully, when to stop and paraphrase text, when to scan for the answer to a question, and when to read headings and summary sections for a quick review. Unfortunately, problems with memory, language, attention, thinking, and reasoning may also impede the reading progress of adolescents with disabilities.

### Writing

Levine (1987) reports writing to be the most common problem of all the communication skills. As we reported earlier, one of the characteristics of adolescence is egocentrism, in which the adolescent frequently exhibits self-conscious behavior. An adolescent with problems in writing, reluctant to create a permanent product that can be seen by others, may exhibit even greater self-consciousness than the typical adolescent. This may result in increased avoidance of the writing process and in fewer written products. The student's writing samples may be characterized by a limited vocabulary and deficient syntax and grammar (Coleman et al., 1987). Written language problems include the areas of handwriting, spelling, text and sentence structure, composition, mechanics, and word usage (Scott, 1991).

Additionally, related problems in spelling, memory, and higher-order thinking may adversely impact the adolescent's performance in writing (Coleman et al., 1987). Sample spelling difficulties may include phonetic spellings, as in *telefone* for *telephone,* or an overreliance on visual cues, as in *exeprience* for *experience*. Memory difficulties can result in problems remembering grammatical, capitalization, and punctuation rules. Abstract thinking skills, necessary for success in writing, may be limited in some students with disabilities, resulting in problems in understanding or producing language.

Ariel (1992) reports that a student's experiential background contributes to the development of written language. Students with disabilities may have limited backgrounds and fewer opportunities to develop written expressive abilities. Similarly, students from diverse cultural backgrounds may have limited knowledge about the experiences of the majority culture being discussed in class, and should be given the encouragement and opportunity to share and express their own experiences in writing.

### Mathematics

Adolescents with mild mental disabilities, learning disabilities, and behavior disorders may experience difficulties in mathematics (Masters et al., 1993). Many secondary students with learning disabilities fail to become proficient in basic fact knowledge in the elementary grades. As a result, these students generally experience greater problems applying computational skills to real life, as in making change, shopping, and budgeting (Schloss, Smith, & Schloss, 1995). Difficulties in memory, reasoning, language, organization, and attention may account for the difficulties in computation, numerical reasoning, and problem solving that some adolescents with mild disabilities seem to experience. Adolescents who have related memory problems may have difficulty memorizing and retrieving math facts and remembering the sequence of mathematical operations (for example, the steps in changing a fraction to a percent, or the steps in solving a word problem).

Students who have difficulties in reasoning will have trouble understanding the abstract concepts of time, money, measurement, algebra, geometry, comparisons/relationships (>, <, =), and word problems ("How do I know whether to add, subtract, multiply, or divide?"). Adolescents with these difficulties may experience problems working independently and generalizing math skills to real-life situations on the job and in the community.

According to Mercer and Mercer (1993), students with learning disabilities who have receptive language problems may have difficulty relating terms to meaning (such as *product, regroup,* and *factor*) and understanding multiple meanings (for example, *reduce* can mean *simplify*). Those with expressive language problems may have difficulty using math vocabulary and verbalizing the steps in a word problem or algorithm (Mercer & Mercer, 1993).

Adolescents with disabilities who lack organization skills may experience difficulty with anything from lining up their problems accurately to organizing the information presented in order to solve a problem. They may make careless mistakes and fail to check their work for accuracy or for the reasonableness of their responses (estimation). Students who have attentional difficulties may be impulsive or distractible. They may have difficulty focusing on the relevant information and screening out the extraneous information. Students with these problems may have difficulty completing multistep computations and attending to essential details in solving word problems.

## Social/Personal Characteristics

Social-skill deficits appear to have a significant impact on the vocational success of students with disabilities (Schloss et al., 1995). Whether students with mild disabilities succeed or fail in regular classes is related to social competence (Epstein & Cullinan, 1988; Polloway, Patton, Epstein, & Smith, 1989).

Gresham (1983) found that students with disabilities interact infrequently and negatively with peers in regular classrooms and are not well accepted by these peers. Unfortunately, many students with mild disabilities are placed in mainstream classes without the necessary prerequisite social skills needed for success, placing them in jeopardy for repeated failure.

Many adolescents with learning disabilities appear to have difficulties in affective and social skills (Bryan, Donahue, & Pearl, 1981; Cruickshank & Paul, 1980). Research has shown that these students are characterized by poor self-concepts, lowered levels of expectations and motivation, and a high degree of learned helplessness (Hiebert, Wong, & Hunter, 1982; Pearl, Bryan, & Donahue, 1980). By late adolescence, there is reason to believe that the social-skill problems of adolescents with learning disabilities have seriously affected their self-concepts and motivation (Alley & Deshler, 1979). Learning disabilities manifested in childhood often persist into adult life and impact the personal (social domain) and work (vocational domain) lives of individuals with learning disabilities (White, 1992).

Social-skill deficits are among the reasons that students are placed in programs for behavior disorders (Epstein, Kauffman, & Cullinan, 1985). Students with emotional problems often exhibit social deficits (Smith & Luckasson, 1992). Adolescents with emotional disabilities have been

© Charles Harbutt/Actuality

*Some adolescents have difficulty relating to peers.*

termed socially inept (Dodge & Murphy, 1984), depressed (Cullinan, Schloss, & Epstein, 1987), less socially accepted (Sabornie, 1985), and unable to develop satisfactory relationships with peers (Epstein et al., 1985). Within the population of adolescents with emotional handicaps, Wagner (1992) found a general disconnectedness from school, high absenteeism, low rates of membership in school groups, and strong affiliations with friends outside of school.

It appears that adolescents who lack people-pleasing skills will have difficulty adjusting to the demands of school, work, and community. Social-skill deficits have also been shown to relate to problems in academic achievement, delinquency, and poor self-concept (Conger & Keane, 1981; Dodge & Murphy, 1984). Efforts to include students with emotional problems in regular education settings have failed for many students, not because of academic deficits but because of social problems.

Students with mental disabilities are likely to also exhibit emotional disabilities (Epstein, Cullinan, & Polloway, 1986; Forness & Polloway, 1987; Polloway et al., 1985). Greenspan and Shoultz (1981) found that individuals with mental disabilities lost their jobs because of an inability to interact effectively with others, not because of an inability to perform occupational skills. It appears that social competence rather than task performance is important for vocational adjustment and, indeed, for adjustment to all facets of adult and community living.

A final comment: As you read this section on characteristics, you probably noticed that the picture presented of adolescents with mild disabilities does not consistently correspond to that of their normally developing peers. Although youth with disabilities move through the same sequence of development, they encounter significantly greater obstacles along the way.

---

**COMPREHENSION MONITORING OF KEY CONCEPTS**

*Characteristics*

1. Adolescents with mild disabilities are those youth between the ages of 11 and 21 who evidence mild learning and/or behavior problems and who require special education services to meet their needs.

2. Although it is inappropriate to make general statements about the characteristics of each and every student with a mild disability, descriptive data suggest similar characteristics among students with mild learning, emotional, and mental disabilities.

3. Cognitive characteristics of adolescents with mild disabilities may include poor problem solving, difficulty with abstract thinking, problems with oral and/or written language, deficient metacognitive skills, and attentional difficulties.

4. Academic problems typical of adolescents with mild disabilities include: reading (vocabulary, word recognition, and comprehension), writing (written expression, grammar, mechanical errors, syntax, and spelling), and math (computation, reasoning, and problem solving).

5. Adolescents with mild disabilities who lack adequate social/personal skills may have poor self-concepts, difficulty interacting with others, lower levels of motivation, and problems adjusting to life's demands.

---

## Problems of Adolescence

In 1940, teachers rated the following as the top discipline problems in the schools: "talking out of turn, chewing gum, making noise, running in the halls, cutting in line, dress-code violations, and littering" (Toch, Gest, & Guttman,1993, p. 34). In 1990, teachers rated the following as the top discipline problems in the schools: "drug abuse, alcohol abuse, pregnancy, suicide, rape, robbery, and assault" (Toch, Gest, & Guttman, 1993, p. 34).

These problems found in today's schools create difficulties for all adolescents, including those with disabilities. Students with disabilities, with their limited academic skills, inadequate reasoning abilities, poor self-concepts, and ineffective interpersonal relationships, are at risk for substance abuse, teen pregnancy, AIDS, suicide, violence, and dropping out of school.

## Substance Abuse

Alcohol-related automobile accidents kill 10,000 young people between the ages of 16 and 24 annually in the United States (Takayama, 1992). Additionally, adolescents who use alcohol and other substances are more likely to commit crimes, practice unsafe sex, drop out of school, contract AIDS, and attempt suicide (Austin, 1988; Bostic, 1994; Goplerud, 1990; Kandel, 1991; *National Drug Control Strategy,* 1995; Newcomb & Bentler, 1991; Rauch & Huba, 1991; Scales, 1991).

Adolescents in the United States use drugs at a higher rate than youth in any other industrialized nation (Johnston, O'Malley, & Bachman, 1994). By age 15, 20% to 25% already have problems with substance usage (Scales, 1991). Approximately 32% of eighth-graders, 40% of tenth-graders, and nearly 50% of twelfth-graders have tried illicit drugs (Johnston et al., 1994). By age 15, 60% to 70% of adolescents have tried alcohol and tobacco (Scales, 1991), with use frequently initiated between sixth and ninth grades (Johnston et al., 1994).

Results from the 1994 national drug use survey of approximately 17,000 eighth-graders, 16,000 tenth-graders, and 15,000 twelfth-graders showed that students abuse alcohol the most, then cigarettes, and third, marijuana (Johnston et al., 1994). Other findings from this survey follow. About 14% of eighth-graders, 23% of tenth-graders, and 28% of twelfth-graders are heavy drinkers (consuming five drinks in a row within two weeks). About 17% of eighth-graders, 25% of tenth-graders, and 19% of twelfth-graders are daily smokers. About 17% of eighth-graders, 30% of tenth-graders, and 38% of twelfth-grade students have tried marijuana at least once (Johnston et al., 1994). In most cases, tenth- and twelfth-graders abuse substances at a higher rate than eighth-graders. However, eighth-graders abuse inhalants more. In this form of substance abuse, called huffing, the young adolescent inhales fumes from gasoline, hair spray, butane, or any number of household items.

Drug use increased from 1993 to 1994, especially in the area of marijuana use, and anti-drug attitudes continue to erode (Johnston, 1994).

**B O X   1 . 1**

### General Findings about Substance Abuse

1. Adolescent males use illicit drugs more than females, although females use stimulants, barbiturates, and tranquilizers at the same level or higher.
2. Males have more occasions of heavy drinking and more frequent use of alcohol than females.
3. There is no difference in the rate of smoking cigarettes between female and male adolescents, although males are more likely to be heavy smokers.
4. In twelfth grade, Euro-Americans (Caucasians) have the highest rate of use on a number of drugs.
5. Across all grade levels, African Americans showed lower usage rates on most drugs.
6. The daily smoking rates of African Americans are one-fifth that of Euro-Americans.
7. Hispanics in eighth grade had the highest rates of use for nearly all drugs, including the most dangerous (such as cocaine, heroin, and crack), and in twelfth grade, on cocaine, crack, and heroin.
8. Native American adolescents display a high incidence of use of cigarettes, alcohol, illicit drugs, and inhalants.
9. Although there are sanctions against drug use in the Asian American culture, substance abuse is on the rise for recent Asian immigrants.

Fewer students in all three grades said that smoking marijuana is harmful and eighth- and tenth-graders perceived a lesser health risk for the use of powder and crack cocaine than in 1993.

Research studies report some demographic differences in substance abuse based on gender and ethnic group (Austin, 1988; Delgado & Rodriguez-Andrew, 1990; Goplerud, 1990; Johnston et al., 1994; Kandel, 1991; McKenry, 1991; Newcomb & Bentler, 1991; Tucker, 1985; Young, 1987). These findings appear in Box 1.1. There is minimal difference in drug use based on size of the community or socioeconomic level, testifying to the widely prevalent use of drugs (Johnston et al., 1994).

In a review of the research on students with disabilities, Genaux, Morgan, and Friedman (1995) concluded that substance abuse is as great a problem among students with disabilities as it is among students without disabilities. However, adolescents with emotional disabilities have higher rates of drug use than students with other disabilities (Devlin & Elliott,

1992; Genaux et al., 1995; Leone, Greenberg, Trickett, & Spero, 1989). Furthermore, Cohen, Brook, and Kandel (1991) report that "some forms of psychopathology, and especially conduct disorder . . . are predisposing factors" (p. 268) for tobacco and other substance abuse. It seems likely that the characteristics of some adolescents with disabilities may place them at greater risk for abuse of controlled substances.

Substance abuse usually proceeds in stages, beginning with the experimentation stage of beer or wine and tobacco use (Cohen et al., 1991; Goplerud, 1990; Rauch & Huba, 1991). The individual then moves to the regular stage of hard liquor use, and next to the serious stage of abuse of tobacco, alcohol, and marijuana. Last, the individual moves to the dependent stage and uses illicit substances. In most cases, use of the gateway drugs, alcohol and tobacco, precedes use of illicit drugs (Califano, 1994; Kandel, 1991).

Movement from the lower to the higher stages of substance abuse depends on family, peer, community, and individual factors (Austin, 1988; Cohen et al., 1991; Tucker, 1985). Lack of parental supervision, parental tolerance of deviant behaviors, and poor parent–child relationships encourages drug use in adolescents. Additionally, fathers who abuse alcohol and mothers who abuse prescription pills are more likely to have children who abuse drugs (Goplerud, 1990). Adolescents with mental retardation are more likely to abuse alcohol and other drugs when they live with family members who are users (Resource Center on Substance Abuse Prevention and Disability, 1995). Adolescents who are members of peer groups that use, tolerate, and supply drugs are at higher risks for illicit substance abuse. High school students listed social pressure from peers and availability of drugs as reasons for increased use of illicit substances (Johnston et al., 1994).

Neighborhoods that condone drug use and provide easy access to drugs promote drug use in adolescents, since adolescents often adopt the standards of adult role models from the community (Males, 1990; Rice, 1990). Individual characteristics that correlate with substance abuse include poor school performance, low school involvement, aggressiveness, and risk-taking tendencies. Research also shows that earlier drug usage is related to future drug problems (Johnston et al., 1994; Kandel, 1991).

As can be seen from the statistics, chances are that as a secondary teacher you will know students who are at risk for substance abuse. Your major role is to refer students suspected of drug abuse for help (Kauffman, 1993; LaChance, 1988). Individual and family counseling are effective interventions for adolescents with problem behaviors (*National Drug Control Strategy*, 1995). The chart in Table 1.3 gives you some information concerning the

**TABLE 1.3**    Symptoms, Characteristics, and Effects of Various Illicit Substances

| Substance | Physical symptoms | Look for | Behaviors |
|---|---|---|---|
| *Hallucinogens* (acids, LSD, MDMA, PCP, mescaline, peyote, psilocybin, STP, DMT) | Mood and perception alterations, possible paranoia, panic, anxiety, nausea, tremors | Liquid capsule, white or brown powder, can be put on paper, stamps, sugar cubes, cigarettes, or joints | Unpredictable behavior, flashbacks, possible emotional instability and psychosis |
| *Stimulants* Amphetamines (bennies, dexies, uppers, black beauties, pep, crack, speed) Nicotine | Loss of appetite, anxiety, irritability, rapid speed, tremors, mood elevation | Pills of varying colors, possible chain smoking, long periods of sleep | Disorientation, severe depression, paranoia, possible hallucinations, increased blood pressure, fatigue |
| *Depressants* Barbiturates, Sedatives, Tranquilizers (downers, ludes, yellow jackets, reds, blues, rainbows) | Decreased alertness and muscle control, intoxication, slurred speech, drowsiness | Capsules of varying colors, longer periods of sleep | Rigidity and painful muscle contractions, emotional dizziness, clammy skin, instability, possible overdose and death, especially when mixed with alcohol |
| *Inhalants* Solvents (gas, glue, nitrites, aerosols) | Euphoria, headaches, nausea, fainting, stupor, rapid heartbeat | Odor of substance on clothing | Damage to lungs, liver, intoxication, drowsiness, poor kidneys, bone marrow, muscular control, suffocation, choking, anemia, possible stroke or sudden death |
| *Narcotics* Heroin (H, smack, junk), Morphine (M, Miss Emma), Dilaudid (Little D), Codeine (School Boy) | Insensitivity to pain, euphoria, sedation, nausea, vomiting, itchiness, watery eyes, running nose | Glassine envelopes, needles and syringes, caps or spoons, tourniquet, needle marks on arms | Lethargy, weight loss, hepatitis, slow and shallow breathing, possible death when combined with barbiturates |
| *Cocaine* (coke, snow, crack) | Short-lived euphoria changing to depression, nervousness, irritability, tightening of muscles | Glassine envelopes, razor, small spoons, odorless, bitter white crystalline powder | Shallow breathing, fever, anxiety, tremors, possible death from convulsions or respiratory arrest |
| *Marijuana* (pot, grass, hashish, joint, reefer) | Altered perceptions, dilated pupils, lack of concentration and coordination, craving for sweets, increased appetite | Plastic baggies, rolling paper, "roach" clips, odor of burnt rope hemp | Psychological dependence, increased heart rate, impaired short-term memory, anxiety, lung damage |
| *Alcohol* (beer, wine, liquor) | Slurred speech, unsteady walk, relaxed inhibitions, slowed reflexes | Smell of alcohol on breath or clothing, hangover, glazed eyes | Accidents, heart and liver damage, addiction, gateway drug |

symptoms, characteristics, and effects of various illicit substances. You should also be aware of other possible symptoms of substance abuse such as (1) a change in a student's school or work attendance or performance, (2) an alteration in personal appearance, (3) a sudden mood or attitude change, (4) a withdrawal from responsibility, (5) unusual patterns of behavior, and (6) a lack of response to environmental stimuli (Coleman, 1986; Florida Hospital, 1987; Kauffman, 1993).

## AIDS

The number of adolescents (13–19 years of age) infected with acquired immunodeficiency syndrome (AIDS) has increased from 1 case in 1981 to 2184 cases from July 1993 through June 1995 [Centers for Disease Control and Prevention (CDC), 1995]. The highest number of diagnosed cases occurs in the 20–29 age group. Since the mean incubation period for the human immunodeficiency virus (HIV) is about ten years (CDC, 1995), many of these adults were infected during their teen years. Thus, the number of reported cases probably does not reflect the seriousness of the problem in adolescence. Further studies and reports show that there are more females, more hemophiliac males, more individuals of color, and more heterosexuals infected with AIDS in the adolescent than in the adult population (CDC, 1992a; Peterson & Bircher, 1988).

Many adolescents are at risk for AIDS because of their practice of unsafe sex, experimentation with drugs, and high abuse of alcohol. A survey of students in grades 9–12 conducted by the Centers for Disease Control and Prevention (1995) found that U.S. teenagers are sexually active and frequently do not use condoms. Of those surveyed, about 54% reported sexual intercourse at least once and 19% reported multiple sex partners; the average age of first sexual experience was 16. While sexual activity is high, only 41% to 45% of the teenagers who were surveyed reported the use of condoms. Both drug and alcohol abuse lead to a lowering of inhibitions for unsafe sex (Rotheram-Borus & Koopman, 1991).

Statistics are not reported separately for students with disabilities. The Family Life Education Curriculum from the Virginia Department of Education (1991) identifies risk factors for HIV infection for students with disabilities. These factors include poor student judgment, poor self-esteem, and the exclusion of many of these students from school sex education programs. In a survey of 2150 school districts, the National School Boards Association (HIV Prevention Education for Exceptional Youth, 1991) found that only 80% of students with learning disabilities, 46% of students with moderate mental retardation, and 49% of the students with emotional disabilities received HIV-prevention education. Bell, Feraios, and Bryan (1991) found that students with learning disabilities felt less in control over exposure to AIDS and indicated less influence on behaviors than a comparable group of adolescents without learning disabilities. For this reason, most authorities feel that teachers must link AIDS education to personal teen behaviors.

Byrom and Katz (1991) have produced a sample AIDS curriculum that can be ordered from the Council for Exceptional Children at 1920 Association Drive, Reston, VA 22091-1589. The curriculum goals include identification of the cause and characteristics, methods of prevention, effects of the disease, and roles and responsibilities of various agencies, and is written for kindergarten through twelfth grade. Lerro (1994), in a special issue of *Teaching Exceptional Children*, identifies sources of materials about AIDS appropriate for adolescents with disabilities.

## Suicide

Depending on the source, suicide is listed as either the second or third leading cause of adolescent death (Psychiatry Star Team, 1995). For every 50 completed, 150 suicides are attempted (Steinberg, 1989). Although more females attempt suicide than males, they are less successful as they often select less lethal means (National Institute of Mental Health, 1995). For example, females may try pills or wrist slashing, while males tend to select guns, ropes, and automobiles. Euro-Americans have higher suicide rates than African Americans, while Native American youth have the highest (Grossman, 1991; Wyche & Rotheram-Borus, 1990).

Students with disabilities are at risk for suicide. Adolescents with schizophrenia have a high rate of suicidal deaths (Gottesman, 1991). Youth with psychotic disorders, conduct disorders, or psychoses are more at risk for suicide (Guetzloe, 1991). Female adolescents with emotional disorders were found to be particularly vulnerable to both suicide ideation (thought) and attempts (Miller, 1994).

Depression, severe drinking and drug abuse, lack of significant friendships, and stressful life situations are frequently linked to suicidal ideation and attempts (Cole, Protinsky, & Cross, 1992; Miller, 1994; Shafi, 1988). The relationship between having a friend who committed suicide and thinking of or attempting suicide has recently received much attention. In an effort to prevent this contagion effect, the American Association of Suicidology has published guidelines for the media to follow in reporting suicidal stories so as not to glamorize the act (Guetzloe, 1991).

Your primary role as a teacher is to detect the presence of any of the indicators of suicidal behavior, to refer the student for immediate help, and to provide emotional support (Guetzloe, 1991; Johnson & Maile, 1987). You should be aware of the following possible indicators (Guetzloe, 1991; Johnson, 1985; Johnson & Maile, 1987; Psychiatry Star Team, 1995): (1) decline in quality of schoolwork, (2) changes in social behavior, (3) unusual neglect of personal appearance, (4) dispensing of personal or favorite possessions as if making "final arrangements," (5) drug or alcohol use, (6) lack of concern about personal welfare, (7) withdrawal from friends and family, and (8) verbal warnings such as "I won't be a problem to you much longer" or "Nothing matters."

You should also be aware of some of the myths and realities of suicide. Table 1.4 contains some of the most common ones, adapted from Capuzzi (1988), Holden (1986), and Steinberg (1989).

**TABLE 1.4** **Myths and Realities of Suicide**

| Myth | Fact |
|------|------|
| Suicide is hereditary. | Suicide can be more prevalent in some families than others, but environmental factors also contribute. |
| Suicide attempts are impulsive reactions to immediate stress. | Suicide attempts are usually well planned, and verbal and behavior cues are given. |
| Suicide is a rich or poor person's curse. | Suicide occurs evenly in all socioeconomic levels. |
| Talking or asking about suicide increases the risk. | Often talking about it gives the adolescent "permission" to ask for assistance. |
| Adolescents who talk about suicide are just trying to get attention; adolescents who really commit suicide don't talk about it. | Talking about it is a verbal cue that the person is at risk. |
| Once an adolescent attempts suicide, he or she won't try it again. | Four out of five adolescents who commit suicide have made at least one previous attempt. |
| Confidentiality must be maintained if you learn of suicide plans. | You have an ethical responsibility to get help for that teenager. |
| Suicide occurs in bad weather, the spring, during holiday periods, or at night. | Suicide can occur at any time. |

## Teen Pregnancy

Approximately 1 million teens become pregnant annually in the United States, a higher number than in any other industrialized nation (Ventura, Taffel, Mosher, Wilson, & Henshaw, 1995). However, pregnancy rates for 18- to 19-year-old teens declined in 1993, the most recent year examined by the Centers for Disease Control and Prevention (Associated Press, 1995). Adolescents who have their first babies between 15 and 17 years of age are more likely to have children at a faster pace and to have more unwanted and out-of-wedlock births (Scott-Jones, Roland, & White, 1989).

About 60% of teen mothers are from the Euro-American culture, 40% from other cultures (Edelman, 1988). When you consider that adolescents of color make up only about 27% of the teenage population, 40% is a high percentage. However, the rate of teenage pregnancy and births correlates more to poverty levels and lack of basic skills than to ethnicity. When the factors of poverty and poor basic skills are controlled, there is no difference in rates of teenage pregnancy between Euro-Americans and other cultures (Edelman, 1988; Scott-Jones et al., 1989; Scales, 1991).

In addition to poverty and poor basic skills, female adolescents who have lower educational expectations and limited life options are at higher risk for pregnancy (Edelman, 1988; Scott-Jones et al., 1989). They often feel that they have less to lose, as they do not have many educational or occupational opportunities to begin with (Hayes, 1987). Many feel that becoming pregnant does not close any doors, since so many of the doors are closed already (Edelman, 1988).

Many adolescents elect to terminate their pregnancies through abortion (Heflin, 1992). Women who obtain legal abortions are predominantly from the Euro-American culture, unmarried, and less than 25 years old (CDC, 1992b). Those who do not terminate their pregnancies are less likely to finish school, less likely to marry, more likely to have subsequent pregnancies, and more likely to be poor (Scott-Jones, 1991). Only about 50% of teenage mothers complete high school (Upchurch & McCarthy, 1990). Two-thirds of Euro-Americans and almost all African Americans remain single (Scott-Jones, 1991). The majority of single mothers younger than 25 live in poverty. Because of poverty, children born to adolescent mothers are more likely than other children to suffer the effects of malnutrition and environmental deprivation (Rice, 1990). Adolescents with disabilities are at high risk for pregnancy because many of these youth have poor basic skills and limited choices.

Parental support and special school programs are essential to meet the needs of pregnant teens. Remaining in school gives the mother more options and the potential to break the poverty cycle (Rice, 1990; Scott-Jones et al., 1989). Scott-Jones (1993) recommends sex education, health education, and career education programs that present adolescents with positive options for adult success.

## Eating Disorders

Anorexia nervosa and bulimia are eating disorders that usually begin during the onset of adolescence. Approximately 1% of adolescent girls develop anorexia nervosa, and about 2% to 3% develop bulimia (Hoffman, 1994). Eating disorders affect females more than males and occur in all socioeconomic levels (Harvill, 1992).

According to the *American Psychiatric Association Diagnostic and Statistical Manual* (DSM-IV-R) (1994), the diagnostic criteria of anorexia nervosa and bulimia include both physical and psychological symptoms. Anorexia is classified as (1) the refusal or failure to make expected weight gain, leading to the maintenance of body weight 15% below that expected for age and height; (2) in females, the absence of at least three consecutive menstrual cycles (primary or secondary amenorrhea); (3) an intense fear of being overweight; and (4) a distorted body image. Even though individuals with anorexia nervosa often show an intense interest in food, cook for others, talk about food, and even hoard it, they refuse to eat for fear of weight gain.

Bulimia is classified as recurrent episodes of binge eating and a feeling of lack of control over food intake. Most of the time, bulimics are within normal weight range. The bulimic individual attempts to prevent weight gain by the use of laxatives or diuretics, diet pills, self-induced vomiting, rigorous exercise, or strict dieting and fasting. In the beginning stages of bulimia, the individual often binges without purging, but in the more severe stages, purging can occur as often as 10 to 12 times a day (Leon, 1991).

Both maladies can affect the electrolyte balance, the organs, the endocrine system, and other physical systems. For example, bulimics often suffer from a lack of potassium, which can cause kidney damage (Harvill, 1992). Death is an outcome in about 10% of cases of anorexia nervosa (Litt, 1991).

There is uncertainty as to the causes of these conditions. However, there appears to be a relationship to certain cultural, family, and individual factors (Fisher & Brone, 1991; Harvill, 1992; Leon, 1991; Litt, 1991). In the U.S. culture, thinness is beautiful. Young girls constantly see commercials in which the thin woman gets the man, the job, the money, and the flashy sports car, and they generally connect these symbols of success with the appearance of the woman. The families of adolescents with eating disorders are frequently overprotective and rigid (Strober & Humphrey, 1987) or chaotic (Harvill, 1992). The adolescent in an overprotective family often cannot develop a sense of personal identity and effectiveness. Frequently, she or he turns to eating to express overt rebellion and anger, as a way to separate from the family. Families of bulimic females have higher rates of eating disorders and substance abuse (Johnson & Connors, 1987) and have problems resolving conflict, generally involving the child (Harvill, 1992).

Such individual characteristics as low self-esteem, feelings of helplessness, fear of becoming fat, and depression characterize many of the students with eating disorders (Hoffman, 1994). Many females with anorexia nervosa tend to be perfectionists, while individuals with bulimia are often impulsive and abuse alcohol and drugs (Hoffman, 1994). There are no separate statistics based on ethnicity or disabilities.

Treatment includes individual and family therapy. Self-help groups such as Overeaters Anonymous are alternative treatments. Although there is not clear evidence as to the most effective intervention, treatment is more successful the earlier it occurs (Harvill, 1992; Hoffman, 1994). As a secondary teacher, you need to refer students you suspect of having eating disorders for professional help.

### Teenage Violence

Violence is becoming a common occurrence in many of our communities. "By age 18 the average child will have seen 26,000 killings on television" (Tuchscherer, 1988). Edelman (1993) cites *TV Guide* as reporting that a violent incident is shown on television on average every six minutes. It is a sad commentary on our society, when children in inner-city communities are more concerned about not what they plan to do *when* they grow up, but what they plan to do *if* they grow up (Kotlowitz, 1992).

Statistics concerning violence are high for teenagers as both perpetrators and victims. While automobile accidents are the leading cause of death for Euro-American teens, homicide is the leading cause of death for teenagers from African American backgrounds (Burbach, 1995; Scales, 1991). Adolescents (ages 12–19) are more likely to be victims of crime than any other age segment of the population (Packer, 1990). One of every 18 youth is assaulted, robbed, or raped—more than double the rate for adults (Packer, 1990). Adolescents between 12 and 14 years of age are physically abused at a higher rate than any other age group (Scales, 1991).

A measure of both community and school violence is the number of juveniles who are in trouble with the justice system. In 1992, about 500,000 juveniles were arrested for homicide, forcible rape, robbery, and assault (Burbach, 1995). Compared to Euro-American youth, males and adolescents of color are more likely to be incarcerated for committing delinquent acts (Farrington, 1987).

Students with disabilities are more frequently members of correctional than school populations (Murphy, 1986). Approximately 27% of adolescents with serious emotional disturbance who have been out of school one year, and 44% who have been out more than one year, have been arrested (Cullinan, Epstein, & Sabornie, 1992).

In addition to the juvenile correctional system, the violence found in many communities is reflected in our schools. Nearly 300,000 high school students are physically attacked each month, and one in five students in grades 9 through 12 carries a weapon (Meek, 1992). In a 1992 survey, 37% of twelfth-graders reported that they had been robbed, 26% that their property had been vandalized, 25% that they had been threatened without a weapon, and 14% that they had been threatened with a weapon (University of Michigan survey, as reported in Toch et al., 1993). Furthermore, in 1989, 5200 secondary teachers were assaulted at school (Packer, 1990). More than 150,000 students stay home from school each day because they are sick of violence and afraid for their safety (Thomas, Williams, & Zonana, 1994).

A report on gun violence in the schools found that in the four years from 1986 through 1990, 71 individuals were killed with guns, 201 were severely wounded, and 272 held hostage (Smith, 1991). It is estimated that about 22% of adolescents bring weapons to school (Walker, Colvin, & Ramsey, 1995). "In the past 20 years, youth have moved from fists to knives, to handguns, to automatic weapons in settling their conflicts" (Walker, Colvin, & Ramsey, 1995, p. 363).

Trends from national data (Moles, 1987) show that junior high schools and schools in large cities have more personal violence than senior high schools or schools in other locations. However, violence is on the rise in both suburban and rural secondary schools (Burbach, 1995).

Arguments between teen gangs are a leading cause of school gun violence (Smith, 1991). In a 1993 survey of 5000 high school students, about 17% of students reported the presence of street gangs in their schools, and of those who reported gangs, 31% indicated seeing teachers attacked or threatened and 79% reported frequent fights between students (Educational Communications, Inc., 1993, as reported in Walker et al., 1995). Teenage gangs exert great influence over their members because the gangs provide the family structure often lacking in the home setting. Being a member of a violent teen gang socializes young adolescents to a life of crime, beginning with theft and moving on to more violent infractions against society. According to a report on National Public Radio (1993), gang members who are still alive at the age of 20 usually have drug problems, are in prison for assault and battery or homicide, and possess few skills. Students with disabilities are especially vulnerable to joining gangs as many demonstrate a greater willingness to conform to peer pressure to engage in antisocial acts (Bryan, Werner, & Pearl, 1982) and a greater inclination toward impulsive behaviors (Blackman & Goldstein, 1982).

Some of the recommendations to increase school safety include locker searches, prohibition of book bags, and random searches using metal detectors (Walker et al., 1995). Full-time police are assigned to many middle schools, junior highs, and senior highs. The National School Safety Center (1995) recommends limiting student movement by requiring hall passes and dispensing them infrequently, training staff to monitor exits, hallways, and entrances, and requiring all visitors to sign in at the office. Other recommendations for keeping schools safe include introducing curricula that teach conflict resolution, involving the public in school activities, improving school leadership skills, promoting systemwide efforts to combat drug abuse in schools and the surrounding communities, eliminating gang activity, implementing a clear, comprehensive code of school conduct, and encouraging students to report weapon violations (Juvenile Justice Bulletin, 1990; *School Violence Alert,* 1995). Some schools are training students as mediators to use active listening, paraphrasing, and other skills to resolve peers' arguments with words, rather than fists (Toch, 1993). Resources for conflict resolution curricula include NAME (National Association for Mediation in Education), 425 Amity Street, Amherst, MA 01002, and Project SMART (School Mediator's Alternative Resolution Team), c/o Victims Service Agency, 50 Court Street, 8th Floor, Brooklyn, NY 11201 (Meek, 1992). For a listing of additional resources, see Meek (1992, p. 52).

As a teacher, you may be assigned such duties as patrolling the halls or cafeterias, or you may be involved in teaching a conflict resolution curriculum. If you promote an atmosphere of high expectations and respect for your students and you provide positive reinforcement of appropriate behaviors, you can prevent many violent discipline problems from occurring in the class (Greenbaum, Turner, & Stephens, 1989).

## Dropouts

In 1993, about 14% of all students dropped out of school (National Center for Education Statistics, 1994). In many states, the dropout rate is more than one in four (McWhirter et al., 1993). Many youth drop out before entering tenth grade (Carnegie Council, 1989). Hispanic youth generally drop out of school more than any other group (National Center for Education Statistics, 1994). Approximately 30% of students with learning disabilities, 50% of students with emotional disabilities, and 31% of students with mental retardation do not complete school (Hebbeler, 1993c). Once students with disabilities drop out, they are less likely than other dropouts to return to high school or to get a GED. Only 2% ever return after dropping out, and only 3% go on to get a GED (Marder, 1992).

Many students who drop out of school come from economically disadvantaged backgrounds. They have a history of poor school performance, low school involvement, poor performance on standardized tests of achievement and intelligence, and negative school experiences (Rice, 1990; Santrock, 1987; Steinberg, 1989; McWhirter et al., 1993). However, roughly 15% of students drop out because they are bored, lack ambition, or because of personal reasons such as wanting to start work (Santrock, 1987). Parents of adolescents with learning disabilities and emotional handicaps report that a high percentage of their children drop out of school because they don't like school and are bored (Wagner, 1991b). Another major reason reported by parents of adolescents with learning disabilities is that their children are not doing well in school, while parents of adolescents with emotional disabilities report that behavior problems interfere with their children's school completion (Wagner, 1991b).

After studying more than 400 students with mild disabilities, Blackorby, Edgar, and Kortering (1991) discovered that African American students and students with behavior disorders were the most likely to drop out. The dropout rate is especially high for students with behavior disorders who have experienced numerous changes in educational service placements, school transfers, and previous releases (dropping out and returning to drop out again) (Kortering & Blackorby, 1992).

Dropouts are more likely to experience unemployment, live at or near poverty levels, be involved in delinquent and criminal activities, and depend on government-subsidized programs (McWhirter et al., 1993). As a teacher, you can play an important role in reducing the number of dropouts. If you select appropriate and motivational curriculum materials, employ effective teaching and management strategies, and show a genuine concern for your students, you will make schools a better place for many adolescents at risk for dropping out of school. Additionally, a curriculum that requires students to identify goals and implement plans for meeting these goals benefits potential dropouts (McWhirter et al., 1993).

Throughout our review of the various problems that affect adolescents, there is a pervasive central theme to the recommended interventions, whether the issue is drug abuse or pregnancy. "The focus for all strategies needs to be on the four senses that matter to youth: a sense of belonging, a sense of usefulness in life, a sense of competency and of being valued by significant others, and a sense of influence and self-empowerment over one's own life" (Arkin & Funkhouser, 1991, p. 92).

**COMPREHENSION MONITORING OF KEY CONCEPTS**

### Problems of Adolescence

*Substance Abuse*

1. Adolescents abuse alcohol the most, then cigarettes, and third, marijuana.

2. Adolescents with disabilities generally abuse drugs at the same rate as adolescents without disabilities. However, those students with behavior disorders have a higher rate of drug use.

3. Students who abuse substances are more likely to be in automobile accidents, commit crimes, drop out of school, contract AIDS, and attempt suicide.

*AIDS*

4. Adolescents are at risk for AIDS because many practice unsafe sex, have inaccurate knowledge about AIDS, and do not change their sexual behaviors based on their knowledge of AIDS.

5. Adolescents with disabilities are at risk for AIDS because they often do not receive HIV-prevention education and frequently make poor decisions about personal behaviors.

6. In comparison with the adult population, more adolescent females, hemophiliacs, individuals of color, and heterosexuals are infected with AIDS.

*Suicide*

7. Suicide is either the second or third leading cause of adolescent death.

8. Students who suffer from schizophrenia, psychotic disorders, conduct disorders, or psychoses are at risk for suicide.

9. As a teacher, you should be able to identify indicators of suicidal behavior, refer the student for help, and provide emotional support.

*Teen Pregnancy*

10. Females who live in poverty and who have poor basic skills, lower education expectations, and limited life options are more likely to become pregnant during the teenage years.

11. The children of teenage mothers are at risk for future school problems.

*Eating Disorders*

12. The individual with anorexia nervosa frequently refuses to eat, while the bulimic individual binges and purges.

13. There is a relationship between eating disorders and cultural, family, and individual factors.

*Teenage Violence*

14. Violence in the community is reflected in the schools in the number of attacks or threats of attack on students and teachers, the amount of property vandalized or stolen, the number of students carrying handguns to school, and the proliferation of gangs.

15. Students with disabilities are at risk for violence, as many demonstrate a greater willingness to conform to peer pressure to engage in antisocial behaviors, and many are members of the delinquent population.

*Dropouts*

16. A high percentage of students with disabilities, especially those with emotional disabilities, drop out of school.

17. Dropouts are more likely to experience unemployment, poverty, criminal activity, and welfare.

18. Most students drop out of school because of poor school performance, minimal school involvement, and negative school experiences.

---

 Now that you have read Chapter 1, reflect on your responses at the beginning of the chapter and complete this post organizer.

1. Look back at your list of characteristics of typical adolescents and those with mild disabilities.
   a. Compare your lists to the characteristics described in Chapter 1.
   b. Evaluate your list for accuracy.
   c. Revise your list as needed.
   d. Share your list with the rest of the class.

2. Develop five questions related to adolescent problems and issues, and interview one adolescent who receives special education services and one who does not. Compare their responses to your questions.

# Regular and Special Education Programs in Middle Schools and High Schools

© Elizabeth Crews

**CHAPTER HIGHLIGHTS**

*Secondary Education Programs*

*Demands and Expectations of the Secondary Setting*

*Secondary Special Education Programs*

*Secondary Program Policies and Their Effect on Students with Mild Disabilities*

*School Reform and Restructuring and the Impact on Secondary Special Education*

*Special Educators in the Secondary Setting*

---

 Before you read Chapter 2, use your prior knowledge to complete this advance organizer.

1. List five demands and expectations that you experienced as an adolescent.

2. Reflect on your own secondary experiences and describe your school's discipline policies and graduation requirements. Discuss your experiences with your peers.

3. Predict the skills and competencies middle and high school students will need in the year 2000.

---

The growth of secondary school programs in the United States during the twentieth century has been impressive. In 1900, only about 10% of adolescents graduated from high school (U.S. Bureau of the Census, 1992), compared to approximately 86% who graduate today (National Center for Education Statistics, 1994). The goals of secondary education and program offerings, which used to be primarily academic, are now more diverse. However, growth has been accompanied by organizational problems and concerns.

The purpose of this chapter is to discuss the typical secondary program and the interfacing of special education programs at the middle and high school levels. First, we examine the history, organization, structure, curriculum, demands, and expectations of the regular secondary setting. Next, we examine secondary special education programs, highlighting the history, the impact of legislation, the organization, structure, and curriculum. Then, we discuss the effect of graduation requirements, discipline policies, and tracking on students with disabilities. Following that, we describe school reform and restructuring and the impact on secondary special education. We conclude with a description of the roles of special educators in the secondary setting.

## Secondary Education Programs

It is essential for special education teachers of adolescents with mild disabilities to have an understanding of the typical school setting. Without an understanding of the history, organization, structure, and curriculum, special education teachers will find it difficult to fulfill the varied roles and responsibilities present in today's middle schools and high schools.

### History of Secondary Education Programs

Our first secondary schools looked much different from those of today. Men from privileged families attended the country's first high school. The goal was to prepare these young men for college and, eventually, for service to state and church (Boyer, 1983). Public high schools did not become popular until 1874, when the Supreme Court of Massachusetts ruled that taxes could be levied to support public high schools. Other states followed, and public high schools began to compete with private academies. At this time, elementary schools usually comprised grades 1–8 and secondary schools grades 9–12. However, considerable criticism was leveled at this 8-4 grade organization (Eichhorn, 1991). Among the critics was Charles W. Eliot, president of Harvard University. Eliot supported an earlier entry and graduation age for the average college student and an introduction of some of the high school subjects into the traditional elementary grades.

As a result of the criticism, the National Education Association (NEA) appointed a number of national committees to consider the direction and organization of public schools (Mason, 1995). One of the recommendations from the national committees was the introduction of middle-level education to serve as a transition between elementary and high schools (Brough, 1995). It was hoped that middle-level education would consider the unique characteristics and needs of young adolescents, prevent school dropout, and help students adjust to high school (Brough, 1995; Clark & Clark, 1994; Mason, 1995). In the early 1900s, many school districts, especially those in urban areas, reorganized their schools into grades 1–6 (elementary), 7–9 (junior high), and 10–12 (high school) (Eichhorn, 1991).

In the late 1950s, with the launch of Sputnik I, the school organization was again questioned. Many argued that a return to a four-year high school would increase academic excellence and that ninth grade with its requirements of a fixed number of credits matched the high school curriculum (Van Til, 1978). Other proponents of a four-year high school argued that biological maturity was occurring at a much earlier age and that, therefore, sixth-graders were more like eighth-graders (Mason, 1995). Additionally, many junior high programs had become narrowly focused on subject matter rather than students, promoted extracurricular rather than intramural activities, and fostered curriculum depth rather than exploration (Cuban, 1992). The junior high had become much like the senior high instead of serving as a transitional bridge between elementary and high school.

The civil rights movement also had an effect on changing the middle-level organization (Eichhorn, 1991; Van Til, 1978). Since middle schools encompass larger geographical areas, it was believed that integrating students at an earlier age, sixth grade instead of seventh, would bring about more racial harmony. By 1970, middle schools had replaced 80% of the nation's 9,500 junior high schools (Wiles & Bondi, 1986). Alexander and McEwin (1989) report that from 1970/71 to 1986/87, the number of schools in the grades 6–8 configuration (middle schools) grew from 1663 to 4329—an increase of 160%.

## Organization, Structure, and Curriculum of Secondary Programs

We concentrate here on the organization, structure, and curriculum of middle schools and high schools. The curriculum of junior highs tends to be similar to that of either middle schools or high schools (Roth, 1991). For example, some junior highs emphasize subject matter and the prerequisites to enter high school. Others emphasize a concern for the whole student and affiliate more with the teaming approach, an organization pattern found in many middle schools.

### Middle Schools

Mason (1995) describes four approaches to scheduling used in most middle schools: (1) self-contained schedules, (2) modular schedules, (3) departmentalized schedules, and (4) block-of-time or interdisciplinary schedules. Self-contained schedules assign students to a single teacher, who then schedules and teaches those students. Mason (1995) notes that this approach is often used for at-risk students or students with special needs.

Modular schedules allow teachers to request the number of 15- or 25-minute periods they will need in a day. Classes may be organized around a brief 15-minute class or a 75-minute laboratory. Departmentalized schedules divide the day into six, seven, or eight standard periods, similar to high school scheduling. With departmentalized scheduling, teachers tend to teach their own isolated subject matter (Clark & Clark, 1994; Mason, 1995).

In the block-of-time or interdisciplinary schedule, students are assigned to teams of teachers who teach different subject matter. The students are often organized by grade-level teams. The teachers share planning periods and hold team meetings to discuss program and student issues. This organization promotes integration of curriculum around interdisciplinary units. For example, at Southwest Middle School in Orange County, Florida, the sixth-grade team of teachers integrated their individual subject areas around the theme of a medieval history unit. The math teachers had students draw angles to make stained glass windows. The science teachers introduced the study of astronomy, a popular science of that period. In language arts, the students designed a castle and wrote about the people who lived in it (see Figure 2.1). In world cultures, the sixth-graders designed a coat of arms for their family and wrote oaths of allegiance.

Self-contained and modular scheduling are less frequently used than departmentalized and interdisciplinary. Approximately 57% of principals who replied to a National Association of Secondary School Principals (NASSP) survey reported that their schools employed teams of students and teachers in interdisciplinary scheduling (Valentine, Clark, Irvin, Keefe, & Melton, 1993).

There are three major curriculum components in middle school: essential skills, subject content, and personal development (Wiles & Bondi, 1986). The academic areas of language arts and mathematics provide essential skill instruction as a part of coursework. Social studies, science, and other subject content areas are also required. To assist in personal development, student activities and clubs are an important part of the program. In

**FIGURE 2.1** Middle School Student's Story

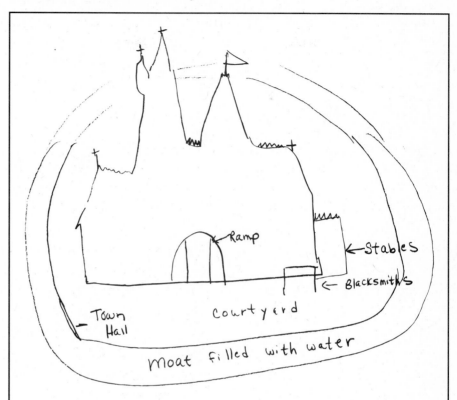

As you can see from my castl, there are many people who live under it's roof or should I say, courtyard. My father, the King, and my mother, the Queen, live there along with my three brothers and two sisters. There are many knights, squires, a blacksmith, three cooks, and many butiful ladies-in-waiting to my mother and sisters. My older brother and I are training to be knights, but my younger brother and sister are both general pests. They try to sail on the moat. Can you imagine with all the garbage and other waste there. Come visit our castl anytime and we'll open the ramp for you.

some middle schools, there are not only guidance counselors, but teacher-based guidance programs. In these teacher-based guidance programs, teachers meet with students on a regular basis to deal with personal and social concerns of adolescents.

The curriculum is also more exploratory in nature and less specialized than the high school curriculum (Lounsberry, 1991; Wiles & Bondi, 1986).

Although the course offerings vary greatly from school to school, often they include art, music, home economics, and industrial arts. Other exploratory electives may encompass a variety of short-term minicourse offerings in computers, drama and speech, health and sex education, and other areas of interest to this age student. Generally, middle school educators oppose interschool athletic contests, but they do occur (Lounsberry, 1991).

### High Schools

In high school, students are organized by grades across subjects while teachers are organized by subjects across grades. Teachers may never see the same student twice during the day, as many of them teach more than 100 students a day. Students may receive instruction from four to seven different teachers daily (Houston, Clift, Freiberg, & Warner, 1988).

High school teachers are assigned to departments based on subject areas. For example, teachers certified in math are members of the math department, while teachers certified in English are members of the English department. Department chairs or faculty frequently operate as isolated entities deciding on courses to offer, course curriculum, and instructors (Siskin, 1991).

Periods, usually 40 to 60 minutes long, divide the day. Recently, some high schools have been experimenting with block scheduling (Orange County Public Schools, 1995). In block scheduling, each class period may last 100 minutes and subjects may vary daily. For example, one of our interns teaches English from 7:15 to 9:06 to her students with mild disabilities on odd days and Learning Strategies from 7:15 to 9:06 on even days in a high school experimenting with block scheduling. Table 2.1 contains suggestions for a sample daily lesson plan for the block schedule.

Most of todays' high schools are comprehensive in that they offer college preparatory, vocational, and general studies curricula. A few school districts sponsor magnet or alternative schools with specialized courses. Typically, about 50% of all students are in the college preparatory track and 20% in the vocational track (Eccles, 1991). Students in the vocational track generally spend some time in general education courses and the rest in specialized courses such as on-the-job training. Students attend the various programs based on their performance on standardized tests and their grade point averages. Eccles (1991) reports that the invalid criteria of racial or ethnic group membership and social status are frequently used for placement.

The high school curriculum is tied to the Carnegie unit. First created as a way for colleges to standardize the evaluation of high school programs, the Carnegie unit is the standard unit used to measure high school work. One Carnegie unit equates to one 40- to 60-minute period per day for 36 to

**TABLE 2.1** **Sample Lesson Plan Ideas for Block Schedules**

| Time | Instructional arrangement | Activity |
|---|---|---|
| 5–15 min. | Individual | Open class with a routine, such as silent reading, journal writing, learning log, vocabulary, skill practice, question of the day, riddle to solve, etc. |
| (Take attendance, collect or check homework, and answer individual questions.) | | |
| 5–15 min. | Group | Help students organize thoughts. |
| (Review previous lesson). | | |
| 5–15 min. | Group | Complete advance organizer. |
| (Preview and share rationale for today's lesson). | | |
| 20–30 min. | Group | Discuss with recorder taking notes on board or computer and distribute to all. |
| | | Lecture with questions. |
| | | Use problem-solving techniques. |
| | | Use Direct Instruction curriculum. |
| (Introduce new content.) | | |
| 20–25 min. | Partner or small group | Skill practice, lab experiments, group projects, peer tutoring, group presentations. |
| (Practice and apply new content with teacher circulating and assisting partners or small groups.) | | |
| 10–20 min. | Individual | Self- or group evaluation, compile information in notebook or portfolio. Write down homework assignment. |
| (End with summary and independent practice.) | | |

*Source:* Adapted from Orange Country Public Schools, 1994.

40 weeks. Thus, a full semester course carries one unit of Carnegie credit. Most states have established a minimum number of Carnegie units for high school graduation (Hall & Gerber, 1985), usually 20 or 21 units (Houston et al., 1988). Carnegie units are usually required in English, mathematics, science, and social studies for graduation. In addition to required subjects, high school students may also choose elective courses.

In a typical high school classroom, the teacher covers a required, predetermined amount of material each semester (Fenzel & Blyth, 1991).

Traditionally, the teacher presents the segmented information in lecture format to large classes of students and measures students' progress on a normative scale. The advent of block scheduling of long periods of time for each class period may change this traditional instructional strategy.

## Demands and Expectations of the Secondary Setting

The transitions from elementary school to middle school to high school often entail drastic changes in the roles, activities, and interpersonal interactions of adolescents. As adolescents face the transition to middle school, they must deal with increased school and parental demands, early pubertal development, and changing peer relationships, all of which lead to transition difficulties. We examine these demands and expectations as they relate to setting, academic performance, social behaviors, and school survival demands.

### Setting Demands

The secondary setting is less personalized and intimate than the elementary setting. Secondary students must organize and retrieve needed materials from lockers, work a combination lock, follow a schedule, and navigate large complex buildings and grounds to adequately function in the secondary setting (Eccles & Midgley, 1989; Robinson, Braxdale, & Colson, 1985).

### Academic Demands

Secondary students must use basic skills as tools. There are substantial reading demands in all content areas, with texts often at high readability levels. Students must be able to integrate basic skills into the writing of term papers and reports. They must be able to sequence thoughts and ideas as they participate in oral activities. They frequently learn information in a whole-class, lecture-type format (Silverman, Zigmond, & Sansone, 1983).

Students are also evaluated differently at the secondary level than at the elementary level (Bursuck, Kinder, & Epstein, 1989; Eccles & Midgley, 1989; Reid & Hresko, 1982; Robinson et al., 1985). Secondary teachers usually have higher standards in grading than elementary teachers. They reward students for individual achievements, and use paper-and-pencil tests to determine student grades. Often students fail before they can do something about it, as monitoring of progress occurs too late for the student to effect grade changes (Reid & Hresko, 1982). The grades of Euro-American boys tend to decline (Fenzel, Blyth, & Simmons, 1991), as do the grades of African American boys and girls, in the middle-level grades (Simmons, Black, & Zhou, 1991).

## School Survival Demands

In a survey of the perceptions of regular and special educators concerning school success, both groups of teachers rated "turning in work on time" as most important for school success (Bursuck et al., 1989). The next three items were "attending class everyday," "accepting consequences of behavior," and "organizing time and paper for studying." All of these fall into the area of school survival skills. Students are expected to develop effective study habits, complete assignments without reminders, and request assistance when needed (Fenzel, 1989; Schumaker, Deshler, Alley, & Warner, 1983).

## Social Demands

Adolescents are expected to participate in extracurricular activities and to identify both overt and covert rules in all classes. They are expected to respond appropriately to feedback, handle feelings of anonymity, and resist inappropriate peer pressures (Fenzel et al., 1991). Students must learn to mingle with students from different ethnic backgrounds and background experiences (Simmons & Blyth, 1987).

---

**COMPREHENSION MONITORING OF KEY CONCEPTS**

### Secondary Education Programs

*History of Secondary Education Programs*

1. More public secondary schools came into existence when the courts ruled that taxes could be levied to support the schools.

2. Proponents for the middle-level configuration of grades 6–8 argue that the ninth-grade curriculum is more like the high school curriculum and that academic excellence is increased when ninth grade is included in high school.

3. Other arguments for a grades 6–8 organization include the earlier maturation of students and more opportunity for racial integration.

*(continued on next page)*

*Organization, Structure, and Curriculum
of Secondary Programs*

4. The most popular organizational structures for middle school are block-of-time or interdisciplinary schedules and departmentalized schedules.

5. Middle school curriculum consists of essential skills, subject content, and personal development.

6. In high school, students are organized by grades across subject areas and teachers are assigned to departments.

7. Course credit is tied to the Carnegie unit, and students are offered college preparatory, general education, and vocational programs in the comprehensive high school.

*Demands and Expectations of the Secondary Setting*

8. Secondary students are expected to navigate through large buildings, to use basic skills as tools for learning, to be independent learners, and to interact appropriately in different settings.

9. The grades of Euro-American boys tend to decline, as do the grades of African American boys and girls, in the middle-level grades.

## Secondary Special Education Programs

Our examination of special education programs at the secondary level begins with a brief history of such programs. We next describe the legislation in special education, vocational education, and vocational rehabilitation that has affected the services for adolescents and adults with disabilities. We conclude with a description of the organization, structure, and curriculum of secondary special education programs. As you read this section, notice how both historical developments and legislative mandates have directly influenced secondary programming in special education, especially the organization, structure, and curriculum.

### History of Secondary Special Education

Before compulsory school attendance, many adolescents with mild disabilities probably did not complete school. As Pritchard (1963) points out, not all forms of retardation were noticeable before the mass general education movement in the 1900s, as it was not unusual to find individuals who could not read or write. In a description of the period between the First and Second World Wars, Cruickshank (1967) found that most students with mild retardation remained in regular classes year after year without learning much.

Once schools began to educate more of the population, school personnel began to distinguish those students who could succeed in the general classroom from those who could not (Winzer, 1993). Many of the students who could not succeed attended special classes or special schools (Sigmon, 1987). Frequently, an adolescent with disabilities was either assigned to the lower track in a secondary school or placed in a segregated setting.

During these years, the focus of most special education programs was on delivering services to students with disabilities in the elementary grades. Many educators believed that working with students earlier would "cure" them of their problems by the time they reached secondary school. In addition, many educators felt that secondary students with disabilities had characteristics or needs similar to those of elementary-level students (Zigmond, 1990).

The push for programs for secondary students with mild disabilities did not receive major impetus until the 1970s. Public Law 94-142, with its provision to educate all handicapped children from age 3 to 21, forced school districts to develop secondary-level special education programs. Until this time, few school districts provided programs for secondary students with learning disabilities (Zigmond, 1990). In a comparison of programs for students with emotional disabilities between 1964 and 1986, Grosenick, George, and George (1987) note the expansion from the original start of programs at only the elementary level to the current inclusion of preschool and secondary school levels. Thus, for many public school districts, programming for secondary students with mild disabilities is a relatively new experience.

## Legislation Impacting Secondary Special Education

Legislation in special education, vocational education, and vocational rehabilitation has impacted curriculum and programs for adolescents and adults with disabilities. The legislation significantly affects secondary special education programming by expanding the environments in which special education services are delivered, emphasizing essential transition services to postschool employment and community living, adding to the traditional list of related services, and increasing accessibility to programs for adolescents and adults with disabilities.

1. Public Law 98-199, the Amendments to the Education for All Handicapped Children Act (EHA) of 1983, authorized funding to create programs for adolescents with disabilities in the transition from school to adult life. The basic tenets of Section 626 of PL 98-199, Secondary Education and Transitional Services for Handicapped Youth, are to improve programs for secondary special education and to assist in the transition process by coordinating education, training, and related services.

2. Public Law 101-476, the Individuals with Disabilities Education Act (IDEA), originally titled the Education of the Handicapped Act Amendments of 1990, mandated
   - education in all settings, such as training centers and the workplace
   - transition services as part of special education and related services
   - inclusion of transition objectives for students with disabilities in the IEP (no later than age 16)
   - the addition of rehabilitation counseling and social work services to the list of related services

3. Public Law 93-112, the Vocational Rehabilitation Act of 1973, resulted in a marked emphasis on services for individuals with disabilities (Rusch & Phelps, 1987). Section 503 addressed the hiring, training, and retention of employees with disabilities, while Section 504 guaranteed program accessibility and eliminated discrimination for individuals with disabilities. Any institution receiving federal funding that violated these mandates would lose its federal financial support.

4. Public Law 101-336, the Americans with Disabilities Act (ADA), expanded the intent of the Vocational Rehabilitation Act of 1973 by specifying and defining the rights of individuals with disabilities in private-sector employment, public services, transportation, and telecommunications.

5. The Carl D. Perkins Vocational and Applied Technology Education Act (1990) mandated that
   - students/families be informed about vocational education opportunities by age 14
   - counseling services and curriculum adaptations be provided to facilitate adjustment to postschool employment
   - a full range of vocational options be accessible to students with disabilities, with vocational education provided in the least restrictive environment for individuals with disabilities who need this service

6. The School to Work Opportunities Act (1993) funded states to institute a performance-based education and training system to prepare students for their first job or to enter postsecondary programs.

## Organization, Structure, and Curriculum of Secondary Special Education Programs

Of the high school population (grades 9–12) of students with disabilities, about 56% are students with learning disabilities, 11% are students with emotional disabilities, and 24% are students with mental disabilities (Wagner, Blackorby, Cameto, Hebbeler, & Newman, 1993). Most of the students with mild disabilities attend comprehensive secondary schools (Hayward, Thorne, & Ha, 1989). Students with learning disabilities and students with emotional handicaps spend about 75% of their time in regular education classes, while students with mental retardation spend only about 44% of their time in regular classes (Wagner, 1993). The courses in the mainstream classes are most often at the basic, remedial, or on-grade level, with very few at the college prep level (Wagner, 1991b; Wagner, 1993). Students with learning disabilities tend to take fewer remedial-level courses than do students with either emotional or mental disabilities. Students with mild disabilities most often enroll in basic or remedial math and science courses. Support for these students while in the regular classroom usually includes monitoring student progress and adapting exams, especially changing the allotted amount of time (Newman, 1993). Virtually all students with disabilities attend schools in which special educators provide consultant services to regular educators (Wagner, 1991b; Cameto, 1993).

Students with mild disabilities also spend time in special education settings, most often in resource rooms with an emphasis on basic skills, assistance in regular education assignments, or in compensatory education (Hebbeler, 1993a). They are most likely to take English, followed by math, social studies, and science, in the special education placement (Newman, 1993). Students with mental disabilities also spend a considerable amount of time in vocational special education classes (Wagner, 1991b; Newman, 1993).

Prevocational education, occupational vocational education, life skills training, and transition planning are important parts of the high school curriculum for special education students (Blackorby, 1993). Prevocational classes include such topics as job-search skills, job-related social skills, and the nature of the world of work and careers. Occupational vocational classes include health-related occupations (such as dental assistant or nursing aide), agriculture (such as horticulture or resource conservation), and occupational home economics (such as child care or food preparation). Life skills training involves home care, meal preparation, money management, and social skills (Cameto, 1993). Transition training involves providing experiences that will assure successful movement from high school to postsecondary education and training, independent living,

**TABLE 2.2** **Percentage of Credits Earned in Various Courses**

| Disability | Academic | Vocational | Life skills | Others | Total credits |
|---|---|---|---|---|---|
| Learning | 55.0% | 24.6% | 5.6% | 14.8% | 22.4 |
| Emotional | 58.2% | 22.8% | 5.5% | 13.5% | 21.8 |
| Mental | 51.9% | 27.3% | 7.3% | 13.5% | 22.0 |

*Source:* From "The Transition Experience of Young People with Disabilities" by M. Wagner et al., 1993, Menlo Park, CA: SRI International (ERIC Document Reproduction ED365 086).

and recreation (Cameto, 1993). See Table 2.2 for a breakdown of credits earned in academic, vocational, life skills, and other courses by students with mild disabilities.

The curriculum is quite different during the last two years of high school than in the first two for students with emotional disabilities and learning disabilities (Wagner, 1993). In grades 9 and 10, these students tend to take academic classes and some vocational classes, mostly in the regular setting. They receive more failing grades and a lower level of support services. In grades 11 and 12, the curriculum is more flexible, and students often enroll in vocational courses, life skills courses, and work-experience (work for pay in real jobs) programs (Blackorby, 1993; Wagner, Blackorby, & Hebbeler, 1993). Students receive more tutoring support, and the rate of failure is lower.

In all grades, students with mental disabilities are enrolled in more prevocational, occupational vocational, and life skills training classes (Blackorby, 1993). They receive consistent support in these classes.

Most high school programs are inclusive (Wagner, 1993). The following factors correlate to the amount of time students with disabilities spend in regular classes (Hebbeler, 1993b; Wagner, 1993; Wagner, Blackorby, Cameto, Hebbeler, & Newman, 1993; Wagner, Blackorby, & Hebbeler, 1993; Wagner & Shaver, 1989):

1. Students at small schools spend more time in the mainstream than students at large schools.

2. Students enrolled in higher-income schools spend more time in regular classes than students enrolled in lower-income schools.

3. Schools that offer support to mainstream students or teachers and provide in-service training to regular education teachers are more successful in integrating their special students.

4. Enrollment in more nonacademic courses leads to greater regular education integration.

5. Students with higher functional abilities and IQ scores spend more time in regular classes.

6. Students in earlier grades spend more time mainstreamed.

7. Students who live in the West North Central regions spend more time in regular classes.

8. Taking an occupation-oriented vocational course leads to greater regular education integration.

---

**COMPREHENSION  MONITORING  OF  KEY  CONCEPTS**

### Secondary Special Education Programs

*History of Secondary Special Education*

1. Before compulsory school attendance, adolescents with special needs probably did not complete high school.

2. When school attendance became compulsory, adolescents with special needs were frequently assigned either to lower-track classes or to segregated settings.

3. Until the passage of PL 94-142, the focus of most special education programs was on elementary-age students.

*Legislation Impacting Secondary Special Education*

4. Federal legislation in special education, such as the Amendments to the Education for All Handicapped Children Act (EHA) and the Individuals with Disabilities Education Act (IDEA), has resulted in the right to a free and appropriate education in the least restrictive environment, nondiscriminatory testing, due process, and transition planning for students with disabilities.

5. Federal legislation in vocational education and rehabilitation, such as the Rehabilitation Act of 1973, Americans with Disabilities Act, Carl D. Perkins Act, and the School to Work Opportunities Act, has assisted adolescents with mild disabilities in receiving vocational education, counseling, training, and transition assistance.

*Organization, Structure, and Curriculum
of Secondary Special Education Programs*

6. Most of the students with mild disabilities attend comprehensive secondary schools.

*(continued on next page)*

7. Students with learning disabilities tend to take fewer remedial-level courses than do students with either emotional or mental disabilities.

8. Students with learning disabilities and students with emotional disabilities spend most of their time in regular academic courses.

9. In the earlier grades, students with learning disabilities and students with emotional disabilities take more academic courses, fail more courses, and receive fewer support services; in the later grades, they take more vocational and life skills courses, fail fewer courses, and receive more support services.

10. Students with mental disabilities spend more time in special education settings and take more prevocational, vocational, and life skills courses.

11. The size of the school, the income level, the amount of support offered to teachers, enrollment in nonacademic courses, IQ scores, grade level, and geographical location affect the success of mainstreaming students with disabilities.

## Secondary Program Policies and Their Effect on Students with Mild Disabilities

In this section, we examine the policies regarding graduation requirements, discipline procedures, and tracking in the secondary school. We discuss, in particular, the effect of these policies on students with mild disabilities.

### Graduation Requirements

As discussed previously, most states require a specific number of Carnegie units for students to graduate from high school and receive a standard diploma. Most states offer several alternatives for students with disabilities to exit high school, including a standard diploma, a special diploma, a certificate of attendance, or a certificate of achievement. A few states require that students with disabilities complete the same number of Carnegie units in courses with the same requirements as students in regular education to earn a standard diploma. However, the majority of states grant students with disabilities a standard diploma even if their course content or course instruction is modified (Bodner, Clark, & Mellard, 1987; Hall & Gerber, 1985). Frequently, local school districts determine the type of diploma and graduation requirements for students with disabilities.

In a review of the laws pertaining to the issuing of diplomas, Kortering, Julnes, and Edgar (1990) note that students with disabilities and their parents must be notified of the type of diploma the students will receive and that reasonable accommodations must be made for them to satisfy standard requirements. The type of diploma awarded often limits the options available to students in postsecondary education and future employment (Hall & Gerber, 1985; Bodner et al., 1987).

In addition to requiring a specific number of Carnegie units for graduation, some states require students to pass a minimum competency test (MCT) for graduation (Bodner et al., 1987). Here again, requirements for students with disabilities vary, with some states requiring that these students also pass an MCT and others exempting them (Education Commission of the States, 1985). Almost all of the states that require students with disabilities to pass the MCT permit adaptations, such as extended time limits, administration in small groups, separate test directions, and administration by special education teachers. The courts have upheld the rights of states to deny a standard high school diploma to students who do not pass a competency test as long as the students receive adequate notice to prepare for the test and the preparation covers material on the test (Kortering et al., 1990; Vitello, 1988). Since graduation requirements vary from state to state, you need to examine the local school district's requirements for issuing a regular diploma.

## Discipline Policies

Many secondary schools expect students with mild disabilities to follow the same code of conduct that the nondisabled population follows. Frequently, students must pass a test regarding school discipline policies. In addition to a code of conduct, some secondary schools use the same schoolwide or teamwide discipline procedures. For example, each teacher assigned to the seventh-grade team may adopt the same rules and consequences for following or not following the rules. Having a consistent set of expectations often benefits students with mild disabilities as they interact with various teachers. Consistent teacher and administrative expectations for both academic and social behaviors is one of the characteristics associated with effective secondary schools (Fenzel & Blyth, 1991).

The most common interventions in secondary schools for antisocial behavior are suspension and expulsion (Coleman, 1986). However, there are legal restrictions on the use of expulsion and suspension for students who are certified as disabled. On January 20, 1988, the Supreme Court issued a ruling in *Honig* v. *Doe* that is binding on all schools in the United States. The case involved indefinite suspension of two California students for dangerous and disruptive conduct, related to their disabilities. The court ruled that PL 94-142 prohibits schools from unilaterally excluding children with disabilities from the classroom for behaviors related to the handicapping condition (Yee, 1989). However, the court further declared that the schools may use the normal disciplinary procedures of "study carrels, timeout, detention, the restriction of privileges, and temporary suspension of up to 10 school days" (Yee, 1989, p. 65).

There is some confusion as to what the 10-day temporary suspension provision actually means. Some school districts interpret it to mean that a 10-day suspension can be dispensed for each incident (Kerr & Nelson, 1989). The Office of Civil Rights offers the opinion that suspensions that total more than 10 cumulative days in a school year violate the rights of students with disabilities (Sarzynski, 1988).

Kerr and Nelson (1989) recommend home visitation, assigned homework, and instruction of parents on how to manage the child during the exclusion period. Unfortunately, in most instances, the school does not institute or monitor a home program during suspension.

## Tracking

Tracking, or stratification, is block scheduling of students based on ability grouping. Schools often use standard reading scores to group students in the middle grades (Epstein & MacIver, 1989). Surveys of middle schools find that most use at least some degree of ability grouping (Braddock, 1990; Valentine et al., 1993). Braddock (1990) reports that about 20% of middle schools assign students to all of their classes according to ability. However, students in middle school are tracked more frequently in reading, math, and English classes (Braddock, 1990).

Ability grouping and curriculum offerings are the two types of tracking dominant in high schools (Games, 1991). Students with high ability enroll in honors English classes, students with average ability in regular English, and students with low ability in basic English classes. Students are also tracked into college preparatory, general education, and vocational programs. As we stated previously, students with mild disabilities are more frequently enrolled in general education and vocational classes (Wagner, 1993). Unfortunately, for many students, once they enter the lower track, they never exit it. Fenzel and Blyth (1991) report that high school students tend to remain in the same track that they were in during middle school.

Logically, it seems that homogeneous grouping should benefit students, as teachers should be able to focus instruction and subject content more appropriately when the class consists of students with similar abilities and skills. However, research does not support this belief (Carnegie Council, 1989; Gamoran & Behends, 1987; Johnson & Markle, 1986). Eccles (1991) reports negative effects for adolescents placed in either general education or vocational tracks. Students in these programs are less prepared to pass college entrance exams as they take few challenging academic courses. Moreover, adolescents in the vocational track are more likely to drop out of high school, even though typically they have higher grade point scores (Eccles, 1991). The Carnegie Council (1989) report on middle school programs describes lower academic tracks or classes as locked into dull, repetitive instructional programs leading at best to minimum competencies. Box 2.1 presents the conclusions reached by Gamoran and Behends (1987) from a review of survey and enthographic research studies on the effects of stratification in secondary schools.

---

**BOX 2.1**

### Effects of Stratification in Secondary Schools

1. Grouping and tracking affect achievement, with students in higher tracks showing higher achievement and greater learning.

2. Grouping and tracking affect subsequent educational attainment. Students in academic tracks are more likely to enroll in colleges and are more likely to receive encouragement from guidance counselors to do so.

3. Instructional strategies differ. In lower-track classes, teachers present simplified concepts at a slow rate and do most of the talking, while students are passive and spend more time off task. Correction strategies also differ. Teachers prompt students in high-level classes to arrive at the correct answer when they respond incorrectly. Conversely, teachers in low-level classes tend to ignore or bypass students when they answer a question incorrectly.

4. Teaching skills differ. More skilled and successful teachers are assigned to higher tracks. Teachers in lower tracks frequently expect less from their students.

5. Tracking polarizes students into pro- and antischool factions. Students in the higher tracks tend to accept the demands of school, while students in the lower tracks often resist school rules and may even attempt to subvert them.

The detrimental effects of tracking for students without disabilities also apply to those students with mild disabilities, as many of these students are tracked into basic and remedial courses. These effects are worth considering as we move toward co-teaching and collaboration with regular education teachers.

---

**COMPREHENSION MONITORING OF KEY CONCEPTS**

### Secondary Program Policies and Their Effect on Students with Mild Disabilities

*Graduation Requirements*

1. Students with disabilities may earn a regular diploma, a special diploma, a certification of attendance, or a certification of achievement.

2. Some states require students with mild disabilities to meet the same Carnegie requirements that regular students meet for graduation. Others offer alternatives for special education students.

3. Alternatives include modified content, modified instruction, and subjects taught by special teachers certified in the content area. In many cases, local education districts decide on graduation requirements.

4. Some states require students with mild disabilities to pass a standard minimum competency test for graduation. Other states exempt students with disabilities, and still others allow the local school districts to decide.

5. The courts have upheld the right of states to deny a standard diploma to students with mild disabilities who have not passed a minimum competency test.

*Discipline Policies*

6. Students with disabilities are expected to follow school discipline policies, and courts have upheld suspensions of up to 10 school days if they do not.

7. Confusion exists as to the meaning of "temporary suspension of up to 10 school days" in the *Honig* v. *Doe* decision.

8. Home visitations, assigned homework, and parental instruction are recommended for students during suspension.

---

*Tracking*

9. Tracking is block scheduling of students based on ability grouping.

10. In middle schools, students are most frequently grouped for instruction in reading, English, and math.

11. In high schools, students are frequently grouped into college, general education, or vocational tracks or, within a subject area, by ability.

12. Research studies show negative effects of tracking on achievement, classroom experiences, educational attainment, and social skills of students in the lower tracks.

---

## School Reform and Restructuring and the Impact on Secondary Special Education

Before we leave our discussion of the secondary program, let's examine the school reform and restructuring movement. We include this section because changes in school policies and procedures could affect the future organization of secondary schools and the special education curriculum. We specifically address *GOALS 2000: EDUCATE AMERICA ACT,* the SCANS Report, the Regular Education Initiative, and inclusive education.

### GOALS 2000

National efforts to promote systematic education reform are embodied in *GOALS 2000: EDUCATE AMERICA ACT* (1994), an education strategy designed to move the nation's schools into the 21st century. *GOALS 2000* is an act to improve learning and teaching by providing a national framework for education reform, and by promoting research and systemic changes needed to ensure equitable educational opportunities and high levels of achievement for all students. Signed into law in March 1994 by President Clinton, it had its beginnings in 1989 when the National Governor's Association and President Bush established six national goals for education (Olson & Platt, 1996). *GOALS 2000* added two additional goals (Goals 4 and 8) to the original six.

It is important to determine the extent to which students with disabilities were considered in the development of this education strategy. As you read the goals and objectives, think about the impact on students with mild disabilities. The year 2000 is established as the target date for each of these eight national education goals.

### Goal 1

All children in America will start school ready to learn.

*Objectives*

- All disadvantaged and disabled children will have access to high-quality and developmentally appropriate preschool programs that help prepare children for school.

- Every parent in America will be a child's first teacher and devote time each day to helping his or her preschool child learn; parents will have access to training and support they need.

- Children will receive the nutrition and health care needed to arrive at school with healthy minds and bodies, and the number of low-birthweight babies will be significantly reduced through enhanced pre-natal health systems.

Goal 1 appears to address special education. It acknowledges the importance of early education experiences, parental involvement, and proper health care, all of which have been priorities in special education. However, it is unclear what "ready to learn" means (Ysseldyke & Algozzine, 1992). In fact, it may mean something different for each child with a disability, depending upon the child's needs and the level of support that child receives.

### Goal 2

The high school graduation rate will increase to at least 90%.

*Objectives*

- The nation will dramatically reduce its dropout rate, and 75% of those students who drop out will successfully complete a high school degree or its equivalent.

- The gap in high school graduation rates between American students from minority backgrounds and their nonminority counterparts will be eliminated.

Goal 2 does not explain how the graduation rate could reach 90% if students with disabilities are included (Ysseldyke & Algozzine, 1992). Furthermore, the goal does not appear to address the problem of the dropout rate in special education. Results of studies have shown that students with disabilities are more likely to drop out than students without disabilities

(Bruininks, Thurlow, Lewis, & Larson, 1988; Owings & Stocking, 1986). Does this mean that the assistance these students are receiving in special education is inadequate to keep them in school? If so, we need to continue to examine our curriculum content and the service delivery systems through which we provide that content.

### Goal 3

American students will leave grades 4, 8, and 12 having demonstrated competency in challenging subject matter, including English, mathematics, science, history, and geography.

*Objectives*

- The academic performance of elementary and secondary students will increase significantly in every quartile, and the distribution of minority students in each level will more closely reflect the student population as a whole.

- The percentage of students who demonstrate the ability to reason, solve problems, apply knowledge, and write and communicate effectively will increase substantially.

- All students will be involved in activities that promote citizenship, community service, and personal responsibility.

- The percentage of students who are competent in more than one language will substantially increase.

- All students will be knowledgeable about the diverse heritage of this nation and about the world community.

It seems unlikely that students with disabilities were included in the development of these objectives. As we stated in Chapter 1, students with disabilities appear to have problems with academics (reading, math, spelling, writing), lack good problem-solving skills, and have difficulty with social interactions. In addition, many students with learning disabilities have language-related problems.

The third objective under Goal 3—to promote citizenship, community service, and personal responsibility—has long been a focus of career education. However, for students with disabilities to be successful, they must be given opportunities within inclusive environments so that they can interact with individuals without disabilities (Ysseldyke & Algozzine, 1992).

### Goal 4

The teaching force will have access to programs for the continued improvement of their professional skills.

*Objectives*

- All teachers will have access to preservice teacher education and continuing professional development activities that will provide them with the knowledge and skills needed to teach to an increasingly diverse student population with a variety of educational, social, and health needs.

- All teachers will have continuing opportunities to acquire additional knowledge and skills needed to teach challenging subject matter and to use emerging new methods, forms of assessment, and technologies.

- States and school districts will create integrated strategies to attract, recruit, prepare, retrain, and support the continued professional development of teachers, administrators, and other educators, so that there is a highly talented workforce of professional educators to teach challenging subject matter.

- Partnerships will be established whenever possible among local education agencies, institutions of higher education, parents, and local business and professional associations to provide and support programs for the professional development of educators.

For teachers of students with disabilities at the secondary level, this means that teachers should be provided with techniques and training in (1) motivating students; (2) managing the academic and social-skill challenges of increasingly diverse groups of students; (3) planning, teaching, and networking collaboratively with other professionals in the school and community, with businesses and agencies, and with parents; and (4) using technology for teaching, maintaining records, and for communicating.

### Goal 5

U.S. students will be first in the world in mathematics and science achievement.

*Objectives*

- Math and science education will be strengthened throughout the system, especially in the early grades.

- The number of teachers with a substantive background in mathematics and science will increase by 50%.

- The number of U.S. undergraduate and graduate students, especially women and minorities, who complete degrees in mathematics, science, and engineering will increase significantly.

In special education, we frequently provide students with mild disabilities with a functional curriculum, which in math could be "managing personal finances" and in science may include "understanding how to safely dispose of engine oil and household cleaning products." For some students with mild disabilities, Goal 5 may be a more realistic expectation if we broaden our definition of math and science to include daily living and occupational skills.

### Goal 6

U.S. citizens will be literate and will possess the knowledge and skills necessary to compete in a global economy and exercise the rights and responsibilities of citizenship.

*Objectives*

- Every major American business will be involved in strengthening the connection between education and work.

- All workers will have the opportunity to acquire the knowledge and skills, from basic to highly technical, needed to adapt to emerging new technologies, work methods, and markets through public and private educational, vocational, technical, workplace, or other programs.

- The number of quality programs, including those at libraries, that are designed to serve more effectively the needs of the growing number of part-time and mid-career students will increase substantially.

- The proportion of those qualified students, especially minorities, who enter college, who complete at least two years, and who complete their degree programs will increase substantially.

- The proportion of college graduates who demonstrate an advanced ability to think critically, communicate effectively, and solve problems will increase substantially.

Goal 6 seemingly embraces an initiative of special education: the successful transition of students from school to the world of work and community living (Will, 1984). However, students with basic academic skills in the bottom fifth of the distribution are 8.8 times more likely to leave school without a diploma (William T. Grant Foundation, 1988). Because many of the jobs included in Goal 6 call for more than a high school education, students with disabilities who do complete a high school education may still be excluded from this goal, since adolescents with disabilities are less likely to enter postsecondary education (Fairweather & Shaver, 1991).

Goal 6 includes an individual's skills in exercising the rights and responsibilities of citizenship. For this goal to be achieved by students with disabilities, we must at the very least reexamine the service delivery system so that students will have opportunities to practice these skills.

### Goal 7

Every school in America will be free of drugs and the unauthorized presence of firearms and alcohol, and will offer a disciplined environment conducive to learning.

### Objectives

- Every school will implement a fair and firm policy on use, possession, and distribution of drugs and alcohol.
- Every school district will develop a comprehensive K–12 drug and alcohol prevention education program, which should be taught as an integral part of health education.
- Every local educational agency will implement a policy to ensure that all schools are free of violence and the unauthorized presence of weapons.
- Parents, businesses, and community organizations will work together to ensure that schools are a safe haven for all children.
- Community-based teams should be organized to provide students and teachers with needed support.
- Every school should work on eliminating sexual harassment.

Goal 7 is appropriate for all students as long as those with disabilities are being included in the overall school program and receive the same opportunities as students without disabilities. In other words, students with disabilities must be included in health education classes and drug and alcohol prevention programs.

### Goal 8

Every school will promote partnerships that will increase parental involvement and participation in promoting the social, emotional, and academic growth of children.

### Objectives

- Every state will develop policies to assist local schools and local educational agencies to establish programs for increasing partnerships that respond to the varying needs of parents and the home, including parents of children who are disadvantaged or bilingual, or parents of children with disabilities.
- Every school will actively engage parents and families in a partnership which supports the academic work of children at home and shared educational decision making at school.

- Parents and families will help to ensure that schools are adequately supported and will hold schools and teachers to high standards of accountability.

Goal 8 directly addresses parents and families of children with disabilities. Special education and vocational education personnel should develop ways to involve parents in their work with community agencies, businesses, employers, and postsecondary institutions. Parents can be important partners in the transition of adolescents with disabilities to postschool employment and postsecondary education opportunities.

Most school reform efforts have not addressed the concerns of students with disabilities (National Council on Disability, 1989). However, if the goals were adapted and given a broader, more inclusive interpretation, they could be appropriate for students with disabilities. If interpreted differently, the eight goals could include initiatives that are important for adolescents with mild disabilities: an emphasis on lifelong learning and preparation for entry into the workforce and the community. However, if they are to be acceptable to the special education community, *GOALS 2000* and all efforts at school reform must become more inclusive of children and youth with diverse needs (Kauffman & Hallahan, 1993).

## The SCANS Report

An initiative that examined "what work requires of schools" is seen in a product of the Secretary of Labor and Secretary's Commission on Achieving Necessary Skills (SCANS). The SCANS Report (U.S. Department of Labor, 1993) represents an examination of changes in the world of work and the implications of those changes for our schools. Although the SCANS Report makes no mention of students with disabilities, it provides a preview of the future world of work that our students will soon be facing.

Currently, more than half our youth leave school without the knowledge and skills needed to secure and hold a job (U.S. Department of Labor, 1993). The knowledge and skills needed include the foundation areas of (1) basic skills (listening, speaking, reading, writing, arithmetic); (2) thinking skills (reasoning, problem solving, making decisions, knowing how to learn); and (3) personal qualities (responsibility, self-esteem, social skills, and self-management). To be successful in the workplaces of the year 2000, students must not only have adequate basic academic skills but also know how to communicate effectively, solve problems, and work cooperatively in teams.

As we reported in Chapter 1, adolescents with mild disabilities frequently have difficulty with basic academics, receptive and expressive language, problem solving, and appropriate interaction with adults and peers. This places them at a serious disadvantage as we move toward the 21st century. Therefore, we need to make some fundamental changes in the way we prepare our youth for transition to the workplace and the community.

In the past, high school graduates who possessed a diploma and a willingness to work were able to make a good start in the U.S. labor market (U.S. Department of Labor, 1993). However, we have learned that to prepare our youth for the changing demands of the workplace, we must make strong connections between education (what they learn in school) and earning a living (know-how needed to handle the challenges of work and life).

> Secondary students often see little connection between what they do in school and how they expect to make a living. They, therefore, invest very little effort in their education. The average American high school junior puts in half of the 60 hours a week that a Japanese peer devotes to schoolwork. (U.S. Department of Labor, 1993, p. 4)

One of the intents of the *GOALS 2000: EDUCATE AMERICA* strategy is to convince our youth that investment in school today will yield results in the workplace and community in the future. We can do this by including basic skills, thinking skills, and personal/social skills within real-life environments, instead of teaching these skills separately and then expecting students to generalize them. This will demonstrate the connection between what students study and its application to the real world. For example, teachers can give students problems to solve in math that relate to mathematical calculations that they may need on a particular job (for example, in building a 12 x 12 foot deck, figuring out how far apart to space boards of a given width). To emphasize ability to interact effectively, the teacher could have teams work together to solve the problem.

In addition to the foundation areas of basic skills, thinking skills, and personal qualities, the SCANS Report recommends that teachers systematically instruct students in four competencies to increase their effectiveness in the workplace: use of resources, interpersonal skills, information, and systems/technology. These competencies may be infused into the curriculum together with the foundation skills. For example, students could be asked to work in groups (interpersonal skills), using a computer (systems and technology), to develop a budget for a family in the year 2000 (allocating resources, thinking skills, and basic skills), compare it to a budget for a family in 1950 (social systems), and then present it in class (personal qualities).

## The Regular Education Initiative

The relationship between regular and special education has received a great deal of attention (Heward & Orlansky, 1992), with some professionals calling for a merger of regular and special education (Stainback & Stainback, 1984). The Regular Education Initiative (REI) was originated in 1986 by Madeline Will, then Assistant Secretary for the Office of Special Education and Rehabilitative Services. The initiative called for a shared responsibility between regular and special education. Although it was called the Regular Education Initiative, regular educators were not consulted or involved.

Advocates for REI claimed that pullout programs in which students were removed from regular classes for instruction in separate special education settings were not effective (Lilly, 1988; Wang, Reynolds, & Walberg, 1986; Will, 1986). Gartner and Lipsky (1987) claimed that there were large numbers of students in regular classrooms who were at risk for failure but were not having their needs met because they did not meet eligibility criteria for special education. Proponents of REI argued that the merging of regular and special education could result in assistance for these students. Advocates of REI also claimed that separate programs stigmatized students, prevented them from being fully integrated into society, and contributed to lower expectations for these students in academic and social-skill functioning (Blackhurst & Berdine, 1993).

Other professionals in special education expressed caution about wholesale acceptance and implementation of the Regular Education Initiative (Hallahan, Keller, McKinney, Lloyd, & Bryan, 1988; Kauffman, Gerber, & Semmel, 1988). They claimed that regular classroom teachers had not been adequately prepared to assume responsibility for students with disabilities, nor had they been consulted about it. They further stated that the curriculum being utilized in regular classrooms might not be appropriate without major adaptations, and that teachers needed systematic instruction in materials modification. Some feared that administrators might try to implement REI without providing essential support services to teachers (Blackhurst & Berdine, 1993). Lieberman (1985) pointed out that there was an advantage in keeping special education as a delivery system: "In regular education, the system dictates the curriculum; in special education, the child dictates the curriculum" (p. 514).

Although there has been much disagreement regarding REI, there are some common points that most special educators support: dissatisfaction with the current regular and special education systems, a need to reexamine our current practices, and an opportunity to work together to improve the options for diverse student populations (Olson & Platt, 1996). In selecting those options, we agree with Blackhurst and Berdine's (1993) term "most facilitative environment" (p. 57), as it focuses on the best setting for a specific individual. Finally, we support Heward and Orlansky's (1992) view that regardless of where services are provided, the quality of instruction is the key variable that contributes to the success of the student.

## Inclusive Education

Inclusive education has replaced the Regular Education Initiative as one of the major educational reform issues facing both regular and special education (Heward, 1996; Olson & Platt, 1996). Although educational programming has traditionally been provided through a variety of service delivery options, there is a movement to educate students with disabilities in regular classrooms. Full inclusion is based upon the premise that students with disabilities should be educated in regular classrooms in their home schools (Hallahan & Kauffman, 1994). Most models advocating full inclusion incorporate the following points (adapted from Sailor, 1991):

1. All students attend the school to which they would go if they had no disability.
2. A natural proportion (representative of the school district at large) of students with disabilities occurs at any school site.
3. A zero-rejection policy exists, so that typically no student would be excluded on the basis of type or extent of disability.
4. School and general education placements are age- and grade-appropriate, with no self-contained special education classes at the school site.
5. Cooperative learning and peer instructional methods receive significant use in general instructional practice at the school site.
6. Special education supports are provided within the context of the general education class and in other integrated environments.

The issue of full inclusion versus a continuum of service options was discussed at the annual conference of the Council for Exceptional Children (CEC) in San Antonio, Texas, in April 1993, resulting in the adoption of the policy statement that appears in Box 2.2. The CEC policy statement calls for a continuum of services, but supports inclusion as a meaningful goal. Implications for secondary schools include obtaining the support and technical assistance necessary to serve an increasingly diverse student population in inclusive settings, and facilitating collaboration among families, educators, businesses, and agencies to prepare children and youth for membership in inclusive communities.

**BOX 2.2**

## CEC Policy on Inclusive Schools and Community Settings

The Council for Exceptional Children (CEC) believes all children, youth, and young adults with disabilities are entitled to a free and appropriate education and/or services that lead to an adult independent living, productive engagement in the community, and participation in society at large.

To achieve such outcomes, there must exist for all children, youth, and young adults a rich variety of early intervention, educational, and vocational program options and experiences.

Access to these programs and experiences should be based on individual educational need and desired outcomes.

Furthermore, students, and their families or guardians, as members of the planning team, may recommend the placement, curriculum option, and the exit document to be pursued.

CEC believes that a continuum of services must be available for all children, youth, and young adults.

CEC also believes that the concept of inclusion is a meaningful goal to be pursued in our schools and communities.

In addition, CEC believes children, youth, and young adults with disabilities should be served whenever possible in general education classrooms in inclusive neighborhood schools and community settings.

Such settings should be strengthened and supported by an infusion of specially trained personnel and other appropriate supportive practices according to the individual needs of the child.

*Source:* From "CEC Policy on Inclusive Schools and Community Settings" by The Council for Exceptional Children, 1993, *Teaching Exceptional Children, 25*(4). Copyright 1993 by The Council for Exceptional Children. Reprinted by permission.

*GOALS 2000,* the SCANS Report, the Regular Education Initiative, and inclusive education all call for change in the preparation of children and youth. These regular education and special education reform movements may impact the organization of secondary special education. Adolescents with mild disabilities may receive services in varied environments, including regular classrooms and the workplace. Regular education and special education teachers may plan and teach cooperatively in inclusive settings with diverse groups of students. Adolescents in middle schools and high schools may complete more assignments in teams through the use of technology. It is imperative that the needs of students with disabilities be addressed in these reform initiatives.

**COMPREHENSION MONITORING OF KEY CONCEPTS**

### School Reform and Restructuring

*GOALS 2000*

1. *GOALS 2000,* an education strategy designed to move the nation's schools into the 21st century, consists of eight goals: starting school ready to learn; increasing the graduation rate; demonstrating competency in challenging subject matter such as English, mathematics, science, history, and geography; providing professional development for teachers; increasing literacy; teaching skills to help students compete in a global economy and exercise rights and responsibilities of citizenship; providing safe schools that are conducive to learning; and promoting partnerships to increase parental involvement.

2. To be acceptable to the special education community, efforts at school reform such as *GOALS 2000* must become inclusive of students with disabilities.

*The SCANS Report*

3. The SCANS Report provides a preview of the future world of work.

4. In order to be successful in the workplaces of the year 2000, students will need to have good skills in basic academics, communication, and problem solving, and will need to know how to work cooperatively in teams.

*The Regular Education Initiative*

5. The Regular Education Initiative (REI) calls for the merger of regular and special education in providing services to students with disabilities by placing fewer students in pullout programs and educating them in regular settings instead.

*Inclusive Education*

6. Full inclusion is based upon the premise that students with disabilities should be educated in regular classrooms in their home schools.

7. The Council for Exceptional Children adopted a policy statement in 1993 that calls for a continuum of services, but supports inclusion as a meaningful goal.

## Special Educators in the Secondary Setting

An important part of our discussion of the secondary program and curriculum includes how you, as a special education teacher, fit into the secondary school environment. As a teacher of adolescents with mild disabilities, you will probably be providing either direct or indirect services or both to students. If you are providing direct services, you directly teach the students, whether in a self-contained, pullout, or mainstream setting. If you are providing indirect services, you assist other teachers or professionals, who, in turn, teach the students. You may consult with these teachers, adapt curricula or materials for them, or serve as a member of an interdisciplinary team. A third option is that you may provide both types of service. Remember, in the comprehensive high school, you will more than likely consult with regular education teachers as part of your responsibilities (Wagner, 1993).

### Teacher as Instructor in a Self-Contained Class

As stated previously, the majority of adolescents with mild disabilities attend regular schools (Wagner, 1993). Since so few students with mild disabilities are enrolled in special schools, we concentrate on the separate class as the self-contained model in this text. In the separate class, students receive "special education and related services for more than 60% of the school day outside the regular classroom. Students may be placed in self-contained special classrooms with part-time instruction in regular class or placed in self-contained classes full-time on a regular school campus" (U.S. Department of Education, 1993, p. 15).

As a secondary teacher in a self-contained setting, you may teach a functional curriculum or a parallel high school curriculum (Clark & Kolstoe, 1990; Zigmond & Sansone, 1986). In a classroom that emphasizes a functional curriculum, your major goal is to teach students such skills as completing job applications and balancing a checkbook, so that they can function as independent adults. In the parallel alternative curriculum, you modify course content and instructional methods, using different materials to present content and offering alternatives to paper-and-pencil tests. As a secondary teacher in a self-contained setting, you may do academic teaching, personal and social teaching, vocational counseling, and guidance (Clark & Kolstoe, 1990).

### Teacher as Instructor in a Pullout Class

Currently, the term *pullout* is frequently used in place of resource room. Popular from the 1960s, a resource room includes students who receive special education and related services between 21% and 60% of the school day (U.S. Department of Education, 1993).

A resource room may either be categorical or noncategorical; that is, you may find students from one category, or you may find students from several categories in the same room (Wiederholt & Chamberlain, 1989). For example, one of our interns teaches two periods of life management skills to students with emotional disabilities (categorical resource room) and two periods of English and one period of social studies to students with mild disabilities (noncategorical resource room) in her high school setting. Of the ten students in the social studies class, two are students with emotional disabilities, three with mental disabilities, and five with learning disabilities.

As a resource teacher, you may find that you tutor your students in content areas corresponding with courses in mainstream classes. Ensminger and Dangel (1992) describe this approach as a type of "study hall with independent assignments and limited verbal exchanges" (p. 2).

Instead of tutoring, you may teach content areas using parallel or standard curriculum. In a survey of 49 state directors, McKenzie (1991) found that 83.7% of the states offered content instruction in secondary learning disabilities classes. You may find that you are teaching basic skills, school survival skills, learning strategies, or a combination of all three (Zigmond & Sansone, 1986). Another option is a work/study program. In this program, you teach mostly specific job-related skills and act as a job coach and supervisor for students during on-the-job experiences.

In a review of research concerning the effectiveness of various types of resource room programs, Wiederholt and Chamberlain (1989) conclude that much of the research is inconclusive. They cite such factors as a paucity of studies investigating secondary resource rooms, lack of detailed description of the subjects, skimpy description of interventions, datedness of many of the studies, and weak research designs as responsible for the inconclusive findings.

## Teacher as Co-teacher

Co-teaching (cooperative teaching) involves general educators and special educators working together jointly to teach heterogeneous groups of students in integrated settings (Bauwens, Hourcade, & Friend, 1989). In co-teaching, two teachers plan and present lessons together and evaluate progress of both regular and special students (Friend & Cook, 1992b). Co-teaching brings together the strengths of two professionals: the regular educator, who knows curriculum content and scope and sequence—the "what" of teaching; and the special educator, who knows ways to individu-

© Nita Winter

*Joint planning time enhances co-teaching efforts.*

alize, to adapt materials and instructional strategies, and to manage disruptive behaviors—the "how" of teaching.

Bauwens and Hourcade (1991) describe three options for co-teaching: team teaching, complementary instruction, and supportive learning activities. In the *team teaching* arrangement, both teachers plan and teach the content lesson. They share equal responsibility for one common body of knowledge. They identify the specific responsibilities for each part. For example, in a team teaching class that we observed, the regular teacher led a discussion of the major characters in the story, while the special teacher led a discussion of the plot.

In the *complementary instruction model,* which Bauwens and Hourcade believe is well suited for the secondary level, the regular education teacher is responsible for teaching the specific subject matter, while the special educator teaches specific strategies or skills, designed to make the students more successful. Each teacher has a separate set of goals. For example, the history teacher teaches European history, while the special educator teaches students to summarize materials, take notes, and organize materials.

In the *supportive learning activities model,* the general educator usually delivers the essential content of instruction, while the special educator implements activities that support or supplement the content learning. For example, the general educator presents various scientific terms to the students, and the special educator then designs a practice activity with flash cards and peer tutoring to help the students learn the terms.

Friend and Cook (1992b) describe the following options for co-teaching:

One teacher teaches the large group while the other teacher circulates around the room, paying particular attention to the needs of the students with disabilities. OR

The teachers divide the class in half, each teaching the same information to a smaller group. OR

One of the teachers provides remediation for students who need it (those with disabilities and those without), while the other provides enrichment for the rest of the class. OR

Both teachers teach the whole group at the same time modeling a skill while the other describes it or both role play for the students or share a presentation. (p. 30)

Co-teaching requires much planning, open communication between the co-teachers, and much compromising. Additionally, the regular educator must show a willingness to share the classroom. A pitfall to avoid is the "paraprofessional trap," in which the special education teacher becomes a classroom helper (Friend & Cook, 1992b).

Redditt (1991) suggests using the techniques of conferencing and referencing to help equalize the roles of the two teachers. In conferencing, the co-teacher who is leading the lesson asks the other teacher for input/ suggestions.

At the conclusion of her presentation on how to determine the amount of discount, in dollar value, for "sale items" being purchased at a store, Ms. Lamb (co-teacher leading the lesson) asks Mr. Arturo (supporting co-teacher) the following:

"Mr. Arturo, do you think this is enough explanation on this concept, or should we spend some more time on it before moving on?"

In referencing, one co-teacher refers to the other co-teacher when speaking to the students. The co-teacher leading the lesson refers to something that both teachers have cooperatively planned for the students.

As Mr. Rogriguez starts the videotape, he comments to the class, "Mr. Saunders and I found this videotape, *Animals in Danger,* in the media center. We thought that it would be a perfect introduction to our new environmental science unit on endangered species."

There is limited research as to the effectiveness of co-teaching at the secondary level. In a survey of four secondary schools in the Maryland system,

Walsh (1991) found that regular education teachers, parents, special education teachers, and special students all agreed that the special students enjoyed going to school more, were happier, and liked school better in co-taught classes than in separate special education class settings. In questions dealing with academic involvement, again all four groups agreed that special education students tried harder in co-taught classes, learned more, and received more homework and schoolwork.

---

**COMPREHENSION MONITORING OF KEY CONCEPTS**

*Special Educators in the Secondary Setting*

1. In providing direct services, special education teachers directly teach the students; in providing indirect services, they work with other teachers or professionals who, in turn, teach the students.

2. Secondary teachers who teach in a self-contained setting generally teach a functional or parallel curriculum.

3. Secondary teachers who teach students in a resource room setting may teach content areas, basic skills, survival skills, learning strategies, or a combination.

4. In a work/study program, special education teachers frequently act as a job coach and supervise students on the job.

5. Resource rooms may be categorical, consisting of students classified in one specific category of special education or noncategorical, open to students with a variety of disabilities.

6. Co-teaching involves general and special educators working together to teach students with mild disabilities and students without disabilities in the mainstream setting.

7. In the team teaching option of co-teaching, both teachers plan and teach the content lesson.

8. In the complementary instruction option, the regular teacher teaches the content lesson and the special educator teaches specific strategies to make the student more successful.

9. In the supportive learning activity option, the general educator teaches the content while the special educator designs activities for the students.

10. Research concerning the effectiveness of the resource room and the co-teaching setting is inconclusive.

Now that you have read Chapter 2, reflect on your earlier predictions and complete this post organizer.

1. Compare the list of demands and expectations of secondary schools that you experienced as a student to those described in the chapter. How closely does your list approximate that in the chapter?

2. Discuss the similarities and differences between your groups' experiences with school discipline and graduation requirements and what was reported in the chapter.

3. Look back at your prediction of skills and competencies needed by students in the year 2000. Compare the items on your list to those listed in the chapter. How accurate were you?

# Assessment for Instructional Planning in Secondary Schools

© Elizabeth Crews

**CHAPTER HIGHLIGHTS**

*Individualized Education Program*

*Informal Assessment*

---

 Before you read Chapter 3, use your prior knowledge to complete this advance organizer. Work in groups to complete this exercise.

1. Trina is a tenth-grade student who has difficulty writing complete sentences, using the correct punctuation, and remembering to indent the first word in a paragraph. Write an objective for one of her areas of difficulty.

2. Name and describe three informal techniques you could use to initially assess secondary students with mild disabilities in order to plan for their instruction, and three different informal techniques you could use to monitor their progress.

---

Instructional planning must be preceded and accompanied by assessment. "Assessment is the process of gathering information, using appropriate tools and techniques" (Hargrove & Poteet, 1984, p. 5). Assessment and planning should lead to decisions about program content and curriculum materials selection. This information should be provided in each student's Individualized Education Program (IEP), which is developed to ensure that students receive an education to address their unique needs, strengths, and weaknesses. The IEP should provide information about the assessment procedures, instructional objectives, teaching strategies, curriculum materials, and modifications required for instructional planning. Currently, there are numerous ways to informally assess secondary students with disabilities and to plan instruction for them.

The purpose of this chapter is to discuss the wide variety of assessment techniques available to plan instruction for secondary students with mild disabilities. We begin with a description of the types of information that should be included in each student's Individualized Education Program. Next, we present a variety of informal assessment techniques, including indirect and direct assessment procedures, used in instructional planning.

## Individualized Education Program

Under the provisions of Public Law 101-476, the Individuals with Disabilities Education Act (IDEA), students with disabilities are required to have an Individualized Education Program (IEP). The IEP (see Figure 3.1) is a written educational plan completed by parents, professionals, and the student when appropriate. We believe that the IEP becomes increasingly important for students with disabilities in the secondary years because the demands of the curriculum increase, while the time remaining for the student to prepare for transition to work and adult life decreases. We also feel it is important to include the secondary student in the IEP process: What better way to help students accomplish their goals than to have them help select them? *The Self-Advocacy Strategy* (Van Reusen, Bos, Schumaker, & Deshler, 1994) teaches students to participate in the IEP process or in any education planning conference. It includes a set of people-pleasing/participation skills along with procedures for students to use in identifying their own strengths, weaknesses, and goals. This strategy is designed to help students improve their organization and communication skills and to increase their self-awareness.

Each state has its own procedures for identifying, assessing, and placing students with disabilities into programs (Masters et al., 1993). However, federal regulations mandate that all IEPs contain certain components: (1) the

**FIGURE 3.1    Individualized Education Program**

A. *Student Information*

Student name: Greg Willis

Date of birth: 8/13/81

Address:    1519 Clearlake Rd.
New Britain, Ct. 06053

Primary language: English

Date: 10/14/96

Ethnic code: 2

Phone: 225-5012

Grade: 10

School: Horace Mann High School

B. *Present Levels of Performance*

| Strengths | Weaknesses |
|---|---|
| PIAT-R - Math 9.0 | PIAT-R - Reading 5.5/SS. 6.5/Spelling 4.7 |
| Brigance - Math 9.8 | Brigance - Word Rec. 6.0, Comprehension 5.0 |
| Career/Voc. Ed. - Managing finances | Social Skills-Following direc., Getting along |
| - Physical, Manual Skills | Career/Voc. Ed - Personal Hygiene, |
| | - Problem Solving |

(Additional pages may be added.)

C. *Long-Range Goals, Short-Term Objectives, and Evaluation Procedures*

| Goals and Objectives | Evaluation Criteria and Method | Date Started | Date Met |
|---|---|---|---|
| Goal: Apply social skills (following directions) with peers and authorities | | | |
| Objectives: Given a set of directions from a teacher, Greg will complete them with 100% accuracy on 3 assignments (continued on next page.) | 100% accuracy (teacher observation) | 10/14/96 | |

(Additional pages would be added with other goals and objectives.)

D. *Services to be Provided*

| Program/Service | Hours per Week | Initiation Date | Duration | Person Responsible/ Where Provided |
|---|---|---|---|---|
| Special Education | 10 | 10/14/96 | 1 year | • Special Education teacher Resource setting |
| Vocational Education | 3 | 10/14/96 | 6 mo. | • Vocational Adjustment Coordinator Job Site |
| Counseling | 2 | 10/14/96 | 1 year | • Counselor Guidance office |

E. *IEP Participants' Signatures*

Parent/Guardian:    James Willis

Teacher(s):    Vivian Heiley

Bradley Ellenburg

LEA Representative:    Robin Huckabay

Student:    Greg Willis

student's present levels of performance, (2) long-range or annual goals, (3) short-term objectives, (4) special education and related services to be provided and who will carry them out, (5) the extent to which the student will participate in regular education programs, (6) projected dates for the initiation and duration of services, (7) objective criteria and evaluation procedures, and (8) a statement of needed transition services, initiated no later than age 16 (Masters et al., 1993). In Chapter 12, we provide a detailed description of the Individualized Transition Plan (ITP), a written, multiagency plan that identifies areas of need for students transitioning from school to work and postschool settings.

## Present Levels of Performance

A student's current functioning is usually documented by using a combination of formal (such as academic achievement tests) and informal (such as student work samples) assessment procedures. Assessment should come from several sources and reflect all aspects of a student's functioning (including attitude/motivation, social, career/vocational, and academic skills). It should be culturally and linguistically unbiased, and be tailored to the particular needs and interests of each individual (for example, assessment of the data-processing skills of an eleventh-grader interested in post-secondary enrollment in a technical school).

On some IEP forms, a student's present level of performance is reported according to category, such as social, career/vocational, and academic skills. Space is provided to write a student's test scores for each category or to write a statement about performance in that area. The following example shows this information for Greg, who is in the tenth grade:

*Social*

- Has difficulty following teacher directions. (Frequently)
- Has difficulty getting along with peers. (Sometimes)
- Gets angry and upset; easily provoked. (Sometimes)

*Career/vocational*

Life Centered Career Education (LCCE) competencies:

- Daily living skills (Has excellent skills in managing finances. Lacks personal hygiene skills.)
- Personal social skills (Has difficulty maintaining interpersonal relationships. Lacks problem-solving skills.)
- Occupational skills (Has excellent physical and manual skills. Has difficulty following directions and being on time.)

*Academic*

- Peabody Individual Achievement Test–Revised (PIAT–R):
  Reading (5.5)*; Math (9.0); Sci./Soc. Studies (6.5); Spelling (4.7)

- Brigance Diagnostic Inventory of Essential Skills:
  Math computation (9.8); Reading–Word recognition (6.0); Comprehension (5.0)

## Long-Range Goals

Long-range goals should be based upon the student's present levels of performance as well as on the student's age, grade, amount of education, strengths and weaknesses, and the student's and family's plans after graduation. They represent the student's most critical needs—those of the highest priority. Long-range or annual goals should be measurable, positive, student-oriented, and relevant (Polloway & Patton, 1993). Although the most valuable sources available to teachers when writing goals and objectives are the student, the family, and the assessment data, other resources are available. These include lists of predetermined curricular areas, minimum student performance standards, or course competencies available in most school districts. Box 3.1 illustrates suggested curriculum frameworks, including a list of 22 skills that students are expected to master in a middle school special education language arts class. You may also select goals and objectives from your school district's curriculum guides, textbooks, commercial programs, or from a scope and sequence chart.

Turnbull, Strickland, and Brantley (1982) suggest establishing three or four goals per subject area to be accomplished over a year's time. Possible goals for Greg are:

- Apply social-skill strategies in situations involving interactions with peers and authorities.

- Read the functional sight vocabulary in the Brigance Diagnostic Inventory of Essential Skills.

- Apply a problem-solving strategy to social and job-related situations.

## Short-Term Objectives

Short-term objectives should represent the specific way in which the student will accomplish a long-range goal. There may be one or more short-term objectives for each long-range goal, with many school districts

---

*5.5 means fifth grade, fifth month.

BOX 3.1

## Curriculum Frameworks for a Middle School Special Education/Language Arts Class

I. Major Concepts/Content

The purpose of this course is to provide instruction in functional and basic communication skills with emphasis upon the Florida Minimum Student Performance Standards. The course should include, but not be limited to, instruction in functional and basic reading, comprehension, vocabulary, literature, listening/speaking skills, study skills, reference skills, thinking, and problem-solving skills that relate to daily living and the world of work/careers. Composition should include writing for a variety of purposes with emphasis on all stages of the writing process (prewriting, drafting, revising, editing).

II. Intended Outcomes

After successfully completing this course, the student will be able to:

1. Develop and demonstrate a knowledge of functional and basic vocabulary.
2. Develop and demonstrate word attack skills for vocabulary usage.
3. Develop and demonstrate literal reading comprehension skills and strategies.
4. Develop and demonstrate inferential reading comprehension skills.
5. Develop and demonstrate evaluative/problem-solving reading comprehension skills.
6. Identify fundamental types of literature.

suggesting at least two objectives for each goal. You should check with your school district and follow their procedures.

Short-term objectives are written statements that should be

1. *Specific and observable.* Skills should be clear and easy to see (for example, reading a list of basic sight words, computing the diameter and radius of a circle).

2. *Measurable.* Skills should be capable of being measured by any evaluator (for example, writing a five-paragraph essay, each paragraph with a topic sentence, three detail sentences, and a clincher sentence).

3. *Meaningful and relevant.* Skills should have meaning for the student. The student who plans to go on to college may need objectives related to

**BOX 3.1**
*(continued)*

7. Relate work of literature to real-life experiences.

8. Compose grammatically correct sentences.

9. Organize objects and information into logical groupings and orders.

10. Write a paragraph expressing ideas clearly.

11. Write for the purpose of supplying necessary information.

12. Write letters and messages.

13. Fill out common forms.

14. Spell correctly.

15. Punctuate correctly.

16. Capitalize correctly.

17. Write legibly.

18. Demonstrate an understanding of the content and meaning of language.

19. Demonstrate functional use of communication that relates to daily living and the world of work/careers.

20. Use syntax appropriate to his/her primary system of communication.

21. Demonstrate knowledge and use of reference, study skills, and test-taking skills.

22. Read as a leisure-time activity.

*Source:* From Curriculum Frameworks: Grades 6–8 (Florida Department of Education, Tallahassee, Florida. Course Number 7810010). Reprinted with permission.

learning test-taking and note-taking strategies, while the student who has difficulty getting along with others may need objectives related to appropriate social-skill interactions. We must show secondary students with disabilities that there is a connection between their needs and the objectives designed for them. Of course, this is best accomplished by including students in the IEP process.

Heward (1996) refers to short-term objectives as the measurable, intermediate steps between the educational performance and the long-range, or annual, goals. Short-term objectives represent the daily activities that enable students to reach their long-term goals (Spruill, 1993). Each short-term objective should contain the condition, learner, target behavior, criterion, and an overlearning component.

1. *Condition.* The conditions under which performance will occur (for example, using a calculator, given eight completed checks, without the use of a dictionary).

2. *Learner.* The name of the student.

3. *Target behavior.* A description of the performance required of the student (for example, write the sums, recite the steps, combine the ingredients in the proper sequence).

4. *Criterion.* How well the task is to be performed. This may be expressed in terms of accuracy (with 5 or fewer errors, with 95% accuracy, with 20 correct); rate (with 20 correct in 1 minute); or time (by Friday, in 5 minutes, within an hour).

5. *Overlearning.* Performance of the objective over time. This may be expressed in terms of days, trials, times, or sessions (for example, for four days, in three trials, five times, or for three sessions).

The following are examples of possible objectives for secondary students with disabilities. Notice that they each contain the five components of a short-term objective.

1. When given a check register with 15 entries and a bank statement with three outstanding checks, Jerome will reconcile his checkbook with 100% accuracy on four assignments.

2. Given a calculator and ten advertisements from the newspaper, Mona will compute the most economical buys with two or fewer errors for three sessions.

3. When given a paragraph, Reggie will type 42 words per minute with no more than 4 errors for three trials.

### Participation in Special Education, Related Services, and Regular Education

This section of the IEP should provide specific information about the services the student will receive and designate who will provide them. For example, in Greg's situation, the special education teacher will spend one period each day on work-related social skills and another on basic functional reading, writing, and spelling in a resource setting. In addition, the vocational adjustment coordinator will train Greg at a job site, a counselor will work with Greg twice a week on interpersonal skills, and Greg will attend a regular class for math each day. The special education teacher will collaborate with each of the others so that all program efforts are related. In conjunction with these efforts, Greg and his family should also be involved.

## Initiation and Duration of Services

Although IEP forms differ from state to state and even from one district to another, there should be a section on the form to record the service provided (such as counseling), the date the service is to begin (9/5/96), and an estimate of how long the service will be needed (one year).

## Objective Criteria and Evaluation Procedures

Most IEP goals and objectives are written for a one-year time period and dates are recorded on the IEP for the start of services. If goals and objectives are accomplished sooner, the date they were met is recorded and new ones are developed and written on the IEP. For each goal and objective listed on the IEP, there is a place to write the criteria for evaluation (such as 4 out of 5 times), the evaluation method (for example, teacher observation with checklist), the date started (9/18/96), and date mastered (12/4/96). Used as an assessment and planning tool, the IEP should serve as an instructional plan that is constantly being changed and updated as teachers monitor the progress of their students.

## Transition Services

The inclusion of a statement about needed transition services is an important addition to the secondary student's IEP. According to the federal definition, transition services are "a coordinated set of activities . . . which promotes movement from school to post-school activities. . . . The coordinated set of activities must: (a) be based upon the individual student's needs; (b) take into account the student's preferences and interests; and (c) must include instruction, community services, the development of employment and other post-school adult living skills and functional vocational evaluation" (34 CFR 300:18). Public Law 101-476 (IDEA) mandated in 1990 that goals and objectives for providing needed transition services for students with disabilities be included in their IEPs by their 16th birthday. This should ensure that a systematic effort will be initiated to prepare the student for the transition from school to adult living and postschool settings. If appropriate, a statement may be added delineating interagency responsibilities before the student leaves the secondary school (National Association of State Directors of Special Education, 1990).

Most school districts are choosing to develop separate Individualized Transition Plans (ITPs) as part of the transition planning process. We have devoted an entire chapter to the important topic of transition planning, and direct you to Chapter 12 for a detailed explanation of the Individualized Transition Plan.

COMPREHENSION MONITORING OF KEY CONCEPTS

*Individualized Education Program*

1. Instructional planning must be preceded and accompanied by assessment. "Assessment is the process of gathering information, using appropriate tools and techniques" (Hargrove & Poteet, 1984, p. 5).

2. Federal regulations require each student with a disability to have an Individualized Education Program (IEP), a written educational plan agreed upon by parents, professionals, and the student when appropriate.

3. The IEP should contain (a) the student's present levels of performance, (b) long-range or annual goals, (c) short-term objectives, (d) special education and related services to be provided and who will carry them out, (e) the extent to which the student will participate in regular education programs, (f) projected dates for the initiation and duration of services, (g) evaluation criteria and evaluation procedures, and (h) a statement of needed transition services, initiated no later than age 16.

4. Long-range goals should be based upon the student's present levels of performance as well as on the student's age, grade, amount of education, strengths and weaknesses, and the student's and family's plans after graduation.

5. Short-term objectives are written statements that should be specific, observable, measurable, meaningful, and relevant, and contain the following components: condition, learner, target behavior, criterion, and overlearning component.

## Informal Assessment

Informal assessment may be accomplished with an array of different techniques and instruments and may be conducted in a variety of settings. Although informal assessment has many purposes, including screening and determining eligibility, we concentrate on informal assessment as it is used for planning and monitoring instruction at the secondary level. For secondary students with mild disabilities, assessment for instructional planning should be functional and meaningful and should focus on all aspects of the student's life (demands of the school curriculum and culture, academics, family and community expectations, preferred ways of learning, student needs, goals, interests, and motivation).

In planning assessment procedures, you should consider the student's age, grade, skills, interests, learning preferences, and IEP goals and objectives. You should also include an analysis of the school environment to identify curriculum demands and expectations and how that environment matches the student's skills and learning preferences.

## Analyze the Environment

Analyzing the environment involves examining the demands and expectations of the curriculum in order to identify the skills and tasks required. Examples of curricular demands are preparing written reports, learning from lectures and audiovisuals, and answering questions in content subject textbooks. Analyzing the environment also includes determining student skills and learning preferences. Examples of student skills are speaking in groups, knowing how to use a computer, and being able to take notes. Student learning preferences include how they learn best, whether they prefer working independently or in groups, and what materials they find most helpful.

Figure 3.2, the Curriculum Analysis Inventory for Secondary Students, and Figure 3.3, the Student Assessment Inventory for Secondary Students, help teachers analyze the environment. The Curriculum Analysis Inventory for Secondary Students examines curricular demands, and the Student Assessment Inventory for Secondary Students examines student skills and learning preferences. The Curriculum Analysis Inventory should be completed by students alone or by students with their teachers at the beginning of the term when content teachers typically explain the requirements of each class. It is sometimes helpful to have students who are in the same classes complete the inventory in pairs or in small groups in the event that there are questions or confusion about requirements. You will notice that the form is divided into two sections. In the first section, the students identify the ways that information is presented in class; in the second section, they check the ways that they are expected to respond. For his science class, Greg has indicated that information is presented through lectures, demonstrations, textbook reading, and cooperative learning. He has marked several ways that students are expected to respond: lab demonstrations, class participation, projects, chapter questions, and tests (multiple choice, matching, fill in the blank, and short answer).

Providing opportunities for assessing the environment as part of the overall assessment process is as important as evaluating your students, because it lets students know what is expected. Frequently, there is a

**FIGURE 3.2**   The Curriculum Analysis Inventory for Secondary Students

Student _Greg W._            Grade _____10_____

Class _Science_            Teacher _Ms. Lee_

**Directions:** The student or student and teacher should complete the inventory for each class that is being taken. Place a check mark by each item that applies.

| **How Information Is Presented** | **How Students Are Expected to Respond** |
|---|---|
| ✓ Lectures | ✓ Demonstrations (lab, art, music) |
| ✓ Demonstration | ____ Homework |
| ____ Discussion | ____ Written reports |
| ✓ Textbook reading | ____ Oral reports |
| ____ Audiovisuals | ✓ Class participation |
| ✓ Cooperative learning | (asking and answering questions) |
| ____ Peer tutoring | ✓ Projects |
| ____ Independent work | ____ Charts, graphs |
| | ____ Products |
| | ✓ Chapter questions in textbook |
| | ✓ Tests |
| |     ✓ Multiple choice |
| |     ✓ Matching |
| |     ____ True/false |
| |     ____ Essay |
| |     ✓ Fill in the blank |
| |     ✓ Short answer |

Comments: _Information is presented through lectures, demonstration, cooperative learning, and textbooks. Students are expected to read, participate in class, complete projects, perform demonstrations, answer chapter questions, and take tests._

*Source:* Adapted from Riegal, R. H., *A Guide to Cooperative Consultation,* © 1988, RHR Consultation Services, 39951 Jason Court, Novi, MI, 48375.

mismatch between curriculum requirements and the skills and learning preferences of the secondary student with mild disabilities. It is helpful as part of the assessment process to identify specifically where that mismatch occurs. After the student has completed the Curriculum Analysis Inventory for Secondary Students, the student, or the teacher and student together, can complete the Student Assessment Inventory for Secondary Students (see Figure 3.3). The inventory is divided into sections that list general academic, social, study, and other skills required of the secondary curriculum. There are also sections for identifying preferred ways of learning, interests, strengths, weaknesses, and comments from previous teachers. You will notice how Greg has marked his strengths. By comparing Greg's Curriculum Analysis Inventory for Secondary Students with his Student Assessment Inventory for Secondary Students, you see that he prefers working alone, yet the science teacher employs cooperative learning. He does not like reading or answering questions in his text, yet the teacher expects it. You have identified a mismatch between curricular expectations and student skills and preferences. More important, Greg has become aware of his preferences for learning and the expectations of his content classes. Knowing these facts will help with the planning of Greg's instructional program. For example, since Greg will need to read and answer questions in his textbook, but has difficulty with this, you may need to teach text comprehension strategies, or utilize compensatory teaching techniques by altering the text or assignment.

## Assess the Student

After completing an analysis of the environment by identifying curricular expectations, student skills and learning preferences, and the relationship between the two, you should informally assess the student. Included are both indirect and direct assessment procedures of students' skills. Indirect assessment is the collection of information about a student (such as interests and aptitudes) from others (such as parents and teachers) or from the students themselves. Direct assessment is the collection of information (for example, a student's written product) by evaluating the student's performance on a task (for example, the conversion of decimals to percentages).

### Indirect Assessment

Checklists, inventories, rating scales, and questionnaires are indirect assessment techniques that rely upon input from a teacher, parent, student, peer, or employer (McLoughlin & Lewis, 1994). For example, information about a student's values, attitudes, and motivation levels, education background, and health history may be best obtained from consulting others.

**FIGURE 3.3**     **Student Assessment Inventory for Secondary Students**

Student __*Greg W.*_____ Grade __*10*_____

**Directions:** The teacher, or teacher and student, should place a check mark by each item that is correct 80% of the time.

**Academic Skills Required**
**of the Curriculum**

____ Writes themes/reports
____ Speaks in groups/classes
____ Uses critical thinking skills
_✓_ Listens attentively
____ Uses good grammar
____ Uses correct punctuation
____ Understands content
     vocabulary
____ Reads content textbooks
     and other materials
____ Asks questions in class
____ Answers questions in class
_✓_ Categorizes
____ Participates in class discussion
____ Demonstrates computation
     skills
_✓_ Solves problems in math

**Social Skills Required**
**of the Curriculum**

____ Has a positive attitude
____ Follows rules
____ Interacts positively with others
_✓_ Pays attention
_✓_ Is punctual
____ Completes assignments
____ Accepts criticism
_✓_ Works independently
____ Works in groups
____ Solves problems

**Study Skills Required**
**of the Curriculum**

____ Takes notes
____ Outlines
____ Is organized
____ Manages time well
____ Has good memorization skills
____ Generalizes information
____ Follows directions
_✓_ Highlights, underlines

**Other Skills Required**
**of the Curriculum**

_✓_ Has good manual dexterity
____ Has good personal hygiene
_✓_ Has job/career goals
____ Has good computer skills

**Learning Preferences**

**Directions:** Check all that apply to how the student learns best.

**Learning modes**

_✓_ See
_✓_ Hear
____ Say

____ Read
____ Write
_✓_ Do (hands on)

**FIGURE 3.3** *(continued)*

**Groupings**

✔ Alone                    ___ With teacher
___ In groups              ___ In school
___ At home                ✔ On the job
___ With tutor

**Materials**

___ Computer               ✔ Overhead projector
✔ Calculator               ___ Tape recorder
___ Videotape              ✔ Games
✔ Concrete objects

**Activities**

___ Takes tests            ___ Works with people
___ Reads textbooks        ✔ Works with hands
___ Writes reports         ___ Does research

**Directions:** Complete the following three sections with comments.

Interests: Math computation and problems; working with his hands building/construction; working with money/finances; sports, especially basketball

Overall strengths and weaknesses: Strengths (math, physical and manual skills, working with money). Weaknesses (problem solving, reading, spelling, following directions, getting along with others).

Comments from previous teachers, including strategies that have proven effective: Using "hands on" activities, concrete objects, games, frequent feedback, shortening assignments, checking for understanding.

*Source:* Adapted from Riegel, R. H. 1988, *A Guide to Cooperative Consultation,* RHR Consultation Services, 39951 Jason Court, Novi, MI 48375. Reprinted by permission.

***Checklists, inventories, and rating scales*** Checklists and inventories usually consist of a set of statements or a list of curriculum competencies, skills, or objectives. The individual completing these instruments marks either Yes or No for each item, circles the numbers of the items that apply to the student, or places a check mark or a similar symbol next to the items that apply. Checklists and inventories provide information about a student's skills. The following are examples of checklist items that an employer could address.

| *Sample checklist items* | *Yes* | *No* |
|---|---|---|
| 1. Pays attention. | _____ | _____ |
| 2. Stays on task. | _____ | _____ |
| 3. Follows directions. | _____ | _____ |
| 4. Gets along with co-workers. | _____ | _____ |
| 5. Is on time. | _____ | _____ |
| 6. Accepts criticism. | _____ | _____ |

Rating scales provide information similar to that obtained with checklists and inventories, but usually call for a range of ratings instead of a simple yes-or-no response. Each item is accompanied by a scale with a range of responses. The individual circles the response that is most descriptive of the student (for example, 1 = poor, 2 = adequate, 3 = excellent). An example of a rating scale for assessing a student's expressive writing is shown in Figure 3.4. Although originally developed for elementary students, this rating scale can be used effectively with adolescents.

***Questionnaires*** Questionnaires, another informal technique, include a series of questions that an individual is asked to complete in writing or in an oral interview. Questionnaires may be structured or open-ended. In a structured questionnaire, the individual may circle Yes or No or choose from a series of statements that best describes the student. Open-ended questionnaires require the respondent to write statements in response to each question.

*Sample structured questionnaire items*

1. When the student doesn't know the meaning of content vocabulary, he/she
   a. asks the teacher.
   b. looks it up.
   c. checks for context clues.
2. When the student misses class, he/she
   a. asks the teacher what he/she missed.
   b. asks a friend for the notes.
   c. makes no attempt to find out what he/she missed.

**FIGURE 3.4    Expressive Writing Rating Scale**

Child _____ Type of writing analyzed _____

Rating Scale:    1        2        3
                poor   adequate   excellent

CONTENT

1  2  3    A. Does the writing clearly communicate an idea or ideas to the reader?
1  2  3    B. Is the content adequately developed?
1  2  3    C. Is the content interesting to the potential reader?

VOCABULARY

1  2  3    A. Does the writer select appropriate words to communicate his/her ideas?
1  2  3    B. Does the writer use precise/vivid vocabulary?
1  2  3    C. Does the writer effectively use verbs, nouns, adjectives and adverbs?
1  2  3    D. Does the vocabulary meet acceptable standards for written English (e.g., "isn't" vs. "ain't")?

SENTENCES

1  2  3    A. Are the sentences complete (subject and predicate)?
1  2  3    B. Are run-on sentences avoided?
1  2  3    C. Are exceptionally complex sentences avoided?
1  2  3    D. Are the sentences grammatically correct (e.g., word order, subject-verb agreement)?

PARAGRAPHS

1  2  3    A. Do the sentences in the paragraph relate to one topic?
1  2  3    B. Are the sentences organized to reflect the relationship between ideas within the paragraph?
1  2  3    C. Does the paragraph include a topical, introductory, or transition sentence?

MECHANICS

1  2  3    A. Are the paragraphs indented?
1  2  3    B. Are the correct margins used?
1  2  3    C. Are capitals used at the beginning of sentences?
1  2  3    D. Are additional capitals used as necessary in the written sample?
1  2  3    E. Is correct end-of-sentence punctuation used?
1  2  3    F. Is additional punctuation used as necessary in the written sample?

HANDWRITING

1  2  3    A. Is the handwriting legible?
1  2  3    B. Is the handwriting neat?

SPELLING

1  2  3    A. Does the writer correctly spell high-frequency, irregular words?
1  2  3    B. Did the writer correctly spell phonetic words?

Notes: Using these guidelines, the teacher can carefully examine a child's written work and pinpoint instructional needs. For example, it might be determined that the child needs instruction on writing complete sentences, using correct punctuation, or proofing for spelling errors. Evaluation of more than one sample would increase the accuracy of these conclusions.

Source: From *Teaching the Mildly Handicapped in the Regular Classroom* (2nd ed.) (pp. 72–73) by J. Q. Affleck, S. Lowenbraun, & A. Archer, 1980, Columbus, OH: Merrill. Copyright 1980 by Bell & Howell and Company. Reprinted by permission.

*Sample open-ended questionnaire items*

1. What are the student's major interests?

2. What work-related behaviors does the student possess that will assist him/her as an employee?

Indirect assessment techniques provide teachers with useful information in developing a student's instructional plan. For example, identifying the work-related social behaviors that a student is lacking allows the teacher to include those social behaviors within social-skills instruction. Finding out what students do when they have difficulty with content vocabulary enables the teacher to reteach strategies or provide additional strategies for vocabulary learning. However, you need to use caution in interpreting results because indirect assessment techniques rely on the perceptions, memory, and judgment of the individual responding and could result in inaccurate information (McLoughlin & Lewis, 1994).

Indirect assessment instruments are available in published form for each academic area, for social/behavior skills, and for vocational skills. Please see McLoughlin and Lewis (1994) or Salvia and Ysseldyke (1991) for a thorough description. Of course, teachers may develop their own items for checklists, inventories, rating scales, and questionnaires, based upon what they want to know about their students.

---

**COMPREHENSION MONITORING OF KEY CONCEPTS**

*Informal Assessment*

1. Informal assessment procedures at the secondary level include analyzing the environment and assessing the student.

2. Analyzing the environment includes identifying both the curricular demands and a student's strengths, needs, and learning preferences, and then determining how the two relate.

3. Assessing the student includes indirect and direct assessment. Indirect assessment is the collection of information (such as interests) about a student from others (such as parents and teachers). Direct assessment is the collection of information (for example, a student's written product) by evaluating the student's performance on a task (for example, the conversion of decimals to percentages).

4. Examples of indirect assessment are checklists, inventories, rating scales, and questionnaires.

5. Checklists and inventories usually consist of a set of statements or a list of curriculum competencies, skills, or objectives.

6. Rating scales are similar to checklists and inventories, but they include a range of ratings.

7. Questionnaires include a series of questions that an individual is asked to complete in writing or in an oral interview.

### Direct Assessment

Several types of direct assessment procedures are available to you for planning initial instruction and monitoring subsequent student performance. Remember, direct assessment involves assigning the student a task and evaluating performance of that task.

***Observation*** "Direct observation of student behavior is the recommended procedure for in-depth study of the possible problem behaviors identified by rating scales, checklists, and interviews" (McLoughlin & Lewis, 1994, p. 268). Observations may be nonsystematic or systematic. Nonsystematic observations consist of observing students during the performance of tasks and noting the way they complete the tasks. Some teachers use index cards or prepare a sheet of paper for each class with the names of students listed. During class, they make notes about behaviors they observe. For example, you may note that when Jesse completes problems in math, he makes random guesses at the answers instead of employing a systematic set of steps to solve the problems. You may notice that Belinda does not start in-class work on time. These observational data are helpful in planning further assessment such as systematic observation.

Systematic observation "requires repeated measures of a specifically defined behavior that is both observable and measurable" (Choate & Miller, 1995, p. 61). This type of observation is often used to assess problem behaviors in the classroom. We will thoroughly describe systematic observation in Chapter 6 as part of our discussion on motivation and management.

For now, let's look briefly at an example of how a teacher might use systematic observation in the classroom. Yvonne's teacher is concerned that Yvonne does not pay attention in math. The teacher selects and clearly defines a target behavior for paying attention (for example, using a calculator and writing answers in her notebook). After providing instruction for 30 minutes, Yvonne's teacher breaks down the last 20 minutes of the class period (independent practice) into 5-minute intervals. The teacher then sets a timer, and when it rings, she looks to see if Yvonne is using her calculator and writing answers to problems in her notebook. If Yvonne is demonstrating the target behavior, the teacher marks an X. If she is not demonstrating the target behavior, the teacher marks an O.

The teacher sets up the following recording system:

Target behavior:   Using a calculator and writing answers to problem in notebook

Time start:        1:30

Time stop:         1:50

Total period:      Twenty minutes

| at 5 min. | at 10 min. | at 15 min. | at 20 min. |
|:---:|:---:|:---:|:---:|
| X | X | O | O |

Notice that the teacher did observe Yvonne exhibit the target behavior the first two times the timer rang, but that she did not see Yvonne use her calculator and write in her notebook the last two times. She found out exactly when Yvonne was paying attention and when she was not. Let's assume that more days of systematic observation reveal the same pattern of behavior. Now, the teacher can hypothesize that Yvonne stops paying attention as the difficulty level of the material increases, or because she is bored or uninterested in the assignment. For the next lesson, the teacher can reteach the material, decrease the number of problems, or have Yvonne complete the assignment with a peer or on the computer and then observe the results. Notice that collection of this information through direct observation is extremely helpful in planning and monitoring instruction.

*Error analysis*  Evaluation of the actual products that students produce is highly useful for teachers as they plan initial instruction and later monitor student progress. A common approach to the evaluation of student products, and an important component of instructional planning and monitoring, is error analysis (Ashlock, 1990; Enright, Gable, & Hendrickson, 1988). Error analysis requires a systematic examination of a student's work for the purpose of identifying error patterns so that faulty, incorrect, or ineffective ways of completing tasks can be altered. Once the error patterns have been identified, the teacher can provide corrective instruction. An error analysis may be conducted in any academic subject area (such as computation errors) and in nonacademic areas as well (such as interviewing for a job). Error analysis holds much promise as an assessment technique in secondary settings because of its clear connection to daily instruction and its immediate benefits to students. Poteet (1995a) suggests that in addition to conducting an error analysis, it is helpful to do a success analysis by identifying the skills the student performs well.

*Math* As far back as 1946, Guiler identified common errors in decimal computation. We believe these areas of difficulty still have relevance for today's secondary students.

1. Adding, subtracting, and dividing decimal numbers
2. Changing fractions to decimals ($\frac{3}{5}$ = .60)
3. Changing mixed numbers to decimals ($7\frac{1}{4}$ = 7.25)
4. Placement of decimal point in multiplication and division of decimals

Roberts (1968) identified common computation errors that are also still relevant today:

1. *Incorrect operation.* For example, the student adds instead of multiplying.
2. *Incorrect number fact.* The student recalls a fact inaccurately, as in 7 + 5 = 11.
3. *Incorrect algorithm.* The student may skip a step or use an incorrect procedure. In the following example, Aida remembered the steps to long division, but when she brought down the number, she brought down both numbers at the same time. This gave her an answer of 299 instead of 268, remainder 6.

3. Arrange this information to reflect a correct computational sequence having a proper unit of expression.

4. Complete the calculation correctly to arrive at an answer. (p. 264)

These four components may be used to analyze a student's problem-solving performance and identify error patterns.

*Reading*  Error analysis in reading usually addresses errors in decoding and comprehension. The most common decoding categories assessed in a student's oral reading sample are:

1. *Additions.* The student adds a word to the text: "The *bright* sun dropped slowly in the sky" for "The sun dropped slowly in the sky."

2. *Substitutions.* The student substitutes another word for the actual word: "The girl ran *quietly* to the waiting taxi" for "The girl ran *quickly* to the waiting taxi."

3. *Omissions.* The student leaves out a word or word part: "Sean smiled at his daughter" for "Sean smiled *benevolently* at his daughter."

4. *Reversals.* The student changes the order of sounds or words: "*Prior just* to dawn, the ship set sail" for "Just prior to dawn, the ship set sail."

In conducting an error analysis of a student's decoding skills, the teacher asks the student to read aloud and marks the types of errors on a duplicate or follow-along copy.

In assessing comprehension errors, the teacher asks questions after the student has read a passage. Typically, questions are asked to assess literal and inferential comprehension. To identify errors in literal comprehension, the teacher asks about the main idea, supporting details, the sequence of events, and the meaning of specific vocabulary. To evaluate inferential thinking, the teacher asks for predictions, implications, and conclusions (McLoughlin & Lewis, 1994). At the secondary level, content texts may be used to determine comprehension of subject area information.

*Spelling*  Many types of work samples (homework, essays, book reports, tests) can provide examples of students' spelling. Miller (1990) and Tindal and Marston (1990) have found certain spelling errors to be common in students' work. These errors include omissions (*chang* for *change; beter* for *better*), transpositions (*handel* for *handle*), and substitutions (*enuff* for *enough; sity* for *city*). Examination of the students' work for these common errors will help the teacher develop one or more instructional strategies in spelling.

*Handwriting* Poor letter formation, spacing, and other associated problems (posture, position of paper, and pencil grip) may be a problem for secondary students. Writing fluency may be an additional area of concern. Salvia and Hughes (1990) found that some 12- and 13-year-olds were writing less than 30 letters per minute. It is important to analyze handwriting errors and correct them as soon as possible before they become permanent habits (such as poor pencil grip or incorrect letter formation) and before they impact other areas (losing points because the teacher cannot read the handwriting). Because secondary students are expected to do a great deal of writing (taking notes from lectures, writing papers, and taking tests), analysis of their handwriting skills for instructional planning is important.

*Written expression* Students are expected to do a great deal of writing at the secondary level. Performing an error analysis of a student's writing sample may reveal valuable information about capitalization, punctuation, spelling, vocabulary, mechanics, grammar, and composition skills. Teachers may define their own categories such as those just listed, or use ideas from published informal assessment materials such as the expressive writing rating scale developed by Affleck, Lowenbraun, and Archer (1980). They recommended a rating of the content, vocabulary, sentences, paragraphs, mechanics, handwriting, and spelling of a student's writing sample.

*Job/work samples* An area important for the assessment of secondary students in vocational education is that of job or work samples and simulations. These simulations of work tasks or activities may or may not represent an actual part of a job (Sitlington & Wimmer, 1978). An error analysis may reveal the job skills that are being performed incorrectly (such as use of a computer) or the work-related social skills that the student is lacking (such as responding to criticism).

*Steps in error analysis* We suggest the following steps for conducting an error analysis of secondary students' work products: (1) Collect work products, (2) Score the products, (3) Identify the errors, (4) Hypothesize reasons for errors, (5) Test hypotheses by looking for similar patterns among correct responses, (6) Accept or revise hypotheses, (7) Teach correction strategies. Let's apply these steps to the writing sample of Zena, a ninth-grade student with a disability, shown in Figure 3.5.

1. *Collect work products.* Examine Zena's writing sample in Figure 3.5. (Note: We show one example to illustrate the steps. When you conduct an error analysis, make sure you collect several different types of writing samples.)

**FIGURE 3.5** **Written Language Sample**

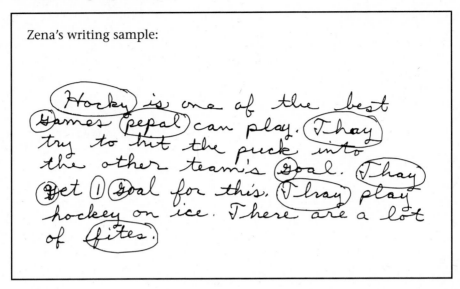

Zena's writing sample:

Hocky is one of the best Games pepal can play. Thay try to hit the puck into the other team's Goal. Thay Get 1 Goal for this. Thay play hockey on ice. There are a lot of fites.

2. *Score the products.* We have marked her paper for spelling, handwriting, and composition errors.

3. *Identify the errors.* Zena has difficulty with spelling (adding or leaving out letters), handwriting (legibility), and composition (all sentences are simple sentences and lack descriptive words).

4. *Hypothesize reasons for errors.* (See step 5.)

5. *Test hypotheses by looking for similar patterns among correct responses.* Spelling errors could be due to carelessness, because she spelled *hockey* incorrectly the first time and correctly the second time. She could be spelling phonetically (*pepal* for *people, thay* for *they,* and *fites* for *fights*). Other, more phonetically regular words are correct (*games, teams, best, lot*). Zena's handwriting is difficult to read because she has problems in letter formation and spacing. Uppercase letters have been used in place of some lowercase letters. Although her sentences are grammatically correct, Zena has difficulty generating enough words. Asked to write five paragraphs, she wrote only five sentences. Her sentences are immature for a ninth-grader (short, simple, declarative sentences), and the vocabulary is limited (lack of descriptive, vivid vocabulary).

6. *Accept or revise hypotheses.* We accept the hypotheses that Zena has difficulty spelling words that are not phonetically regular (spelling), that she has problems with letter formation and spacing (handwriting), that she

has difficulty generating enough words when she writes, and that her writing and vocabulary lack maturity (composition).

7. *Teach correction strategies.* Zena needs to be taught strategies to assist her in the areas identified in step 6, and she should be instructed in an overall error-monitoring strategy.

**Portfolio assessment** Paulson, Paulson, and Meyer (1991) define portfolio assessment as "a purposeful collection of a student's work that exhibits the student's efforts, progress, and achievements in one or more areas" (p. 60). It provides an excellent means of monitoring/evaluating a student's progress in the curriculum. Portfolio assessment in reading or English may include a collection of books read, student reviews of plays, comparisons between books and movies, book reports completed, reflections on literary works, reading logs, audio- and videotapes, and writing samples. A math portfolio may contain a record of the student's performance on in-class and homework assignments, pictures or diagrams drawn by the student and used to solve math problems, and a section in which the student reflects on how a particular math concept applies to real life. Rakes (1995) suggests having students summarize lab experiments in science, and react to one or two historical characters or events each week in history. In social studies, the examination of topics in current events provides a means for students to react to real-life issues in journal format in their portfolios. In art, music, and vocational education, it is interesting to observe the evolution of a student's work throughout the year. Portfolio assessment is ongoing, allowing both teacher and student to see the progress that is being made and to identify where the problem areas are so that they may be addressed immediately.

Paulson et al. (1991) recommend that portfolios

1. Specify the criteria for selecting contents and include student input.
2. Specify criteria for evaluation.
3. Include a student reflection component.

*Specify the criteria for selecting contents and include student input.* Some teachers give students a list of required components (related to IEP and curriculum objectives), but then encourage students to generate their own additional components. In this way, you maximize students' contributions to their own learning. Paulson et al. (1991) suggest that when deciding upon the contents of the portfolio, you should consult the scope and sequence of the course, choose the most critical goals, and then think of two or three kinds of student work samples or products that would best demonstrate those goals.

*Specify the criteria for evaluation.* Teachers may develop their own criteria for evaluation. These criteria may change as the school year moves on and the student progresses. For example, in assessing writing skills, you may initially look to see if students can get a few thoughts down on paper. Later, you may assess whether they can generate several complete sentences in the form of a paragraph. Still later, you may assess whether your students can write several paragraphs about a topic using correct punctuation, grammar, and self-reflection. Table 3.1 illustrates one way that a student's writing may be evaluated. This type of assessment provides teachers with information about the skills that students have mastered as well as about their attitudes and interests.

**T A B L E  3 . 1**  **Evaluation Criteria for Written Products**

| Area to be assessed | Points |
|---|---|
| 1. Punctuation | 10 |
| 2. Capitalization | 10 |
| 3. Appearance (margins, neatness) | 10 |
| 4. Accuracy of information | 20 |
| 5. Quantity (number of words) | 10 |
| 6. Grammar | 10 |
| 7. Content (interest, creativity) | 15 |
| 8. Reflection on one's work | 15 |
| Total points possible | 100 |

| Grade | Points |
|---|---|
| A+ | 98–100 |
| A | 94–97 |
| A– | 91–93 |
| B+ | 88–90 |
| B | 84–87 |
| B– | 81–83 |
| C+ | 78–80 |
| C | 74–77 |
| C– | 70–73 |
| | Below 70: Redo |

*Source:* Adapted from *Effective Instruction of Difficult to Teach Students,* by L. Idol and J. F. West (Ed.), Austin, TX: PRO-ED, p. 22. Reprinted by permission.

*Include student reflection.* By involving students in reflection about their work, we give them opportunities to become actively involved with their own learning and to take responsibility for their progress. By reading student comments, we gain insights into what students believe to be important.

In summary, a portfolio (1) provides a comprehensive view of student performance in context; (2) involves the student as a participant in assessment, instead of the object of assessment; and (3) assists the student to become more independent and self-directed (Paulson et al., 1991).

***Criterion-referenced testing***  Of the variety of informal assessment measures at our disposal, criterion-referenced tests (CRTs) are the most commonly used (Meier, 1995). CRTs assist teachers in planning for instruction and in monitoring progress (McLoughlin & Lewis, 1994). In criterion-referenced testing, a student's performance is compared with a preestablished criterion or standard—not to the performance of others, as in norm-referenced testing. This means that each student "is compared against his or her own previous performance levels" (Ysseldyke & Algozzine, 1984, p. 345).

The criterion or standard that is used in criterion-referenced testing may be an objective written or selected by the teacher, or a skill taken from a curriculum scope and sequence chart (Overton, 1992). Scope refers to the breadth of the academic content, and sequence refers to the order. For example, fractions appear on the scope and sequence charts for both elementary and secondary levels. In the primary grades, students may cut a pie into different sections to show ½, ⅓, or ¼, whereas in middle school, students may convert fractions to decimals in order to solve complex problems. Thus, the topic may be the same (fractions), but the scope or breadth is different for each grade level. Sequence refers to the order in which we teach skills. For example, first we teach addition of like fractions, next addition of unlike fractions, then addition of mixed numbers without regrouping, and finally, addition of mixed numbers with regrouping.

Criterion-referenced tests emphasize mastery. The results tell us what skills the student can and cannot perform. For example, in one section of the Comprehensive Inventory of Basic Skills (Brigance, 1983), which addresses the topic of locating and explaining the purpose of the parts of a book (table of contents, index, glossary), the student locates and describes the purpose or use of each part. As the student finds the specific part and writes the purpose, the teacher scores the responses for accuracy, and determines which items were not mastered. These become the student's next instructional objectives. For example, one objective states:

> By _____, when given a book that has different parts, _____ will locate parts and indicate the functions of the following parts (list as appropriate). (p. K-6)

**TABLE 3.2** **Commercially Published Criterion-Referenced Tests**

| Test | Academic area grades | |
| --- | --- | --- |
| 1. Brigance Diagnostic Comprehensive Inventory of Basic Skills (Brigance, 1983) | Reading, writing, spelling, listening, math, and study | K–9 |
| 2. Brigance Diagnostic Inventory of Essential Skills (Brigance, 1981) | Reading, writing, spelling, math, vocational, health, functional, and study skills | 4–12 |
| 3. Multilevel Academic Skills Inventory (Howell, Zucker, & Morehead, 1982) | Reading and math skills | 1–9 |
| 4. System FORE (Bagai & Bagai, 1979) | Reading, math | 1–12 |
| 5. Enright Diagnostic Inventory of Basic Mathematics Skills (Enright, 1983) | Math computation skills | 1–9 |

Notice that with criterion-referenced assessment, there is a close connection between assessment and instructional planning, as assessment leads directly to the development of instructional objectives.

Criterion-referenced tests are readily available in commercial form and may also be developed by teachers to assess student performance on some aspect of the curriculum. Criterion-referenced tests are available in most academic areas and can be used to assess academic, survival, and vocational skills. Table 3.2 contains a list of commercially published CRTs.

We recommend the following four steps when using criterion-referenced tests for instructional planning (Olson and Platt, 1996): (1) Select the test. (2) Administer the test. (3) Select the expected level of mastery. (4) Identify the objectives.

*Select the test.* Once you determine a student's area(s) of weakness (such as math computation), you can select or develop a criterion-referenced test. If Ruby has difficulty with computation, you could administer the ENRIGHT®, one of the BRIGANCE® inventories, or construct your own test. It is important to examine the scope and sequence of a test when making your selection to ensure that the skills you want to test can be measured with that test. Then, administer that section of the test to the student. Table 3.3 contains a sample employment scope and sequence from the vocational section of the BRIGANCE® Diagnostic Inventory of Essential Skills (Brigance, 1981).

**TABLE 3.3    Sample Employment Scope and Sequence Chart**

| Assessment | Page | |
|---|---|---|
| V–4 | 259 | **Job interests and aptitudes:** (Space is not provided for recording the results. A copy of the assessment may be filed in this record book, if needed or appropriate.) |
| V–5 | 260 | **Health and physical problems/handicaps:** (Space is not provided for recording the results. A copy of the assessment may be filed in this record book, if needed or appropriate.) |
| V–6 | 261 | **Application for a social security number:**  Completes:<br><br>1. Name  2. Name at Birth  3. Place of Birth  4. Mother's Maiden Name  5. Father's Name<br>6. Date of Birth  7. Age  8. Sex  9. Race  10. Previously Applied?<br>11. Mailing Address  12. Today's Date  13. Telephone Number  14. Signature |
| V–7 | 262 | **Choosing a career:** (Space is not provided for recording the results. A copy of the assessment may be filed in this record book, if needed or appropriate.)<br><br>Notes: |
| V–8 | 263 | **Employment signs:** Number of 20 signs read:  __/20  __/20  __/20  __/20  __/20<br><br>1. APPLICATIONS  8. EMPLOYMENT AGENCY  15. EQUAL OPPORTUNITY EMPLOYER<br>2. RECEPTIONIST  9. PERSONNEL OFFICE  16. PART TIME HELP WANTED<br>3. HELP WANTED  10. PERSONNEL MANAGER  17. APPLY AT PERSONNEL OFFICE<br>4. APPLY HERE  11. NO HELP WANTED  18. NO UNAUTHORIZED PERSONS . . . .<br>5. EMPLOYEES ONLY  12. APPLY AT OFFICE  19. ALL VISITORS . . . .<br>6. JOB INFORMATION  13. DIRECTOR OF PERSONNEL  20. APPLICATIONS ACCEPTED . . . .<br>7. EMPLOYMENT OFFICE  14. AUTHORIZED PERSONNEL ONLY<br><br>Notes: |
| V–9 | 264 | **Employment vocabulary:** Number of 25 words matched to definitions:  __/25  __/25  __/25  __/25  __/25<br><br>1. appearance  9. fringe benefits  17. references<br>2. application  10. gross income or pay  18. reliable<br>3. deductions  11. interview  19. salary<br>4. employee  12. net income or pay  20. seniority benefits<br>5. employer  13. overtime pay  21. state income tax<br>6. equal opportunity employer  14. pay period  22. trainee or apprentice<br>7. federal income tax  15. personal data  23. unemployment compensation<br>8. FICA tax  16. personnel manager  24. union<br>  25. union dues<br><br>Notes: |

| Assessment | Page | |
|---|---|---|
| V–10 | 265 | **Employment abbreviations:** Number of 55 abbreviations read: __/55 __/55 __/55 __/55 __/55 __/55 |

1. Agcy.
2. am
3. appt.
4. bd.
5. ben.
6. betw.
7. Co.
8. Col. grad.
9. Corp.
10. deliv.
11. Dept.
12. EOE
13. eve.
14. exp.
15. exper.
16. Excell.
17. F/T
18. furn.
19. Gen.
20. hr.
21. hi-schl. grad.
22. HSG
23. immed.
24. ins.
25. lic.

26. M/F
27. min.
28. mgmt.
29. mgr.
30. mo.
31. Nat'l
32. nec.
33. ofc.
34. oppty.
35. pd.
36. perm.
37. ph.
38. pm
39. pos.
40. pref.
41. pref'd
42. P/T
43. Refs.
44. Refs req'd
45. rm.
46. sal.
47. temp.
48. trnee.
49. transp.
50. w/
51. wk.
52. wkly.
53. wknds.
54. yr.
55. yrs.

Notes:

| V–11 | 266 | **"Help wanted" advertisements:** Number of 7 responses correct: __/7 __/7 __/7 __/7 __/7 __/7 |

Notes:

| V–12 | 267 | **Simple application for employment:** Completes: |

1. Name
2. Social Security Number
3. Address
4. Phone
5. Education
6. Work Experience
7. References
8. Signature
9. Date

Notes:

| V–13 | 268 | **Complex application for employment:** Completes: |

1. Personal
2. Education/Training
3. Employment Record
4. Military
5. Health
6. References
7. Signature and Date

Notes:

| V–14 | 269 | **Job interview questions:** (Space is not provided for recording the results. A copy of the assessment may be filed in this record book, if needed or appropriate.) |

Notes:

| V–15 | 272 | **Job interview preparation rating scale:** (Space is not provided for recording the results. A copy of the rating may be filed in this record book, if needed or appropriate.) |

| | | |
|---|---|---|
| V-16 | 273 | **Job interview rating scale:** (Space is not provided for recording the results. A copy of the rating may be filed in this record book, if needed or appropriate.) |
| V-17 | 274 | **W-4 form:** Completes:<br>1. Names  2. Social Security Number  3. Home Address  4. Marital Status<br>5. Exemptions  6. Signature  7. Date<br>Notes: |
| V-18 | 275 | **Future time on clock:** Figures future time on clock for:<br>hours  half hours  quarter hours  five minutes  minutes<br>Notes: |
| V-19 | 276 | **Past time on clock:** Figures past time on clock for:<br>hours  half hours  quarter hours  five minutes  minutes |
| V-20 | 277 | **Time duration on clock:** Figures time duration for:<br>hours, not past noon  hours, past noon  half hours  quarter hours  quarter hours and half hours |
| V-21 | 278 | **Payroll deductions:** Number of 9 responses correct: ___/9  ___/9  ___/9  ___/9  ___/9 |
| V-22 | 280 | **Federal income tax return—form 1040A:** Completes:<br>A. Name  E. Presidential Election Campaign Fund  9. Dividends  12a. Credit for Contribution to Candidates  12c. Earned Income Credit  15. Total<br>B. Address  F. Filing Status  10. Unemployment Compensation  12b. Total Fed. Tax Withheld  13. Total  16. Refund<br>C. Soc. Sec.  G. Exemptions  11. Adj. Gross Income  14a. Tax  17. Balance Due<br>D. Occupation  7. Wages  14b. Advance Earned Income Credit  H. Signature<br>8. Interest  I. Date |
| V-23 | 281 | **Unemployment compensation form:** Completes:<br>1. Name and Social Security Number  6. Dependents under 18  10. Leave of Absence<br>2. Address  7. Disabled Children  11. Other Compensation<br>3. Date of Birth  8. Dependents 18+ Who Are Full-Time Students  12. Self-Employment<br>4. Signed Statement and Date  9. Reasons for Refusing Full-Time Work  13. Present Business Involvement<br>5. Listing of Previous Jobs  14. Pension<br>Notes: |

*Source:* From *Essential Skills Record,* BRIGANCE® *Diagnostic Inventory of Essential Skills* by Albert Brigance (Ed.), 1981, North Billerica, MA: Curriculum Associates®, pp. 28, 29, 30. Reprinted by permission.

*Administer the test.* Careful attention to the contents of the test enables teachers to administer only those sections that are pertinent to the student. In addition, unlike the administration of a standardized test, the administration of a criterion-referenced test is flexible, meaning you can make modifications as you test. Felicia's teacher wanted to find out if she could fill out a *basic* application for employment, so the teacher administered that section of the BRIGANCE® Diagnostic Inventory of Essential Skills. Felicia began to complete this section so well that her teacher stopped her and quickly moved on to the *complex* application for employment.

It is common to find suggestions for administration in most CRTs. These include the materials you will need, the time you should allow, and the criteria for acceptance. However, these do not have to be rigidly adhered to, and often leave decisions up to the discretion of the individual administering the test. For example, a teacher of a student from a different cultural background may modify the criterion for mastery on a task that includes unfamiliar vocabulary or expressions.

*Select the expected level of mastery.* One of the concerns associated with criterion-referenced tests is establishing a criterion (Witt, Elliott, Gresham, & Kramer, 1988). This problem has received considerable attention from experts in the field, and we share some of their suggestions with you. Hofmeister and Preston (1981) recommend five guidelines for selecting a criterion, which we paraphrase as follows:

1. Make the criterion different for different subject matter (math, science, English).

2. For most skills, use a range of 80–100%. Increase this to 95–100% for skills involving personal safety.

3. For total recall items, such as completion, use 80%. For recognition items, such as multiple choice, make the criterion higher.

4. Use the performance of others to help set the criterion (identify how well peers perform the task).

5. Ask experts in an academic content area to specify the minimum criterion for acceptable performance.

Shapiro (1989a) recommends the following ways to determine mastery:

1. Use a normative comparison of performance by using a task that 80% of the class has mastered (peer assessment).

2. Associate your criterion for a task with your school's grading policy (95–100%, mastery; 85–94%, average; 75–84%, needs improvement, further instruction).

3. Use a criterion that is easily understood by the student and capable of being charted (4/6 items correct = student continues with the objective; 6/6 items correct = student moves on to a new objective).

Evans and Evans (1986) offer additional considerations in the form of questions that are important to ask:

Does passing the test mean that the student is proficient and will maintain the skills?

Is the student ready to progress to the next level in the curriculum?

Will the student be able to generalize and apply the skills outside the classroom?

Would the student pass the mastery test if it were given at a later date? (p. 10)

*Identify the objectives.* Instructional objectives may be identified by determining which skills the student has not mastered. This is accomplished by comparing the student's score to the preestablished criterion. For example, if a task requires Angelo to complete his name, address, and social security number on an application for employment, and he does this with 100% accuracy, you would assume that he has mastered that skill (particularly if he does this consistently on several different applications). If another task requires him to record his previous work experience along with the dates of employment, and he does so with only 70% accuracy, then he has not mastered the skill, and you would target this as an objective for instruction. For example: "Given an employment application from Mario's Pizza Place, Angelo will complete in writing the work experience section with 95% accuracy." Some of the commercially available CRTs have objectives written for each skill. If a student does not meet the mastery level, the teacher can simply transfer the objective to the IEP or weekly lesson plan.

A commonly used method in assessment is to teach, test, reteach (if necessary), and retest (Meier, 1995). Criterion-referenced testing provides a means of accomplishing this because assessment is so closely tied to the curriculum. Witt et al. (1988) identify some advantages and disadvantages of criterion-referenced testing. The strengths of criterion-referenced testing include the ability to (1) identify a student's skills, (2) decide what to teach next, and (3) monitor a student's progress. Limitations of CRTs include problems with (1) constructing CRTs, (2) establishing a criterion for acceptable performance, and (3) creating parallel test forms.

***Curriculum-based assessment*** Curriculum-based assessment is "the practice of obtaining direct and frequent measures of a student's performance on a series of sequentially arranged objectives derived from the curriculum used in the classroom" (Blankenship & Lilly, 1981, p. 81). It enables us to identify a student's instructional needs by assessing targeted curriculum skills (Choate, Enright, Miller, Poteet, & Rakes, 1995). There is wide support for curriculum-based assessment (CBA) as a strategy for decision making for students who have difficulty with academics (Shinn, Rosenfield, & Knutson, 1989). With curriculum-based assessment, you use the actual curriculum of the local school to assess students. Choate et al. (1995) state that "useful assessment is so interwoven with instruction that it defies separation" (p. xii). Thus, there is a direct link between assessment (testing) and instructional planning (teaching).

CBAs are initially given to establish the beginning point of instruction and then readministered periodically to monitor student progress (Guernsey, 1990). They may be developed for curriculum material from any subject area. For example, you may develop a CBA to assess reading comprehension skills within an English literature class. To do this, you would select reading passages from different parts of the text you are using and develop a set of comprehension questions for each passage.

Shinn et al. (1989) point out that "to ensure continuing student progress, we must assess student progress frequently and systematically" (p. 313). The teacher selects relevant skills from the curriculum, gives the student informal tests that assess performance of these skills, and develops instructional objectives (Blankenship, 1985). Short, timed skill probes selected from the student's curriculum are frequently used to establish a baseline, then later utilized as a measure against which to judge the student's progress.

Some states, such as Louisiana, require that curriculum-based assessment be conducted before referring a student for special education (Meier, 1992). This assists in the decision of whether a student's difficulties "are curriculum and/or teaching related or if the child in fact learns differently from his normally achieving peers" (Gickling & Thompson, 1985, p. 207). Even though CBAs are used to help determine eligibility, they are more commonly used by teachers during instruction (Meier, 1995).

We like the way Blankenship (1985) has identified steps to use in developing a CBA. We have modified and condensed some of her steps and have provided explanations of each step, along with examples from her article, "Using Curriculum-Based Assessment Data to Make Instructional Decisions."

1. *List the skills in the curriculum material selected, decide if all the important skills are included, and verify the appropriateness of the sequence of skills.* Look over the skills in the curriculum you are using. Make sure they correspond to the objectives you have selected and written in the IEPs for your stu-

**TABLE 3.4  Partial Skills List for a Metric Measurement Chapter**

| Skill | Page number/ number of items | Total number of items |
|---|---|---|
| *Centimeter* | | |
| 1. Given a metric ruler, measure a variety of objects and express their lengths in centimeters. | 178/8 179/6 198/2 200/1 | 17 |
| 2. Given a metric ruler, draw lines to specified lengths in centimeters. | 179/4 | 4 |
| *Conversion problems* | | |
| 1. Given numbers expressed in meters, write the same quantities expressed in centimeters. | 180/3 198/1 | 4 |
| 2. Given numbers expressed in centimeters, write the same quantities expressed in meters. | 180/1 | 1 |
| 3. Given numbers expressed in centimeters, write the same quantities expressed in meters plus centimeters. | 180/3 | 3 |
| 4. Given numbers expressed in kilometers, write the same quantities expressed in meters. | 181/2 198/1 | 3 |
| 5. Given numbers expressed in meters, write the same quantities expressed in kilometers. | 181/1 | 1 |
| 6. Given numbers expressed in meters, write the same quantities expressed in kilometers plus meters. | 181/1 | 1 |

*Source:* From "Using Curriculum-Based Assessment Data to Make Instructional Decisions," by C. Blankenship, 1985, *Exceptional Children, 52*(3), p. 235. Reprinted by permission.

dents. Check to make sure there are no gaps between skills. Revise the skills list if necessary by adding, deleting, or changing the sequence of skills. Blankenship gives an example of a list of skills included in a metric measurement chapter (Table 3.4) and reports that the teacher (Paterson, 1981), who wanted to develop a CBA for this curriculum material, found the skills list to be satisfactory.

2. *Write an objective for each skill listed.* As you write objectives for the skills on the list, make sure you include the five components: condition, learner,

target behavior, criterion, and overlearning. Blankenship (1985) reports that Paterson (1981) wrote an objective for each skill, an example of which follows:

> On two occasions, given a metric ruler and two lines of different lengths, the students will write their appropriate lengths in centimeters, scoring at least 3 out of 4 items correct. (p. 236)

3. *Develop items to assess each objective and prepare testing materials.* Make sure you include a sufficient number of items to complete an adequate assessment of each skill. In addition, you also need to develop parallel forms of your test so that you can conduct repeated assessments over a period of time. Then, decide what types of materials you will use to assess each skill. Paterson (1981) used worksheets containing a few items to assess each skill, with parallel forms to assess students on different occasions. She decided to use four items for each skill. She included two of the items on one test and two items, measuring similar skills, on a parallel form of the test.

4. *Plan how to give your CBA and administer before beginning instruction.* Paterson (1981) chose to give her CBA to her math class on two separate days (January 5 and 6), before beginning her unit on metric measurement. Blankenship (1985) reports that Paterson did this to assess her students' skills in metric measurement, group her students for instruction, and monitor their progress after instruction.

5. *Examine the results.* Studying the results will help you decide which students already know the skills, which students are ready to learn the skills, and which ones need instruction in prerequisite skills before beginning instruction in the target skill. Paterson (1981) used the method shown in Table 3.5 to report her students' scores. This method enabled her to select the students who could already measure and draw lines and were thus ready to learn metric conversion.

Notice in Table 3.5 that Pam was the only one who had mastered the prerequisite skills of measuring and drawing lines in centimeters. On January 5, Pam scored 2 correct and 0 incorrect on measuring lines. On January 6, she scored 2 correct and 0 incorrect on measuring lines, resulting in a total of 4 out of 4 correct. Pam was also able to draw lines correctly 3 out of 4 times, demonstrating that she had mastered both prerequisite skills. She was ready to learn about conversion. Paterson (1981) discovered that Isaac and Scott had not mastered measuring and drawing lines in centimeters, so she decided that she needed to teach that skill to them. They lacked the essential prerequisite skills of measuring and drawing lines.

Guernsey (1990) recommends the use of a chart to report results for individuals or large groups. "Because test items and learning objectives are

**Table 3.5** **Results of CBA Given Prior to Instruction**

| Date | Centimeter | | Conversion problems | | | | | |
| | Measure lines | Draw lines | 1 | 2 | 3 | 4 | 5 | 6 |
|---|---|---|---|---|---|---|---|---|
| *Isaac* | | | | | | | | |
| 1/5 | 1/1 | 0/2 | 0/2 | 0/2 | 0/2 | 0/2 | 0/2 | 0/2 |
| 1/6 | 1/1 | 0/2 | 0/2 | 0/2 | 0/2 | 0/2 | 0/2 | 0/2 |
| *Scott* | | | | | | | | |
| 1/5 | 0/2 | 1/1 | 0/2 | 0/2 | 0/2 | 0/2 | 0/2 | 0/2 |
| 1/6 | 0/2 | 0/2 | 0/2 | 0/2 | 0/2 | 0/2 | 0/2 | 0/2 |
| *Pam* | | | | | | | | |
| 1/5 | 2/0 | 1/1 | 1/1 | 0/2 | 0/2 | 0/2 | 0/2 | 0/2 |
| 1/6 | 2/0 | 2/0 | 1/1 | 2/0 | 0/2 | 0/2 | 0/2 | 0/2 |

*Note:* Scores reported as number of correct answers/number of incorrect answers. Boxed items indicate scores requiring further student instruction on the skills being tested.
*Source:* From "Using Curriculum-Based Assessment Data to Make Instructional Decisions" by C. Blankenship, 1985, *Exceptional Children, 52*(3), p. 234. Reprinted by permission.

closely allied, by recording student scores under each objective the teacher can tell at a glance who has mastered the material, who needs entry level instruction, and who may lack prerequisite knowledge for instruction" (p. 17).

6. *Readminister the CBA after instruction.* After providing instruction to your students, you should give them a test on the material you have just covered. This will help you determine which skills to work on next. Paterson (1981) rechecked Isacc and Scott on measuring and drawing lines (prerequisite skills) and found that they were ready to begin instruction on conversion.

Frequent measures on items from the original skill list should be conducted after instruction has occurred. After you have finished teaching the entire chapter, unit, or list of skills, readminister the entire CBA. Use this information to determine overall performance of students and to target specific students for remediation or additional practice.

Poteet (1995b) states that curriculum-based assessment facilitates both student and program evaluation, assists teachers in determining what to teach, and increases student achievement. CBA can be used to place students in curriculum materials and to individualize instruction (Blankenship & Lilly, 1981). It provides a direct link between assessment and instructional planning.

---

**COMPREHENSION MONITORING OF KEY CONCEPTS**

*Direct Assessment*

1. Examples of direct assessment are observation, error analysis, portfolio assessment, criterion-referenced testing, and curriculum-based assessment.

2. Observations may be nonsystematic or systematic. Nonsystematic observations consist of observing students during the performance of tasks and noting the way they complete the tasks. Systematic observation "requires repeated measures of specifically defined behavior that is both observable and measurable" (Choate & Miller, 1995, p. 61).

3. Error analysis requires a systematic examination of a student's work for the purpose of identifying error patterns so that faulty, incorrect, or ineffective ways of completing tasks can be altered.

4. An error analysis can be conducted in math, reading, spelling, handwriting, written expression, or with job samples.

5. The steps in error analysis are (1) collect work products, (2) score the products, (3) identify the errors, (4) hypothesize reasons for errors, (5) test hypotheses by looking for similar patterns among the correct responses, (6) accept or revise hypotheses, and (7) teach correction strategies.

6. Portfolio assessment is "a purposeful collection of a student's work that exhibits the student's efforts, progress, and achievements in one or more areas" (Paulson et al., 1991, p. 27).

7. In criterion-referenced testing, a student's performance is compared with a preestablished criterion or standard. The steps include (1) selecting the test, (2) administering the test, (3) selecting the expected level of mastery, and (4) identifying the objectives.

8. Curriculum-based assessment (CBA) is "the practice of obtaining direct and frequent measures of a student's performance on a series of sequentially arranged objectives derived from the curriculum used in the classroom" (Blankenship & Lilly, 1981, p. 81).

9. The steps in curriculum-based assessment are as follows: (1) List the skills in the curriculum material selected, decide if all the important skills are included, and verify the appropriateness of the sequence of skills. (2) Write an objective for each skill listed. (3) Develop items to assess each objective and prepare testing materials. (4) Plan how to give your CBA and administer before beginning instruction. (5) Examine the results. (6) Readminister the CBA after instruction.

 Now that you have read Chapter 3, reflect on your earlier responses at the beginning of the chapter and complete this post organizer.

1. Trina is a 10th-grade student who has difficulty writing complete sentences, using the correct punctuation, and remembering to indent the first word in a paragraph. Write an objective for one of her areas of difficulty. Describe how the objective you wrote *before* you read the chapter differs from the one you just wrote.

2. Name and describe three ways you could informally assess secondary students with mild disabilities in order to plan for their instruction and three different ways you could monitor their progress. Did you answer this question with different suggestions this time?

# Diverse Populations in the Secondary Schools

© Kathy Sloane/Jeroboam

**CHAPTER HIGHLIGHTS**

*Characteristics/Cultural Values*
*Instructional Considerations*
*Issues*

---

 Before you read Chapter 4, complete this advance organizer by discussing the following questions with a peer.

1. What are some of your cultural values?

2. What can influence cultural values?

3. What are the four basic approaches to multicultural education?

4. How do you plan to incorporate multicultural education into the curriculum?

---

Imagine yourself as a newly arrived immigrant, sitting in a high school class in Sydney, Australia. Your teacher has just asked you to interpret the popular lyrics of an Australian song (now the national anthem): "Waltzing Matilda, waltzing Matilda, you'll come a waltzing Matilda with me" (Fuld, 1966). You reply that it's obviously about a man and woman dancing. The teacher frowns and asks a native student sitting next to you. The student answers correctly. You are confused, because you understood the teacher, as he spoke English even though he had an accent. Unfortunately, you lack the knowledge of Australian culture needed to answer the question correctly. In Australia, Matilda is not only the name of a woman but a knapsack that bounces, or waltzes, as one walks. This little example shows how difficult it can be to comprehend a passage without adequate cultural information. Thus, it is not surprising that adolescents from diverse cultural backgrounds may have difficulty in school, since the culture of our schools is intertwined mostly with the Euro-American culture. School values such as independence, individual achievement, competition, future orientation, and the informal classroom atmosphere are derived from the beliefs and values of the Euro-American culture (Olson & Platt, 1996). However, we are starting to realize that awareness of only one culture limits schools in meeting the needs of students

By the year 2000, the "minority" population will increase from 30% to 50% in the public schools (Quality Education for Minorities Project, 1990). The U.S. Census Bureau (1991) predicts that by the year 2010, children of color will be a majority in New York, Texas, and Florida. In the 1992 Civil Rights survey, approximately 33% of elementary and secondary students with mild disabilities were from the minority populations of African Americans, Asian Americans, Hispanic Americans, and Native Americans (U.S. Department of Education, 1994). Thus, as a teacher of adolescents with mild disabilities, you need to be aware of and incorporate cultural differences into your secondary curriculum. In this chapter, we examine the African American, Asian American, Euro-American, Hispanic, and Native American cultures. We use the term *Euro-American* to describe North Americans of European ancestry because, as M. S. Poplin stated during a speech in 1992, we are all immigrants to this country and Euro-Americans form a cultural group just as African Americans or Hispanics do. In examining these cultures, we will describe general characteristics, instructional considerations, and issues.

Cultural differences are not the only differences we could address. Individuals also differ in intelligence, sexual orientation, disabilities, and religious upbringing. We choose to address cultural differences in this chapter because we agree with Briganti's statement (1989, p. 12) that "the more information we have about a student's cultural group, the easier it is to develop accurate interpretations of individual behavior."

## Characteristics/Cultural Values

The purpose of this section is to share some characteristics of the various cultures—not to validate stereotypic beliefs, but to assist you in better understanding and interacting with students of color. An awareness of other cultures is necessary before teachers can consider cultural differences in their curriculum (Locke, 1988). Understanding a person's culture may explain some behaviors and help with planning and instruction. For example, many teachers from the Euro-American culture demand eye contact from their students. A teacher who understands that youth from the African American, Asian American, Hispanic, and Native American cultures are often taught to avoid direct eye contact will not consider such avoidance as disrespectful.

We do not mean to imply that all people from a particular culture share the same values or characteristics. In reply to the statement that "all Indians are good trackers," Jim Chee, a fictional Navajo policeman popularized by Tony Hillerman (1990), comments "some Navajos are good at tracking and some aren't" (p. 239). We must never overlook individuals within a group. Families and individuals experience their culture in personal ways (Derman-Sparks, 1989). Thus, individuals should be viewed as *influenced* by their culture, but not *defined* by it (Hyun & Fowler, 1995).

Ortiz (1993) cautions that we need to learn about the student's contemporary culture. Many adolescents of color are totally acculturated into the values of the Euro-American or majority society. Such variables as proximity, time, age, and birthplace determine the degree of acculturation (Leung, 1989). The common practice of newly arrived immigrants' moving into inner cities among people of their own culture hinders acculturation, as they tend to have fewer opportunities to interact with people from other cultures. First-generation immigrants usually adhere to their customs more than second and third. Immigrants who arrive in a new country when they are older usually are steeped more in their traditional culture than are immigrants who arrive when they are younger or who are born in the newly adopted country. Moreover, socioeconomic status and educational level of families may affect beliefs as much as culture does (Hyun & Fowler, 1995). For example, African Americans from higher socioeconomic levels frequently have different beliefs and values than do those from lower socioeconomic levels.

We do not mean to imply that differences are deficits. As Adgar, Wolfram, and Detwyler (1993) state in their discussion of cultural diversity, differences should not be equated with deficits, but cultural differences should be acknowledged honestly. Here we discuss cultural influences on child-rearing and socialization practices, learning styles and school achievement, and communication styles. In particular, we discuss the African American, Asian American, Euro-American, Hispanic American, and Native American cultures.

### Child-Rearing and Socialization Practices

Adolescents from the African American culture are often members of an extended family, relying on relatives for care and teaching of appropriate skills. It is not unusual for grandparents to be raising children (Lum, 1986), and often the family is matriarchal. For many adolescents, the church is a part of the extended family and an integral aspect of family life (Hale-Benson, 1986). The minister is frequently considered the most influential member of the community (Randall-David, 1989).

African American parents often socialize their children to attribute negative attitudes of Euro-Americans toward them as evidence of prejudice (Simmons et al., 1991). They are taught that such prejudice does not mean that they are defective, and thus should not affect self-esteem. Recent studies indicate that African American adolescents frequently separate school achievement from self-esteem (Hare & Castenell, 1985; Mboya, 1986; Spencer, 1991). Consequently, many adolescents may do poorly in school and still maintain a positive self-concept (Ogbu & Matute-Bianchi, 1986; Simmons et al., 1991).

As in the African American culture, child-rearing is a shared experience in the Asian American culture. The extended family including aunts, uncles, and grandparents is the primary socialization unit. The family is overindulgent in raising children until the preschool years, when children are expected to assume responsibilities and do chores to help the family (Chinn & Plata, 1987).

The family is also the basic social unit. The child's duty is to respect the family and never do anything to dishonor it. Individual needs and desires are subjugated to the family's needs and desires. Asian parents teach children to conform to the family's wishes and not to question or discuss matters with adults (Shimabukuro, 1993). They are also taught that their behavior is a direct reflection on the family. Along with conformity, parents teach children respect for their parents, elders, and other authority figures. Often families view a handicapping condition as a stigma to the family (Chan, 1987; Chinn & Plata, 1987; Leung, 1989).

In the Euro-American culture, only the immediate family of mother, father, and siblings is usually involved in child-rearing, often due to the high mobility of each generation (Anderson, 1988). Children are socialized to become independent, and parental pride is frequently measured by children's displaying independent behaviors early. It is expected that once adolescents enter the world of work, they will not live with the immediate family.

The Hispanic culture views child-rearing as an extended family experience. The family unit often consists of the nuclear family of mother, father, and siblings, the extended family of relatives, and close family friends (Ramirez & Castaneda, 1974). Older siblings often take care of younger siblings. For example, Mexican American students are frequently absent from school to help at home (Briganti, 1989). Many Hispanic mothers who must work leave their children with a family member whenever possible (Hernandez & Estrada, 1992). The strong ties of family, relatives, and friends promote a tradition of working together for the good of the family and the group (Briganti, 1989). The culture socializes children differently depending on their gender. Boys are given more and earlier independence than girls, and males enjoy rights and privileges denied females (Baruth & Manning, 1992). Children are also socialized to show respect for older family members and other adults in authority (Briganti, 1989; Zirpoli & Melloy, 1993).

As in many other cultural groups, Native American adolescents place a high priority on the family. Grandparents play an important role in the socialization of youth (Lum, 1986). Many Native Americans live with grandparents or other family members for extended periods (Ramirez, 1993). As with Mexican American families, high school students may stay at home during a family crisis as family matters are given priority over school attendance (Sanders, 1987). Individuals are frequently defined by their family and may introduce themselves by talking about their family and family background, instead of their individual accomplishments or feelings (Hillerman, 1990). As in the Asian American culture, youth are taught to respect their elders. Sharing with others is promoted, as many Native Americans feel that the willingness to share is more important than accumulating private wealth (Lewis & Ho, 1989).

## Learning Styles and School Achievement

Many African Americans have high motoric activity and preference for oral/aural modalities (Hale, 1982). Manning (1993) relates that African American students frequently perform better in a cooperative, informal, and loosely structured environment with teachers and students working together to achieve common goals.

African American adolescents have high achievement orientations, but often reduce their aspirations when faced with discrimination, school inequality, and prejudice (Ogbu, 1987). They often feel that investing time and energy in schoolwork is fruitless as there is no economic payoff

(Brookins, 1991; Ogbu, 1987). Peer pressure against exhibiting "white-oriented" studious behavior frequently discourages motivation in African American adolescents (Brookins, 1991). In grades 6 and 7, African American males are involved in "more problem behavior, more dating behavior and interactions, think it more positive to be a member of their own gender, are more resistant to acting like the opposite sex, care more about being good at sports, are more satisfied with their looks and less self-conscious" than Euro-American males and females and African American females (Simmons et al., 1991, p. 500). Both African American boys and girls show decreases in grade point averages and like school less at the junior high level than they did at the elementary level (Simmons et al., 1991).

A feature of the Asian American culture is the emphasis families place on educational attainment (Kitano, 1987; Shimabukuro, 1993). They believe that hard work in education leads to future success and honor for the family. Their Confucian work ethic is similar to the Protestant work ethic (Sue & Padilla, 1986). Often Asian American students are less likely to ask questions during class and tend to function well in a well-structured, quiet learning environment in which definite goals are established (Baruth & Manning, 1992).

Euro-Americans are often competitive, value independence, and are future oriented. Euro-Americans believe that the individual is the most basic social unit and that individual rights are extremely important (Anderson, 1988). They frequently associate success with material wealth and possessions (Zirpoli & Melloy, 1993). Many Euro-Americans value education and strive to achieve because they feel that education is essential for a productive and successful future. The school culture tends to reflect the values of the Euro-American culture (Olson & Platt, 1996).

Cooperation is favored over competition, and group attainment is emphasized in both the Hispanic and Native American cultures (Zirpoli & Melloy, 1993). This feeling of obligation toward the group leads many Hispanic and Native American adolescents to avoid recognition for accomplishments at the expense of peers (Baruth & Manning, 1992; Ramirez, 1993). They feel that behavior that brings attention to an individual is egotistical (Dillard, 1983).

Navajo adolescents learn early that serious learning is private and, therefore, do not exert their best efforts when tested (Sleeter & Grant, 1988). Many Native American youth are taught to value quiet and stillness and to learn by observing their elders. After their elders demonstrate a task repeatedly, they are given the opportunity to try it (Zirpoli & Melloy, 1993). Many adolescents are shy, unassertive, and passive (Dillard, 1983).

## Communication Styles

The African American culture has several unique expressive communication styles. Many African Americans exhibit a spiraling storytelling style, with frequent departures from an initial point, but with a return to make a whole (Hilliard, 1989). *Playing the dozens, woofing,* and *signifying* are other communication patterns that may lead to misunderstanding by people of other cultures.

Playing the dozens is a "high form of verbal warfare and impromptu speaking" (Littlejohn & Henderson, 1992, p. 84). The exchange usually takes place in front of an audience, which encourages the contestants to continue to make humorous offensive remarks. The following dialogue illustrates the game.

*One speaker:* "Your mama is so fat that she uses ponds because bathtubs are too small."

*Another speaker:* "Oh, yeah, your mama is so fat that she washes only once a month. It costs a lot to drive to the ocean."

Woofing is another form of seemingly aggressive communication that involves a trading of insults and a challenge to fight. A person displays a physically defiant, challenging stance to shout down or intimidate another. However, according to Littlejohn and Henderson (1992), woofing is actually a substitute for physical aggression in settling arguments. Signifying is a communication technique used to avoid answering a question, disclosing personal information, or the intrusive questioning of others. For example, instead of asking her date what he does for a living directly, a woman may say "My, that's a mighty fine house you have. You must own a bank, right?" (Littlejohn & Henderson, 1992, p. 82).

The communication style of Asian Americans is characterized by formality of speech, silent pauses for thinking, indirect expressions of feelings and thoughts, sanctity of private thoughts, and harmony (Fukuyama & Inoue-Cox, 1992; Yee, 1988). Often age, gender, rank, and occupation dictate communication patterns. Asian Americans generally use titles, especially when addressing elders or those of high rank, and frequently avoid using the personal pronouns me and I.

Asian Americans consider silences and long pauses in a conversation as virtuous and necessary for thinking. Silence following an active verbal response may also indicate disagreement (Hyun & Fowler, 1995). Asian Americans often converse in circles as they "loop" around the subject several times before resolving an issue (Fukuyama & Inoue-Cox, 1992). This hesitancy is seen in the unwillingness of the speaker to share his or her inner experiences and thoughts. People of other cultures frequently misunderstand the hesitancy of Asian Americans to disagree directly or say "no" in a conversation when it might cause embarrassment to either speaker or listener. They often say "yes" to reinforce that they hear you, and "no" through hesitation, ambiguity, or leaving the situation (Fukuyama & Inoue-Cox, 1992).

Generally the Euro-American culture promotes an informal and direct communication style. When speaking to others, direct eye contact is maintained. Generally, Euro-Americans actively engage in conversations, do not avoid disagreements, and feel free to disclose personal information. They usually expect a listener to do more than listen, requiring periodic reassurances that the listener is paying attention (Hillerman, 1990).

Nonverbal communication styles seem to be similar across the various groups that comprise the Hispanic population (Hernandez & Estrada, 1992). In speaking to an elder, children are taught to avoid prolonged eye contact as a sign of respect. They need little personal space and tend to sit and stand closer to people during conversations. They may greet even a slight acquaintance with an embrace or kiss on the cheek (Briganti, 1989; Hernandez & Estrada, 1992). Exuberance is also seen in the verbal communication style of many Hispanics. Interruptions are not considered impolite, and one does not need to wait for a pause to interject conversation (Zirpoli & Melloy, 1993). However, Grossman (1990) finds that many Hispanics are not direct and forthright in asking for help, especially from teachers, and that they frequently avoid expressing personal opinions about controversial issues.

Many Native Americans rarely sustain eye contact and prefer to maintain some distance when conversing (Reifel, 1992). A nod of the head or a gentle handshake are preferred greetings (LaFromboise, 1982; Reifel, 1992). Additionally, they place great importance on establishing a rapport at the beginning of a conversation, rather than hurrying interactions. They may sit with their eyes closed and simply listen and think about what others have to say (Zirpoli & Melloy, 1993). They consider constant interruptions, quick questions, and short answers as rude behaviors (LaFromboise, 1982). As a sign of respect, Native Americans do not argue with or criticize parents or others. Often, to maintain respectful relationships, they refrain from expressing their feelings (Zirpoli & Melloy, 1993). They work hard at maintaining agreement, because they feel that to disagree with someone symbolizes an assertion of ego and individuality and creates disharmony (Brown, 1991). Therefore, they may agree to something and then not follow through, a behavior that people from other cultures often view as dishonest and untrustworthy.

**COMPREHENSION MONITORING OF KEY CONCEPTS**

### Characteristics/Cultural Values

1. As of 1992, approximately one-third of elementary and secondary students with mild disabilities were from the minority populations of African Americans, Asian Americans, Hispanic Americans, and Native Americans.

2. Many adolescents of color are totally acculturated into the values of the Euro-American or majority society. Such variables as proximity, time, age, and birthplace determine the degree of acculturation.

3. Extended families are the rule in many cultures, with grandparents and aunts and uncles helping to socialize children.

4. Cooperation and group attainment are often valued over competition and individual attainment in the Hispanic and Native American cultures, while competition, independence, and future orientation are often valued in the Euro-American culture.

5. African American students frequently perform better in a cooperative, informal, loosely structured environment with teachers and students working together to achieve common goals.

6. Playing the dozens (a "high form of verbal warfare and impromptu speaking"), woofing (a trading of insults and a challenge to fight), and signifying (to avoid the answer to a question, the disclosing of personal information, or the intrusive questioning of others) are communication patterns found in the African American culture.

7. The communication style of Asian Americans is characterized by formality of speech, silent pauses for thinking, indirect expressions of feelings and thoughts, sanctity of private thoughts, and harmony.

8. Generally, Euro-Americans actively engage in conversations, do not avoid disagreements, feel free to disclose personal information, and usually expect a listener to demonstrate in some way that he or she is paying close attention to the conversation.

9. Exuberance is seen in the verbal communication style of many Hispanics, and interruptions are not considered impolite.

10. Native Americans consider constant interruptions, quick questions, and short answers as rude behaviors.

## Instructional Considerations

In this section, we examine materials, curriculum, and teaching strategies that consider cultural diversity in the education of adolescents with mild disabilities. Through the wise selection of materials, curriculum, and teaching strategies, we feel that teachers will be more sensitive to the needs of students of color in special education settings.

### Materials

You may be limited in the selection of materials, as many states have a state-adopted list of texts for use in the schools. However, you always have the option of including multicultural materials in your selection of supplemental materials, whether you are teaching from a basic content-area text or from the Learning Strategies Curriculum (Deshler & Schumaker, 1988). For example, if you are teaching about westward expansion, you may include supplemental texts about Euro-American pioneer women, Native Americans, and African American cowboys in your reading selections. Some guidelines for the selection of multicultural materials follow (Austin, 1990; Dean, Salend, & Taylor, 1993; Garcia & Malkin, 1993; Klein, 1985; Nauman, 1987).

1. *Select books that aim at a worldview.* Books should incorporate the history, heritage, language, and traditions of various groups. For example, avoid books that equate only Euro-Americans with advanced civilizations and people of color with primitive or quaint civilizations.

2. *Select books that have accurate illustrations and are factually correct.* Do the nonwhite characters just have their faces tinted? Do the faces of the nonwhite characters look stereotypically alike, or do they possess unique characteristics? Are there any people of color at all in the text?

3. *Select books that have more recent publication dates.* In most cases, more recent copyright dates reflect more current viewpoints of cross-cultural awareness. Many of the minority theme books that began appearing in the mid-1960s were written by Euro-Americans and reflect their viewpoints.

4. *Select books written and/or illustrated by authors from various cultures.* A person who grew up in a ghetto may be able to present a more realistic and authentic picture of ghetto life than one who has never had those experiences.

5. *Select books that show adolescents of different cultures in various activities.* Find youth of various cultures engaged in science, math, and academic activities as well as sports activities.

6. *Select books that use language with care.* Check for sexist language. For example, is *man* used as a generic term? Are *savage, backward,* or similar adjectives used to describe groups of people? In a summary of a study of *Roget's Thesaurus,* Klein (1985) reports that the word *whiteness* has 44 pleasing and favorable synonyms, while the word *blackness* has 60 distinctly unfavorable synonyms.

7. *Select books that show adolescents in a variety of relationships.* Many books depict people of color in subservient roles, dependent on others to solve their problems, while they depict European males as powerful decision makers. Many books depict females as being successful because of their relationships with males or their physical appearance, not their intelligence or initiative.

8. *Select books that represent different perspectives.* It is easy to add supplemental books that bring in the perspective of different cultures and are not written solely from the Euro-American male viewpoint. For example, Katz's book *The Black West* (1987) provides an African American perspective on settling the West.

Perhaps the most important guideline to remember in the selection of books is to "never select a book which would give pain to even one child" (Klein, 1985, p. 14). Box 4.1 contains a list of teacher materials that may help you add more multicultural materials to your curriculum. Please note in particular the magazine *Teaching Tolerance,* which is free of charge for teachers. Box 4.2 presents an annotated list of high-interest, low-reading-level books and favorite teen books. The teen books are identified based on a survey of 4000 adolescents (International Reading Association, 1992).

## Curriculum

Multicultural education is "a reform movement designed to bring about educational equity for all students, including those from different races, ethnic groups, social classes, exceptionality, and sexual orientations" (Banks, 1992, p. 21). Banks (1989) identifies four basic approaches for infusing multicultural education into the curriculum. In the *contributions* approach, students learn about ethnic groups at specific times of the year. For example, students study African Americans during Black History month and Asians during the Chinese New Year. Usually, the heroes and cultural elements selected for study are based on mainstream criteria. Thus, teachers generally select Martin Luther King, Jr., and Shirley Chisholm for study rather than Malcolm X and Angela Davis, who are more controversial. The contributions approach is the one used most often in the schools to integrate ethnic content.

BOX 4.1

## Teacher Materials

Banks, James A. (1991)
*Teaching Strategies for Ethnic Studies*, 5th edition
Allyn & Bacon
Available from Materials and Services Center
P.O. Box 802
Edmonds, WA 98020
This book contains information concerning the historical background and current demographics of African Americans, Native Americans, Euro-Americans, Hispanic Americans, and Asian Americans. Examples of activities and multicultural units are also presented, along with an annotated bibliography of books for teachers and students.

Caduto, Michael J., & Bruchac, Joseph (1988)
*Keepers of the Earth: Native American Stories and Environmental Activities for Children*
Fulcrum Publishing
350 Indiana St., Suite 350
Golden, CO 80401
The teacher's guide plus book includes traditional Native American stories and activities for using the stories, which can be adapted for younger adolescents.

Chase, Josephine, & Parth, Linda (1979)
*Multicultural Spoken Here: Discovering America's People Through Language Arts and Library Skills*
Goodyear Publishing Co.
1640 Fifth St.
Santa Monica, CA 90401
These materials include word searches, recipes, maps, vocabulary words, and much more about Native Americans, African Americans, Asian Americans, Mexican Americans, and Euro-Americans.

Cheung, King-kok, & Yoji, Stan (1988)
*Asian American Literature: An Annotated Bibliography*
The Modern Language Association of America
10 Astor Place
New York, NY 10003
This bibliography is a comprehensive guide to Asian American literature.

Empak Publishing Co.
212 E. Ohio Street
Chicago, IL 60611
This company offers products such as timelines, posters, books, and videos concerning African American history.

**B O X   4 . 1**
*(continued)*

Harvey, K. D., Jarjo, L. D., & Jackson, J. K. (1990)
*Teaching about Native Americans* (Bulletin No. 84)
National Council for the Social Studies
3501 Newark St. NW
Washington, DC 20016
The book contains an excellent chapter on Resources for Teachers and Students. It also includes lesson plans on diversity, adaptations, and discrimination.

*The History of the Civil Rights Movement* (1990)
Silver Burdett Press
Division of Paramount Publishing
P.O. Box 2649
Columbus, OH 43216
Each of the nine books in this series focuses on a different African American figure in the civil rights movement: Ella Baker, Stokely Carmichael, Fannie Lou Hamer, Jesse Jackson, Martin Luther King, Jr., Malcolm X, Thurgood Marshall, Rosa Parks, and A. Philip Randolph.

Katz, William L. (1987)
*The Black West*
Open Hand Publishing, Inc.
P.O. Box 22048
Seattle, WA 98122
This book explores contributions of African American settlers in the West.

Lanker, Brian (1989)
*I Dream a World: Portraits of Black Women Who Changed America*
Stewart, Tabori & Chang, Inc.
575 Broadway
New York, NY 10012
The book contains excellent photographs and biographical profiles.

Martinez, Julio A., & Lomeli, Francisco A. (1985)
*Chicano Literature: A Reference Guide*
Greenwood Press
88 Post Rd. W., Box 5007
Westport, CT 06781
This resource contains biographies of Mexican American writers and a useful chronology of Chicano literature.

National Black Child Development Institute
*The Spirit of Excellence: Resources for Black Youth*
1023 15th St. NW, Suite 600
Washington, DC 20005
The series of four resource guides contains annotated citations of books, records, and audiovisual materials for African American adolescents.

*(continued on next page)*

**BOX 4.1**
*(continued)*

Nauman, A. K. (1987)
"School Librarians and Cultural Pluralism"
*The Reading Teacher, 41*(2), 201–205
This article includes a list of both elementary and secondary supplemental books for a multicultural collection.

*Teaching Tolerance*
Published since 1991
400 Washington Ave.
Montgomery, AL 36104
Published twice a year, this *free* magazine covers issues and information about students of color, students with disabilities, students of various religions, and students with different sexual orientations. It offers a wealth of teaching resources and ideas for incorporating multicultural education and tolerance into the curriculum. Additionally, it identifies student materials.

Thompson, Dennis (1991)
*The Black Artist in America: An Index to Reproductions*
Scarecrow Press, Inc.
Division of Grolier Education Corporation
52 Liberty St., Box 4167
Metuchen, NJ 08840
This reference guide identifies African American artists and locates reproductions of their work. Among the artists are Joshua Johnson, Romare Bearden, and Betty Saar.

Tiedt, P. L., & Tiedt, I. M. (1990)
*Multicultural Teaching: A Handbook of Activities, Information, and Resources,* 3rd edition
Allyn & Bacon
11 Tenth St.
Des Moines, IA 50309
This book contains suggestions for activities that may be adapted for adolescent learners with special needs.

Waldman, Carl (1985)
*Atlas of the North American Indian*
Facts on File Inc.
460 Park Ave. South
New York, NY 10016
This atlas provides a historical overview for teaching about Native Americans, with excellent maps.

**BOX 4.2**

## Materials for Students

READERS HOUSE/LVNYC
Attn: Publishing Department
121 Avenue of the Americas
New York, NY 10013
Available from this source are a multicultural series of selections at grades 3–6 reading level, interest level grade 7 to adult. Examples include:

Anaya, Rudolfo A. (1989). Writers' Voices selected from *Bless Me, Ultima*. The story of a Chicano boy in New Mexico. It also includes an article about Chicano history in the United States.

Angelou, Maya. (1989). Writers' Voices selected from *I Know Why the Caged Bird Sings* and *The Heart of a Woman*. An autobiographical sketch of Angelou's family tree. Also included are articles on Joe Louis and desegregation.

Erdrich, Louise. (1989). Writers' Voices selected from *Love Medicine*. Describes the life of two Native American families in North Dakota. It also includes articles about Native Americans and the Vietnam War.

Kingston, Maxine Hong. (1990). Writers' Voices selected from *China Men* and *The Woman Warrior*. This autobiographical work tells about a Chinese American family. It also includes a history of Chinese immigration.

Also available from this source are videotapes of the lives of famous authors such as Alex Haley and Alice Walker.

Teens' Favorite Books: Young Adults' Choices, 1987–1992
International Reading Association
Newark, Delaware 19714

Bethancourt, T. Ernesto. (1987). *The Me Inside of Me*. Lerner. This book is about a Mexican American teenager who begins a new phase of life with a new knowledge of who he is.

Highwater, Jamake. (1988). *I Wear the Morning Star*. Harper & Row. The third book in the Ghost Horse trilogy, this describes the cruelty and prejudice faced by Sitko Ghost Horse, a Native American, who is forced to assimilate into the Euro-American culture of the twentieth-century.

Hortze, Sollace. (1990). *A Circle Unbroken*. Clarion. Set in 1840 in Missouri, this novel describes the emotional predicament of a girl captured by the Sioux and then returned to her Euro-American family as a teenager.

*(continued on next page)*

**BOX 4.2**
*(continued)*

Hudson, Jan. (1992). *Dawn Rider*. Philomel. A Blackfoot girl reveals her secret knowledge of horses as she attempts to save her people.

Hudson, Jan. (1991). *Sweetgrass*. Philomel. Well-researched history is woven into this coming-of-age story of a 15-year-old Blackfoot girl living in Montana.

James, J. Alison. (1992). *Sing for a Gentle Rain*. Atheneum. In this fantasy, a thirteenth-century Anasazi Native American girl tries to battle the drought. This novel helps teenagers understand that different cultures value different skills.

Myers, Walter Dean. (1990). *Scorpions*. HarperCollins. Jamal Hicks, a seventh-grader, faces the daily challenges of living in the violent inner city.

Paulsen, Gary. (1992). *Canyons*. Delacorte. A 14-year-old Euro-American boy discovers the skull of an Apache boy. The writer then tells a parallel story about the lives of the two boys.

Sanfield, Steve. (1991). *The Adventures of High John the Conqueror*. Orchard. Sanfield retells folktales of High John the Conqueror, an African American slave, as he outwits his Old Master. Each story begins with an explanation of the customs. The result is a good history of the lives of slaves and their masters.

Smith, K. (1991). *Skeeter*. Houghton Mifflin. The book tells about the relationship between Skeeter, an elderly African American man, and two 16-year-old boys.

Terry, Wallace (1987). *Bloods: An Oral History of the Vietnam War by Black Veterans*. Random House. Twenty African American veterans share their experiences in the Vietnam War.

Yep, Laurence. (1987). *Mountain Light*. HarperCollins. A sequel to *The Serpent's Children*, it chronicles 19-year-old Squeaky Lau's immigration to America in search of gold.

In the *ethnic additive* approach, ethnic content is added to the existing curriculum. For example, a teacher presenting a unit on the westward movement in U.S. history might include a section on the Utes. As in the contributions approach, Banks notes that one of the disadvantages of this approach is its Eurocentric perspective. Thus, in the previous example, only Euro-Americans moved from the East to the West; the Utes were already in the West.

In the *transformation* approach, educators incorporate different ethnic perspectives on issues, events, and times in the curriculum. For example, in studying about the battle at the Alamo, a teacher introduces the viewpoints not only of the Texans who fought there, but also of the Mexicans who fought there and the Native Americans who were living in the mission at the time.

In the *social action* approach, students learn to make decisions about important social problems and issues. A sample activity reflective of this approach is to have students analyze their history text for racial and prejudicial comments and then write to the publisher concerning the misrepresentation of minority cultures.

An integral part of any multicultural education curriculum is teaching students to accept and appreciate individual differences. Dean et al. (1993) recommend that teachers emphasize the following points: (1) Every culture is valuable. (2) There are similarities among cultures. (3) Cultural diversity is an integral and ongoing part of the curriculum. (4) Individual behavior varies within cultures. (5) Families and individuals experience their cultures in personal ways.

## Teaching Strategies

Educators have identified generic teaching strategies that are effective for students with disabilities from diverse cultures (Baker, 1990; Briggs, 1991; Brown, 1991; Chan, 1987; Dean et al., 1993; Franklin, 1992; Hilliard, 1989; Johnson, 1991; Moll, 1988; Ruiz, 1989; Shan & Bailey, 1991; Zanger, 1990). We present seven such techniques that we feel will help you meet the needs not only of adolescents of color, but of adolescents from all cultures who may be at risk.

1. *Personalize the content.* You may want to utilize students as resources and as examples. When studying a unit on poetry, one of our senior interns had students bring in examples of their favorite rap pieces and then analyze the rhyming patterns. Another intern, in a lesson on marine life, asked tenth-grade students to compare their individual heights to that of five marine mammals. You may also want to capitalize on students' interests by having them complete an interest inventory at the beginning of the year. In addition to sharing group expectations, letting students select individual goals for the day and tell how they have reached those goals personalizes the content. Franklin (1992) finds that many African American students seek teacher attention, support, and recognition.

2. *Emphasize the importance and relevance of the content.* Share the reasons for studying a particular topic with your students. Indicate its relevance to the world of work and to the needs of adult wage earners in addition to what is needed for today, as emphasized in the SCANS Report (see

*Middle school students participate in a cultural celebration.*

Chapter 2). For example, you may want to connect discussion of nutrition, math, and labor unions to current baby-sitting jobs and to future jobs involving child care. Baker (1990) encourages her at-risk high school students to ask questions such as "Why are we doing this?" and "How can I use this information after I graduate?" If neither she nor her students can answer the questions satisfactorily, she changes the content of the lesson.

3. *Build on students' experiences and everyday situations.* Previewing is an effective way to connect content with past experience. After checking titles, headings, and pictures, let students predict the content of a story. Ask students what they already know and present them with an overview. In *The OLE Curriculum* developed for Hispanic special education students, teachers identify the central idea of a text, ask students about their experiences, discuss the experiences, make predictions, and then compare the action of the text to these personal experiences (Ruiz, 1989).

4. *Explain information using both analytical and holistic approaches.* Most often teachers present information step by step or present the particulars of a problem instead of the global characteristics, while many students focus in on the global (Hilliard, 1989). For example, in a discussion of the major political, economic, and social traditions in American history

class, Mr. Jonas discusses each of them separately as they affected American society. In contrast, Ms. Junifer discusses all three traditions at once and compares and contrasts their effects on American society.

5. *Use a variety of methods and activities.* If you use cooperative group and peer learning activities along with teacher-directed instruction, you are catering to the cooperative nature of many cultures. Briggs (1991) recommends that you give well-structured assignments and assure that group membership remains the same for at least three months if you plan to use cooperative groups for LEP (limited English proficient) students with disabilities. For Native Americans whose culture teaches learning through observation, Johnson (1991) recommends teacher modeling as an effective teaching strategy. Using a variety of methods also caters to the numerous learning styles found in the classroom.

6. *Use a variety of materials.* Videodiscs, films, videotapes, and other visual aids, along with guest speakers from diverse cultures, enrich the learning experience for students of color. Display ethnically diverse bulletin boards, posters, and calendars. Using combinations of oral, print, and visual media along with singing and movement enhances the performance of African American students (Franklin, 1992). Concrete images benefit Chinese exceptional students, who often need external visual cues to understand stimuli (Chan, 1987). Using a variety of materials also appeals to the numerous learning styles found in the classroom.

7. *Evaluate student progress in many ways and give frequent feedback.* Students from different groups enter school with different cultural expectations of displaying knowledge. Many Native American students are unaccustomed to answering teacher questions in the "spotlight" in front of other students (Villegas, 1991). Asian American adolescents also feel uncomfortable with teacher questioning. The Hispanic adolescent does not like to receive recognition at the expense of peers. Therefore, teachers must use a variety of methods to evaluate students. Besides the traditional paper-and-pencil tests, other evaluation techniques include examination of students' daily work samples, analysis of students' answers to oral and written questions, and systematic observation of students' task performances during class (see Chapter 3). Daily feedback and positive notes on individual assignments encourage students who value more immediate feedback than nine-week grades. Grades may be based on projects, oral presentations, literature logs, portfolios, or any combination. Some teachers add points for attendance and participation to their grades. Brown (1991) suggests that you may wish to present a model of an acceptable finished product to increase the comfort level of students whose culture does not promote risk-taking behaviors.

If you are working in a co-teaching model, you may suggest to the regular educator some test adaptations, such as letting students who fail a test retake it without penalty or letting you read the items on the test to a group of students. One co-teaching pair selected questions written by students in cooperative groups to include on the nine-week history exam. During the review sessions, the teachers discussed the questions and the answers with the class.

---

## COMPREHENSION MONITORING OF KEY CONCEPTS

### Instructional Considerations

1. Teachers can better meet the needs of students of color who have disabilities by selecting multicultural supplemental books and adding cultural sensitivity to the curriculum and instructional strategies.

2. When selecting supplemental books, check for evidence of a worldview, accurate illustrations, recent publication dates, works by authors of color, depictions of adolescents engaged in various types of activities and relationships, appropriate language, and a variety of perspectives.

3. The four basic approaches to multicultural education are the contributions approach, the ethnic additive approach, the transformation approach, and the social action approach.

4. In the contributions approach, the contributions of ethnic groups and persons are studied at specific times of the year; the ethnic additive approach adds ethnic content to the existing curriculum; the transformation approach incorporates ethnic perspectives into the curriculum; the social action approach actively involves students in making decisions about cultural problems and issues.

5. Effective teaching strategies include personalizing the content, emphasizing the importance and relevance of the content, building on the experiences of students, presenting information both globally and analytically, using a variety of methods, activities, and materials, and evaluating the progress of students in a variety of ways.

## Issues

Early special education treatment of students with disabilities from various cultural groups mirrored society's treatment. Cultural bias in assessment, a lack of instructional quality, and a mismatch between minority cultures and the school's culture have contributed to the overrepresentation of students of color in the special education population (Grossman, 1990; Sue & Padilla, 1986). Today, an awareness of this discrimination is leading to changes in assessment procedures, consideration of language differences, and alteration of instructional techniques before a student of color is staffed into a special education setting. Now, students are tested with both formal and informal assessment procedures and in their native or primary language. Many school districts require alternative methods of assessment and instruction before considering special education placement for students of color.

Even with these safeguards, the field is just beginning to answer the challenge of how to ensure that cultural differences are considered before special education placement. In a study of adolescents with disabilities, about 29% of African American adolescents were enrolled in classes for students with mental disabilities while only 21% of Euro-Americans were enrolled in these classes (Newman, 1992). In this section we examine in more detail the issues of assessment, bilingual education, and racism, all of which may lead to more students of color being placed in special programs.

### Assessment

Students from cultural groups other than Euro-Americans may perform inadequately on assessment devices, especially standardized tests, because of (1) limited language proficiency, (2) unfamiliarity with test content, (3) assessment by examiners who lack social and cultural sensitivity, (4) poor test-taking strategies, (5) unfamiliarity with test conditions, and (6) lack of motivation (Duran, 1989; Nuttall, Landurand, & Goldman, 1984). Even when standardized tests are administered in a student's native language, they are frequently inappropriate, as they are often normed on monolingual English-speaking children and then translated into Spanish or normed on speakers who did not learn English as a second language (Schiff-Myers, Djukic, McGovern-Lawler, & Perez, 1994).

An awareness of the inequity of certain testing procedures with students from diverse cultural backgrounds is documented in an examination of the litigation surrounding assessment. Litigation has produced mandates requiring educators to test students in their native language, to select evaluation procedures that consider cultural background, and to accurately discriminate the normal process of learning English from a handicapping condition. PL 94-142 mandates the following requirements concerning educational assessment: (1) Assessment procedures must not discriminate against students because of cultural differences. (2) No single test or procedure may be used as the sole criterion for placement decisions. (3) Assessment must be conducted in the child's primary language. (4) A multidisciplinary team of trained personnel must administer and interpret the evaluation procedures. (5) Due process procedures must be followed in conducting the assessment, including securing parental consent prior to assessment. (6) Students categorized as having disabilities must be reevaluated every three years.

In response to the problems of assessment and to the legislative mandates, many school districts are attempting to use assessment procedures other than standardized tests for staffing students into special education programs and for designing Individual Education Programs (IEPs). Patton (1992) recommends the use of observations, checklists, interview techniques, and evaluation of student products or portfolio assessment for determining giftedness in African American students. Dean et al. (1993) recommend ongoing assessments of real learning experiences that are directly linked to instruction. To avoid test bias, Nuttall et al. (1984) suggest a global approach to cross-cultural assessment. In this approach, language dominance, adaptive behavior, and sociocultural background are considered in the multifactored assessment. Prior to assessment, the student's proficiency in English and the native language is assessed. Then, qualified examiners observe the student in various settings, interview the parents, conduct medical examinations, and assess the student using informal reading and math inventories in both the native language and English.

Similar to the global approach, Rydell (1990) identifies three types of data collection procedures appropriate for assessment of students from diverse cultural backgrounds: (1) interview-based assessment, (2) observation-based assessment, and (3) curriculum-based assessment. Such items as the frequency of school changes, the consistency of a student's academic performance from year to year, and the extent of learning problems in native schools are often included in interviews with parents and teachers. Cloud (1991) recommends using a questionnaire to collect information about the home environment and family members. Some sample items adapted from the Home Background Questionnaire (Cloud, 1991) are: (1) What is the birthplace of the parents (guardians)? (2) What language do the parents (guardians) speak in the home most of the time? (3) What language does the student most often speak with parents (guardians)? siblings? friends? (4) How many years of instruction has the student received in a language other than English?

Observation-based assessment procedures involve such measurements of behavior as anecdotal records, event recording, duration, interval recording, and time sampling. With anecdotal records, the observer attempts to write down what happened before, during, and after the behavior, either at the time or immediately afterwards. With the other techniques, the observer watches the behavior as it occurs, marking each time the behavior happens (event recording), the length of the behavior (duration), or whether the behavior occurs within a particular interval (interval recording) or after a particular interval (time sampling). For more detailed descriptions of these systematic observational techniques, please refer to a behavior management text (such as Alberto & Troutman, 1995; Zirpoli & Melloy, 1993). In curriculum-based assessment, specialists examine a student's skills as they relate to the demands of the curriculum. See Chapter 3 for a discussion of observation-based and curriculum-based assessments.

Another approach recommended for students from diverse cultural backgrounds is dynamic assessment (Duran, 1989; Patton, 1992). Dynamic assessment involves a test–train–test cycle. As the student attempts to solve an unfamiliar problem (test), he or she is provided immediate feedback and cues on how to improve performance (train) and then is presented with the problem again (test). Using a preestablished hierarchy of "most general" to "most specific" cues and hints, the examiner counts the number of hints and cues required before the student can solve the task. A lower number of cues results in an evaluation of greater learning potential.

Recognizing the importance of cultural and linguistic considerations before a student is considered for special education placement, Ortiz & Garcia (1988) recommend a prereferral process. In this prereferral process, verification must exist that "(a) the school's curriculum is appropriate, (b) the child's problems are documented across settings and personnel, not only in school, but also at home, (c) difficulties are present both in the native language and in English, (d) the child has been taught but has not made satisfactory progress, (e) the teacher has the qualifications and experience to effectively teach the student, and (f) instruction has been continuous, appropriately sequenced, and has included teaching of skills prerequisite to success" (p. 15).

Even though alternative assessment procedures are often recommended as a solution to assessment bias, they are not foolproof. Many of the assessment procedures have not been empirically validated. For example, dynamic assessment procedures have not been subjected to intensive research studies (Duran, 1989). Moreover, an exact method is lacking for measuring if students are ready for assessment in English or the native language (Figueroa, 1989). A summary of assessment reports dealing with Hispanic special education students by the Texas and California Handicapped Minority Research Institutes found that (1) language proficiency of students is frequently not considered, (2) most testing is done in English, (3) English-language problems are misinterpreted as handicaps, (4) home data are not used in assessment, (5) the same few tests are used, and (6) reevaluations usually lead to more special education (Figueroa, Fradd, & Correa, 1989).

## Bilingual Education

Many adolescents of different ethnic groups have limited English proficiency (LEP). It is not uncommon for a newly arrived immigrant to lag behind in all academic subject areas, except math, because they do not understand English. Learning another language generally occurs on two levels: the basic interpretative communication skills (BICS) level and the cognitive academic language proficiency level (CALP) (Cummins, 1984). BICS involves everyday, social, conversational language, whereas CALP encompasses the language skills necessary for academic and cognitive progress in a second language. Learning everyday, conversational, social language is easier because a person is able to rely on context-embedded situations (Cummins, 1984). For example, in a conversation, the speaker and listener usually know the topic, watch body language, and can guess at unknown vocabulary words from the context. In contrast, language skills required in the classroom are often context-reduced (Cummins, 1984). Students are usually given minimal context clues when they are listening to a history lecture or reading a chapter in a history text. Generally, conversational language can be mastered within one or two years, whereas the context-reduced language of classroom instruction and written texts takes between five and six years (Villegas, 1991).

It is difficult to discriminate between bilingual students with limited English proficiency and those with language disorders (Figueroa et al., 1989; Mercer & Rueda, 1991). Bilingual students with limited English proficiency will probably attain proficiency after receiving bilingual education services, whereas students with language disorders need long-term special education services (Schiff-Myers et al., 1994). Bilingual students who are most likely in need of special education services are those who have problems in cognitive academic language proficiency (Sue & Padilla, 1986). They may have adequate social communication skills in English, but poor cognitive, academic language skills in English; or they may have developed adequate social communication in the native language, but poor cognitive, academic language skills in both the native language and English (Sue & Padilla, 1986). In their discussion of the language-minority student, Gersten and Woodward (1994) contend that many bilingual students are staffed into special education placements because they have been exposed to a variety of regular education bilingual models. They feel that this inconsistency in their background education makes the students at risk for special education services. For example, because of the extreme mobility of many bilingual students, they may be exposed to either the native-language emphasis or the sheltered-English model of instruction. In the native-language emphasis, the teacher teaches content information in a student's primary language until he or she exhibits an adequate grasp of English. In the sheltered-English or structured-immersion model, the teacher teaches content information with adaptations in the English language.

Bilingual students have been receiving special education services only since the 1970s. Federal legislation such as PL 90-247 and PL 94-142 and litigation were instrumental in establishing these programs. Ortiz (1984) describes four types of service delivery options for exceptional bilingual students: (1) the bilingual support model, (2) the coordinated services model, (3) the integrated bilingual special education model, and (4) the bilingual special education model. Ambert and Dew (1982) originated the first three models and Ortiz and Yates (1982), the fourth.

In the *bilingual support model,* bilingual paraprofessionals join English-speaking special educators in teaching special students. The paraprofessional provides native-language instruction in areas specified on the IEP while the special educator teaches basic skills in English. In the *coordinated services model,* a bilingual teacher teams with a monolingual special education teacher to deliver instruction. The bilingual teacher provides instruction in the basic skill areas in the native language plus services designated on the IEP under native language; the special educator provides English as a second language (ESL) training plus services designated on the IEP under English. In the *integrated bilingual special education model*, a dually certified teacher provides instruction in the basic skill areas in the native language and provides ESL training. The teacher is trained separately in both special education and bilingual education. The *bilingual special education model* is also based on dually certified teachers, but these teachers are trained in bilingual special education and develop competencies specific to instructing exceptional bilingual students—many of whom, according to Ortiz, are yet to be identified.

Currently, misidentification, misplacement, and poor academic performance of students within the special education setting plague programming

**BOX 4.3**

## Suggested Strategies for Teaching Language-Minority Special Learners

1. Present lessons that focus on interesting and relevant topics.

2. Create a positive and accepting atmosphere and show respect for bilingual students.

3. Give students opportunities to volunteer, but do not require participation. Accept all verbal responses in the beginning stages of communication and allow students more time to respond to questions.

4. Plan highly contextualized lessons to give students clues to meaning. For example, teach vocabulary in context, not isolated lists, and group together related concepts.

5. Remind students of knowledge or prior experiences that relate to the text selection or lesson objectives.

6. Use visuals and gestures to provide context clues. Make copies of your notes and give to students, or tape important lectures.

7. Use cooperative learning activities in which bilingual students have opportunities to interact with other students who speak the same language.

8. Monitor and evaluate the progress of students in a variety of ways, including curriculum-based, portfolio, and other alternative procedures (see Chapter 3).

9. Use the student's primary language by including bilingual supplemental books, such as bilingual dictionaries.

10. Check frequently for understanding. Remember to use specific questions, such as "Who has an example of supply and demand?" and to avoid general questions such as "Do you understand?" Rephrase directions instead of repeating them.

11. Teach test-taking strategies, including familiar testing vocabulary (such as *circle* and *choose*), the meaning of questions (*why* calls for a reason), using time wisely, and skipping problems when stuck (*ESOL*, 1991).

12. Teach an integrated curriculum. Gersten and Woodward (1994) recommend integrating the traditional task-analysis approach found in special education settings with the literature-based (whole-language) instruction found in regular education settings.

13. In the vocational curriculum, emphasize the grammatical structure, vocabulary, and appropriate expressions of specific job situations.

14. Reinforce vocational skills through practice in real-life settings.

for language-minority exceptional students (Ruiz, 1989). In a review of reports from two research institutes dealing with special education interventions offered to Hispanic students with disabilities, Figueroa et al. (1989) found that "whole-language emphasis, comprehensible input, cooperative learning, and student empowerment are more successful than traditional behavioristic, task-analysis driven, worksheet-oriented special education classes" (p. 176). Ruiz (1989) concurs with this finding and encourages a holistic curriculum, more "typical of a gifted program than a remedial program" (p. 140) to teach oral language and literacy skills to language-minority special learners. Some specific suggestions for teaching students with limited English proficiency are found in Box 4.3. These suggestions are adapted from the writings of Briganti (1989), Briggs (1991), Brown (1991), and Kerka (1992).

## Racism

Racism is a conscious or unconscious belief that human races have distinct characteristics and that one's own race is superior and has the right to rule others (Banks, 1991; McKissack & McKissack, 1990). Racism involves both prejudice and discrimination (Gollnick & Chin, 1990). Prejudice is an opinion formed without taking the time and care to judge fairly before the facts are known (McKissack & McKissack, 1990). Prejudice becomes discrimination when members of a particular race or group are denied certain types of employment, housing, political rights, educational opportunities, or social interactions.

Racism is not a new concept. In the early part of this century, immigrants from eastern and southern Europe faced prejudice and discrimination (Mizell, 1992), forcing many of them to relinquish their accents, their names, and their heritage to adopt the more successful, majority culture. However, since the 1950s, the term *racism* has focused on prejudice and discrimination against people of color (Gollnick & Chin, 1990).

People of color are more likely to be poor, unemployed, incarcerated, and locked out of the political system (Sleeter & Grant, 1988). For example, the poverty rate of African Americans is nearly three times that of Euro-Americans ("Report: American Remains Separate and Unequal," 1993). Housing is more segregated today than in 1960, and schools are more segregated than in 1970 (Sleeter & Grant, 1988). About 67% of all African American students attend predominantly Black schools, and 70% of all Hispanics attend predominantly Latino schools (Mizell, 1992). Racism in schools is evident in the following practices (Garibaldi, 1989; Gay, 1989; Murray & Clark, 1990):

1. *Teachers and administrators have lower expectations for students of color.* Research studies show that teachers expect that students of color will demonstrate less ability, display poorer academic performance, exhibit more disruptive behaviors, and come from more dysfunctional homes than Euro-American students (Garibaldi, 1989; Scales, 1992). These lower expectations are typified in the disproportionate number of students of color assigned to special education or low-track classes. Gay (1989) recommends the total elimination of tracking because it currently serves as "a process for the legitimation of the social inequalities that exist in the larger society" (p. 175). Lower expectations are also manifested in teachers' interactions with students (Hilliard, 1989). Teachers demand less from the students, accept more low-quality or more incorrect responses, give fewer prompts to elicit the correct response, give briefer and less informative feedback, and allow less opportunity to practice independently (Brophy, 1979; Gamoran & Behends, 1987).

2. *Teachers interact and communicate differently with students of color.* Teachers ask fewer and lower-level questions, give less time for student responses, and make less encouraging responses to students of color than to Euro-American students (Gay, 1989). A study conducted by the U.S. Commission on Civil Rights (1983) found that both elementary and secondary teachers directed more praise, asked more questions, and built on spoken contributions of their Euro-American students more than they did for their Mexican American students. Moreover, punishment is often harsher for minority students (Murray & Clark, 1990).

3. *The curriculum is less demanding for students of color.* Secondary schools offer less extensive and less demanding science and math programs to African American and Hispanic students (Oakes, 1990). Only one out of five African Americans takes physics and only 7% major in sciences within American high schools (Tobias, 1992). Moreover, the National Survey of Science and Mathematics Education found that middle schools and junior highs offer fewer math and science courses in schools with high concentrations of minority populations (Tobias, 1992). Spencer and Dornbush (1990) refer to the "dynamic of substituting warmth and affability for challenge as a form of racism without racists" (p. 125).

4. *Bias is often shown in the selection of materials and personnel.* Classroom materials often omit authentic images of different cultures and lifestyles. Many districts fail to hire or practice token hiring of racial minority teachers and other school personnel (Murray & Clark, 1990). Students of color often suggest that there should be more teachers of color and more courses that help them understand their own histories and cultures and differences among cultures (*Voices from the Inside*, 1992).

**COMPREHENSION MONITORING OF KEY CONCEPTS**

*Issues*

1. Litigation has promoted alternative assessment measures for staffing and for designing IEPs for students of color.

2. Some of these alternative assessment procedures include interviews, observation-based assessment, curriculum-based assessment, and dynamic assessment.

3. Alternative assessment procedures have not been validated or subjected to intensive research studies.

4. Two levels of language proficiency are BICS (the basic interpretative communication skills, or social language) and CALP (the cognitive academic language proficiency level, or school language).

5. Bilingual students who are in need of special education lack proficiency in cognitive academic language.

6. The bilingual support model, the coordinated services model, the integrated bilingual special education model, and the bilingual special education model are used to deliver services to bilingual students with disabilities. In the bilingual support model, the teacher works with a paraprofessional; in the coordinated services model, the bilingual educator and monolingual special educator work as a team; in the integrated bilingual special education model, a dually certified teacher, trained separately in bilingual and special education, provides instruction; in the bilingual special education model, a dually certified teacher trained in bilingual special education provides instruction.

7. Racism is a conscious or unconscious belief that human races have distinct characteristics and that one's own race is superior and has the right to rule others. Since the 1950s, racism has focused on prejudice and discrimination against people of color.

8. Racism in the schools is evidenced by lower teacher and administrator expectations of students of color, by different communication and interactions with students of color, in the offering of a less demanding curriculum for students of color, and in the selection of materials and personnel.

As a special educator, you may face discrimination toward your students with disabilities whether they are of color or not. Hopefully, this chapter has increased your awareness of cultural diversity, the issues, and effective strategies for dealing with adolescents of color. Teachers do make a difference. A good teacher might have prevented the incident related in the following poem:

Six humans trapped by happenstance
In bleak and bitter cold,
Each one possessed a stick of wood
Or so the story is told.

Their dying fire in need of logs
The first man held his back
For of the faces around the fire
He noticed one was Black.

The next man looking across the way
Saw one not of his church
And couldn't bring himself to give
The fire his stick of birch.

The third one sat in tattered clothes
He gave his coat a hitch.
Why should his log be put to use
To warm the idle rich?

The rich man just sat back and thought
Of the wealth he had in store
And how to keep what he had earned
From the lazy, shiftless poor.

The Black man's face bespoke revenge
As the fire passed from his sight.
For all he saw in his stick of wood
Was a chance to spite the White.

The last man of this forlorn group
Did nought except for gain.
Giving only to those who gave
Was how he played the game.

Their logs held tight in death's still hands
Was proof of human sin.
They didn't die from the cold without.
They died from the cold within.

*Anonymous*

Now that you have read Chapter 4, reflect on your responses to the items at the beginning of the chapter and complete this post organizer.

1. What additional cultural values did you think of as you read the chapter?

2. Did you identify variables such as proximity, time, age, birthplace, socioeconomic status, and educational level that influence cultural values?

3. Compare the four approaches to multicultural education that you identified with those identified by Banks. How closely did you agree?

4. Compare your plan for incorporating multicultural education into the curriculum with the materials and instructional strategies lists. Describe the items that are the same and those that are different.

# Communication and Collaboration in the School, Home, and Community

© Nita Winter

**CHAPTER
HIGHLIGHTS**

*Communication*

*Collaborative Consultation*

*Working with Families, Support Personnel, and Community Agencies*

---

 Before you read Chapter 5, use your prior knowledge to complete this advance organizer.

1. Generate a list of communication skills that you think are essential to building and maintaining good relationships with others, performing successfully in your academic program in college, and/or being an effective teacher.

2. Construct your own definition of collaboration. Now think of a current collaborative relationship you have with someone (such as working on a project with a classmate or completing a task at work). Describe the steps you have followed in collaborating successfully with this individual.

3. As a special education teacher, predict the ways that you will be involved with families of secondary students with mild disabilities, community service agencies, and other professionals in the school.

---

During the past decade, there has been increasing emphasis on educating students with mild disabilities in regular classroom settings. In fact, in the United States, more than two-thirds of students with disabilities receive the majority of their education in regular classrooms (West & Cannon, 1988). The movement toward integrating students with mild disabilities into regular classrooms has altered the roles and responsibilities of teachers. Special educators, who in the past had sole responsibility for educating students with disabilities, are now sharing that responsibility with regular educators (Lewis & Doorlag, 1995), who are in turn participating in Individualized Education Program (IEP) development and adapting methods to ensure mastery of the goals listed in the IEP (Gans, 1985). Additionally, regular classroom teachers are expected to interact in new ways with students' families and other professionals such as school psychologists, social workers, and special educators (Heron & Harris, 1993).

These changes are prompting regular and special education teachers to develop alternate ways to communicate and collaborate regarding the educational programs of students for whom they share responsibility. The purpose of this chapter is to discuss a broad array of issues and strategies regarding communication, collaborative consultation, and interactions with other professionals, families, and community service personnel to help you maximize the success of students with mild disabilities in secondary schools.

## Communication

Communication is a dynamic process in which individuals share ideas, information, and feelings (Morsink, Thomas, & Correa, 1991). Developing, refining, and perfecting your communication skills may enhance many aspects of your performance as a professional in the school and community. According to Lang, Quick, and Johnson (1981), good communication is purposeful, planned, personalized, open, and clear.

1. *Purposeful.* Make your intention clear: "I will open the conference and state the reason for the meeting."
2. *Planned.* Think about what is being communicated: "I want to let the family know why I am concerned about Josh."
3. *Personalized.* Relate to the audience's background: "I'll refer to our conversation last month when we first met to discuss Josh and his progress in school."
4. *Open.* Communicate an open, inquiring, receptive attitude: "I'll ask the family members to share what they have noticed."
5. *Clear.* Use words that others can understand and that are a part of their language: "I'll remember not to use acronyms like IEP, WISC-R, LD."

**BOX 5.1**

### Communiqué from a Superintendent

#### *Halley's Comet*

A school superintendent told his assistant superintendent the following: "Next Thursday at 10:30 A.M. Halley's comet will appear over this area. This is an event that occurs only once every 75 years. Call the school principals and have them assemble their teachers and classes on their athletic fields and explain this phenomenon to them. If it rains, cancel the day's observation and have the classes meet in the auditorium to see a film about the comet."

The memo from the assistant superintendent to the principals stated: "By order of the superintendent of schools, next Thursday at 10:30 Halley's comet will appear over your athletic field. If it rains, then cancel the day's classes and report to the auditorium with your teachers and students. You will be shown films, a phenomenal event which occurs only once every 75 years."

The announcement principals made to teachers was: "By order of the phenomenal superintendent of schools, at 10:30 next Thursday Halley's comet will appear in the auditorium. In case of rain over the athletic field, the superintendent will give another order—something which occurs once every 75 years."

Teachers told their students: "Next Thursday at 10:30 the superintendent of schools will appear in our auditorium with Halley's comet, something which occurs every 75 years. If it rains, the superintendent will cancel the comet and order us all to our phenomenal athletic field."

Students reported to their parents: "When it rains next Thursday at 10:30 over the school athletic field, the phenomenal 75-year-old superintendent will cancel all classes and appear before the whole school in the auditorium accompanied by Bill Halley and the Comets."

Source Unknown

## Need for Effective Communication

Many experts believe that communication skills are the keys to success (Dettmer, Thurston, & Dyck, 1993) and are the most important skills that individuals can possess (Gutkin & Curtis, 1982). We tell our students as they enter our professional preparation program that most of their problems will be problems in communication. We like to share a humorous example with them (see Box 5.1) to illustrate how important it is to be clear, concise, and accurate.

Friend and Cook (1992a) point out the increasing emphasis on communication skills in the effective schools research and in many of the nation's professional preparation programs. Future teachers may audio- or videotape their teaching and then evaluate their own communication effectiveness. Role plays provide excellent opportunities for practicing the use of communication, and offer an opportunity for feedback from peers.

Communication skills form the building blocks of successful collaboration (Knackendoffel, Robinson, Deshler, & Schumaker, 1992). Effective communication skills enable you to listen better, understand the feelings of others, solve problems collaboratively, persuade others, and influence productive change.

## Interpersonal Communication Skills

Interpersonal communication skills include nonverbal and verbal communication, listening, reflecting, pausing, questioning, and summarizing. Each of these skills may be used to strengthen your communication efforts with other professionals, families, students, and community contacts.

### Nonverbal Communication

It has been said that up to 90% of a message may be communicated through nonverbal behaviors and vocal intonation (Morsink et al., 1991). Similarly, Mehrabian and Ferris (1967) found that the content of a message is represented by the following breakdown: 7% verbal, 38% vocal, and 55% facial expressions. *Observing* the nonverbal communication of others may help you understand what they are feeling. *Using* nonverbal communication techniques may help you better communicate your message while showing interest and involvement. Friend and Cook (1992a) describe nonverbal cues that include (1) body movements (facial expressions, eye contact, posture, and gestures), (2) vocal cues (quality and pacing), and (3) spatial relations (proxemics, or the distance between you and others). Cultural differences are also part of nonverbal communication. We address these differences later in the chapter.

*Body movements.* Consider how your body language communicates messages to a listener. You can use a variety of facial expressions, eye communication, posture, and gestures such as nodding your head or moving your hands to enhance your communication efforts.

Ms. Nolan stood up, walked to the door, and greeted Mr. and Mrs. Dalton with a broad smile and a handshake. She gestured to a table where they all sat down. She leaned forward in her chair, making eye contact as she asked them how they had enjoyed their daughter Linda's last English composition. She continued her eye communication and nodded frequently in acknowledgment as they commented about it.

Ms. Nolan's nonverbal behaviors showed that she was emotionally present and listening. She communicated a warm and caring attitude with her facial expressions, posture, and gestures and let the parents know that she was ready to interact with them.

*Vocal cues or paralanguage.* Hybels and Weaver (1986) describe the components of paralanguage as rate (speed), pitch (high or low), volume (loudness), and quality (pleasing or unpleasing). You can use your voice effectively by speaking clearly and audibly. Your pace should be moderate, not too fast, slow, or monotonic. You can vary your pitch and volume to make a point and maintain interest. Warmth, enthusiasm, and concern can be communicated through your voice quality. In the preceding example, Ms. Nolan could use paralanguage by injecting enthusiasm into her praise of Linda's past work and then change to a more serious, concerned tone as she begins to discuss Linda's current difficulties.

*Spatial relations·or proxemics.* Proxemics refers to the space or distance that we put between ourselves and others, and is different for each of us. The personal space you are comfortable with may be influenced by the age, gender, race, and size of the other person (Olson & Platt, 1996). Sensitivity to proxemics will help you when you have to set up a room for a team meeting or parent/teacher conference at your school. You should choose a meeting area that allows sufficient room around the table for people to feel comfortable with their amount of personal space.

### Verbal Communication

We would like to make an initial point about verbal communication before we look at the specific components of listening, reflecting, pausing, questioning, and summarizing. Verbal communication should be clear, specific, and concrete. Just as in the instructional language you use with your students, you need to be precise in the language you use with other adults and avoid the use of vague terms. *Some, things, a little, might, few,* and *much* are vague terms too frequently used in secondary settings (Florida Performance Measurement System, 1984, p. 151). Consider the following example from a member of a school problem-solving committee:

A. "Some of us thought we might be able to help Jeremy if we didn't give him so many math problems—maybe fewer would make a difference."

B. "The outcome of our team meeting about Jeremy was to limit the number of math problems to 15 a class period for the next two weeks and then reassess the situation."

Notice that Statement A contains vague terms; it is not concrete or specific enough to communicate exactly what was decided. Statement B specifies the decision that the team made and includes a plan to reexamine the situation at a predetermined time.

*Listening.* "Listening, by itself, is believed to be the most effective tool for influencing others" (Knackendoffel et al., 1992, p. 9). Hybels and Weaver (1986) indicate that approximately 53% of the time that we spend in communicative situations is spent listening. Yet how many of us have received formal training in listening?

Gordon (1974) describes two styles of listening: passive and active. *Passive listeners* may use nonverbal techniques such as body language to communicate interest (leaning forward, making eye contact, nodding, exhibiting facial expressions that are encouraging and indicate interest). During passive listening, you may also inject words or phrases that encourage the speaker: "Mm-hm," "Right," "Yeah," "Yes," "Go on," "I see." Although passive listeners are relatively silent, you can see the positive effect they could have on speakers such as parents who want to express their frustration about their child.

*Active listeners* are involved to a much greater extent. These listeners make comments, ask questions, and relate experiences of their own to the situation (Turnbull & Turnbull, 1986). Gordon (1974) recommends three steps in active listening: (1) Listen to what the speaker says. (2) Restate or echo the feelings. (3) Infer the reason for the feelings.

*Teacher 1:* "I can't stand it! I don't understand why Brian continues to skip."

*Teacher 2:* "You sure sound upset that he keeps missing school."

*Teacher 1:* "It's getting serious, he's running out of time, and I don't know what to do."

*Teacher 2:* "It sounds like you are worried that if he misses much more, he won't be able to graduate."

In this example, Teacher 2 listens to what Teacher 1 says, restates the feelings, and infers the reason for Teacher 1's concern.

***Reflecting.*** "Reflecting statements involve the mirroring back of feelings and content to the sender in order to communicate an understanding of one's frame of reference and feelings" (Morsink et al., 1991, p. 145). Two types of reflecting statements are paraphrases and reflections of emotions (Knackendoffel et al., 1992). When you *paraphrase,* you restate the content of the speaker's message in your own words. You do not parrot or editorialize—you simply translate the statement into your own words. Consider this exchange between two teachers.

*Science teacher:* "I don't know how I'm going to be part of a collaborative team and meet weekly, when I hardly have time to prepare and grade all my students' labs as it is."

*English teacher:* "So you're worried about how you're going to find the time to be part of this collaborative team when you're already stretched to the limit."

*Science teacher:* "Right. They want to meet on Thursday at 1:00, which is my most demanding time of the day, right between my two toughest classes."

*English teacher:* "So the meeting time is the main source of your problem."

*Science teacher:* "Exactly."

*Reflections of emotions* focus on the speaker's feelings. These statements reflect the person's emotions rather than the actual words. They let the speaker know you understand, and they encourage the speaker to continue sharing concerns with you. Following are some examples: (1) "You look pretty upset about what is going on with Melanie." (2) "It sounds like you've really gone out on a limb for that student." (3) "Wow, it seems like you've really gone above and beyond on this project." Reflections of emotions should be stated in a nonjudgmental manner; they should recognize, not reject, what the speaker is experiencing.

***Pausing.*** Pausing after you speak is an effective technique for encouraging responses from your listener(s). We call this *wait time* when we use it with children and adolescents in school. Pausing after you make a comment or ask a question with parents and other professionals will indicate to them that you are waiting for a response.

Friend and Cook (1992a) warn against using interruptions, overtalk, and reduced verbal spacing because they undermine and have a negative impact upon communication. *Interruptions* occur when one speaker begins speaking while another is still talking or during a brief pause. *Overtalk* occurs when both speakers are talking at the same time until one gives up the conversation to the other. *Reduced verbal spacing* refers to the practice of beginning to talk when another speaker is still talking or clipping off the last word or two of the previous speaker's statement. Communication is more effective when you use pauses during conversations and provide speakers with adequate verbal space.

**Questioning.** An important part of verbal communication is questioning. In their *Collaborative Problem Solving—Teaming Techniques Series*, Knackendoffel et al. (1992) recommend the use of informational questions (open-ended, close-ended, and indirect questions) and clarifying questions (used to refine what has been said).

*Informational questions.* Questions that seek information may be open-ended, close-ended, or indirect.

*Open-ended questions* generate a great deal of information and conversation. They cannot be answered yes or no; instead, they encourage an elaborated response. Open-ended questions frequently begin with *what, why,* or *how,* as in the following examples:

- "What are your greatest concerns about Libby?"
- "Why do you think she isn't doing her homework?"
- "How has Sam's family reacted to his problem?"
- "What do you think about Rudy's program?"
- "What solutions has the ninth-grade team tried so far?"

*Close-ended questions* are used to collect specific information; they are useful when you are seeking specific facts. They can be answered yes or no, or with a brief phrase. Close-ended questions frequently begin with *who, how many/often, is/are, does/do,* or *will.*

- "Who would be the best teacher to place him with for math?"
- "How many days was he absent during the last grading period?"
- "Is she chronically late for class?"
- "Does she typically do this at home, too?"
- "Will he interact with the other students if we place him on their team?"
- "Who would be the best teacher to place him with for math?"

*Indirect questions* ask for information without actually asking a question. Thus, they do not end with a question mark even though they require a response. Indirect questions may begin with phrases such as *I imagine, I wonder,* or *You probably*.

- "I imagine you have tried charting Gina's time on task before."
- "I wonder if peer tutoring would be effective with Naomi."
- "You probably contacted Vince's job coach at Wendy's to check on his punctuality and attendance."
- "I wonder if Lashon's parents have been called."
- "I imagine you have encountered this kind of resistance to new ideas before."

*Clarifying questions.* Clarifying questions are used to collect more information about a speaker's comments. They require the speaker to provide more details and to be more specific.

- "Could you give us some examples of Wanda's lack of interest?"
- "You mentioned that Nathan is uncooperative. What does he do and say that gives this impression?"
- "I'm not sure I understand. What does Marva do that annoys the other students?"
- "I remember you stated that Monty's family was going to participate. In what ways did they agree to help?"
- "At our last meeting, you said that Cindy never follows directions. You didn't mention it this time. Is that still true, or has there been a change?"

***Summarizing.*** Summarizing is a technique used to pull ideas together, tie up loose ends, highlight the main points, and ensure that there is a common understanding of what has been presented. It is an excellent way to conclude a conference, meeting, or problem-solving session. Following are some sample summarizing statements:

- "Let's go over what we've covered."
- "Does that about sum up what we've agreed to do?"
- "What else did we discuss? What have I left out?"
- "This is my understanding of the strategies we're going to try with Chris."
- "These five topics represent the solutions that we've generated."

### Barriers to and Strategies for Effective Communication

Knowledge of the potential roadblocks to effective communication may help you avoid some of the common pitfalls that interfere with and impede good, sound communication. In addition, awareness of effective communication techniques may enhance your professional interactions with families, in the school, and in the community. Table 5.1 summarizes the do's and don'ts of effective communication.

### Cultural Considerations

A discussion of communication would not be complete without addressing how cultural and linguistic differences among the professionals in the schools may affect communication about school issues and students. We have described the communication styles of different cultural groups in Chapter 4. Our intent in this chapter is to relate and apply this information to interactions with families and with other professionals.

Professionals from different cultural groups and with different language patterns may be challenged as they interact to solve school problems. For example, to a speaker of English, a speaker of a language that is more circular may seem rambling. To the other speaker, the speaker of English may appear to be clipped and less descriptive. An awareness of these differences will help you as you interact with other professionals and with families.

#### Communication Styles

In previous sections, we have presented techniques that are believed to exemplify effective communication skills. Be aware however, that deviations from these exemplary practices may be due to differences in cultural orientation toward communication rather than a lack of skills in communication. At the same time, bear in mind that the following general descriptions will not apply to all members of each cultural group discussed.

*Asian Americans.*  As we described in the previous chapter, many Asian Americans talk or "loop" around a subject before resolving an issue (Fukuyama & Inoue-Cox, 1992). It is helpful to know that the Asian American communication style may be characterized by silence, long pauses, and some hesitancy. As members of a school problem-solving team, they may need to talk about a problem for a considerable length of time before coming to any conclusions.

*Hispanic Americans.*  The nonverbal communication style of many Hispanic Americans includes a low requirement for personal space and a tendency to

**TABLE 5.1** **Do's and Don'ts of Effective Communication**

| Do | Don't |
|---|---|
| Listen, attend, and show interest to the speaker. | Rehearse what you want to say while another person is talking. |
| Use nonverbal communication while a speaker is talking: body language that shows interest, eye contact, and positive facial expressions. | Look down at your notes, lean back in your chair, avert your gaze, frown, scowl, or look bored and uninterested. |
| Vary your pitch and volume, speak clearly and audibly, and maintain a calm, pleasant voice quality. | Speak in a monotone, mumble, shout, sound abrasive or sarcastic. |
| Honor the amount of personal space each person requires. | Invade a person's comfort zone by sitting or standing too close. |
| Be clear and precise, use language that is specific and concrete, avoid using jargon and acronyms. | Use vague, ambiguous terms, examples that are not meaningful to the listener(s), and jargon and acronyms related to your discipline. |
| Use both passive and active listening techniques. | Sit passively without interacting and encouraging the speaker. |
| Use paraphrases and other reflective techniques to indicate interest and involvement. | Speak in judgmental terms or editorialize about the content of the speaker's statement. |
| Use reasonable-length pauses between your statements and those of the other speaker. | Interrupt, talk over, or invade the verbal space of the other speaker. |
| Use a variety of questions to collect and clarify information: open-ended, close-ended, indirect, and clarifying. | Restrict yourself to one type of question or fail to ask questions at all. |
| Conclude conferences and meetings with a summarization to highlight main points and to clarify what was decided. | Leave a meeting or conference without getting closure and coming to a common understanding. |

sit and stand close to others during communication exchanges. Furthermore, interrupting is not considered inappropriate (Zirpoli & Melloy, 1993). As participants on school problem-solving teams, they may not wait for a pause to interject a comment.

*Native Americans.* It has been noted that many Native Americans work for harmony and agreement, a characteristic that may enhance collaborative efforts on school committees. They view interruptions as rude (LaFromboise, 1982). In examining communication styles, Reifel (1992) found that Native Americans rarely make eye contact and prefer more personal space when carrying on a conversation. Because they put great stock in building rapport, Native American teachers may spend considerable time making family members comfortable at the beginning of a conference, or may take extra time with introductions and conversation at the initiation of a meeting with colleagues.

*African Americans.* Nonverbal and verbal communication styles of African Americans may include the avoidance of eye contact during conversations or presentations and an active, lively conversational style that includes interruptions intended to encourage the speaker. Such verbal encouragers, may enhance exchanges with family members during conferences and encourage colleagues to interact during problem-solving committee meetings.

*Euro-Americans.* The communication style of Euro-Americans tends to be informal, with a preference for more personal space and a tendency to make direct eye contact. They may prefer listeners to encourage or reassure them that they are listening and paying attention (Hillerman, 1990). Thus, Euro-American members of problem-solving committees may look to other members of the committee for nonverbal (nods, eye contact) and verbal ("Mm-hm") cues to show that their points are being understood. When they make suggestions to parents at conferences, they may look for signs of comprehension (nods) and agreement ("Yes").

### Intercultural Communication and Collaboration

Effective intercultural communication and collaboration among professionals necessitates an awareness and an appreciation of each other's beliefs and styles of communicating. As we move toward the 21st century, we are encountering a more diverse student population. It is because the student population is becoming more culturally and linguistically diverse that we need individuals from varied backgrounds, who understand diversity, to help develop instructional programs for our heterogeneous student population in the secondary schools.

Correa (1989) recommends the use of a culture broker—someone who provides each of the individuals involved with an understanding of the other's perspective.

The students in Ms. Perez's special education class are experiencing difficulty in many of their other classes. They do not meet their responsibilities in sticking to deadlines, completing assignments, and asking for clarification when they are confused about something. Ms. Rogers (seventh grade science teacher) cannot understand why Ms. Perez (special education teacher) continues to "indulge and enable" the students in her special education class. Ms. Martinez (another faculty member on the school problem-solving team) sees that the indulging behavior may stem from Ms. Perez's cultural beliefs. Ms. Perez admits that she believes it is important to "mother and indulge" these students who have so many problems. Ms. Martinez also understands the confusion of Ms. Rogers, who is trying to assist these students to function independently and self-sufficiently, skills seen as important in the school culture.

Ms. Martinez becomes the culture broker, and she works with Ms. Rogers and Ms. Perez on the school problem-solving committee by blending the school culture perspective and the Hispanic-American culture perspective into the problem-solving process. This and similar efforts will help develop the type of shared understanding that will lead to successful intercultural communication and collaboration among families and professionals.

---

**COMPREHENSION MONITORING OF KEY CONCEPTS**

### Communication

1. Effective communication is purposeful, planned, personalized, open, and clear.

2. Interpersonal communication skills include both nonverbal and verbal communication.

3. Nonverbal communication consists of body movements, vocal cues or paralanguage (rate, pitch, volume, and quality), and spatial relations or proxemics (distance between ourselves and others).

4. Verbal communication techniques include listening, reflecting, pausing, questioning, and summarizing.

5. Open-ended questions often begin with *what, why,* or *how;* generate a great deal of information; and cannot be answered yes or no.

*(continued on next page)*

6. Close-ended questions are likely to begin with *who, how many/ often, does/do,* or *will;* are useful when seeking specific facts; and can often be answered yes or no.

7. Indirect questions ask for information without actually asking a question.

8. Clarifying questions require the speaker to provide more information or to be more specific.

9. Effective intercultural collaboration among professionals requires an awareness and appreciation of each other's beliefs and styles of communicating.

## Collaborative Consultation

In a dynamic field, constantly undergoing reform and restructuring, school professionals continue to explore alternative methods of providing special education services to students with disabilities. An alternative that is enjoying increased attention and support is that of collaborative consultation. Idol, Nevin, and Paolucci-Whitcomb (1994) define collaborative consultation as

> an interactive process that enables groups of people with diverse expertise to generate creative solutions to mutually defined problems. The outcome is enhanced and altered from original solutions that group members would produce independently. (p. 1)

### Rationale for Collaborative Consultation

There are many reasons for incorporating collaborative consultation into the schools. The field of education is moving toward increased integration and inclusion of students who are educationally heterogeneous and diverse (Bauwens et al., 1989), necessitating collaboration among professionals in the schools. Many regular educators are unprepared to meet the educational needs of heterogeneous student populations (Margolis & McGettigan, 1988) and increasingly diverse groups of children and adolescents (Reynolds, Wang, & Walberg, 1987). Regular content teachers may lack the resources to meet the needs of students in more diverse classrooms. Collaborative consultation appears to have great potential for assisting teachers with the integration of students with varying academic abilities, including those who qualify for special education services (Bauwens et al., 1989). A recurring national school reform theme focuses on developing alternatives in schools and districts for meeting the needs of *all* students. Collaborative consultation may provide school district personnel with the support and knowledge they need to meet the needs of the changing student population.

There is concern about the number of students being referred for testing and possible placement in special education. Collaborative consultation emphasizes the prevention of learning and behavior problems by meeting the needs of students prior to referral and possible placement. Gable, Young, and Hendrickson (1987) report studies that have shown that the use of consultation may contribute significantly to reducing the number of students referred for special education and may facilitate the sharing of expertise among regular and special educators.

## Functions and Purposes of Collaborative Consultation

Collaborative consultation may be carried out in a variety of ways and in a number of different contexts. We focus on collaborative consultation first as a *problem-solving and decision-making process* and second, as a *service delivery model*.

When professionals engage in problem solving and decision making, they are providing indirect services because although they work on problems involving students, they do not work directly with students. Indirect services are provided by special education teachers working with regular education teachers individually or in teams to meet the needs of exceptional students (Ysseldyke & Algozzine, 1990). For example, at Martin Luther King, Jr. Middle School, Mr. Lauver (English teacher) and Ms. Jackson (special education teacher) serve on the school problem-solving committee to solve problems and make decisions about students.

When collaborative consultation is used as a service delivery model, special education professionals may provide indirect services (such as consulting teacher). For example, at Hillsborough High School, Ms. O'Leary (special education teacher) assists Mr. Jenkins (history teacher) by developing glossaries and study guides for his students in history.

Another way that collaborative consultation is used as a service delivery model is through co-teaching. Ms. Palmer (science teacher) and Ms. Ortiz (special education teacher) work together to co-teach the science class and to design curriculum units to supplement the science textbook that has a readability level that is too demanding for some of the students.

### Problem-Solving and Decision-Making Process

When collaborative consultation is used for problem solving, two or more individuals or a team may work to prevent and/or remediate learning and behavior problems. These individuals or teams may meet *formally* (as in a decision-making team) or *informally* (as when two teachers have identified a need to work together). For example, the Teacher Assistance Team (TAT) is a prereferral system (Chalfant, Pysh, & Moultrie, 1979) that meets formally to review teacher referrals, collect information, brainstorm solutions, and make recommendations for the referring teacher to try. The team may work on both prevention and remediation of students' difficulties. In contrast, Ms. Ivers and Mr. Sing may meet informally to assist Judd, who is having difficulty completing the lab work in Mr. Sing's class. They will identify the problem, generate some alternative solutions, implement a plan, decide who will monitor aspects of the plan, and then evaluate the results. In this way, they are working on remediating Judd's problems with the lab work.

You will find a number of different terms used to describe collaborative consultative efforts. Zins, Curtis, Graden, and Ponti (1988) include the terms *prereferral intervention, teacher assistance teams, intervention assistance teams,* and *teacher support teams* in the category of school-based consultation. The intent of each of them is to work together in a collaborative manner through formal, structured stages to solve problems and make decisions about students. "These approaches tend to reduce the number of inappropriate referrals, provide support to students, and expand the instructional alternatives that teachers have at their disposal" (Olson & Platt, 1996, p. 161). Descriptions of some of the various types of teams that use collaborative consultation are provided in Table 5.2. For further information, please consult the special series provided in *Remedial and Special Education*, Volume 11, Number 1 (January/February 1990).

A number of problem-solving programs and formats are suggested in the literature (Idol et al., 1994; Knackendoffel et al., 1992; Sugai & Tindal, 1993; Thurston, 1987). All of them contain similar elements, including (1) identification of the problem, (2) description of possible solutions, (3) implementation of a plan, and (4) evaluation of the results. Figure 5.1 contains an example of a form containing these elements—a Cooperative Planning Guide (Olson & Platt, 1996) that is completed collaboratively by the regular and special education teacher. Steps include defining and analyzing the problem and implementing and evaluating a plan. Notice how specific the teachers must be in analyzing the problem ("List the factors in the environment which may be contributing to the problem"), implementing a plan ("List and prioritize five recommendations"), and in evaluating the plan ("Specify how each recommendation will be monitored and evaluated").

**T A B L E  5 . 2  Types of Teams That Use Collaborative Consultation**

| | |
|---|---|
| Teacher Assistance Teams | . . . where problem-solving teams are formed by representative classroom teachers who serve in an advisory or facilitative capacity to other teachers in the same building. |
| Intervention Assistance Teams | . . . where teams are formed on an as-needed basis and because each member has expertise in a particular type of teaching or child management strategy; members may come from both within and outside of an individual building. |
| School-Based Resource Teams | . . . where teams are formed within a building, and like intervention assistance teams, are formed to solve a particular type of problem; any type of professional may serve on the team including classroom teachers, administrators, and support staff. |
| Student Support Teams | . . . where teams are formed specifically for an individual student and team members have responsibility for the educational program of that individual student. |
| Child Study Teams | . . . where teams are formed specifically for an individual student, as with student support teams, but the sole purpose of the team is to study the student and the presenting problems; often used as placement teams in special education. |

*Source:* "Collaborative Consultation in the Education of Mildly Handicapped and At-Risk Students" by J. F. West and L. Idol, 1990, *Remedial and Special Education, 11*(1), p. 26. Copyright 1990 by PRO-ED, Inc. Adapted and reprinted with permission.

### Service Delivery Model

Collaborative consultation may also be used as a service delivery model for students with disabilities (West & Idol, 1990). Used this way, collaborative consultation is carried out by a consulting teacher (indirect services), a resource/consulting teacher (indirect and direct services), or a co-teacher (indirect and direct services). Service delivery models were introduced in Chapter 2 in the section Special Educators in the Secondary Setting.

***Consulting teacher.*** The consulting teacher model of service delivery is "a process for providing special education services to students with special

**FIGURE 5.1** **Cooperative Planning Guide**

### Cooperative Planning Guide

Student's name: __Marcus Wyler__                    Date: __"/10__

1. Define the problem.

   Marcus doesn't pay attention in science class and this affects his performance on tests and projects.

2. Analyze the problem:
   a. List the factors in the environment which may be contributing to the problem.

   • The pace is fast.
   • The class is large.
   • The class is primarily lecture.

   b. List the behaviors of the student which may be contributing to the problem.

   • He doesn't come to class prepared with pencil and paper.
   • He doesn't watch when information is put on the board.
   • He doesn't write anything down, so he probably doesn't study.

   c. Discuss the student's strengths.

   • He likes working with peers.
   • He has excellent attendance.
   • He learns well from visuals.

3. Implement a plan:
   a. List and prioritize five recommendations.

   • Award points for coming prepared (1) D.W.
   • Present material on transparencies when possible (4) D.W.

   b. Go back and write the initials of the person responsible for implementing each recommendation next to that recommedation.

   • Cue him when to write something down (3) D.W. & J.H.
   • Teach him to take notes. (2) J.H.
   • At the end of a class, review the key points of the presentation and let him compare his notes to a peer's (5) D.W.

4. Evaluate the plan:
   For each recommendation listed in 3(a), specify how it will be monitored and evaluated.

   • Science teacher will keep a record of points earned.
   • Special education teacher will check notes for technique and science teacher for content.
   • Science teacher will keep track of the effectiveness of cueing.
   • Science teacher and special education teacher will check notes for evidence of materials presented on transparencies.
   • Science teacher and special education teacher will check notes for key points.

Special education teacher: __Judy Hernandez__
Science teacher: __Don Whitley__
Comments: __Let's meet next Thursday after school to review Marcus's progress.__

*Source:* From *Teaching Children and Adolescents with Special Needs* by J. Olson and J. Platt, 1996, Columbus, OH: Merrill/Prentice Hall. Reprinted by permission.

needs in which special education teachers, general education teachers, other school professionals, or parents collaborate to plan, implement, and evaluate instruction conducted in general classrooms for the purpose of preventing or ameliorating students' academic or social behavior problems" (Idol, 1986, p. 2). The responsibilities of the consulting teacher may include (1) providing inservice training to teachers; (2) making observations in the school and community; (3) assisting teachers to adapt curriculum and instruction, design materials and units, assess students, monitor student progress, and manage behavior; (4) supporting and assisting teachers in their interactions with families; (5) sharing and modeling effective teaching strategies; and (6) serving as a member of a school problem-solving/decision-making team. The consulting teacher provides indirect services with the intent of empowering others. Consulting teachers must possess excellent interpersonal communication skills, the ability to work collaboratively as a member of a team to generate ideas and solve problems, and knowledge of the regular education curriculum and how to adapt and supplement it.

***Resource/consulting teacher.*** The resource/consulting teacher provides both direct and indirect services. Direct services are provided through instruction of students with mild disabilities in a pullout or resource program. In secondary schools, resource teachers may teach content subjects (such as math or English), learning strategies (test taking, note taking), social/personal skills (resisting peer pressure, conversation skills), and/or employability skills (job-seeking skills, interviewing skills). Indirect service, or consultation, is provided when the resource/consulting teacher offers assistance to teachers who have students with disabilities in their classrooms (McKenzie, 1972). This assistance may include (1) suggestions for addressing academic and behavior difficulties of students, (2) ideas for adapting the curriculum and modifying instructional materials, (3) provision of staff development for other teachers, and (4) strategies for interacting with families of students with disabilities.

The roles and responsibilities of the resource/consulting teacher are varied and many. It is challenging to provide direct teaching to students (resource) and still find the time to assist other professionals and families (consulting) with their concerns about secondary students with mild disabilities.

***Co-teaching.*** The co-teaching (cooperative teaching) service delivery model can be used to provide both direct and indirect services to secondary students with mild disabilities. Co-teaching is "an educational approach in which general and special educators work in a co-active fashion to jointly teach academically and behaviorally heterogeneous groups of students in educationally integrated settings" (Bauwens et al., 1989, p. 18). The duties of a special education teacher in co-teaching differ from those of a resource/consulting teacher in terms of the setting in which services are provided. Co-teachers provide instruction to students with disabilities in the regular classroom. Resource/consulting teachers teach students with disabilities in pull-out programs. In Chapter 2 we discussed co-teaching as a direct service by describing the three options of co-teaching: team teaching, complementary instruction, and supportive learning activities. In this chapter we focus on the consultative functions of co-teachers, referred to as indirect services.

In providing indirect services, the special education and regular classroom teacher (1) engage in planning and problem-solving sessions regarding their students' needs, (2) adapt and develop instructional materials, and (3) conference with families. Because co-teachers deliver instruction together, they have the advantage of being equally familiar with the students and with how those students respond in class.

*Math co-teacher:* "Did you notice the way Melinda looked as we were going over the math homework?"

*Learning disabilities co-teacher:* "Yes, she seemed very confused. Maybe we should spend some extra time with her tomorrow to make sure she understands. We may have to break it down for her."

*Math co-teacher:* "Good idea! That may do it. And if the three who were absent today are back tomorrow, what do you think about including them in the same review session? Then she won't think we're singling her out."

*Learning disabilities co-teacher:* "Great. I know Rob will be back. I'm not sure about Marie and Larita."

To effectively implement co-teaching as an indirect service model requires adequate planning time, consistent support from administrators and other faculty members, and excellent communicative and collaborative skills.

## Benefits of Collaborative Consultation

There are significant benefits to collaborative consultation as a problem-solving/decision-making process and as a service delivery model. These benefits can be realized by special educators, regular educators, other school personnel, students and their families, and members of the community.

1. Collaborative consultation provides adult professionals, who have expertise related to students' needs, with a systematic approach to solving problems (Cook & Friend, 1990).

2. Through the collaborative efforts of regular and special educators' expertise, more students are impacted than when students receive only pullout instruction (Idol, 1988). From a monetary point of view, this is attractive to schools, in that the number of students receiving assistance can be increased without raising the cost (Idol-Maestas, 1983).

3. Data indicate that consultation is an effective means of increasing the academic and social skills of students with mild handicaps (Idol-Maestas, 1983; Knight, Meyers, Paolucci-Whitcomb, Hasazi, & Nevin, 1981).

4. Communication is greatly enhanced among special and regular educators, speech/language pathologists, guidance counselors, social workers, parents, and community agencies (Wilber, 1992).

5. Collaborative consultation has been suggested for students with limited English proficiency (Harris, 1991).

6. "When educators collaborate, instructional services are based on academic and social learning needs rather than on a special education label" (Wilber, 1992, p. 6).

7. Through collaborative consultation, with its reliance on shared expertise, group members are likely to acquire the skills of others (Idol et al., 1994, p. 9).

8. Collaborative consultation has been researched at the secondary level (Patriarca & Lamb, 1990; Tindal, Shinn, Walz, & Germann, 1987). The Florida Department of Education (1989) reported an improvement in the communication between regular and special education teachers.

9. Collaborative consultation has been suggested as a way to assist in transition planning (Sileo, Rude, & Luckner, 1988).

10. Adults who engage in collaborative consultation experience a *"process gain* (generating new ideas through group interaction that are not generated while working alone) or *collective induction* (inducing general principles that none induce alone)" (Thousand & Villa, 1990).

11. Collaborative consultation appears to improve services for students with mild disabilities and those at risk for failure (Schulte, Osborne, & McKinney, 1990).

12. Parents benefit from consultation efforts because of the instructional assistance and monitoring of progress provided to students by consulting teachers (Idol-Maestas, 1983).

It appears that when special and regular educators share their expertise with one another, students with and without disabilities are the beneficiaries. Outcomes are enhanced when two or more people engage in problem solving/decision making. Collegial interactions encourage mutual reinforcement and support.

## Roadblocks to Collaborative Consultation and Recommended Strategies

Regardless of how collaborative consultation is implemented, it has the potential for dramatically changing the roles and responsibilities of school professionals. Not surprisingly, it has met with some resistance. Karp (1984) defines resistance as an individual's "ability to avoid what is not wanted from the environment" (p. 69). Although there is a demonstrated need for collaborative consultation, much resistance and many roadblocks to its use have been documented in the literature. We describe six of these potential roadblocks and suggest strategies for overcoming them.

### 1. Fear of Failure

Reluctance to implement collaborative consultation may be due to a fear of trying something new and failing. Teachers may view the added expectations and the changing roles and responsibilities that accompany this innovation as beyond their capabilities, and doomed to fail. Such fear may be experienced by professionals engaged in collaboration when they are expected to acquire different philosophies or learn new ways of interacting (Idol et al., 1994). Fortunately, there are ways to cope with fear.

*Strategy: Systems change.* Hall and Hord (1984) suggest that the implementation of collaboration, or any innovation, requires movement through a series of seven stages, from a basic awareness to a higher level of understanding and acceptance. Their model is helpful for understanding the developmental nature of change (Idol et al., 1994). In coping with the fear and uncertainty that some professionals may have about collaborative consultation, it is helpful for them to determine where they, as individuals and as team members, fall on the continuum of change. Different strategies can then be implemented to move to the next stage. The seven stages are as follows:

1. *Awareness.* "I really haven't been involved in collaborative consultation."
2. *Informational.* "Tell me more about collaborative consultation."
3. *Personal.* "Well, just what is my role going to be?"

4. *Management.* "How will I implement collaborative consultation?"

5. *Consequence.* "Now, let me see how this is going to impact me."

6. *Collaboration.* "By working cooperatively on this, we can succeed."

7. *Refocusing.* "This is going well, but I have an idea for making it even better."

**Strategy: No-fault teaming.** When two or more people work together to try something new, it is helpful to adopt the concept of "no-fault teaming" (personal communication, Terri Ward). The idea is that people will work together to try something new, and if it does not work, nobody is to blame. This approach reduces fear and encourages active experimentation with new concepts.

### 2. Lack of Time

Insufficient time to participate in consultation is cited as a major reason for resource teachers' lack of involvement (Idol-Maestas & Ritter, 1985; McLoughlin & Kelly, 1982). Lack of time may be one of the greatest barriers to integrating consultation into the roles and responsibilities of the special educator (Idol, 1986). Special education teachers who provide direct services to students and are also expected to provide consultation services may find "time to consult" particularly difficult.

**Strategy: Allotment of time.** Engage in proactive planning by allotting sufficient consulting time for special and regular education teachers and other professionals. West and Idol (1990) report several strategies that have been successfully implemented in elementary, middle, and junior and senior high school settings. We present an adapted version of their work in Box 5.2.

### 3. Differences in Background and Training

Historically, the roles and responsibilities of special and regular educators have been different, as has the training. Typically, special educators are trained to teach in individualized instructional settings with limited numbers of students and to modify curricula to accommodate the needs of learners with disabilities. The training of regular educators emphasizes meeting a wide variety of demands in a regular content classroom with large numbers of students while following a specified curriculum. This differential training may cause each to doubt the credibility of the other in suggesting realistic solutions for students.

Collaboration has traditionally been initiated by and associated with special education, even though the intention has been to involve all school

**BOX 5.2**

### Strategies for Increasing Consulting Time

1. Have the principal or other support staff member teach a period each day on a regular basis.

2. Cluster students for independent assignments and study activities in large rooms with fewer staff supervising.

3. Ask a business or community organization that has adopted your school to supply a permanent floating (no cost) substitute.

4. Use teaching assistants or volunteers to supervise at lunch and as classes change.

5. Ask the principal to assign a specific time each week for professionals to collaborate.

6. Use part of regularly scheduled inservice days for collaborative teams to meet, or designate a half day each month without students (third Monday afternoon of each month) to use for collaboration.

*Source:* "Collaborative Consultation in the Education of Mildly Handicapped and At-Risk Students" by J. F. West and L. Idol, 1990, *Remedial and Special Education, 11*(1), p. 30. Copyright 1990 by PRO-ED, Inc. Adapted and reprinted by permission.

professionals. Many teacher preparation programs in special education offer a course in collaboration with parents and professionals, whereas most regular education programs do not. This differential training reinforces the level of preparedness of special educators and the lack of preparedness of regular educators to engage in consultation (Pugach & Johnson, 1988).

***Strategy: Mutual language, communication, respect, and ownership.*** Methods to "even the playing field" for professionals who have received different training and who are consequently approaching consultation with different perspectives include:

1. Using a common language that is easily understood by all participants (avoiding jargon, acronyms, and vocabulary specific to one person's experiential background, but not to others').

2. Using effective communication techniques as described at the beginning of the chapter (such as active listening, reflecting statements, nonverbal techniques, questions, and providing adequate verbal space).

3. Showing respect for others' knowledge, valuing their expertise, and pooling the talents of all team members.

4. Developing an attitude of shared ownership for ideas and activities, and assuming joint responsibility, accountability, and recognition for problem resolution (Phillips & McCullough, 1990).

***Strategy: Staff development.*** Another technique to overcome differences in background and training is to arrange for appropriate staff development activities (such as communication and collaboration, problem solving, and coordination of instructional programs). Participation in training provides the knowledge, understanding, and skills that are needed.

***Strategy: Preservice and inservice preparation.*** An additional proactive solution for dealing with differences in background and training is to coordinate the preservice and inservice programs of special and regular education. Joint preservice and inservice training in a core of essential competencies has been recommended for special and regular educators in order to provide for better transition to actual school situations, improve collaborative problem-solving skills, and support students at risk in the regular classroom (West & Cannon, 1988).

***Strategy: Technical skills and personal qualities.*** The competencies presented in Box 5.3 are derived from the work of Friend and Cook (1992a), Idol et al. (1994), and Little (1982), in combination with our own ideas. They represent the types of technical skills and personal qualities that are likely to facilitate effective collaboration for all professionals engaging in collaborative consultation regardless of field, background, and training.

### 4. Lack of Parity among Professionals

Pugach and Johnson (1989) state that parity is an essential ingredient of collaboration, but unfortunately, have found that most of what is written describes the assistance that regular classroom teachers receive from specialists. Often, special educators designated as consultants have been perceived by regular educators as experts who possess distinct training and expertise (Johnson, Pugach, & Hammitte, 1988). If consultation is implemented within a hierarchical structure, with classroom teachers perceived as having less expertise, then the success of the consultative effort is likely to be limited (Johnson et al., 1988). The contributions of the regular educator in terms of large class instruction and regular education curriculum must be considered and valued. "The needs of the regular educator must be viewed as different, not deficient" (Gans, 1985, p. 195).

Conversely, special education teachers may experience turf battles with regular educators who may be unwilling to share their classroom and

**BOX 5.3**

## The Top Ten Technical Skills and Personal Qualities of Effective Collaborators

*Technical Skills*

*Effective collaborators typically know how to*

1. Manage resistance
2. Facilitate change
3. Resolve conflict
4. Adapt curriculum and instruction
5. Use principles of effective instruction
6. Manage the learning environment
7. Use effective communication skills
8. Monitor student progress
9. Work as a member of a team
10. Engage in problem solving

*Personal Qualities*

*Effective collaborators typically are*

1. Respected by others
2. Socially competent
3. Warm, sensitive, understanding
4. Flexible
5. Risk-takers
6. Knowledgeable and experienced
7. Good listeners
8. Confident
9. Able to think on their feet
10. Energetic

students during co-teaching. In these cases, special education teachers may be relegated to the role of paraprofessional. Again, collaborative efforts must be viewed as a two-way proposition.

Margolis and McGettigan (1988) found that "people commonly withdraw from participation in decision-making groups when they think their knowledge is less than that of other members" (p. 19). To ensure that there is parity in consultation efforts, each member of a team must be treated with respect and made to feel that his or her ideas are important.

***Strategy: Training in communication and collaborative consultation.*** To ensure that there is parity in a co-teaching situation in the classroom, teachers need to communicate openly about their roles and responsibilities. It may be helpful to provide training in effective communication skills, collaborative consultation skills, and systems change for all participants. This training could include

1. Techniques for effective verbal and nonverbal communication
2. Strategies for co-teaching
3. Roles and responsibilities of co-teachers
4. Problem-solving strategies
5. Strategies for managing resistance
6. Instructional techniques for addressing academic diversity in content classes
7. Multilevel participatory planning and decision making
8. Systems change

### 5. Adherence to Tradition

Traditionally, the provision of services to students with disabilities has been the responsibility of special education and not a shared partnership with regular education (Pugach & Johnson, 1988). For many, collaborative consultation represents a significant change in direction from what has been done in the past, and may prompt professionals to say, "Why change? We've always done it this way."

***Strategy: Overcoming inertia.*** Convincing professionals to give up the comfort of their current practices may be accomplished in the following ways:

1. Share student outcome data and highlight the benefits for students, teachers, and families when collaborative consultation is implemented.
2. Move slowly and systematically, and actively involve all participants from the beginning (Friend & Bauwens, 1988).
3. Secure support from the school administration, faculty, and staff.
4. Employ the concept of no-fault teaming.
5. Build on existing strengths and skills of participants.

6. Provide incentives (such as visits to other schools, attendance at conferences, a stipend for instructional materials, or an additional planning period) to individuals willing to participate in innovative projects.

### 6. Lack of Administrative Support

Lack of administrative support has been found to be the major roadblock to the development and implementation of collaborative consultation between special and regular educators (Nelson & Stevens, 1981). The support of administrators is necessary for effective consultation programs (Graden, Casey, & Christenson, 1985; Idol-Maestas & Ritter, 1985). Active, visible participation of administrators is needed in designing and implementing consultation efforts (Phillips & McCullough, 1990).

*Strategy: Involving administrators.* Teachers can guide and encourage administrators to become more involved by (1) inviting them to sit in on collaborative problem-solving sessions; (2) sharing student successes that have resulted from collaborative efforts; (3) encouraging administrators to visit their classrooms to observe the benefits of co-teaching; (4) sharing testimonials that focus on the use of collaboration among parents and professionals and highlight the benefits for students, teachers, and families; and (5) keeping them informed of needs related to collaboration (such as the need for joint planning times for regular and special education teachers).

District- and building-level administrators can promote and establish collaborative consultation by involving all stakeholders. Suggestions for school administrators include the following:

1. Promote a climate that is conducive to collaboration.

2. Take a leadership role in promoting collaborative consultation, and model collaboration for faculty and staff.

3. Have a clear understanding of the basic principles of collaborative consultation and facilitate similar understanding by others (as by providing speakers, written information, visits to other sites, and ample opportunities for dialogue)

4. Develop an awareness of probable roadblocks to consultative efforts and of effective solutions for managing them.

5. From the beginning, include faculty and staff in participatory planning and decision making. Secure their ownership.

6. Provide necessary staff development training for all participants.

7. Know how to plan, finance, implement, and evaluate collaborative consultation.

8. Provide incentives and support for professionals engaging in collaborative consultation.

**COMPREHENSION MONITORING OF KEY CONCEPTS**

*Collaborative Consultation*

1. Collaborative consultation is "an interactive process that enables groups of people with diverse expertise to generate creative solutions to mutually defined problems. The outcome is enhanced and altered from original solutions that group members would produce independently" (Idol et al., 1994, p. 1)

2. Collaborative consultation is used for problem solving and decision making, and as a service delivery model.

3. When used for problem solving and decision making, collaborative consultation involves two or more people or a team working to prevent, remediate, and solve students' problems.

4. When used as a service delivery model, collaborative consultation is carried out by a consulting teacher (indirect services), a resource/consulting teacher (direct and indirect services), or a co-teacher (direct and indirect services).

5. Direct services are provided when a special education teacher directly teaches students with disabilities.

6. Indirect services are provided by special education teachers working with regular education teachers to meet the needs of students with disabilities.

7. The consulting model includes conducting inservice sessions, making observations, adapting and designing materials, monitoring student progress, interacting with families, sharing effective teaching strategies, and serving on a school problem-solving committee.

8. The resource/consulting teacher model requires special education teachers to teach students in a pullout program and to provide consultative services to regular classroom teachers.

9. The co-teaching model requires the special education teacher to co-teach with a regular classroom teacher in a content class, and to plan, problem-solve, adapt materials, and interact with families and regular classroom teachers.

10. Roadblocks to collaborative consultation include fear of failure, lack of time, differences in background and training, lack of parity among professionals, adherence to tradition, and lack of administrative support.

*(continued on next page)*

> 11. Strategies for managing roadblocks include systems change, no-fault teaming, allotment of time to consult, use of mutual language, staff development, coordination of preservice and inservice preparation programs, and training in communication and collaborative consultation.

## Working with Families, Support Personnel, and Community Agencies

In this section, we use the terms *parents* and *families* interchangeably. We believe *families* to be a more accurate and inclusive term, because the caregivers in many cultural groups include more than the mother and father, extending to stepparents, foster parents, aunts, uncles, grandparents, guardians, older siblings, and others. *Support personnel* include related services personnel and other members of the school and district faculty and staff. *Community agencies* represent the members of the community who are involved in the education of our children and youth. They may include prospective employers, job coaches, and members of agencies that interact with the schools. We believe in the statement "It takes a whole community to educate a student."

### Communication and Collaboration with Families

Current legislation (including PL 101-476, the Individuals with Disabilities Education Act) mandates parent involvement in the development, implementation, and evaluation of the IEP, and includes other provisions for parent involvement. However, maximizing the opportunities for enhanced home/school cooperation and collaboration involves more than simply meeting a mandate. It takes a systematic and ongoing effort.

All stakeholders benefit from home/school collaboration—students, families, schools, and community. Research has demonstrated that parent involvement with the schools has improved students' opportunities for success in school (Epstein, 1989) and improves their achievement (Henderson, 1987; Rich, 1987). Additionally, students have higher attendance rates and lower suspension rates (Dettmer et al., 1993). With parent involvement, test scores, attitudes, and rate of homework completion also appear to improve (Christenson & Cleary, 1990). Comer (1989) reports a decrease in school failure when parents and community members with diverse areas of expertise collaborate, and when parents and school personnel collaborate.

Home/school involvement has a positive affect on families by making them feel part of the team or partnership that is helping to plan the adolescent's school program and eventually his or her transition to work or school, and to community living. Teachers, as well, benefit from opportunities to collaborate with the adolescent's family members, because they provide a source of valuable information. Schools and districts benefit because home/school collaboration increases parental advocacy for school programs and improves attitudes toward school (Dettmer et al., 1993).

## Barriers to Home/School Collaboration

Barriers to home/school collaboration efforts have been reported by both families and teachers.

### Barriers for Families

1. Families sometimes find it difficult to keep the lines of communication flowing on a consistent basis.

2. Philosophical and cultural differences, as well as confusion about school language (use of jargon and acronyms), may impede communication efforts.

3. Families with adolescents with special needs may avoid interactions with the school because of a fear of negative reports of the adolescent's progress, an overwhelming feeling of helplessness about the adolescent's problems, or negative feelings about school in general, perhaps stemming from their own school experiences.

4. Many families perceive professional educators as "the experts" and consequently doubt their own abilities to contribute to a home/school collaborative relationship.

### Barriers for Teachers

1. Many teachers report apathy, indifference, and a lack of cooperation on the part of families. In reality, the lack of involvement could be due to family work schedules, lack of transportation, miscommunication, or overloaded, overwhelmed family members.

2. There is a tendency to blame parents for the problems of students (Leitch & Tangri, 1988).

3. Teachers state that schools are not changing in relation to societal changes, such as the increasing numbers of women entering the workforce (Olson & Platt, 1996) and the prevalence of single-parent families (Ascher, 1987; Peterson, 1987), many of them headed by women. Leitch and Tangri (1988) report a comment from a teacher that illustrates this problem: "Families today are just not like we used to know them . . .

times and people have changed but the public school system hasn't changed . . . we need a system that fits new needs" (p. 73).

4. Many teachers report a lack of time and resources to communicate and collaborate effectively with families, stating that they already have difficulty meeting their existing consultative responsibilities with other professionals in the school.

5. Teachers of junior high students cited inadequate planning, and staff members' lack of coordination in using one another as resources, as barriers to home/school collaboration (Leitch & Tangri, 1988).

### Strategies for Home/School Collaboration

Home/school partnerships can be enhanced with (1) effective conferencing techniques, (2) home/school communication systems, (3) education, training, and support for families, and (4) strategies for interacting with families from diverse backgrounds.

#### Conferences

The educational programs of adolescents with mild disabilities can be positively affected by communication between adolescents' families and their teachers. Parent/teacher conferences provide an excellent method for school personnel to communicate (Smith et al., 1995). Blalock, Polloway, and Patton (1989) describe three types of conferences: (1) procedural conferences for planning and review of programs, including the Individualized Education Program (IEP) and the Individualized Transition Plan (ITP); (2) crisis conferences in response to an immediate problem (such as an attendance problem, failure to complete homework, or disruptive behavior in class); and (3) routine conferences, such as those scheduled at the end of a grading period or to accompany an Open House at the school. For all conferences, you need a set of procedures to follow before, during, and after the conference (see Box 5.4).

*Before the conference.* Careful advance planning for a conference allows you to determine exactly what you want to accomplish. In addition to handling the logistics (such as what participants to include, when and where to hold the conference, and what student data to collect), you need to establish the purpose of the conference, and decide what you want to contribute and what you want to learn from other participants. For example, suppose you want to have a conference for the purpose of discussing with Lonny's family (mother and grandmother) his failure to complete his math homework. You decide you will show samples of Lonny's daily work in math, a

**BOX 5.4**

## Conference Procedures

### Before the Conference

1. Identify the purpose of the conference.
2. Contact and invite family members and other participants, and communicate the purpose, time, place, and anticipated length of the conference.
3. Collect and review all pertinent information (student work samples, comments from other teachers, and other data about pupil performance).
4. Decide what you are going to contribute and what you want to learn from other participants.
5. Plan the setting (room arrangement and seating) and an agenda.

### During the Conference

1. Create a positive, open, accepting atmosphere, and take time to establish rapport with participants.
2. Introduce participants, and state the purpose of the meeting clearly and concisely.
3. Use effective communication skills (active listening; reflecting statements; pauses; open-ended, close-ended, indirect, and clarifying questions; and summarizing).
4. Take notes during the conference, preferably with a predeveloped form.
5. Listen carefully to comments from family members, and include their input.
6. At the end of the conference, restate what was decided, and check your statements for accuracy with other participants.
7. Close the conference by thanking participants, planning follow-up, and scheduling another meeting if one is necessary.

### After the Conference

1. Review your notes.
2. Send a note of thanks to participants, with a brief description of what occurred and a reminder about any assignments that were given.
3. Evaluate the conference. (Did you accomplish your purpose? Did everyone participate? Were the recommendations generally acceptable to everyone? Do you need to follow up with anyone?)
4. Make arrangements for another meeting if necessary.

© Lila Weisbrot/The Image Works

*Student progress is shared with parents during a conference.*

description of his performance on tests, and his homework grades. You will ask his mother and grandmother to provide information about Lonny's attitude and ability in math, what he does when he gets home from school that might be keeping him from his math, and any other information that might contribute to solving the problem. You will ask his other teachers to describe his performance in their classes.

Many teachers like to send family members and other conference participants an information form to be completed prior to the conference. The form may include questions about the family's perceptions of the adolescent's interests, ambitions after graduation from high school, academic performance, and social interactions with others. Similar forms may be given to other participants, such as co-teachers, counselors, and transition specialists. When used at the conference, the comments that participants have written on these forms may provide an excellent way to initiate conversation and contribute needed information about the student.

*During the conference.* You begin a conference by introducing participants, taking time to establish rapport and make people comfortable, and then stating the purpose of the conference. It is helpful to open the conference with positive statements about the student. Throughout the conference, you should use the effective communication techniques described at the beginning of this chapter.

Thurston (1987) recommends that consultants utilize a problem-solving method called POCS (problem, options, consequences, and solution) by taking notes on ideas generated during problem-solving meetings (see Figure 5.2). Whether you use a predeveloped form like POCS or the Cooperative Planning Guide in Figure 5.1, or a form that you have developed, it is vital to include input from family members and other participants. At the end of the conference, you may refer to the form to restate what was decided and check with participants for accuracy. Then close the conference and schedule another meeting if needed.

Figure 5.2 shows that the conference participants reached agreement on how to solve Lonny's problem of not completing his math homework. It was decided that his mother would provide him with uninterrupted time to work on math homework each night, his math teacher would give him additional instruction and a peer to work with during math, and Lonny would sign a contract agreeing to these terms.

*After the conference.* It is important to follow up with conference participants with a thank-you, a summary of what was decided, and a reminder about the next meeting. To help with future meetings, you may reflect on the strong and weak points of the conference to evaluate its effectiveness.

Please review the information about communication presented at the beginning of this chapter. These techniques can enhance your communication efforts with families during procedural, crisis, and routine conferences.

### Home/School Communication

There are a variety of home/school communication techniques designed to enhance the communicative and collaborative interactions of families and teachers. They include written communication (newsletters and bulletins, progress reports and notes, student assignment notebooks, academic or behavior contracts), verbal communication (telephone calls, answering machines, homework hotlines), formal parent involvement tools, and family education workshops.

*Written communication.* A number of types of written communication are appropriate for use with adolescents in middle schools or senior high schools.

*1. Newsletters and bulletins.* Although they do not provide families with specific information about their adolescent, newsletters are an excellent means of communicating about school events; upcoming test dates; extracurricular activities; dates and times of Open House, Parent Conference nights, and PTA meetings; when report cards will be issued; and career days, when

**FIGURE 5.2** The POCS Method of Problem Solving

---

Lonny Smith

Problem:
Lonny does not complete his math homework.

Expected Outcome:
Lonny will complete his math homework.

| Options | Consequences |
|---|---|
| 1. Use a contract. | Everything is specified. |
| 2. Provide additional instruction. | May improve math skills. |
| 3. Give peer assistance during math. | May provide extra support. |
| 4. Assign fewer problems. | May not address math difficulties. |
| 5. Provide quiet time for homework. | Could help concentration. |
| 6. Withhold privileges. | May not address the problem. |

Chosen Solution:
Lonny will be given additional instruction in math by his teacher and peer support during math class. Lonny's mother will provide uninterrupted time for math homework. Lonny, his teacher, and his mother will sign a contract agreeing to these terms.

Responsibilities and Commitments:
Ms. Elder, math teacher, will provide instruction and support. Mrs. Smith, Lonny's mother, will supervise homework completion. Lonny Smith, student, will meet the terms of the contract.

Follow-up Date and Time:
February 23  -  3:00 p.m.

---

*Source: Survival Skills for Women: Facilitator Manual* by L. Thurston, 1987, Manhattan, KS: Survival Skills Education and Development. Reprinted with permission. (Note: Handwritten information has been added.)

representatives visit from colleges and vocational training centers. Some newsletters contain articles of interest to parents, such as how to help prepare your adolescent for the transition from middle school to high school, or an explanation of the new schoolwide discipline program. You may also include secondary students in the development of newsletters by creating student sections or columns for them to complete. Some schools send out newsletters that are produced entirely by students, who identify topics, conduct interviews, write articles, secure advertisers, and print copies.

Bulletins may be used to announce upcoming events, such as meetings and workshops. In early September, a bulletin was sent home from Crosby High School announcing a meeting of all families whose sons and daughters were planning to graduate in June. The purpose of the meeting was to review graduation requirements and procedures and to present options after graduation.

*2. Progress reports and notes.* Teachers may enhance communication and collaboration with families of adolescents with mild disabilities by sending home periodic progress reports to document performance in pullout and inclusive classes. These reports may be in the form of a checklist, a series of comments, or both.

Some teachers may prefer to send informal notes home to families periodically. The notes may take the form of a thank-you for attending a conference or parent workshop, for serving as a resource on a topic and speaking to a class, or for supporting the teacher regarding a problem at school.

*3. Student assignment notebooks.* Teachers may communicate with families by requiring students to keep assignment notebooks or planners, which contain daily work, homework assignments, and project deadlines. This helps families monitor what students are doing in school and informs them about work to be completed at home. Some notebooks may contain a place for comments from teachers and family members. Figure 5.3 shows an example of a student planner.

*4. Academic or behavior contracts.* Teachers may use contracts to specify the expected outcomes for student academic and/or social behavior. A contract is a written agreement among the student, family member(s), and teacher(s) detailing the responsibilities of all parties (Olson & Platt, 1996). Consistent communication is needed among all concerned for contracts to be successful. Families may help by supervising completion of the terms of the contract at home (such as finishing homework) and by providing incentives (home reinforcers). Home reinforcers that may be rewarding to

**FIGURE 5.3** **Student Planner**

| | M | T | W | Th | F |
|---|---|---|---|---|---|
| English | Read short story P. 83 | Work on Report | Answer questions P. 96 | Study for test | — |
| Science | Prepare for lab work | Write up lab results | Read Chapter 6 | Answer questions P. 121 | Work on science project |
| Math | Do problems P. 71 | Stay after school for Math Club | Study for quiz | Do problems P. 79 | Study Chapter 5 |
| Learning Strategies | Practice test-taking strategies | → | → | → | Complete Worksheet |
| Physical Education | Prepare for fitness test | → | → | Design a fitness log | — |
| Band | Practice for the football game | → | → | → | — |

Comments: _____

_____

_____

_____

adolescents who meet the terms of their contract might include use of the car, money, tapes/CDs, an extended curfew, food, or going out with friends.

*Verbal communication.* The following forms of verbal communication have been successful with students in secondary schools.

*1. Telephone calls and answering machines.* Personal calls to families for the purpose of providing praise, discussing a problem, or asking for help may prove very effective. However, frequent calls between home and school place excessive demands on teacher time (Salend, 1990). Telephone answering machines provide an effective alternative. Chapman and Heward (1982) found that recorded messages resulted in a significant increase in parent-initiated contacts with teachers. Recorded messages may be used to inform families about assignments, meetings, and school events. For example, on Monday, Mr. Harvey typically records a message for the families of students in his history class to give them an overview of what to expect for the week:

Today we reviewed the main events of the Civil War and discussed its impact on the Southern economy. We have now completed Chapter 9 and are getting ready for a test on Friday. Please review the questions at the end of the chapter along with the names and dates of the battles of the Civil War. For the next two days, we are going to be discussing how the leaders of those times may have responded to some of our current national and world problems.

There is a one-hour documentary about the Civil War called, "The War between the States" on Wednesday night at 9:00 on Channel 2. Please try to watch it with your son or daughter if you can. We will discuss it in class on Thursday.

In addition to general messages, Minner, Beane, and Prater (1986) recommend that teachers record individualized messages to parents using a code system. For example, a message to the family of a middle school student said:

Student 10's class work in English has really improved. Class assignments and essays have been excellent—well written and free of spelling and grammatical errors. Now let's work on meeting deadlines for book reports. There is another one due next Tuesday.

Families can record messages back to teachers, and then teachers can follow up (Salend, 1990). This exchange serves to keep the lines of communication open without taking a great deal of time.

*2. Homework hotlines.* Teachers may also offer a "homework hotline" to students and their families. The math teachers at South Lake Middle School decided to take turns staffing a hotline for two hours each evening. From 7:00 until 9:00 P.M., one of the math teachers was available by phone for questions from students and parents.

A more elaborate, computer-based system called TransParent Model (Baush, 1989) provides information over the telephone about homework assignments. Families can access the line at any time to get information (Dettmer et al., 1993).

### Education, Training, and Support for Families

Family members may find support through parent education programs, training, and professional organizations and publications. You need to be aware of these resources, so that you can inform families about their availability.

***Parent education programs and training.*** Just as teachers need to participate in inservice training to improve their skills and competencies in teaching and to learn effective ways to collaborate with families, so do parents need periodic training to improve their parenting skills and learn new ways of coordinating their efforts with school professionals. In addition, many families have problems with the same academic content with which their adolescents are struggling. Parents frequently become frustrated when they cannot explain academic content or answer questions. There are a variety of programs offered by school districts to provide assistance to families in coping with problems of adolescents, and in particular of adolescents with mild disabilities, many of which focus on interactions with school programs. Find out what is available in your school and district, publicize it in your monthly newsletter to families, and announce it at PTA and Open House functions. Following are some examples:

1. *Family Math,* offered in the evening, involves parents and their children and adolescents, working as a team, in a hands-on approach to math concepts and logical thinking (Lueder, 1989).

2. *Family literacy programs* have been designed to enable parents to assist their children with academic work (Nuckolls, 1991).

3. *Evening computer literacy programs* have been offered to parents and students so that they can learn computer skills together (Dettmer et al., 1993).

The Billings Demonstration Program (Hartwell, Kroth, & Wiseman, 1983), which focused on parents and teachers of junior and senior high school students, improved home/school communication, attitudes, and participation of students in school. Lombardino and Mangan (1983) found that after receiving training in language programming, parents became effective instructors for their own children. We recommend that you become involved in training programs with families and that you keep parents informed of training opportunities.

***Professional organizations and publications.*** Membership in national organizations and state and local affiliates provides a variety of services to both professionals and families who work with adolescents with mild disabilities. The Council for Exceptional Children, the Learning Disabilities Association of America (formerly called the Association for Children and Adults with Learning Disabilities), and the Association for Retarded Citizens are organizations that hold conferences and meetings, publish journals and newsletters, and provide training and materials for home and school use.

Locally, many communities have Parent to Parent organizations that feature speakers, parent support groups, materials, workshops, and monthly newsletters. Some school districts provide information about the types of family support groups that are available in the area.

Publications provide articles that can be extremely useful to parents. Topics may include collaborative efforts of families and school professionals, parent advocacy, and tips for effective parenting. Examples of publications for parents are *The Exceptional Parent*, a monthly publication that focuses on family issues and concerns, and *Newsbriefs*, a newsletter published by the Learning Disabilities Association of America.

### Strategies for Interacting with Families from Culturally Diverse Backgrounds

Language and cultural differences can become barriers to effective home/ school communication and collaboration. Stein (1983) noted that Hispanic parents of mainstreamed students may be less likely to participate in IEP meetings because they trust the decisions of school personnel, or as Herrera-Escobedo (1983) found, they do not want to infringe on the role of the teacher or principal. There are various strategies that you can use to improve communication and collaboration with families from culturally diverse groups:

1. Recognize cultural differences and develop an awareness of how they affect home/school interactions (Cross, 1988).

2. Utilize other minority parents as liaisons with the parents with whom you interact (Salend, 1990).

3. Include a culture broker (Correa, 1989) in interactions with families from culturally diverse groups to assist the individuals involved in understanding the others' perspectives.

4. Adapt collaborative efforts to include activities that are culture specific (Cross, 1988).

5. Include members of the community representative of various cultures at school events and activities to promote an awareness and acceptance of diversity.

6. Explore your own cultural beliefs, such as your definition of family, what you think of as attractive long-term goals, and what you think of as problem behaviors (Cross, 1988).

7. Mobilize the support of community leaders and other individuals who are significant in the family's life (Salend, 1990).

8. Consistently practice effective verbal and nonverbal communication in all interactions with families.

## Coordination with Support Services and Community Agencies

Teachers and parents are not solely responsible for communicating and collaborating to help solve the problems of adolescents with mild disabilities. Other resources are available in the form of school support services and agencies.

### *Support Services*

In addition to the teachers who provide consultative services in the school, a variety of school support personnel contribute to the collaborative process. They include administrators, counselors, school psychologists, social workers, educational diagnosticians, curriculum specialists, speech/language pathologists, physical and occupational therapists, transition specialists, and job coaches. The titles may differ from state to state, but the responsibilities are similar.

These school professionals contribute to the home/school collaborative process by (1) participating as members of school problem-solving committees, (2) providing needed services to students, (3) coordinating services among professionals, (4) planning, implementing, and evaluating educational programs, (5) networking with business and community agencies, and (6) maintaining effective communicative/collaborative interactions with families. The following example illustrates how school, business, and community collaboration worked for one family.

> Nick, age 14, came to school each day and promptly fell asleep in his first class. The rest of the day, he had difficulty paying attention and completing his assignments. Ms. Rose contacted his mother, Mrs. Girard. She explained that she works at night and leaves Nick and his 8-year-old sister at a sitter's. When she gets out of work at 2:00 A.M., she goes to the sitter's, wakes them up, and takes them home. By then, they are usually wide awake. When Nick and his sister get up in the morning, he fixes breakfast and makes their lunches.
>
> The social worker visited the home and found that there was rarely anything for breakfast or lunch. Mrs. Girard met with the school problem-solving committee and a plan was developed. The social worker enrolled Nick and his sister in their school breakfast and lunch programs. The counselor contacted Mrs. Girard's employer, who was able to change her hours so that she could work during the day. Nick's program was reviewed with assistance from the principal, educational diagnostician, curriculum specialist, and his special education teacher and content teachers, and some changes were made.

Nick began to pay attention, complete assignments, and improve his grades. He eventually became a tutor for a younger student, which improved his standing with his peers.

### Community Agencies

A multitude of agencies provide services to students with disabilities. For example, a variety of services are available for students with disabilities after they graduate from high school—rehabilitation services, adult day-care programs, and vocational-technical training centers (Cegelka & Greene, 1993). The Education and Human Services Consortium (Melaville & Blank, 1991) recommends that health, education, and human services collaborate in providing services to students instead of operating independently and sometimes unsuccessfully. Because of the documented need, interagency cooperation is now a part of the Carl D. Perkins Vocational Education Act (PL 98-524), the Rehabilitation Act Amendments of 1986 (PL 99-506), and the Education Act Amendments of 1986 (PL 99-457).

A detailed description of interagency cooperation and coordination is presented in Chapter 11 (Career Education, Vocational Development, and Work-Related Social Skills) and Chapter 12 (The Transition Planning Process). In this chapter, we suggest some initial steps toward building collaborative relationships with community agencies:

1. Develop partnerships with local community agencies and businesses to facilitate transition of students from school to work, and as part of career and vocational education. Invite representatives of these organizations to speak at school.

2. Include members of community agencies (human services, health, vocational rehabilitation) and parents on school improvement and restructuring committees, and as participants in school events, PTA meetings, receptions, and graduation.

3. Develop short- and long- range plans with agencies.

4. Encourage a local business or community agency to adopt your school. Prepare an adoption certificate, and invite the local newspaper to come to school and photograph the adoption ceremony. Include your "parent" business or agency in all school events, and publicize their contributions to the school.

5. Swap newsletters with businesses and community agencies.

6. As part of Career Day, invite business and community members to participate.

7. In transition planning, collaborate with all stakeholders to improve the coordination of services for students.

---

**COMPREHENSION MONITORING OF KEY CONCEPTS**

*Working with Families, Support Personnel, and Community Agencies*

1. Barriers to collaborative consultation for families include philosophical and cultural differences, problems with school jargon, negative feelings about school, and doubts about their abilities to collaborate with school "experts."

2. Barriers to collaboration for teachers include the belief that parents are apathetic, schools' failure to change in relation to societal changes, lack of time and resources, and lack of coordinated planning with other staff members.

3. Home/school partnerships can be enhanced with effective conferencing; home/school communication techniques; education, training, and support for families; and strategies for interacting with families from culturally diverse groups.

4. Home/school communication techniques include written communication (newsletters and bulletins, progress reports and notes, student assignment notebooks, and academic and behavior contracts) and verbal communication (telephone calls, answering machines, and homework hotlines).

5. Education, training, and support for families may include parent education programs, training, professional organizations, and publications.

6. In addition to teachers and families, support services and community agencies provide resources for collaborating to solve the problems of adolescents with disabilities.

---

 Now that you have read Chapter 5, use the information you have gained to complete this post organizer.

1. Generate a list of communication skills that you believe are essential to building and maintaining good relationships with others, performing successfully in your academic program in college, and/or being an effective teacher.

2. Compare the definition of collaboration that you developed before reading the chapter to the definition in the chapter. Would you modify your definition in any way? Think back to the collaborative relationship you identified before reading the chapter (such as working on a project with a classmate or completing a task at work). Compare the steps you followed in collaborating successfully in that situation to the ideas in the chapter. How could you improve your collaborative efforts?

3. Describe five strategies that you think are essential for enhancing your interactions with families, support personnel, and community agencies.

# Motivating Secondary Students

© Don Melandry/Jeroboam

 Before you read Chapter 6, use your prior knowledge to complete this advance organizer.

1. Share with a peer what motivates you to study for an exam or to attend classes.

2. Identify teacher behaviors that you feel foster a positive classroom climate.

3. Discuss the pros and cons of using group contingencies for motivation.

Adelman and Taylor (1983) portray a highly motivated student as looking forward to an activity, asking about it, and showing a willingness to participate in it, whereas an unmotivated student shows disinterest and avoidance of an activity. Unfortunately, many secondary students with mild disabilities fit the latter description. Borich (1988) defines motivation as "what energizes or directs a learner's attention, emotions, and activities "(p.1). Feather (1982) has proposed a conceptual model of motivation that includes the factors of expectation and value. According to this model, students become actively involved when they expect to be successful with reasonable effort and when they value the reward associated with successful task completion.

In her discussion of motivation in the special education classroom, Cohen (1986) contrasts the traditional behavioral approach, prevalent in many special education classrooms, with the intrinsic approach. In the behavioral approach, teachers attempt to motivate students through the use of positive reinforcers and external environmental events. The ultimate goal is for students to learn to manage their own behaviors. However, Cohen contends, teachers often do not reach the goal of teaching students self-management, and frequently, students do not generalize these procedures to nonstructured settings.

The intrinsic approach, in contrast, acknowledges the role of a person's experiences, perceptions, and emotions (Cohen, 1986). The psychological needs of self-determination, competence, and relatedness to others affect a person's motivation (Deci & Chandler, 1986; Deci, Hodges, Pierson, & Tomassone, 1992). Self-determination involves a feeling of control and ownership. Competence involves a feeling of achievement, success, and accomplishment. Relatedness to others involves positive interactions and feelings. In a study examining the effect of self-determination and competence on motivation to achieve, Deci et al. (1992) discovered that junior and senior high school students with learning disabilities and those with emotional disabilities believed that competence-related and autonomy-related variables were important motivational factors.

In this chapter, we examine motivation strategies—such as positive reinforcement—that are typically aligned with behavioral, or external, approaches to motivation, and strategies—such as goal setting—that are typically aligned with intrinsic approaches. In addition, we include other strategies—such as modeling an enthusiasm for learning—that are not so easily categorized. We have selected strategies based not on their affinity with any particular theory or philosophy, but on their effectiveness with adolescents with mild disabilities. Just as with instructional strategies, it is our belief that special education teachers need to utilize a variety of motivation strategies to meet the individual needs of adolescents with mild disabilities. Thus, we discuss a wide range of motivation strategies: providing students with choices, modeling an enthusiasm for learning, giving students a rationale for learning, varying instructional procedures, selecting interesting and relevant materials, promoting expectations for success, involving students in goal setting, and establishing a positive classroom climate. We also discuss ways of using the traditional management strategies of positive reinforcement, contingency contracts, group contingencies, and self-management to increase student motivation.

To paraphrase Griffin (1988), in his discussion of underachievers in secondary schools, teachers can create conditions that stimulate a desire to learn and grow and that persistently invite students to be motivated. We, as teachers, can create the conditions, but ultimately, students create the motivation.

## Providing Students with Choices

Choices capitalize on students' interests, and as we all know, the more we are interested in a topic, the more motivated we are to explore it. Moreover, incorporating choices into the curriculum matches a student's need for self-determination, or control over the learning environment, and the need for competence—needs that underlie intrinsic motivation (Adelman & Taylor, 1990). Jones and Jones (1990) recommend that teachers give students choices about "(1) what material to work on, (2) when work will be accomplished, (3) how it will be completed, (4) the level of difficulty of the assignment, (5) self-correcting and self-monitoring of work, and (6) individual goal setting" (p. 180). As an example, Figure 6.1 is a form that lists assignments that students can select to show that they know the information after reading a chapter in a social studies or science text.

Deci and colleagues (1992) found that teachers who gave students choices of prestated consequences increased their students' intrinsic motivation and self-regulation of inappropriate behaviors. Choice statements may present the student with the appropriate behavior and some type of unpleasant option (Olson & Platt, 1996). For example, Mr. Hernandez issued the following choice statement to a student: "Samantha, your responsibility is to work, not sleep in class. I am not going to keep waking you up. You have a choice either to begin working or to receive an office referral. It's your choice." Hopefully, this statement will motivate Samantha to avoid the prestated consequence of an office referral and to begin work.

We have found that once the statement is issued, it is best to leave the immediate area and give the student some time to think about the choice. This also avoids a direct confrontation and allows the student to save face

**FIGURE 6.1** **Alternative Assignments**

Name _____ Date _____

I will do _____ of these to show I understand the material
found in Chapter _____ of _____.

_____ 1. Take a test.

_____ 2. Design a report of the major points using a videodisc
and bar-coder software program.

_____ 3. Create and answer your own end-of-chapter questions.

_____ 4 Write an introduction to and summary of the chapter.

_____ 5. Complete _____ worksheets.

_____ 6. Discuss the major points with two other students on a
tape recorder.

_____ 7. Complete a journal highlighting the relevant points.

_____ 8. Create a poster with definitions of the major
vocabulary terms.

_____ 9. Your option as approved by the teacher: _____
_____.

or even mumble nasty things out of your hearing range (or, at least, you
can pretend they are out of your hearing range). An appropriate choice
leads to a quiet comment, "Samantha, I see you made a wise decision." An
inappropriate choice leads to follow-through of the consequence, "I'm
sorry, Samantha, that you made that choice. We're all responsible for our
behavior. You force me to write the referral." Giving students continuous
feedback concerning their effectiveness in making good choices or decisions is essential in promoting motivation (Adelman & Taylor, 1990).

## Modeling an Enthusiasm for Learning

Your own enthusiasm for a task is often evident to students. Task-attraction
and task-challenge behaviors motivate students to become involved in
class activities (Florida Performance Measurement System, 1984). Task-

attraction statements are statements that describe the interest and attractiveness of the task. An example of a task-attraction statement is "I also enjoyed reading *Our Town* because it reminds me of some of the people I knew in my small hometown in Illinois. In fact, Howey acts just like one of my high school friends, who . . ." A task-challenge statement indicates "to the students that an exercise or activity will be hard to do" (Florida Performance Measurement System, p. 157). Ms. Homes used a task-challenge statement when she told students, "Deciding what to do after you graduate from high school is probably one of the most difficult decisions you will make, so be certain to ask questions during our unit on career options."

Brophy (1987) recommends that teachers share their interests in books, articles, TV programs, or movies connected to subject areas. For example, Mr. Horne had students watch a videotape of "Eyes on the Prize," one of his favorite TV shows, during his unit on the civil rights movement. Ms. Herman spends time every Monday having students check out the weekly TV listings for programs that correspond to their content-area classes.

Responding to students' questions with curiosity is another way to model enthusiasm and a positive attitude for learning (Jones & Jones, 1990). Mr. Shane models enthusiasm and a positive attitude in this reply to a student's question: "I don't know the answer, but I'd like to find out. Why don't you look it up and share it with us? It sounds as though the answer will be very interesting."

In addition, Hill (1989) recommends that teachers model a commitment to continuous learning. He describes how effective teachers find time to browse in the library when they assign library work for students.

## Sharing Rationales

Lenz, Alley, and Schumaker (1987) discovered that secondary students are more motivated to learn strategies when they are shown the benefits for school, employment, and life in general. Sharing objectives, setting forth their importance, and showing how they are integrated with other elements of the curriculum often help students see the value of the subject matter (Drayer, 1979). The acknowledgment of students' feelings is important to include in a rationale when the teacher expects that students will not be interested in the assignment or may find it boring (Deci & Chandler, 1986). The statement "I know this may not seem to be a very interesting activity, but students in the past found that it improved their job-interviewing skills and helped them get summer jobs" may motivate students to undertake the task.

Zigmond, Sansone, Miller, Donahue, and Kohnke (1986) recommend the following rationales to legitimize learning for secondary students:

1. They need the skills to get a job.
2. They need the skills to perform on the job.
3. They need the skills to survive as an adult.
4. They need this particular skill before other, more desirable skills can be learned.
5. They need the skills to be mainstreamed into a particular regular class.
6. They need the skills for college or some type of postsecondary training.
7. They need the skills to complete the courses and earn the credits required for high school graduation.
8. They need the skills to enjoy or participate in a desired leisure-time activity.
9. They need the skills to function like their normal peers.
10. They need the skills to participate in extracurricular school activities. (p. 17)

When teachers cannot think of a reason that students must learn the information, they may wish to put students in small groups to brainstorm the reasons (Jones & Jones, 1990). Then students and teachers can come up with the rationale together. Ms. Murphy found it helpful to place the responsibility for identifying the rationale for studying global problems such as water resources upon her students. She opened the lesson by asking "Why do you think we need to learn about water resources? In what ways can you use information about water resources in this class, other classes, and outside of school, now and in the future?"

## Using a Variety of Procedures

Presenting information in many different ways, using different instructional arrangements, providing for active student involvement, and giving students alternative ways of showing they know the information are very motivational techniques (Brophy, 1987; Meier, 1995; Morsink, 1984). During review, sometimes Mr. Simons asks individual students to summarize the information, sometimes he presents the information in a game format with students racing against time to answer questions, and sometimes he presents the major points on a transparency. We discuss various instructional arrangements, active participation, and alternative evaluations for students extensively in Chapter 7.

Using a variety of instructional methods also accommodates different learning styles, or ways that students approach learning. Learning-style in-

© Nita Winter

*Middle school students enjoy expressing themselves in a variety of ways.*

struction is based on the belief that students' learning styles can be assessed and matched to specific teaching methods, and that this match, in turn, enhances learning. For example, several students in Mr. Camp's class appeared to learn information better visually, so he taught some of the information about the Civil War using videotapes and photographs. Other students appeared to learn information better auditorily, so he presented part of the information through lecture and discussion.

Basing decisions about instruction on the idea of learning styles is very controversial. Proponents, such as Dunn, McCarthy, and Lazear, propose that it is easy to assess and teach learning styles. In particular, the model of Dunn and Dunn (1978) considers the effects on learning of many different elements—environmental (sound, light, temperature, and physical design), emotional (motivation, persistence, responsibility, and structure), sociological (colleagues, self, pair, team, authority, and varied), physical (perceptual, intake, time, and mobility), and psychological (analytic, global, cerebral preference, reflective, and impulsive). According to Dunn (1990), students with disabilities reveal no psychological preferences and usually require multisensory instruction.

McCarthy (1987) identifies imaginative learners, analytic learners, commonsense learners, and dynamic learners in her 4MAT model of learning styles. According to McCarthy, the imaginative learner needs personal involvement in the learning experience and learns through social interactions; the analytic learner wants to know what experts think and learns by thinking through ideas; the commonsense learner wants to know how things work and learns through hands-on activities; and the dynamic learner enjoys being involved with a variety of activities and learns through self-discovery.

Lazear (1991) views learning styles within Gardner's multiple intelligences model. The multiple intelligences are verbal/linguistic, logical/mathematical, visual/spatial, body/kinesthetic, musical/rhythmic, interpersonal, and intrapersonal intelligence (Gardner, 1983). Verbal/linguistic intelligence is related to words and language; logical/mathematical is related to numbers and the recognition of abstract patterns; visual/spatial includes the ability to create mental images; body/kinesthetic includes physical movement and body awareness; musical/rhythmic is related to recognition and sensitivity to rhythms and beats; interpersonal relies on relationships and communications; and intrapersonal centers on metacognition and inner awareness (Lazear, 1991). According to Gardner (1983), most people possess all of these intelligences but at various competence levels.

Identification of learning styles and concomitant matching of instructional procedures have historically appealed to special educators, beginning with the visual and auditory subtests of the Illinois Test of Psycholinguistic Ability (ITPA) (Kirk, McCarthy, & Kirk, 1968). Even though research failed to support modality assessment and instruction using the ITPA, Arter and Jenkins (1977) found that 99% of the special education teachers they surveyed still felt modality identification was a critical factor in the selection of instructional techniques. Although the notion of different learning styles is intuitively appealing, empirical evidence is not supportive. In their review of the research with special education students, Kavale and Forness (1990) concluded that modality-based or learning-style instruction holds "little promise for special education, " as "evidence indicates essentially no effect for modality teaching" (p. 360). Snider (1992) concurs with this conclusion, as she found that research failed to support modality and modality matching.

However, research does show that including novel elements in a lecture (Brophy, 1987) and using a variety of activities (Kuykendall, 1992), whether aligned with learning styles or not, does increase motivation. Consideration of the concepts of learning styles and multiple intelligences produces a curriculum rich with a variety of activities and instructional arrangements. For example, Maker, Nielson, and Rogers (1994) organized activities matched to the various intelligences to develop a thematic unit on "Connections" within the topic of Native Americans in North Carolina:

(a)  An activity they selected for verbal/linguistic intelligence was "Create your own symbolic alphabet or icons that reflect current cultural values."

(b)  For logical/mathematical intelligence—"Create a code. Send a message in the code. Evaluate the effectiveness of your code."

(c)  For visual/spatial intelligence—"Create an original work of art inspired by your Native American Studies."

(d)  For body/kinesthetic intelligence—"Use your body to create a nonverbal interpretation of an event from Native American history."

(e)  For musical/rhythmic intelligence—"Create an original work of music inspired by your Native American studies."

(f)  For interpersonal intelligence—"Create an original way to communicate with others that is inspired by your studies of Native Americans."

(g)  For intrapersonal intelligence—"Visualize yourself as a Native American personality. Create a legend you would want to pass down to your descendants." (p. 15)

This list of activities provides many interesting and varied suggestions for teaching about Native Americans in North Carolina. Undoubtedly, all students can benefit from these activities, whether or not learning styles can be assessed or matched to specific instructional strategies.

---

**COMPREHENSION MONITORING OF KEY CONCEPTS**

*Providing Students with Choices*

1.  Incorporating choices into the curriculum capitalizes on students' interests and on their need for self-determination and competence.

2.  Teachers can incorporate choices into the curriculum by letting students decide on activities, tasks, and requirements, and even on consequences for inappropriate behaviors.

3.  Choice statements for motivating students to stop inappropriate behaviors often consist of presenting the student with the appropriate behavior and some type of unpleasant option.

4.  Giving students continuous feedback concerning their effectiveness in making good choices or decisions is essential in promoting motivation.

*(continued on next page)*

### Modeling an Enthusiasm for Learning

5. Using task-attraction and task-challenge statements; sharing interests in books, articles, and other media; responding to students' questions with curiosity; and modeling a commitment to continuous learning are ways for teachers to show enthusiasm for learning.

6. Task-attraction statements are statements that describe the interest and attractiveness of the task.

7. Task-challenge statements alert the students that the activity will be difficult.

### Sharing Rationales

8. Rationales for motivating students may include (a) sharing the benefits of learning information or skills for school, employment, and life in general, (b) sharing objectives and their importance and relationships; and (c) acknowledging the feelings of students.

### Using a Variety of Procedures

9. Using a variety of procedures means presenting information in many different ways, using different instructional arrangements, providing for active student involvement, and giving students alternative ways to show they know the information.

10. The belief that a student's learning style can be assessed and matched to a particular teaching method is very controversial, with equivocal empirical evidence.

11. Dunn and Dunn believe that environmental, emotional, sociological, physical, and psychological elements affect learning; McCarthy posits imaginative, analytic, commonsense, and dynamic learning styles; Gardner identifies multiple intelligences.

12. Even though the notion of learning styles is controversial, the idea that teachers should include a variety of instructional procedures and activities is valid.

## Selecting Interesting and Relevant Materials

Secondary students tend to enjoy materials that they can relate to and that deal with adolescence (Zigmond, Sansone et al., 1986). Brophy (1987) recommends that materials include people, fads, or events prominent in the news or in the youth culture. Kaywell (1992) has published an annotated guide to young adult literature that addresses AIDS, alcohol and drugs, eating disorders, suicide, and other problems of adolescents. The guide provides descriptions of 900 titles.

Often, driver's training manuals, sports or fashion magazines, newspapers, TV programs, and movies pique students' interests more than text materials. One of our student interns motivated her high school students with mild disabilities to read the story of Frankenstein by showing a videotape first. If the local newspaper is too difficult for students to read, you may wish to order *News for You* (New Reader's Press, P.O. Box 131, Syracuse, NY 13210). This high-interest low-vocabulary newspaper is published weekly and contains major news stories, feature stories, sports stories, crossword puzzles, and cartoons.

Another consideration in the selection of motivational materials is to evaluate if the subject matter seems mature (Zigmond, Sansone et al., 1986). Using newspapers as a source of math problems and job applications to develop reading and writing skills are examples of using mature materials to teach basic skills. Technology has created many interesting and relevant materials for teacher use, including videodiscs and CD-ROMs. Please see Chapter 4 and Chapters 7–12 for detailed descriptions and examples of various student materials.

## Promoting Expectations for Success

In much of the motivational research conducted with students with mild disabilities, results show that students often expect failure and feel that successes are due to luck or fate, beyond their control (Cooley & Ayres, 1988; Dohm & Bryan, 1994; Licht & Kistner, 1986). Since they do not expect to succeed, students with mild disabilities are often bored, alienated, and lacking in motivation for schoolwork (Adelman & Taylor, 1983; Murtaugh & Zetlin, 1989). Conversely, motivation research shows that an individual who (a) attributes success to sufficient ability and reasonable effort and (b) attributes failure to either insufficient effort or inappropriate strategies is more motivated to try challenging tasks (Licht & Kistner, 1986).

Brophy (1987) suggests the following strategies for maintaining successful expectations: (1) Program for success. (2) Teach performance appraisal, self-reinforcement, and goal setting. (3) Help students understand the linkage between effort and outcome. (4) Provide remedial socialization. In programming for success, Brophy urges teachers to control task difficulty by presenting instruction at the student's level, and to prepare the student for the task through the sharing of objectives. In performance appraisal, he recommends teaching students to judge their performances by comparing them to absolute standards or to their own previous progress. In teaching students the relationship between effort and outcome, he suggests portraying skill development as improvement in small steps and as domain-specific so students understand that some skills are easier to master than others. For remedial socialization, he recommends makeup exams, performance contracts, additional instruction, additional practice opportunities, and attribution retraining.

Attribution retraining means helping students understand that outcomes are related to performance—that increased effort promotes increased successes and that failure is often due to poor effort or inappropriate strategies (Licht & Kistner, 1986). The basic procedure is to give students effort ("You really do try to concentrate on the task") and ability ("You're very talented at this") feedback statements while they perform tasks, and at the same time encourage the students to internalize these interpretations (Dohm & Bryan, 1994). Comments such as "I can tell you spent a lot of time on that report" and "You've really been working hard" convey to the student that success is connected to effort or hard work. When a student's response is incorrect, the feedback should be nonevaluative and portray the failure in terms of the problem to be solved (Deci & Chandler, 1986). If James receives a poor rating in his work/study setting, the teacher might say, "Let's talk about what you might do next time to better handle an irate customer. What strategies do you think you might try?" This type of feedback connects failure to inappropriate strategies and concentrates on problem solving.

Dohm and Bryan (1994) report the success of attribution training, combined with teaching particular task strategies, in leading students with disabilities to persist longer on a task, acquire adaptive attributes, and make greater performance gains in reading and math tasks. In Box 6.1, we share strategies to help students focus on ability and effort instead of luck as reasons for success.

## Setting Goals

Research shows that students with mild disabilities are motivated to achieve goals that they have set either in cooperation with the teacher or alone. High school students with learning disabilities who set their own perfor-

**B O X   6 . 1**

| **Ways to Program Students for Success** |
| --- |

*Help students attribute their success to ability by . . .*

displaying students' work.

emphasizing students' strengths.

promoting cooperative learning.

praising students' achievements.

reinforcing students' beliefs in their abilities.

*Help students attribute their success to effort by . . .*

individualizing instruction.

emphasizing the importance of effort.

providing feedback about students' use of effort.

guiding students to analyze their own use of effort.

reinforcing students' use of effort.

*Decrease the probability that students will attribute their success to luck by . . .*

showing all of your students you believe they have ability.

showing all of your students you believe they are capable of effort.

attributing students' successes to ability and effort.

attributing students' failures to lack of effort, not bad luck.

asking questions that students can answer by thinking instead of guessing.

*Source:* Adapted from "Attribution Processing: The Way in Which Students React to Success and Failure Has a Substantial Effect on Subsequent Efforts to Learn" by R. Wheeler, 1988, *The Middle School Journal, 19*(4), p. 27. Reprinted with permission.

mance goals improved math computation performance more than students with assigned goals (Fuchs, Bahr, & Rieth, 1989); adolescents with mental disabilities displayed improved production rates and quality level in a work setting when they set their own goals (Gajar, Goodman, & McAfee, 1993); high school students with behavior problems learned more and felt more positive about school when they participated in setting goals and selecting strategies for reaching the goals (Maher, 1987). Goal-setting activities had a positive impact on the completion of project-type assignments for students with disabilities (Lenz, Ehren, & Smiley, 1991). Teaching students about goals led to more active participation and goal setting during IEP planning (Van Reusen, Deshler, & Schumaker, 1989; Van Reusen & Bos, 1994).

Following are some general guidelines for teaching students to develop their own goals:

1. *Help students recognize weaknesses and strengths.* Cohen (1986) recommends that teachers have students read about individuals they admire and compare their qualities and, from this comparison, identify what qualities they would like to acquire. For students of color, it is important to identify famous individuals from their culture who have achieved their goals (Kuykendall, 1992). In *The Self-Advocacy Strategy* (Van Reusen et al., 1994), which is one of the motivation strategies in the curriculum component of the Strategies Intervention Model (Deshler & Schumaker, 1988), teachers give students an inventory sheet to assist them in identifying their strengths, weaknesses, and preferences for learning. Kuykendall (1992) suggests that students list qualities or characteristics that they possess that may help them reach their goals and then specify things that could keep them from meeting them.

2. *Teach students to select clear, specific goals that may be accomplished in a short time frame and are of moderate difficulty.* Specific goals may encompass academic, vocational, or any other curriculum areas. For example, an appropriate academic goal is "to complete all homework assignments on time for one week" rather than "to study more for the entire year." An appropriate vocational goal is "to initiate one friendly conversation a day with a coworker" rather than "to get along with co-workers better." Jones and Jones (1990) suggest that adolescents set academic goals for nine weeks to correlate with report cards. In *The Self-Advocacy Strategy,* teachers present students with lists of relevant reading, writing, math, study skills, social skills, and vocational skills to assist them in writing goals.

3. *Teach students to select activities or sequential strategies to reach their goals.* As part of their planning, Lenz, Ehren, and Smiley (1991) had students list the key steps required to reach the goal of successful completion of an assignment. They included (a) specifying time for the completion of each step, (b) telling how the teacher plans to evaluate the project, (c) checking the availability of special materials, and (d) checking whether the assignment has to be completed at any particular location. In *The Self-Advocacy Strategy,* teachers provide students with a form listing suggested activities (reading, listening, writing reports), materials (games, calculator, computer, movies), learning preferences (large group, small group, one-on-one), and test preferences (multiple-choice, essay, take-home) that they may select to reach their goals.

4. *Teach students to monitor goal attainment.* In *The Self-Advocacy Strategy,* students write the skill they wish to learn and the date for achieving the

skill, such as "I plan to learn the keyboard skills (skill) by May (month)." Then the students monitor whether they have met the goal by that date. If the goal is not met, teachers should teach students to handle failure in a positive manner. They may teach students to make adjustments, revise goals, and/or set a new timetable for achieving their goals. It is important for students to realize that they can learn from their mistakes.

Figure 6.2 is a sample goal sheet that incorporates these guidelines. Notice that the goal sheet includes strategies for achieving the goal and a criterion for monitoring whether the goal has been met.

**FIGURE 6.2 A Sample Goal Sheet**

Student Name _____

Goal (something you would like to have, become, or accomplish by the end of the nine weeks):

_____

_____

_____

| Help: | Hinder: |
|---|---|
| List qualities or characteristics that will help you reach your goal: | List things that could possibly hinder or limit your efforts to reach your goal: |

Strategies for achieving this goal:

1. _____

2. _____

3. _____

I will know my goal is reached when _____

_____ .

*Source:* Adapted from *Improving Black Student Achievement by Enhancing Student Self-Image.* by C. Kuykendall, p. 60. Copyright 1989, National Education Service, Bloomington, IN. Reprinted with permission.

## Establishing a Positive Classroom Climate

It is important to establish a positive classroom climate when teaching adolescents with disabilities. However, you must remember that you are a professional and a student advocate, but not a pal. Some ways that you may establish a positive climate are by being fair and consistent, sharing expectations, implementing rules, modeling respect for students, and participating in dialogue journals.

### Fairness and Consistency

Being fair and consistent is difficult as it is human nature to like some students better than others. However, it is important to remember that the rules and procedures apply to everyone, not just to the student who always seems to be getting into trouble. Questions you can ask to check on fairness and consistency are (1) Am I writing more referrals for one particular student? If so, why? (2) Am I following through after I give a command or request? Students are quick to point out inconsistent teacher behavior. Instead of becoming defensive when they do, sometimes, a simple response such as "You're right; I'm sorry; I need to work on that" will satisfy students that you are trying to be fair and consistent.

### Expectations

Sharing expectations is another way to build a positive classroom climate. Students are often more comfortable and willing to take risks if they understand what is expected of them. Sprick (1985) recommends that secondary teachers share their expectations with students, prompt the students to follow the expectations, and then give them feedback on how well they have followed the expectations. At the beginning of class, Mr. Lucas reminds students that he expects them to take notes during the lecture, to listen and not interrupt others, and to raise their hands to ask questions. Throughout the lesson, Mr. Lucas prompts students, if necessary, to follow these expectations: "Lillie, I appreciate the comment, but next time let's wait until Juan is finished talking." At the end of the lesson, Mr. Lucas provides feedback to the students by telling them how they did: "I want to thank you today for your attention. I noticed you all took notes and remembered to raise your hands for questions. Let's work on listening to others without interrupting tomorrow." Or he may ask the students how they felt they did: "How do you think the lesson went? Did you have a chance to talk without being interrupted? What should we work on tomorrow?" Sharing expectations is an easy technique to use as it fits nicely into the opening and closing sections of a lesson. Hill (1989), in his discussion of effective strategies for teaching students of color, emphasizes the importance of communicating to these students that you as a teacher expect that they can and will learn.

## Rules

Having rules is another way to build a positive classroom climate. Farris (1990) found that her middle school students developed a sense of ownership and empowerment when they were involved in rule making. Adelman and Taylor (1990) recommend that students help decide consequences for misbehavior. They argue that student involvement motivates students to make a commitment to what is decided. Thus, Mr. Hermosa had his middle school students suggest four rules necessary to maintain order in the class. He and the students then identified positive consequences for following the rules and negative consequences for not following the rules. The students suggested that he give them a warning or reminder before he instituted any of the negative consequences. The rule plan is found in Box 6.2.

## Respect

You often model respect for students in the way you communicate with them. Are you being sarcastic at the expense of an individual student? Do you listen as they talk instead of working on attendance or other activities

---

**BOX 6.2** | **Rule Plan**

### Suggested Rules

- Be prepared for class.
- Respect others' belongings.
- Use appropriate language.
- Complete all assignments on time.

### Consequences

- Use positive attention, use positive comments, or give out homework passes.
- First, issue a warning statement; second, talk to students privately; third, write referrals.

at the same time? Do you ever say "Thank you" or "You're right, I made a mistake"? Do you ever apologize when you were unreasonable or very angry? Greeting students at the door sets a positive mood and gives you an opportunity to show respect for their thoughts and feelings. Moreover, it is a way for you to build rapport as you give individual attention or individually acknowledge students by name with a simple greeting or personal comment.

### Dialogue Journals

Dialogue journals provide opportunities for students to share personal problems with the teacher and opportunities for the teacher to give individual attention to students. Dialogue journals involve two-way written communication between the teacher and students. Gaustad and Messenheimer-Young (1991) recommend that students initiate the topics and that teachers respond to each entry in a personal and positive way without correction of grammatical errors, spelling mistakes, or the quality of writing. They have found that students are willing to correct the quality of writing when teachers comment that they cannot decipher the journal entry. Often students write in dialogue journals to begin the class. The routine of entering the room, sitting down, and writing in a journal for 10 minutes occupies students while they are waiting for you to begin class or for the bell to ring.

Instead of asking students to write anything they wish in their journals, you can introduce a more structured dialogue journal by asking students to give you written feedback at the end of class. One of the authors ends her university classes by asking students weekly to respond in their journals to two questions: (1) Is there any information you do not understand? (2) Do you have any concerns? She then replies to individual students' comments and returns the journals.

---

**COMPREHENSION MONITORING OF KEY CONCEPTS**

*Selecting Interesting and Relevant Materials*

1. Students' interests and maturity of subject matter should be considered in the selection of interesting and relevant materials.

*Promoting Expectations for Success*

2. Motivation research shows that individuals who attribute success to sufficient ability and reasonable efforts, and failure to

either insufficient efforts or inappropriate strategies, are more motivated to try challenging tasks.

3. Strategies for maintaining successful expectations include (a) program for success; (b) teach performance appraisal, self-reinforcement, and goal setting; (c) help students understand the linkage between effort and outcome; and (d) provide remedial socialization.

4. In attribution retraining, teachers convey to students that increased effort promotes increased success and that failure is often due to poor effort or inappropriate strategies.

### Setting Goals

5. Research shows that students with mild disabilities are more motivated to achieve goals that they have set themselves or in cooperation with the teacher.

6. Some guidelines for teaching students to develop their own goals are:(a) Help students recognize their weaknesses and strengths. (b) Teach students to select clear, specific goals that may be accomplished in a short time frame. (c) Teach students to select activities or sequential strategies to reach their goals. (d) Teach students to monitor goal attainment.

### Establishing a Positive Classroom Climate

7. Some ways that you can build a positive classroom climate with students are being fair and consistent, sharing expectations, implementing rules, modeling respect for students, and participating in dialogue journals.

8. Questions you can ask yourself to check on fairness and consistency are (a) Am I writing more referrals for one particular student? If so, why? (b) Am I following through after I give a command or request?

9. Secondary teachers can share their expectations with students, prompt the students to follow the expectations, and then give them feedback on how well they have followed the expectations.

10. Dialogue journals involve two-way written communication between the teacher and students, usually with the students initiating the topics and the teacher responding to them.

## Using Management Techniques

Basing their approach on the behavioral model, teachers often use management techniques such as positive reinforcement, contingency contracting, group contingencies, and self-management to increase appropriate behaviors and to motivate students. Positive reinforcement, contingency contracts, and group contingencies rely on extrinsic approaches with the teacher manipulating the environment, whereas the goal of self-management is to teach students to manipulate their own environment.

### Positive Reinforcement

Positive reinforcement motivates adolescents by adding interest or excitement to the classroom routine (Emmer, Evertson, Clements, & Worsham, 1994). Positive reinforcement is the contingent presentation of a stimulus following a response that increases the probability of the response occurring again in the future. For example, if James finishes his assignment on time with no more than two errors, he receives an A. A grade of A is positively reinforcing to James only if he continues to finish any new assignments on time and accurately. Positive reinforcement may include the dispensing of material rewards, social reinforcers, and activity or privilege reinforcers.

Before we discuss each of these reinforcers separately, there are some caveats regarding their use. Sometimes it is difficult to identify appropriate reinforcers for particular students. Asking the student or having the student select from a menu of choices may help in this identification. Sometimes reinforcement systems are so complex and require so much recordkeeping that they tend to manage the teacher, instead of the teacher managing the system. Another concern arises from research findings that receiving an external reward actually reduces the likelihood that the rewarded activity will occur once the reinforcer is withdrawn (Deci & Chandler, 1986; Emmer et al., 1994). Emmer and associates (1994) suggest using rewards only when the subject matter or activities are not highly interesting to the students or are highly repetitive. With these caveats in mind, we discuss reinforcers appropriate for secondary students.

### *Material Rewards*

Material incentives include rewards such as food, objects, games, or tangible items of value to students (Emmer et al., 1994). Grades are tangible rewards that are natural consequences in the environment, as teachers are required to grade student performance. Grades are more motivating when they are linked to a student's achievement and competence (Emmer et al.,

1994). Evaluating students in many different ways and sharing expectations for grades are ways to link grades to competence (see Chapter 7).

In addition to grades, we are continuously surprised by the successful use of stickers, certificates, and even stars to motivate some middle school students with disabilities. Other material incentives recommended for adolescents include the following (Alberto & Troutman, 1995; Emmer et al., 1994; Griffin, 1988; Morsink, 1984; Olson & Platt, 1996; Zigmond, Sansone, et al., 1986):

1. Coupons from fast food restaurants
2. NFL- or NBA-labeled pencils, pens, and erasers
3. Cosmetics
4. Free soda or popcorn snack
5. Certificates of achievement
6. Discarded classroom materials
7. Homework passes
8. Posters of sport or rock stars

As you can see from the list, material incentives may be expensive and may create problems in their dispensing. You should always pair the giving of material incentives with social recognition or praise.

### Social Reinforcers

Even though research shows that secondary teachers use less specific praise than elementary-level teachers, specific praise can still be a powerful reinforcer for adolescents (Morsink, 1984). Specific praise statements should include both an evaluative comment and informative feedback. A statement such as "Well done, Sam, you completed all eight items correctly" is appropriate for secondary students.

For many secondary students, private praise or group praise is better than public or individual. Mr. Kernshaw stops by individual students' desks and comments on their work during independent practice. After asking students to turn to page 35 in their science book, Ms. Littlejohn thanks those students who followed the direction with "I appreciate the group of students who turned to page 35 in their science books. Thank you."

Some secondary students may not accept even private praise (Sprick, 1985). When this occurs, it is best to remain calm and examine the effect on the behavior. Sometimes, students say "I don't care what you think" and yet perform the task. Continue with the positive comments, as "every student needs to learn that he has enough self-worth to accept recognition from someone else" (Sprick, 1985, p. 44).

Emmer and associates (1994) caution about praising efforts of secondary students. They maintain that praising effort only, and not accomplishment, conveys to the students that they are not competent.

Feedback other than specific praise may also be a powerful motivator for secondary students. Positive recognition, graphing, and progress reports are examples of other types of feedback. Positive recognition may be a smile, a nod, or even a positive signal to students. Ms. Tyler writes positive statements on homework sheets and reports. From the bar graph she created, Rosa notes that she has a perfect record for punctuality at the job site.

Blumberg (1986) used a Daily Progress Report with low achievers and disruptive students in junior high school settings. Each teacher marked the chart with comments concerning behaviors and academic performance of students. The report was then shared with parents, who were given the opportunity to mark on the chart and share their concerns. Use of the Daily Progress Report resulted in improved grades and an increase in appropriate school behaviors. A sample progress report similar to the Daily Progress Report is found in Figure 6.3.

### Activity and Privilege Reinforcers

A privilege or activity reinforcer permits students to do something special or enjoyable. Some appropriate activities or privileges for adolescents include the following (Alberto & Troutman, 1995; Emmer et al., 1994; Griffin, 1988; Morsink, 1984; Olson & Platt, 1996; Zigmond, Sansone et al., 1986):

1. Free time with choice of activities
2. Pizza or ice cream party
3. Use of media equipment (such as videotape or computer)
4. Hall pass to media center
5. Free time to play tapes or CDs
6. Schedule own lessons
7. Plan next field trip
8. Extra time for lunch or a break
9. Read a magazine
10. Talk to a peer
11. Make a card, poster, or banner using the computer
12. Play a computer game with a friend

The lottery system, designed by Canter (1986), is an effective procedure to use with secondary students to dispense either tangible or activity reinforcers. To set up a classwide lottery system, identify behaviors or class rules

**FIGURE 6.3    Sample Progress Report**

Student name **Sunny Ortiz**        Date **10/14**

To Teacher:    Please evaluate _____**Sunny**_____ on the following behaviors
in your class by marking a P for Poor, F for Fair, G for Good,
and E for Excellent.

To Student:    Please present this form to each of your teachers at the
beginning of class. Return the form to Mrs. Williams.

| Periods | First | Second | Third | Fourth | Fifth | Sixth |
|---|---|---|---|---|---|---|
| Timeliness (on time) | G | | | | | |
| Preparedness (brought supplies) | P | | | | | |
| Academic Work | G | | | | | |
| Conduct | F | | | | | |
| Grades | B | | | | | |
| Teacher Initials | L.R.O. | | | | | |
| Homework Assignments | pgs. 100–105, Items 10–15 | | | | | |

**BOX 6.3**

### Sample Lottery System

You will earn chances for the room lottery held every Friday by

1. Returning homework on time.
2. Bringing in supplies (paper and pencil).
3. Participating in cooperative groups.
4. Scoring 85% or above on assignments.
5. Turning in assignments on time.

Tickets will be given out at the end of class. Write your name on your tickets and drop them into the lottery container.

On Friday, two winners will be drawn. Being a winner entitles you to draw a card to determine which prize you have won. Each card has a number from 1 to 7, representing the numbers of the prizes. However, one card has all seven numbers, which allows you to win all seven prizes.

Additionally, the person with the highest number of tickets earned in a week automatically gets to pick a card.

The prizes for this week include homework passes, NFL pencils, a selection of CDs on loan during free time, fast food restaurant coupons, early dismissal for lunch, and options you negotiate.

and reward students for displaying appropriate behaviors with old movie tickets or slips of paper. Students write their names on the tickets and place them in a container. At the end of the week, you draw out the name of the winner. The winner wins the lottery prize of either a tangible or activity reinforcer for the week. Box 6.3 displays a sample lottery system.

### Contingency Contracts

In a contingency contract, the student and the teacher record the expected behavior and the reinforcer in a written document. The behavior may be academic or affective. Contracting is often effective with adolescents because it requires student commitment and goal setting. Ms. McCabe used the contract shown in Figure 6.4 to increase the independent work of her students with emotional disabilities.

Zirpoli and Melloy (1993) have developed a flowchart of the steps for negotiating a contract with adolescents based on the work of Welch and Holborn (see Figure 6.5). Notice that different procedures are followed depending on whether the answer to each question is Yes or No.

**FIGURE 6.4    Sample Independent Contract**

> As a class, we agree to try the following strategies before asking the teacher for help:
>
> _____ 1. Reread the problem.
>
> _____ 2. Look up any unknown vocabulary word in the dictionary.
>
> _____ 3. Try to do the next problem.
>
> _____ 4. Reread the text information.
>
> _____ 5. Think about specific questions to ask.
>
> _____ 6. Politely ask another student the specific questions.
>
> _____ 7. Use computer tools (speller, thesaurus, grammar check).
>
> I agree to try Items _____.
>
> Signed: _____
>              (student's signature)
>
> I, Ms. McCabe, will help _____ if he or she has tried _____ items as soon as it is possible for me to break away from other instruction.
>
> Signed: _____
>              (teacher's signature)

## Group Contingencies

Group contingencies are frequently powerful reinforcers as adolescents enjoy working with peers and working in groups (Alberto & Troutman, 1995). In group contingencies, reinforcement is given to the entire group based on the performance either of individuals or of the group as a whole. An example of an individual earning the reward for the group is if Mr. Sims says that Jane must score 80% on the spelling quiz for the whole class to receive free time. Stating that everyone must score 80% on the spelling quiz for the whole class to receive free time is an example of an incentive based on the performance of the group as a whole. The class may vote on the reinforcers in an attempt to select the most popular ones.

To use group contingencies, you must be certain each student can perform the behavior and that there is not an individual who becomes the

**FIGURE 6.5    Sample Flowchart for Developing Contingency Contracts**

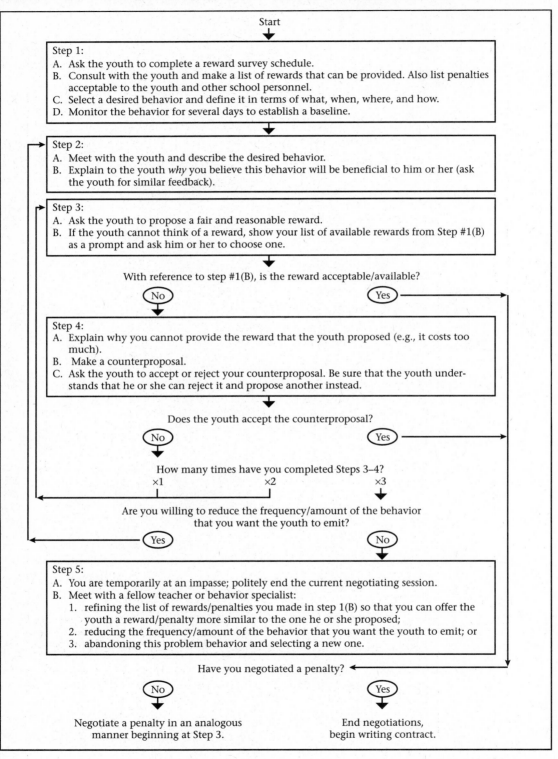

scapegoat or the saboteur. If Jane is not capable of earning 80% on that particular spelling quiz, you are setting Jane up for failure and possibly verbal abuse from her peers. Teaching students cooperative behaviors, and sharing reasons for helping peers, limits singling out students as scapegoats. To prevent a student from sabotaging the group effort, simply remove the student from the group contingency and design a more individualized plan for that student.

Another adaptation that may be necessary for an effective group contingency is to keep the name of the individual who is earning the group reward a secret. That way students will focus not on helping or pressuring Jennifer, but on everyone, as no one knows who will be earning the rewards for the class. You may select the name of the student at random or you may target a particular student. Ms. Sauers kept the names of the students who were earning the reward for the group secret as a way to motivate middle school students to participate in an English grammar class. Every 15 minutes, she drew out a slip of paper with the name of a student from the container of students' names. If two out of the three students whose names were drawn had participated appropriately during class, she gave 10 minutes of free time for the entire class just before the end of the 50-minute period.

Dividing students into teams that compete against a specific criterion to earn reinforcements capitalizes on peer relationships. For example, Ms. Herbst identified "talkouts and interruptions" as a problem in her ninth-grade class. During her baseline count, she found that students were averaging about 15 talkouts and interruptions each 50-minute period. She divided her class into two teams and explained that for each day team members talked out or interrupted others less than 8 times, they earned a letter for their team. The team who spelled out the word "Homework" first earned 20 homework points toward their nine-week grades.

## Self-Management

Self-management is any type of intervention that involves students assuming control over their own behaviors. Self-management is particularly effective for adolescents as it allows them to be in control of the environment and gives them a sense of power and competence (Carter, 1993; Jones & Jones, 1990).

*Source for Figure 6.5:* Adapted from "Contingency Contracting with Delinquents: Effects of a Brief Training Manual on Staff Contract Negotiation and Writing Skills" by S. J. Welch and S. W. Holborn, *Journal of Applied Behavior Analysis,* 1988, *21,* 357–368. Department of Human Development, University of Kansas, Lawrence, Kansas 66045. Reprinted with permission.

Research shows that various self-management techniques have improved the problem-solving and occupational skills of adolescents with learning disabilities (Shapiro, 1989b); the math, reading, and spelling accuracy and productivity of middle school adolescents with behavior disorders (Carr & Punzo, 1993); the comprehension of new reading passages by middle school students with mild disabilities (Malone & Mastropieri, 1992); and the completion, accuracy, and neatness of creative writing assignments by high school students with learning and behavior problems (Glomb & West, 1990). Rooney and Hallahan (1988) found that adolescents who self-managed their attention behaviors during seatwork even influenced teacher behaviors. Teachers initiated assistance less frequently and interacted with these students for shorter periods of time as students were maintaining high levels of attention without teacher assistance. Thus, self-management appears to motivate students in both academic and social areas and to influence teacher behaviors.

The component skills of self-management usually include self-monitoring or recording, self-instruction, self-reinforcement, and self-evaluation. During self-monitoring, students keep track of their own behaviors as they mark whether the behaviors occurred. Self-instruction involves teaching students to verbalize thoughtful internal statements to control their behaviors. In self-reinforcement, students choose the reinforcer and administer it. In self-evaluation, students compare behavior against a preset standard to see if the criterion is met (Cole, 1987).

Self-management plans may include some or all of these component skills. Here we suggest how all the different components can be used in a self-management plan that includes the following steps: (1) Identify and define behaviors (usually done in self-monitoring and self-instruction). (2) Design data-collection procedures and forms (self-monitoring). (3) Select the criterion for the behavior (self-evaluation). (4) Establish a verbalization technique (self-instruction). (5) Select a reinforcer (self-reinforcement). (6) Plan for generalization (all of the components).

### Step 1. Identify and Define Behaviors

Since the ultimate goal is for students to track behavior, behaviors must be specific, observable, and occur frequently enough to merit intervention. For example, identification of a behavior such as "be a good worker" is not specific enough; "be punctual for work every day" is much clearer. In teaching adolescents self-management strategies for job success, Montague (1987b) defined eye contact specifically as "looking directly into the eyes of the other person for at least 3 seconds while listening or talking" (p. 76). Suggested behaviors for adolescents to self-monitor include "on-task behavior, out-of-seat behavior, assignment completion and accuracy, attendance, punctuality, homework completion and accuracy, use of appropriate language, inappropriate verbalizations, classroom rule compliance, and appropriate socialization with peers" (Polirstok, 1989, p. 119).

Schloss (1987) had adolescents complete a self-audit form to assist in the identification of appropriate on-the-job behaviors. The students (1) identified their behaviors that co-workers or supervisors did not like, (2) listed how often good workers performed these behaviors, (3) estimated how often they thought they exhibited the behaviors, and (4) identified how often they would like to exhibit the behaviors. Modeling examples and nonexamples of the behavior and then asking students to discriminate between them assures that students can identify the behaviors. For example, a teacher may model appropriate social interactions by smiling, talking in a pleasant tone, and using polite language. Conversely, the teacher may demonstrate inappropriate social interactions by frowning, shouting, or using impolite language. Then students discuss which behaviors represent appropriate interactions and why.

### Step 2. Design Data-Collection Procedures

Teachers can teach students to use event recording, time sampling, or permanent product recording to track behaviors (Alberto & Troutman, 1995). In event recording, the student marks whether the behavior occurred. For example, Towanda marks every time she talks out. In time sampling, the student marks at specific times whether the behavior is occurring. For example, after a 30-second timer beeps, Hector marks whether he is paying attention. In permanent product recording, students are presented with a list of questions that they check off. For example, after completing a job application, Tony marks (1) if he remembered to capitalize proper nouns, (2) if he wrote in complete sentences, (3) if he looked up any words he couldn't spell, and (4) if he proofread the work before turning it in. All forms should have a place for the date and a key for coding.

Here again, you need to model marking the recording form and arrange for students to practice marking in role-playing situations before they use it in other classes or at the work site. Often, simply viewing the form leads to improvement just because the student is presented with a visual picture of progress.

### Step 3. Select the Criterion

Next, you select the criterion for acceptable performance of the behavior and teach students to self-evaluate using the criterion. There are no hard and fast rules for selecting the criterion for any behavior. Remember,

Schloss used the behaviors of co-workers to set the standard for on-the-job behavior. Polirstok (1989) recommends that you rate the behavior first and explain your rating system to the students before you have the students attempt to evaluate. A technique to measure whether students are evaluating their performance correctly is to check the match between your recording and students' recordings.

Videotapes may facilitate student evaluations of their own behavior (Osborne, Kiburz, & Miller, 1986). Ms. Kulack videotaped two adults as they role-played a job interview. She then led the students in a critique of the interview. Next, she videotaped pairs of students and had them self-evaluate their performances.

### Step 4. Establish a Verbalization Technique

Self-verbalizations take many forms. You can teach students to use a problem-solving procedure (Zirpoli & Melloy, 1993), cognitive cuing (Montague, 1987b), coping statements (Forman, 1993), or cognitive rehearsal strategies (Alberto & Troutman, 1995).

A common *problem-solving procedure* has students ask and answer specific questions: (1) What's my problem? ("I don't seem to make eye contact when my supervisor talks to me. During my weekly review, she mentioned this and I noticed it too.") (2) What's my plan? ("When I come into work everyday, I'll look her in the eye as I say 'Good Morning.'") (3) Am I following it? ("My count shows I am.") (4) Did I do it correctly? ("The supervisor congratulated me on maintaining eye contact during our last weekly review.")

Miller, Osborne, and Burt (1987) taught students with behavior disorders a similar procedure. When students were off task, they either wrote or read a mediation essay (Blackwood, 1970) that they had previously written with the teacher. The essay consisted of answers to the following questions: "(1) What did I do wrong? (identifies the target behavior). (2) Why shouldn't I do it? (relates behavior to negative consequence). (3) What should I do? (suggests appropriate alternative behavior). (4) What will happen if I try an alternative behavior (relates behavior to positive consequence)" (Miller et al., 1987, p. 19).

Montague (1987b) uses *cognitive cuing* in the form of questions that remind students to complete tasks or use certain skills. For example, when Eddie was asked to take responsibility for closing Jack's Burger House, Montague and Eddie listed his duties in a logical order, and then formulated questions that corresponded to the duties: "Did I turn off the outside light?" "Did I lock the front door?" and so on. Eddie memorized the questions and then answered each one as he closed the restaurant. Glomb and West (1990) distributed cue cards with the mnemonic CAN on desks to remind students to check for completion, accuracy, and neatness of their creative writing assignments.

When students use *coping statements,* they make positive, thoughtful, internalized statements or acknowledge their mistakes and attempt to pinpoint corrections. Jones and Jones (1990) recommend that teachers initially provide students with specific statements to use. For example, a teacher taught students frustrated by the math assignment to say, "I can do this if I slow down and relax," or if they lost a computer game, "It's okay I didn't win the game; next time I'll listen more carefully."

*Cognitive rehearsal strategies* for adolescents are usually adapted from the training procedure of Meichenbaum and Goodman (1971). For example, to teach a specific coping statement, first you model the statement (" I can do this if I slow down and relax"), then the student overtly says the statement under your direction, then the student says it alone, and last, the student moves to private speech.

### Step 5. Teach Self-Reinforcement

Alberto and Troutman (1995) recommend beginning with teacher management of reinforcement and then gradually shifting to students. Montague (1987b) describes a self-reinforcing procedure to encourage neat appearance and being on time, two necessary job skills. The student prepares a checklist of these two behaviors, and puts a token in a jar for each behavior successfully completed. At the end of the week, tokens are exchanged for money. Most self-management systems use self-reinforcement, but some use self-punishment in the form of giving up or losing something. For example, in the self-management procedure previously described, the student now removes a token each time either of the behaviors is not completed successfully.

### Step 6. Plan for Generalization

To ensure that self-management techniques will generalize to other situations requires training. You must teach your students to use them in different settings and with different teachers. Polirstok (1989) identifies the following factors as contributing to generalization of self-management procedures:(1) Emphasize that students are in control of their own behaviors.(2) Select powerful reinforcers. (3) Design portable plans that are easily imported to other settings. (4) Encourage other teachers, parents, and peers to encourage and praise students for following their plans.

**COMPREHENSION MONITORING OF KEY CONCEPTS**

*Using Management Techniques*

1. Positive reinforcement is the contingent presentation of a stimulus following a response that increases the probability of the response occurring again in the future.

2. Some caveats to the use of positive reinforcement are the difficulty of selecting appropriate reinforcers, the complexity of managing the reinforcement system, and the maintenance of the behavior once the reward is withdrawn.

3. Material incentives include rewards such as food, objects, games, or tangible items of value to students.

4. Specific praise statements, which are powerful reinforcers for adolescents, should include both an evaluative comment and informative feedback.

5. Private praise or group praise is better than public or individual praise for many adolescents.

6. A privilege or activity reinforcer permits students to do something special or enjoyable.

7. Contingency contracting is writing the behavior and the reinforcer into a written document negotiated by the student and the teacher.

8. In group contingencies, reinforcement is given to the entire group based on the performance either of individuals or of the group as a whole.

9. Adaptations for group contingencies include removing students who are trying to sabotage the group effort, keeping the name of the individual or individuals earning the reward for the group secret, and dividing the group into teams.

10. Self-management involves students assuming control over their own behaviors; it is particularly effective for adolescents because it allows them to control their environment and gives them a sense of power and competence.

11. The component skills of self-management usually include self-monitoring or recording (students record their behaviors), self-instruction (students verbalize internal statements to control their behaviors), self-reinforcement (students choose the

reinforcer and administer it), and self-evaluation (students judge whether criterion is met).

12. In designing a self-management plan, teachers (a) identify and define behaviors, (b) design data-collection procedures and forms, (c) select the criterion for the behavior, (d) establish a verbalization technique, (e) select a reinforcer, and (f) plan for generalization.

 Now that you have read Chapter 6, reflect on your earlier predictions and complete this post organizer.

1. What did you list as motivating factors? Did you mention any of the motivation factors such as providing choices or setting goals?

2. Compare the teacher behaviors that you discussed as promoting a positive classroom climate with those discussed in the chapter. Which ones did you mention?

3. Revise your list of pros and cons for using group contingencies. What new ones did you add? How do they compare to those listed in the chapter?

# PART TWO

# Effective Instructional Interventions for Inclusive and Pullout Settings

© Alan Dorow/Actuality

# Basic Principles of Effective Teaching

© Billy E. Barnes/Jeroboam

*Before Instruction: The Preactive Phase*

*During Instruction: The Interactive Phase*

*After Instruction: The Reflective Phase*

 Before you read Chapter 7, use your prior knowledge to complete this advance organizer. Select two peers to work with you.

1. What are some decisions teachers need to make before they begin instruction?

2. Develop a teaching routine for high school students with mild disabilities following the framework recommended in the teacher effectiveness research.

3. Develop a teaching routine for middle school students with mild disabilities based on suggestions found in the social constructivist literature.

4. Discuss two different ways to evaluate students.

Teachers make many decisions as they prepare and present instruction. In fact, Jackson (1968) estimated that teachers make more than 1300 decisions daily. We use an adaptation of the instructional cycle created by Costa and Garmston (1985) as we discuss the various decisions that teachers make in *developing an instructional plan*. Teachers make these decisions in both inclusive and pullout settings—whether they share responsibility with the regular educator or assume direct responsibility for instruction.

The three phases of the instructional cycle are *preactive* (before instruction), *interactive* (during instruction), and *reflective* (after instruction). During the preactive phase, teachers make decisions about student characteristics, stages of learning, instructional alignment, allocated learning time, objectives, subject matter content, materials, and instructional arrangements. During the interactive phase, teachers concentrate on instructional language, engaged learning time, teaching routines, feedback, and management of student behavior. During the reflective phase, teachers examine learner progress and lesson effectiveness, teach students to evaluate, and also self-evaluate. For purposes of discussion, we examine each of these areas separately. However, in reality, they often overlap in the development of an instructional plan (see Box 7.1).

## Before Instruction: The Preactive Phase

During the preactive phase, teachers make a variety of decisions. These decisions concern student characteristics, stages of learning, instructional alignment, allocated learning time, objectives, subject matter content, materials, and instructional arrangements.

### Student Characteristics

In Chapter 3, we discussed ways to assess students' skills and interests, which assist teachers in making decisions about instruction. Certainly, the IEP reflects a student's level of performance and essential goals and objectives for the student. Teachers should also consider motivation, participation, behavior, and prior knowledge (Muth & Alvermann, 1992). For example, if you are teaching a group of unmotivated students with poor reading skills, you may plan to present oral instruction and hands-on cooperative activities. If you are teaching a group of motivated students with good reading skills who have difficulty with cooperative behaviors, you may plan more teacher-directed instruction using a textbook.

**BOX 7.1**

---

**Basic Instructional Cycle**

---

*Before Instruction: The Preactive Phase*

Student Characteristics

Stages of Learning

Instructional Alignment

Allocated Learning Time

Objectives

Subject Matter Content

Materials

Instructional Arrangements


*During Instruction: The Interactive Phase*

Instructional Language

Engaged Learning Time

Teaching Routines

Feedback

Management of Student Behavior


*After Instruction: The Reflective Phase*

Student Evaluation

Teacher Self-Evaluation

---

## Stages of Learning

Stages of learning influence the selection of objectives, teaching strategies, and materials. In the Strategies Intervention Model geared for adolescents with mild disabilities, Deshler and Schumaker (1988) recommend different instructional procedures for acquisition and generalization learning stages. In a discussion of integrated technology and media, Hasselbring and Goin (1993) attribute poor use of technology to a lack of consideration of the different learning stages. These learning stages include acquisition, fluency or proficiency, maintenance, and generalization (White & Haring, 1976).

During acquisition, students wrestle with new content as they concentrate on accuracy. When learning to type, a student concentrates on such target behaviors as placing fingers correctly on the keys, hunting for the correct keys, and moving the correct finger to strike the keys. Using direct teaching procedures, the teacher models finger placement, prompts students to find the correct keys, and provides immediate feedback. Additionally, the teacher selects diagrams of the keyboard and perhaps, a tutorial software program. Haring and Eaton (1978) suggest strategies such as modeling, immediate feedback, and question-asking during this stage.

Once students acquire a skill, they move into the fluency stage and concentrate on performing the skill at a faster rate so it becomes an efficient skill. In the typing example, the behaviors change from hitting the correct keys to hitting the correct keys at a faster rate. To use a skill like typing efficiently, the learner must move beyond the hunt-and-peck method. The teacher now spends less time in direct instruction and designs practice activities for the students. The teacher selects easy sample materials for the students to type and perhaps, a drill-and-practice software program. During this stage, Haring and Eaton (1978) recommend flash cards, drill activities, and external reinforcers for motivation. In the learning strategies curriculum, Deshler and Schumaker (1988) recommend easy materials for practice during the fluency stage.

Once students develop fluency, they move into the maintenance stage. During this stage, teachers usually provide distributed practice activities so that students can master the skill. In the typing example, the teacher selects short lessons for practice. Hasselbring and Goin (1993) recommend the same drill-and-practice software as they suggest for the fluency stage. In much subject content, students maintain skills as they are learning new ones. For example, in math, Juan maintains his knowledge of subtraction as he is learning the new, more advanced skill of division.

In generalization, students apply the information to real-life situations and experiences. In the typing example, students now concentrate on the content of the typed paragraph, instead of thinking about the mechanics of typing. The teacher provides application experiences for the students, such as requiring them to type résumés or reports. Deshler and Schumaker (1988) recommend grade-level material for practice at this stage. Students now participate in software simulations and produce information using word processors and databases (Hasselbring & Goin, 1993). Teachers frequently overlook this stage and do not provide enough opportunities or instruct students in how to generalize behaviors to other situations and settings.

## Instructional Alignment

Instructional alignment is the degree of congruence among instructional objectives, instructional procedures, and evaluation (Cohen, 1987). What teachers intend to teach should match what teachers teach and what they

**TABLE 7.1** Instructional Alignment

| Objective | Instruction | Assessment |
|---|---|---|
| A. Presented with six paragraphs, students will identify whether the paragraph is narrative, informative, or descriptive, missing no more than one for three sessions. | Teacher defines each type of paragraph with examples. During teacher-led practice, students identify the type of paragraph. | Teacher presents six paragraphs and students identify the type of paragraph from the three options. |
| B. Presented with six paragraphs, students will identify whether the paragraph is narrative, informative, or descriptive, missing no more than one for three sessions. | Teacher defines each type of paragraph with examples. During teacher-led practice, students identify the type of paragraph. | Teacher tells students to write a narrative paragraph, a descriptive paragraph, and an informative one. |

assess (West, Idol, & Cannon, 1989). Table 7.1 contains an example and nonexample of instructional alignment.

Notice in example A, students identify the different types of paragraphs during instruction and again during assessment. In example B, students identify the different types of paragraphs during instruction, but during assessment they must write a sample of each paragraph. In example B, the teacher is assessing students without regard to the objective and the instructional activity. Nowhere in the objective or during instruction did the teacher ask students to write paragraphs. Cohen (1987) found that students who experience academic difficulty have more problems with lack of instructional alignment than do those who do not experience academic problems.

The idea of instructional alignment matches closely the philosophy of curriculum-based assessment (CBA) described in Chapters 3 and 11. As in CBA, there is alignment between assessment and instruction so that measurement of student progress is more reliable and valid (Deno, 1987).

### Allocated Learning Time

Academic learning time often consists of two components: (1) the amount of time teachers allocate to instruction (allocated learning time) and (2) the amount of time that students actively engage in academic activity (engaged learning time) (Rieth, Polsgrove, & Semmel, 1981). Researchers have found that both components correlate significantly to academic achievement (Berliner, 1984; Delquadri, Greenwood, Stretton, & Hall, 1983; Denham &

**TABLE 7.2**  **Typical Schedule**

| | |
|---|---|
| 2 minutes | Greet students, take attendance, collect homework |
| 5 minutes | Introduce lesson |
| 15–20 minutes | Present major content of lesson |
| 10–15 minutes | Involve students in practice activities |
| 6 minutes | Do student evaluation, discuss homework assignment, summarize lesson |
| 1 minute | Prepare students to leave |
| 1 minute | Dismiss students |

Lieberman, 1980; Stallings, Needels, & Staybrook, 1979). Before instruction, teachers deal mostly with allocated learning time.

Schedules and timesaving routines are two ways to ensure that most class time is allocated to instruction. A typical schedule for either a 40- or 50-minute period appears in Table 7.2.

Many teachers who manage time efficiently also list a daily schedule or agenda on the board before students enter the class. The schedule informs both students and the teacher of the focus of the day's lesson and often serves to keep both on track. For example, Ms. Palm wrote the following schedule on the board:

*March 25, 1996*

Review homework

Review individual goals

Present mapping technique

Practice mapping technique

Fill in progress charts

Assign homework, p. 34

Teachers who have routines for turning in assignments, sharpening pencils, dispensing hall passes, taking attendance, and returning homework can allocate more time to instruction. In her class, Ms. Johnson prepares materials ahead, marks places in the teacher's guide with sticky notes for quick reference, and sets up multimedia materials either before class or when students are busy working in small groups or on individual tasks.

To minimize loss of instructional time as students transition from one task to another, Englert, Tarrant, and Mariage (1992) suggest that teachers share behavioral expectations for each activity and inform students that the lesson is ending. They also suggest that teachers scan and circulate among students during transitions. These techniques not only promote increased instructional time, but frequently prevent problem behaviors from occurring.

## Objectives

As we stated in Chapter 3, an objective must contain the learner, the target behavior, the condition, the criterion, and an overlearning component. Identification of objectives serves as the first step in lesson planning and relates to annual goals. With the help of objectives, teachers plan more efficiently, monitor student progress effectively, and alter instruction when needed (Christenson, Thurlow, & Ysseldyke, 1987). For example, consider the following objective: Given a worksheet with 10 paragraphs, students must identify whether each is an example of a narrative, descriptive, or expository paragraph with 90% accuracy for three worksheets." With this objective, the teacher has decided to monitor student performance by means of a worksheet and to accept the criterion of 90% mastery demonstrated three times. The teacher has also decided to emphasize recognizing paragraphs as opposed to writing them. Schloss, Smith, and Schloss (1995) suggest that objectives should reflect students' interests and abilities. In Chapter 3, we discussed how assessment of students' skills and interests leads to objectives.

## Subject Matter Content

Subject matter falls into the categories of concepts, rules, laws, lawlike principles, and value judgments (Florida Performance Measurement System, 1984). The subject matter for teaching concepts includes definitions, examples and nonexamples, and attributes. A quick check of a teacher's guide will assist in identifying subject matter content. For example, if you are teaching the concept of a compound sentence, you will find the definition on page 130 in the Instructor's Manual for *The Sentence Writing Strategy* (Schumaker & Sheldon, 1985). The manual defines a compound sentence as a "sentence with two or more independent clauses." You will also find examples of compound sentences ("The students finished class, and they went to lunch") on page 151, and nonexamples ("The men and women met at the station and went to dinner") on page 152. Attributes may include that compound sentences contain coordinating conjunctions and at least one comma or semicolon.

Engelmann and Carnine (1982b) posit that some subject matter contains such basic concepts that definitions are superfluous. Instead, they recommend the selection of examples and nonexamples. For instance, it is much easier to teach the basic concept *on* through the example of placing an object on the table, than by defining *on*. Both concepts and basic concepts are present in any subject area. Table 7.3 presents the various types of subject matter with sample content.

Popular subject matter for adolescents also includes learning and metacognitive strategies. Subject matter in this area usually consists of steps to help students learn how to learn. The teacher's manual often specifies the steps, as in the following example from *The Paraphrasing Strategy*: "(1) Read a paragraph. (2) Ask yourself, 'What were the main idea and two details?' (3) Put the main idea and details into your own words" (Schumaker, Denton, & Deshler, 1984).

Frequently, teachers must decrease subject matter complexity. One way to decrease the difficulty of subject matter is to check a student's understanding of the prerequisite skills (Silbert, Carnine, & Stein, 1990). For example, consider the objective "Given a worksheet with 10 paragraphs, students must identify whether each is an example of a narrative, descriptive, or expository paragraph with 90% accuracy for three worksheets." Before you introduce the three types of paragraphs, you must make certain that students understand the basic components of a paragraph. Other techniques that decrease the complexity of subject matter are procedural facilitators, anticipation of student errors (Rosenshine, 1990), and selection of easy materials for practice (Deshler & Schumaker, 1988).

Procedural facilitators are prompts that help students successfully complete a task (Scardamalia & Bereiter, 1985). A teacher who provides students with cue cards to remind them of the steps of a strategy is using a procedural facilitator. Anticipating student errors becomes easier as the teacher gains experience. Effective teachers often point out the most difficult step of a process or material to prevent students from making anticipated errors. For example, Ms. Plumber is anticipating student errors when she tells students that a common error in the calculation of averages is to forget to divide.

## Materials

School districts frequently select texts and materials from state-adopted lists for teacher and student use. However, individual teachers may select and adapt materials to supplement instruction. With wise selection and effective adaptations of materials, you can motivate reluctant students, bring in multicultural information, and individualize the curriculum. In this section, we examine the selection and adaptation of materials appropriate for both inclusive and pullout settings.

**TABLE 7.3** Types of Subject Matter Content

| Sample Subject Content | Definition | Areas | Essential Components | Example |
|---|---|---|---|---|
| Basic concept | Abstract or generic idea | All subject matter | Usually just examples/nonexamples | That color is red. |
| Concept | Abstract or generic idea | All subject matter | Definition, examples (attributes, nonexamples) | An atom is the smallest particle of an element that can exist either alone or in combination. |
| Rule | A prescribed guide for action | Mostly language arts, math | Identify rule, examples, application | If the word ends in a silent *e*, try a long vowel sound. |
| Law | Principle that explains physical behavior | Mostly natural sciences | Identify law, describe cause and effect, use linking/words, apply | If opposite poles of a magnet attract, then the north pole should move toward the south pole of the magnet. |
| Lawlike principle | Principle that explains human or animal behavior | Social studies | Same as law | If you follow the rules, you will earn points. |
| Value judgments | Evaluation of something's worth | Literature, art, self-help, social skills | Develop criteria, compile facts, compare the two | *A Wrinkle in Time* was an excellent book. |

### Selection of Materials

Supplemental instructional materials include visual materials, functional materials, multimedia packages, and computer software. Transparencies that highlight the key concepts of a lecture, videodiscs, CD-ROMs, filmstrips, films, and videotapes are examples of visual materials that often make complicated concepts easier for students to understand. Two- and three-dimensional models, role plays, and demonstrations make materials more concrete (Olson & Platt, 1996). One of our senior interns showed middle school students his completed portfolio required in a college class. This provided students with a concrete model of a portfolio. Another intern involved students in role plays as they acted out word problems in math.

Functional materials, such as newspapers, job applications, recipes, television guides, and menus, that depict normal life events enhance text information. In their recommendations for restructuring secondary special education programs, Kortering and Elrod (1991) note the importance of including materials that "embed knowledge-based information into pending normal life events such as puberty, job changes, job promotions or demotions, and community events" (p. 150).

Teachers and students can use software programs such as Print Shop (Brøderbund), which combines both text and graphics, to create posters, transparencies, and other materials to enhance lesson presentations. Teachers and students can also use videodisc and CD-ROM technology to create multimedia presentations. We discuss this technology further in Chapter 8.

Many computer software programs are currently available for student use. *Tutorial* software is best for students who are acquiring a skill. Generally, a tutorial program introduces the content, prompts students, gives them opportunities to produce the content, and provides both informational and reinforcing feedback. Most programs also adjust explanations at the point of a student's misunderstanding and branch out to an alternate presentation (Church & Bender, 1989). *Drill-and-practice* software provides extra opportunities for students to practice skills and gives them immediate feedback for correct and incorrect responses. *Simulation* software presents controlled replications of real-world events that are difficult or impossible to teach about in the classroom, such as driving a car (Church & Bender, 1989). The software requires student interactions as they attempt to solve problems. Many newer software programs combine tutorial, drill-and-practice, and simulation activities in one program. In other chapters, we discuss specific software programs.

Materials do not have to be expensive. It is easy to pick up free menus from restaurants, and often companies will furnish free products. Ms. Rodriguez went to the local paper company and they gave her discarded colored paper that did not meet production quality. Holcomb (1989) suggests that teachers select public-domain software and shareware to boost classroom computer resources. Public-domain software, or "freeware," is not copy-protected, and may be copied often. It is free. FrEdWriter is an example of a public-domain word processing program developed especially for educational use; it is available in both English and Spanish versions. With share ware, users pay a moderate fee (usually $20 or less) if they choose to keep the product (Holcomb, 1989). See Box 7.2 for a list of sources for low-cost software and free materials.

Some guidelines for selecting appropriate materials for students with disabilities follow (Church & Bender, 1989; Fitzgerald, 1990; Lewis, Heflin, & DiGiani, 1991; Stewart, 1990):

1. *Select materials that are age-appropriate and on the students' academic level.* This is difficult to do for secondary students, as their reading levels are frequently below their maturity levels. An easy way to check maturity level of a text is to examine the illustrations. Are they immature and inappropriate for older students? To try for a better match between reading and maturity levels, you can select high-interest/low-level books. These books control the vocabulary of the text and yet maintain mature interest levels. Check publications by Benefic Press (10300 W. Roosevelt Rd., Westchester, IL 60153), Reader's Digest Services (Educational Division, Pleasantville, NY 10570), and Fearon Publishers (6 Davis Drive, Belmont, CA 94002).

2. *Select materials that you can integrate into the curriculum.* Do the materials match the IEP objectives and provide practice for meeting those objectives? As mentioned previously, functional materials such as menus, recipes, and newspapers are easy to integrate into different curriculum objectives. To integrate software programs into the curriculum, teachers need to direct students to the relevant information on the software program and summarize the learning experiences for them (Church & Bender, 1989).

3. *Select materials that are easy for students to use.* This is particularly important for material that is selected to give students practice with previously taught content. Materials that provide step-by-step explanations and strategies are easier for students to follow as they perform the task. Check readability, organizational format, and supporting graphics in a text. Check software programs to see if they allow teachers to enter simpler content, edit old content, or adjust selected presentation features such as sound, speed of presentation, or number of items. For example, the software program Punctuation Put-On (Sunburst) allows modification of the options and passages. Lee (1987) also suggests selecting software that requires minimal keyboard skills.

**BOX 7.2**

## Sources for Low-Cost Software and Free Materials

Educational Resources
2360 Hassell Rd.
Hoffman Estates, IL 60195
800/624-2926
(Apple II, Macintosh, IBM, TRS-80, Commodore)

Free Publications from U.S. Government Agencies
Library Unlimited
P. O. Box 3988
Englewood, CO 80155-3988

Free Resource Builder for Librarians and Teachers
McFarland and Company, Inc., Publishers
Box 611
Jefferson, NC 28640

Guide to Free Computer Materials (updated yearly)
Educators Progress Service, Inc.
214 Center St.
Randolph, WI 53956

Innovative Software Solutions for Special Education
Laureate
110 E. Spring St.
Winooski, VT 05404

The Public Domain Exchange
2074C Walsh Ave., Dept. 634
Santa Clara, CA
800/331-8125 or 408/496-0624
(Apple II family and Macintosh)

The Specialware Directory: A Guide to Software for Special Education
LINC Associates, Inc.
3857 N. High Street
Columbus, OH 43214

4. *Select materials that include some sort of monitoring system.* Many commercial materials produce charts or graphs for students to use in monitoring their progress and grading their own products. For example, *The Sentence Writing Strategy* of the Learning Strategies Curriculum (Schumaker &

Sheldon, 1985) contains progress charts that students can use to set goals and monitor their progress. Many software programs provide feedback regarding both correct and incorrect responses (Lee, 1987). Materials that contain these features promote self-management skills, and save time for teachers.

5. *Select materials that are free of gender and cultural bias.* Materials can be used to teach students to recognize and celebrate the diversity and variety of individuals (Olson & Platt, 1996). Be certain to select materials that depict people from different cultures and women and men in a variety of roles. Please refer to Chapter 4 for a more thorough discussion of this topic.

Even with careful selection of materials, you may find that they are inappropriate for the student or you may find that your co-teacher does not wish to use them. In such cases, you may have to adapt materials. Burnette (1987) reports that special education teachers modify approximately 40% of their instructional materials. Common problems of commercial materials include complicated written directions and inappropriate or confusing content. With adaptations, you can individualize materials and assist mainstreamed students.

### Adaptation of Materials

Some adaptations for written *directions* include the following:

1. *Highlight or underline the important words in the directions.* For example, in the following directions, the teacher has underlined the verbs and highlighted the types of paragraphs for emphasis:

> Read the topic sentences below and identify whether each topic sentence would introduce a **N**arrative, **D**escriptive, or **E**xplanatory paragraph. Explain your choice."

Gallagher (1988) recommends that teachers underline each direction in a different color.

2. *Write the directions in steps.* For example, the preceding directions might appear as:
   a. Read each sentence.
   b. Identify whether it would introduce a Narrative, Descriptive, or Explanatory paragraph.
   c. Explain your choice.

3. *Add examples, pictures, or diagrams to the directions* (Meier, 1992). For example:

   a. Read each sentence.

   b. Identify whether it would introduce a

      Narrative ("I am an only child.");

      Descriptive ("The score was tied with a minute to go just as Stockton lobbed the ball to Malone."); or

      Explanatory ("To complete an application, first read the form.") paragraph.

   c. Explain your choice.

4. *Simplify directions by using shorter sentences, more familiar vocabulary, and active verbs.* For example:

Read each sentence. Mark an *N* if the sentence begins a Narrative paragraph. Mark a *D* if the sentence begins a Descriptive paragraph. Mark an *E* if the sentence begins an Explanatory paragraph. Then, explain your choice.

5. *Use a combination of 1–4, above.* For example, you may want to highlight and add steps.

6. *Go over the directions orally in class with students.* After the students have read the directions, check their comprehension with specific questions, and ask them to repeat or rephrase the directions.

*Content* adaptations frequently involve altering the content of worksheets or text materials. Sometimes, however, changing the content of an assignment is not a viable alternative for students with disabilities in an inclusive setting, as some regular educators oppose the diluting of content information. Therefore, in this section, we discuss some adaptations that change the content and others that leave the content intact.

1. *Shorten the assignment.* One way to shorten an assignment is to offer students the choice of doing either the odd- or even-numbered problems. This selection often motivates students to complete a task.

2. *Highlight essential information in the content section.* It is easy to draw yellow felt pen lines through essential parts of the printed text in regular textbooks (Meier, 1995).

3. *Provide clues for students to answer questions at the end of the chapter.* Write the page number of the answer next to the question. You can also rearrange the questions so that they appear in the same sequence as the answers found in the chapter.

4. *Discuss the first example with the students, or complete the first example.* If the response type changes, do the first example of each different type of

item. Mr. Riviera prepared a worksheet with true or false items followed by fill-in-the-blanks. He completed the first true or false item and the first fill-in-the-blank item with the students.

5. *Prepare questions ahead or identify critical information for the students on a written guide or outline before requiring them to read the information.* The written guide alerts students to relevant information and provides them with a learning set.

6. *Read the content on tape.* Edwards (1983) suggests that teachers read the exact text for individuals with good listening skills. He recommends that teachers paraphrase and highlight picture, map, and graph cues for students with low-level listening skills. Riegel, Mayle, and McCarthy-Henkel (1988) recommend that the reader identify the name of the text-book, author, and chapter at the beginning of the tape, followed by directions telling the students that they may stop the tape at any time to answer questions or write notes. They also recommend that the reader emphasize italicized words, read the end-of-chapter questions before reading the chapter itself, read the entire meaning of abbreviations (*e.g.* is read "for example"), and summarize the main idea of a visual aid immediately after it is mentioned in the text.

7. *Change the physical appearance of the material.* Adequate white space, boxes around different items, and answer lines or squares are some changes that simplify worksheets without changing the content. In Figure 7.1, a special educator changed only the physical appearance of a spelling assignment required in the regular class.

## Instructional Arrangements

Depending on objectives, activities, subject matter content, and student needs, teachers may organize students into large groups, small groups, peer groups, and individual arrangements for instruction. The selection of the instructional arrangement should meet the needs of students as identified on the IEP and should address cultural diversity.

### Large Group Arrangement

Special education teachers in pullout settings often use whole group instruction when they teach learning strategies. For example, Ms. Dumar teaches content from the Learning Strategies Curriculum to 20 students with mild disabilities during sixth period. Traditionally, regular educators in secondary inclusive classes present content information in a large group format. Large group instruction is an efficient use of teacher time, as one

**FIGURE 7.1** **Adaptation of Spelling Assignment**

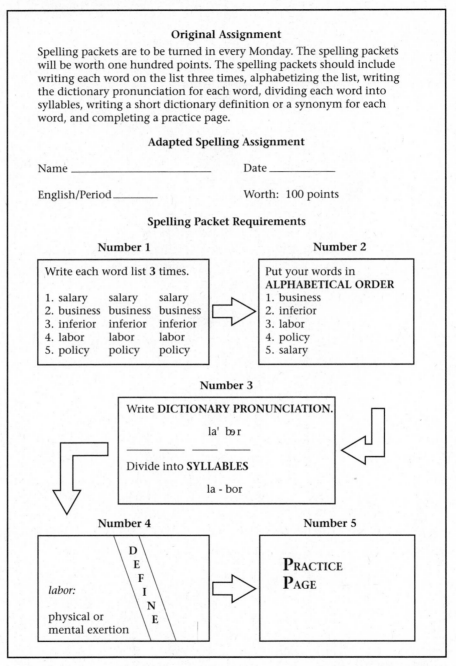

### Original Assignment

Spelling packets are to be turned in every Monday. The spelling packets will be worth one hundred points. The spelling packets should include writing each word on the list three times, alphabetizing the list, writing the dictionary pronunciation for each word, dividing each word into syllables, writing a short dictionary definition or a synonym for each word, and completing a practice page.

### Adapted Spelling Assignment

Name _____     Date _____

English/Period _____     Worth: 100 points

### Spelling Packet Requirements

**Number 1**

Write each word list **3** times.

1. salary    salary    salary
2. business  business  business
3. inferior  inferior  inferior
4. labor     labor     labor
5. policy    policy    policy

**Number 2**

Put your words in **ALPHABETICAL ORDER**
1. business
2. inferior
3. labor
4. policy
5. salary

**Number 3**

Write **DICTIONARY PRONUNCIATION.**

la' bər

Divide into **SYLLABLES**

la - bor

**Number 4**

*labor:*

physical or mental exertion

DEFINE

**Number 5**

PRACTICE PAGE

*Source:* Created by Susan Miller, Orange County Public Schools, Orlando, Florida. Reprinted by permission.

teacher can serve many students as they listen to lectures; participate in group discussions; view videodiscs, films, or videotapes; listen to guest speakers; or watch demonstrations.

Computers can be used effectively in whole class instruction for presenting demonstrations, simulations, and multimedia information. For example, the videodisc program Mastering Fractions, used during whole group instruction to teach fractions to secondary students with disabilities, demonstrated positive effects on student achievement (Woodward & Gersten, 1993). A large TV can be converted into a computer monitor with appropriate cabling, or an LCD projection panel device can be placed on top of an overhead projector to project the computer image on a screen (Roblyer, 1989).

Co-teaching is a strategy that can be used effectively to teach students with disabilities in a large group setting. In co-teaching, regular educators are often responsible for the content of the lecture, and special educators for adaptations that make the lecture more appropriate for students with disabilities. Co-teaching was discussed extensively in Chapters 2 and 5.

Mercer and Mercer (1993) suggest the following guidelines for accommodating students with special needs in a large group setting: (1) Keep instruction short—not more than 30 minutes in sixth and seventh grades and not more than 40 minutes in eighth through twelfth grades. (2) Actively involve all students. (3) Use visual aids. (4) Use frequent change-ups, such as telling a joke, allowing students to stretch, or other variations. (5) Share behavioral expectations with students. Roaming during a lecture, asking frequent questions, and connecting the content with student experiences are other effective strategies.

### Small Group Arrangements

Teachers normally provide small group instruction to two to five students when they want to work closely with students and supply frequent feedback (Bos & Vaughn, 1994). Teachers may use small groups to reteach content to those students who did not master the information during whole group instruction. In addition, secondary teachers often place students in small groups for practice activities and cooperative projects. For example, Mr. Germaine first lectures about circuits and then places students in groups to design a circuit board. Ms. Sims first discusses propaganda and then places students in groups to find examples of propaganda in the newspaper. Teachers should maintain flexible small groups, monitor the groups, and place group members in close proximity.

Computers can be used in small group instruction to provide more practice and to allow students to work on projects together. During group

© Nita Winter

*Secondary students enjoy working cooperatively in groups.*

projects using the computer, Roblyer (1989) suggests that teachers assign each student a role. For example, one student reads the instructions and directs the work, another student serves as the keyboarder and enters the commands, and a third student acts as the recorder for the group's observations and findings.

### Peer Group Arrangements

Peer tutoring and cooperative learning are two instructional arrangements in which peers work independently and learn from one another. Peer tutoring usually consists of one person acting as the tutor and the another as the student. Cooperative learning involves peers working together to solve problems or share information. Both peer tutoring and cooperative learning are often recommended to help special students succeed in the mainstream setting. Studies have shown peer tutoring to be effective for secondary students with mild disabilities in a mainstream social studies classroom (Maheady, Sacca, & Harper, 1988), in ninth- and tenth-grade math classes (Maheady, Sacca, & Harper, 1987), and in seventh- through eleventh-grade computational math (Kane & Alley, 1980).

In a review of research on the effects of cooperative learning on students with disabilities, Tateyama-Sniezek (1990) reported inconclusive findings on the use of this strategy to increase academic achievement of students with disabilities in inclusive settings. However, the secondary population was included in only 7 of the 12 studies reviewed. When Stevens and Slavin (1991) reviewed some of the same studies, they concluded that the components of individual accountability and group rewards were necessary for cooperative learning to have a positive effect on achievement.

Whether a teacher uses peer tutoring or cooperative learning, the guidelines are similar.

1. *Select the students.* Maheady et al. (1988) paired students with mild disabilities with "normal" students in a social studies class. For tutors, select students who have demonstrated initial acquisition of the skill and who are eager to participate (Chiang, Thorpe, & Darch, 1980; Scruggs, Mastropieri, & Richter, 1985). Johnson and Johnson (1986) and Slavin (1988a) recommend that teachers assign students of various ethnic backgrounds and ability levels to different cooperative groups. The recommended size of the cooperative group is three to five members of various ethnic backgrounds and ability levels (Johnson & Johnson, 1986).

2. *Prepare materials.* Often the teacher prepares the materials, especially for peer tutoring. For example, Maheady et al. (1988) prepared the study guides and the Friday quizzes. For cooperative groups, you may prepare questions or worksheets, or assign topics. For example, O'Melia and Rosenberg (1994) prepared homework material consisting of eight computation and two story problems related to the daily math lesson for their Cooperative Homework Teams project. Of course, with either arrangement, students may prepare the materials.

3. *Define students' roles.* In their Classwide Peer Tutoring procedure, Maheady et al. (1988) specified the roles of both tutor and tutee. After the teacher instructed the students for two days, the students worked together for two days before their Friday exam. Using the study guide, the tutor dictated the question and followed a feedback procedure of saying "That's right" when the peer's answer was correct . When the answer was incorrect, the tutor said "That's wrong" and repeated the correct answer; then the tutee repeated and wrote the correct answer. If the answer was wrong again, the tutee had to write the correct answer three times.

In cooperative learning groups, Johnson and Johnson (1986) recommend assigning of the roles of checker, accuracy coach, summarizer, elaboration seeker, and reporter. The checker makes certain all students understand the information; the accuracy coach corrects any errors; the summarizer restates the major conclusions or answers of the group; the elaboration seeker asks members to relate new and past information; and the reporter writes down the information.

4. *Train students for their roles.* Slavin (1988b) stresses that teachers should make students understand that "putdowns, making fun of teammates or refusing to help them are ineffective ways for teams to be successful and not acceptable kinds of behavior" (p. 52). Maheady et al. (1988) used role-play sessions to teach students the procedures. You may also need role-play sessions to teach students how to relate in socially appropriate ways with others. Some cooperative behaviors for role-play sessions include listening to others' opinions, complimenting each other's ideas, making constructive comments, and speaking in a pleasant voice (Olson & Platt, 1996).

5. *Provide motivation.* Both peer tutoring and cooperative group arrangements are motivating because they give students more opportunities to participate in an activity. Awarding contingent points, conducting weekly competitions among teams, and recognizing group effort also motivate students. In the Classwide Peer Tutoring system, tutees earned 3 points for each correct answer and 2 points when they corrected an error. Tutors earned up to 10 bonus points for accurate dictation of questions, appropriate error correction procedures, accurate delivery of points, and supportive and complimentary feedback (Maheady et al., 1988). Slavin (1988a) recommends free time or bonus points as motivation for appropriate group participation.

Two cooperative group arrangements created by Slavin and his colleagues at Johns Hopkins University involve placing the students on teams to provide motivation. In one arrangement (STAD, or Student Teams–Achievement Divisions), the teacher divides the class into five-member teams. The teacher instructs the students for two days. Then the students study the material together with the other team members for two days, and on Friday they take a quiz on the material. Each individual scores points for the team based on the quiz scores.

In the other team cooperative group arrangement, Teams–Games–Tournaments (TGT), students compete for points during a Friday tournament instead of a Friday quiz. Students performing at similar skill levels and representing different teams are assigned to each tournament table. For example, students who are top performers for each team are at one table, the middle performers are at one table, and the poorest performers are at one table. Each student answers questions on flash cards in a game format. Slavin (1988b) recommends awarding 6 points to the student who answers the most questions and 2 points to the student who answers the fewest questions at each table.

In the Cooperative Homework Teams (O'Melia & Rosenberg, 1994), middle school students were given points for the completion and accuracy of math homework assignments. The mean individual scores were then converted to team mean scores.

Friedman (1986) suggests the use of relay teams as they race to complete practice items in the least amount of time using software programs. In this format, the teacher places two computers in the front of the room. A member from each team completes one problem and then rushes back to the group. The team to complete the most problems correctly on the computer within a set amount of time wins the race.

Group effort may be recognized by posting each team's score. Maheady et al. (1987) announced weekly results and outstanding individual performances in the school's weekly bulletin. They also posted students' scores on a laminated scoreboard. O'Melia and Rosenberg (1994) presented certificates to those teams that met or exceeded preselected criteria.

6. *Evaluate both the product and the process.* Since peer arrangements involve the teaching of both academic and cooperative skill, provisions should be made for evaluation of both the group product and the process. Slavin (1988a) suggests giving a group grade based on an average of the individual performances of all group members. Johnson and Johnson (1986) emphasize the need for individual accountability in any group project. They suggest that a way to ensure this accountability is to select only one student's product to represent the group effort. All students receive a grade based on that one student's project. Of course, the selection is kept secret until the project is due, although the students are informed of the grading procedures at the beginning of the project.

Some teachers also give grades for appropriate group participation. You may have students self-evaluate the group process by answering such questions as, What was a helpful action? What was not a helpful action? What might be done differently next time? (Schniedewind & Salend, 1987). Maher (1984) suggests tutor support conferences in which students can discuss concerns and difficulties.

### Individual Arrangements

Students may also work independently, on a computer, or with the teacher or a paraprofessional in individual instructional arrangements. Students work independently to practice a previously taught skill or to research a paper or project. Computer use on an individual basis is preferable when (1) a student needs self-paced time and personalized feedback to assure mastery, (2) a student does not like to make mistakes in front of others, or

(3) a student is writing his or her own program, word-processing a report, or creating a personal computer-generated product (Roblyer, 1989).

A teacher or paraprofessional may work with one student when that student is having difficulty learning in small groups, needs assistance with specific aspects of the assignment, or is on a different skill level than the rest of the class (Polloway, Patton, Payne, & Payne, 1989). Teachers also monitor and help individual students during independent practice time.

An individual instructional arrangement is not to be confused with individualization. Individualization can occur during small group and large group instruction. Stevens and Rosenshine (1981) define individualization as "a characteristic of effective instruction if the term implies helping each student to succeed, to achieve a high percentage of correct responses, and to become confident of his or her competence" (p. 3).

## COMPREHENSION MONITORING OF KEY CONCEPTS

### *Before Instruction: The Preactive Stage*

1. Teachers should consider IEP objectives and students' interests, motivation, prior knowledge, participation, and behaviors when planning.

2. In the acquisition stage of learning, students concentrate on accuracy; in the fluency stage, they concentrate on speed; in the maintenance stage, they concentrate on mastery; in the generalization stage, they apply their knowledge to new situations.

3. Techniques for the acquisition stage include modeling, prompting, questioning, and immediate feedback with tutorial types of materials; techniques for the fluency stage include drill-and-practice activities and reinforcement plus drill-and-practice software; techniques for the maintenance stage include distributed practice; techniques for the generalization stage include application activities and simulation-type software.

4. Instructional alignment is the amount of agreement among objectives, instructional procedures, and evaluation techniques.

5. Scheduling academic activities, establishing timesaving routines, and monitoring transition activities are three ways to increase allocated learning time.

6. An objective includes the learner, the target behavior, the condition, the criterion, and an overlearning component.

7. Subject matter falls into the categories of concepts, rules, laws, lawlike principles, and value judgments, plus learning and metacognitive strategies.

8. To decrease the complexity of subject matter content, teachers can identify prerequisite skills, provide procedural facilitators, anticipate student errors, and select easy practice materials.

9. Guidelines for selecting materials include choosing materials that (a) are age-appropriate and on the students' academic level, (b) can be integrated into the curriculum, (c) are easy for students to use, (d) include some sort of monitoring system, and (e) are free of gender and cultural bias.

10. Teachers often adapt written directions by (a) highlighting, (b) writing the directions in steps, (c) adding examples, pictures, or diagrams, (d) simplifying sentences and vocabulary, and (e) going over the directions orally.

11. Some content adaptations involve altering the content, such as shortening an assignment; others, such as putting boxes around some of the information, leave the content intact.

12. The selection of an instructional arrangement—large group, small group, peer group, or individual—depends on objectives, activities, subject matter, and student needs.

13. The large group arrangement is appropriate for discussions, demonstrations, and videotapes, while the small group arrangement is frequently used to reteach content to those students who did not master the information during whole group instruction or for practice activities and cooperative projects.

14. Peer group arrangements provide students with opportunities for frequent responding and for learning from one another, while individual instruction is used when a student is having difficulty learning in small groups, needs assistance with specific aspects of the assignment, or is on a different skill level than the rest of the class.

## During Instruction: The Interactive Phase

During the interactive phase, teachers must attend to several factors, including instructional language, engaged learning time, teaching routines, feedback, and management of student behavior. In this section, we discuss all but managing behavior, which was included in our discussion of motivation in Chapter 6.

## Instructional Language

In a study of the instructional ecology of 52 secondary programs for students with mild disabilities, Rieth, Polsgrove, Okolo, Bahr, and Eckert (1987) found that resource room teachers spent 19.5% of their time answering student requests for clarification concerning assignments. They concluded that students must have difficulty understanding the directions or instructional content of the assignment. You need to be aware of your instructional language as you are giving directions and explanations. A teacher must often adapt the vocabulary, sentence structure, and auditory nature of instructional language for students with mild disabilities and those from culturally diverse backgrounds.

Providing short definitions of difficult, unfamiliar vocabulary words or connecting new words to previous student knowledge are effective adaptations. For example, during a teacher-led discussion, one of our senior interns recorded difficult words on the board with short definitions and had students add them to their personal glossaries. Another intern highlighted the word *condensation* by underlining *condense* and drawing a picture of a can of condensed milk, which students recalled was thicker than homogenized milk. In this way, the teacher connected a new term, *condensation,* with a familiar item, a can of condensed milk. Vocabulary maps also enhance vocabulary development. Students or the teacher can design the maps, which include the word, a short definition, and a picture (see Figure 7.2).

Instructional language should also indicate a clear signaling of transitions (Brophy & Good, 1986). Positive repetition of directions and positive attention for students who follow the directions can assist in transitions (Canter, 1986). For example, Mr. Janus used the effective technique of positive repetition and attention when he told his students, "Please put away your journals and turn to page 35 in the science text. I can see that all the people in this row have put away their journals. I certainly appreciate everyone turning to page 35."

Visual cues aid in the understanding of instructional language. They include writing assignments on the board, listing the key points of a lecture on a transparency, placing the steps of a procedure on poster board, and completing the first problem as a group on an independent practice task. Briggs (1991) recommends that teachers use gestures and simple diagrams

**FIGURE 7.2    Sample Vocabulary Map**

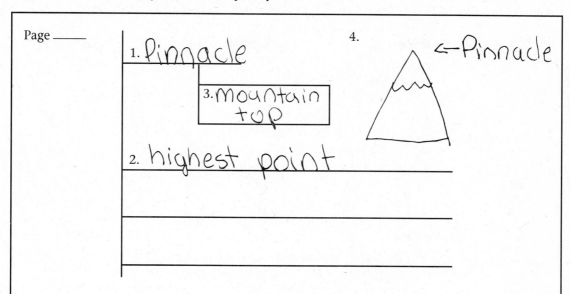

1. Locate the vocabulary word in the text.
2. Pronounce the word.
3. Locate and discuss the definition.
4. Write the word in blank 1.
5. Write the definition in blank 2.
6. Think of 1 or 2 words that will help you remember the definition.
   Write the words in box 3.
7. Draw a picture that will help you remember the word in space 4.

*Source:* Frame and steps are from "Vocabulary Overview Guide: A Metacognitive Strategy to Improve Vocabulary Comprehension and Retention" by E. M. Carr, 1985, *Journal of Reading*, pp. 684–689. Copyright by the International Reading Association. Reprinted by permission. (Actual example is from the work of a secondary student in a learning disabilities class who wishes to remain anonymous.)

to assist students with limited English proficiency. For example, a teacher might move around the class nervously to illustrate pacing.

By using frequent comprehension checks, you can determine whether students understand instructional language. Ask specific questions, such as "What is the first step of the paraphrasing strategy?" instead of "Do you understand?" Checking the syntax of sentences is another strategy for clarifying instructional language (Olson & Platt, 1996). An active sentence such as "Jim drove the car" is easier to understand than a passive sentence such as "The car was driven by Jim" (Wiig & Semel, 1984). Notice, that in the active sentence, the sequence has the subject acting on the verb ("Jim drove"); in the passive sentence, students must reverse the order of "driven by Jim" to "Jim drove."

In a summary of research on effective instructional language at the junior and senior high school levels, Brophy and Good (1986) identified the frequent use of "uh," vague terms, mazes, and discontinuity as interfering with the clarity of instructional language. Vague terms included words such as "might, little, more, maybe, probably, few, as you know" (p. 355). Mazes are false starts or halts in speech. Mr. Mark used a false start when he began, "This technique will help you find, or rather remember . . ." Saying "find" is the false start as he should have just stated, "This technique will help you remember . . ." Discontinuity disrupts the flow of an idea by inserting irrelevant content or relevant content at the wrong time. An example of discontinuity is, "Today, in science, we are discussing mass. Did anyone see the Magic and the Bulls play last night?" Asking about the Magic and the Bulls is not relevant to the discussion of mass.

## Engaged Learning Time

Engaged learning time is the amount of time that students actively engage in academic activities (Rieth, Polsgrove, & Semmel, 1981). Although active student participation correlates significantly with achievement, many researchers report that secondary students with disabilities are engaged most often in seatwork. Moreover, secondary teachers teach students on a one-to-one basis as they complete worksheets. Rieth, Polsgrove, et al. (1987) found that secondary students with mild disabilities actively engaged in written or oral responses only 36.7% of the time; they engaged in such passive responses as silent reading and attending to task directions 33.4% of the time. Ensminger (1991) reported similar results in his observation of secondary students in ten metropolitan high schools. He found a "study hall" environment in which most students were individually completing textbook assignments or engaged in tutorial instruction with limited verbal exchanges. In observations of LD resource rooms, Zigmond (1993) found students engaged in seatwork 85.7% of the time and teachers engaged in teaching only 26.5% of the time. Questioning and active student participation are ways to increase engaged learning time of adolescents with disabilities.

### Questioning

Asking frequent questions of students keeps them alert, accountable, and on task (Graham, 1985). Teachers also use questions to monitor and adjust instruction (Christenson, Ysseldyke, & Thurlow, 1989). In a teacher-directed lesson, questioning often proceeds in the following cycle: (1) Teacher asks a question and waits; (2) a student responds; (3) teacher gives feedback. Sometimes, in the cycle, the teacher asks other questions to prompt students to respond. In a teacher-facilitated lesson, questioning often proceeds in the following dialogue cycle: (1) Teacher or student asks a question and waits; (2) a student responds; (3) another student comments on the response; (4) a student asks another question; (5) teacher or student gives feedback.

Questions are used to determine prior knowledge ("What do you already know about condensation?"); to check understanding ("Why did Madelyn turn down Jesse's offer?"); to lead students to become independent learners ("What do you think might be a good question to ask?"); or to check recall of teacher-presented information ("What's the definition of condensation?"). In the preceding examples, you probably noticed the presence of low-level ("What's the definition of condensation?") and high-level ("Why did Madelyn turn down Jesse's offer?") questions. Low-level questions correspond to the knowledge stage of Bloom's cognitive-development hierarchy (Bloom, Englehart, Furst, & Kratwohl, 1956). Usually requiring only one- or two-word answers, they measure student recall of facts, information, and definitions (Meier, 1995). Numerous studies show that low-level, fast-paced questions that produce many correct student responses are effective for students in learning factual information (Christenson et al., 1987; Rosenshine & Stevens, 1986). In contrast, high-level questions correlate with the levels of application, analysis, synthesis, and evaluation of Bloom's taxonomy. In answering high-level questions, students must perform such tasks as applying, comparing, contrasting, and judging information. Both students and teachers have a more difficult time with high-level questions (Meier, 1995).

Another factor to consider in the questioning cycle is wait time, or the amount of time that an individual waits for a response after asking a question. Tobin (1987) suggests that wait time depends on the type of question, with less wait time required for low-level questions. A 3-second pause is frequently recommended for low-level questions, and 10 to 20 seconds for high-level questions (Northwest Regional Educational Library, 1990).

### *Active Participation*

As you will recall, the small group instructional arrangements of cooperative learning and peer tutoring actively involve students. However, even if you do not use cooperative learning or peer tutoring, you can engage the students during instruction and practice activities. Instructional pausing is an effective way to involve students during a lecture. Hawkins (1988) found that the procedure was very successful in teaching verb usage to adolescents with behavior disorders. In this procedure, the teacher presents the content for about 4 minutes and then asks students in pairs to discuss and check their understanding of the content for about 3 minutes.

Beattie and Algozzine (1982) found that different types of practice tasks promote more active participation. They compared the impact of a worksheet and a game activity on students with mental disabilities and found that the game activity was more effective.

Often teachers engage students in practicing concepts after they teach them. For example, Ms. Samuels, when teaching English to tenth-graders with mild disabilities, first discussed finding the main idea of newspaper articles with the whole group. Then, as a practice activity, she asked students in groups of three to find the main idea in two other articles.

## Teaching Routines

The teacher effectiveness literature (Rosenshine & Stevens, 1986; Ysseldyke, Thurlow, & Christenson, 1987) and the social constructivist literature (Englert et al., 1992) provide special educators with a basis for designing teaching routines. The teacher effectiveness literature highlights an active, directive, involved teaching style, with the teacher in charge. The teacher presents the information, provides feedback and correction, gives students many opportunities to respond and practice the tasks, and conducts frequent reviews. Teachers follow teaching routines, and frequently a script, as they present the content. The major belief of this direct instruction model is that students with disabilities do not develop insights on their own (Vockell & Mihail, 1993). Instead, teachers must teach the information systematically and not incidentally (Isaacson, 1989). These direct instruction techniques appear in the special education curriculum packages of Corrective Reading by Engelmann and colleagues and the Learning Strategies Curriculum by Deshler and colleagues (Poplin, 1988).

The social constructivist literature highlights meaningful contexts, classroom dialogues, responsive instruction, and classroom communities (Englert et al., 1992). These teaching practices are exemplified in whole-language or literature-based teaching, reciprocal teaching, and the Foxfire approach. Although literature-based teaching, reciprocal teaching, and the Foxfire approach do not delineate a standard teaching routine, they all emphasize the importance of connecting learning to student experience (Newman, 1985; Reid & Stone, 1991), the need to make learning a cooperative experience (Hilke, 1990; Johnson & Johnson, 1983; Newman, 1985;

Slavin, 1988a), the empowerment of students by involving them in planning and implementing instruction (Adelman & Taylor, 1986; Cohen, 1987; Deci & Chandler, 1986), and the need to present learning in meaningful contexts (Poplin, 1988; McNutt, 1984). The teacher's role is more of a facilitator as students take over the major responsibilities.

Researchers report positive results for both the direct instruction techniques based on the teacher effectiveness literature and the teaching principles based on the social constructivist literature. Such direct instruction programs as the Learning Strategies Curriculum increases students' mastery of how to learn (Hock, 1988), and the Corrective Reading curriculum increases student mastery of basic skills (Polloway, Epstein, Polloway, Patton, & Ball, 1986; Gregory, Hackney, & Gregory, 1982; Gersten & Maggs, 1982). Research has also shown that the reciprocal teaching approach based on the social constructivist philosophy is effective with junior high students using expository or informational text in remedial reading classes (Brown & Palincsar, 1982; Palincsar & Brown, 1984). Englert et al. (1992) suggest that effects may differ depending on whether the task involves basic skills or higher-order learning. They recommend approaches embodying the social constructivist principles for higher-order learning. In a review of the teacher effectiveness research, Rosenshine and Stevens (1986) note that the direct instruction techniques are best for teaching well-structured subjects. We believe that no one approach is likely to meet the needs of all adolescents with mild disabilities. Therefore, we discuss each approach in turn, with examples.

### Direct Instruction Model

Effective teachers using the direct instruction approach usually follow the teaching routine presented in Box 7.3. A teacher opens the lesson with an advance organizer; presents new information, either through demonstration or questioning techniques (body); leads the students in practice with prompts, corrections, and repetitions (guided practice); assigns sufficient practice activities so that students can achieve overlearning and mastery (independent practice); and closes the lesson with a post organizer. We will discuss each of these steps, using examples adapted from a lesson plan prepared by a student intern, Traci Myers, for teaching the concept of equilateral, isosceles, and scalene triangles during the acquisition stage.

1. *Begin with an advance organizer.* Advance organizers may consist of an activity for obtaining student attention, a statement of the lesson objectives, a confirmation of the teacher's expectations, or a presentation of a graphic organizer (Putnam & Wesson, 1990). A rationale is also important to include for secondary students, as sharing the usefulness of a lesson

**BOX 7.3**

## Direct Instruction Model

1. *Advance Organizer*
   Gain attention.
   Conduct review of prerequisite learning.
   Give overview.
   Share and relate objective to real-life experiences.
   Share purpose and importance of lesson.
   Present expectations.
   Set goals.

2. *Body*
   Present new information.
   Check for prior knowledge.
   Conduct lecture/discussion (questioning).
   Model/demonstrate.
   Monitor comprehension (questioning).
   Promote active student involvement.

3. *Guided Practice* (teacher-directed)
   Ask questions.
   Incorporate error-correction procedures.
   Include cued choral responding.
   Expect high frequency of student response.
   Require 80% and above accuracy.
   Ensure active student involvement.

4. *Independent Practice*
   Arrange small cooperative groups.
   Assign individual activity.
   Monitor progress.
   Develop advanced practice and generalization to other areas.
   Require 90%–100% accuracy.

5. *Post Organizer*
   Conduct review.
   Summarize.
   Preview tomorrow's lesson.

promotes student motivation (Lenz, Alley, & Schumaker, 1987). In our example, the teacher begins with an overview, expectations, rationale, and review:

"Today we are going to discuss three different types of triangles. First we will discuss the different triangles and practice identifying them, and then you will complete a worksheet. I expect you to raise your hand if you have any questions and to score at least 85% on the independent activity. Learning about different types of triangles should help you progress to higher math and to meet one of your IEP math objectives. Before we discuss different triangles, what is the definition of a triangle?"

2. *Present the new information.* New information can be presented through demonstration, modeling, or questioning. Throughout the body of the lesson, the teacher constantly monitors student comprehension, continuing with the lesson or changing it depending on this feedback. In our example, the teacher follows this outline when presenting the new information:

1. On overhead, show transparency of and read definition of equilateral triangle.
2. Show concrete (three-dimensional models) and semi-abstract (pictures) examples.
3. Have students write down definition and draw an example.
4. Ask questions about the definition, and point out the relationships between definition and example.
5. Show examples and nonexamples, and ask students questions relating to definitions.
6. Proceed in the same manner with an isosceles triangle and then a scalene triangle.
7. Point out the similarities and differences among the three triangles.

She continuously asks questions to check for comprehension of information and gives feedback.

3. *Lead the students in practice.* Often the practice involves questions presented at a fast pace with active student responding. The teacher provides for many successful repetitions of the task and prompts correct answers (Rosenshine & Stevens, 1986). The teacher continues to give feedback for correct and incorrect responses. In our example, the teacher involves the students in practicing identification of the three types of triangles:

"Now that we have discussed each type of triangle, let's see how well you can identify the three different types. Take out a blank sheet of paper. Rip it into three equal parts. On one piece, write *equilateral,* on another write *scalene,* and on the third piece, write *isosceles.* I will show you a picture of a triangle. When I say *now,* hold up the paper with the correct name on it."

She holds up a picture of a triangle and says "now." Students hold up their papers. She then gives feedback, explaining or asking students to defend why an answer is correct or incorrect.

4. *Assign the student independent tasks and activities.* Now, instead of the teacher guiding the students, students work independently. This is an ideal time for teachers to help individuals and to check individual comprehension. Individual practice is aligned with the objective, guided practice, and the evaluation. If the students do not complete the task during class, it may be a homework assignment.

> The teacher passes out a worksheet with pictures of 20 triangles and has students label whether the triangles are equilateral, isosceles, or scalene. She checks for comprehension by checking worksheets. She assigns peer tutors to those students having problems or students who do not score 85%. (If students do not finish in class, the assignment becomes homework.)

5. *Present the post organizer.* The post organizer ends the lesson. The teacher may summarize the lesson, or a student may summarize, or the teacher may ask questions to lead the students in summarizing the lesson. Teachers often give a preview of the next lesson at this time. Rosenshine and Stevens (1986) recommend that teachers write the main points of the lesson on the board and divide students into groups to summarize the main ideas to each other.

> The teacher concludes the lesson by reviewing the definitions of the three types of triangles through questioning. She then lets the students know how they met the behavioral expectations identified at the beginning of the lesson with statements such as "Thank you for remembering to raise your hands."

Once the students have mastered the skill of identifying the three types of triangles, Ms. Myers plans generalization activities such as a homework assignment that requires students to find examples of these figures in the home and work environment.

### Social Constructivist Approach

As noted previously, there is not a specific framework or model to follow in teaching a lesson based on the social constructivist philosophy. Instead, the lesson demonstrates responsive instruction, meaningful context, classroom dialogues, and classroom communities. Our example from this philosophy involves teaching students how to generate information-seeking questions to assist in comprehension of social studies text information.

1. *Link the information to meaningful context.* Information is not presented in isolation, but linked to authentic and purposeful contexts (Altwerger,

Edelsky, & Flores, 1987; McNutt, 1984). The emphasis is on relating learning to something meaningful in the student's life (Ensminger & Dangel, 1992). Teachers ask students to identify why it is important to study the information in an attempt to connect academic learning to prior knowledge and purpose.

> The teacher asks students why they think they should learn how to generate information-seeking questions. She then has the students generate questions concerning familiar everyday events, using prompts such as "If you want to know the hours that the motor vehicle department is open, you call the information desk and ask _____. What other questions might you ask? What if you wanted to find out information about a rock concert? What questions might you ask?"

2. *Use classroom dialogues.* Classroom dialogues are discussions about cognitive processes and learning strategies (Englert et al., 1992). Teachers model their thinking processes, engage students in talking about their own cognitive processes, and then transfer control of the dialogue to the students. The teacher eventually wants students to apply the processes internally without the teacher present by asking such questions as "What am I supposed to do? Do I understand? How am I doing?" (Englert et al., 1992, p. 77).

> The teacher models her thought processes concerning the asking of information-seeking questions: "First, I need to read the heading of the passage. Hmmm, the effects of World War I on France. Let's see, I think a good question might be, What were the effects of the war on France? Reading the first paragraph, my question is, Why was France so unstable after the war?"
> The teacher then engages students in a dialogue: "Does anyone else have a question to ask?" Eventually, the students will ask the questions without teacher modeling.

3. *Demonstrate responsive instruction.* Teachers demonstrate responsive instruction when they react to the needs, capabilities, and interests of individual learners (Poplin, 1988). Students are more motivated when they participate in decision making, because they feel ownership and responsibility for their learning (Deci & Chandler, 1986). Teachers who incorporate students' ideas and examples into their lesson presentations, and who respond to students' mistakes as opportunities for constructing new knowledge and meanings, are demonstrating responsive instruction (Englert et al., 1992). In the Foxfire pedagogy, teachers share predetermined objectives with the students, but the students decide how to reach the objectives (Ensminger & Dangel, 1992).

The teacher asks students whether they want her to write their information-seeking questions on the board. She uses Jason's suggestion to write *who, what,* and *when* on the board to remind students of the types of questions they may ask. She leads students to self-evaluate their questions, as she makes no judgmental comments about them.

4. *Use classroom community activities.* Classroom communities allow students not only to learn from teachers but also to collaborate and talk with peers. Classroom communities may involve (1) groups of students completing projects, (2) peers critiquing each other's work, or (3) students studying together and assisting one another. In the Foxfire approach, Ensminger and Dangel (1992) relate how the activities from the classroom community expanded into activities for the surrounding community. In their example, groups of students with learning disabilities improved writing skills by designing holiday cards. The groups then sold the cards and purchased items for children at a local shelter for the homeless.

The teacher divides students into groups of three and asks each group to read a selection and prepare information-seeking questions to ask other students.

## Feedback

We have discussed feedback indirectly in the two different teaching routines. However, feedback is such a critical teaching behavior that we feel it deserves further discussion. Feedback behaviors are defined as "any statements or questions by the teacher used to provide information about the correctness or incorrectness of their [students'] classwork, such as seatwork, group work, response to teacher questions, etc." (Kea, Schumaker, & Deshler, 1987, p. 12). Rieth, Bahr, Polsgrove, Okolo, and Eckert (1987) found that secondary students with mild disabilities in resource settings benefited from a great deal of feedback.

Kea et al. (1987) recommend different forms of feedback depending on whether a teacher is commenting on a reply to a question or on a student's task performance. If a student answers a teacher's question correctly in a quick and firm manner, they suggest a brief acknowledgment without further elaboration ("That's correct, John. That sentence is an example of a complex sentence.") If the student gives an incorrect or incomplete answer, or fails to respond to the question, they recommend probing, providing clues, repeating or rephrasing the question, or allowing more time for the student to answer. An example of this type of correction is "No, John, look at the sentence again. Remember our definition of a complex sentence."

When giving feedback on task performance, they recommend either positive feedback for correct answers or corrective feedback for incorrect ones. The positive feedback should include three appropriate aspects of the performance. Mr. Jackson is identifying three correct behaviors when he says to John, "You have used the correct punctuation for that complex sentence. You have written a very descriptive independent clause, and you have selected an appropriate subordinating conjunction."

For corrective feedback on errors during task performance, the teacher asks questions, makes suggestions for improvement, and requires the student to correct the error. Mr. Jackson is demonstrating corrective feedback when he says, "John, you have written a very descriptive independent clause. However, your dependent clause seems to be missing some words. Does the sentence make sense to you with those words missing? I think if you add the words it will improve the sentence. Why don't you do that now?"

Collins, Carnine, and Gersten (1987) found that both quick, basic feedback and elaborated feedback successfully increased student performance on reasoning tasks. However, elaborated feedback produced the greatest gains in skill acquisition.

---

**COMPREHENSION MONITORING OF KEY CONCEPTS**

*During Instruction: The Interactive Phase*

1. Teachers should (a) adapt the vocabulary, sentence structure, or auditory nature of instructional language for students with mild disabilities, (b) clearly signal transitions, and (c) check frequently for student comprehension.

2. Frequent use of "uh," vague terms, false starts in speech (mazes), and insertion of relevant content at the wrong time or irrelevant content (discontinuity) interferes with clarity of instructional language.

3. Engaged learning time is the amount of time that students actively engage in academic activities.

4. Questioning and active student participation are ways to increase engaged learning time of students, which is important for academic achievement.

5. Questions are asked to determine prior knowledge, to check understanding, to encourage independent learners, and to check recall.

*(continued on next page)*

6. In the direct instruction approach influenced by the teacher effectiveness literature, teachers are in charge as they present information, provide feedback and correction, give students opportunities to respond, and conduct frequent reviews.

7. The social constructivist literature highlights meaningful contexts, classroom dialogues, responsive instruction, and classroom communities.

8. The teaching routine for the direct instruction approach consists of an advance organizer, teacher presentation of new information in the body of the lesson, guided practice, independent practice, and a post organizer.

9. A teaching routine based on the social constructivist literature includes linking the information to meaningful contexts using classroom dialogues, demonstrating responsive instruction, and using classroom community activities.

10. When students answer oral questions correctly, offer a quick, firm acknowledgment; when students answer incorrectly, probe, provide clues, rephrase or repeat questions, or allow more response time.

11. When giving feedback on correct task performance, offer three positive comments; when students make mistakes, ask questions, make suggestions for improvement, and require students to correct the error.

## After Instruction: The Reflective Phase

In the reflective phase of instruction, teachers evaluate learner progress and lesson effectiveness. Students may also self-evaluate. Competent teachers also self-evaluate to refine their instructional practices at this time (Posner, 1996; Reynolds, 1992). Since we have discussed student self-evaluation extensively in Chapter 6, we do not discuss it again here.

### Student Evaluation

The techniques used for evaluation often influence a student's success. As stated previously, aligning evaluation with curriculum content ensures that teachers are testing students based on what they teach (Cohen, 1987). In working with students with mild disabilities, teachers need to make certain the criterion of evaluation is clear (Tiedt & Tiedt, 1986). There are a variety of ways for students to show they know the information, and there are alternative grading practices (Bigge, 1988; D'Alonzo, 1983; McKenzie & Houk, 1993; OCPS/FDLRS, 1988). Test adaptations are also often necessary.

### Specific Criteria

Presenting students with an acceptable completed project or an expert product is one way to ensure that they know the expectations of an assignment. Johnson (1991) noted that seeing a completed expert project is helpful for Native Americans, who often do not exhibit risk-taking behaviors and are hesitant to complete a nonstructured assignment. Asking a student for permission to make a copy of an acceptable completed project for use with other classes is easy to do. Ms. White made a copy of Jim's term paper on Edgar Alan Poe for the other students to refer to as they were working on their term papers. Mr. Simmons shared his narrative paragraph with the students before asking them to write one.

Another technique that incorporates specific criteria and student self-evaluation is to present students with a checklist of questions with their point values. The students then check to be certain they have answered all the questions before they turn in a project or paper. For example, the following two items might appear on a checklist:

1. Did you identify the resources and their locations? (10 points)
2. Did you make fewer than 5 spelling errors? (5 points)

By checking these questions, the student knows to include both the resources and their locations and to check the report for spelling errors.

Evaluation criteria should also include a description of the requirements for high versus low scores (Archbald, 1992). For example the Adams County School District scored essays for organization, sentence structure, usage, mechanics, and format, using a 1–5 scale for each (see Archbald, 1992). To receive a score of 5 on organization, students were given the following criterion: "The essay is well-organized. It is coherent, ordered logically, and fully developed." At the other extreme was the criterion for a score of 1: "Little or nothing is written. Essay is disorganized and poorly developed. Does not stay on topic" (Archbald, 1992, p. 284).

### Variety of Outputs

Teachers at the secondary level tend to evaluate students on the basis of test scores. Yet there are many other ways for students to show they know the information. Some students may prefer to do projects, complete homework assignments, or share information orally instead of taking written exams.

You may select alternative evaluation techniques for students, or you may let students choose. For example, one of our interns gave students a choice of a final exam or a project that involved a weekly write-up of their classwork. For those students who chose the write-up, she included specific questions to answer. She also required them to reflect on how they might use the information to better their lives. With another class, she shared her objectives and let the students choose ways to show her that they had met the objectives. The students had to write up their ideas for teacher approval. In Chapter 6, we presented some alternative assignments for students to select to display their knowledge.

If homework assignments are part of your evaluation procedures, you may want to ensure that homework is appropriate for the ability and maturity level of the student, focused on fluency and maintenance tasks, closely tied to the subject matter currently being studied in the classroom, related to previous instruction and guided practice activities, quickly checked and returned to students, and graded with comments (Butler, 1987; Cotton, 1988; Foyle & Bailey, 1986; Jongsma, 1985; Rosenberg, 1989). Effective teachers assign homework only after they have taught the content.

### Alternative Grading

Grading is the most common system used to communicate student evaluations (Bigge, 1988). Multiple grades, contracting for grades, and basing grades on a variety of assignments are alternative grading practices. Assigning one grade for content and another grade for grammatical errors is an example of using multiple grades. Some teachers assign a grade for an original assignment and then average that grade with one given when the student redoes the assignment. For example, a student who scores 70% on the original assignment (7 out of 10) and redoes the assignment with a score of 90% (9 out of 10) receives a final score of 80% (16 out of 20). Contracting for grades involves a student and teacher agreeing to the requirements necessary for an A, the requirements necessary for a B, and so forth. For example, Mr. Smith requires a final report and a final exam for an A grade, but only a final report for a B grade. Some teachers also add a criterion measure to the contract. In the preceding example, Mr. Smith now requires a final report of a grade no lower than an A and a final exam of a grade no lower than a B for the student to earn an A.

Teachers who give points or percentages for different activities are basing grades on a variety of assignments. For example, Mr. Smith counts the two exams as 50%, participation as 10%, and the two projects as 40% of the total grade. You may let the students decide how much each item is weighted in the final grade.

O'Melia and Rosenberg (1994) describe the use of peer teams to cooperatively grade and correct individual homework assignments. Each day the teacher selects different checkers who, using answer sheets, grade each team member's homework. The teacher records the grades and returns the papers. Students help each other correct errors and then return the corrected papers to the teacher. The teacher awards daily points to individuals for completion and correct answers and then converts the individual scores to team scores. This grading procedure increased both completion and accuracy of homework assignments for seventh- and eighth-graders with learning disabilities and those with emotional disabilities (O'Melia & Rosenberg, 1994).

### Test Adaptations

Since secondary teachers in the regular classroom most often select exams as the means to assess students' knowledge and understanding of information, we present the following suggestions for test adaptations (D'Alonzo, 1983; ESOL, 1991; McKenzie & Houk, 1993; Meier, 1995; OCPS/FDLRS, 1988; Sugai & Tindal, 1993).

1. Give students the test orally and allow them to answer the questions either orally or in writing. When students choose to answer the items orally, ask a volunteer or peer to write down the answers, or allow students to record their answers on a tape recorder.

2. Give an open-book test or a take-home test for short-answer and essay responses. Allow students to use notes during the tests.

3. Give choices as to which questions to answer or as to how many points the test is worth.

4. Announce or write on the board at regular intervals the amount of time remaining for the test. For example, every twenty minutes, Mr. Osborne writes down the time left in the period.

5. Let students know how many points each question is worth. This allows students to budget their time appropriately. Ms. Gregory reminds students to spend more time on the questions worth 20 points than on those worth 10.

6. Administer practice tests. Provide students with out-of-use exams.

7. Give students study guides, a written outline, or a review sheet several days before giving the exam.

8. Allow students to answer questions directly on paper. Many students have difficulty transferring answers to answer sheets.

9. Provide a word bank for fill-in-the-blank items. For example, Mr. Jones lists the following possible answers for the fill-in-the-blank questions:

North America, South America, Australia, Asia, Europe, Antarctica, Africa. Students can select from these options to answer the test item "We live on the continent of _____."

10. Let students retake an exam for a better grade. The student may drop the lower grade or average the two scores together.

11. Give students visual cues on the test. For example, type or print the test with lots of white space. Break matching sections or fill-in-the-blank questions into blocks of five items. Boldface important vocabulary in the stem of the item, such as "The **causes** of the **Civil War** included . . ." Figure 7.3 presents an example of a modified quiz with visual cues.

12. Give examples on the test so that students will know how to respond. This helps particularly when students have trouble understanding the vocabulary of the question. A question using this technique is "Identify and describe the components of a narrative poem, beginning with (1) the plot." The student now knows that "plot" is one of the components.

13. Number answers to multiple-choice questions. Students frequently confuse the letters *b* and *d*. Numbers are much easier to discriminate.

14. Check the format for multiple-choice and matching questions. Keep all the options for the multiple-choice questions on the same page as the stem of the question. Keep all matching items on one page so students do not have to flip pages back and forth.

## Teacher Self-Evaluation

In a literature review of the qualities of a competent teacher, Reynolds (1992) found that successful educators reflect on what was successful and unsuccessful in their teaching and use that information to refine their instructional practices. Reflection occurs both during their interaction with students and after the lesson is finished.

Competent educators use multiple forms of gathering data for reflection (Taylor & Valentine, 1985). They may mentally replay the lesson or student interaction, actually review a videotaped lesson to assess their teaching methods, keep a journal of thoughts and feelings, or ask a colleague to act as a coach, observing and giving feedback. We include a section titled "Your Evaluation of the Lesson" on our lesson plan form for student teachers. This self-evaluation enables our students to assess the positive aspects of the lesson and suggest adaptations and modifications for improvement. Reflective thinking allows teachers to act in deliberate and intentional ways, devise new ways of teaching, and create meaning from classroom experiences (Posner, 1996; Reynolds, 1992).

**FIGURE 7.3**  **Modified Quiz**

QUIZ #1                    NAME _____ DATE _____

**I. Match the numbers on the map to the place names below:**

_13_ 1. Arctic Circle

____ 2. France

____ 3. Italy

____ 4. Atlantic Ocean

____ 5. Switzerland

____ 6. Norway

____ 7. Africa

____ 8. Spain

____ 9. Netherlands

____10. North Sea

____11. Strait of Gibraltar

____12. Great Britain

____13. West Germany

____14. Mediterranean Sea

**II. Fill in the blanks:**

15. Norway, Sweden, Finland, and Denmark make up [_____].

16. [_____] is the largest country in Western Europe.

17. The countries of Spain, Italy, and Greece are located on [_____].

18. Switzerland, Austria, and Luxembourg are said to be [_____] because they have no coastline.

19. The [_____] Mountains separate Spain and France.

20. Because of the [_____], much of Western Europe has a maritime climate.

Source: Developed by Michael W. Kunze, Orange County Public Schools, Orlando, Florida. Reprinted by permission.

**COMPREHENSION MONITORING OF KEY CONCEPTS**

*After Instruction: The Reflective Phase*

1. Expert products and evaluation checklists are two ways to inform students of the evaluation criteria.

2. Projects, homework assignments, and student choices are options other than tests for students to demonstrate knowledge.

3. Multiple grades, contracting for grades, and basing grades on a variety of assignments are examples of alternative grading practices.

4. Test adaptations are frequently necessary as exams are often used by secondary teachers to assess a student's knowledge and understanding of information.

5. In addition to evaluating students, competent educators reflect on their own successes and failures and use this information to change their instructional strategies.

 Now that you have read Chapter 7, reflect on your earlier responses at the beginning of the chapter and complete this post organizer.

1. Look back at your list of the decisions teachers make before beginning instruction. Which decisions did you forget? Did you add any additional ones? If so, describe them.

2. Look back at the teaching routine that you developed for high school students with mild disabilities following the framework recommended in the teacher effectiveness research. How would you change it after reading the chapter?

3. Reexamine the teaching routine that you developed for middle school students with mild disabilities based on suggestions found in the social constructivist literature. How would you change it after reading the chapter?

4. Compare your two ways of evaluation with those described in the chapter. How are they the same? How do they differ?

# Academic Content

**CHAPTER HIGHLIGHTS**

*The Secondary Academic Curriculum*
*Academic Content Area Instruction*
*Using Technology to Teach Academic Content*
*Alternatives for Enhancing Academic Content*
*Activities and Materials for Academic Content*

 Before you read Chapter 8, use your prior knowledge to complete this advance organizer.

1. Identify the different curriculum content that is taught in the middle school and high school.

2. With a peer, discuss some alternative ways to teach content.

3. Identify two ways to use technology to teach content areas.

4. With a peer, discuss three alternatives for enhancing academic content.

In this chapter, we discuss secondary curriculum and methodology for teaching academic content. Poteet (1995a) describes curriculum as a "set of courses and instructional experiences offered to students" (p. 3). Curriculum answers the questions of *what, when,* and *whom.* The *what* is the scope of the curriculum, the *when* is the sequence, and the *whom* is the target population (Meier, 1995). For example, the scope (*what*) of the curriculum for eighth-grade math found in *Mathematics in Action* includes multiplying whole numbers, dividing whole numbers, and fraction concepts (Hoffer et al., 1991). The sequence (*when*) indicates that "understanding subtraction concepts using models" is introduced in first grade while "understanding subtraction concepts without models" first appears as part of the curriculum in sixth grade. The target audience (*whom*) is students in regular education classes, as *Mathematics in Action* is often adopted as the basal math text. If you are employed in an inclusive setting, you will probably interact with an educator who is an expert at identifying the *what* and *when* of the curriculum.

Sources of curriculum include curriculum guides or standards, teachers' manuals, scope and sequence charts from texts, and criterion-referenced tests such as the BRIGANCE® Diagnostic Inventory of Essential Skills. In a survey of 341 special education teachers, 48% of whom taught at the secondary level, Sands, Adams, and Stout (1995) found that teachers ranked professional judgments, IEPs, student and teacher needs, and the general education curriculum as their primary choices for sources of curriculum.

Once the curriculum content has been identified, you need to identify the *how,* or methodology, for teaching that content. The *how* includes teaching strategies, materials, and activities. Here again, you may examine curriculum guides or teachers' manuals to assist you in the selection of teaching methods. If you are employed in an inclusive setting, the *how* is your area of expertise in teaching students with disabilities.

In this chapter, we first discuss the academic curriculum content found in secondary schools and then discuss the strategies for teaching secondary students with mild disabilities in academic subject areas. Our discussion of curriculum includes both the general education curriculum and the special education curriculum. In our discussion of instructional strategies, we examine the textbook approach, the unit approach, the use of technology, and alternatives for enhancing academic content. Finally, we conclude with a list of activities and materials for teaching academic subjects.

## The Secondary Academic Curriculum

In her description of curriculum, Meier (1995) moves from a broad to a narrow perspective—from curriculum as a "list of required courses and subjects" to "the content of a specific course or subject area" to "the content of instruction for a particular day or lesson" (p. 127). Usually, state and local education agencies determine the broad content of required courses and subjects for grade levels or graduation; local school district administrators and teachers determine the specific subject area course or curriculum; and individual teachers determine the content of instruction for a particular day or lesson.

Special education curriculum generally breaks down to four different orientations (Sands et al., 1995, p. 69): "(a) Basic skills models that primarily emphasize the remediation of academic deficits, (b) Social skills and life-adjustment models, (c) Learning strategies models, and (d) Functional orientations of vocational training and adult outcomes." This chapter is devoted to academic curriculum; the other orientations are discussed in Chapters 9–12.

Secondary students with disabilities may participate in the regular education academic curriculum, in a parallel academic curriculum, or in a remedial academic curriculum. In the regular education academic curriculum, students usually take credits in English, math, science, and social studies. The parallel curriculum often modifies the content demands of the regular education courses, while the remedial curriculum presents basic skills instruction in reading, math, and spelling. As noted in Chapter 2, students with learning disabilities and those with emotional disabilities tend to be in an academic curriculum for the first two years of high school and then participate in more flexible curricula in their last two years, while students with mental disabilities tend to participate more in functional and vocational curricula (Blackorby, 1993). Of course, the emphasis in all special education curricula is on leading students to a successful transition from school to postschool experiences.

## Regular Education Curriculum

The core subjects of writing, math, and reading, which form the basis of the elementary school curriculum, usually appear at the secondary level as tools for learning. Writing is used to express knowledge, math is used to solve problems and make practical decisions, and reading is used to gain information and meaning from texts. For example, writing at the secondary level includes such skills as organization, editing, and proofreading to develop a topic. In math, students are expected to use the basic skills of addition, multiplication, subtraction, and division to solve problems. Box 8.1 contains a list of expected reading skills for math, social studies, and science. Notice the emphasis on vocabulary, analysis of information, directions, and graphics.

At the middle school level, curriculum is usually divided into core, or basic, and exploratory courses (Clark & Clark, 1994). The core consists of

| | |
|---|---|
| **B O X 8 . 1** | **Required Reading Skills in Content Areas** |

*Math*

1. Analyze information from tables, formulas, and equations.
2. Read word problems.
3. Follow directions.
4. Read diagrams and graphs.
5. Read and understand specialized math vocabulary terms:
   a. technical words (arc, linear)
   b. words with special math meanings (prime, natural, square)
   c. process words (times, subtract, column)

*Science and Health*

1. See relationships.
2. Read charts, tables, graphs, and formulas.
3. Vary rate of reading according to purpose.
4. Read directions accurately.
5. Evaluate, draw conclusions, and make judgments.
6. Read and locate information from government publications and bulletins.
7. Fuse reading skills with steps in the scientific process.

*Social Studies*

1. Understand cause-and-effect structures.
2. Understand sequence of events.
3. Read and identify similarities and differences.
4. Follow directions.
5. Make inferences.
6. Read for main ideas and supporting details.
7. Read and differentiate fact from opinion.

courses in reading/language arts, social studies, mathematics, and science. The exploratory curriculum centers on essential and elective or enrichment courses in the fine arts, industrial arts, technology, and other areas. The idea behind the exploratory curriculum is for students to explore their aptitudes, interests, and special talents (Clark & Clark, 1994).

Although school districts vary in their selection of regular education curriculum sequences, some general themes can be identified for the subject matter of English, math, social studies, and science at the secondary level. Glatthorn (1988) identified the following themes of the grade 5–12 English curriculum: literature, language, composition, speaking and listening, critical thinking, and vocabulary development. The National Council of Teachers of Mathematics (NCTM) (1989) emphasizes the need for problem solving as the top priority in all math programs at both the elementary and secondary levels. This priority of regular education is reflected in an increase in problem-solving components in mathematics texts (Resnick & Resnick, 1985). Goals such as learning to reason and communicate mathematically are emphasized in all math content (NCTM, 1989).

In social studies, the typical themes are "World cultures and western hemispheres for Grade 6, World geography or history for Grade 7, American history for Grade 8, Civics or world cultures for Grade 9, World history for Grade 10, American history for Grade 11, and American government for Grade 12" (Polloway & Patton, 1993, p. 360). The National Council for Social Studies has identified the motifs of concern for self, others, ethics, and the world as appropriate for developing meaningful social studies instruction at the middle school level. Based on these motifs, Levy (1991) identifies the following general objectives of the secondary social studies curriculum: "(a) to develop problem-solving and decision-making skills that incorporate high ethical standards, (b) to develop skills and values associated with democratic citizenship, (c) to develop attitudes that reflect an awareness of the pluralistic, interdependent, and changing nature of the world community" (p. 8).

Although there is no generally accepted curriculum sequence in science education, science programs typically include subject matter from the areas of life science, physical science, and earth science (Polloway & Patton, 1993). Life science encompasses the study of living things, as in biology and ecology. Physical science is the study of nonliving things, as in chemistry and physics. Earth science includes the study of geology and astronomy. Most science curriculum objectives revolve around "the acquisition of relevant content and knowledge, the development of various inquiry-related skills, and the nurturing of a scientific attitude" (Polloway & Patton, 1993, p. 334).

Instead of isolated subject areas comprising the regular education curriculum, experts, particularly in the middle school setting, are suggesting an integrated approach (Rhodes & Dudley-Marling, 1988; Newman & Church, 1990). In this approach, subject matter is not presented in isolation; instead math, English, social studies, and science objectives focus on a central theme. For example, in the medieval history unit described in

Chapter 2, the math teacher had students draw angles to make stained glass windows, while the language arts teacher asked students to write about castle life. Kataoka and Lock (1995) present an integrated curriculum in teaching about whales and hermit crabs in their science program. Some activities included animal measurement in math, poetry books for reading, careers related to marine biology for social studies, and graphics of shoreline and ocean for computer studies. This type of curriculum enhances the skills and knowledge of students in a variety of disciplines (Levy, 1991).

## Parallel Curriculum

Many students with disabilities participate in the regular academic curricula as they attend regular classes. In the inclusive model, the special educator adjusts and alters some of the instructional strategies so that students can meet the general goals and objectives. However, some students with mild disabilities enroll in a parallel curriculum. Often this curriculum presents the learner with fewer instructional areas and less complexity (Bigge, 1988). It is a content-centered substitute that allows students to gather information through methods other than reading (Wiseman & Hartwell, 1979). Frequently, students master fewer skills and objectives. Many states have basic textbooks for secondary students with mild handicaps that parallel the regular secondary content in social studies, science, English, and math content.

Perhaps the most widely recognized parallel curriculum is the Parallel Alternate Curriculum (PAC) model developed at Arizona State University as part of the network of Child Service Demonstration Centers (Wiseman & Hartwell, 1979) funded by the federal government to study secondary programs for students with learning disabilities. The PAC program modifies mainstream content demands and presents required high school courses using taped books, videotaped materials, movies, lectures, and discussions (Ariel, 1992). You may want to check with your school district or state Department of Education for parallel curriculum programs.

## Remedial Curriculum

It is also possible to find remedial materials to teach academic content at the secondary level. Corrective Mathematics (Engelmann & Carnine, 1982a), Corrective Reading (Engelmann, Becker, Hanner, & Johnson, 1988, 1989), and Corrective Spelling through Morphographs (Dixon & Engelmann, 1980) are remedial programs that can be used in a secondary setting. These remedial programs concentrate on basic skills instruction rather than on using reading, math, and written expression as tools for gaining and expressing information. Corrective Mathematics is a remedial program in basic math for students who have not mastered the basic skills of addition, subtraction, multiplication, and division. The program, designed for students in third through twelfth grade, also includes higher-level operations and story problems. Corrective Reading is designed for students in grades 4 through 12 who have not mastered decoding and comprehension skills. Corrective Spelling through Morphographs is for students in fourth grade and above and covers more than 12,000 words. The program emphasizes basic units of meaning, or morphographs, that are always spelled according to specific rules. Students learn to generalize these rules to new words.

## Functional Curriculum

The functional curriculum includes skills and learning experiences that assist students in the areas of personal/social, daily independent living, and occupational adjustment (Clark, 1994). It is sometimes referred to as life skills instruction (Brolin, 1993; Clark, 1991). Although functional curriculum is not a new concept, its emphasis has moved from experiences appropriate only for students with severe disabilities to those with mild disabilities. The curriculum emphasizes practical skills relevant to the "real world" (Meier, 1995) and answers the question "Will I need it when I'm 21?" (Burns & Shipstead, 1989). Instead of practicing decimals with worksheets, students practice decimals in the daily living activity of writing checks and balancing a checkbook. Materials such as calculators and newspapers are often a part of the functional curriculum.

In the Dubuque Iowa Community schools, functional life skills content is integrated into the high school science curriculum (Helmke, Havekost, Patton, & Poloway, 1994). The course, Science for Living, integrates 28 major life demands—such as "planning nutrition and diet, exercising, using medicine, administering simple first aid, knowing how the body fights disease, and recognizing signs of health problems" (p. 53)—with basic science content.

Some curriculum models and curriculum packages include the Community-Referenced Curriculum (Smith & Schloss, 1988), Community Living Skills Taxonomy (Dever, 1988), Hawaii Transition Project (1987), and Life Centered Career Education curriculum programs (Brolin, 1993). See Box 8.2 for examples of functional skills adapted from the Academy of Life Centered Career Education (as printed in the 1994 Specialized Curriculum for Exceptional Learners Instructor's Manual) and Bender and Valletutti (1982).

BOX 8.2

## Sample Functional Skills

### Math

1. Comparing weight and height measurements of an individual from year to year
2. Comparison shopping for cheaper products
3. Budgeting expenses
4. Computing weekly net pay
5. Computing interest payments on loans

### Reading

1. Using a phone directory to locate a person's phone number
2. Reading labels on prepared foods to check nutritional values
3. Ordering food from a restaurant menu
4. Locating information in a driver's education manual
5. Checking the TV listings for descriptions and times of programs
6. Identifying fact and fiction in written advertisements

### Writing

1. Completing catalog forms
2. Writing letters to the editor
3. Composing accurate phone messages
4. Filling out job applications, credit card applications, and other forms
5. Using word processing programs

### Social Studies

1. Identifying major points on a city map
2. Identifying key national political figures such as the president, senators, and representatives
3. Describing cultural characteristics of family background
4. Comparing features of community transportation systems

**BOX 8.2**
*(continued)*

---

*History*

1. Discussing major historical events of the community
2. Naming and understanding the reason for major holidays
3. Identifying individual basic rights
4. Learning the national anthem

*Science and Biology*

1. Planting a garden
2. Caring for houseplants
3. Developing nutritional menu plans
4. Calculating fat grams

---

The Individuals with Disabilities Education Act (IDEA) mandates addressing functional curriculum needs through transition planning for all students by age 16 (see Chapter 12). The functional curriculum centers around the roles of the student as a resident of the home, a learner in the school setting, a participant in the community, a consumer of goods and services, a worker, and a participant in leisure experiences (Bender & Valletutti, 1982). The purpose is to create independent learners who can function in postsecondary settings. We discuss functional curriculum at greater length in Chapters 11 and 12.

---

**COMPREHENSION MONITORING OF KEY CONCEPTS**

*The Secondary Academic Curriculum*

1. Curriculum answers the questions *what* (scope), *when* (sequence), and *whom* (target audience).
2. Methodology or instructional strategies answer the question *how*.
3. Some sources of curriculum include curriculum guides or standards, teachers' manuals, scope and sequence charts from texts, and criterion-referenced tests.

*(continued on next page)*

4. Special education curriculum generally breaks down to four different orientations: "(a) Basic skills models that primarily emphasize the remediation of academic deficits, (b) Social skills and life-adjustment models, (c) Learning strategies models, and (d) Functional orientations of vocational training and adult outcomes" (Sands et al., 1995, p. 69).

5. In regular secondary education, academic curriculum centers on using reading, math, and writing as tools for learning.

6. General themes exist in each of the subject areas of English, math, social studies, and science at the secondary level.

7. The special education curriculum may include the general academic curriculum, parallel curriculum, remedial curriculum, and functional curriculum.

8. Parallel curriculum contains less complexity and fewer skills than the regular curriculum and modifies the content demands, especially in the area of reading.

9. Remedial curriculum emphasizes basic math, reading, and language arts skills.

10. Functional curriculum prepares students in the areas of personal/social, daily living, and occupational adjustments. It emphasizes practical skills necessary for independent living.

## Academic Content Area Instruction

In this section, we examine two different methods of teaching academic content to secondary students: the single textbook approach and the unit teaching approach. These approaches may be used to teach a variety of subject areas, including English, math, social studies, and science.

### The Single Textbook Approach

Teachers often use grade-level texts to teach academic information to students with mild disabilities. Grade-level texts frequently pose problems for students with mild disabilities as they often contain many abstract concepts and difficult vocabulary, are poorly organized, repeat information infrequently, and present numerous facts and ideas in a relatively small space (Olson & Platt, 1996). In an examination of ten American history texts at the eighth-grade level, Kinder, Bursuck, and Epstein (1992) found that all were rated one or more years above grade level in readability, only 30% reviewed information from the previous chapter, and only 5% had questions at the beginning of the chapter to prepare the reader for gaining information. McLeod and Armstrong (1982) report that middle school, junior high, and high school teachers of students with learning disabilities find that most mathematics texts do not provide enough practice activities for their students.

Even with these problems with content-area texts, students and teachers often select them. Secondary teachers selected teacher adaptation of mainstream texts as the primary approach for teaching math to students with learning disabilities (McLeod & Armstrong, 1982), while middle school students with learning disabilities selected the basal reader as their favorite approach to reading over four other choices (Reetz & Hoover, 1992). Since both teachers and students often select texts for the teaching of content subjects, we discuss two approaches to use with a textbook. One involves selecting considerate texts (Armbruster & Anderson, 1988); the other is a four-step plan of preparation, readiness, guided reading, and follow-up.

### *Select Considerate Texts*

A considerate text is a text that can be read, understood, and learned from with relative ease. Armbruster and Anderson (1988) suggest that teachers select a considerate text on the basis of *structure, coherence,* and *audience appropriateness.*

*Structure* is the arrangement of ideas in a text. Research shows that a reader remembers more information and engages in higher-level cognitive processing when a text is well organized (Armbruster & Anderson, 1988). Well-organized texts depict important information using titles, previews, and pointer words ("first") or phrases ("the third step"). Well-organized texts also use textual cues such as highlighting and consistent structure to organize information. For example, a text that discusses each planet in our solar system is consistent if the information about the different planets is similarly organized. If the section on Saturn includes information about the planet's size, its physical structure, its distance from the sun, and its ability to sustain life, then the section on Earth should include the same information in the same order.

A *coherent* text is one in which ideas are connected together logically and explicitly so that students do not have to guess at the connection. For example, a student must make the connection that mammals have hair and are warm-blooded from the following two sentences: "A dog is a mammal. A dog has hair and is warm-blooded." However, with the sentence "A dog is a mammal because a dog has hair and is warm-blooded," the student does not have to make the connection because the connection is explicitly stated.

*Audience appropriateness* refers to the match between the main ideas of the text and the reader's level of knowledge and skills. Research shows a strong correlation between reading comprehension and memory, on the one hand, and a student's knowledge of the topic and vocabulary, on the other (Armbruster & Anderson, 1988). A considerate text elaborates or gives detailed explanations of topics that are typically unfamiliar to students and defines unfamiliar vocabulary.

Box 8.3 presents some questions you can ask to check if the content-area text you are using or plan to use is considerate. The questions deal with structure, coherence, and audience appropriateness.

### Use Four-Step Plan

We recommend a four-step plan adapted from Brown (1991) for teaching students with disabilities to comprehend content from a text. The four steps are (1) preparation, (2) readiness, (3) guided reading, and (4) follow-up. We first discuss each step in turn and then present an extended example in which a teacher uses this four-step approach to teach secondary students with mild disabilities from a tenth-grade physical science text.

***Step 1: Preparation.*** In the preparation step, the teacher identifies the objectives for the lesson, the information to emphasize, and the adaptations that may be necessary for the students to learn the information. The teacher also completes a task analysis of the independent practice items to determine how the student must demonstrate knowledge of the information.

The teacher begins by examining both the teacher's guide and the student's text. Teachers' guides often state the objectives, list key concepts, and define vocabulary terms and identify discussion questions. They frequently include test items, and sometimes the guides even identify material that may cause problems and the common mistakes that students make. The student's text shows how the information is presented and lists questions or independent exercises for the students to complete.

A check of both the teacher's guide and the student's text suggests adaptations that may be necessary. For example, a check of the teacher's guide in a geometry textbook recommends that teachers bring in three-dimensional models to supplement the textbook presentation of parallel relationships. Besides adding concrete materials, common adaptations include adding more guided practice activities, organizing concepts into steps, highlighting key concepts in students' texts, relating content to students' experiences,

**BOX 8.3**

## Suggestions for Evaluating Textbooks

(A "yes" answer to each question denotes a considerate text.)

### Questions Dealing with Structure

1. Are the headings and subheadings organized consistently with subject information?
2. Is the information organized in the same manner for all similar topics?
3. Do headings specifically tell the reader about the content of the section?
4. Are pointer words such as *first, second,* and *third* used to designate a sequence or listlike pattern?
5. Are pointer phrases such as *in contrast* and *on the other hand* used to signal a compare/contrast organization?

### Questions Dealing with Coherence

1. Are explicit or obvious connectives such as *because, since,* and *therefore* used to explain a relationship?
2. Are pronoun references clear?
3. Are shifts in topic smooth?
4. Are chronological sequences presented in the same order as their actual occurrences in time?
5. Are graphic aids clearly related to the text?
   a. Do they aid in understanding the information?
   b. Are they clearly referenced so the reader can find them?
   c. Are they easy to read and interpret?
   d. Are they clearly titled or labeled?

### Questions Dealing with Audience Appropriateness

1. Do detailed explanations accompany unfamiliar topics?
2. Is unfamiliar vocabulary defined?
3. Is adequate background information provided?
4. Is the text appropriate for the reader's level of knowledge and skills?

adding more independent practice activities using content enhancement, reading text as a group, and paraphrasing the text information.

***Step 2: Develop readiness.*** Next, the teacher tries to activate prior knowledge before students read the text. The teacher may attempt to activate background knowledge by presenting the students with an overview and asking them to discuss the information. For example, Putnam and Wesson (1990), in their inquiry lesson plan, began by presenting two food chain charts to students. They then asked the students in pairs to discuss what the charts meant and, after the teacher posed some questions, to write a hypothesis.

Another way to activate prior knowledge is to use prediction activities (Ogle, 1986; Ruiz, 1989) and the PreReading Plan (PReP) (Langer, 1981). Ruiz recommends the following prediction routine for students with disabilities from diverse cultures. First, teachers identify the major idea of the lesson. Then, they ask the students to share any similar experiences of their own and to predict what they will learn. In other prediction routines, students discuss what they know before they begin the lesson, identify what they have learned at the end, and then compare the two (Orange County Public Schools, 1986).

In the PReP technique, the teacher selects a key word or phase or shows a related picture before instruction begins, to stimulate group brainstorming. The teacher then asks the students to "Say anything that comes to mind associated with the word, phrase, or picture." Next, the teacher asks questions, such as "What made you think of that word?" that require students to explain their associations. In the final step, the teacher asks such questions as "Are there any new ideas after our discussion?" With this question, the students can modify and rethink the linkages between their prior knowledge and the new information presented by other students.

Cooper (1986) recommends bringing in concrete objects, showing a film, or presenting role-playing simulations to help build background information for the Native American student who may not have the necessary prior knowledge to understand text information. For example, a teacher may bring in pioneer tools and clothing to help build background for a unit on the westward movement (Brown, 1991). The teacher who uses vocabulary maps (see Chapter 7) and introduces new vocabulary terms also builds a student's background knowledge. Graham and Johnson (1989) recommend that teachers present an outline of important facts and concepts, with their relationships, to introduce science and social studies materials.

***Step 3: Guided reading.*** Cooper (1986) suggests that teachers now introduce the organization of the text, focus the students' attention on pictures, ask students to predict questions that the text will answer, pose purpose-setting questions, pair students with reading partners, and prepare students to summarize materials. Smith and Schloss (1990) suggest silent reading, questions and discussion, and then purposeful oral rereading at this step.

Ellis and Lenz (1987) suggest a student self-monitoring strategy during reading. Identified by the mnemonic FIST, students taught this strategy ask questions as they read textbook passages:

F = First sentence in the paragraph is read.

I = Indicate a question based on information in the first sentence.

S = Search for the answer to the question.

T = Tie the answer to the question with a paraphrase.

Mercer and Mercer (1993) suggest that teachers teach students a skimming strategy to identify the main ideas of a chapter: (1) Read the title and headings. (2) Reach the first few paragraphs. (3) Read the first sentence of each subsequent paragraph since this is where the main idea is usually found. (4) Read the captions and study illustrations. (5) Read the conclusion or summary at the end of the chapter.

We suggest the following procedures as you guide the students through the reading of the text:

1. Have the students first read the questions that they are expected to complete at the end of the selection.

2. Write the questions on the board or on a transparency and ask students if they think they know any of the answers.

3. Write down the students' answers.

4. Before asking the students to read a section silently, examine the headings and subheadings with them.

5. Have students read the section orally.

6. Discuss the selection, relating the information to student experiences if possible.

7. During the discussion, bring in concrete materials if necessary, or have the students perform the activity that is described.

8. Direct students to see if the reading has answered any of the questions previously written on the board.

9. Continue with the next section, repeating Steps 4–8.

10. At the end of the lesson, summarize the major information and the answers to the questions.

Another instructional technique that can be used during students' reading of the text is reciprocal teaching. Reciprocal teaching is "a dialogue between teachers and students for the purpose of jointly constructing the meaning of the text" (Palincsar, 1986, p. 119). At first, the instruction is teacher-directed, but then the teacher acts more as a facilitator as students ask each other questions and assist one another in constructing meaning from the text (Olson & Platt, 1996). We discuss reciprocal teaching extensively in Chapter 9.

***Step 4: Follow-up.*** Cooper (1986) identifies follow-up activities as a reinforcement, extension, or application of the concepts and skills. Reinforcement requires that the students practice the skill. With extension and application, the students use the concept or skill in a different way. Brown (1991) recommends that follow-up activities build on students' interests, skills, and talents and that the activities include written, oral, and visual experiences.

The components of this four-step plan have a strong research basis. Active participation, activating students' background knowledge, encouraging students to generate questions and predictions, and relating content to students' interests are effective strategies for teaching secondary students with mild disabilities.

### Sample Science Content Lesson Using the Four-Step Plan

***Step 1: Preparation.*** Mr. Robertson turns to the teacher's guide for the tenth-grade text *Physical Science: Investigating Matter and Energy* (Marshall & Jacobs, 1987) and finds the following objectives for Chapter Two:

1. To define volume, graduated cylinder, and meniscus.
2. To state the fact that 1 milliliter is the same as 1 cubic centimeter.
3. To measure liquid volumes. (p. 7)

He decides to teach all the objectives. He rewrites them to add criterion, condition, and overlearning. For example, he changes Objective 3 to read "Presented with a worksheet, the students will measure liquid volume correctly 7 out of 8 times for two lessons." He then completes a task analysis of the chapter test and finds questions that require students to remember the definitions of graduated cylinder and meniscus (Objective 1), to measure liquid volumes (Objective 3), and to write the answer in either mL or cc (Objective 2).

Mr. Robertson then reads the student's text selection and discovers what information is presented, and how. Definitions of the terms, procedures for measuring liquid volume, two pictures of cylinders containing water, and four independent practice problems are included. From a task analysis of the practice items, he finds that students must read the volume in two different cylinders for two of the problems, and in two other problems they must draw and shade in each of the pictured cylinders when the volume is specified.

He also identifies the following adaptations that he will need to make in the text information for the students: (1) Simplify vocabulary, using student's restatement of text definitions. (2) Simplify measuring concepts, using steps. (3) Bring in more concrete examples of cylinders, including everyday kinds of cylinders. (4) Add more measuring activities. (5) Add more guided practice items. (6) Add more independent practice items to the four items in the text.

***Step 2: Develop readiness.*** Before asking students to read the text, Mr. Robertson brings in the students' background information by asking questions about familiar measures, such as "How do we measure weight? When someone asks you how much you weigh, you say 'I weigh 120 (what?).'" He continues to activate students' background knowledge by discussing liters that are in their experience, so he brings in a two-liter plastic soda bottle. He asks students how much soda is in the bottle. He also brings in familiar types of graduated cylinders, such as a shot glass and a glass measuring cup.

***Step 3: Guided reading.*** During this step, Mr. Robertson has students read the first three paragraphs, which contain the definitions of volume and graduated cylinder (see Objective 1) and the relationship of milliliters and cubic centimeters (see Objective 2). He stops the oral reading and discusses with the students the definitions of the terms, pointing out the picture of the graduated cylinder. He asks the students to define the terms in their own words as he writes their definitions on a transparency. He then asks students to copy these definitions in their glossaries. He again brings in the everyday examples of the two-liter soda bottle, the shot glass, and the glass measuring cup, along with other graduated cylinders from the science lab, as the group discusses graduated cylinders and the use of liters and cubic centimeters in measuring the amount of liquid.

The students then return to reading the next section of the text to find the definition of meniscus (see Objective 1). Mr. Robertson directs the students' attention to the picture of a meniscus and cylinder in the text. He shows an acetate of two other cylinders for the students to practice labeling meniscus.

The students then read the final selection, which in paragraph form tells students how to measure the volume of liquid in a cylinder and how to read the scales from different sizes of graduated cylinders (see Objective 3). Mr. Robertson supplements this text material by dividing the procedure into steps with pictures. For example, he writes the first step on the acetate—"Look at the long lines next to each other on a graduated cylinder"—and draws a cylinder with lines. He then writes each of the following steps and asks students to come up with illustrations to go along with the steps. After listing the steps with illustrations, he models how to measure the volume of a cylinder.

He then divides the students into pairs and gives each pair a cylinder filled with water that they must measure using the steps. They write down the volume. He continues to fill and empty the cylinders, giving the students more practice items as they continue to read and write down the volume. Finally, he tells the students to empty their cylinders and to fill them up so that they have 2 centimeters of water, 25 centimeters, and 10 milliliters. He circulates around the room to check each pair. He then gives them pictures of these same cylinders and directs them to shade in specified volumes.

*Step 4: Follow-up.* To reinforce measurement skills, Mr. Robertson has the students independently complete a worksheet, which assesses their knowledge of definitions, the relationship between millimeter and cubic centimeter, and measuring volume. The worksheet contains five fill-in-the-blank items requiring definition and relationship answers and eight items requiring the students to shade in the amount and to read the volume. Then Mr. Robertson directs the students in groups of three to review the definitions written in their glossaries, to summarize how to measure volume, and to include the summary in their science journals. For homework, he asks students to interview their parents or others on their use of volume measurements.

## The Unit Teaching Approach

The unit teaching approach is not built around a specific textbook; instead, multiple texts are often used. Thematic units are frequently used at the secondary level. Swicegood and Parsons (1991) describe a thematic unit for students with disabilities as an approach that "integrates reading, writing, and speaking experiences at a remedial level while fostering active and strategic study of the content" (p. 112).

The University of Kansas Center for Research on Learning has designed graphics and a teaching routine to assist teachers using this approach (Lenz, 1992). The two graphics are the Unit Organizer and the Expanded Unit Map (see Figures 8.1 and 8.2).

**FIGURE 8.1** Unit Organizer

NAME _____
DATE _____

BIGGER PICTURE
Regions of the World

LAST UNIT/Experience
Grasslands

CURRENT UNIT
Deserts

NEXT UNIT/Experience
Forests

UNIT MAP

is about . . .

Different types of barren regions where water is scarce.

Chapter 10

such as — Tropical Deserts

such as — Temperate Deserts

such as — Cold Deserts

such as — Semi-arid Deserts

| | | |
|---|---|---|
| 4/17 | Introduce unit organizer | |
| 4/18 | Describe types of deserts | |
| 4/19 | Read pp. 1–6 in Chapter 10 | |
| 4/20 | Make desert collages | |
| 4/21 | Show video on deserts | |
| 4/24 | Discuss pp. 7–12 | |
| 4/26 | Complete a cloze activity on desert types | |
| 4/27 | Read pp. 12–18 | |
| 4/28 | Discuss cold deserts | |
| 4/17 | Construct a bulletin board of cold desert climate, vegetation, and animals | |
| 5/1 | Write a journal entry called: "One Day in the Gobi Desert" | |
| 5/2 | Review | |
| 5/3 | Test | |

Unit Self-test Questions

1. In what ways do tropical, temperate, cold, and semi-arid deserts differ?
2. How do desert plants get water?
3. How do desert animals withstand the extreme heat of the desert?
4. What are three examples of desert vegetation?

UNIT
RELATIONSHIPS

compare/contrast

cause/effect

descriptive

*Source:* The Unit Organizer Routine (Instructor's Manual) by B. K. Lenz, J. A. Bulgren, J. B. Schumaker, D. D. Deshler, and D. A. Boudah. Copyright © 1994 Edge Enterprises. Reprinted by permission. The Unit Organizer and Expanded Unit Map are instructional tools developed at the University of Kansas Center for Research on Learning.

# FIGURE 8.2 Expanded Unit Map

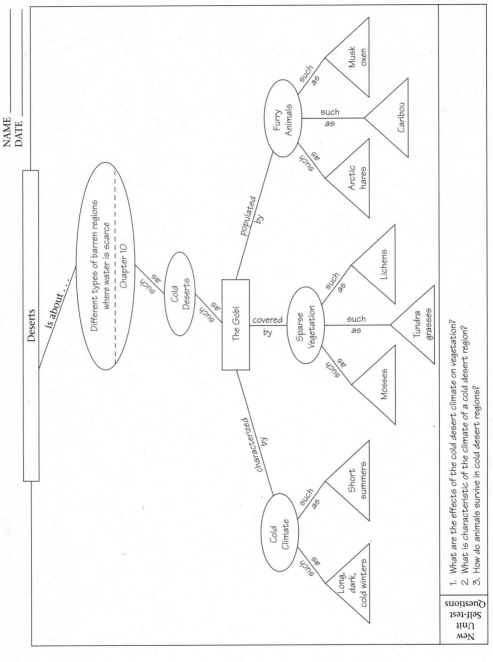

*Source: The Unit Organizer Routine (Instructor's Manual)* by B. K. Lenz, J. A. Bulgren, J. B. Schumaker, D. D. Deshler, and D. A. Boudah. Copyright © 1994 Edge Enterprises. Reprinted by permission. The Unit Organizer and Expanded Unit Map are instructional tools developed at the University of Kansas Center for Research on Learning.

The Unit Organizer (Figure 8.1) is "a graphic worksheet used by the teacher and students to chart, monitor, and review the direction of a unit" (Lenz et al., 1994, p. 1). It contains the major topics, subtopics, and connecting words or phrases. The connecting words or phrases show relationships among topics and subtopics. For example, in Figure 8.1, the main topic Deserts leads to four subtopics or certain types of deserts: tropical, temperate, cold, and semi-arid. The connecting phrase "such as" connects the topic Desert to each of the subtopics or certain types of deserts. The Unit Organizer also contains a schedule of tasks and activities developed by the teacher, self-test questions developed by both teacher and students, and unit relationships, which can be specified by the teacher or by both teacher and students.

The Expanded Unit Map takes each subtopic of the unit and expands on it. For example, in Figure 8.2, we have expanded on the subtopic "cold deserts." Again, connecting phrases are used to indicate the relationships between the subtopic and the details.

Three different teaching routines accompany the visuals: one for introducing the unit (Cue), one for daily instruction (Do), and one for follow-up (Review) (Lenz et al., 1994). The reader is referred to the Content Enhancement Series (Edge Enterprises, Inc.) on unit organization for further information.

In using the unit teaching approach, the basic steps are (1) think about and choose possible topics, (2) construct the unit content, (3) plan activities and experiences, and (4) evaluate both content and process. We will discuss each of these steps in turn.

### Think About and Choose Possible Topics

As previously mentioned, usually state and local education agencies identify the curricular requirements for various grade levels. For example, "Man's Relationship to the Environment" is a general theme in an eleventh-grade history course, "The Human Body" is a general topic found in a middle school science program, and "More Colorful Writing" is a general theme found in a tenth-grade English course (Orange County Public Schools, 1986).

Swicegood and Parsons (1991) suggest that students decide on the final topic selection. We find that it is easier for students to do this if the teacher first tells a little bit about each topic and then asks students to share the information they already know. For example, after Ms. Corso read a brief newspaper article about global warming and another article about the works of Thoreau, the students in her varying exceptionalities history class selected People's Relationship to the Environment as the topic for their next unit.

### Construct the Unit Content

Next, the students and you may wish to devise the subtopics together and then ask similar general questions about each of these subtopics. For example, Ms. Corso and her students identified pollution, the growth of industries, exploitation of energy sources, misuse of natural resources, and the population growth as subtopics to study more extensively in their exploration of People's Relationship to the Environment. They then devised the following questions to answer about each of the subtopics: (1) How has ____ affected the environment? (2) How has _____ changed over the years? (3) What are some of the benefits of _____, if any? (4) What types of problems have been created by _____? (5) What do scientists think will happen in the future? (6) How might we solve these problems? The students then divided into cooperative groups to research questions concerning the subtopic of their choice.

You may also create a content outline or lead the students to decide as a group the questions they would like to answer about the topic (Swicegood & Parsons, 1991). Newspapers, easy-to-read texts, videotapes, and encyclopedias are good resources.

### Plan Activities and Experiences

Activities may include (1) speaking and listening activities, such as debates, role plays, and interviews; (2) organizational activities, such as outlining, note taking, and self-talk; (3) reading activities, such as assisted reading, and constructing tree diagrams and webs; and (4) written expression activities, such as journals and diaries, shared writing, and research papers (Swicegood & Parsons, 1991).

After researching their assigned topics, Ms. Corso and her students talked about possible activities. The cooperative group presenting information on pollution decided to monitor the hallways near the class and chart the amount of litter on the ground at various times of day. The group examining the growth of industries decided to interview a couple of business executives to get their perspectives on the relationship between their companies and the environment. The group investigating population growth decided to research and chart the population growth of their own high school over the previous four years.

After deciding on activities, the next step is to brainstorm with students ways for them to share their information. Options may include oral reports, written reports, posters, role plays, and models. For example, the group that was studying pollution in Ms. Corso's class decided to report the answers to their questions and other information in a "Don't Pollute" newsletter.

### Evaluate Content and Process

Swicegood and Parsons (1991) suggest the use of alternative evaluation procedures to measure both the content and the process of student learning. These evaluation procedures may include "traditional tests and grades, rating scales, teacher-made surveys, holistic scoring of writing, types of questions and points raised, comparing of work samples over time and anecdotal logs on the class" (p. 116).

If you select a traditional paper-and-pencil test, you may want to have cooperative groups each turn in five exam questions derived from the general questions they address. These questions, in turn, are included in a study guide. Lenz (1992) suggests that students answer self-test questions and even create their own visual representation of a unit. The students can also use the questions to prepare for the quizzes and tests, and to close the unit.

Here again, the unit teaching approach contains teaching techniques that we know are research-based. Active participation, meaningful learning, student-generated questions, and integration of content are supported in the research literature.

---

**COMPREHENSION MONITORING OF KEY CONCEPTS**

### Academic Content Area Instruction

1. Single texts or multiple texts may be used in teaching content to secondary students with mild disabilities.

2. Two alternatives for the single textbook option are selecting considerate texts and following a four-step plan.

3. Teachers evaluate structure, coherence, and audience appropriateness to select a considerate text.

4. A structured text is one that displays a well-organized arrangement of ideas; a coherent text is one in which ideas are connected together logically and explicitly so that students do not have to guess at the connection; audience appropriateness checks the match between the main ideas of the text and the reader's level of knowledge and skills.

5. The steps of the four-step plan are (1) preparation, (2) developing vocabulary and background, (3) guided reading, and (4) follow-up.

6. The unit teaching approach integrates subject matter around a theme or focus and engages students in active and strategic study of content.

*(continued on next page)*

7. Steps for creating a unit are choosing a topic, constructing the unit content, planning activities and experiences, and evaluating the content and process of student learning.

8. If the procedures of active participation, meaningful learning, student-generated questions, and activation of students' prior knowledge are employed, then either the single textbook approach or the unit teaching approach is supported in the teacher effectiveness research literature.

## Using Technology to Teach Academic Content

Teachers can use software programs, videodiscs, and CD-ROMs to create multimedia presentations that supplement and enhance instruction in the content areas. Multimedia involves "the integration of visual, graphic, audio, and textual information through the control of a computer" (Speziale & LaFrance, 1992, p. 31). It makes your computer act more as a television set.

Multimedia applications should be integrated into the lesson. Roblyer (1989) suggests that teachers first review their curriculum and identify topics or skills that warrant the use of multimedia applications, based on the following characteristics: (1) They are difficult for students to understand; (2) they present hurdles for students that interfere with the major objectives of the lesson, such as too much calculation, handwriting, and other skills irrelevant to meeting the major objectives; (3) they require extensive homework; (4) they present uninteresting or tedious materials; or (5) they require materials that are not available.

### Computer Software

There are many software programs available for the production of transparencies, banners, posters, and other visuals to assist in teacher presentation of content information. CrossMaster (Focus) is a software program that automatically builds puzzles from words and clues provided by the teacher. Print Shop (Brøderbund), and Create with Garfield (DLM) are examples of programs that combine both text and graphics to create visuals to enhance any lesson presentation. PowerPoint (Microsoft) can be used to create transparency masters, several small versions of the transparencies, or an outline on a single page for students to follow along during the lesson. When using transparencies, star important points, underline details, and expose only one line of information at a time (Lambie, 1983).

© Kent Reno/Jeroboam

*Secondary students use computers to prepare reports.*

Slide Shop (Scholastic) and VCR Companion (Brøderbund) are user-friendly programs that allow teachers to create either text or graphic screen slides, with color and special effects, to produce a slide show (Szulanczyk, 1992). The slide show is transferred to videotape simply by connecting a single cable from the computer to a videocassette recorder.

Software such as Decisions, Decisions (Tom Synder Productions) is designed to help teachers effectively use one computer to teach historical or contemporary issues in a dynamic "you are there" format. A teacher can present the program to a large group of students by connecting the computer to a large television monitor or to an LCD panel for overhead projection.

## Videodisc

A videodisc looks like an old-fashioned record. Videodiscs come in either 8- or 12-inch formats and store both video and audio information that cannot be erased. The videodisc can store up to 30 minutes of full motion video or 54,000 still images, and up to one hour of audio, on each side of the disc (Salpeter, 1990). In many programs, a variety of software and print documentation accompanies the videodisc. Woodward and Gersten (1993) list the following advantages of videodisc technology: (1) inclusion of both visual and narrative presentations, (2) relative ease of use, (3) the ability to embed effective instruction principles into the presentation, and (4) facilitation of group instruction. Bottge and Hasselbring (1993) found that a videodisc program that involved students in solving real-world problems increased the ability of ninth-grade students in remedial math classes to generalize these problem-solving skills to other tasks.

A videodisc series recommended for students with disabilities is Mastering Fractions (System Impact), which incorporates the effective teaching strategies of mastery learning, guided practice, and well-structured sequences to teach fractions. Woodward and Gersten (1993) describe a sample lesson involving a 3-minute presentation of the concept of reducing fractions with computer graphics and narration.

> The videodisc program presents a set of two to four guided practice problems. Each set is a still frame, and the teacher advances to the next frame when all the students are ready. Students copy the problems from the screen onto paper at their desks and work the problems; the teacher then presents the next frame showing the same problems and their answers. The videodisc then shows another set of problems or presents a "decision menu" for the teacher, directing her to different sections of the videodisc depending on student performance over the set of guided practice problems. (p. 144)

Woodward and Gersten report positive results for the program in increasing the math skills of secondary students with mild disabilities.

Unlike Mastery Fractions, most current videodisc programs function as instructional supplements, with teachers clicking on pictures or audio clips in the videodisc program to enhance their lectures (Woodward & Gersten, 1993). A videodisc series recommended as a supplement for students with special needs is ABC News Interactive (Hasselbring & Goin, 1993). The U.S. government, communism, AIDS, substance abuse, teen sexuality, and the lives of famous people are some of the topics found in this ABC series.

You operate a videodisc in the same fashion as a videocassette by connecting the videodisc player to a television monitor. However, unlike a videocassette recorder, which requires rewinding and pausing to find a particular section, frames in a videodisc can be easily accessed and frozen on the screen, and can be played in any order. Standard remotes are used to access numbered frames, freeze numbered frames, and step forward and backward. For example, if you are presenting information on animal behaviors, you can turn to the list of images and video clips in the directory or teacher's guide and choose visuals and audio to enhance the presentation. Simply use the buttons on the remote control to jump to the frame numbers listed in the directory. You can click on these pictures to hear an audio clip of a loon's mating call, see a video clip of two elks in ritual battle, or view a still shot of a rhinoceros caring for its young. In addition to frame numbers, many directories now include bar codes, similar to the food labels at supermarkets. Instead of using the remote, you simply pass a pen-shaped scanner over the bar code that is printed next to the object's description. A teacher can position the videodisc player and television monitor in front of the room for group instruction and, with the remote or bar-code scanner, operate the program from a distance while monitoring and giving feedback to individual students (Woodward & Gersten, 1993).

Instead of searching through the guide each time to find a video or audio clip, you can use software such as Bar'N'Coder (Pioneer) to enter into the computer ahead of time a sequence of bar codes or frame numbers from the videodisc. For example, if you are presenting a lecture on substance abuse, using Bar'N'Coder, you can select items from the videodisc program of ABC News Interactive to supplement your lecture simply by entering the bar codes of the items you want into the computer's database and printing your list of bar codes. Now, using your computer printout of bar codes, you simply scan the appropriate bar code to call up a graph of the number of teenagers who abuse alcohol as you discuss the prevalence of alcohol abuse.

## Hypermedia

You can use HyperCard (Apple), AmigaVision (Commodore), or LinkWay (IBM) hypermedia programs to create a multimedia lesson using a computer. These tools allow you to combine text, graphics, animation, movie clips, and sound in the presentation of information.

Hypermedia programs link together a variety of electronic devices, including television monitors, videodiscs, CD-ROMs, videocassette recorders, and, of course, the computer (Byrom, 1990). They let you create a deck or stack of screens or cards that are interrelated and cross-referenced by hot spots or buttons on each card (Ray & Warden, 1995). Buttons link information between cards. "These buttons may be programmed to perform several functions, such as: move to another screen, launch another application, play a sound, start an animation, keep a running test score, or play a Quick-Time movie, videodisc or CD-ROM" (FDLRS/TECH, 1994). For example, in a history lesson on the Civil War, you can create a map of the country on the first card or screen, with buttons located at Atlanta, Gettysburg, and other battle sites. A click on one of these buttons leads to another card or screen. A click on Atlanta, for example, might call up information on Sherman and his forces, while a click on Gettysburg leads to a screen showing a picture of Lincoln and an audio of the Gettysburg Address taken from a videodisc. A click on Sherman, in turn, could lead to a quick written profile on the man. Thus, hypermedia lets you access information in a non-sequential fashion.

## CD-ROM

Similar to an audio CD, a 4¾-inch CD-ROM (Compact Disc–Read Only Memory) can hold up to 250,000 pages of text or 74 minutes of high-fidelity sound (Male, 1988). Data are stored digitally and then played back via a computer interface (Hasselbring & Goin, 1993). Nothing can be written on the disc. Specialized retrieval software allows users to search quickly through a large amount of material. Entire sets of encyclopedias, references, periodicals, and newspapers are frequently stored on CD-ROMs (Lathrop, 1992).

For example, one CD-ROM disc, Compton's Multimedia Encyclopedia (Encyclopedia Britannica), contains the complete 26-volume *Compton's Encyclopedia*—9 million words, 32,000 articles, 15,000 pictures and diagrams, 60 minutes of sound, and 800 maps—plus the *Merriam-Webster Intermediate Dictionary*. Multimedia tools, including Picture Explorer, Idea Search, Title Finder, Topic Tree, U.S. History Timeline, Word Atlas, Science Feature Articles, Research Assistant, and On-line Notebook, help users find what they want (FDLRS/TECH, 1991). With these features, you can browse through pictures, find summaries of significant historical events, zoom in on any geographical area, explore science topics with graphics, animation, sound, and special summaries, and find about 300 thought-provoking, research-oriented questions designed to develop writing and critical thinking skills. What a boon to make your academic content lessons more exciting, interesting, and current.

---

**COMPREHENSION MONITORING OF KEY CONCEPTS**

### Using Technology to Teach Academic Content

1. Multimedia involves "the integration of visual, graphic, audio, and textual information through the control of a computer" (Speziale & LaFrance, 1992).

2. Teachers can use software programs to create transparencies, banners, posters, and supplemental visual materials.

3. A computer can be connected to a large television monitor or to an LCD panel for overhead projection to present a program to the whole class.

4. The standard videodisc can store full motion video, still images, and audio on both sides of the disc.

5. Teachers can operate a videodisc by connecting the videodisc player to a television monitor and using a standard remote to access numbered frames in a nonsequential manner.

6. Software programs such as Bar'N'Coder integrate computer and videodisc applications allowing teachers or students to print bar codes that are then scanned to access videodisc frames.

7. Hypermedia programs can be used to produce a multimedia lesson using decks or stacks of screens.

8. A single CD-ROM (Compact Disc-Read Only Memory) can hold an entire set of encyclopedias, references, periodicals, or newspapers, stored digitally and accessed via a computer interface.

## Alternatives for Enhancing Academic Content

Whether they are teaching from a single text or multiple texts, as in the unit teaching approach, teachers can assist students in learning content information through the use of maps, concept diagrams, reconstructive elaborations, text outlines, study guides, procedural facilitators, and visual depictions. Frequently referred to as content enhancements, these techniques supplement the teaching of math, language arts, social studies, and science. They help students organize, comprehend, and remember content information (Bulgren, Deshler, & Schumaker, 1993). In a review of the use of seven types of content enhancements with adolescents with learning disabilities, Hudson, Lignugaris-Kraft, and Miller (1993) concluded that "even with the limitations in mind, content enhancements and effective teaching practices can be used throughout an effective instructional cycle to improve the performance of all students in content classes" (p. 125).

### Maps

Figures 8.3 and 8.4 present two types of maps: a story map and a semantic map. Both maps are visual representations that show relationships among conceptual ideas. Maps usually have boxes, arrows, lines, and other figures.

A story map provides students with a visual guide to help them understand, recall, and retell narrative stories. Students are reminded to sequence the action section of the map in chronological order. Story maps help students organize information and find specific content, and are effective for cooperative learning activities. In Figure 8.3, we provide a completed sample story map for *The Monkey's Paw* (Jacobs, 1937).

**FIGURE 8.3** Story Map

Title: The Monkey's Paw

Setting: Home

Characters: Herbert—son              Sergeant Morris—a friend

Ms. White—mother         Ms. Samson—plant manager

Mr. White—father

Problem: Power of paw to grant three wishes is misused

Event 1  Family told story of power of the paw

Event 2  Family given paw

Event 3  Father wishes for $5000—first wish

Event 4  Gets $5000 from son's death

Event 5  Mother wishes for son back—second wish

Event 6  Son returns from grave

Event 7  Father uses third wish for him to rest in peace

Solution: Paw is destroyed as it destroyed the family

*Source:* Based on information from *The Monkey's Paw: A Story in Three Scenes* by W. W. Jacobs, 1937, New York: Samuel French.

A semantic map is effective for any type of information that can be outlined or for teaching vocabulary and key words. The major idea or topic appears in the center box, subtopics are in the next boxes, and last, details are arranged under each subtopic. In Figure 8.4, for example, the main topic is energy, one of the subtopics is sources, and one of the details under that is fossil fuels. Scanlon, Duran, Reyes, and Gallego (1992) recommend

**FIGURE 8.4** **Semantic Map**

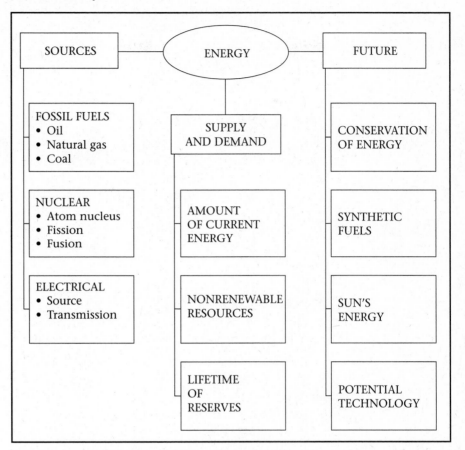

*Source:* Based on information from *Global Science* by John W. Christensen, 1991, Dubuque, IA: Kendall/Hunt.

that students create a semantic map by predicting text content, reading the content, and then comparing the two. This technique involves the following six steps:

*1. Plan.* The teacher first reads the content material and completes a sample preliminary map indicating the relationships among the concepts. The concepts may be stated explicitly or implicitly in the text.

*2. Brainstorm.* The teacher now presents the topic to the students. In our example (Figure 8.4), the topic is energy. The students discuss the meaning of the topic and then generate and list concepts that they feel are related. In our example, the students identified details such as fossil fuels, conservation of energy, and the sun's energy. All the while, the teacher shares information, encourages predictions, and remains non-judgmental. If a concept is inaccurate, the teacher urges the students to reevaluate their thinking after they read and review the information.

*3. Clue the list.* The students skim the text to find other important information that they may have omitted. The teacher prompts them to check pictures, titles, highlighted words, and other text features. These ideas are added to the previous list. After checking the text, the students added nuclear, electrical, oil, and other items to the list on energy.

*4. Develop the map.* The teacher then directs the students to group the ideas together and to identify a labeling term for each cluster. The teacher takes the ideas and makes a map. During the discussion, the teacher should attempt to gain a consensus regarding the map's appearance. In our example, the students agreed on three major clusters or subtopics: sources, supply and demand, and future. After seeing the map with the subtopics and details, they grouped together further details. For example, they grouped oil, natural gas, and coal, which they found in the text under fossil fuels.

*5. Read.* Using the map as a guide, the students read to justify, confirm, or modify their predicted relationships. Scanlon et al. (1992) suggest that the teacher now encourage the students to take notes.

*6. Review.* The teacher asks students to see if any changes are needed in the map after reading the content. They may use additional resources such as an encyclopedia or related texts to justify any modifications and to confirm their information. The teacher again attempts to gain a consensus until all disagreements are resolved.

Scanlon and associates have used this strategy effectively with secondary students with learning disabilities in grades 6–8 and 10–12. Students demonstrated greater recall and comprehension of content-area concepts from social studies, science, and vocational texts (Scanlon et al., 1992).

### Concept Diagrams

A Concept Diagram is an instructional graphic that displays complex, abstract information and relationships among pieces of information. The Concept Diagram includes a definition of the concept, examples and nonexamples, and attributes or characteristics.

Figure 8.5 presents a sample Concept Diagram. The targeted concept (fraction) and the overall concept (number) appear in the first box, identified by the numbers 1 and 2. Key words (such as numerator), examples (½), nonexamples (⅒), and characteristics (denominator is zero) associated

**FIGURE 8.5** **Concept Diagram**

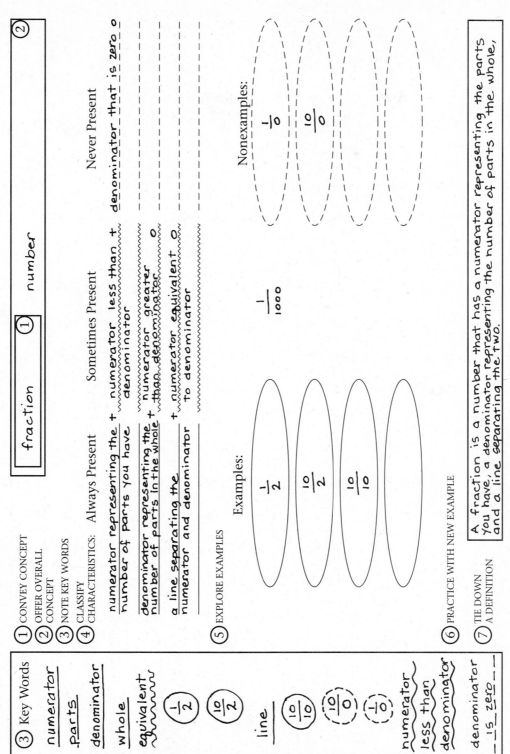

Source: Adapted from *The Concept Mastery Routine* by J. A. Bulgren, D. D. Deshler, and J. B. Schumaker. Copyright © 1993 Edge Enterprises. Reprinted by permission.

with fractions appear in the box at the left, identified by the number 3. Notice that characteristics are marked with solid lines if they are always present, wavy lines if they are sometimes present, and dashes if they are never present. Teachers may select key words from textbooks, supplementary books, or other resources, or elicit them from students.

Characteristics are classified (number 4) according to whether they are always present (numerator representing parts), sometimes present (numerator less than denominator), or never present (denominator that is zero). Examples (such as $\frac{1}{2}$) and nonexamples (such as $\frac{1}{0}$) are listed under number 5. Examples must contain all of the "always present" characteristics and none of the "never present"; they may or may not contain one or more of the "sometimes present" characteristics. Nonexamples omit one or more of the "always present" characteristics and may have one or more of the "never present" characteristics. A definition of the concept (A fraction is a number . . .) is written in the last box on the page, identified by the number 7.

If students are unsure about whether something is an example or nonexample of the concept, they may write the term in the open space of the diagram. Notice that in this example, students questioned if $\frac{1}{1000}$ was a fraction. Now students must decide whether $\frac{1}{1000}$ is an example or nonexample of a fraction by checking the characteristics. If they decide that $\frac{1}{1000}$ has a given characteristic, they place a + by that characteristic. If they decide that $\frac{1}{1000}$ does not have the characteristic, they place a 0 by it. Notice, in Figure 8.5, the students have placed a + after the three characteristics listed as always present, a + and two 0s next to the characteristics listed as sometimes present, and a 0 after the characteristic listed never present. Therefore, they decide that $\frac{1}{1000}$ is a fraction, because all of the "always present" characteristics were marked, some of the "sometimes present," and none of the "never present."

Before working with students, teachers should read materials and collect information about a concept and then construct a preliminary or draft Concept Diagram that they follow as they interact with students to complete a Concept Diagram.

Bulgren et al. (1993) recommend a Concept Mastery teaching routine to accompany the Concept Diagram. We present a skeleton outline of their steps. The reader is referred to *The Concept Mastery Routine* guidebook published by Edge Enterprises, Inc., for the scripted version.

*1. Cue.* The teacher presents, gives a rationale for, and specifies the behaviors of the routine. The teacher may present a blank Concept Diagram to each student.

*2. Do.* The teacher and students cooperatively construct the Concept Diagram as they follow the linking steps with the mnemonic CONCEPT:

*C*onvey the concept name.

*O*ffer the overall concept name.

*N*ote key words. (Elicit from students which ones are characteristics, examples, and nonexamples.)

*C*lassify the always, sometimes, and never present characteristics.

*E*xplore examples and nonexamples of the concept by comparing to characteristics.

*P*ractice with new examples suggested by teacher to check understanding of the concept.

*T*ie down the definition using the names of the targeted concept and overall concept and the always present characteristics.

*3. Review.* The teacher checks students' understanding of the concept with such questions as "What did we learn about [the concept] today?"

You can use the Concept Diagram and the teaching routine in an interactive manner with students after they have read an assignment about the concept, heard a lecture, or seen a film to guarantee that they are ready to participate. Students need an adequate amount of prior knowledge about the concept to be active participants.

## Reconstructive Elaborations

Reconstructive elaborations involve the development of strategic pictures to make content more familiar and meaningful to students for more efficient retrieval and recall of information (Mastropieri & Scruggs, 1989). Developed by Mastropieri and Scruggs, the technique has also been termed keyword mnemonics when the strategy calls for developing keywords in addition to the pictures. Mastropieri and Scruggs (1989) report that the technique "enhances the learning of science, abstract and concrete English vocabulary, U.S. history, and social studies content, including information on transportation and natural resources" (pp. 391–392). King-Sears, Mercer, and Sindelar (1992) found that secondary students with learning disabilities and students with behavior disorders increased their recall of tenth-grade-level science vocabulary words using this strategy. The strategy was effective whether the students or the teacher created the pictures.

Figure 8.6 displays an example of using reconstructive elaborations to teach the science terms *deciduous* and *evergreen*. The first step is to decide on

**FIGURE 8.6** **Reconstructive Elaboration**

DECIDUOUS (Decide)            Shed leaves in fall
EVERGREEN (Evergreen)        Stay green all year

*Source:* "Reconstructive Elaborations: Strategies for Adapting Content Area Information" by M. A. Mastropieri and T. E. Scruggs, 1989, *Academic Therapy, 24*(4), pp. 391–405. Copyright 1989 by PRO-ED, Inc. Reprinted by permission.

the critical pieces of information that students need to know. A check of the teacher's guide, worksheets, and supplementary materials provides the information. In Figure 8.6, Mastriopieri and Scruggs (1989) decided that students needed to know that deciduous trees shed leaves in the fall and that evergreen trees stay green all year.

The second step is to decide on the type of reconstruction that is necessary to make the material more meaningful and familiar. The authors suggest that a keyword and a picture are necessary if students are not familiar with the material, while a pictorial representation alone suffices for familiar terms. Since *deciduous* is such an unfamiliar term, the authors decided to use the familiar and meaningful keyword *decide,* which sounds like the targeted word, along with a picture. Because students were familiar with the term *evergreen,* they included only a picture.

The third step is to decide on the elaboration to link the pieces of information together. In the case of *deciduous* in Figure 8.6, the authors created an interactive illustration of the tree and the keyword *decide,* with the deciduous tree saying "It's cold. . . ." In the case of *evergreen,* the authors created a picture of an evergreen tree saying "I'm always green. . . ." You can use stick figures, line drawings, or magazine pictures to draw the illustrations.

The last step involves teaching students the retrieval of thinking back to the keyword or the pictorial representation and the interactions in the picture. For example, to assist students in recalling the definition of *deciduous,* you may say, "Think back to the keyword *decide;* now think about the interactions in the picture."

## Text Outlines and Study Guides

Text outlines and study guides provide students with an overview and an organization for gaining information. An outline of the major points in a lecture is an effective way to begin a lesson. Darch and Gersten (1986) found that high school students with learning disabilities recalled more information when the teacher used a text outline plus direct instruction procedures compared to when the teacher developed student motivation, highlighted the relevance of the passage, offered a general introduction to the concepts, and discussed the new vocabulary to introduce content information.

You can prepare a general topic outline and direct students to take notes using the outline during the lecture. You can also divide students into cooperative groups and have them complete a general topic outline while reading the chapter. For example, Ms. Mays prepared the following outline for students to complete while listening to her lecture on France after World War I.

I. Losses for France after the war
 A. Land _____
 B. Loss of men _____
 C. Destruction _____
II. Benefits to France after the war
 A. _____
 B. _____

Under the first general topic of losses, she provided keywords for the students to listen for during the lecture to help them identify the three major losses. Under the second general topic, she just listed A and B to cue students into listening for two benefits France gained from the war.

Students can also complete study guides alone or in cooperative groups. Riegel et al. (1988) recommend different levels of study guides depending on a student's reading level. Box 8.4 displays three different levels of study

**BOX 8.4**

## Study Guides

### Sample Independent Study Guide

*Define the following terms:*

1. Axis
2. blitzkrieg
3. neutral
4. isolation

*Answer the following questions:*

1. What happened on December 7, 1941?
2. Describe two factors that contributed to war in Europe.

### Sample Prompted Study Guide

*Define the following terms:*

1. Axis (page 123)
2. blitzkrieg (page 130)
3. neutral (page 129)
4. isolation (page 125)

*Answer the following questions:*

1. What happened on December 7, 1941? (page 132)
2. Describe two factors that contributed to war in Europe. (pages 121 & 122)

### Sample Directed Study Guide

*Define the following terms:*

1. Axis (page 123)—Germany and its allies
2. blitzkrieg (page 130)—lightning warfare
3. neutral (page 129)—to take no side between nations at war
4. isolation (page 125)—a belief that a nation should not become involved in foreign (other countries') problems

*Answer the following questions:*

1. What happened on December 7, 1941? (page 132) The Japanese bombed Pearl Harbor, Hawaii.
2. Describe two factors that contributed to war in Europe. (pages 121 & 122) Economic factors and political conditions contributed to war in Europe.

guides. The *independent* study guide identifies crucial information for the student to find and assumes that the student has good reading and study skills. Students must be able to use the index, skim and scan for information, and make inferences (Riegel et al., 1988). The *prompted* study guide identifies crucial information and provides prompts for the students in locating the information. The *directed* study guide identifies, provides prompts for, and defines the crucial information. Riegel et al. (1988) suggest rewriting definitions using simpler vocabulary.

## Procedural Facilitators

We discussed procedural facilitators in Chapter 7 as a means to decrease the complexity of subject matter and to increase students' self-learning. Procedural facilitators are prompts that help students successfully complete a task (Scardamalia & Bereiter, 1985). Box 8.5 displays a procedural facilitator for math. Ms. Hopkins had her students copy the steps in rounding to the nearest hundred, with the examples, into their math notebooks along with other procedures. Students numbered this procedure and added it to their table of contents. Whenever students experience difficulty with mathematical procedures that she has previously taught, she directs them to their math notebooks.

Montague and Leavell (1994) found that junior high students with learning disabilities who used a story grammar cue card generally showed increases in quality and length of stories. Students checked off the following questions listed on the card before they turned in their compositions: (1) Did you include when and where in the story? (2) Did you include the thoughts and feelings of the characters? (3) Did you include the problem and the plan? (4) Did you include an ending?

---

**BOX 8.5** | **Procedural Facilitators**

*Rounding Hundreds*

1. Underline the number in the tens column.   (3<u>4</u>5)  (7<u>6</u>8)
2. Ask yourself is that number 5 (tens) or above.   (3<u>4</u>5 = No)   (7<u>6</u>8 = Yes)
3. If Yes, add another hundred to the current hundred.   (<u>7</u>68 = 800)
4. If No, the current hundred remains the same.   (<u>3</u>45 = 300)

NOTICE WHEN YOU FINISH, THE NUMBER HAS 0 TENS AND 0 ONES.

## Visual Depictions

Visual depictions are graphic structures that help organize information, making it easier to learn (Crank & Bulgren, 1993). Hudson, Lignugaris-Kraft, and Miller (1993) recommend their use as advance organizers, for presenting information during the lesson, for guided practice, and for independent practice. We discuss four visual display formats: hierarchical/central, directional, comparative, and representative structures (Crank & Bulgren, 1993; Hudson et al., 1993). *Hierarchical/central* structures focus on a major topic, with all other information flowing outward from this topic. Semantic maps and unit visuals are examples of this structure. *Directional* displays present information in a sequence. They include timelines, flowcharts, and cause-effect depictions (Crank & Bulgren, 1993). *Comparative* visuals compare and contrast relationships between two or more concepts. *Representative* structures consist of "diagrams, pictures, and concrete models that illustrate relationships among objects or parts of objects" (Hudson et al., 1993, p. 111). See Figure 8.7 for examples of the four types of visual depictions.

---

### COMPREHENSION MONITORING OF KEY CONCEPTS

*Alternatives for Enhancing Academic Content*

1. Maps, Concept Diagrams, reconstructive elaborations, text outlines, study guides, procedural facilitators, and visual depictions assist students in learning content information, whether teachers are teaching from one text or multiple texts as in the unit method.

2. Maps are visual representations that usually have boxes, arrows, lines, and other figures to show relationships between conceptual ideas.

3. A Concept Diagram contains a definition of the concepts, examples, nonexamples, keywords, and characteristics. As presented here, it is the visual part of the Concept Mastery Routine designed by Bulgren et al. (1993).

4. Reconstructive elaborations involve the development of strategic pictures to make content more familiar and meaningful to students for more efficient retrieval and recall of information.

5. A keyword and a picture are necessary if students are not familiar with the material, while a pictorial representation suffices for familiar terms in reconstructive elaborations.

*(continued on page 313)*

**FIGURE 8.7    Sample Visual Depictions**

A.   Hierarchical/Central

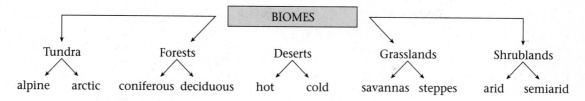

B.   **Directional**

ECOLOGICAL SUCCESSION

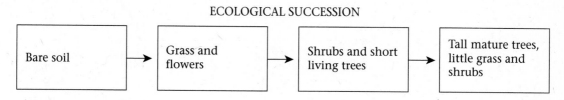

C.   **Comparative**

|  | *Aztecs* | *Incas* | *Mayas* |
|---|---|---|---|
| Major dates | 1200–1521 | 1450–1532 | 200–800 |
| Location | Central plateau of Mexico | Andes mountains of Ecuador and Peru | Yucatan peninsula of southern Mexico and Guatemala |
| Characteristics | Dark skins, coarse hair, broad faces | Thick hair, copper-colored skin, black eyes, short | Short, dark skins, black hair, round heads |
| Habitat | Adobe houses with thatched roofs | Granite houses with thatched roofs | Rectangular or oval huts with walls of poles, some covered with mud, thatched roofs |
| Occupation | Farmers, miners, warriors | Farmers, warriors | Farmers |
| Food | Maize, beans, squash, tomatoes, chili peppers, chocolate | Potatoes, maize, guinea pigs, dogs, llamas, beer | Maize, beans, squash, chili peppers |
| Transportation | People carried goods, canoes | Superb system of roads, runners, llamas to carry light loads, balsa boats | Canoes |

*(continued on next page)*

**FIGURE 8.7** *(continued)*

|  | *Aztecs* | *Incas* | *Mayas* |
|---|---|---|---|
| Government | Autocracy—emperor elected by nobles and descendant of the gods | Despotism—all powerful emperor, four distinct ruling classes, nobility, common people, and slaves | Independent villages |
| Religion | Large-scale human sacrifices, dominant force in daily life | Animal sacrifices; Sun God, ancestor of Inca rulers, built temple of sun gleamed with gold and precious stones | Human sacrifices, humans descended from moon and sun, ruler priest group |
| Accomplishments | One of two places agriculture invented, highly developed military organization, large populated cities, built large flat-topped pyramids crowned with temples | Master road builders, good communications, strong political and social system, priests performed trephining, skillfully ruled conquered territory | Calendar, sophisticated number system, performed brain operations, outstanding in astronomy and arithmetic, built high stone pyramids with small temples on top |
| Language | Used symbols and pictures (rebus writing) | Oral language only, no written language, system of writing numbers, used knotted string to recite history | Advanced written language of pictographs and ideographs |
| Reason for end | Conquered by the Spaniard Hernando Cortés in 1521, European diseases | Conquered by Francisco Pizarro 1500s | People abandoned the great cities one by one |

D. **Representational**

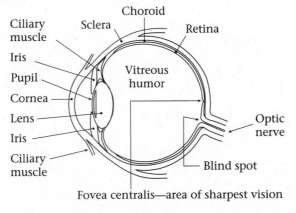

Fovea centralis—area of sharpest vision

6. Text outlines and study guides provide students with an overview and an organization for gaining information.

7. An independent study guide identifies crucial information for the student to find and assumes that the student has good reading and study skills; a prompted study guide identifies crucial information and provides prompts for the students in locating the information; a directed study guide identifies, provides prompts for, and defines the crucial information for the student.

8. Procedural facilitators are prompts that decrease the complexity of subject matter and increase student self-learning.

9. Visual depictions are graphic structures that can consist of four formats: hierarchical/central, directional, comparative, and representative.

## Activities and Materials for Academic Content

In this section, we discuss some activities and materials for content-area teaching for secondary students with mild disabilities. We suggest these activities as substitutes for worksheets. You should select them based on their appropriateness for the objectives of the lesson.

### Activities

1. Check the newspaper ads for five occupations and have students in cooperative groups calculate monthly salaries. Have students rank the occupations in order by salary. Part-time occupations or summer jobs may be substituted.

2. Using coupons cut from Sunday's paper and the food sales in Thursday's paper, let students calculate their savings.

3. Adopt a class at an elementary school. Write books for the class.

4. Adopt a group of residents at a retirement home as pen pals. Exchange letters and cards. Students may use Print Shop to personalize the cards.

5. Tap into the e-mail in the school mainframe. Communicate with another class in another state through the e-mail. Kidmail by CUE contains disks that can be sent between correspondents without telecommunications equipment (Messerer & Learner, 1989). It is in the public domain and is free.

6. Tap into Web 66 (http://web66.coled.umn.edu/), a registry run by the University of Minnesota, Minneapolis, College of Education. You need a Macintosh connected to the Internet and Web-browsing software such as Netscape or Mosaic. About 874 elementary and secondary schools in the United States are registered.

7. Give students unfinished word problems and have them add the questions (Drayer, 1979). For example: Astronaut High School won the football game by 15 points. The opposing team scored 17 points.

8. Have students keep a black book of steps of different math algorithms that they can refer to when they are stuck.

9. As part of a closing activity of a lesson, have students write on poster board or an acetate the major points of the lesson.

10. Using road maps, have students calculate the distances between cities. Then give the students the amount of gas used by different automobiles and have them calculate the gas mileage for each car.

11. Bring in empty food boxes or cans and have students read and compare the ingredients. For example, have them read which has more sugar, a box of gelatin dessert or a box of dry whipped topping mix.

12. Have students write letters to enter contests. Many contests require students to express ideas or opinions. Search through newspapers and magazines, and be alert to radio and television contests (Polloway & Patton, 1993).

13. Divide students into cooperative groups and give them catalogs and an imaginary $300 to spend. The group who spends closest to that amount is recognized.

14. Have students calculate different facts about themselves, such as height, weight, head circumference, waistline measurement, length of thumb, number of words read in a minute, or other measurable quantities (Mercer & Mercer, 1993).

15. Divide students into cooperative groups and have them locate items in the room by measuring them. For example, one problem might read: Find an item in the class that is only one inch long.

16. Use calculators with students in a game format. For example, give students a list of operations to perform within a particular time. The first person to finish with the correct answers wins.

17. Have students examine the ads in the yellow pages of the phone directory and compare the information. For example, restaurant ads often give the location, the hours, and the type of food served.

18. Have students write away for free materials. Free material catalogs, such as *Free Stuff for Kids,* may be available in the school's media center.

19. Have students read the lyrics of a popular song and then paraphrase the song in their own words.


## Software Materials

*Program Name:* Reading Realities: At-Risk Series
*Computer Platform:* Apple II Series, MS-DOS
*Publisher:* Teacher Support Software

The series is a reading comprehension program especially written for at-risk students. Developed specifically for teens who are reading at the second- to sixth-grade level, it helps them become better readers, writers, and thinkers. The program contains three packages: Real Life Issues, such as alcohol, drugs, teen pregnancy, and living with a disability; Career Preparation, which provides information about a variety of careers such as secretary, hairdresser, photographer, and teacher; and Jury Series, which includes actual court cases decided by the students. The program also includes a management system, a speech option, a list of creative extension activities, an annotated list of teenage books, and hotline numbers.


*Program Name:* Reading for Information
*Computer Platform:* IBM
*Publisher:* IBM

The series includes reading selections that span a variety of topics, including science, health, biology, reading maps, reading checkbook pages, reading theater tickets, and many other topics. The program also includes a student monitoring system.


*Program Name:* The Carmen Sandiego series: Where in the World Is Carmen Sandiego? Where in the USA? Where in Europe? Where in Time?
*Computer Platform:* Apple II Series, Macintosh, IBM, PC/Tandy
*Publisher:* Brøderbund

Students practice reading, language arts, social studies, problem solving, world history, and geography as they attempt to find Carmen Sandiego, the ex-secret agent turned thief, and her gang. Students use cues from world atlases and world maps as they research the whereabouts of Carmen and her gang. The program provides excellent opportunities for cooperative learning activities.

*Program Name:* Survival Math
*Computer Platform:* Apple II Series, Commodore, TRS 80
*Publisher:* Sunburst
Four simulations assist students in applying math concepts such as unit prices, percent discounts, area, perimeter, and units of measure to everyday life. In Travel Agent Contest, students plan a budget for a trip. Smart Shopper Marathon involves best buys, Hot Dog Stand requires students to run a concession stand during a football game, and Foreman Assistant involves students in managing the construction of a playroom.

*Program Name:* Math Shop
*Computer Platform:* Apple II Series, Macintosh, MS-DOS
*Publisher:* Scholastic, Inc.
Students practice a wide range of math skills and apply math concepts as they wait on customers in the ten shops. Students choose the shops to work in and serve customers as they ring up sales and make change. The program offers a variety of simulations, allows for automatic adjustment of skill levels, and provides clues for wrong answers. Blackline masters for activities are included.

*Program Name:* Math Blaster Mystery
*Computer Platform:* Apple II Series, MS-DOS
*Publisher:* Davidson
Students become mathematical detectives as they develop strategies for solving word problems and apply higher-order thinking skills. For example, in one of the four activities, Weigh the Evidence, students must determine which three of four numbered weights total a given number and move and stack the weights on another scale with the greatest value on the bottom. The program provides for student recordkeeping, and teachers can enter their own word problems and can create and print out tests and worksheets.

*Program Name:* Timeliner
*Computer Platform:* Apple II Series, Macintosh, MS-DOS
*Publisher:* Tom Snyder Productions
Using this program, students create a timeline that is one day up to many years long. The program places the events in chronological order and can merge events on different timelines. Individual students or the entire class can create the timelines. Sample timelines are included. The program is easy to use and requires little training for independent use.

*Program Name:* Hyperstudio 3.1
*Computer Platform:* Apple II Series, Macintosh
*Publisher:* Roger Wagner Publishing
This hypermedia-based program allows students and teachers to build interactive lessons and presentations by combining text, graphics, animation, movie clips, and sound in the presentation of ideas and information. Hyperstudio can interact with laserdisc players, CD-ROMs, and audio and video digitizers.

*Program Name:* National Gallery of Art
*Computer Platform:* Macintosh
*Publisher:* Voyager
This videodisc includes more than 1600 masterpieces—paintings, drawings, sculptures, and prints—by famous artists. The companion software lets students easily organize and view works of art by artist, nationality, period, style, date, medium, or subject. Students or teachers can create slide lists for lectures or presentations.

*Program Name:* Hurricane Hugo
*Computer Platform:* IBM
*Publisher:* Turner Educational Services
Hurricane Hugo is a multimedia authoring tool that prompts students to question, research, and organize data and assess opinions. Lesson plans are provided for teachers. The program contains CNN news footage, interviews, footage from news sources, and advanced computer animation.

*Program Name:* Operation Frog
*Computer Platform:* Apple II Series
*Publisher:* Scholastic
Using this computer simulation, students dissect and reassemble a frog. Documentation includes activities, worksheets, experiments, a collection of facts, and vocabulary and reference guides.

*Program Name:* A Field Trip to the Rain Forest
*Computer Platform:* Apple II Series, Macintosh
*Publisher:* Wings/Sunburst
With this simulation software, students explore the environment of the Central American rain forest. Students learn about animals and plants that survive in the ecosystem by day or by night.

✔ Now that you have read Chapter 8, reflect on your earlier predictions and complete this post organizer.

1. Look back at your description of middle and high school curriculum content. Compare your descriptions with those in the chapter. Which types of curriculum did you identify or omit?

2. In your suggestions for teaching content, did you think about a single text, the unit method, and content enhancements? Meet with the same peer again and see if you can describe techniques for teaching using a single text, the unit method, and content enhancements. You may even want to see if you can design a reconstructive elaboration.

3. Compare your two ways to use technology with those discussed in the chapter.

4. How do your alternatives for enhancing content compare with those in the chapter?

# Cognitive Strategies

© Nita Winter

**CHAPTER
HIGHLIGHTS**

*Cognitive Strategy Instruction*

*Metacognition*

*Cognitive Behavior Modification*

*Reciprocal Teaching*

*Task-Specific Strategy Instruction*

*Activities and Materials for Cognitive Strategy Instruction*

 Before you read Chapter 9, use your prior knowledge to complete this advance organizer.

1. Predict the types of instructional techniques you might use to teach a lesson using the principles of cognitive strategy instruction.

2. To find out about your own metacognitive awareness skills, read a passage from a previous section of this textbook. As you read it, try to observe what you do as you read. For example: Do you look back at words you have just read? Do you think about other things when you read? Do you look at and read each word? Do you think about each word, or do you put words together in groups? Do you know what you are reading? Write down everything you notice about your reading.

3. To find out about your own metacognitive monitoring skills, try this activity. If you were to read the same passage again, what would you do to

improve your reading of it? For example: Would you look back or adjust your pace? Would you pause to paraphrase what you had just read? Would you underline sections of text? Write down any adjustments you would make.

4. Design a metacognitive activity for a secondary student in the content area of your choice.

---

Special education teachers in secondary schools are expected to teach basic skills, content knowledge, social responsibility, and problem solving to their students within increasingly diverse and competitive learning environments. Among the eight national education goals (GOALS 2000, 1994) for the year 2000, we seek the attainment of a high school graduation rate of at least 90%, demonstration of students' competency in challenging subject matter (including English, mathematics, science, and history), and readiness for responsible citizenship and productive employment (Houck, 1993). With these and other challenges facing us and our students, we need instructional approaches that will allow us to create strategic learning environments that facilitate the development of independent, strategic learners and problem solvers.

In this chapter, we discuss the use of cognitive strategies to teach adolescents with mild disabilities to become strategic information processors and problem solvers. First, we provide the rationale for using cognitive strategies, along with the principles of strategic instruction. Then, we describe how cognitive strategies are taught through the use of metacognition, cognitive behavior modification, reciprocal teaching, and task-specific strategies. At the end of the chapter, we suggest activities and materials to complement the teaching of cognitive strategies.

## Cognitive Strategy Instruction

The use of cognitive strategy instruction finds its roots in the field of cognitive psychology. Learners are seen as active participants in acquiring and processing information, rather than as passive recipients of information (Paris & Byrnes, 1989). Cognitive strategies are the "behaviors of a learner that are intended to influence how the learner processes information" (Mayer, 1988, p. 21). For example, Jason may use the cognitive strategy of writing a long-distance phone number five times to help him memorize it, while Jenny may use the cognitive strategy of clustering, so the phone number is processed as 203 225 05 31. Thus, cognitive strategy instruction empowers students by giving them techniques or methods for acquiring, remembering, and demonstrating information in order to solve problems.

## Rationale and Description

Cognitive strategy instruction is designed to improve students' academic and social-skill performance in and out of school settings (Clark, Deshler, Schumaker, Alley, & Warner, 1984). Cognitive strategies provide students with a set of self-instructional steps that assist them in addressing a specific need (such as writing an essay) and in learning, organizing, retaining, and expressing information.

Frequently, students with learning disabilities appear to lack cognitive skills, or the effective use of these skills, to meet academic and social demands (Ellis, 1986). Students with learning disabilities, mild mental disabilities, or behavior problems often fail to take an active role in their own learning, and frequently fail to develop strategies that could be used to complete tasks (Torgesen, 1982). Others may actually use strategies, but may not choose them wisely (as in repeating a long list of words over and over in order to memorize it instead of using mnemonics or visual imagery).

Jones, Palincsar, Ogle, and Carr (1987) indicate that if students do not already possess a strategy for completing certain tasks, then teaching an appropriate strategy is likely to improve achievement, especially for less proficient students. Since low-achieving students are not likely to develop cognitive strategies spontaneously, it is important to provide specific strategy instruction (Jones et al., 1987). In studies demonstrating effective learning of strategies, teachers implemented a well-designed instructional sequence that included direct instruction of students in the use of self-instruction (Ellis, 1983; Schmidt, 1983). Thus, cognitive-strategy instruction offers promise for students with mild disabilities to set goals, devise strategies, and monitor their own progress (Meese, 1994).

Knowing how to use a cognitive strategy does not necessarily mean that students know why the strategy is useful or how to evaluate its effectiveness (Billingsley & Wildman, 1990). Students need to know (1) what the strategy is for, (2) how, when, and where to use the strategy, (3) why the strategy is important and useful, and (4) how to evaluate its effectiveness (Winograd & Hare, 1988). This knowledge is critical to generalization efforts. Studies have shown that cognitive strategy training has a significant impact on academic performance when generalization of the training to natural environments occurs (Ellis, 1983; Schmidt, 1983). Wong (1986) found that when generalization is an integral part of the training, students' application of the strategy training has been positive.

In Chapter 7, we presented examples of direct instruction and social constructivist teaching routines. Direct instruction is characterized by an active, direct, involved teaching style, with the teacher systematically presenting information, providing feedback and correction, giving many opportunities for practice, and conducting frequent reviews. Social constructivist teaching practices are characterized by a facilitative teaching style, with the teacher connecting learning to students' experiences, empowering students by involving them in planning and implementing instruction, and presenting learning in meaningful contexts.

You will note that cognitive strategy instruction includes elements of both direct instruction and social constructivist teaching practices. Educators do not have to choose between instructed (direct instruction) and constructed (constructivism) knowledge (Harris & Pressley, 1991); cognitive strategy instruction uses both. Teachers begin by systematically teaching, providing practice, and giving feedback. Then, they activate students' prior knowledge and involve them in planning, instruction, and self-evaluation. Thus, cognitive instruction is an integrated approach to teaching and learning.

## Strategic Planning and Teaching

In classrooms where strategic teaching and learning are taking place, both teachers and students are constantly thinking and making decisions related to strategy selection, application, and evaluation. If you walked into a secondary classroom in which a teacher was using cognitive strategy instruction, you might see the teacher (1) tailoring instruction to students' needs and difficulties, (2) modeling the use of strategies by "thinking aloud," (3) making certain that students understand the task and the application and significance of the strategy to the task, (4) maintaining active involvement of students, (5) providing experiences to help students create their own strategies, (6) assisting students to personalize the strategies they use, and (7) providing feedback regarding students' use of strategies. In that same classroom, you would see students, as strategic learners, (1) applying strategies to various academic content, (2) actively participating and monitoring their own progress, (3) interacting with teachers and with each other, and (4) taking responsibility for their own learning by utilizing the principles of self-instruction, self-evaluation, and self-regulation. Remember to look for these teacher and student behaviors as we describe metacognition, cognitive behavior modification, reciprocal teaching, and task-specific strategies later in this chapter.

In describing strategic planning and teaching, we borrow from the ideas of Jones et al. (1987), along with the principles of effective teaching (Englert et al., 1992) presented in Chapter 7.

1. *Strategic teachers spend time thinking/reflecting about instructional planning and teaching.* Ms. Benavidez thinks about the upcoming unit in her literature class involving teaching students to identify the elements and organization of a short story. She reflects on ways to motivate her students' interest, introduce the topic, organize her instruction, present her lessons, and evaluate her students' performance. She develops an outline to organize her content.

2. *Strategic teachers focus on students' prior learning experiences.* Ms. Benevidez thinks of ways to activate her students' prior knowledge about short stories. She decides she will ask them to recall stories they have read or heard and to think about why they liked them, who was in them, and what they were about.

3. *Strategic teachers possess a wide variety of strategies and explain to students the purpose and significance of each strategy.* Ms. Benevidez thinks about the strategies and the graphic structures (such as interaction frames) that would be appropriate for analyzing and organizing the elements in a short story.

4. *Strategic teachers are rich in content knowledge.* Reflecting on the content of her literature class and outside resources, Ms. Benevidez plans ways to relate this unit on short stories to previous units, use the district adopted text with possible modifications, and bring in other content sources to gain maximum student interest and participation. She also thinks about the English classes her students have already taken in order to connect the experiences in her class with previous learning.

5. *Strategic teachers know how to achieve a balance between strategies and content.* Ms. Benevidez balances her lesson in a manner that includes direct teaching of content (elements and organization of a short story) and the presentation of one or more strategies (interaction frame) to facilitate acquisition of that content in a meaningful way.

6. *Strategic teachers understand learner characteristics.* Knowing that many of her students have difficulty organizing information, paraphrasing what they read, identifying the main idea, and summarizing information, Ms. Benevidez predicts the difficulties that they may encounter (in understanding, appreciating, and interpreting short stories, as well as writing their own short stories).

7. *Strategic teachers are knowledgeable about the organization of instructional materials and curriculum.* Ms. Benevidez looks over the literature textbook and identifies ways in which she could make the material easier for her students to acquire, organize, and retain (such as modeling how to identify the elements of a story, using "think aloud" techniques to summarize the story, and using content enhancement routines, outlines, and study guides).

8. *Strategic teachers actively collaborate with their students in selecting, applying, and monitoring the use of strategies to meet specific goals.* Ms. Benevidez thinks about how she will determine what her students already know about short stories, help them set goals for the unit, and discuss possible strategies to help them achieve their goals.

Figure 9.1 contains an example of what Ms. Benevidez modeled for her students. She showed them how to use an interaction frame to organize the important elements of a short story and eventually summarize the story. She taught her students by explaining the rationale for using the interaction frame, completing the interaction frame while "thinking aloud," actively involving the students during the process by asking them questions, providing feedback to students as they made suggestions, developing guided and independent practice opportunities, and discussing other situations in which they could utilize this organizational strategy. Notice that by completing the elements in the interaction frame, the students were able to construct a summary.

As you read the next sections on metacognition, cognitive behavior modification, reciprocal teaching, and task-specific strategies, notice that the strategic planning and teaching behaviors previously described are included in each of them. Metacognition is the knowledge (awareness) and control (monitoring) that individuals have over their own learning. Cognitive behavior modification teaches self-regulation and problem solving. Reciprocal teaching involves gaining meaning from text through the use of dialogues. Task-specific strategy instruction involves learning how to learn—how to plan and complete a task, monitor progress, and make adjustments and modifications. Although there are some differences among these four approaches, the many similarities qualify each of them as a form of cognitive-strategy instruction

Each approach (1) has a set of steps or procedures, (2) utilizes cognitive modeling, (3) actively involves students, (4) includes practice and feedback, (5) incorporates a gradual transfer of strategy ownership and regulation, and (6) promotes generalization. Table 9.1 provides a comparison of metacognition, cognitive behavior modification, reciprocal teaching, and task-specific strategy instruction in terms of definition, components, instructional procedures, instructional approach, and content taught.

**FIGURE 9.1    Interaction Frame Used with Literature/Short Story**

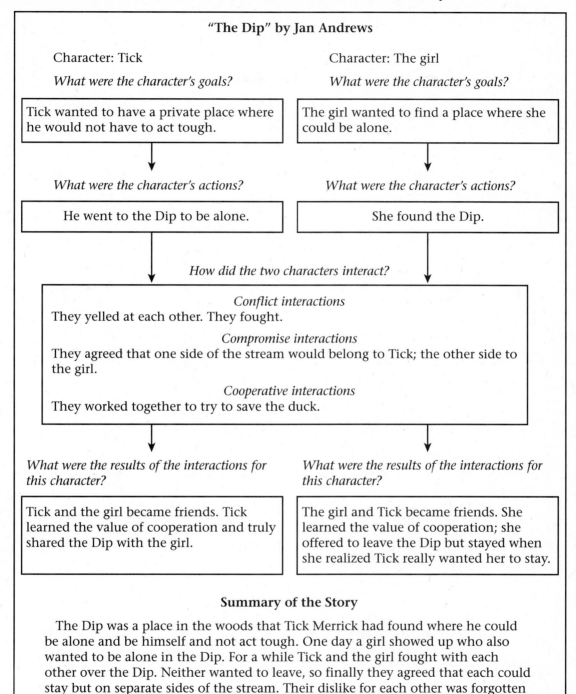

"The Dip" by Jan Andrews

Character: Tick

*What were the character's goals?*

Tick wanted to have a private place where he would not have to act tough.

Character: The girl

*What were the character's goals?*

The girl wanted to find a place where she could be alone.

*What were the character's actions?*

He went to the Dip to be alone.

*What were the character's actions?*

She found the Dip.

*How did the two characters interact?*

*Conflict interactions*
They yelled at each other. They fought.

*Compromise interactions*
They agreed that one side of the stream would belong to Tick; the other side to the girl.

*Cooperative interactions*
They worked together to try to save the duck.

*What were the results of the interactions for this character?*

Tick and the girl became friends. Tick learned the value of cooperation and truly shared the Dip with the girl.

*What were the results of the interactions for this character?*

The girl and Tick became friends. She learned the value of cooperation; she offered to leave the Dip but stayed when she realized Tick really wanted her to stay.

**Summary of the Story**

The Dip was a place in the woods that Tick Merrick had found where he could be alone and be himself and not act tough. One day a girl showed up who also wanted to be alone in the Dip. For a while Tick and the girl fought with each other over the Dip. Neither wanted to leave, so finally they agreed that each could stay but on separate sides of the stream. Their dislike for each other was forgotten when they found an injured duck and tried to nurse it back to health together. The duck did not survive, but Tick and the girl had learned the value of cooperation and found they had become real friends.

*Source:* Reprinted with permission of the National Education Association.

**TABLE 9.1**    **Comparison of Cognitive Approaches**

| | Metacognition | Cognitive behavior modification | Reciprocal teaching | Task-specific strategy instruction |
|---|---|---|---|---|
| Definition | The knowledge (awareness) and control (monitoring) that individuals have over their own thinking and learning. | A technique in which the teacher models his or her thinking processes while performing a task; then the student practices overtly and covertly by him- or herself. | An interactive teaching strategy that takes the form of a dialogue between teachers and students to jointly construct the meaning of text. | Learning *how* to learn and perform. Focus on tasks and curriculum demands. |
| Components | Active involvement of students. Systematic steps or procedures. Cognitive modeling. Self-awareness. Self-monitoring. Gradual transfer of ownership and regulation. Generalization. | Active involvement of students. Systematic steps or procedures. Cognitive modeling. Guided practice. Verbalizations. Overt and covert processing. Gradual transfer of ownership and regulation. Generalization. | Active involvement of students. Systematic steps or procedures. Instruction in useful strategies. Guided interactive instruction. Well-informed learners. Readable, meaningful practice materials. Scaffolding. Cognitive modeling. Gradual transfer of ownership and regulation. Generalization. | Active involvement of students. Systematic steps or procedures. Cognitive modeling. Overt and covert processing. Guided and independent practice. Gradual transfer of ownership and regulation. Generalization. |
| Instructional procedures | Identify task. Determine student's performance. Select a strategy. Teach the strategy. Provide practice. Provide feedback. Teach generalization. | Explain strategy. Share rationale. Perform task while thinking aloud. Have student perform task overtly and covertly. Provide feedback. | Teach summarizing, question generating, clarifying, and predicting. Read title, ask for predictions. Read a segment of text. Ask a question about content. Summarize/ask for elaborations. Discuss clarifications. Discuss predictions regarding next segment. Provide feedback. | Pretest. Describe/obtain commitment. Model. Verbal practice. Controlled practice and feedback. Advanced practice and feedback. Confirm acquisition and obtain generalization commitment. Generalization. |
| Instructional approach | Integration of direct instruction and constructivism. | Integration of direct instruction and constructivism. | Integration of direct instruction and constructivism. | Integration of direct instruction and constructivism. |
| Content | Academic subjects. Social behaviors. | Academic subjects. Social behaviors. | Academic subjects. | Academic subjects. Social behaviors. |

> ### COMPREHENSION MONITORING OF KEY CONCEPTS
>
> #### *Cognitive Strategy Instruction*
>
> 1. Cognitive strategies are the "behaviors of a learner that are intended to influence how the learner processes information" (Mayer, 1988, p.21).
> 2. Cognitive strategy instruction is designed to improve students' academic and social-skill performance in and out of school settings.
> 3. Students with learning disabilities, mild mental disabilities, or behavior problems often fail to take an active role in their own learning, and frequently fail to develop strategies that could be used to complete tasks.
> 4. Students need to know the purpose of a strategy; how, when, and where to use it; why it is useful; and how to evaluate its effectiveness.
> 5. Cognitive strategy instruction includes elements of both direct instruction and social constructivist practices.
> 6. In classrooms where strategic teaching and learning are taking place, both teachers and students are constantly thinking and making decisions related to strategy selection, application, and evaluation.
> 7. Strategic teachers (a) spend time thinking about planning and teaching, (b) focus on students' prior learning experiences, (c) possess a wide variety of strategies and explain to students the purpose and significance of each strategy, (d) are rich in content knowledge, (e) know how to balance strategies and content, (f) understand learner characteristics, (g) know instructional materials and curriculum, and (h) collaborate with students in selecting, applying, and using strategies.

## Metacognition

Metacognition is the general knowledge (awareness) and the control (monitoring) that individuals have over their own thinking and learning (Flavell, 1976; Paris, Lipson, Jacobs, Oka, Debritto, & Cross, 1982). Although metacognition is presented as a separate section in this chapter, metacognitive tactics (e.g., self-awareness, self-monitoring, self-questioning, self-instruction) are present within all of the cognitive strategies we discuss.

## Description

Awareness, the first part of metacognition, involves a learner's knowledge about his or her cognitive resources and the relationship between those capabilities and the demands of a task (Olson & Platt, 1996). For example, Jarrod finds his biology text difficult to follow and is aware that he has difficulty understanding and remembering what he reads. Frequently, when he gets to the bottom of a page, he cannot remember what he just read. Jarrod is demonstrating knowledge and awareness about his comprehension skills (metacognitive awareness).

Monitoring, the second component of metacognition, involves the self-regulation skills that enable a person to adjust, correct, monitor, and control his or her cognitive activities (Olson & Platt, 1996). Active monitoring of cognitive activities is necessary for efficient learning (Baker & Brown, 1980). For example, Jarrod finds that if he pauses after each paragraph to paraphrase what he just read, and rereads the paragraph if needed, he can then generate a summary statement at the bottom of the page. Jarrod is demonstrating control and regulating his actions. Notice how he initially demonstrates an awareness of his comprehension difficulties with the biology text (metacognitive awareness), and then exercises *control* over the situation by pausing, rereading, paraphrasing, and summarizing (metacognitive monitoring).

Wong (1986) found that students who think they are in control of their environment appear to be the most successful learners. Wong indicates that remedial programs for students with learning disabilities should include a metacognitive component to help them become independent learners. Students with mild disabilities can become more active, involved learners, better equipped to deal with the demands of the secondary curriculum, if systematically taught a series of metacognitive strategies, shown how and where to use them, and reinforced for using them and applying them across situations and settings.

## Steps in Implementing Metacognitive Instruction

We stated earlier that cognitive strategies include specific steps or procedures. A review of the metacognitive research indicates the presence of specific steps that appear to be part of instruction in metacognitive skills. The following steps are adapted from Olson and Platt (1996), Palincsar and Brown (1987), Pressley, Borkowski, and O'Sullivan (1984), and Seidenberg (1988). You should use these to help your students increase awareness and control over their own learning.

1. *Identify the problem.* Through discussion with the student, jointly determine the problem.

*Mrs. Jonas:* "Liz, I notice that you've had difficulty on your first two tests. What do you think might be the problem?"

*Liz:* "I seem to be having trouble getting all the information when you lecture in class."

2. *Determine the student's performance.* Assess the student's skills with a pretest, test or quiz, interview, work samples, or self-report.

*Mrs. Jonas:* "Tell me exactly what you do during class."

*Liz:* "I listen and take notes."

*Mrs. Jonas:* "Good. However, you're having trouble getting all the information in the lectures, so let's take a look at your notes."

*Liz:* "Here are my notes from last week's classes."

*Mrs. Jonas:* "I see. You have missed some of the major concepts and many of the details. If you compare your notes to my lecture notes and outline, you will see what I mean."

3. *Select a strategy to facilitate completion of the task and explain the benefits to be expected.* Decide on a strategy and discuss how it will help.

*Mrs. Jonas:* "I have a note-taking strategy that will help you get the information from my lecture. It should help you organize and remember the information presented, and manage the content more effectively. I think you'll find that your grades will improve."

4. *Explicitly teach the strategy.* Model the strategy while thinking aloud. Work interactively with the student to model and rehearse the use of the strategy. Teach the student to be aware of when he or she is using the strategy effectively.

(Teacher modeling while thinking aloud)

*Mrs. Jonas:* "I am going to think aloud while I show you how to take notes. I will watch this video on amphibians and take notes just the way you should during one of my lectures. I'll take notes on the overhead projector, so you can watch what I do.

"Let's see. I'll divide my paper into two columns. I'll write the information from this videotaped lecture/presentation in the column on the right, and I'll go back later and use the column on the left to jot down definitions, or questions that I have about the lecture.

"Hmm. That sounds like a main topic, so I'll write that down. I'll put it in the column on the right. I need to remember to use abbreviations when I can, because that will help me work faster. Uh oh, I didn't hear that word. I need to leave a blank space, so I'll remember to check with someone. Then I'll fill it in later."

(Teacher and student working interactively)

*Mrs. Jonas:* "Let's see. I'll try to write that term, but I'm not sure how to spell it. Liz, what should I do?"

*Liz:* "Go back later, look it up or ask someone, and check to see if you spelled it right. Correct it if you need to."

*Mrs. Jonas:* "Excellent suggestion. Hmm. These points sound like details. Liz, where do we write them?"

*Liz:* "Under the major concept they describe."

*Mrs. Jonas:* "Good. Now, am I doing this right? Yes, I've got my two columns, I'm using abbreviations, I'm remembering to put details under the main points. Liz, in what other ways can I tell I'm using this strategy effectively? Remember to think out loud."

*Liz:* "I know I'm doing this right because I've got the teacher's ideas in the column on the right, and my own questions, comments, and definitions in the column on the left. . . ."

5. *Provide guided practice.* Schedule practice sessions with the student in which you ask him or her to use the strategy. Have him or her use self-monitoring to check the use of the strategy.

(Teacher presenting information in lecture form, and student using the strategy while thinking aloud)

*Liz:* "OK, I need to draw a line to divide my paper into two columns. I'll write the teacher's ideas on the right, and my questions and comments on the left.

"Let's see. Did I remember to use abbreviations? Have I left blanks in the places where I missed words. . . .?"

6. *Provide feedback.* Provide specific, positive, corrective, and elaborated feedback regarding the successful selection and use of the strategy.

*Mrs. Jonas:* "Liz, I'm pleased that you're using the two-column note-taking strategy when you need to. You are remembering to record my comments on the right and yours on the left. Your use of abbreviations seems to be helping you work faster and record more information. You are constantly checking to make sure you are using the strategy correctly. Remember to indent your details under your main concepts. It will help you see how they are related."

7. *Teach generalization of the strategy.* Show students how to apply the strategy to other classes (such as English or driver education), materials (such as textbooks), situations (such as conducting an interview for the school paper), and settings (such as jotting down an employer's comments about the procedures needed to complete an assignment at work). Conduct frequent discussions about when and where the strategy can be applied.

*Mrs. Jonas:* "You've done a great job with the note-taking strategy in my biology class. Where else do you think you could use it?"

*Liz:* "I've been using it to take notes from my English book. I think I could use it in math, too, because the teacher puts a lot of work on the board."

After the teacher has taught these seven steps, students should be able to adjust, monitor, and control their own cognitive activities. In other words, there is a gradual transfer of ownership. Metacognitive interventions give students control over their cognitive processing by transitioning from "other regulation" (in this case, the teacher) to self-regulation (the student) (Reeve & Brown, 1985). Figure 9.2 contains an example of a self-monitoring form that students can use to record their use of a strategy. Such a form is extremely helpful for strategy generalization.

---

### COMPREHENSION MONITORING OF KEY CONCEPTS

#### *Metacognition*

1. Metacognition is the general knowledge (awareness) and the control (monitoring) that individuals have over their own thinking and learning.
2. Metacognitive tactics include self-awareness, self-monitoring, self-questioning, and self-instruction.
3. Remedial programs for students with learning disabilities should contain a metacognitive component to help them become independent learners.
4. The following steps can be used to implement metacognitive instruction: (a) Identify the task. (b) Determine the student's performance. (c) Select a strategy to facilitate completion of the task and explain the benefits to be expected. (d) Explicitly teach the strategy. (e) Provide guided practice. (f) Provide feedback. (g) Teach generalization of the strategy.

*(continued on page 333)*

**FIGURE 9.2** **Self-Monitoring for Strategy Generalization**

Name ___Liz McIntire___    Week of ___March 6–10___

Directions:   Write "Yes" in the box if you needed and used a strategy.
Write "No" in the box if you did not need to use a strategy.

Class                                   Dates

|  | Mon. | Tues. | Wed. | Thurs. | Fri. |
|---|---|---|---|---|---|
| Biology | No | Yes | Yes | Yes | Yes |
| English | Yes | Yes | Yes | Yes | Yes |
|  |  |  |  |  |  |
|  |  |  |  |  |  |

Directions:   Write the name of your class, assignment, strategy, where you used it,
and your results.

| Class/Assignment | Stategy Used | Where Applied | Results of Using the Strategy |
|---|---|---|---|
| Biology / Lecture | Note taking | In class/ homework | Good – I passed open-note quiz |
| English / Textbook | Note taking | In class/ homework | Good – I outlined two chapters |
|  |  |  |  |
|  |  |  |  |

*Source:* Adapted from "Generalization and Adaptation of Learning Strategies to Natural Environments: Part 2: Research into Practice" by E. S. Ellis, B. K. Lenz, and E. J. Sabornie, 1987, *Remedial and Special Education, 8*(2), 6–23.

> 5. Metacognitive interventions give students control over their cognitive processing by helping them transition from "other regulation" (teachers, parents, peers) to "self-regulation" (student).

## Cognitive Behavior Modification

Cognitive behavior modification (CBM) combines behavioral, social, and cognitive learning theories. In this technique, the teacher first models his or her thinking processes in the performance of a task; then, the student practices overtly with assistance, and eventually covertly (internalizing the procedure) by him- or herself. Cognitive behavior modification interventions are characterized by (1) active participation of students in learning, (2) overt verbalization, (3) systematic, discrete steps, (4) modeled strategies, and (5) planned, reflective responses (Ryan, Short, & Weed, 1986). CBM involves an analysis of the task and of the thinking processes involved in performing the task (Bos & Vaughn, 1994).

Cognitive behavior modification teaches problem solving to students and relies on self-regulation and self-evaluation (Harris & Pressley, 1991). CBM has been used to teach learning strategies and has improved both academic and social behavior of students (Williams & Rooney, 1986). It provides the opportunity for students to take responsibility for their own learning and to control their own behavior (Meichenbaum, 1980).

CBM training approaches include modeling, self-instructional techniques, and evaluation of performance (Meichenbaum, 1977, 1983). The procedures used in cognitive behavior modification training can be adapted to fit a variety of tasks (Meese, 1994), situations, and settings.

### Components of Cognitive Behavior Modification

Cognitive behavior modification incorporates the components of systematic steps or procedures, cognitive modeling, guided practice, and verbalization (Bos & Vaughn, 1994; Lloyd, 1980; Olson & Platt, 1996). These components can be used to teach both academic and social skills.

#### Systematic Steps or Procedures

In cognitive behavior modification, students typically follow a series of steps or procedures to complete a task involving the particular skill or content being taught. The seven steps, along with examples, will be discussed in the next section.

### Cognitive Modeling

Showing students how to talk to themselves is an effective way to teach many academic and social skills (Meese, 1994). Cognitive modeling is the primary means of instruction in cognitive behavior modification (Bos & Vaughn, 1994). Teachers model the actions needed to perform a task (for example, the actions involved in skimming include reading the title, headings, captions, and summary); but more important, teachers "think aloud" their unobservable thought processes ("I know I can figure out what the main idea of each paragraph is. I'm going to do this by reading the first sentence in each paragraph, because the first sentence usually contains the main idea"). Modeling your actions and sharing your thoughts through self-talk are effective ways to teach academic (reading for information) and social (such as accepting criticism) skills.

### Guided Practice

Students can be taught to imitate the teacher's self-talk or verbalizations (Alberto & Troutman, 1995) through guided practice. Initially, students perform "out loud" the same task that was modeled by the teacher (overt verbalization). Eventually, the students perform the task to themselves through private speech (covert verbalization). There is also a shift from external guidance, provided as the teacher assists students in performing the task, to internal guidance in which the students complete the steps alone.

### Verbalization

Verbalization includes self-instruction, self-evaluation, self-regulation, and self-reinforcement. Self-instruction is the use of overt verbalization, faded to covert verbalization, in the completion of a task. ("I need to remember to read the captions and look at the illustrations.") Self-evaluation refers to judging the quality or acceptability of a behavior (Paris & Oka, 1986). ("I do better when I read the boldface headings before I read the first sentence in each paragraph.") Self-regulation involves monitoring one's own actions and thoughts in the performance of a task. As students monitor their own progress, they can decide if the strategy is working and change it if it is not. ("I'm not getting the main idea of each section by studying the captions and illustrations and reading the headings. I think I need to read the first and last sentences and the summary.") Self-reinforcement is the self-selection and self-administration of a reinforcer contingent upon meeting a performance standard (Hughes, Ruhl, & Misra, 1989). ("Good, I'm getting much faster at skimming to find the main idea of a passage.")

Meichenbaum (1977) recommends numerous ways for teachers to encourage students to use verbalization. Teachers can (1) model self-statements in the completion of their own tasks, (2) begin with tasks with which students are somewhat familiar and add other tasks later, and (3) use cue cards to assist students in remembering the steps or procedures.

## Steps in Implementing Cognitive Behavior Modification

We have adapted the techniques of Meichenbaum and Goodman (1971) and Meichenbaum (1977) and recommend the following procedures:

1. Explain the strategy.

   "Jamal, you seem to have a hard time taking tests. I have a strategy that other students have tried and it has worked for them. It includes thinking out loud about the test and following some steps."

2. Share the rationale.

   "This strategy has raised the test scores of other students. I think you would improve your test-taking skills by using it. Remember, you have to pass the high school competency test in order to graduate, and using this strategy combined with studying may help you do it."

3. Perform the task for the student while thinking aloud (cognitive modeling).
   a. Define the problem.

      "What am I supposed to do when I take a test?"

   b. Focus attention and guide responses.

      "Let's see . . . take my time—look over the entire test before beginning. Read the directions slowly and carefully, and follow the steps to the test-taking strategy."

   c. Use self-reinforcement.

      "Good, I'm doing OK. I should be all right on this test."

   d. Use coping skills.

      "If I don't know the answer to a question, I'll put a mark next to it and come back to it after I've finished the rest of the test."

4. Have the student perform the task under the direction of the teacher (overt, external guidance). Prompt and guide the student if necessary.

   "What do you do first? What will you do if you don't know an answer?"

5. Have the student perform the task while instructing himself/herself aloud (overt self-guidance). Be sure to listen as the student practices. Provide positive and corrective feedback.

6. Have the student whisper the instructions while performing the task (faded, overt self-guidance). Listen and observe the student and provide feedback.

7. Have the student perform the task while guiding his or her actions through private speech (covert self-instruction). Watch what the student does.

---

**COMPREHENSION MONITORING OF KEY CONCEPTS**

*Cognitive Behavior Modification*

1. Cognitive behavior modification (CBM) is a technique in which the teacher first models his or her thinking processes in the performance of a task, and then the student practices overtly with assistance, and eventually covertly (internalizing the procedure) by him- or herself.

2. The components of cognitive behavior modification include systematic steps or procedures, cognitive modeling, guided practice, and verbalization.

3. Seven steps are recommended for implementing cognitive behavior modification: (a) Explain the strategy. (b) Share the rationale. (c) Perform the task for the student while thinking aloud. (d) Have the student perform the task under direction of the teacher. (e) Have the student perform the task while instructing himself/herself aloud. (f) Have the student whisper the instructions while performing the task. (g) Have the student perform the task covertly.

---

## Reciprocal Teaching

Reciprocal teaching is an interactive teaching strategy that takes the form of a dialogue between teachers and students for the purpose of jointly constructing the meaning of text (Palincsar, 1986). In reciprocal teaching, students and teachers take turns being the teacher, with each individual taking responsibility for leading the dialogue on part of the passage that they are trying to comprehend and remember (Reeve & Brown, 1985). Reciprocal teaching promotes comprehension of text, comprehension monitoring, and self-questioning through interactive discussions about text.

Reciprocal teaching originates from metacognitive, schema (prior knowledge), and active processing theories and has two main conceptual bases: scaffolding and self-questioning (Ashman & Conway, 1989). Scaffolding refers to a temporary support, much like the scaffolding that is used in the construction of a building. Once the building is completed and can stand on its own, the scaffolding is removed. Similarly, when students are acquiring a skill, they may temporarily benefit from supports (reminders of the steps to follow, prompts about questions they could ask themselves, or cue cards containing the steps of a strategy) from the teacher. Once they have attained the skill, the supports (e.g., reminders, prompts, or cue cards) can be removed.

Self-questioning can be used in three ways during reciprocal teaching (Ashman & Conway, 1989). Students can use self-questioning to monitor their own behavior ("What do I need to do first?"), to activate prior knowledge ("What do I already know about this topic that would help me?"), and to generate higher-order questions ("What questions could I ask myself about what was presented on this topic?").

Initially, instruction in reciprocal teaching is teacher-directed, but eventually a student assumes the teacher's role, while other students respond to that student's questions and comments. Reciprocal teaching is used with individuals or with small groups of students, with lessons lasting for about 30 minutes over a 20-day period (Palincsar & Brown, 1986, 1988).

In a series of studies, Brown and Palincsar (1982) and Palincsar and Brown (1984) used a structured dialogue to teach four strategies to junior high students who had adequate decoding skills but poor reading comprehension. The four strategies were summarizing, generating questions, clarifying, and predicting. The students' scores on reading passages improved, with some students reaching the skill levels of their normally achieving peers (Seidenberg, 1988). Comprehension of material presented in regular classes also improved, illustrating that reciprocal teaching produced generalization (Olson & Platt, 1996). When correctly implemented, reciprocal teaching has been effective for teachers working in group settings, in peer tutoring arrangements, in lecture situations, and with reading materials from all content areas (Masters et al., 1993).

## Components of Reciprocal Teaching

The components of reciprocal teaching are instruction in useful strategies, guided interactive instruction, well-informed learners, and readable, meaningful practice materials.

### Instruction in Useful Strategies

Reciprocal teaching involves instruction of students in the use of four strategies: summarizing, question generating, clarifying, and predicting. There is strong evidence that application of these strategies is effective in enhancing reading comprehension (Palincsar, 1986). Notice how the strategies focus on metacognitive skills (awareness and monitoring).

*Summarizing.* Students are taught to identify and paraphrase main ideas in text.

*Question generating.* Students are shown how to ask themselves questions about the content.

*Clarifying.* Students are taught how to identify when there has been a breakdown in comprehension and how to take action to restore meaning (for example, realizing that you do not understand, and rereading or looking back).

*Predicting.* Students are shown how to hypothesize the next event in the text.

### Guided Interactive Instruction

At the beginning of a reciprocal teaching activity, the teacher assumes the leadership role by providing instruction in the four strategies just described: leading the dialogue, asking questions, and making summary statements. Students respond to the teacher's questions and elaborate on the teacher's summary, clarifications, and predictions. Gradually, students assume leadership of the dialogue while the teacher provides support and assistance, perhaps by prompting, encouraging, or providing additional modeling of the strategies. This gradual transfer of control from teacher to students is referred to as scaffolding and is a characteristic of metacognitive strategy instruction.

Remember that one of the goals of cognitive strategy training is to actively involve students in the performance of a task. Brown and Palincsar (1982) compared student performance at the first reciprocal teaching dialogue sessions, when the teacher was in control, with performance at the end, when students had taken control. They found that nonquestions were reduced from 19% to 0% and student responses needing clarification decreased from 36% to 4%.

### Well-Informed Learners

Studies indicate that when students are shown the value of what they are learning, told where and when they can apply the skills being taught, and instructed in how to manage and monitor the skills, they acquire the skills more readily (Palincsar, 1986). Informed training provides students with the rationale for the activities they are asked to do, and helps students understand the significance of the strategy and its potential benefits (Olson & Platt, 1996). Therefore, each day at the beginning of the reciprocal teaching dialogue, teachers should review the strategies, explain why they are important, and discuss opportunities for generalization of the strategies beyond that day's lesson.

In addition, graphing the results of comprehension tests and audio-taping reciprocal teaching sessions help demonstrate to students that using reciprocal teaching leads to positive results (Palincsar & Brown, 1984). Students are able to view firsthand the results of their efforts. This may be particularly helpful for students with a history of academic difficulty and for students with mild disabilities.

### Readable, Meaningful Practice Materials

Researchers in strategy instruction have recommended that practice materials provide readers with the opportunity to read without encountering decoding problems (Deshler, Alley, Warner, & Schumaker, 1981). Palincsar (1986) suggests using material that can be read at 80 words per minute with no more than two errors.

Practice materials should be meaningful, relevant, and functional. Palincsar (1986) recommends selecting materials that are representative of the type of material that students are expected to read in school. At the secondary level, using materials from students' content-area classes may help with the transfer of skills.

## Steps in Implementing Reciprocal Teaching

We combine the suggestions of Masters, Mori, and Mori (1993), Palincsar (1986), and our own in presenting steps for implementing reciprocal teaching.

1. Review the four strategies of summarizing, question generating, clarifying, and predicting along with why they are important and the context in which they are useful. This explanation is reviewed frequently with the students.
2. Read the title and ask students to predict what they will learn.
3. Read a segment of text orally or have the students read it silently (depending on the decoding skills of the students).
4. Ask a question about the content.
5. Summarize the section and ask students to elaborate on the summarization.

6. Discuss any clarifications that students made.

7. Discuss predictions regarding the next segment of text.

In the beginning, the teacher leads the discussion, and initiates and sustains the dialogue. Eventually, the teacher's role is transferred to the students, and the teacher participates as a coach. Box 9.1 includes a sample scripted reciprocal teaching lesson that follows the seven steps for implementing reciprocal teaching.

---

**BOX 9.1**

**Sample Scripted Reciprocal Teaching Lesson**

1. Review the strategies and discuss why they are important and the context in which they are useful.

   *Ms. Johnson:* "Today we will be using our summarizing, questioning, clarifying, and predicting strategies again. Why are these important for us to use?"

   *Lucas:* "They help us understand and remember what we read and study in class."

   *Carol:* "The questioning strategy has helped me get better grades on tests."

   *Ms. Johnson:* "These are great reasons for using the strategies. Where else besides this class have you used the strategies?"

   *Mike:* "I use the prediction and summarization strategies in English and History," and so on.

2. Read the title and ask students to predict what they will learn.

   *Ms. Johnson:* "The title of today's chapter is 'Fats and Oils.' What do you think we'll be learning about?"

   *Sheila:* "A lot is being written about the fat content of foods and how that affects health. I think it will focus on what foods are high in fat and what foods are not."

   *Ms. Johnson:* "Good prediction. Anything else?"

   *Lashon:* "I bet we'll get some information about cholesterol."

   *Ms. Johnson:* "Another prediction that makes sense. Let's read."

3. Read a segment of text orally or have the students read it silently (depending upon the decoding skills of the students).

   Ms. Johnson asks the students to read silently a segment of text that describes the functions of body fat.

4. Ask a question about the content.

   *Ms. Johnson:* "I would like to know what some of the functions of fat are."

**BOX 9.1**
*(continued)*

*Wilma:* "*Fat* supplies us with energy."

*Ms. Johnson:* "Yes. How so?"

*Wilma:* "The body stores fat. Then when we need it, like when we don't get enough fat in our diet, it's there as a source of energy."

*Ms. Johnson:* "Good answer. What is another function of fat?"

*Carol:* "Fat acts as padding."

*Ms. Johnson:* "Right. How does this work?"

*Mike:* "Fat surrounds the heart, kidneys, and other organs and holds them in place. It protects them."

*Ms. Johnson:* "Exactly. Does anyone else have a question?"

*Lashon:* "Does this mean fat is good? I thought fat was bad."

*Mike:* "I think too much fat is bad, but some fat is good and is needed."

5. Summarize the section and ask students to elaborate on the summary.

   *Ms. Johnson:* "I will summarize what we just read. Every part of the body contains some fat. Body fat serves several important functions. It is an energy source, storing fat for later use. It provides insulation and padding and actually protects the organs that it pads from blows. Fat transports some vitamins through the body. Some fat in the diet is important, but most people eat too many fatty foods."

6. Discuss any clarifications that students made.

   *Ms. Johnson:* "Let's clarify Lashon's point about whether fat is good or bad. Mike had a good response. Look back in the passage we just read and see if you can find something to support what Mike said."

   *Lucas:* "Mike said some fat is good, but we shouldn't have too much of it. The text says fat has some important functions and you just summarized them. It also says that eating too many fatty foods may cause heart disease and weight problems."

   *Ms. Johnson:* "So . . ."

   *Lucas:* "So we should have some fat in our diets, but not too much. We should watch the kinds of food we eat."

   *Ms. Johnson:* "Excellent clarification."

7. Discuss predictions regarding the next segment of text.

   *Ms. Johnson:* "I think the next section will give us some information about the types of food that are high in fat and the types that are low in fat. Anyone have another prediction?"

This sample lesson shows the teacher in the lead. Eventually, the students would function in the role of the teacher.

**COMPREHENSION MONITORING OF KEY CONCEPTS**

*Reciprocal Teaching*

1. Reciprocal teaching is an interactive teaching strategy that takes the form of a dialogue between teachers and students for the purpose of jointly constructing the meaning of text.

2. Reciprocal teaching originates from metacognitive, schema (prior knowledge), and active processing theories, and has two main conceptual bases: scaffolding and self-questioning.

3. The components of reciprocal teaching are instruction in useful strategies, guided interactive instruction, well-informed learners, and readable, meaningful practice materials.

4. Reciprocal teaching involves instruction of students in the use of four strategies: summarizing, question generating, clarifying, and predicting.

5. The steps for implementing reciprocal teaching are (a) review the strategies of summarizing, question generating, clarifying, and predicting, (b) read the title and ask for predictions, (c) have students read a segment of text orally or silently, (d) ask a question about the content, (e) summarize the section and ask for elaborations, (f) discuss any clarifications that students made, and (g) discuss predictions regarding the next segment of text.

## Task-Specific Strategy Instruction

The intent of task-specific strategy instruction is to teach students to approach a task in a strategic manner by teaching them how to learn and how to perform (Schmidt, Deshler, Schumaker, & Alley, 1989). Task-specific strategy instruction focuses on tasks (such as taking tests) and on the demands of the curriculum (such as passing content-area and high school competency tests). Through instruction in task-specific strategies, teachers actively involve students in learning, and involve them in setting their own goals (Olson & Platt, 1996).

Emphasis on task-specific strategy instruction is related to the nature of cognitive deficits that many adolescents with learning disabilities display (Ellis, Deshler, & Schumaker, 1989). Problems in executive functioning (ability to create and apply a strategy to complete a task) were found in more than 50% of the 318 adolescents with learning disabilities who were studied by Warner, Schumaker, Alley, and Deshler (1980). However, once taught a task-specific strategy, many students improved in school (Schumaker, Deshler, Alley, Warner, & Denton, 1982) in their test scores and grades. Students have been taught and have successfully applied a variety of task-specific strategies across situations (academic and social), settings (home, school, work, and community), and content areas (including English, science, mathematics, and history).

A strategy is an individual's approach to a task, including how a student thinks and acts when planning, executing, and evaluating a task (Lenz, Clark, Deshler, & Schumaker, 1988). A strategy is a tool that the student can use to analyze the demands of a task, facilitate completion of the task, and help monitor progress along the way (Lenz & Bulgren, 1995). As in previously described cognitive and metacognitive instruction, students progress from following the teacher's directions, cues, and prompts to incorporating and applying the strategy in a self-directed, planned manner (Paris & Cross, 1983). Ellis et al. (1987) offer the following recommendations:

1. *A strategy should contain a set of steps leading to a specified outcome.*
   Each step should begin with a verb or word that relates to the action being cued. For example, RAP is a paraphrasing strategy for reading comprehension (Schumaker et al., 1984):

   *R*ead a paragraph.

   *A*sk yourself what are the main idea and details.

   *P*ut the main idea and details in your own words.

2. *A strategy should cue the use of cognitive strategies and metacognitive processes.* When they use RAP, for example, students monitor their own performance during the reading of text by asking themselves

   "Do I know the main idea of this paragraph?"

   "Have I said it in my own words?"

   "Do I know what to do next?"

3. *A strategy should contain no more than seven steps.* Limiting the steps to a reasonable number ensures that the strategy will be learned and applied.

4. *A strategy should include a remembering system to facilitate recall.* Mnemonics such as RAP are helpful reminders for students.

5. *A strategy should be task-specific rather than situation- or content-specific.* Learning strategies should focus on tasks or curriculum demands, such as preparing for tests, monitoring errors in written work, or writing a theme. These skills are used in a variety of situations across content areas.

© Elizabeth Crews

*A teacher uses "think aloud" as she demonstrates a learning strategy.*

## Critical Features of Task-Specific Strategy Instruction

In surveying the literature on strategy instruction, we find a number of specific features that are characteristic of task-specific strategy instruction. We present suggestions from Ellis, Deshler, Lenz, Schumaker, and Clark (1989), Harris and Pressley (1991), Mercer and Mercer (1993), and Roehler and Duffy (1984), in combination with our own recommendations.

1. Teachers involve students in planning their instructional programs and in setting their own goals and objectives, and they explain the purpose and benefits of specific strategies in relation to students' needs and the demands of the secondary curriculum.

2. Teachers help students analyze their belief systems about themselves as ineffective learners and create new belief systems in which they see themselves as independent problem solvers.

3. Teachers use critical teaching behaviors during instruction such as utilizing advance and post organizers, clarifying expectations, modeling, actively involving students, monitoring student performance, ensuring mastery, and promoting generalization.

4. Teachers describe and model the physical and mental actions involved in using a strategy.

5. Teachers provide instruction in strategies regularly and with intensity.

6. Teachers reinforce and emphasize personal effort. Ellis, Deshler, Lenz, Schumaker, and Clark (1989) use the following formula:

   *Appropriately chosen strategy + Personal effort = Successful problem solving*

7. Teachers emphasize covert processing. Roehler and Duffy (1984) call instruction that emphasizes covert processing "direct explanation" (p. 265); that is, teachers directly teach students the covert processes involved in a task.

8. Teachers provide ample opportunities to practice strategies on a variety of materials across situations, settings, and content areas.

9. Teachers and students identify a variety of contexts within which a strategy can be independently applied in order to promote generalization of strategies.

10. Teachers provide for cooperative planning and teaming among special education, regular education, family, and community participants.

11. Teachers show students how to analyze problems and develop their own strategies (an executive skill) independent of teacher assistance.

## The Strategies Intervention Model

The University of Kansas Institute for Research in Learning Disabilities (now the Center for Research on Learning) was established in 1978 to study the needs of adolescents with learning disabilities and of other low-achieving students. Deshler and Schumaker and their colleagues developed the Strategies Intervention Model specifically for secondary students with learning disabilities. Their research has impacted programs nationwide and increased the knowledge base about secondary programming. Their findings are applicable to all adolescents with mild disabilities (including those with mild mental and emotional disabilities) because of the heterogeneous nature of learning disabilities (Mercer & Mercer, 1993).

We present this model because of its specific focus on the demands of the secondary curriculum, its attention to the characteristics of adolescents with mild disabilities, its learning strategies curriculum materials, and its emphasis on strategic instruction. Space does not permit us to describe the numerous other strategy interventions available in the literature. For additional information on models of strategy instruction, we direct the reader to the work of Archer and Gleason (1992), Derry and Murphy (1986), Ellis (1993), Gaskins and Elliot (1991), Graham, Harris, and Sawyer (1987), Paris (1988), Pressley et al. (1990), Roehler and Duffy (1984), and Wong (1986).

The goal of the Strategies Intervention Model is "to teach adolescents with learning disabilities strategies to facilitate their acquisition, organization, storage, and retrieval of information, thus allowing them to cope with the demands of social interaction" (Alley & Deshler, 1979, p. 8). The Strategies Intervention Model consists of three components: the Strategic Curriculum Component (what strategies are taught), the Strategic Instruction Component (how strategies are taught), and the Strategic Environment Component (how the environment is arranged to enhance strategic performance). (See Box 9.2.)

---

**BOX 9.2**

### Strategies Intervention Model Components

#### *Strategic Curriculum Component*

The Strategic Curriculum Component of the Strategies Intervention Model specifies WHAT will be taught to the low-achieving or at-risk student. This component consists of four types of strategies.

*Learning Strategies:* designed to teach the student how to cope with the academic demands encountered across a variety of school, home, community, and employment settings. These learning strategies teach the student how to respond to critical reading , writing, listening, remembering, and test-taking demands.

*Social Skill Strategies:* designed to teach the student how to interact appropriately across a variety of situations and settings. Strategies such as resisting peer pressure, accepting criticism, negotiating, following directions, and asking for help are included.

*Motivation Strategies:* consists of strategies that enable the student to become active in planning the direction of his or her life. Strategies that teach the student how to set, monitor, and attain goals related to important areas of his or her life and then communicate these goals to others are included.

*Executive Strategies:* designed to teach the student how to independently solve problems and generalize learning. These strategies are taught to students after instruction in three to five learning strategies.

**BOX 9.2**
*(continued)*

## *Strategic Instruction Component*

The Strategic Instruction Component includes procedures for HOW strategies should be taught to students. In addition, it includes procedures for the effective delivery of content to low-achieving and at-risk students.

*Acquisition Procedures:* provides teachers with a sequenced set of steps for teaching the strategies to mastery.

*Generalization Procedures:* provides teachers with a sequenced set of steps for teaching and ensuring generalization and maintenance of newly-acquired strategies to other settings and situations.

*Strategic Teaching Behaviors:* provides teachers with the critical teaching behaviors that should be infused throughout all steps and phases of strategy and content instruction to promote maximum learning by low-achieving and at-risk students.

*Content Enhancement Procedures:* provides teachers with routines and devices for delivering subject-matter information in a manner that can be understood and remembered by students.

## *Strategic Environment Component*

The Strategic Environment Component deals with how to manage and organize educational settings and programs in a manner that will effectively promote and prompt strategic learning and performance.

*Teaming Techniques:* consists of methods related to teaching teachers, students, parents, and other professionals how to work as a team in order to bring about maximum student learning.

*Management Techniques:* consists of methods related to how to manage materials, time, instructional arrangements, and student behavior in a manner that promotes student independence and success.

*Evaluation Techniques:* consists of systems related to evaluating student performance, program performance, and teacher performance and providing feedback about progress to those involved in a manner that will promote student learning and success.

*Development Techniques:* consists of methods related to systematically implementing program components and developing strategies responsive to student needs.

*Source:* From *The Strategies Intervention Model: Planning for a Strategic Learning Environment,* 1990, Lawrence: University of Kansas Institute for Research in Learning Disabilities. Reprinted with permission.

### Strategic Curriculum Component

The strategic curriculum component focuses on content and consists of four types of strategies: *learning strategies* (such as self-questioning, note taking, and error monitoring), *social-skill strategies* (following rules, accepting criticism, and resisting peer pressure), *motivation strategies* (goal setting), and *executive strategies* (adapting, choosing, and developing strategies).

The learning strategies curriculum, in turn, is divided into three strands: the *acquisition strand,* which assists students in acquiring information from printed materials; the *storage strand,* which helps students store and retrieve information; and the *expression and demonstration of competence strand,* which helps students with writing, error monitoring, organization, and test taking (see Box 9.3).

**BOX 9.3**

---

### Learning Strategies Curriculum

#### Acquisition Strand

*Word Identification Strategy:* teaches students a problem-solving procedure for quickly attacking and decoding unknown words in reading materials, allowing them to move on quickly for the purpose of comprehending the passage.

*Paraphrasing Strategy:* directs students to read a limited section of material, ask themselves the main idea and the details of the section, and put that information in their own words. This strategy is designed to improve comprehension by focusing attention on the important information of a passage and by stimulating active involvement with the passage.

*Self-Questioning Strategy:* aids reading comprehension by having students actively ask questions about key pieces of information in a passage and then read to find the answers for these questions.

*Visual Imagery Strategy:* designed to improve students' acquisition, storage, and recall of prose material. Students improve reading comprehension by reading short passages and visualizing the scene which is described, incorporating actors, action, and details.

*Interpreting Visuals Strategy:* designed to aid students in the use and interpretation of visuals such as maps, graphs, pictures, and tables to increase their ability to extract needed information from written materials.

*Multipass Strategy:* involves making three passes through a passage for the purpose of focusing attention on key details and main ideas. Students survey a chapter or passage to get an overview, size up sections of the chapter by systematically scanning to locate relevant information which they note, and sort out important information in the chapter by locating answers to specific questions.

### Storage Strand

*First-Letter Mnemonic Strategy:* designed to aid students in memorizing lists of information by teaching them to design mnemonics or memorization aids, and in finding and making lists of crucial information.

*Paired Associates Strategy:* designed to aid students in memorizing pairs or small groups of information by using visual imagery, matching pertinent information with familiar objects, coding important dates, and a first-syllable technique.

*Listening and Notetaking Strategy:* designed to teach students to develop skills which will enhance their ability to learn from listening experiences by identifying the speaker's verbal cues or mannerisms which signal that important information is about to be given, noting key words, and organizing their notes into an outline for future reference or study.

### Expression and Demonstration of Competence Strand

*Sentence Writing Strategy:* designed to teach students how to recognize and generate four types of sentences: simple, compound, complex, and compound-complex.

*Paragraph Writing Strategy:* designed to teach students how to write well-organized, complete paragraphs by outlining ideas, selecting a point-of-view and tense for the paragraph, sequencing ideas, and checking their work.

*Error Monitoring Strategy:* designed to teach students a process for detecting and correcting errors in their writing and for producing a neater written product. Students are taught to locate errors in paragraph organization, sentence structure, capitalization, overall editing and appearance, punctuation, and spelling by asking themselves a series of questions. Students correct their errors and rewrite the passage before submitting it to their teacher.

*Theme Writing Strategy:* teaches students to write a five-paragraph theme. They learn how to generate ideas for themes and how to organize these ideas into a logical sequence. Then the student learns how to write the paragraphs, monitor errors, and rewrite the theme.

*Assignment Completion Strategy:* teaches students to monitor their assignments from the time an assignment is given until it is completed

*(continued on next page)*

**BOX 9.3**
*(continued)*

and submitted to the teacher. Students write down assignments; analyze the assignments; schedule various subtasks; complete the subtasks, and ultimately, the entire task; and submit the completed assignment.

*Test Taking Strategy:* designed to be used by the student during a test. The student is taught to allocate time and read instructions and questions carefully. A question is either answered or abandoned for later consideration. The obviously wrong answers are eliminated from the abandoned questions and a reasonable guess is made. The last step is to survey the entire test for unanswered questions.

*Source:* From *The Strategies Intervention Model: Planning for a Strategic Learning Environment,* 1990, Lawrence: University of Kansas Institute for Research in Learning Disabilities. Reprinted with permission.

### Strategic Instruction Component

The strategic instruction component focuses on the effective delivery of instruction. It consists of *acquisition procedures, generalization procedures, strategic teaching behaviors,* and *content enhancement procedures.*

**Acquisition procedures.**   The purpose of these acquisition procedures is to give students the knowledge, motivation, and practice necessary to learn and apply a strategy. The acquisition phase consists of seven steps, or stages:

*Stage 1. Pretest*

- Determine the student's current habits regarding a specific task by administering a pretest.
- Communicate results to the student, pointing out effective and ineffective practices.
- Present an alternative to the student's current strategy or lack of strategies.

*Stage 2. Describe the strategy and obtain commitment to learn*

- Orient the student to the new strategy.
- Provide the rationale for learning the strategy and explain the benefits of using the strategy.
- Share results that others have had.
- Describe situations in which the strategy can be used.

- Describe the steps to the strategy.
- Obtain student's commitment to learn the strategy.*
- Ask the student to write goals for learning the strategy.

*Stage 3. Model the strategy*

- Model the entire strategy while thinking aloud.
- Enlist student involvement.
- Provide feedback.

*Stage 4. Provide verbal practice*

*Verbal rehearsal*

- Conduct rapid-fire verbal rehearsal by asking the students to name the steps of the strategy.

*Verbal elaboration*

- Ask students what the steps mean (have them elaborate).
- Ask students when, where, and why they would use the strategy.

*Stage 5. Provide controlled practice and feedback*

- Have students practice the strategy using controlled materials (in which the complexity and level have been reduced).
- Provide feedback and assistance.
- Have students practice until they reach a specified criterion.

*Stage 6. Provide advanced practice and feedback*

- Have students practice the strategy using grade-level materials (similar to what is used in content classes and other natural environments).
- Provide feedback and assistance.
- Have students practice until they reach a specified criterion (both speed and accuracy are stressed).

*Stage 7. Confirm acquisition and obtain generalization commitments*

- Determine the student's progress by administering a posttest.
- Share the results of the student's posttest.
- Obtain the student's commitment to generalize the strategy.

---

*Deshler and colleagues typically include "obtaining commitment to learn the strategy" in the Pretest stage, but indicate it may be included in the Describe stage instead. It has been our firsthand experience working with adolescents that it should be included in the Describe Stage *after* the strategy has been described.

***Generalization procedures.*** Although generalization is included as a separate stage within the strategic instruction component of the Strategies Intervention Model, it is promoted and encouraged throughout the seven stages of acquisition. The four phases of generalization are as follows:

*Phase 1. Orientation*

- Describe various contexts (in and out of school) in which the strategy can be applied.
- Discuss the cues that students will encounter in various settings that will remind them to use the strategy.
- Identify specific content classes in which students will use the strategy.

*Phase 2. Activation*

- Prompt students to use the strategy in other situations, settings, and assignments.
- Explain the strategy to classroom teachers.
- Assist classroom teachers to prompt and reinforce strategy use.
- Develop a method of monitoring students' use of the strategy in content classes.
- Provide feedback to students.
- Ask content teachers for feedback.
- Evaluate the effectiveness of the application of the strategy.

*Phase 3. Adaptation*

- Identify situations, settings, and assignments in which the strategy may have to be adapted/modified.
- Enlist suggestions from content teachers.
- Show students how to adapt/modify the strategy.
- Monitor progress of students' use of the modified strategy.

*Phase 4. Maintenance*

- Conduct periodic probes to determine continued use of the strategy in a variety of settings.
- Enlist support from content teachers in monitoring long-term use of the strategy.
- Assist students in setting goals and planning methods of evaluation of strategy use.

As reported throughout this chapter, cognitive strategy instruction involves a great deal of self-monitoring and self-recording. Ellis et al. (1987)

developed a method of self-monitoring and recording for strategy generalization which we have modified (see Figure 9.2, p. 332). Notice how use of this form can assist students in pinpointing where and when they have applied a strategy and how effective their efforts were.

*Strategic teaching behaviors.* The Strategic Instruction component of the Strategies Intervention Model includes a set of strategic teaching behaviors to be infused throughout all steps and phases of strategy and content instruction. The premise is that students learn more effectively when teachers use advance and post organizers, communicate rationales and expectations, review and check for understanding, ensure intensity of instruction, monitor progress, provide feedback, and require mastery. You will notice that these strategic teaching behaviors are similar to those presented in our discussion of the effective teaching research in Chapter 7.

*Content enhancement procedures.* The last component of Strategic Instruction is the use of content enhancement procedures. These are planning and teaching routines for presenting content in a manner that can be organized, understood, and remembered by students. The use of content enhancement procedures is based upon the premise that students learn more when (1) they are actively involved, (2) abstract concepts are presented in concrete forms, (3) information is organized for them, (4) relationships among pieces of information are made explicit, and (5) important information is distinguished from unimportant information (Lenz, Marrs, Schumaker, & Deshler, 1993). We provide examples in our discussion of content in Chapter 8.

### Strategic Environment Component

The Strategic Environment Component focuses on how to manage and organize programs and materials, and consists of teaming, management, evaluation, and development techniques. *Teaming techniques* bring together students, parents, teachers, administrators, and other professionals in order to achieve maximum benefits for students. Roles and responsibilities are carefully defined, and collaboration is emphasized. *Management techniques* are used to manage time, materials, and individuals in a manner that promotes student learning and performance. *Evaluation techniques* provide feedback about student, teacher, and program effectiveness. *Development techniques* are used for the ongoing development of strategies that are responsive to student needs.

Netherton, Wickham, Gipson, Platt, and Corrales (1992) have developed a resource book for teachers to use with middle and high school students in the instruction of learning strategies. Its primary purpose is to provide teachers with an easy-to-use source of visual displays that are correlated to each of the learning strategies. For more information about the Strategies Intervention Model, contact Dr. Donald Deshler or Dr. Jean Schumaker, University of Kansas, Center for Research on Learning, 3061 Dole Center for Human Development, Lawrence, Kansas 66045.

### Sample Learning and Motivation Strategies

Each of the following strategies should be taught using the acquisition and generalization procedures and the strategic teaching behaviors.

*Self-Questioning Strategy.* Schumaker, Deshler, Nolan, and Alley (1994) have developed a strategy to help students meet the reading demands of elementary, secondary, and postsecondary settings. The Self-Questioning Strategy requires students to generate questions, predict answers to them, and find the answers as they read a passage. The mnemonic for this strategy is ASK IT:

*A*ttend to clues as you read.

*S*ay some questions.

*K*eep predictions in mind.

*I*dentify the answers.

*T*alk about the answers.

*Test-taking strategy.* Hughes, Schumaker, Deshler, and Mercer (1988) have developed a strategy to provide students with a comprehensive routine to use when taking tests in a variety of test-taking situations across content areas. The mnemonic for this strategy is PIRATES; notice that the substeps also have mnemonics of their own.

*P*repare to succeed.
- *P*ut name and PIRATES on the test.
- *A*llot time and order.
- *S*ay affirmations.
- *S*tart within two minutes.

*I*nspect the instructions.
- *R*ead.
- *U*nderline what and where.
- *N*ote special requirements.

*R*ead, remember, reduce.

*A*nswer or abandon.

*T*urn back.

*E*stimate.
- *A*void absolutes.
- *C*hoose the longest choice.
- *E*liminate similar choices.

*S*urvey. (p. 98)

***Self-advocacy strategy.*** Van Reusen, Bos, Schumaker, and Deshler (1994) have developed a motivation strategy that students can use when preparing for and participating in education or transition planning meetings. Students use SHARE behaviors during the meeting to assist them with their interpersonal skills.

*S*it up straight.

*H*ave a pleasant tone of voice.

*A*ctivate your thinking.
- Tell yourself to pay attention.
- Tell yourself to participate.
- Tell yourself to compare ideas.

*R*elax.
- Don't look uptight.
- Tell yourself to stay calm.

*E*ngage in eye communication.

They use I PLAN when planning for and participating in these meetings.

*I*nventory your
- strengths.
- areas to improve or learn.
- goals.
- choices for learning or accommodations.

*P*rovide your inventory information.

*L*isten and respond.

*A*sk questions.

*N*ame your goals. (pp. 129–130)

## Activities and Materials for Cognitive Strategy Instruction

In this section, we suggest activities and materials to complement the teaching of cognitive strategies. These activities should be used to support and supplement your teacher-directed instruction (modeling while thinking aloud, overt and covert responding, and so on).

## Activities

1. Have students use techniques such as K-W-L (K = what they know, W = what they want to learn, L = what they learned) across content areas, with educational videotapes and television programs, and in conjunction with guest speakers and field trips.

2. Bring in magazine and newspaper articles that students will find interesting and that relate to the content you are teaching, and have students write summary statements.

3. Have students modify story grammar elements to develop a set of components that will work with content-area topics such as global warming or overpopulation (for example, topic, definitions of terms, problems, options, possible results).

4. To work on note taking: Using the overhead projector, model how to take notes while watching a videotape. Students can watch the video and see what you write down. When the videotape is over, go back and "think aloud" why you wrote what you did.

5. To work on sentence writing: Bring in copies of magazines, tabloids, or ads from the newspapers, or show videotapes of commercials, and have students write simple, compound, and complex sentences about something they read or see.

6. To work on self-questioning: Have students follow a current events topic in the news and on television that relates to a content area in school (such as social studies). Have them practice generating questions, predictions, and facts about the topic and relate it to what is being studied in school.

7. To work on paraphrasing: Have students paraphrase easy, motivating, and interesting material before they paraphrase difficult content texts. Use cartoons, articles from magazines (such as *Auto Trader* or *Sports Illustrated*), school bulletins and newsletters, catalogs, a segment from the evening news, or television commercials.

8. Have students work in groups to develop an interaction frame to accompany a textbook chapter or topic (see Figure 9.1).

9. Give practice in self-monitoring by having students write a goal (for example, homework completion, scores on math quizzes, number of words written) and then chart their progress each day toward achieving that goal.

10. Assess the metacognitive awareness and monitoring skills of your students by asking them to describe their own thoughts and actions while performing a task (such as reading a passage). Then ask them to suggest ways to improve their performance (strategies they might try or adjustments they might make).

## Software Materials

*Program Name:* Building Better Sentences: Creating Compound and Complex Sentences
*Computer Platform:* Apple
*Level:* Middle School
*Publisher:* Media Materials, Inc.
*Strategies:* Sentence Writing and Error Monitoring

This program is designed to provide practice in sentence composition and is effective for working on sentence writing and error monitoring strategies. Students can create simple and complex sentences using adverb and adjective clauses. The program provides students with rules and examples of the various sentence types.

*Program Name:* Developing Writing Skills
*Computer Platform:* Apple (64K), Macintosh (128K), IBM PC (64K)
*Level:* Intermediate–High School
*Publisher:* Intellectual Software
*Strategies:* Sentence Writing and Paragraph Writing

This is a three-disk program covering word choice, sentences, and paragraphs. Lessons are easy to read and assume little previous knowledge of topics covered. Students learn to use specific words, well-constructed sentences, and coherent paragraphs through a tutorial and drill exercise program.

*Program Name:* Building Memory Skills
*Computer Platform:* Apple (48K), IBM
*Level:* Middle School to Adult
*Publisher:* Microcomputer Education, Inc.
*Strategies:* Memory, Mnemonics

This program requires a sixth grade-reading level. The teacher may need to review vocabulary needed for concept development in the program. The program introduces students to techniques for remembering information. Techniques for memorization such as attention, association, visualization, and organization are presented in an interactive manner throughout the program.

*Program Name:* How to Identify the Main Idea
*Computer Platform:* Apple
*Level:* Middle and High School
*Publisher:* Science Research Associates, Inc.
*Strategies:* Paraphrasing and Summarizing

This combined computer/worktext program helps students identify stated and implied main ideas. The program provides practice with materials in science, social studies, and literature. There are 18 examples per subject area on three reading levels. Junior high (reading level grades 7–9), and senior high (reading level grades 9–12) versions are available. Important points are highlighted on the screen. This program is best suited for higher-functioning students who need work in regular content-area texts.

*Program Name:* Urban Reader
*Computer Platform:* Apple (64K)
*Level:* Middle and High School
*Publisher:* Educational Publishing Concepts, Inc.
*Strategies:* Paraphrasing
This program is a high-interest/low-readability comprehension program for students in urban settings in grades 7–12. Selections are approximately 300 words in length and are written on reading levels 4–9. Students read passages and answer questions. If a question is answered incorrectly, the program takes the student back to the part of the story where the correct answer can be found, and an explanation is given for why it is the correct answer. The program includes a recordkeeping system and colorful graphics.

*Program Name:* Examine the Stem
*Computer Platform:* Apple (48K)
*Level:* Middle and High School
*Publisher:* Tom St. Clair (public domain software)
*Strategies:* Word Identification
This program describes the parts of a word and shows how to separate the root word from its suffix and/or prefix. The student divides the word using the pencil that appears on the screen. This program is easy to follow, has good graphics, and includes corrective feedback.

*Program Name:* Skills for Successful Test Taking
*Computer Platform:* Apple (48K), IBM PC and PS/2
*Level:* Middle School–Adult
*Publisher:* MCE, Inc.
*Strategies:* Test Taking
The program provides interactive learning activities that improve test-taking skills. It includes standard tests and provides sample questions. The tutorial emphasizes the importance of preparation, reading and following of directions, and student attitudes. The program contains pre- and post-tests. The program reading level is grades 6–7.

*Program Name:* Test Taking Made Easy
*Computer Platform:* Apple (48K), IBM PC and PS/2
*Level:* Middle–High School
*Publisher:* MCE, Inc.
*Strategies:* Test Taking

The program is a high-interest/low-vocabulary program designed to improve test-taking skills. The reading level of this program is third grade, while the interest level is grade 7 to adult. Specific techniques are included for answering true-false, multiple-choice, and fill-in-the-blank questions. Students respond by typing in a word or letter. The program prints out a description of students' specific strengths and weaknesses.

## COMPREHENSION MONITORING OF KEY CONCEPTS

### *Task-Specific Strategy Instruction*

1. A strategy is an individual's approach to a task, including how a student thinks and acts when planning, executing, and evaluating a task.

2. Task-specific strategies typically (a) contain a set of no more than seven steps, (b) cue cognitive and metacognitive processes, (c) include a remembering system, and (d) are task-specific rather than situation- or content-specific.

3. Characteristic features of task-specific strategy instruction are that teachers: (a) involve students in planning, (b) help students analyze their belief systems, (c) use critical teaching behaviors, (d) describe and model strategies, (e) reinforce student efforts, (f) emphasize covert processing, (g) provide practice opportunities, (h) promote generalization of strategies, (i) provide for cooperative planning with others, and (j) show students how to develop their own strategies.

4. The Strategies Intervention Model focuses on directly teaching strategies to students, having students practice strategies with controlled materials, and then having students apply the strategies to regular classroom content materials and generalize their use.

5. The Strategies Intervention Model consists of three components: the strategic curriculum component (what strategies are taught), the strategic instruction component (how strategies are taught), and the strategic environment component (how the environment is arranged to enhance strategic performance).

6. The strategic curriculum component consists of learning strategies, social-skill strategies, motivation strategies, and executive strategies.

*(continued on next page)*

7. The strategic instruction component consists of acquisition procedures, generalization procedures, strategic teaching behaviors, and content enhancement procedures.

8. The strategic environment component consists of teaming, management, evaluation, and development techniques.

*A final note:* In this chapter, we have presented information about cognitive strategies and have shown you how to implement strategy instruction by using metacognition, cognitive behavior modification, reciprocal teaching, and task-specific strategy instruction. There is overlap among these approaches, as all of them incorporate metacognitive tactics, actively involve students, are taught systematically with steps or procedures, utilize scaffolding with the gradual transfer of strategy regulation, incorporate cognitive modeling, and promote generalization.

Remember, good cognitive strategy instruction is not the memorization of steps to be carried out in a mechanistic way. Good strategy instruction involves making students aware of strategies, how and why they work, and when and where to use them (Harris & Pressley, 1991). We urge you to add cognitive strategy instruction to your repertoire of effective techniques for adolescents with mild disabilities.

---

 Now that you have read Chapter 9, reflect on your earlier responses at the beginning of the chapter and complete this post organizer.

1. Describe and give examples of the types of instructional techniques you might use to teach a lesson using the principles of cognitive strategy instruction.

2. Think back to the metacognitive activity at the beginning of the chapter in which you read a passage, wrote down what you noticed about your reading, and then indicated what you would do to adjust your performance of the task. What additional knowledge have you gained about your reading from the information in this chapter? What strategies could you use to monitor your own comprehension that are different from those you identified before reading the chapter?

3. Now that you have thought about your metacognitive awareness and monitoring skills, think about how to teach students to improve their own metacognitive awareness and monitoring performance. Design a metacognitive activity for a secondary student in the content area of your choice. Be sure to include both awareness and monitoring activities.

---

# CHAPTER 10

# School Survival and Study Skills

© Kathy Sloane/Jeroboam

 Before you read Chapter 10, use your prior knowledge to complete this advance organizer.

1. Working in a small group, discuss the reasons for including instruction in school survival and study skills in the middle school and high school curriculum.

2. Working with your group again, focus on school survival skills. First define school survival skills, and then list the five that you think are the most essential in order to succeed at the secondary level.

3. Working alone this time, identify the specific study skills that you possessed when you began attending secondary school. Which study skills were you lacking, and how did you handle the situation?

In this chapter, we present student-directed strategies and skills called school survival and study skills. These skills represent what students can use independently to ensure success both within and outside the school setting. They include the school survival skills of teacher-pleasing/class-participation behaviors and organizational skills, and the study skills of listening, note taking, textbook usage, and test taking. A secondary school program that includes school survival and study skills can provide adolescents with mild disabilities with the self-confidence and skills to function effectively in postsecondary education or employment.

## Introduction and Rationale

As adolescents enter secondary settings, they face new academic challenges and complex setting demands. They are expected to navigate large school buildings, arrive in class on time with the appropriate materials and supplies, acquire and retain academic content from class lectures and presentations, adjust to the varied requirements and teaching styles of several different teachers, exhibit good work habits, and make good grades (see Chapter 2). To successfully meet these challenges and handle the setting demands, they need school survival and study skills.

*School survival skills* refer to the expectations that teachers have for students—the behaviors that increase the opportunity for academic success in educational settings (Brown, Kerr, Zigmond, & Harris, 1984). Often they fall into the categories of teacher-pleasing behaviors, class participation, and organization skills. Specific skills related to these categories include showing an interest in school, complying with teacher directions and requests, demonstrating good work habits, attending class, monitoring assignments, and taking an active role in one's own learning (Bursuck, Kinder, & Epstein, 1989; Zigmond, Kerr, Schaeffer, Brown, & Farra, 1986). These skills are also expected by employers in work settings.

*Study skills* are those competencies associated with acquiring, recording, organizing, synthesizing, remembering, and using information (Devine, 1987; Hoover, 1988). Study skills include listening, note taking, outlining, textbook usage, test taking, reference skills, and others that are needed for success in academic settings (such as math class) and nonacademic settings (such as the work place). Study skills represent the key to independent learning by helping students acquire and use information effectively (Bos & Vaughn, 1994).

Students with mild disabilities need to learn school survival skills in order to interact and participate in class, complete assignments, organize their time and materials, and work independently to complete homework.

They must also be taught study skills to help them first acquire and retain academic content through listening, note taking, and textbook usage, and then demonstrate knowledge of academic content in test taking. Through instruction in study skills, students learn systematic approaches for completing classroom tasks and strategies for compensating for deficiencies in basic skills (Silverman, Zigmond, & Sansone, 1981).

---

### COMPREHENSION MONITORING OF KEY CONCEPTS

#### Introduction and Rationale

1. To successfully handle the academic challenges and complex setting demands of secondary schools, adolescents with mild disabilities need school survival and study skills.

2. School survival skills refer to the expectations that teachers have for students—the behaviors that increase the opportunity for academic success in educational settings. School survival skills include showing an interest in school, complying with teacher directions and requests, demonstrating good work habits, attending class, monitoring assignments, and taking an active role in learning.

3. Study skills are those competencies associated with acquiring, recording, organizing, synthesizing, remembering, and using information. Study skills include listening, note taking, textbook usage, test taking, and others that are needed for success in both academic and nonacademic settings.

4. Students with mild disabilities need to learn school survival skills in order to interact and participate in class, complete assignments, organize their time and materials, and work independently to complete homework.

5. Students with mild disabilities need to be taught study skills to help them (a) acquire and retain academic content through listening, note taking, and textbook usage, and (b) demonstrate knowledge of academic content through test taking.

---

## School Survival Skills

The success of students with mild disabilities in regular content class (such as being prepared for and participating in class discussions) and real-life situations (such as interacting on the job and in the community) would be enhanced if these students independently used school survival skills or strategies. In this section, we focus on teacher-pleasing behaviors, class-participation skills, and organization skills (time, materials, and assignments).

## Teacher-Pleasing Behaviors/Class-Participation Skills

Teacher-pleasing behaviors are those that help students cope with the rules and demands in their classes and that cause teachers to view them more positively (Zigmond, 1990). Many students learn these skills incidentally, by observing. They come to class prepared and on time, make eye contact, ask and respond to questions in class, look interested and involved in the lesson, and comply with requests and directions. Many students with mild disabilities, however, do not learn and display these behaviors spontaneously. Instead, they appear uninterested and uncooperative, and may actually alienate the teacher. Teacher-pleasing/class-participation strategies can and have been taught to adolescents with mild disabilities.

Ellis (1989) has designed a number of specific strategies to help students with mild disabilities learn and exhibit school survival skills. These strategies include SLANT, RELATE, PREP, and PREPARE. SLANT and RELATE teach students to display an interest, participate, and interact appropriately in class. PREP and PREPARE help students take an active role in their own learning and demonstrate good work habits. The strategies all involve acronyms to help students remember the behaviors. SLANT stands for:

S  =  Sit up.

L  =  Lean forward.

A  =  Act like you're interested.

N  =  Nod your head.

T  =  Track the teacher with your eyes.

Suggestions for "Act like you're interested" include asking and answering questions, maintaining eye communication, writing down key information presented by the teacher, and referring to handouts, textbooks, or outlines provided by the teacher.

A strategy that can be used along with SLANT to increase a student's verbal participation during content classes is RELATE (Ellis, 1989). Students learn how to use "alert" words that signal important information, such as reasons, examples, or comparisons, and learn how to contribute by asking questions or making comments (Meese, 1994).

R = Reveal reasons.
Listen for alert words such as "prior to" and the reasons. Paraphrase the reasons back to the teacher.

E = Echo examples.
Listen for alert words such as "for example" and the examples. Paraphrase the examples back to the teacher.

L = Lasso comparisons.
Listen for alert words such as "similarly" and the comparisons. Paraphrase the similarities and/or differences back to the teacher.

A = Ask questions.
Ask yourself if the information makes sense. If not, ask a question at an appropriate pause.

T = Tell the main idea.
Listen for alert words such as "in summary." Listen for a main-idea statement. Paraphrase the main idea.
*or*
Tell what you think the main idea is and see if others agree with you.

E = Examine importance.
Ask the teacher to say what is most important.
*or*
Decide what you think is most important. Tell what you think is most important and see if others agree with you.

Notice the metacognitive nature of the strategy as students listen for "alert" words (awareness) and ask themselves questions (monitoring). RELATE can be used independently by a student or in small groups, by systematically following the six steps.

The PREP strategy (Ellis, 1989) is designed to help students prepare for class. We share the PREP strategy along with our own descriptors.

P = Prepare materials for class.
Bring textbook, notebook, pen/pencil, homework, study guide.

R = Review what you know.
Write at least three items known about the topic.

E = Establish positive mindset.
Write a positive statement about yourself.

P = Pinpoint goals.
Write a question about the topic and your participation goals.

Ellis (1989) reports that students who have used his class participation and preparation strategies have come to class better prepared and have increased their academic responding time during class.

The PREPARE strategy (Ellis & Lenz, 1987) is designed to help middle school students prepare for class. It is suggested that students write the steps on an index card and carry it with them throughout the school day (Rafoth & Leal, 1993). We present the PREPARE steps with our own descriptors.

P = Plan locker visits.
    Decide when you can get to your locker (for example, before first, third, and sixth periods, and after lunch).

R = Reflect on what you need and get it.
    Decide which books, assignments, homework, and supplies you need.

E = Erase personal needs.
    Put aside your personal problems before going to class.

P = Psych yourself up for the class.
    Decide what you want to accomplish and set a goal for the class you are going to. Focus on the positive and tell yourself you can do it.
    P = Pause for an attitude check.
    S = Say a personal goal related to the class.
    Y = Yoke in your negative thoughts.
    C = Challenge yourself to good performance.

A = Ask yourself where the class has been and where the class is going.
    Think back about what you have been doing in the class. Ask yourself how what you are doing now fits into what you have done.

R = Review notes and study guides.
    Look back at your notes to remind yourself what was covered during the last class and how that ties in with today's class.

E = Explore the meaning of the teacher's introduction.
    Focus on the class introduction and decide what the class will be about today.

---

**COMPREHENSION MONITORING OF KEY CONCEPTS**

*Teacher-Pleasing Behaviors/Class-Participation Skills*

1. Teacher-pleasing behaviors/class participation skills are those that help students cope with the rules and demands in their classes and that cause teachers to view them more positively.

2. SLANT (Ellis, 1989) is a strategy to help students with mild disabilities exhibit teacher-pleasing behaviors in content classes.

3. RELATE (Ellis, 1989) is a strategy to increase a student's verbal participation during content classes.

4. PREP (Ellis, 1989), a class preparation strategy, has helped students come to class better prepared and has increased their academic responding time during class.

5. PREPARE (Ellis & Lenz, 1987) is a strategy developed for middle school students to help them prepare for class.

### Organization Skills

Many students with mild disabilities lack the organization skills that many other students seem to pick up on their own. However, in order to successfully negotiate the demands of secondary school programs, students need to have an organization system. In this section, we share strategies for completing assignments, managing time, and managing materials.

#### *Completing Assignments*

A student's failure to complete work on time leaves teachers with a poor impression of the student's attitude toward school, and may result in poor grades (Schaeffer, Zigmond, Kerr, & Farra, 1990). WATCh is a strategy developed by Glomb and West (1990) to help students with behavior disorders complete their assignments thoroughly, accurately, neatly, and on time.

W = Write down the assignment, the due date, and any special requirements in an assignment planner.

A = Ask yourself if you understand the assignment, and ask for clarification if necessary.

T = Task-analyze the assignment and schedule the task over the days available to complete the assignment.

Ch = Check each task as you do it with CAN (substrategy):
    C = Completeness
    A = Accuracy
    N = Neatness

Another four-step strategy to help students complete their assignments thoroughly, accurately, and on time was developed by Archer and Gleason (1994) as part of their Skills for School Success series.

Step 1:   Plan it.
- Read the directions carefully.
- Circle the words that tell you what to do.
- Get out the materials you need.
- Tell yourself what to do.

Step 2:   Complete it.
- Do all the items.
- If you can't do an item, ask for help or go ahead to the next item.
- Use HOW.

Step 3:   Check it.
- Did you do everything?
- Did you get the right answers?
- Did you proofread?

Step 4:   Turn it in.

HOW in step 2 is a substrategy to help students complete their written assignments neatly and in an organized manner: H = Heading, O = Organized (with adequate margins and spacing), and W = Written neatly.

Frequently students in middle and high school are given assignments or projects at the beginning of a grading period that are not due until the middle or end of the 6- to 9-week period. If teachers do not provide checkpoints along the way, students should independently set these dates for themselves. For example, if a research report is due in six weeks, students might identify their own intermediate steps and design the following schedule for themselves:

Week 1    Use the class text and notes in combination with a visit to the media center to reflect on possible topics for the project.

Week 2    Select the topic and collect information about the topic. Read through the information and make notes.

Week 3    Organize the information collected, make an index card for each reference, and make an outline of the report.

Week 4    Use the computer, write the first draft of the report.

Week 5    Edit, use spell-check, and finalize the report on the computer. Complete a bibliography.

Week 6    Proofread the report, make final adjustments, and hand it in.

Because students with mild disabilities, who tend to lack organizational skills, may find long-term projects overwhelming, they should break tasks down into smaller, more easily achieved steps. In this way, they have a better chance of completing the assignment accurately and on time.

***Completing homework.*** For students in middle and high school, homework is important to academic achievement and school success (Mercer & Mercer, 1993). Homework gives students the opportunity to practice previously presented material, preview and review content, and complete projects and other assignments. Homework appears to play a significant role in a student's overall success in a given subject, and may affect the student's relationship with the classroom teacher (Lombardi, 1995).

Students should ask themselves a series of questions before, during, and after their completion of homework.

### Before

1. Do I understand the homework assignment?
2. What do I need to ask the teacher before I leave class?
3. What information and materials will I need in order to complete the homework assignment?
4. How much time should I allot to the completion of this assignment?
5. Is the homework assignment a review of something taught, a preview of a new lesson, preparation for a test, or a long-term project?
6. When is this homework assignment due?

### During

1. Am I doing this correctly? Should I check with anyone?
2. How am I doing on time?
3. Do I have all the necessary resources to complete this assignment?
4. What else do I have to do for tomorrow?
5. Where shall I put this assignment so I will remember to take it with me tomorrow?

### After

1. Did I choose a good place to work?
2. Was I able to concentrate?
3. Did I work quickly and accurately?
4. How will this assignment count toward my grade in the class?
5. Was the assignment easy or difficult?
6. What could I have done to improve my completion of this homework assignment?

Seman (1995, p. 53) has devised a strategy to help students self-monitor their homework completion.

H  =  Have a regular time and place to work each day.

O  =  Organize a monthly, weekly, and daily calendar.

M  =  Mark each assignment in a separate notebook or on the calendar.
    R  =  Read directions for each assignment.
    A  =  Ask the teacher if you don't know what to do.
    T  =  Take all necessary materials home.
    E  =  Examine the calendar daily.

E  =  Elect to do the shortest assignment.

W  =  Write the amount of time given to complete it.

O  =  On with it.

R  =  Record with a check mark when items are done.

K  =  Keep homework in an assigned place (get signature if necessary).

### Managing Time

Adolescents with mild disabilities frequently fail to finish assignments, turn in incomplete assignments, and are late for class or appointments (Masters et al., 1993). Many of these difficulties are due to ineffective and inefficient use of time.

*Analyzing use of time.* The first step in improving students' use of time is having them analyze how they are currently spending their time. Students should record for one week what they do from the time they get up in the morning until they go to bed at night. Students can use a preprinted chart as shown in Figure 10.1. After completing this activity, they will be able to decide whether they are using their time effectively.

*Prioritizing use of time.* After the analysis is complete, students may decide to change their priorities. If they are spending too much time watching TV, they may take some of their TV time and put it into homework, job, working out, or activities with friends.

*Setting time management goals.* Once students have decided on priorities for using their time, they are ready to set goals. Adam sets the goal "By the end of the first week of the grading period, I will be spending more time on homework than on watching TV." Some students find it helpful to set up a daily "To Do" list consisting of "Must Do," "Should Do," and "Nice to Do" goals. For example, Adam decides that on Monday, he "must" finish his history report because it is due on Tuesday, he "should" read the next chapter in biology, and it would be "nice" to put new speakers in his car (see Figure 10.2).

**FIGURE 10.1 Time Analysis Chart**

Name: _Adam Preston_      Date: _Jan. 22-28_

*Directions:* For one week, write down what you do each hour from the time you get up in the morning until you go to bed at night.

| Time | Monday | Tuesday | Wednesday | Thursday | Friday | Saturday | Sunday |
|------|--------|---------|-----------|----------|--------|----------|--------|
| 6:00–7:00 A.M. | Eat/get ready | Eat/get ready | Eat/get ready | Eat/get ready | Eat/get ready | Sleep | Sleep |
| 7:00–8:00 A.M. | Walk to bus/ Ride bus | Walk to bus/ Ride bus | Walk to bus/ Ride bus | Walk to bus/ Ride bus | Walk to bus/ Ride bus | Sleep | Sleep |
| 8:00–9:00 A.M. | English | English | English | English | English | Eat/get ready | Eat/get ready |
| 9:00–10:00 A.M. | Math | Math | Math | Math | Math | Work | Church |
| 10:00–11:00 A.M. | History | History | History | History | History |  | Work |
| 11:00–12:00 P.M. | P.E. | P.E. | P.E. | P.E. | P.E. |  |  |
| 12:00–1:00 P.M. | Lunch | Lunch | Lunch | Lunch | Lunch |  |  |
| 1:00–2:00 P.M. | Biology | Biology | Biology | Biology | Biology |  |  |
| 2:00–3:00 P.M. | Voc. Ed. | Voc. Ed. | Voc. Ed. | Voc. Ed. | Voc. Ed. |  |  |
| 3:00–4:00 P.M. | Ride bus/ walk from bus | Ride bus/ Walk from bus | Ride bus/ Walk from bus | Ride bus/ Walk from bus | Ride bus/ walk from bus |  |  |
| 4:00–5:00 P.M. | Watch TV | Shoot baskets | Watch TV | Watch TV | Hang out with friends | Hang out with friends | Watch TV |
| 5:00–6:00 P.M. | Watch TV | Watch TV | Hang out with friends | Watch TV | Hang out with friends | Go out to eat | Watch TV |
| 6:00–7:00 P.M. | Eat dinner | Eat dinner | Eat dinner | Eat dinner | Eat dinner | Hang out | Eat dinner |
| 7:00–8:00 P.M. | Dishes/chores | Dishes/chores | Dishes/chores | Dishes/chores | Dishes/chores | Basketball Game and | Dishes/chores |
| 8:00–9:00 P.M. | Talk on phone | Watch TV | Watch TV | Watch TV | Go out | Hang Out | Watch TV |
| 9:00–10:00 P.M. | Nothing | Watch TV | Nothing | Homework |  |  | Nothing |
| 10:00–11:00 P.M. | Homework | Homework | Homework | Sleep |  |  | Homework |
| 11:00–12:00 A.M. | Sleep | Sleep | Sleep | Sleep |  |  | Sleep |

**FIGURE 10.2  Daily Goals**

> ## "To Do" List
>
> ### <u>Monday</u>
>
> #### <u>Must Do</u>
> 1. Fill in schedule for the week.
> 2. Finish history report for Tuesday.
> 3. Bring in an article to discuss in biology.
>
> #### <u>Should Do</u>
> 1. Read next chapter in biology.
> 2. Write an essay for extra credit to raise my English grade.
> 3. Get started on vocational education project.
>
> #### <u>Nice to Do</u>
> 1. Work overtime to make some extra money.
> 2. Put new speakers in the car.

***Scheduling use of time.*** Students should set up a weekly schedule to keep track of what they need to do. For example, after examining his time analysis chart, Adam could design a weekly schedule to include more time for homework and less time for watching TV.

In addition to using a weekly schedule, students may find it helpful to follow some general scheduling guidelines. We present ideas from Langan (1982) and Bos and Vaughn (1994), along with our own recommendations for students to use when setting up their schedule.

1. Schedule regular times to work on school assignments, and plan them in blocks of about one hour.

2. When working on assignments for more than an hour, plan short breaks, particularly when working on the computer.

3. Work on assignments before and after going to class: before, to read and prepare for the class; and after, to review what was presented and to get ready for the next class.

4. Prioritize your assignments, working on the most pressing requirements first, as indicated on your "Must Do" list.

5. Work on your most difficult and challenging assignments when you are most alert.

6. Conduct cumulative reviews so that you avoid cramming for tests, and distribute review sessions over several days.

7. Try to plan a balanced schedule with time allotted to family activities, recreation with friends, working out at the gym, and after-school work (paid or unpaid).

8. Prepare a written schedule each week. Use abbreviations for subjects and words (such as Eng. for English, pp. for pages, ? for questions).

9. Keep your schedule flexible. Make changes as needed.

10. Cross off items as you complete them, or make notes on your schedule at the end of each day or week.

***Monitoring use of time.*** Once students have created their schedules, they should monitor their progress. Students should check off items as they are completed, note their progress, and write notes explaining partial completion of an item or a change of item in cases where something else takes priority.

Some students prefer to use a monthly assignment calendar on which they record upcoming tests, projects, and school activities (see Figure 10.3). Keeping a calendar or planner may help students use their time more effectively and complete more assignments.

### Managing Materials

Many students have no system for organizing materials (Archer & Gleason, 1995). In middle and high school, students are expected to store notes, handouts, homework, and other materials for each class together, take assignments and materials back and forth from school, and quickly retrieve necessary materials during classes. One method of organization that may help adolescents is the use of a notebook.

Three-ring binders can be used for storing weekly schedules or assignment calendars, notebook paper, graph paper, handouts, notes, school newsletters/notices, vocabulary lists or glossaries, study guides, and outlines or syllabi. The notebook should contain paper separated by tabbed dividers for each class or subject. Pens, pencils, a calculator, and computer disks can be stored in a plastic pouch which can be inserted into the binder. To reinforce the use of binders, teachers may award points toward the grade in the class to those students who use and maintain notebooks.

**FIGURE 10.3** Monthly Assignment Calendar

| Monday | Tuesday | Wednesday | Thursday | Friday | Saturday | Sunday |
|---|---|---|---|---|---|---|
| | | | 1<br>Study for Math test | 2<br>Math test<br>Basketball Game | 3 | 4 |
| 5 | 6<br>Choose topic for Science report | 7 | 8 | 9<br>Go to media center & collect info. for science report. | 10<br>School fundraiser | 11 |
| 12 | 13<br>Turn in Outline for science report | 14 | 15<br>Meet with study group & study for English test | 16<br>English Test<br>Basketball Game | 17 | 18 |
| 19 | 20<br>Turn in first draft of science report | 21<br>History test | 22 | 23 | 24<br>Work Overtime | 25 |
| 26 | 27<br>Final draft of science report due. | 28 | | | | |

Students can monitor their own organization skills by completing a brief checklist for each of their classes on a daily basis. This type of activity gives students with organization problems a better perspective on their ability to organize materials independently. The checklist in Figure 10.4 can be reproduced for each class. Students can use the blank lines to write in any special materials (such as calculator for math, dictionary for English, swimsuit and towel for physical education, lab book for science) that may be required.

We have presented a variety of school survival skills (teacher-pleasing behaviors, class participation skills, and organization skills) that will help your students meet the complex demands of the secondary school setting. During the middle and high school years, you can assist your students to move from dependence to independence in learning and to become good

**FIGURE 10.4 Daily Checklist**

Class _____ Date _____

*Directions:* Write "yes" in the space next to each item that you remembered to bring to class. Do this for each day of the week. Write "no" if you did not bring the item.

|  | M | T | W | Th | F |
|---|---|---|---|---|---|
| • Assignment calendar or weekly schedule | | | | | |
| • Homework assignment | | | | | |
| • Three-ring notebook with paper | | | | | |
| • Textbook | | | | | |
| • Pen/pencils | | | | | |
| • _____ | | | | | |
| • _____ | | | | | |

*Note:* For classes in which there was no homework assigned, write N/A for not applicable.

planners and decision makers. At the beginning of the school year, and again at the start of each new grading period, you should state your expectations to your students and teach the skills necessary for students to be successful and function independently in the school environment.

Teacher-pleasing behaviors, class-participation skills, and organization skills are critical for school success and must be taught directly, modeled, practiced with frequent feedback, and monitored. After you have instructed students in these skills, you should continue to promote their application and reinforce their use.

---

**COMPREHENSION MONITORING OF KEY CONCEPTS**

### Organization Skills

*Completing Assignments*

1. Many students with mild disabilities lack the organization skills that many other students seem to pick up on their own.

2. WATCh (Glomb & West, 1990) is a strategy that has been used to help students with behavior disorders complete their assignments thoroughly, accurately, neatly, and on time.

3. Plan it, Complete it, Check it, Turn it in (Archer & Gleason, 1994) is a strategy to help students complete their assignments thoroughly, accurately, and on time. It includes a substrategy HOW to help students complete their written assignments neatly and in an organized manner.

4. Because students with mild disabilities, who tend to lack organizational skills, may find long-term projects overwhelming, they should break tasks down into smaller, more easily achieved steps in order to complete the assignment accurately and on time.

5. For students in middle and high school, homework is important to academic achievement and school success.

6. Homework gives students the opportunity to practice previously presented material, preview and review content, and complete projects and other assignments.

*Managing Time*

7. Adolescents with mild disabilities frequently fail to finish assignments or turn them in incomplete, are late for class or appointments, and experience difficulty organizing tasks.

8. Students can improve their use of time by (a) analyzing how they are currently spending their time, (b) prioritizing their time, (c) setting time management goals using "To Do" lists, (d) setting up a weekly schedule, and (e) monitoring their progress by checking off items as they are completed.

9. Some students prefer to use a monthly assignment calendar on which they record homework assignments, upcoming tests, projects, and school activities.

*Managing Materials*

10. In middle and high school, students are expected to store together notes, handouts, homework, and other materials for each class, take assignments and materials back and forth from school, and quickly retrieve necessary materials during classes.

11. Three-ring binders can be used for storing weekly schedules or assignment calendars, notebook paper, graph paper, handouts, notes, school newsletters/notices, vocabulary lists or glossaries, study guides, and outlines or syllabi.

## Study Skills

Studies have shown that students with mild disabilities are not actively involved with learning because they lack the skills for active engagement (Gleason, 1988). These students typically lack the organizational and study skills necessary to meet the demands of the secondary setting (Deshler, Schumaker, Alley, Warner, & Clark, 1982; Deshler & Schumaker, 1988). In this section, we focus on listening, note taking, textbook usage, and test taking—that is, on study skills and strategies that can be used independently by students.

### Listening

Students spend more than half of their time in school listening, and once they are out of school, listening continues to be important (Mandlebaum & Wilson, 1989). Students in middle and high school must be able to follow oral directions given by six or seven different teachers each day. "It has been widely noted that listening skills, which are critical to efficient student learning, are typically not systematically taught and that many students with handicaps do not learn such skills without specific instruction" (Mandlebaum & Wilson, 1989, p. 454). For secondary students, listening skills are those skills needed to understand lectures and other oral and audio presentations in school (such as a history lecture, directions from the proctor during the high school competency test, or audiotapes), and oral directions or presentations out of school (such as instructions from an employer at work, directions from an official at the motor vehicle department during the road test, or instructions from parents about what time to be home with the car). Devine (1987) and Lerner (1985) suggest that listening skills can be improved through systematic teaching and practice.

### Purposes for Listening

Wolvin and Coakley (1985) and Wallace, Cohen, and Polloway (1987) suggested five purposes for listening: discrimination, comprehension, therapy, analysis, and appreciation. Following are examples of these.

*Discrimination* means distinguishing among words and phrases—for example, telling the difference among similar-sounding words in English class.

*Comprehension* is identifying and using literal and interpretive information. An example of literal comprehension is getting the main idea and details from a lecture in science class about ozone depletion. An interpretive example is figuring out that your boss sounds stressed and wants you to work late.

*Therapy* refers to helping individuals work their way through a problem. For example, you use reflective or active listening when you listen to a friend who needs to talk through a problem and respond, "Yeah, I see your point, you're in a really tough situation."

*Analysis* involves comparing, contrasting, categorizing, predicting, hypothesizing, determining fact or opinion, and generalizing. Examples of analysis are predicting what will come next in a lecture or what the topic will be in tomorrow's social science class.

*Appreciation* refers to listening for pleasure at a personal level, such as enjoying the vocal arrangement of a piece of music or listening to a stand-up comedian.

### Pre-Listening Strategies

Adaptating the work of Barker (1971), Nichols and Stevens (1957), and Taylor (1964), Alley and Deshler (1979) suggest the following pre-listening techniques.

*Mental preparation.* Before they attend class, students should practice the three Rs of listening preparation: review, read, and relate. That is, they should *review* previous notes, *read* about the topic that is going to be covered, and *relate* the topic to what they already know. Students can find out what the topic is going to be by looking over the notes from the last class or last chapter in the textbook, checking the class outline or syllabus, or searching for clues in the classroom (such as an outline on the chalkboard or overhead, a handout, or a bulletin board or poster). Lynn looked at the class outline and found that her math teacher would be discussing how to balance a checkbook. She reviewed her notes from the last class and read the chapter on money and budgeting.

*Physical preparation.* Students should come to class with the materials they will need and sit where they will be able to concentrate and pay attention. Lynn brought her notebook and notes, her math book, a pen, a pencil with eraser, and a check register. She sat in front where she could see and hear and avoid distractions.

*Vocabulary preparation.* If the topic of the class is known ahead of time, students can ask for a study guide, outline, or handout listing vocabulary and definitions. Otherwise, they can check the chapter for terms and their meanings. Lynn looked over the math chapter and consulted the glossary in the back of the book for assistance. When she got to class, she noticed four additional terms and their definitions on the board, so she copied them in her notes.

### Listening Strategies

*TQLR.* Tonjes and Zintz (1981) designed the TQLR technique to help students become better listeners.

T = Tuning in

Q = Questioning

L = Listening

R = Reviewing

Adolescents can use this technique with oral presentations/lectures, or with conversations. *Tuning in* helps establish the topic, or purpose for the verbal communication, and helps establish a focus for the presentation. Tony determined that the English teacher was going to explain how to write a business letter. In the *questioning* step, he thought of questions to ask (How is a business letter different from a letter he would write to a friend? In what situations would he need to write a business letter?). Then he focused on *listening* to find the answers to his questions as the teacher explained different reasons for writing business letters (such as a letter of inquiry about a job or a letter of resignation). In the final *reviewing* step, Tony went over what he heard during the English teacher's presentation to be sure that he remembered the important points (the reasons for writing business letters, the parts to a business letter, the differences between a business letter and a friendly letter). In the absence of teacher direction, students can use this technique independently to improve the quality of information they receive verbally.

*Verbal and nonverbal cues.* Alley and Deshler (1979) suggest that students should listen for verbal cues during an oral presentation. These may include statements like "The three reasons hypothesized for the disappearance of the dinosaurs are . . . ," "The most important point I will make in this presentation is . . . ," or "The best way to solve this algebraic equation is to. . . ." Students should pay attention to the teacher's pace, volume, pauses, and stress on words and phrases. Students should also watch for nonverbal cues, including eye contact, hand signals, facial expressions, and posture.

*Main ideas and supporting details.* Students should listen for main ideas and details. This requires direct teaching and practice and is essential for note taking, listening comprehension, and test-taking success. Students can independently ask themselves the following questions:

- What is the speaker's purpose?
- What is the speaker's message?
- What are the main points of the lecture?
- How has the speaker organized the content? Has the speaker stated a main idea followed by details or examples? Has the speaker given all the main ideas first with the intention of restating them with details later?
- Are the main ideas stated sequentially?

Once students can identify the major and supporting points, they may want to highlight main ideas and details in different colors in their notes, underline main ideas with one line and details with two, or develop another way to call attention to them.

*Questioning and summarizing.* Students can be instructed to list five to ten questions before the lecture/presentation. During the presentation, the students listen for the answers to those questions. After the presentation, students can compare responses with one another. This technique can be practiced independently by students once they become accustomed to beginning each class by generating their own questions about a topic. In addition to questioning, good listeners take advantage of pauses in an oral presentation to summarize the main points. Summary statements keep listeners alert, help them answer their own questions, and assist them in re-membering information later. Summarizing is one of the best methods students can use to review (Devine, 1987).

*Critical listening.* High school students need to be able to listen to speakers in a critical manner. Students should focus on listening for a speaker's bias, use of emotionally charged words, slanted language, preference for fact or opinion, and emotional appeals (Devine, 1987). This skill is helpful for students as they transition from school to work and life.

*Listening actively.* Students in secondary school should always listen actively—that is, listen with paper and pen/pencil. The paper can be in the form of a notebook, study guide, outline, or handout. If they listen actively, students are more likely to remember what was presented and to jot down questions regarding what was said. Whether students tell or write main points, fill in blanks, or jot down items that puzzle them is less important than that they do respond during the presentation (Devine, 1987).

Students need to learn and practice how to listen. Table 10.1 contains descriptions of poor listening habits and what students can do to change them.

## Note Taking

Students who do not take notes forget almost 80% of a lecture within two weeks (Pauk, 1989). The act of taking notes appears to promote deeper mental processing of content (Smith & Tompkins, 1988) and assists students in retaining information. Instruction in note taking may be particularly appropriate for students with learning disabilities, who often have difficulty organizing academic content (Saski, Swicegood, & Carter, 1983). With systematic instruction and practice, students with learning disabilities can acquire note-taking skills (Gearhart & Weishahn, 1984).

Note taking is the primary means of gaining content from lectures (Suritsky & Hughes, 1991) and thus is essential for secondary students, who receive information primarily through lecture presentations. Once students have been taught how to take notes, they can independently record information for later retrieval on tests or for use in completing assignments.

### Twenty Tips for Note Taking

Whatever specific method or format is used for taking notes, you may want to share the following general suggestions with your students to help them organize, understand, and retain information.

**TABLE 10.1** Poor Listening Habits and How to Change Them

| Poor listening habits | Poor listeners . . . | Good listeners . . . |
|---|---|---|
| Criticizing a speaker | criticize the speaker's voice, clothes, or looks. Therefore, they decide that the speaker won't say anything important. | realize that a lecture is not a popularity contest. Good listeners look for the ideas being presented, not for things to criticize. |
| Finding fault with the speaker | become so involved in disagreeing with something the speaker states that they stop listening to the remainder of the lecture. | listen with the mind, not the emotions. Good listeners jot down something they disagree with to ask the speaker later, then go on listening. |
| Allowing yourself to be distracted | use little distractions—someone coughing, a pencil dropping, the door opening and closing—as an excuse to stop listening. | filter out distractions and concentrate on what the speaker is saying. |
| Faking attention | look at the speaker but don't listen. They expect to get the material from the textbook later. | understand that speakers talk about what they think is most important. Good listeners know that a good lecture may not contain the same information as the textbook. |
| Forcing every lecture into one format | outline the lecture in detail. The listener is so concerned with organization that he misses the content. | adjust their style of note-taking to the speaker's topic and method of organization. |
| Listening only for facts | only want the facts. They consider everything else to be only the speaker's opinion. | want to see how the facts and examples support the speaker's ideas and arguments. Good listeners know that facts are important because they support ideas. |
| Listening to only the easy material | think it is too difficult to follow the speaker's complicated ideas and logic. A poor listener wants entertainment, not education. | want to learn something new and try to understand the speaker's point. A good listener is not afraid of difficult, technical, or complicated ideas. |
| Calling a subject boring | decide a lecture is going to be dull and "tune out" the speaker. | listen closely for information that can be important and useful, even when a lecture is dull. |
| Overreacting to "push button" emotional words | get upset at words which trigger certain emotions—words such as communist, income tax, Hitler, or abortion. Emotion begins and listening ends. | hear these same words. When they do, they listen very carefully. A good listener tries to understand the speaker's point of view. |
| Wasting thought speed | move along lazily with the speaker even though thinking is faster than speaking. A poor listener daydreams and falls behind. | use any extra time or pauses in the lecture to reflect on the speaker's message. They think about what the speaker is saying, summarize the main points, and think about the next points. |

*Source:* From *Better Study Skills for Better Grades and Real Learning. ICPAC Information Series* (p. 5) by Indiana College Placement and Assessment Center and Indiana University Student Academic Center, 1993, Bloomington, IN: ICPAC. Reprinted by permission.

1. Before going to class, review notes from the previous class, review vocabulary or special terms, read assigned pages, and think about the topic that will be covered.

2. Use a looseleaf notebook so that you can keep notes, handouts, and tests in order and together. You can take out materials, add materials, and move them around as needed.

3. Divide your notebook into different sections for each class, or use a different notebook for each class.

4. Bring materials to class each day (looseleaf notebook, pens, pencils, highlighters, calculator, or other required materials).

5. Sit in the front where you can see and hear, away from distractions, and pay close attention.

6. Write the name of your class and the date at the top of the paper, and number each page.

7. Write on only one side of the paper.

8. Write quickly, but clearly and legibly. Do not write everything the teacher says, just key words and phrases.

9. Write a main idea. Then indent details under the main idea in outline form. Add an example of your own or one of the teacher's. Skip a line or two before moving on to another idea.

10. Leave a blank column on your paper to record your own questions and ideas. Take advantage of pauses in the presentation to make your own notes.

11. Put a question mark by items that you do not understand, and ask the teacher for clarification.

12. Put a blank where you missed a word and check on it later.

13. Use a marking system to distinguish main ideas from details and examples, perhaps by drawing a box around main ideas and underlining, highlighting, or color coding certain items.

14. Use abbreviations:

    | | | |
    |---|---|---|
    | ex. or e.g. | = | example |
    | def | = | definition |
    | info | = | information |
    | # | = | number |
    | cont'd | = | continued |
    | etc. | = | and so forth |
    | impt | = | important |
    | ref | = | reference |
    | p | = | page |

| wd | = | word |
| vs | = | versus |
| > | = | greater than |
| < | = | less than |
| + | = | plus or add |
| – | = | subtract or take away |
| i.e. | = | that is |
| s | = | summary |
| & | = | and |

15. Listen and look for verbal and nonverbal cues:
    - Points that are repeated
    - Key points ("The most important point to remember is . . .")
    - Words and definitions
    - A change in the speaker's volume, rate, and posture
    - Gestures used to emphasize points
    - Information that is written on the board or overhead
    - Directions for an assignment
    - Lists ("The five types of . . .")
    - Use of absolute words (all, always, never, none, best)
    - Words and phrases that signal or alert you to something:
        - "In conclusion"
        - "In summary"
        - "Finally"
        - "For example"
        - "In comparison"
        - "Prior to"
        - "The opposite of"
        - "Similarly"
        - "Remember"

16. After the class, fill in any missed information, and ask the teacher to clarify anything you did not understand.

17. Compare your notes with those of a friend. Check for accuracy and consistency. Consult your textbook if needed.

18. Make sure your notes are organized chronologically in your notebook along with supporting handouts.

19. As soon after class as possible, examine your notes and check to see how they support, supplement, and/or explain the information in your textbook.

20. Review your notes before the next class. Cumulative review assists with understanding, retention, and test preparation.

### Note-Taking Methods

Students can use a variety of formats to take notes from lecture presentations and textbooks. "No evidence points to the consistent significant superiority of one technique over another" (Devine, 1987, p. 173). We believe that students need to be instructed in a number of different formats and procedures so that they can select what best meets their needs. We present Pauk's (1978) method of recording, reducing, reciting, reviewing, and reflecting; the Directed Notetaking Activity of Spires and Stone (1989); and the Guided Lecture Procedure (Kelly & Holmes, 1979) for use with lecture presentations. We also describe Horton, Lovitt, and Christensen's (1991) columnar note taking from texts and Archer and Gleason's (1994) method for taking notes from written material.

***Record, reduce, recite, review, and reflect.*** Pauk (1978) stresses that the note-taking format itself does not automatically lead to learning, but is simply a vehicle for organizing the real process of learning. He emphasizes the process the student goes through in completing five important steps.

Record    The student actively listens and records the speaker's ideas.

Reduce    The student rereads all of his/her notes and reduces the facts, ideas, and words of the speaker into concise summaries written in the student's own words.

Recite    The student covers the notes and recites them out loud in his/her own words in order to commit them to memory.

Review    The student reviews his/her notes briefly before each class, and thoroughly in preparation for a test.

Reflect    The student reflects on the information gained from the lecture, on how it relates to other information from the text and from the student's own experiences, and on the note taking process that made the lecture more meaningful.

Pauk recommends using a 6-inch column on the right to record the lecture presentation and a 2½-inch column on the left to reduce ideas, recite, review, and reflect. Notice how the student uses metacognitive monitoring skills in this process of note taking.

***The Directed Notetaking Activity.*** In their Directed Notetaking Activity, Spires and Stone (1989) incorporate a metacognitive emphasis by including self-questioning and self-monitoring. They use a split-page method, in which students divide their paper into two columns. The left column, about one-third of the page, is used to record the main concepts. The right column, about two-thirds of the page, is used for definitions, examples, and support-

**FIGURE 10.5** **Split-Page Method of Note Taking on a Lecture about Biological Diversity**

| | |
|---|---|
| Definition of biological diversity | The variety of different species, genetic variability among individuals within each species, and a variety of ecosystems. |
| Three related concepts: | 1. Genetic diversity<br>2. Species diversity<br>3. Ecological diversity |
| - Genetic diversity | The variability in the genetic makeup of individuals within a single species. |
| - Species diversity | The variety of species in different parts of the Earth. |
| - Ecological diversity | The variety of biological communities that interact with one another and their non-living environments. |

ing details. See Figure 10.5 for an example of how a student might use the split-page method of note taking in a lecture about biological diversity.

Students are also taught a self-questioning procedure to use before, during, and after a lecture (similar to a directed reading activity). This procedure serves to assess their interest in and experience with the topic (before taking notes), their level of involvement with the lecture (while taking notes), and their evaluation of their performance of the task (after taking notes). Some sample questions follow:

*Planning (before taking notes)*

How interested am I in this topic?

If my interest is low, how do I plan to increase interest?

Do I feel motivated to pay attention?

What is my purpose for listening to this lecture?

*Monitoring (while taking notes)*

Am I maintaining a satisfactory level of concentration?

Am I taking advantage of the fact that thought is faster than speech?

Am I separating main concepts from supporting details?

What am I doing when comprehension fails?

What strategies am I using for comprehension failure?

*Evaluating (after taking notes)*
Did I achieve my purpose?

Was I able to maintain satisfactory levels of concentration and motivation?

Did I deal with comprehension failures adequately?

Overall, do I feel that I processed the lecture at a satisfactory level?
(Spires & Stone, 1989, p. 37)

Students are instructed in this procedure using Pearson's (1985) model of explicit instruction, which is similar to metacognitive and learning strategy instruction presented in Chapter 9. The directed note-taking activity incorporates a metacognitive emphasis by making students *aware* of their interest and experience with the topic and by requiring them to *monitor* their performance.

**Guided Lecture Procedure (GLP).** The Guided Lecture Procedure (GLP) (Kelly & Holmes, 1979) is a note-taking strategy that involves students actively during lecture presentations. The GLP is divided into three parts.

*Before the lecture.* Before the lecture begins, students are told the objectives of the lecture and are given time to write them down.

*During the lecture.* During the first part of the lecture, students listen, but do not take notes. Approximately halfway through the lecture, the teacher stops and the students write, in shortened form, everything they can recall from the presentation.

*After the lecture.* Following completion of the last part of the lecture, students work in small groups with the teacher as a facilitator, discuss the entire lecture, and take notes. At this stage, the actual lecture notes are developed. After completion of the small group activity, the students reflect on the lecture and on the GLP process. Then they summarize the main points of the lecture without referring to the notes that they developed in their groups (Cheek & Cheek, 1983).

Notice that this note-taking procedure incorporates many of the principles of the social constructivist model, as the teacher acts as a facilitator and students assume responsibility for their own learning. Metacognitive skills are also involved, as students summarize and monitor their understanding of the lecture and the GLP process.

© Erika Stone

*Students work together to outline a chapter.*

***Taking notes from written material.*** Archer and Gleason (1994) have developed a method for taking notes from written material that, like the columnar method, focuses on paragraphs (see Figure 10.6).

1. Students leave the left margin of the paper empty.

2. In the center of the paper, they write the heading or subheading and page number.

3. Students take notes on each paragraph. First they write the topic of the paragraph and then, indented under the topic, they list important details.

4. When the notes have been completed and checked for accuracy, students go back and write a question for each paragraph in the left-hand margin.

5. The questions in the left-hand margin can be used for studying.

**FIGURE 10.6**   Note Taking from Written Material

<table>
<tr>
<td valign="top">

<br><br><br><br><br><br><br>

What are

the characteristics

of mammals?

<br><br><br><br><br><br><br><br>

Where do

mammals

live?

<br><br><br><br><br><br>

What do

mammals

eat?

<br><br><br><br><br>

What does the

skeleton of a

mammal do?

</td>
<td valign="top">

Taking Notes on Written Material

1. Write down the heading or subheading and the page number.
2. Take notes on each paragraph.
   a. Write a word or phrase that tells about the whole paragraph.
   b. Indent and write the important details that you should remember from the paragraph.

Example Notes

      Mammals (p. 156)

Characteristics of mammals

    —have backbones

    —nurse their young

    —have hair

    —are warm-blooded

    —have more well-developed brains than other animals

Where mammals live

    —most live on land and have four legs

    —some live in trees in forest or jungle

    —dolphins, whales, porpoises, and manatees live in water

    —gophers and moles live underground

What mammals eat

    —plants (herbivorous)

    —animal flesh (carnivorous)

    —insects (insectivorous)

The skeleton of mammals

    —provides framework for body and protects organs

    —is attached to muscles

    —contains more than 200 bones

Guidelines for Good Note Taking

> 1. Write your notes in your own words.
> 2. Make your notes brief.
> 3. Use abbreviations and symbols.
> 4. Be sure you understand your notes.

</td>
</tr>
</table>

*Source:* Adapted from *Skills for School Success* by A. I. Archer & M. M. Gleason Copyright © 1989  Curriculum Associates, Inc.. Adapted by permission.

## COMPREHENSION MONITORING OF KEY CONCEPTS

### Study Skills

*Listening*

1. For secondary students, listening skills are those skills needed to understand lectures and other oral presentations in school and oral directions or presentations out of school.

2. Adolescents may have occasion to use listening for five purposes: discrimination, comprehension, therapy, analysis, and appreciation.

3. Pre-listening strategies include mental preparation prior to listening, physical preparation, and vocabulary preparation.

4. TQLR (Tonjes & Zintz, 1981) is a technique to help students become better listeners during oral presentations, lectures, and conversations.

5. Listening strategies include (a) listening for verbal cues and watching for nonverbal cues, (b) listening for main ideas and supporting details, (c) generating questions and summaries during a lecture presentation, (d) listening critically for emotionally charged words, slanted language, fact, opinion, and emotional appeals, and (e) listening actively, with paper and pen/pencil.

*Note Taking*

6. The act of taking notes seems to promote deeper mental processing of content and assists students in retaining information.

7. Note taking is the primary means of gaining content from lectures and thus is essential for secondary students, who receive information primarily through lecture presentations.

8. Tips for effective note taking include (a) having the appropriate materials, (b) sitting where you can see and hear, (c) using a split-page method with the speaker's ideas on one side and your notes on the other, (d) using highlighting, underlining, color coding, and abbreviations, and (e) reviewing your notes after each class and before the next class for the purpose of cumulative review.

9. Pauk (1978) recommends using a 6-inch column for recording the lecture presentation, and a 2½-inch column for reducing, reciting, reviewing, and reflecting during note taking.

> 10. The Directed Notetaking Activity (Spires & Stone, 1989) uses a split-page format on which students record main concepts (left side) and definitions, examples, and supporting details (right side). Students ask themselves questions before, during, and after taking notes.
>
> 11. The Guided Lecture Procedure (Kelly & Homes, 1979) is a note-taking strategy in which students are told the objectives of the lecture, listen to the speaker, and work in groups to generate the lecture notes.

## Textbook Usage

Many secondary students with disabilities experience difficulty reading (Schloss et al., 1995) and comprehending content-area textbooks (Meese, 1994). Therefore, you may need to facilitate your students' learning from text. In Chapter 8 we discussed teaching using a single text. Here we present specific strategies to assist students in acquiring information independently from content-area texts. Notice the metacognitive features in each of these strategies—SCROL, CAN-DO, skimming, and scanning—evidenced by the emphasis on awareness (what the student already knows) and monitoring (self-questioning and self-monitoring).

### *SCROL*

Grant (1993) offers a textbook strategy that focuses on how to use text headings to improve reading and learning from content textbooks.

S = Survey. The student reads the headings and subheadings and asks, "What do I already know about this topic? What information might the writer present?"

C = Connect. The student asks, "How do the headings relate to one another?" and writes down keywords from the headings that might provide connections.

R = Read. The student reads the segment under the heading, paying particular attention to words and phrases that express important information about the heading.

O = Outline. The student writes the heading and outlines the major ideas and supporting details in the segment without looking back at the text.

L = Look back. The student looks back at the heading segment, checking the outline for accuracy and correcting inaccuracies.

### CAN-DO

Ellis and Lenz (1987) developed a strategy to help students learn content information. Notice how CAN-DO can be used with textbooks. For example, students in middle and high schools are frequently assigned textbook chapters to read independently. Then the teacher assigns end-of-chapter questions to answer and eventually tests the students on the material. The CAN-DO textbook strategy may facilitate organization and memorization of information because of its emphasis on (1) making decisions about what items to list, (2) noting the main ideas and details with a graphic organizer (tree diagram), (3) describing how items are related, and (4) requiring that information be overlearned.

C = Create a list of items to be learned.

A = Ask yourself if the list is complete.

N = Note the main ideas and details, using a tree diagram.

D = Describe each component and how it relates to others.

O = Overlearn main parts, then supporting details.

Ellis and Lenz (1987) modified the CAN-DO strategy so that it could be used with textbooks in technical classes for learning machine and equipment parts.

C = Create a list of parts for the machine or piece of equipment.

A = Ask yourself if the list is complete.

N = Note if these parts contain smaller parts within.

D = Describe each part and how it relates to the machine.

O = Overlearn the main parts and then the smaller parts.

### Skimming

Skimming is an excellent tool for students to use to quickly identify the main ideas of a chapter in a content-area textbook. We have paraphrased the steps recommended by Mercer and Mercer (1993) and provided examples:

1. Read the title and headings (for example, *"Saving the Environment"*).
2. Read the introduction (the first few paragraphs).
3. Read the first sentence of each subsequent paragraph, since this is where the main idea is usually found. ("Many of the nation's coastal regions were hit hard by storm damage during the country's most active tropical storm season of the century.")

4. Read captions and study illustrations ("Volunteers do their part at the beach to prevent further hurricane damage" under a picture of people building a retaining wall where there is evidence of beach erosion).

5. Read the conclusion or summary at the end of the chapter. ("In conclusion, steps must be taken now to prepare for. . . .")

### Scanning

Scanning is a helpful strategy that students can use to rapidly locate specific information (such as the definition of a term) in a content-area text by quickly reading key sentences, words, and phrases. Again, we have paraphrased the steps recommended by Mercer and Mercer (1993) and provided examples:

1. Think of the specific question to be answered. (For example, "When did the Spanish-American War begin?")

2. Estimate the form in which the answer will appear (in this case, a date).

3. Use the expected form of the answer as a clue to locate it (a four digit number).

4. Look for clues by moving the eyes quickly over the pages until a section is found that appears to contain the answer. Then read more carefully. ("There is a table containing historic events and their dates in the chapter.")

5. Find the answer, write it, and stop reading. ("The date that the Spanish-American War began is in the table. I'll write it down.")

## Test Taking

By the time they are adolescents, students are expected to pass classroom content tests, high school minimum competency tests, and entry exams related to postsecondary education, training, and the military. In secondary schools, scores on tests often comprise the major portion of students' grades (Archer & Gleason, 1995). Because success in mainstream content classes and in real-life settings is frequently measured in terms of grades on tests, it is essential to provide assistance to students in test taking. When students in special programs are instructed in test taking, their performance in the regular classroom improves (Scruggs & Marsing, 1987). We present strategies that your students can use independently to prepare for and take tests. In Chapter 7 we discussed test adaptations that teachers can make.

### General Test-Preparation Strategies

Students may find it helpful to follow a set of procedures or guidelines as they prepare for tests.

1. Find out when tests will be given in each content class and record the dates on the class outline/syllabus or on your calendar/planner.

2. Start preparing ahead of time by conducting a cumulative review. Read over class notes, handouts, and chapters after each class, going back to the first set each time so that by the time you are ready for your test, you have reviewed most of the material several times.

3. Ask your teacher what the test will include (such as information from notes and text) and what types of items will be asked (such as completion or multiple choice).

4. Find out how much time you will be given to take the test, and if you will be penalized for guessing.

5. Find out if you may use notes or your textbook during the test, and if any of the tests will be take-home tests.

6. Ask the teacher to provide a study guide, conduct a review session, or administer a practice test before the test.

7. Ask the teacher to share tests from the previous year as examples of what to expect.

8. Predict the questions that may be asked by reviewing your notes for clues (items that the teacher suggested you mark with an asterisk or emphasized more than once) and by looking over study guides, handouts, or class activity sheets.

9. Work with a study group to share information, identify major concepts, predict questions, develop mnemonics, and review.

10. Maintain a positive attitude. Good test preparation + use of test-taking strategies + a positive attitude = good test performance.

### Specific Test-Preparation Strategies

In addition to following general procedures in preparing for tests, students may want to employ specific test-preparation strategies.

***EASY.*** Ellis and Lenz (1987, p. 99) developed a strategy for students to use independently to prepare for tests by organizing and prioritizing information. Notice the metacognitive nature of the strategy as students use self-questioning and self-reinforcement.

E  =  Elicit "Wh" questions (who, what, when, where, why) to identify important information.

A  =  Ask yourself which information is the least troublesome.

S  =  Study the easy parts first and the hardest parts last.

Y  =  Say "Yes" to self-reinforcement.

**RCRC.** Archer and Gleason (1994) have devised a study strategy that students can use independently to prepare for content tests by verbally rehearsing information from textbooks, notes, or class handouts. This strategy can be used on a daily basis, thus encouraging students to conduct a cumulative review after each class instead of waiting until just before the test to cram.

R  =  Read.
Read a small section of material from texts, notes, or handouts, then read it again.

C  =  Cover.
Cover the material so that you cannot see it.

R  =  Recite.
Tell yourself what you have read.

C  =  Check.
Uncover the material and check to see if you are right.

### General Test-Taking Strategies

By the middle school years, most tests require students to read directions and questions and to work independently (Ritter & Idol-Maestas, 1986). Therefore, they need systematic procedures for taking tests. We provide two options here: SPLASH and SCORER. Notice how each one emphasizes the importance of (1) previewing the test before beginning, (2) skipping difficult questions and returning to them later, and (3) checking over the entire test before turning it in.

**SPLASH.** Simmonds, Luchow, Kaminsky, and Cottone (1989, p. 101) devised the following method for taking tests. This method can be used for all types of questions and content.

S  =  Skim the entire test.
Note the easy and hard parts, directions, and point values so that you can best allocate the available time.

P  =  Plan your strategy once you have a general idea of the test.

*L* = Leave out difficult questions in a planned manner.
(Teachers may want to cue students to mark with an asterisk items they skip over.)

*A* = Attack immediately those questions you know.

*S* = Systematically guess after exhausting other strategies.
(Here teachers must first instruct students to look for clues and answers on the test to help answer unknown questions. If there is no penalty for guessing, students should be told to guess the best choice after eliminating incorrect choices.)

*H* = House cleaning.
Leave 5%–10% of your allotted time to make sure all answers are filled in, clean up erasures, and check answers.

***SCORER.*** Carmen and Adams (1972) developed this well-known test-taking strategy that students can use independently as a self-instructional approach to test taking.

*S* = Schedule time.
Preview the entire test for types of items, point values, and number of items.

*C* = Clue words.
Look for words that provide clues, such as *always, never, usually*.

*O* = Omit difficult questions.
Put a mark by difficult items and move on to easier items. You can return to the difficult questions later.

*R* = Read carefully.
Read all the directions and all parts of questions carefully.

*E* = Estimate your answer.
On items requiring calculations, estimate the answer first before completing the calculation in order to avoid careless errors and eliminate obviously incorrect responses.

*R* = Review your work.
Go back over the entire test and answer all abandoned items.

### Format-Specific Test-Taking Strategies

Students should familiarize themselves with general rules for approaching and answering the following types of test items: multiple choice, true–false, completion, matching, and essay. Before beginning any test, students should read the entire test, decide which question types to answer first, and after examining how many points each section is worth, determine how many minutes they will spend on each section of the test. We present suggestions based on the work of Langan (1982), Meese (1994), and Hughes, Schumaker, Deshler, and Mercer (1987), as well as our own recommendations.

*Multiple Choice*

1. Read the directions and each question carefully.

2. Underline key words in the directions (such as *Choose the best answer*) and in the questions (*all, never, sometimes*).

3. Cross out the alternatives that you know are obviously incorrect.

4. Read the question in its entirety with each of the remaining alternatives. Treat each alternative as a true-false item and decide if it is true or false. This helps you identify the best possible answer.

5. If you still cannot determine the answer, try the following:
   - Choose the longest alternative.
   - Avoid alternatives that include absolute words such as *always, never, every, all, none.* Instead, choose alternatives with qualifiers, such as *usually, sometimes, probably, often.*
   - Eliminate alternatives that are similar or identical.

6. Change answers only if you have a good reason for doing so.

*True–False*

1. Read the directions and each question carefully.

2. Underline key words in the directions (such as *Write "+" if the question is true, and "–" if the question is false*) and in each question (*never, always*).

3. Remember that questions with absolutes—such as *always, never, no one,* and *only*—are frequently false.

4. Remember that questions with qualifiers—such as *probably, most, sometimes,* and *usually*—are frequently true.

*Completion*

1. Read the directions carefully, checking to see if you can write one, two, or several words in the blank.

2. Look for clues, such as whether *a* or *an* precedes the blank. This tells you whether your completion item begins with a consonant or a vowel.

3. Read the question carefully to make sure that your answer makes sense and is grammatically correct.

4. If you think of more than one answer when you read the question, jot down your ideas in the margin and read the question again to see which one sounds best.

*Matching*

1. Read the directions carefully. Some matching questions require you to draw a line from the item in one column to a matching item in another column. Other matching questions require you to write the letter or number of an item in one column next to the item it describes in the other column. Check the directions to determine if you can use an item more than once.

2. Check to see if there are the same number of items in each column.

3. Read the items in each column before beginning to match items in order to get a sense of the alternatives.

4. Begin by answering the items you are sure of.

5. Cross out each alternative as you use it, thereby eliminating choices.

6. Go back to see if you have used all of the alternatives.

*Essay*

1. Read the directions carefully, and read each question in its entirety to be sure you answer each part.

2. Take note of the test vocabulary used in each question (see Table 10.2) and make sure you write the type of response that the question requires.

3. Make a brief outline before writing your response.

4. Write a clear and thorough response.

5. Proofread your essay for organization, accuracy, spelling, and grammar.

In this section of the chapter, we have provided study skills for improving the listening, note-taking, textbook usage, and test-taking skills of adolescents. These skills are most effectively acquired and practiced when students are (1) systematically taught through active demonstration and modeling by the teacher, (2) given ample practice opportunities with specific feedback, (3) provided with frequent prompting and reinforcement by the teacher, and (4) carefully monitored to ensure correct application of the study skill strategies.

---

### COMPREHENSION MONITORING OF KEY CONCEPTS

**Study Skills**

*Textbook Usage*

1. Many secondary students with disabilities experience difficulty reading and comprehending content-area textbooks.

**TABLE 10.2** **Test Vocabulary**

| | | |
|---|---|---|
| 1. | Apply | Using example, explain how an idea or concept would work. |
| 2. | Compare | Show similarities and differences of two or more things. |
| 3. | Contrast | Highlight just the differences of two or more concepts. |
| 4. | Define | Provide a general description of the concept. |
| 5. | Discuss | Provide a more detailed description, including pros and cons. |
| 6. | Evaluate | Discuss the concept including your opinion and the facts to support the opinion. |
| 7. | Explain | Tell why something occurred. |
| 8. | Illustrate | Use examples, including diagrams and pictures, to further explain your idea. |
| 9. | Justify | Offer reasons and provide facts to support your statements. |
| 10. | Outline | Condense material into major topics with their subpoints underneath. |
| 11. | Relate | Show the connection between several thoughts and ideas. |
| 12. | Solve | Arrive at a desired outcome using facts and knowledge. |
| 13. | State | Offer main point without providing details. |
| 14. | Summarize | Bring knowledge together with emphasis on main points only. |

*Source:* From *Teaching Children and Adolescents with Special Needs* (2nd ed.) (p. 299) by J. L. Olson & J. M. Platt, 1992, Englewood Cliffs, NJ: Merrill/Prentice-Hall.

2. Students who are familiar with the way a textbook is organized may find it easier to locate, comprehend, and remember information.

3. SCROL (Grant, 1993) is a textbook strategy that focuses on how to use text headings to improve reading and learning from content textbooks.

4. CAN-DO (Ellis & Lenz, 1987) is a strategy for learning content information.

5. Skimming can be used to identify the main ideas of a chapter in a content-area textbook.

6. Scanning can be used to rapidly locate specific information in a content-area text by quickly reading key sentences, words, and phrases.

*(continued on next page)*

*Test Taking*

7. Adolescents are expected to pass classroom content tests, high school minimum competency tests, and entry exams related to postsecondary education, training, and the military.

8. General test preparation strategies include (a) finding out when tests will be given, (b) finding out what to expect on the test, (c) making use of study guides, review sessions, and practice tests, (d) predicting the questions that may be asked, (e) working with a study group, and (f) maintaining a positive attitude.

9. EASY (Ellis & Lenz, 1987) is a strategy for preparing for tests by organizing and prioritizing information.

10. RCRC (Archer & Gleason, 1994) is a study strategy for preparing for content tests by verbally rehearsing information from textbooks, notes, or class handouts.

11. SPLASH (Simmonds et al., 1989) and SCORER (Carmen & Adams, 1972) are methods that students can use independently while they are taking tests.

12. Before beginning any test, students should read the entire test, decide which question types to answer first, and after examining how many points each section is worth, determine how many minutes they will spend on each section of the test.

13. Students should familiarize themselves with general rules regarding specific types of test items (multiple choice, true–false, completion, matching, and essay).

 Now that you have read Chapter 10, reflect on your earlier responses at the beginning of the chapter and complete this post organizer.

1. Return to your small group, and review the reasons you gave for including instruction in school survival and study skills in the middle and high school curriculum. What additions would you now make?

2. Work with your group again, and focus on school survival skills. How would you modify your list of the five skills most essential to success at the secondary level?

3. Working alone, look back at your own list of study skills that you lacked when you began secondary school. How would you have handled the situation differently now that you have read the chapter?

# PART THREE

# Instruction in Functional and Lifelong Learning Skills

© Bob Daemmrich/The Image Works

**CHAPTER 11**   Career Education, Vocational Development, and Work-Related Social Skills

**CHAPTER 12**   The Transition Planning Process

# Career Education, Vocational Development, and Work-Related Social Skills

© Steve Takatsuno/Jeroboam

**CHAPTER HIGHLIGHTS**

*Career Education*

*Vocational Education*

*Work-Related Social Skills*

---

 Before you read Chapter 11, use your prior knowledge to complete this advance organizer.

1. In your own words, explain what career education is and at what grades it should be taught.

2. If you were assessing an adolescent's vocational skills, what would you look for and how would you assess them? Give examples of both formal and informal assessment.

3. Identify five work-related social skills that you feel are needed for an adolescent to be successful in work and life.

---

**A** text on teaching adolescents with mild disabilities would not be complete without addressing the career, vocational, and work-related social skills of youth with learning and behavior problems. Adolescents must prepare for future employment and must have marketable skills in order to compete in the workforce of the 21st century. They must possess daily living skills (balancing a checkbook, living within a budget), personal/social skills (accepting criticism from employers, interacting appropriately with peers), and occupational skills (filling out a job application, completing a task accurately and in a timely manner).

In this chapter, we present suggestions for assisting students to attain their highest level of economic, personal, and social fulfillment by providing strategies to help them meet a variety of societal roles and prepare for gainful employment. First, we describe career education and provide examples of how to infuse it into the existing curriculum. Next, we discuss vocational education, including preparation (in school), training (out of school), services, models, programs, and resources. Finally, we present work-related social skills, which are essential for locating, obtaining, and keeping a job.

## Career Education

The term *career education* may be misleading because it is frequently viewed only as preparation for work. It actually includes the much broader focus of preparation for the roles of consumer, citizen, and family member, as well as worker. "Life-centered competencies and life span developmental skills go beyond the vocational development tasks described in occupational development and career maturity literature" (Clark, Carlson, Fisher, Cook, & D'Alonzo, 1991, p. 111). Career education prepares individuals for participation in all aspects of life, including home, school, occupation, and community (Brolin, 1995). It is a total person approach to education that lends itself well to the preparation of *all* students in practical, meaningful, and functional skills.

Because of its broad focus, career education typically begins at birth and continues throughout the life span. In their article "A Nation at Risk or a Policy at Risk? How about Career Education?" Elrod and Lyons (1987) recommend (1) infusing career education components into the regular curriculum, (2) increasing career exploration opportunities, (3) providing career counseling in high schools, and (4) offering alternative diplomas (a regular diploma with a vocational education endorsement).

## Historical Development

Career education began as a movement for the general population of students in 1971 when Sidney Marland, then Commissioner of Education, declared career education to be the top priority of the U.S. Office of Education (Halpern, 1992; Marland, 1971). In the early 1970s, many national leaders were expressing concern about the high dropout rate of students, believing it to be due primarily to the failure of schools to provide the knowledge and skills needed for future adult functioning (Brolin, 1995). Career education was suggested as a possible solution. In 1974 the Office of Career Education was created within the U.S. Office of Education, giving priority to career education as a critical need. This office existed under the direction of Dr. Kenneth B. Hoyt until 1982 (Brolin, 1993).

During the 1970s, the career education movement broadened its focus to include the needs of individuals with disabilities. The Division on Career Development, known today as the Division on Career Development and Transition, was formed in 1976, and became the Council for Exceptional Children's 12th division. This division has conducted conferences, issued position statements, organized state units, and published journals, documents, and newsletters highlighting career education issues. The passage of P.L. 95-207, the Career Education Implementation Incentive Act, in 1977 ensured the inclusion of individuals with disabilities as an appropriate target group for services, and helped states to infuse career education into the school curriculum.

## Definition

According to the Council for Exceptional Children (1978), career education is

> the totality of experiences through which one learns to live a meaningful life . . . providing the opportunity for children to learn, in the least restrictive environment possible, the academic, daily living, personal-social, and occupational knowledge and skills necessary for attaining their highest level of economic, personal, and social fulfillment. The individual can obtain this fulfillment through work (both paid and unpaid) and in a variety of other societal roles and personal life styles. (p. 64)

Brolin (1995) considers career education to be "a lifelong process that infuses a careers emphasis in all subjects, grades K–12, including job training, apprenticeship programs, mentoring, career exploration, and the nonpaid work done as a family member, citizen, and leisure seeker" (p. 53). Most authorities suggest that career education be infused into the ongoing program of each student beginning in elementary school and continuing throughout adulthood. If career education is effectively infused into the curriculum, there is a greater probability that when students with disabilities leave school, they will be better prepared to assume their varied roles as young adults in their communities.

## Description

Career education can be distinguished from vocational education, transition, supported work, and other related concepts in eight ways (Brolin, 1989, p. 783):

1. *"Career education interfaces education with work."* Productive work activity, paid and unpaid, is one of the expectations of adulthood. A major feature of career education is its focus on the classroom as a workplace (Hoyt, 1993). Teachers can prepare students in elementary and secondary classrooms for the various roles and settings in which productive work activity occurs. For example, you can set up volunteer projects (unpaid work) or initiate projects in which students perform a service for pay (paid work). Students in one of the junior high schools with which we work adopted grandparents at a local senior center. The students made lunch for their adopted grandparents, took them fishing, wrote them letters, and visited them regularly to talk or play games with them. Students at a local high school initiated a program in which they prepared and served lunch to the school faculty, staff, and administration every day. Students at another high school contracted with a local business to help them with printing and mailing a brochure. These examples illustrate some of the unpaid and paid work experiences that you can arrange for students while they are still in school. The school curriculum provides the opportunity to teach many cognitive, affective, and psychomotor skills needed for various work roles (Brolin, 1989).

2. *"Career education is a K–12+ effort that involves all possible school personnel."* Adolescents begin developing a work personality in early childhood. Teachers throughout the K–12+ curriculum should assist students in developing positive work attitudes, habits, values, interests, and a willingness to assume responsibility. Activities may include anything from learning how to take turns and put things away in the early grades, to completing and following through on assignments in a timely manner at the middle and high school levels. Administrators and staff members can reinforce respon-

© Harriet Gans/The Image Works

*A guest speaker shares career options with students.*

sible behavior (attendance and punctuality), good decision making (completing homework assignments), and positive attitudes (getting along with adults and peers). Guidance counselors can assist students with the selection of classes and with planning for postsecondary training, work, and transition to the community.

3. *"Career education is an infusion concept."* We believe that career education should be taught by integrating concepts into the curriculum rather than by offering career education as a separate course. For example, the career education competency of "achieving independence" can be taught in math class by teaching students how to develop a budget and balance a checkbook; in English class by teaching how to write letters of inquiry and complaint; in social science by teaching good citizenship skills and civic responsibility; in health and science by teaching fitness, nutrition, and respect for the environment. By using role playing, simulations, and hands-on activities, teachers can relate their instruction to the career education competencies needed for success at home (managing personal finances), in school (communicating with others), on the job (exhibiting appropriate work habits and behaviors), and in the community (engaging in leisure/recreational activities).

4. *"Career education does not replace traditional education or subject matter."* Career education does not replace traditional education—it enhances academic learning and subject matter. When teaching fractions, for example, you can enhance instruction by using practical, meaningful career education examples. You could ask students to determine the construction materials needed and the cost to complete the building of a deck using fractions as your units of measurement; the amounts of various ingredients used in a specific recipe; or the number of beats given to whole notes, half notes, and quarter notes in a musical arrangement. We believe teachers can relate academics to career competencies without changing what they are already teaching.

5. *"Career education conceptualizes career development occurring in stages."* Career education is generally conceptualized as a progression of four interrelated stages:

*Career awareness* occurs during the elementary school years and involves making students aware of work (paid and unpaid) and of how students might fit into it someday. Activities may include guest speakers (parents, community volunteers, representatives of various vocations) who describe what they do in their paid and unpaid work; visits to workplaces (fire station, police station, hospital, bank, day-care center); and class activities (journal writing, group discussions, art and drama, role playing). At this stage, it is important to show students that paid and unpaid work can be a source of personal satisfaction.

*Career exploration* takes place during the middle school/junior high years and involves assisting students to explore their interests, abilities, and skills related to their future roles as employees, citizens, family members, and participants in leisure/recreation activities. Activities may include hands-on experiences (participation in voting during mock elections or participation in individual and team sports), assessment of interests and aptitudes (completion of interest inventories and aptitude tests), and community service projects (helping to build a school playground at a local elementary school or volunteering to pick up litter at a local park).

*Career preparation* is emphasized during the high school years and focuses on making decisions/planning/preparing for work, or for additional schooling after high school, and for living in the community as a responsible citizen and family member. At this stage, there is special emphasis on identifying students' strengths, weaknesses, preferences for learning, and future goals. It is important at this stage to help students match their interests, characteristics, and skills with appropriate roles for the future. Activities may include career counseling (assisting with career choices, job selection and placement, and training needs, or helping to recommend and secure appropriate postsecondary training options), career and vocational assessment strategies (informal and formal assessment instruments to determine students' personal/social skills, daily living skills, and vocational skills), and maintaining a meaningful, functional curriculum related to future roles in the community (infusing career competencies, such as exhibiting appropriate work habits and behaviors, within subject matter).

*Career assimilation* usually involves the transition of students into postsecondary training or gainful employment, although it can also take place during the secondary years. Many students with mild disabilities may need placement, follow-up, and continuing education, and this need may extend for several years. At this stage, it is important to make sure that students have mastered career education competencies. Activities can include assisting students with job placement (assessing students' strengths and skills and helping to find an employment situation that is an appropriate match); conducting follow-up evaluations (observing students on the job and talking to employers); providing additional training (assisting students to develop satisfactory social relationships, helping students manage finances, and prompting students to participate in leisure activities); working closely with families (checking on students' skills in managing finances, caring for personal needs, and getting around the community); and interacting with agencies (helping students to access community resources and other supportive services). Career assimilation integrates all previous stages and addresses lifelong learning needs.

6. *"Career education requires a substantial experiential component."* Many students with disabilities learn better with a hands-on approach. Career education competencies can be best achieved through actual experiences within subject-matter classes. For example, in teaching a student to manage personal finances, you could set up a bank in the classroom, issue checkbooks to students, set up simulations in which they have to live within a budget, and use advertisements from the newspaper for comparative shopping. These experiences would be meaningful and relate to students' future needs.

7. *"Career education focuses on the development of life skills, affective skills, and general employability skills."* Life skills such as caring for personal needs, cooking, cleaning, managing money, and caring for children are important for successful life adjustment. Affective skills such as getting along with others, using good communication skills, and making thoughtful decisions are critical for students entering the world of work and community living.

General employability skills such as being prompt and dependable, following directions, and accepting criticism are needed for success in the workplace. Opportunities for practicing these skills should be provided for students throughout the K–12 curriculum.

8. *"Career education requires the school to work more closely with the family and community resources."* As Brolin (1989) points out, "The majority of learning occurs outside school" (p. 784). It is critically important to work with families and contacts within community agencies, for these are the individuals who impact a student's lifelong learning opportunities. Teachers should develop a positive, cooperative relationship with these important resource people early, and maintain it throughout the postsecondary years. Activities could include having parents and individuals from the community as guest speakers, sponsors of athletic activities, volunteers, chaperons, and pen pals. For example, you could ask members of a local business to communicate regularly through e-mail with students in a middle or high school class, and enlist the participation of volunteers from a local corporation to come to a middle school once a week during their lunch hour to tutor students. Activities could also involve sending students out into the community for hands-on experiences. For example, you could arrange for high school students to shadow a variety of individuals in different vocations as they go about their work, and then have them return to school to share their experiences with one another.

Families can be helpful in securing employment for their adolescents through the friends and family network, and in monitoring the attainment of daily living and social skills. Your knowledge of cultural differences will be particularly helpful as you interact with parents and extended family members, and work cooperatively with them to help students acquire lifelong learning skills and paid employment.

---

### COMPREHENSION MONITORING OF KEY CONCEPTS

#### Career Education

1. Career education prepares individuals for participation in all aspects of life, including home, school, occupation, and community.

2. Career education is a total person approach to education that lends itself well to the preparation of *all* students in practical, meaningful, and functional skills.

*Historical Development*

3. Career education began as a movement for the general population of students in 1971 when Sidney Marland, then Commissioner of Education, declared career education to be the top priority of the U.S. Office of Education.

4. During the 1970s, the career education movement broadened its focus to include the needs of individuals with disabilities.

5. The passage of P.L. 95-207, the Career Education Implementation Incentive Act, in 1977 ensured the inclusion of individuals with disabilities as an appropriate target group for services, and helped states to infuse career education into the school curriculum.

*Definition*

6. Career education begins at birth and continues throughout the life span, preparing individuals for all aspects of life.

7. Brolin (1995) considers career education to be "a lifelong process that infuses a careers emphasis in all subjects, grades K–12, including job training, apprenticeship programs, mentoring, career exploration, and the nonpaid work done as a family member, citizen, and leisure seeker" (p. 53).

*Description*

8. Career education occurs in four stages: career awareness, career exploration, career preparation, and career assimilation.

9. Career awareness takes place during the elementary years and focuses on making students aware of paid and unpaid work options.

10. Career exploration occurs during middle/junior high school and involves having students explore their interests, abilities, and skills as workers, citizens, family members, and leisure activity participants.

11. Career preparation is emphasized during high school and focuses on making decisions/planning/preparing for work, for schooling after high school, and for community living.

12. Career assimilation involves transitioning students into post-secondary training or gainful employment.

13. Career education requires the school to work closely with families and the community.

### Life Centered Career Education Model

In the previous sections, we emphasized the importance of infusing career education throughout the curriculum. The Life Centered Career Education (LCCE) model (Brolin, 1993), originally developed in the 1970s by Brolin and colleagues, has evolved over the past 20 years as a model that is practical, meaningful, and related to the real world. The LCCE model suggests that transitional programming begin at the elementary level with the development of a work personality and the skills needed for successful adult functioning (Brolin, 1993). The LCCE model incorporates (1) the four stages of career development (career awareness, exploration, preparation, and assimilation); (2) three curriculum areas consisting of 22 major life-skill competencies and 97 subcompetencies, (3) a K–12+ focus; (4) the significant involvement of school, family, and community resources; (5) and preparation for all of life's roles (Brolin, 1995).

Figure 11.1 illustrates how the stages of career development and the LCCE competencies are integrated into an academically oriented curriculum. Notice that basic academic skills are emphasized more at the lower grade levels, while the more functional skills are the focus at the higher grade levels.

Of course, in addition to the academic focus during the elementary grades, career education activities are also included. The lower half of the figure illustrates the substantial collaborative effort needed throughout the curriculum as part of the career education focus.

#### *Career Education Competencies*

The 22 competencies and 97 subcompetencies are organized into the areas of daily living, personal/social, and occupational skills. Daily living skills include competencies that prepare individuals for successful adjustment to the challenges of community living (managing finances and exhibiting responsible citizenship). Personal/social skills include competencies that allow individuals to be successful in work and other settings (communicating with others, making friends, and accepting criticism). Occupational guidance and preparation skills include competencies that prepare students to explore, seek, secure, and maintain an occupation (identifying the requirements of specific jobs, applying for a job, and working at a satisfactory rate). Table 11.1 lists the 22 competencies and 97 subcompetencies and shows how they are distributed across the three areas.

#### *Planning Career Education Lessons and Activities*

The Life Centered Career Education competencies can be infused into any content class or subject-matter area. We present two examples of lesson plans illustrating how you can incorporate daily living, personal/social,

**FIGURE 11.1** **Curriculum/LCCE Transition Model**

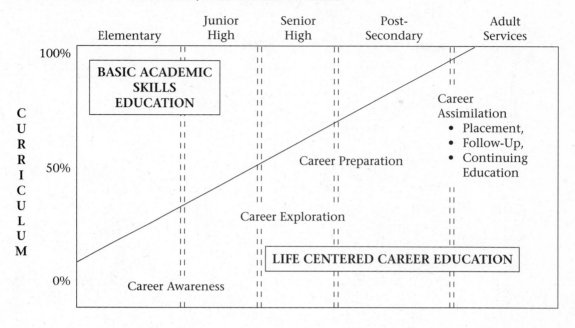

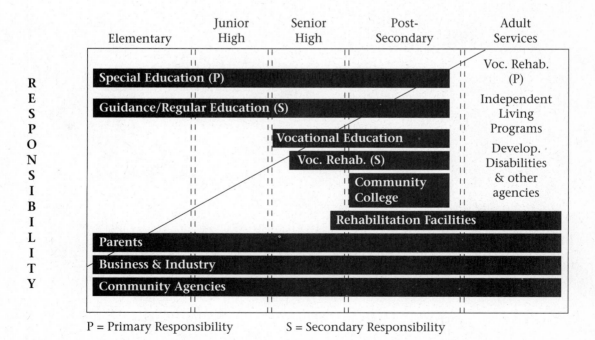

P = Primary Responsibility    S = Secondary Responsibility

*Source:* From *Life Centered Career Education: Professional Development Activity Book* (p. 43) by The Council for Exceptional Children. Copyright 1993 by The Council for Exceptional Children. Reprinted by permission.

**TABLE 11.1   Life Centered Education Competencies**

| Curriculum area | Competency | Subcompetency: The student will be able to: | |
|---|---|---|---|
| DAILY LIVING SKILLS | 1. Managing Personal Finances | 1. Count money & make correct change | 2. Make responsible expenditures |
| | 2. Selecting & Managing a Household | 7. Maintain home exterior/interior | 8. Use basic appliances and tools |
| | 3. Caring for Personal Needs | 12. Demonstrate knowledge of physical fitness, nutrition & weight | 13. Exhibit proper grooming & hygiene |
| | 4. Raising Children & Meeting Marriage Responsibilities | 17. Demonstrate physical care for raising children | 18. Know psychological aspects of raising children |
| | 5. Buying, Preparing & Consuming Food | 20. Purchase food | 21. Clean food preparation areas |
| | 6. Buying & Caring for Clothing | 26. Wash/clean clothing | 27. Purchase clothing |
| | 7. Exhibiting Responsible Citizenship | 29. Demonstrate knowledge of civil rights & responsibilities | 30. Know nature of local, state & federal governments |
| | 8. Utilizing Recreational Facilities & Engaging in Leisure | 33. Demonstrate knowledge of available community resources | 34. Choose & plan activities |
| | 9. Getting Around the Community | 38. Demonstrate knowledge of traffic rules & safety | 39. Demonstrate knowledge & use of various means of transportation |
| PERSONAL/SOCIAL SKILLS | 10. Achieving Self-Awareness | 42. Identify physical & psychological needs | 43. Identify interests & abilities |
| | 11. Acquiring Self-Confidence | 46. Express feelings of self-worth | 47. Describe others' perception of self |
| | 12. Achieving Socially Responsible Behavior—Community | 51. Develop respect for the rights & properties of others | 52. Recognize authority & follow instructions |
| | 13. Maintaining Good Interpersonal Skills | 56. Demonstrate listening & responding skills | 57. Establish & maintain close relationships |
| | 14. Achieving Independence | 59. Strive toward self-actualization | 60. Demonstrate self-organization |
| | 15. Making Adequate Decisions | 62. Locate & utilize sources of assistance | 63. Anticipate consequences |
| | 16. Communicating with Others | 67. Recognize & respond to emergency situations | 68. Communicate with understanding |

| | | | | |
|---|---|---|---|---|
| 3. Keep basic financial records | 4. Calculate & pay taxes | 5. Use credit responsibly | 6. Use banking services | |
| 9. Select adequate housing | 10. Set up house-hold | 11. Maintain home grounds | | |
| 14. Dress appropri-ately | 15. Demonstrate knowledge of common illness, prevention & treatment | 16. Practice personal safety | | |
| 19. Demonstrate marriage responsibilities | | | | |
| 22. Store food | 23. Prepare meals | 24. Demonstrate appropriate eating habits | 25. Plan/eat balanced meals | |
| 28. Iron, mend & store clothing | | | | |
| 31. Demonstrate knowledge of the law & ability to follow the law | 32. Demonstrate knowledge of citizen rights & responsibilities | | | |
| 35. Demonstrate knowledge of the value of recreation | 36. Engage in group & individual activities | 37. Plan vacation time | | |
| 40. Find way around the community | 41. Drive a car | | | |
| 44. Identify emotions | 45. Demonstrate knowledge of physical self | | | |
| 48. Accept and give praise | 49. Accept & give criticism | 50. Develop confidence in oneself | | |
| 53. Demonstrate appropriate behavior in public places | 54. Know important character traits | 55. Recognize personal roles | | |
| 58. Make & maintain friendships | | | | |
| 61. Demonstrate awareness of how one's behavior affects others | | | | |
| 64. Develop & evaluate alternatives | 65. Recognize nature of problem | 66. Develop goal-seeking behavior | | |
| 69. Know subtleties of communi-cation | | | | |

*(continued on next page)*

**TABLE 11.1** *(continued)*

| Curriculum area | Competency | Subcompetency: The student will be able to: | |
|---|---|---|---|
| OCCUPATIONAL GUIDANCE AND PREPARATION | 17. Knowing & Exploring Occupational Possibilities | 70. Identify remunerative aspects of work | 71. Locate sources of occupational & training information |
| | 18. Selecting & Planning Occupational Choices | 76. Make realistic occupational choices | 77. Identify requirements of appropriate & available jobs |
| | 19. Exhibiting Appropriate Work Habits & Behaviors | 81. Follow directions & observe regulations | 82. Recognize importance of attendance & punctuality |
| | 20. Seeking, Securing & Maintaining Employment | 88. Search for a job | 89. Apply for a job |
| | 21. Exhibiting Sufficient Physical-Manual Skills | 94. Demonstrate stamina & endurance | 95. Demonstrate satisfactory balance & coordination |
| | 22. Obtaining Specific Occupational Skills | | |

and occupational skill competencies into your content-area instruction—one for math and the other for American government. In Box 11.1, we show you how to infuse managing personal finances (daily living skill), achieving independence (personal/social skill), and identifying remunerative aspects of work (occupational guidance and preparation skill) into a math lesson on decimals and percent by teaching students how to calculate sales tax. In Box 11.2, we show you how to infuse exhibiting responsible citizenship (daily living skill), acquiring self-confidence (personal/social skill), and selecting and planning occupational choices (occupational guidance and preparation skills) into an American government lesson on social security.

During the math lesson, in addition to working on multiplying numerals by decimals and percents, you would stress with students the necessity of being able to calculate sales tax for (1) planning purchases and working within a budget (daily living skill of managing personal finances); (2) knowing how much they actually have to pay (personal/social skill of achieving independence); and (3) deciding what is affordable for them, given a potential job they might have (occupational guidance and preparation skill of identifying the remunerative aspects of work).

| 72. Identify personal values met through work | 73. Identify societal values met through work | 74. Classify jobs into occupational categories | 75. Investigate local occupational & training opportunities | |
|---|---|---|---|---|
| 78. Identify occupational aptitudes | 79. Identify major occupational interests | 80. Identify major occupational needs | | |
| 83. Recognize importance of supervision | 84. Demonstrate knowledge of occupational safety | 85. Work with others | 86. Meet demands for quality work | 87. Work at a satisfactory rate |
| 90. Interview for a job | 91. Know how to maintain post-school occupational adjustment | 92. Demonstrate knowledge of competitive standards | 93. Know how to adjust to changes in employment | |
| 96. Demonstrate manual dexterity | 97. Demonstrate sensory discrimination | | | |
| There are no specific subcompetencies as they depend on skill being taught | | | | |

*Source: Life Centered Career Education: A Competency-Based Approach* (4th ed., pp. 12–13) by D. E. Brolin, 1993. Copyright 1993 by The Council for Exceptional Children. Reprinted by permission.

During the American government lesson, in addition to working on the United States social security system, you would stress with students the necessity of being able to use their knowledge about social security for (1) knowing the nature of the federal government as it relates to social security (daily living skill of exhibiting responsible citizenship); (2) knowing how the social security system works and its impact on them (personal/social skill of acquiring self-confidence); and (3) deciding whether a potential job is covered by social security (occupational guidance and preparation skill of selecting and planning occupational choices).

As you teach content lessons and infuse career education competencies within them, you can develop your own lesson plans, as we did in our examples, or you can use the curriculum materials available commercially. The LCCE includes a curriculum guide, a trainer/implementation manual, curriculum-based assessment measures, activity books with more than 1000 lesson plans and instructional objectives, and a competency rating scale. Whether you select the LCCE, another commercial program, or design your own, we urge you to assist students to become productive, well-adjusted, competent adults after they leave school by implementing comprehensive career education within your instruction.

**BOX 11.1** | **Incorporating LCCE Competencies into a Math Lesson**

Title/Topic:   Calculating sales tax

Purpose:   To practice multiplying with decimals and percents using the real-life skill of calculating sales tax.

Objectives:   After instruction, students will verbally state what sales tax is and explain the reason for it with 90% accuracy.

After discussion, students will verbally state the sales tax rate in their state with 100% accuracy.

When asked, students will verbally explain how sales tax is used and name at least four types of items that are taxed with 90% accuracy.

Given receipts for five different items, students will verbally state which items have been taxed with 100% accuracy.

Given a variety of different purchases, students will calculate on paper the sales tax using multiplication with 100% accuracy.

Procedures:
1. Preview the lesson by explaining to students that they will be using a skill they have been working on in math to help them with a real-life situation.
2. Review with students how to multiply by decimals and percents.
3. Introduce the topic of sales tax, including its definition, the reason for it, the rate in their state, uses of sales tax, and types of items taxed.
4. Provide receipts for specific items, such as clothing, groceries, stereo components, and cars, and have students determine which items are taxed.
5. Show students how they can compute sales tax by multiplying using decimals and percents.
6. Give students advertisements from the newspaper and have them select items that would be taxed.
7. Have students calculate the sales tax on each item and explain their work.
8. Discuss with students how the cost of items, plus sales tax, impacts what they can afford to buy in relation to the jobs they have.

Materials:   Math books, paper, pencils, sample receipts, and newspaper ads.

Evaluation:   Teacher evaluation of students' verbal responses and written work for accuracy and understanding.

**BOX 11.2**

## Incorporating LCCE Competencies into an American Government Lesson

Title/Topic: Social Security in the United States

Purpose: To discuss the passage of the Social Security Act in 1935, several facts about social security, and the uses of social security cards today.

Objectives: Using the textbook, students will verbally define the Social Security Act of 1935 and state three ways that social security programs have changed with 90% accuracy.

After instruction, students will verbally state who is covered by social security and name three benefits of social security with 95% accuracy.

When asked, students will verbally state at least two potential jobs that are covered by social security with 95% accuracy.

Using sample forms, students will record their social security number in the appropriate space on the form with 100% accuracy.

Procedures:
1. Preview the lesson by describing how an act passed by Congress in 1935 impacts all of us today.

2. Go over the section in the American Government textbook that explains the passage of the Social Security Act by the United States Congress in 1935.

3. Find examples in the textbook of how social security programs have changed since 1935.

4. Discuss what the Social Security Act provides, including the benefits you receive when you retire or when you cannot work for a certain length of time because you are injured or ill.

5. Discuss with students who is covered by social security and how that impacts future employment (you are covered in the military and in most jobs in which you work for yourself or for others).

6. Using the overhead projector, show a sample of a social security card and discuss when you might need to show it, such as when you begin a job or claim benefits.

7. Have students examine their own cards. Then ask them for examples of where they might be asked to

*(continued on next page)*

**BOX 11.2**
*(continued)*

write their social security number, such as on school forms, income tax forms, job applications, and automobile insurance forms.

8. Have students work in groups. Give them sample income tax, job application, school, medical, band, and insurance forms and ask them to fill in their social security number in the correct area.

9. Preview the next lesson, which will include social security contributions, benefits (survivor, retirement, and disability), and Medicare.

Materials: American Government textbook, transparency of a social security card, the students' cards, sample forms, paper, pencils, overhead projector, and transparency markers.

Evaluation: Teacher evaluation of students' verbal responses and written work for accuracy and understanding.

## COMPREHENSION MONITORING OF KEY CONCEPTS

### Life Centered Career Education Model

1. The Life Centered Career Education model incorporates the stages of career development, three curriculum areas consisting of 22 life-skill competencies and 97 subcompetencies, a K–12+ focus, and involvement of school, family, and community.

2. The three curriculum areas of the LCCE are daily living skills, personal/social skills, and occupational skills

3. Daily living skills prepare individuals for successful adjustment to community living (managing finances and exhibiting responsible citizenship).

4. Personal/social skills prepare individuals for success in work and other settings (such as communicating with others, making friends, and accepting criticism).

5. Occupational guidance and preparation skills prepare individuals to explore, seek, secure, and maintain an occupation (such as applying for a job and working at a satisfactory rate).

6. Career education can be infused into any content class or subject matter area.

> 7. The LCCE includes a curriculum guide, a trainer/implementation manual, curriculum-based assessment measures, activity books more than 1000 lesson plans and instructional objectives, and a competency rating scale.

## Vocational Education

In the preceding sections, we have described career education, an essential ingredient in the preparation of our nation's youth with disabilities for their numerous roles in life. In this section, we discuss vocational education, a vital element in the preparation of adolescents with disabilities for one specific role—that of gainful employment.

> Imagine schools where the curriculum is so relevant to students' future goals that discipline problems decrease dramatically, teenagers who were never successful in traditional classrooms become focused and excited about learning, and teachers find that their job can, indeed, be fun and rewarding—the way they envisioned it when they chose their profession! (Williamson, 1994, p. 11)

Employment is an important outcome and critical aspect of education and transition for most adults (Bullis & Gaylord-Ross, 1991). Vocational training and transitional services are needed for successful transition to employment and adult living. Unfortunately, postschool and employment outcome studies show that many students with mild disabilities leave high school without training and services and are, therefore, unemployed or employed part-time to a greater extent than students without disabilities (Edgar, 1987, 1988; Frank, Sitlington, & Carson, 1991; Gerber & Brown, 1991; Haring & Lovett, 1990; Haring, Lovett, & Smith, 1990; Roessler, Brolin, & Johnson, 1990; Siegel & Gaylord-Ross, 1991).

In 1986, the Senate Subcommittee on Employment of the Handicapped Report showed that 67% of Americans with disabilities from age 16 to 64 were not employed. Moreover, 75% of those who were employed were working part-time, and 67% of those who were not employed stated that they wanted to work (Karge, Patton, & De la Garza, 1992). Follow-up studies of students with mental disabilities or learning disabilities (Roessler et al., 1990) have found low rates of employment among those with disabilities during the first year after leaving high school. Employment outcome studies of students with behavior disorders have found that approximately 50% are employed, earning minimum wage or less and working in service occupations or as laborers (Frank et al., 1991), and about 33% are not involved in any job or training program (Neal, Meadows, Levine, & Edgar, 1988).

These studies paint a bleak picture for adolescents with mild disabilities who exit high school to face the demands of independent living, employment, and postsecondary education and training. To compound the problem, it appears that students with mild disabilities may not have access to appropriate vocational education opportunities. Hoffman et al. (1987) surveyed adults with learning disabilities and found that they had received limited vocational education during and after high school. The National Longitudinal Transition Study found that postschool outcomes appear to be better for adolescents who complete high school, receive vocational education in high school, spend more time in regular education classes, and participate in school and community activities (Wagner, 1993). Special education teachers, other professionals, and parents must make a concerted effort to include vocational education, regular class participation, and school and community activities in programs for adolescents with disabilities.

## Definition

Access to appropriate vocational education enhances employment outcomes for students with disabilities (Benz & Halpern, 1987; Hasazi, Gordon, & Roe, 1985; Hasazi, Johnson, Hasazi, Gordon, & Hall, 1989; Wagner, 1991b). It is essential to include vocational education (occupational guidance and preparation) in your planning with regular education personnel, vocational education personnel, students, families, and support service personnel.

Vocational education is "education designed to develop skills, abilities, understandings, attitudes, work habits and appreciations needed by workers to enter and make progress in employment on a useful and productive basis" (American Vocational Association, 1968, p. 12). In other words, vocational education is a series of experiences designed to provide students with the skills needed for gainful employment. This is accomplished through vocational assessment, counseling, education, and training, and through job placement and follow-along services (Masters et al., 1993). According to Kokaska and Brolin (1985), the vocational education process for students with disabilities should result in their acquiring the following six vocational competencies:

1. Know and explore occupational possibilities.

2. Select and plan occupational choices.

3. Exhibit appropriate work habits and behaviors.

4. Exhibit sufficient physical/manual skills.

5. Obtain a specific occupational skill.

6. Seek, secure, and maintain employment.

The first two competencies relate to possible occupations. Vocational education typically prepares students in the occupational areas of (a) agriculture and agribusiness, (b) home economics, (c) technical occupations, (d) health occupations, (e) trades and industrial occupations, (f) business and office occupations, and (g) marketing and distributive occupations (Masters et al., 1993). The next four competencies relate to the specific skills that individuals need in order to obtain and keep a job.

## Vocational Assessment

Vocational assessment is used for screening, program placement, planning, monitoring progress, and for program evaluation (Cobb & Larkin, 1985). Vocational assessment is the ongoing, systematic process of gathering information about an individual's aptitudes, skills, interests, and work-related behaviors, which allows professionals to make decisions about curriculum, materials, instructional strategies, and necessary modifications. Vocational assessment and the integration of vocational assessment into the school curriculum should be seen as integral components of a comprehensive and effective educational curriculum (Niles & Tiffany, 1990) and linked to the goals and techniques of instruction and to service delivery and intervention (Cobb & Larkin, 1985). Veir (1987) suggests that a comprehensive assessment profile can provide information about a student's:

- functional academic skills
- abilities
- entry-level skill needs
- learning styles
- needs for modifications in materials, curriculum, and equipment
- interests
- psychomotor skills and dexterity
- goals and objectives
- work habits
- work attitudes
- previous work experiences
- education and training needs

- employment potential
- needs for support services

Vocational assessment may be conducted by special needs coordinators, vocational education personnel, special education personnel, regular education personnel, parents/families, school psychologists, bilingual educators, and guidance counselors. It is important that these individuals work as a team and that they are familiar with the characteristics and needs of adolescents with mild disabilities, the regular education curriculum, and vocational course content and programs.

Two basic types of assessment can provide you, other professionals, parents, and students with information for setting vocational goals and objectives, and for developing an instructional plan in vocational education. These types are formal and informal assessment measures.

### Formal Assessment

Formal assessment involves the use of standardized, commercially produced instruments, which allows comparison of a student's performance to that of a norm group. Formal assessment is used for placing students in programs, identifying strengths and weaknesses, and identifying current levels of functioning. It provides an excellent means of determining which areas to assess further and which informal assessment procedures to use. Examples of formal assessment in the areas of vocational education include the following:

*Aptitude tests and interest inventories.* The Occupational Aptitude Survey and Interest Schedule—2 (OASIS–2) (Parker, 1991a, 1991b) can be used as an aptitude and interest measure to assist students with vocational decision making. The Aptitude Survey measures six aptitudes related to the skills and abilities required for the jobs listed in the *Dictionary of Occupational Titles* (U.S. Department of Labor, 1977). The *Interest Schedule* measures 12 interest areas related to the occupations listed in the *Guide to Occupational Exploration* (Harrington & O'Shea, 1984).

*Rating scales.* The Prevocational Assessment and Curriculum Guide (PACG) (Mithaug, Mar, & Stewart, 1978) is a standardized rating scale that assesses functioning in school and workshop settings. The Vocational Assessment and Curriculum Guide (VACG) (Rusch, Schutz, Mithaug, Stewart, & Mar, 1982) is a standardized rating scale that addresses functioning in vocational settings, primarily service occupations. The AAMD Adaptive Behavior Scale (School Edition) (Nihira, Foster, Shellhaas, & Leland, 1981) is a standardized rating scale that measures daily living and social functioning.

The Vineland Adaptive Behavior Scales (Sparrow, Balla, & Cicchetti, 1985) are standardized rating scales that assess daily living skills, communication, socialization, and motor skills.

***Basic and functional skills tests.*** The Adaptive Behavior: The Street Survival Skills Questionnaire (SSSQ) (Linkenhoker & McCarron, 1985) is a standardized instrument that tests students' knowledge of basic concepts, functional signs, time, money, measurement, tools, domestics, public services, and health and safety. The Social and Prevocational Information Battery (SPIB) (Halpern & Irvin, 1986) is available in forms for students with mild and moderate disabilities. The test measures job search skills, job-related behavior, banking, budgeting, purchasing, home management, functional signs, hygiene and grooming, and health care.

***Computer programs for vocational assessment.*** The Apticom Program (Vocational Research Institute, 1989) measures vocational aptitudes using limited reading and in a computer format. The Talent Assessment Program (TAP) (Instant Report, 1988) is a screening instrument in a computerized format that provides information about training and/or jobs that may be appropriate for the individual. The MESA Program (Valpar International, 1982) is a computer program, in both norm-referenced and criterion-referenced forms, that provides vocational screening. The McCarron–Dial Work Evaluation System (McCarron & Dial, 1976) offers a computerized component that relates assessment findings to jobs that may be within the capabilities of the individual.

Use of these formal measures, or others like them, will provide information regarding intellectual functioning, academic achievement, aptitudes and interests, social maturity, and performance of occupational, daily living, and functional skills. Remember, formal assessment measures should be selected carefully, taking into consideration (1) the characteristics of the student and the environment, (2) the reliability, validity, and characteristics of the test instruments, and (3) the linguistic and cultural backgrounds of the norm group and the students being tested.

### Informal Assessment

During the past several years, some of the most rapidly developing assessment approaches in special education have focused on student performance within the context of services, such as classroom instruction, curriculum, home, and job (Greenwood & Rieth, 1994). These approaches are referred to as informal assessment procedures. Unlike formal assessment, which compares a student's performance to that of other students, informal assessment compares a student's performance to "preestablished standards or goals considered acceptable" (Meier, 1995, p. 93). Informal assessment can be used for screening and placement, but it is more commonly used to establish the beginning point of instruction; set goals; determine students' needs, strengths, and weaknesses; analyze environmental and task demands; and monitor student progress. There is overlap among informal assessment measures. For example, many types of informal assessment, such as curriculum-based vocational assessment, criterion-referenced testing, and rating forms, include a scope and sequence of skills. These skills represent the behaviors necessary for adequate performance of a given task. Note that curriculum-based vocational assessment, criterion-referenced testing, and rating forms can be used both for initial assessment of skills and for monitoring progress.

There are also differences among informal measures. For example, in addition to assessing students' skills, community-based assessment is used to collect information about employment opportunities, job skill requirements, working conditions, salaries, and training requirements. These factors are not included in the other types of informal assessment we describe.

We present six types of informal measures and describe each one separately. You may find yourself using them at different times or in combination.

***Curriculum-based vocational assessment (CBVA).*** Curriculum-based vocational assessment (CBVA) is the ongoing process of collecting data while the student is engaged in vocational education activities (Stodden, Ianacone, Boone, & Bisconer, 1987). CBVA procedures can be used to identify the career and vocational needs of students by observing their performance of tasks from career and vocational curricula (Stodden et al., 1987). CBVA links assessment directly to the vocational curriculum used in the classroom (Masters et al., 1993). "Useful assessment is so interwoven with instruction that it defies separation" (Choate et al., 1995, p. xii). CBVA involves selecting skills from the curriculum, giving students informal measures that assess the performance of these skills, and developing instructional objectives (Blankenship, 1985).

Four features that are characteristic of curriculum-based vocational assessment are that it (1) assists educators in planning a student's vocational program, (2) views assessment as an integral part of a student's vocational education program, (3) ensures that the individuals conducting CBVA activities are also responsible for the students' vocational instruction, and (4) uses direct methods to determine student achievement and monitor progress in the vocational education program (Schloss, Smith, & Schloss, 1995).

Swisher and Clark (1991), in collaboration with vocational instructors, designed a curriculum-based vocational assessment program by identifying the generalizable and vocational skills in business, consumer/home economics, and industrial technology classes. Then they developed a series of sequential, work sample activities that could be provided to students over a 90-hour time span. This effort resulted in the development of the Practical Arts Evaluation System (PAES), "an invaluable tool in the education and transition planning for students with special needs" (Swisher & Clark, 1991, p. 14). The PAES program consists of curriculum materials, activity units, data collection forms, computer scoring forms and software, and on-site training (Brolin, 1995). Please consult Chapter 3 for a detailed explanation of the six steps involved in developing your own curriculum-based assessment.

***Criterion-referenced testing.*** In criterion-referenced testing (CRT), a student's performance is compared with a preestablished criterion or standard, not to the performance of others, as in norm-referenced testing. Criterion-referenced testing "reflects the extent to which a student has mastered content taught within a short instructional sequence" (Greenwood & Rieth, 1994, p. 109). Since criterion-referenced testing assesses student performance of skills, the results assist teachers in deciding what skills have been mastered and what skills may need to be taught or retaught.

Examples of commercial criterion-referenced tests that are appropriate for use in the vocational instruction of adolescents are the Brigance Diagnostic Inventory of Essential Skills (Brigance, 1981) and the Brigance Inventory of Life Skills (Brigance, 1995). You can set your own expected level of mastery for the skills that you are interested in assessing, or you can use the mastery level recommended in the Brigance inventories. In Chapter 3 of this text, we discussed in detail the four steps to follow when assessing students with criterion-referenced tests (select the test, administer the test, select the expected level of mastery, and identify your objectives).

For example, Mr. Willis used a question from the Vocational section of the Brigance Inventory of Essential Skills (select the test) to determine if Phil could complete a W-4 form. He asked Phil to fill in the blank sections on the form (administer the test). Mr. Willis set the criterion at 100% because of the need to complete this form accurately (select the expected level of mastery). Based upon Phil's performance of the task, he wrote, "Given a W-4 form, Phil will write his name, social security number, address, marital status, exemptions, signature, and date with 100% accuracy" (identify your objectives).

***Community-based assessment.*** Community-based assessment is a type of behavioral assessment that focuses on skills (such as interviewing for a job or getting along with co-workers) that enable individuals with disabilities to function as independently as possible in inclusive settings (for example, on the job or at an automated teller machine). This type of assessment is performance-based, and results in information about students' functional skills in natural settings. Note how this aspect is similar to situational assessment.

Another aspect of community-based assessment, in addition to assessing students' skills, is collecting information about employment opportunities, job vacancies, job skill requirements, working conditions, salaries, and education/training requirements (Berkell & Brown, 1989). You can access this type of information through government offices, civic organizations, community agencies, and the chamber of commerce.

*Rating forms.* Rating forms are assessment instruments that provide specific information regarding a student's strengths and weaknesses. They may take the form of rating scales, inventories, or checklists. Stodden et al. (1987) recommend the use of academic and vocational rating forms. They can be used as part of curriculum-based vocational assessment because students are rated on skills and behaviors that are in the curriculum being taught.

For example, Figure 11.2 shows an academic rating form for Shelley, completed by her English teacher. The front of the form indicates Shelley's level of interest and aptitude and describes the modifications that were made to meet her needs. On the back of the form, the teacher rates Shelley's work-related behaviors, generalizable skills (generalized outcomes), and specific skills (specific outcomes). You will notice, under work-related behaviors, that Shelley works well with peers and authorities, shows initiative, and exhibits appropriate behavior and manners. However, she has difficulty completing her work accurately and in a timely manner, and lacks confidence. Under generalized outcomes, she understands and follows directions and locates information, but she has difficulty with capitalization, punctuation, and the completion of forms. An analysis of specific outcomes confirms what was found under generalizable outcomes, but the information is presented in greater detail.

Figure 11.3 shows Shelley's vocational rating form in computer technology, which was completed jointly by two of her teachers (computer and vocational). These teachers rated her work-related behaviors in a similar manner to that of the English teacher. Under generalized outcomes, they found her strengths to be in following written directions, knowledge of the keyboard, proper care of hardware and software, and an appreciation of the uses and benefits of computer technology; however, she still needs to work with flowcharts, programming, and electronic communication. The specific outcomes column shows that she needs instruction and practice in using commands and graphics, editing capitalization and punctuation errors, and using e-mail.

Veir (1987) suggests the use of a student inventory to collect assessment information. You can use this type of inventory form to assess how students prefer to receive information in class (such as cooperative learning, lecture, discussion) and how they prefer to complete assignments (written reports, oral reports, media projects). Once you have assessed students' learning preferences, you should identify how various teachers present information in their classes. This can be done with a course description inventory form (lecture, overhead projector or chalkboard, and so on). Using these assessment procedures will help you determine if there is a match between learning preferences and methods of instruction, and assist you in developing the IEP and ITP.

*Checklists.* Checklists are informal observation instruments that list the behaviors necessary for adequate performance of a given task. They can be used for the initial skills assessment and for monitoring progress. For example, Mr. Edmund designed a checklist of the items included on most job applications and used it to assess whether students completed each section of the application correctly. Ms. Lewis compiled a list of work-related social behaviors that she believed to be essential for success on the job, and used this list to monitor the social skills of her students.

*Situational assessment.* Clark and Kolstoe (1990) state that situational assessment is probably the most common type of assessment used in high school occupational or prevocational programs. Although situational assessment is most frequently associated with on-the-job observation, it need not be restricted to work situations. It can be used as part of career education and transition assessment as well. Some of the skills we can observe at work can also be observed at home, at school, or in community situations. For example, Joel's supervisor, special and vocational education teachers, and parents responded to the following questions:

1. Does Joel assume responsibility?
2. Does Joel get along with others?
3. Does Joel relate well to authority?
4. Does Joel complete tasks in a timely manner?
5. Does Joel work independently?
6. Does Joel ask questions when he is having difficulty?
7. Does Joel implement suggestions or corrections made by others?
8. Does Joel follow a specific set of steps to solve problems?

# FIGURE 11.2 Academic Rating Form

*Directions*

1. Fill in student information below.

2. Follow steps A–C to complete rating charts on page 2 of this form.

A. Use the blank spaces (up to 41) at the bottom of each column for additional behavior/performance competencies relevant to your curricular area.

B. Please circle the appropriate category:
   P = Proficient—can perform with 90% accuracy
   M = Proficient with modification—can perform with *instructor assistance.*
   N = Not proficient
   (do not circle when information was not evaluated/covered)

C. Complete the totals and percentages at the bottom of each column.

3. Rate overall student performance.

4. Add modifications and comments (see below).

5. Obtain appropriate signatures.

6. Return to assessment coordinator.

Student: __Mathews__  __Shelly__  __M.__  __Adams H.S.__  __16 / 10__  (9 weeks)  18 weeks
         Last Name   First Name   MI   School      Age/Grade   Length of Stay (circle one)

ASSESSMENT ENVIRONMENT: English
VOCATIONAL INSTRUCTOR: __T. Brown__  __J. Brown__
ASSESSMENT COORDINATOR: __V. Hall__  __V. Hall__

DATES ATTENDED: Entry _____   Exit _____

As related to your course, circle the student's overall:  Interest . . . (high) medium low   Aptitude . . . high (medium) low

COMMENTS:
- use of visuals, demonstration, and monitoring of progress appears to be helpful.
- Shelly has a positive attitude.

MODIFICATIONS:

Setting: English class

Content: Writing letters, memos with correct punctuation.

Teaching Method: Use of overhead projector and computer with demonstration, practice, feedback.

Materials/Equipment: Computer, transparencies, overhead projector

__Shelly Mathews__   __9-3-96__
Student signature    Date

__Ann Howard__   __9-3-96__
Instructor signature   Date

ACADEMICALLY-RELATED RATING FORM

Page 2

Assessment Environment: English

## I WORK RELATED BEHAVIORS

| Level | I WORK RELATED BEHAVIORS |
|---|---|
| Ⓟ M N | 1 Display initiative |
| Ⓟ M N | 2 Exhibit a desire to improve |
| Ⓟ M N | 3 Display integrity |
| P Ⓜ N | 4 Exhibit self-confidence |
| Ⓟ N | 5 Display frustration tolerance |
| Ⓟ M N | 6 Exhibit flexibility |
| Ⓟ M N | 7 Make judgments and decisions |
| Ⓟ M N | 8 Problem solves effectively |
| Ⓟ M N | 9 Relate with peers/co-workers |
| Ⓟ M N | 10 Relate with teachers/supervisors |
| Ⓟ M N | 11 Cooperate as a team member |
| Ⓟ M N | 12 Accept constructive criticism |
| Ⓟ M N | 13 Work unsupervised |
| P Ⓜ N | 14 Complete tasks accurately |
| P Ⓜ N | 15 Complete tasks in a timely manner |
| Ⓟ N | 16 Seek assistance appropriately |
| Ⓟ M N | 17 Display appropriate habits/manners |
| Ⓟ M N | 18 Display appropriate appearance |
| Ⓟ M N | 19 Comply with attendance regulations |
| Ⓟ M N | 20 Practice punctuality |
| Ⓟ M N | 21 Display appropriate conduct |
| Ⓟ M N | 22 Use and care of materials/equipment |
| P Ⓜ N | 23 Comply with safety precautions |
| P M N | 24 |
| P M N | 25 |
| P M N | 26 |
| P M N | 27 |
| P M N | 28 |
| P M N | 29 |
| P M N | 30 |
| P M N | 31 |
| P M N | 32 |
| P M N | 33 |
| P M N | 34 |
| P M N | 35 |
| P M N | 36 |
| P M N | 37 |
| P M N | 38 |
| P M N | 39 |
| P M N | 40 |
| P M N | 41 |

TOTAL: 17 3 3
Number of P/M (Add: P + M) = 20
Total (Add: P + M + N) = 23
% P/M (Divide: P + M/P + M + N) = 87 %

## II GENERALIZED OUTCOMES

| Level | II GENERALIZED OUTCOMES |
|---|---|
| P Ⓜ N | 1 Use sentences/phrases to express thoughts |
| Ⓟ M N | 2 Understand/follow oral directions |
| Ⓟ M N | 3 Understand/follow written directions |
| Ⓟ Ⓜ N | 4 Give oral directions |
| Ⓟ N | 5 Use punctuation correctly |
| P Ⓜ N | 6 Use capitalization/usage correctly |
| Ⓜ N | 7 Locate information in different sources |
| Ⓜ N | 8 Write clear/logical letters/memos |
| Ⓜ N | 9 Write clear/logical directions |
| Ⓟ N | 10 Complete forms correctly |
| P M N | 11 |
| P M N | 12 |
| P M N | 13 |
| P M N | 14 |
| P M N | 15 |
| P M N | 16 |
| P M N | 17 |
| P M N | 18 |
| P M N | 19 |
| P M N | 20 |
| P M N | 21 |
| P M N | 22 |
| P M N | 23 |
| P M N | 24 |
| P M N | 25 |
| P M N | 26 |
| P M N | 27 |
| P M N | 28 |
| P M N | 29 |
| P M N | 30 |
| P M N | 31 |
| P M N | 32 |
| P M N | 33 |
| P M N | 34 |
| P M N | 35 |
| P M N | 36 |
| P M N | 37 |
| P M N | 38 |
| P M N | 39 |
| P M N | 40 |
| P M N | 41 |

TOTAL: 6 1 3
Number of P/M (Add: P + M) = 7
Total (Add: P + M + N) = 10
% P/M (Divide: P + M/P + M + N) = 70 %

## III SPECIFIC OUTCOMES

| Level | III SPECIFIC OUTCOMES |
|---|---|
| Ⓟ Ⓝ | 1 Expand sentences with words/phrases/clauses |
| Ⓟ Ⓝ | 2 Use singular/plurals correctly in writing |
| Ⓟ Ⓜ N | 3 Use singular/plurals correctly in speech |
| Ⓟ M N | 4 Use homonyms correctly |
| Ⓟ M N | 5 Use synonyms correctly |
| Ⓟ M N | 6 Use antonyms correctly |
| P Ⓜ N | 7 Write clear/logical sentences/phrases |
| P Ⓜ N | 8 Use correct punctuation to end sentences |
| P Ⓜ N | 9 Punctuate a series of words correctly |
| P Ⓜ N | 10 Punctuate dates correctly |
| P Ⓜ N | 11 Punctuate addresses correctly |
| P Ⓜ N | 12 Punctuate time correctly |
| Ⓟ Ⓝ | 13 Abbreviate days of the week correctly |
| Ⓟ Ⓝ | 14 Abbreviate months of the year correctly |
| Ⓟ M N | 15 Arrange words in alphabetical order |
| Ⓟ M N | 16 Arrange info. in chronological order |
| Ⓟ M N | 17 Locate words in a dictionary |
| P Ⓜ N | 18 Locate information in a telephone book |
| P Ⓜ N | 19 Use an index to locate information |
| P Ⓜ N | 20 Write letter requesting information |
| P Ⓜ N | 21 Answer letter requesting information |
| P Ⓜ N | 22 Write consumer request/complaint letter |
| P Ⓜ N | 23 Complete demographic information on forms |
| Ⓟ M N | 24 Abbreviate titles |
| P M N | 25 |
| P M N | 26 |
| P M N | 27 |
| P M N | 28 |
| P M N | 29 |
| P M N | 30 |
| P M N | 31 |
| P M N | 32 |
| P M N | 33 |
| P M N | 34 |
| P M N | 35 |
| P M N | 36 |
| P M N | 37 |
| P M N | 38 |
| P M N | 39 |
| P M N | 40 |
| P M N | 41 |

TOTAL: 12 8 6
Number of P/M (Add: P + M) = 18
Total (Add: P + M + N) = 24
% P/M (Divide: P + M/P + M + N) = 75 %

Source: From Curriculum-Based Vocational Assessment: A Guide for Addressing Youth with Special Needs by R. A. Stodden, R. N. Ianacone, R. M. Boone, and S. W. Bisconer. Copyright © 1987 Centre Publications. Reprinted by permission.

# FIGURE 11.3 Vocational Rating Form

*Directions*

1. Fill in student information below.

2. Follow steps A–C to complete rating charts on page 2 of this form.

A. Use the blank spaces (up to 41) at the bottom of each column for additional behavior/performance competencies relevant to your curricular area.

B. Please circle the appropriate category:

   P = Proficient—can perform with 90% accuracy

   M = Proficient with modification—can perform with *instructor assistance*.

   N = Not proficient

   (do not circle when information was not evaluated/covered)

C. Complete the totals and percentages at the bottom of each column.

3. Rate overall student performance.

4. Add modifications and comments (see below).

5. Obtain appropriate signatures.

6. Return to assessment coordinator.

Student:  Mathews          Shelly       M.       Adams H.S.        16/10        9 weeks    18 weeks

       Last Name        First Name     MI        School          Age/Grade       Length of Stay (circle one)

ASSESSMENT ENVIRONMENT: Computer technology

VOCATIONAL INSTRUCTOR: T. Brown  J. Brown

ASSESSMENT COORDINATOR: V. Hall  V. Hall          DATES ATTENDED: Entry _____ Exit _____

As related to your course, circle the student's overall:     Interest . . . high   medium   low        Aptitude . . . high   medium   low

MODIFICATIONS:

COMMENTS:

Setting: Computer Tech.

- Great attitude

Content: Word processing, E-mail

- Work in graphics is improving

Teaching Method: "Hands on," direct teaching, practice

- Is beginning to use E-mail daily

Materials/Equipment: Computer hardware, software

T. Brown  B. Rogers        9-4-96
Instructor signature        Date

Shelly Mathews        9-4-96
Student signature        Date

Assessment Environment: Computer Technology

VOCATIONALLY-RELATED RATING FORM

Page 2

| I WORK RELATED BEHAVIORS | Level |
|---|---|
| 1 Display initiative | P M N |
| 2 Exhibit a desire to improve | P M N |
| 3 Display integrity | P M N |
| 4 Exhibit self-confidence | P M N |
| 5 Display frustration tolerance | P M N |
| 6 Exhibit flexibility | P M N |
| 7 Make judgments and decisions | P M N |
| 8 Problem solves effectively | P M N |
| 9 Relate with peers/co-workers | P M N |
| 10 Relate with teachers/supervisors | P M N |
| 11 Cooperate as a team member | P M N |
| 12 Accept constructive criticism | P M N |
| 13 Work unsupervised | P M N |
| 14 Complete tasks accurately | P M N |
| 15 Complete tasks in a timely manner | P M N |
| 16 Seek assistance appropriately | P M N |
| 17 Display appropriate appearance | P M N |
| 18 Display appropriate habits/manners | P M N |
| 19 Comply with attendance regulations | P M N |
| 20 Practice punctuality | P M N |
| 21 Display appropriate conduct | P M N |
| 22 Use and care of materials/equipment | P M N |
| 23 Comply with safety precautions | P M N |
| 24 | P M N |
| 25 | P M N |
| 26 | P M N |
| 27 | P M N |
| 28 | P M N |
| 29 | P M N |
| 30 | P M N |
| 31 | P M N |
| 32 | P M N |
| 33 | P M N |
| 34 | P M N |
| 35 | P M N |
| 36 | P M N |
| 37 | P M N |
| 38 | P M N |
| 39 | P M N |
| 40 | P M N |
| 41 | P M N |

TOTAL: 19 3
Number of P/M (Add: P + M) = 20
Total (Add: P + M + N) = 23
% P/M (Divide: P + M/P + M + N) = 87 %

| II GENERALIZED OUTCOMES | Level |
|---|---|
| 1 Relate computer hardware/software | P M N |
| 2 Describe computer system components | P M N |
| 3 List common uses of computers | P M N |
| 4 Compare computer to calculator | P M N |
| 5 Compare computer to electronic game | P M N |
| 6 Explain ways computers affect people | P M N |
| 7 Identify computer related occupations | P M N |
| 8 Identify computer related references | P M N |
| 9 Describe limitations of computers | P M N |
| 10 Describe computer use in society | P M N |
| 11 Identify effect on employment | P M N |
| 12 Identify keyboard letters/numbers | P M N |
| 13 Identify special purpose keys | P M N |
| 14 Identify cursor movement techniques | P M N |
| 15 Describe proper care of soft/hardware | P M N |
| 16 Explain simple error messages | P M N |
| 17 Describe standard flow chart symbols | P M N |
| 18 List languages/applications | P M N |
| 19 Compare computer languages | P M N |
| 20 Explain concept of programming | P M N |
| 21 Follow written directions | P M N |
| 22 Describe electronic communication | P M N |
| 23 Identify binary number system | P M N |
| 24 Explain data processing functions | P M N |
| 25 Define data base and its use | P M N |
| 26 Identify job opportunities | P M N |
| 27 Name entry level skills in computers | P M N |
| 28 Cite use in processing information | P M N |
| 29 Differentiate micro/mini/mainframe | P M N |
| 30 Define and relate input/output | P M N |
| 31 Explain need for precise language | P M N |
| 32 Explain need for precise instructions | P M N |
| 33 Describe how computers process data | P M N |
| 34 Differentiate Logo/Pilot/BASIC | P M N |
| 35 Define BASIC statements/comments | P M N |
| 36 | P M N |
| 37 | P M N |
| 38 | P M N |
| 39 | P M N |
| 40 | P M N |
| 41 | P M N |

TOTAL: 23 9 3
Number of P/M (Add: P + M) = 32
Total (Add: P + M + N) = 35
% P/M (Divide: P + M/P + M + N) = 91 %

| III SPECIFIC OUTCOMES | Level |
|---|---|
| 1 Use correct keyboard letters/numbers | P M N |
| 2 Use correct keyboarding skills | P M N |
| 3 Use common special purpose keys | P M N |
| 4 Control cursor movement effectively | P M N |
| 5 Demonstrate care of sof/hardware | P M N |
| 6 Insert disk/turn on computer | P M N |
| 7 Stop/escape/continue prepared program | P M N |
| 8 Boot a program | P M N |
| 9 Run program from catalog or menu | P M N |
| 10 Operate printer/load paper/print data | P M N |
| 11 Operate computer devices | P M N |
| 12 Use drill and practice program | P M N |
| 13 Use simulation program | P M N |
| 14 Use problem-solving program | P M N |
| 15 Use computer as word processor | P M N |
| 16 Use data based program | P M N |
| 17 Use utility program | P M N |
| 18 Edit syntax errors | P M N |
| 19 Edit spelling/punctuation | P M N |
| 20 Use electronic communication program | P M N |
| 21 Read a flow chart | P M N |
| 22 Copy a simple program from disk | P M N |
| 23 Save a simple program | P M N |
| 24 Initialize a disk | P M N |
| 25 Delete all/part program from disk | P M N |
| 26 List and use basic statements | P M N |
| 27 List and use basic commands | P M N |
| 28 Use looping commands | P M N |
| 29 Use branching commands | P M N |
| 30 Create graphic designs | P M N |
| 31 Write simple text program | P M N |
| 32 Write multiple input procedures | P M N |
| 33 Use text/graphics/sound | P M N |
| 34 Debug a program | P M N |
| 35 | P M N |
| 36 | P M N |
| 37 | P M N |
| 38 | P M N |
| 39 | P M N |
| 40 | P M N |
| 41 | P M N |

TOTAL: 19 5 6
Number of P/M (Add: P + M) = 24
Total (Add: P + M + N) = 34
% P/M (Divide: P + M + M + N) = 71 %

Source: From Curriculum-Based Vocational Assessment: A Guide for Addressing Youth with Special Needs by R. A. Stodden, R. N. Ianacone, R. M. Boone, and S. W. Bisconer. Copyright © 1987 Centre Publications. Reprinted by permission.

433

For students with learning disabilities, it is important to know how their cognitive, perceptual, interpersonal, and motor skills affect them in their work environments (Hursh, 1989). The evaluator can observe how the student follows instructions, adjusts to demands, interacts with others, and uses supports or accommodations to compensate for the disability (Hursh, 1989).

In situational vocational assessment, supervisors observe students in both training and actual work activities using rating forms or applied behavior analysis techniques. McLoughlin and Lewis (1994) suggest that although situational assessment is broad and includes a variety of topics, observations and ratings should be as objective as possible. Rating forms are used to describe where a student falls on the continuum and what additional training a student may need. Applied behavioral analysis is used when continuous measurement of behaviors is needed (such as number of words per minute typed on the computer).

Situational assessment provides a unique opportunity to observe students in natural, real-life settings performing actual tasks. Because it provides a degree of realism not possible with other assessment techniques, it offers the opportunity for training at the time assessment occurs, and for more relevant instructional planning.

*Work samples.* Work samples, formal (commercial) or informal (developed locally), are vocational assessment techniques that simulate actual jobs (Berkell & Brown, 1989). They are "well-defined, and standardized simulations of a job, or part of a job, using the performance requirements and materials, tools, equipment, and supplies that are found in the actual job in the business or industry setting" (Hursh, 1989, p. 208).

A work sample evaluation could involve a student in a word processing or filing activity, food preparation, or medical lab work. Work samples provide meaningful assessment information because actual work behaviors, interpersonal skills, attitudes, vocational potential, and other skills can be observed. Work samples are useful for exploring new occupations to which the student may not have been previously introduced, for orienting the student to specific work demands, and for evaluating skills and aptitudes for working with specific materials and equipment (Hursh, 1989). Work sample evaluations can be adapted or tailored to the needs of students with mild disabilities. For example, you can modify directions by shortening or changing the sequence; allow the student to practice using the tools and materials before evaluating; or develop visual or auditory cues if needed.

Work samples are available through a variety of commercial sources, such as Comprehensive Occupational Assessment and Training System (COATS), Valpar Component Work Sample Series, McCarron-Dial Work Evaluation System, and Testing, Orientation, and Work Evaluation in Rehabilitation (TOWER), to name a few. For a thorough listing, we refer you to the work of Clark and Kolstoe (1990), who suggest that if you decide to purchase commercial samples, you should consult McCray's (1980) *Suggested Guidelines for Evaluating Work Samples*. If you develop your own work samples, Sitlington (1979) offers the following suggestions:

1. *Determine your work samples.* Survey your community to see which jobs are feasible for your students. Decide which of these jobs can be represented in a work sample format.

2. *Perform a job analysis.* Conduct an analysis that includes job tasks (following directions, measuring, estimating, basic math skills), work requirements (punctuality, working with others, working on weekends) physical demands (lifting heavy loads), and environmental conditions (working outdoors).

3. *Construct the work sample.* Design and sequence the job tasks, and then develop instructions, practice opportunities, and methods for evaluating quality, rate, and accuracy.

4. *Put together a work sample manual.* Include instructions for the student and the evaluator to follow.

5. *Establish norms.* Select norm groups that are similar to the population with whom your students will be competing for jobs. Standard scores and percentile scores can be used to set up norm tables.

6. *Include reliability and validity.* To determine consistency, use test/retest reliability. For validity, decide whether the job activities are realistically included in the work sample and if students who perform well on the sample also do well on the actual job the sample represents.

Work samples, whether formal or informal, should reflect the needs of the local job market and community, and be valid, reliable, and appropriate for adolescents with disabilities in terms of their academic, social, and vocational skills. Perhaps a combination of commercial and locally developed work samples may provide the best solution, considering economic factors, personnel, the characteristics of the population, and local job opportunities (Berkell & Brown, 1989).

---

### COMPREHENSION MONITORING OF KEY CONCEPTS

#### Vocational Education

1. Employment outcomes and follow-up studies indicate that many students with disabilities leave high school without adequate training and services, and thus many are unemployed or are employed only part-time.

*(continued on next page)*

*Definition*

2. Vocational education is "education designed to develop skills, abilities, understandings, attitudes, work habits and appreciations needed by workers to enter and make progress in employment on a useful and productive basis" (American Vocational Association, 1968, p. 12).

3. Vocational education prepares students in agriculture and agribusiness, home economics, technical occupations, health occupations, trades and industrial occupations, business and office occupations, and marketing and distributive occupations.

*Vocational Assessment*

4. Vocational assessment is the ongoing, systematic process of gathering information about an individual's aptitudes, skills, interests, and work-related behaviors, which allows professionals to make decisions about curriculum, materials, instructional strategies, and necessary modifications.

5. Formal vocational assessment includes aptitude and interest inventories, rating scales, basic and functional skills tests, and computerized assessment programs.

6. Informal vocational assessment includes curriculum-based vocational assessment (CBVA), criterion referenced tests (CRTs), community-based assessment, rating forms, situational assessment, and work samples.

## Vocational Preparation

The intent of vocational preparation is to provide adolescents with the skills and experiences they will need for employment. Offered through vocational education (in-school) and vocational training (out-of-school), these skills and experiences prepare students for unskilled, semiskilled, and skilled occupations, such as data processing, retail occupations, or electrical work, within a variety of settings (comprehensive high school or area vocational center). Additionally, vocational preparation involves a multitude of different services, from special vocational education services to interagency collaboration to vocational student organizations. Effective vocational preparation includes the contributions of many, varied service providers (occupational specialist, special education teacher, job coach, agencies, and so on). Vocational preparation also requires careful planning and is delivered through a variety of programs and models, with a rich selection of resources and materials.

### Vocational Education

Vocational education is typically provided as in-school instruction in seven program areas (Clark & Kolstoe, 1990, pp. 219–220):

*Vocational agriculture and agribusiness*

Horticulture

Farm mechanics

Fertilizers and insecticides

Animal husbandry

*Marketing and distributive occupations*

Wholesale occupations

Retail occupations

Warehousing

*Health occupations*

Nurse's aide

Practical nurse

*Vocational home economics*

Industrial sewing

Commercial food preparation

*Business and office occupations*

Word processing

Data processing

Computer operator

Bookkeeping

*Technical occupations*

Electronics

Printing

Graphics

*Trades and industrial occupations*

Building trades (carpentry, plumbing, electrical, etc.)

Heating and refrigeration

Tool and die

Manufacturing and processing

Instruction centers around employability skills, and often takes place in classes or labs that are designed to simulate actual work settings for each of the seven areas. The goal is for students to generalize the skills learned in class to the actual work environment.

***Settings.*** Vocational education at the secondary level may be offered in different settings: comprehensive high schools, area vocational centers, vocational high schools, and general high schools (Clark & Kolstoe, 1990; Hasazi & Cobb, 1988).

*Comprehensive high schools* are large high schools offering at least five vocational education program areas on the same campus on which college preparatory and general education programs are provided. The largest percentage of vocational education programs are provided in this type of setting.

*Area vocational centers* offer only vocational education programs and are located in regional centers that serve surrounding school districts. They may provide both secondary and postsecondary training programs. Students in eleventh and twelfth grades attend their home schools for half a day and are transported to the vocational center for the other half.

*Vocational high schools* are separate facilities that serve students in ninth through twelfth grades who are interested in a primarily vocational curriculum. Students can acquire all the academic credits they need for a high school diploma at this school through vocationally related academic coursework. These schools typically serve local school districts on a regional basis.

*General high schools* offer fewer than five vocational education program areas. Frequently, they provide industrial and practical arts, and, in rural areas, agriculture, and business and office occupations.

**Special vocational education.** Students with disabilities who receive vocational education in any of the previously mentioned settings are entitled to a variety of specialized services (Hasazi & Cobb, 1988). Additionally, school districts receiving federal funds for vocational education must provide students and their families with information about the vocational education programs available prior to ninth grade (Carl D. Perkins Act, PL 98-524). This gives students and their families time and information so that they can make informed choices about vocational education program options.

Special vocational education services may take the form of special education teachers assisting vocational instructors to adapt instruction and modify the curriculum, equipment, or tasks for students with mild disabilities. Because modifications are made, students can remain in regular vocational classes. Another approach is to have vocational resource teachers provide instruction around reading, math, and safety concepts specifically related to the vocational curriculum (Hasazi & Cobb, 1988). It is important that these resource teachers have the skills to adapt curricula and design strategies to accommodate students' needs. A third approach is to provide vocational education in separate classrooms using the same curriculum as in the vocational classroom, but at a less intense pace. Unfortunately, this approach increases the degree of isolation experienced by students and teachers (Nacson, 1982).

**Postsecondary vocational education.** Postsecondary vocational education programs include noncollegiate programs offered in community colleges, junior colleges, and vocational technical schools. They are usually two-year programs leading to an associate degree in various technical areas (Hasazi & Cobb, 1988). Additionally, many of these programs provide support services for students with disabilities while they are enrolled in the program.

### Vocational Training

Vocational training is achieved through out-of-school work experience programs that complement classroom learning in actual work settings (Clark & Kolstoe, 1990). Students are paid minimum wage or above, and are closely supervised as they implement classroom instruction in real work situations. Although many excellent vocational training programs and materials have been developed to simulate working environments, some experiences cannot be taught or even anticipated in the classroom. They must be taught and handled on the job. Thus, a vocational training component, such as an apprenticeship (out-of-school work experience), is essential to effective vocational preparation.

Apprenticeship programs offer students with mild disabilities on-the-job training. Many apprenticeships are in construction trades, while others are available in metalworking and graphic communications (Evans & Herr, 1978). What makes these programs attractive is the employer's commitment to providing training, time, and resources.

### Vocational Services

Services are available to ensure that vocational preparation is successful for adolescents with mild disabilities. They include employment and training agencies, interagency collaboration, vocational service providers, and student organizations.

***Employment and training agencies.*** Using funds from the Job Training Partnership Act (JTPA) of 1983, employment and training agencies provide placement and training for students with disabilities. Training may include assistance with job-seeking, on-the-job training, vocational training, bilingual training, and follow-up services (Tindall, 1985).

***Interagency collaboration.*** The development of interagency agreements among vocational education, special education, vocational rehabilitation, adult education, community colleges, employment and training agencies and private industry councils can help to ensure employment as an outcome for adolescents with mild disabilities. These agreements should specify the roles and responsibilities of all parties, the services each partner will provide, and provisions for monitoring and evaluating the agreement.

*Vocational service providers.* Effective vocational preparation involves the services of many providers. We include examples from Brown and Retish (1987) and Gajar, Goodman, and McAfee (1993), along with our own.

*Guidance counselors* at both the secondary and postsecondary levels provide career counseling (career awareness and career planning) to students and their families.

*Occupational specialists* assist students with decision-making and employability issues, and may serve as a liaison among the school, community, and job.

*Work experience teachers* work primarily at the high school level, and arrange work experiences so that students can try out the world of work.

*Work evaluators* provide assistance from middle school through postsecondary education in identifying students' strengths and specifying the training needed to improve students' limitations.

*Rehabilitation specialists* facilitate transition from school to work through career counseling, skill evaluation, placement, and referral for further services.

*Special education teachers* may coordinate the special and vocational services needed by adolescents with disabilities, which may involve direct service to students, consultation with vocational education teachers and other professionals, communication with families, and interaction with job sites and community agencies.

*Job coaches* are those individuals who help students obtain and retain a job by training, supervising, evaluating, supporting, and counseling them. Job coaching is an important element of supportive employment.

*State employment agencies* list jobs, evaluate the qualifications of applicants, and try to match applicants with available positions.

*Social services* are state-supported agencies that provide counseling and help clients establish linkages with other agencies and needed services.

The ability to access service providers and their services is an important skill for adolescents with mild disabilities to acquire so that they can utilize the support services that are available. Part of vocational preparation should include direct teaching, practice, and coaching in how to access these service providers.

*Student organizations.* Participation in secondary and postsecondary student organizations helps adolescents expand their experiences in vocational programs (Berkell & Brown, 1989). Organizations such as the Distributive Education Clubs of America (DECA), Future Farmers of America (FFA), Future Data Processors (FDP), Health Occupations Student Association (HOSA), and numerous others provide additional vocational experiences, serve as a support mechanism for members, and offer opportunities for the development and enhancement of leadership, social, and interpersonal skills.

## Instructional Planning, Models, Programs, and Resources

Effective instruction in vocational education includes thorough planning and a careful selection of models, programs, and resources. Please note the continual emphasis on collaboration, teaming, and communication.

### Vocational Planning

Vocational planning focuses on job placement, job training, and job supervision and follow-up. It may involve a special education teacher, work/study coordinator, vocational education teacher, prevocational or vocational coordinator, job placement specialist, vocational adjustment counselor, and/or job coach. Successful planning requires communication among these specialists and with parents, as well as collaboration with business and industry, employment and training agencies, and other community resources.

**Job placement.** Job placement strategies include job-seeking, job development, and job analysis.

*Job-seeking.* The "job club" strategy was developed by Azrin and Besalel (1980) as an alternative to traditional job-seeking activities. It involves group meetings in which individuals receive social support from their job-seeking peers (Elksnin & Elksnin, 1988). Participants are shown how to obtain leads through an informal job information network (friends, relatives, former employers, other job-seekers). Individuals are taught how to (1) consult existing ads, (2) design their own situation-wanted advertisements that promote their personal qualities (dependability, willingness to learn) instead of formal qualifications, (3) conduct themselves appropriately in an interview, (4) initiate telephone inquiries to employers, (5) keep records related to their job-seeking efforts, and (6) form and use carpools.

Research examining the effectiveness of job clubs for adults with disabilities has been positive (Elksnin & Elksnin, 1988; Jacobs, Kardashian, Kreinbring, Ponder, & Simpson, 1984). Sarkees and Scott (1985) recommend the job club technique for high school students with disabilities. Other job-seeking approaches include contacting high-probability employers, making presentations to organizations to which employers belong, using resources in the community, and encouraging students' attempts to find jobs (Clark & Kolstoe, 1990).

*Job development.* Job development involves developing a pool of job alternatives. To develop the pool, Clark and Kolstoe (1990) recommend using a community survey that can be mailed to potential employers, and supplemented with information from the job service center, the chamber of commerce, and other organizations.

*Job analysis.* A job analysis involves determining the specific requirements and demands of a job. Figure 11.4 shows a job analysis report (Bragman & Cole, 1984) that includes physical demands, environmental conditions, communication skills, intellectual skills, and work situations. Notice how this information could assist in matching an individual to a job.

**Job training.** For successful job training, Moon, Goodall, Barcus, and Brooke (1986) recommend job orientation and assessment, initial training and skill acquisition, and skill generalization and maintenance/fading. They recommend the following to job coaches:

*Job orientation and assessment*

■ Conduct a job analysis and then a task analysis of all job tasks.

■ Demonstrate and model job skills and work-related skills

■ Have the student perform job tasks and provide immediate reinforcement.

*Initial training and skill acquisition*

■ Use behavioral analysis training by identifying reinforcers and then eventually fading them.

■ Record the student's performance of targeted skills.

■ First stress accuracy and then build fluency.

■ Identify problem areas and provide training.

*Skill generalization and maintenance/fading*

■ Determine a schedule for fading out.

■ Make sure that job skills have been established and maintained for some time.

■ Gradually withdraw or fade out.

■ Train co-workers and supervisors to provide support.

**FIGURE 11.4  Job Analysis Report**

1. Job title _____

2. Description of duties _____

   _____

3. Tools needed _____

4. What kind of job is it?
   ____ Clerical
   ____ Sales
   ____ Agriculture
   ____ Service
   ____ Self-employment
   ____ Factory

5. Job level
   ____ Skilled
   ____ Semiskilled
   ____ Unskilled

6. Experience
   ____ Required
   ____ None required

7. Employment
   ____ Full time
   ____ Part time
   ____ Seasonal

8. How many people employed?
   ____ Male
   ____ Female

9. What tests are given?
   ____ Employment service tests
   ____ Company made test
   ____ Other
   ____ None

10. What kinds of licenses are required?
    ____ Driver's license
    ____ Health certificate
    ____ Other

11. Must the employee fill out a written report? ____ Yes ____ No

12. Must the employee belong to a union?
    ____ Yes    ____ No

13. How are employees found?
    ____ Employment service
    ____ Help wanted ads
    ____ Labor unions
    ____ People come in
    ____ Referral by friends
    ____ Other

14. Do you have plenty of workers available?
    ____ Shortage
    ____ Steady supply
    ____ More than enough

15. How are employees paid?
    ____ Hourly
    ____ Weekly
    ____ Monthly
    ____ Piecework

16. Does the employee
    ____ Work alone
    ____ Work with others

17. What are the working conditions?
    ____ Inside
    ____ Wet
    ____ Noisy
    ____ Dirty
    ____ Day work
    ____ High places
    ____ Outside
    ____ Dry
    ____ Quiet
    ____ Clean
    ____ Night work
    ____ Low places
    ____ Neither

(continued on next page)

**F I G U R E  1 1 . 4**  *(continued)*

18. Does this job require
    ____ Standing
    ____ Sitting and standing
    ____ Both
    ____ Lifting
    ____ Carrying
    ____ Moving about
    ____ Driving

19. How much education is required?
    ____ No formal education
    ____ Little formal education
    ____ Elementary school completion
    ____ Some high school
    ____ High school diploma

20. How much on the job training is given?
    ____ None
    ____ Less than 6 weeks
    ____ 6 weeks to 6 months
    ____ Apprenticeship

21. How much adjustment to change is required?
    ____ None      ____ Some
    ____ Little     ____ Frequent

22. Is there much pressure on the job?
    ____ None      ____ Some
    ____ Little     ____ Great

23. How much supervision is the employee given?
    ____ None      ____ Some
    ____ Little     ____ Much

24. Does the employee handle money?
    ____ Yes       ____ No

25. How much memory is required?
    ____ None
    ____ Little
    ____ Memory for oral directions
    ____ Much

26. Does the employee meet the public?
    ____ No
    ____ Seen by the public
    ____ Talks to public
    ____ Works with public all the time

27. How much reading is required on the job?
    ____ None
    ____ Little
    ____ Addresses
    ____ Sales orders
    ____ Patterns
    ____ Directions
    ____ Bulletins
    ____ Letters

28. How much arithmetic is required?
    ____ None          ____ Dividing
    ____ Little         ____ Measurements
    ____ Counting       ____ Sales slips
    ____ Adding         ____ Invoices
    ____ Subtracting    ____ Other
    ____ Multiplying

29. How much writing is required?
    ____ None
    ____ Listing
    ____ Sales orders
    ____ Production records
    ____ Information to be read by others

30. What kind of speaking is required?
    ____ Little
    ____ Giving messages
    ____ Asking for materials or tools
    ____ Giving directions

31. How much strength is required?
    Hands: ____ None   ____ Little
           ____ Some   ____ Great
    Arms:  ____ None   ____ Little
           ____ Some   ____ Great
    Legs:  ____ None   ____ Little
           ____ Some   ____ Great
    Back:  ____ None   ____ Little
           ____ Some   ____ Great

32. Other pertinent information:

*Source:* From *Career Development and Transition Education for Adolescents with Disabilities* by G. M. Clark and O. P. Kolstoe. Copyright © 1990 by Allyn & Bacon. Reprinted by permission.

***Job supervision and follow-up.*** Job supervision generally requires monitoring and assessing the progress of students. Clark and Kolstoe (1990) suggest:

1. Scheduled and unscheduled visits to follow up on the worker's performance.
2. Scheduled visits to address problems (chronic tardiness for work).
3. Unscheduled visits to deal with crises (a physical confrontation between the worker and a co-worker).
4. Scheduled or unscheduled visits after the student no longer requires training and is employed.

### Vocational Training Models

Vocational training can be provided in a variety of ways. Gajar et al. (1993) describe the most common models.

***Work adjustment training.*** Work adjustment training involves teaching students work behaviors that are common to most jobs, such as punctuality and accepting constructive feedback or criticism. Instruction usually occurs in a classroom or a simulated work setting, but the work is not paid, actual employment. Generalization of skills is difficult because of the differences between the training environment and the actual employment environment. Targeted prevocational and extravocational skills are more apt to be generalized if actual work situations are involved, such as part-time jobs.

***Work experience.*** Work experience, which is usually not paid, gives students some experience in a job so that they can judge the suitability of that vocational area for them. Part of career exploration, work experience is effective when it is integrated with the rest of the vocational program and when specific training goals have been identified.

***Work/study.*** Used at both secondary and postsecondary levels, work/study divides the student's day into a combination of classes and paid work in the community. In other words, work/study programs provide vocational education (in-school instruction) and vocational training through paid work (out-of-school experience). The work/study model is most effective when the student is engaged in an actual job that is closely related to the area of vocational training.

***Generalized skills training.*** During the middle school and early high school years, it is helpful to provide training in specific skills that can be applied to a number of occupations. For example, students may be taught office skills, such as word processing, accounting, management skills, and operation of office equipment. These skills are not tied to a specific job, but are appropriate for a variety of occupations. This type of training is helpful as career/vocational awareness and exploration activities.

***Specific skills training.*** Offered at the secondary and postsecondary levels in vocational education classrooms, specific skills training provides training in skills that are needed for specific types of jobs, such as food preparation, plumbing, office management, or electrical work. This type of training is designed for employment in a particular job category, but with a variety of different employers. Specific skills training is most effective when students participate in related work experience and apply the skills on the job.

***Employment site instruction.*** The purpose of employment site instruction is to provide vocational training on the job. The employment site instruction model, which includes support from special and vocational educators, can be used to help individuals with mild disabilities learn a new job, or to help workers update and improve their existing skills. This use of supported employment facilitates the acquisition and generalization of work-related social skills and job skills.

### Vocational Programs

Numerous vocational programs are available in the literature. Readers are directed to consult the myriad articles and textbooks written on this topic, since it is not within the scope of this chapter to report on all of them. We do, however, highlight three research-based programs to give you an idea of some of the types of programs available and what is included in each.

*Supported Employment* (Rusch, 1990)

| | |
|---|---|
| Population: | Adults with disabilities |
| Goal: | Competitive employment |
| Components: | Enclaves (small groups of workers placed in a work situation) with support provided by a specialist |
| | Individual training provided by a job coach |
| | Mobile work crews with disabilities and their trainers who work at various job sites and are integrated with workers who do not have disabilities |

*Career Ladder Program* (Siegel, 1988)

| | |
|---|---|
| Population: | High school seniors with mild disabilities |
| Goal: | Assisting students to obtain and retain specific jobs |

Components:   Work/study programs with students placed and supervised in paid work situations

Employment skills workshops that offer instruction in work-related skills

Ongoing career development support

Assistance from a transition specialist who works closely with employers at work sites

*Community-Based Employment* (Stodden & Browder, 1986)

Population:   Adults with learning and mental disabilities

Goal:   Competitive employment

Components:   Direct observation of skills to identify strengths and skills needed

Preemployment training of work adjustment skills

Work experience through volunteer work supported by job coaches

On-site competitive work training through placement of workers in jobs with job coaches

Supported employment with job coaching provided for one year

Notice the emphasis in all three programs on supported employment through job coaching, collaboration with employers, and assistance from other specialists. These vocational programs also include training in specific job skills and in work-related skills (such as getting along with coworkers and accepting criticism). Finally, note that program goals typically target competitive employment and independence.

### Vocational Resources and Materials

Numerous vocational training materials are available in the area of occupational guidance. We provide several examples, and suggest that you consult your university, local school district's instructional materials center, or regional service agency for others.

***Dictionary of Occupational Titles (DOT).*** The DOT is an index of occupations and jobs available through the U.S. Department of Labor (1977). It lists the performance requirements and working conditions for specific jobs in approximately 20,000 occupations. Each title specifies job purpose, description, requirements, procedures, and worker functions. The DOT is helpful for job placement.

***Dictionary of Worker Traits (DWT).*** The DWT includes information about the characteristics that workers should have for various occupations, including aptitude, interests, temperament, physical demands, environmental conditions, general education development, and vocational preparation needed (Kerns & Neeley, 1987). Worker traits are provided for all the occupations listed in the DOT. The DWT is used in job placement, vocational assessment, and in IEP planning.

***Encyclopedia of Careers and Vocational Guidance.*** This three-volume set identifies occupations by code number based on the DOT (Hopke, 1984). It provides information on career planning, finding a job, career opportunities, and specific occupational information (Greenan, 1989). With more than 900 occupations listed and described, it is helpful for vocational assessment and planning.

***Guide for Occupational Exploration (GOE).*** The GOE organizes the occupations listed in the DOT into the following interest areas: artistic, plants and animals, protective, mechanical, industrial, business detail, selling, accommodating, humanitarian, leading/influencing, physical, and performing (Greenan, 1989). It also includes information about the requirements of specific occupations so that individuals can compare their interests and skills with job requirements. The GOE is used in career/vocational exploration and placement.

***Vocational-Technical Education Consortium of States (V-TECS) Curriculum.*** Approximately 140 V-TECS catalogs provide job descriptions and technical requirements for more than 350 job titles listed in the DOT. The catalogs describe worker tasks, standards of performance, and duties. The V-TECS curriculum is helpful in career/vocational curriculum planning.

***Employability enhancement materials.*** Developed at the Arkansas Research and Training Center in Vocational Rehabilitation at the University of Arkansas-Fayetteville, these materials include the following:

- Employability Maturity Interview (EMI) is a structured interview to measure readiness for vocational planning.

- Work Performance Assessment (WPA) is a work simulation that measures a student's response to supervisors' requests.

- Job-Seeking Skills Assessment focuses on a student's ability to complete job applications and interviews. Skills are taught with Job Application Training (JAT) and Getting Employment Through Interview Training (GET-IT).

***Computer programs for vocational training.*** The following two programs are particularly useful:

- Practical Assessment Exploration System (PAES) involves placing students in simulated work situations in the classroom, where they complete activities in business, consumer/home economics, and industrial technology (Brolin, 1995). Contents include curriculum materials, units, software, and computer scoring forms. This program can be used in career/vocational exploration and vocational training.

- A Day in the Life, a sophisticated software program developed at Pennsylvania State University (1993), teaches literacy skills, critical for employability, using job-related problem-solving activities (Brolin, 1995). The five job areas of food services, health, maintenance, retail, and clerical are integrated with life skills, basic skills, and critical thinking. This program is helpful for vocational curriculum planning and training.

---

**COMPREHENSION MONITORING OF KEY CONCEPTS**

### Vocational Preparation

1. Vocational preparation is provided through vocational education (in-school experiences such as classes or labs) and vocational training (out-of-school experiences such as paid work).

2. Vocational education is typically provided as in-school instruction in seven areas: (a) vocational agriculture and agribusiness, (b) marketing and distributive occupations, (c) health occupations, (d) vocational home economics, (e) business and office occupations, (f) technical occupations, and (g) trades and industrial occupations.

3. Vocational education at the secondary level may be offered in different school settings: comprehensive high schools, area vocational centers, vocational high schools, and general high schools.

4. Special vocational services may involve the special education teacher assisting the vocational education teacher in adapting instruction and modifying curriculum; instruction by the vocational resource teacher in content areas related to the vocational curriculum; or instruction in vocational education in separate classrooms using the same vocational curriculum, but at a slower pace.

*(continued on next page)*

5. Vocational training is accomplished through out-of-school work experience, such as apprenticeship programs, that complement classroom learning.

6. Vocational services for adolescents with disabilities may be provided through employment and training agencies, interagency collaboration, vocational service providers, and student organizations.

7. Vocational service providers include guidance counselors, occupational specialists, work experience teachers, work evaluators, rehabilitation specialists, special education teachers, job coaches, state employment agencies, and social services.

### Instructional Planning, Models, Programs, and Resources

8. Vocational planning focuses on job placement, job training, and job supervision and follow-up.

9. Vocational training models are many and varied; they include (a) work adjustment training, (b) work experience, (c) work study, (d) generalized skills training, (e) specific skills training, and (f) employment site instruction.

10. Examples of specific vocational programs are Supported Employment (Rusch, 1990), the Career Ladder Program (Siegel, 1988); and Community-Based Employment (Stodden & Browder, 1986).

11. Vocational resources and materials include the Dictionary of Occupational Titles (DOT), the Vocational-Technical Education Consortium of States (V-TECS) curriculum, employability enhancement materials, and computer programs for vocational training.

## Work-Related Social Skills

Essential to a chapter discussing career and vocational needs is a discussion of work-related social skills. As one reads the vocational research literature (Hill, Wehman, Hill, & Goodall, 1986; Neubert, Tilson, & Ianacone, 1989; Salzberg, Lignugaris-Kraft, & McCuller, 1988; Wilgosh & Mueller, 1993), the importance of social skills in securing and maintaining a job in the world of work is apparent.

Gajar and associates (1993) posit that teaching appropriate work-related social skills is especially difficult because of the subtle discriminations and incidental learning involved. They relate that it is much easier to teach such task-production skills as cooking fries following a 12-step procedure than it is to teach employees to discriminate between a kidding comment and a caustic insult. Often, individuals with disabilities cannot interpret the social norms of a workplace and then analyze whether their behaviors match these norms. For example, the simple awareness of providing treats for an individual's birthday as part of the social process may go unnoticed by the worker with disabilities. In the rest of this chapter, we discuss the rationale, specific skills, instructional strategies, and curriculum packages for teaching work-related social skills.

## Rationale for Teaching Work-Related Social Skills

The vocational literature, surveys of adolescents and employees with disabilities, employer surveys and interviews, and the job demands of the 21st century demonstrate the importance of work-related social skills for successful employment. In a summary of their research studies, Wilgosh and Mueller (1993) reported that skills related to production and social awareness facilitated the hiring of workers, including those with disabilities. In a review of 13 studies over a 35-year period from 1951 to 1986, Salzberg et al. (1988) found that social factors such as not following instructions and responding inappropriately to criticism, bizarre and aggressive behavior, and inadequate or offensive verbal repertories contributed to the job loss of workers with mental disabilities. Hill et al. (1986) found that people with mental disabilities most frequently were dismissed from jobs because of attitude problems and negative social reactions. Neubert et al. (1989) found that more than two-thirds of all problems of workers with mild disabilities were related to work adjustment skills, including social skills deficits.

Employer and employee surveys also support a need for social skills training for successful transition to the world of work. Approximately 82% of successfully employed individuals with disabilities identified their training in social skills in high school as valuable for maintaining a successful job experience (Hudson, Schwartz, Sealander, Campbell, & Hensel, 1988). In a survey of items related to successful employment, more than 130 secondary school students with mental disabilities or learning disabilities rated the item "works well with others" among the top three (Burnham & Housley, 1992). Both successfully employed individuals and employers regard interpersonal skills such as communication of ideas as important to current job success (Campbell, Hensel, Hudson, Schwartz, & Sealander,

1987). Twenty-five employers of employees with mental disabilities included the social skills of "communicating effectively" and "getting along with the public" among those crucial skills expected by employers (Burton & Bero, 1984).

Jobs in the future will demand even more social skills as the focus turns to an increased use of teams in the workplace. With the higher productivity and product quality of the team approach, employers view qualified employees as those who are able to make decisions and display good interpersonal skills, rather than those with occupation-specific skills (American Society for Training and Development, 1989; Carnevale, Gainer, & Meltzer, 1988). These interpersonal skills include the ability to judge appropriate behavior, cope with undesirable behavior in others, deal with ambiguity, listen, share responsibility, and interact easily with others (Carnevale et al., 1988).

## Identification of Work-Related Social Skills

Attempting to find a consensus on the identification of work-related social skills is no easy matter. In a discussion of social skills in general, Schloss, Schloss, Wood, and Kiehl (1986) found that the prevalent definitions either relied on a broad basis of social competence or on discrete, situation-specific responses. McFall (1982) conceptualized a two-tiered model of social competence and social skills: "[Social competence] involves a value-based judgment by an observer concerning the effectiveness of an individual's performance in a specific task . . . [while] social skills are the specific component processes that enable an individual to behave in a manner that will be judged as competent" (p. 23). In other words, social competence is the overall effectiveness of social behavior, while skills are the strategies and tactics individuals use to negotiate daily social tasks such as making requests. A person who is socially competent perceives and interprets social situations and knows how to change his or her behavior when a situation changes (Cartledge, Stupay, & Kaczala, 1986; Chadsey-Rusch, 1986).

Additionally, Chadsey-Rusch (1986), in a review of work-related social skills research, found that researchers classified social skills in various categories. For example, Cartledge (1989) identified three categories of needed social skills: task-related behaviors, social communication skills, and decision-making skills. Task-related behaviors referred to an individual's overall work maturity and included following directions, staying on task, attending, volunteering, and completing tasks. Social communication skills formed the basis for interpersonal relationships and involved greeting others, conversing, listening to others, smiling, and complimenting others. Decision-making skills included accurately perceiving personal or social situations and then behaving appropriately.

With these various ways of viewing social skills in mind, we identify the following work-related social skills as necessary for job success: (1) understanding and following directions and instructions (Foss, Auty, & Irvin, 1989; Montague, 1987a; Mueller, Wilgosh, & Dennis, 1989; Test, Farebrother, & Spooner, 1988; Whang, Fawcett, & Mathews, 1984); (2) asking questions and requesting assistance (Foss et al., 1989; Montague, 1987a; Test et al., 1988); (3) accepting criticism from supervisors and co-workers (Cheney & Foss, 1984; Foss et al., 1989; Montague, 1987a; Mueller et al., 1989; Scott, Ebbert, & Price, 1986; Whang et al., 1984); and (4) getting along and conversing with co-workers and supervisors (Burton & Bero, 1984; Cheney & Foss, 1984; Mueller et al., 1989).

Social behaviors may differ from setting to setting. For example, Salzberg et al. (1988) found that the social behaviors required of food service workers differed from those required of janitors and maids. White and Thurston (1992) suggest surveying supervisors in local employment settings to identify the social behaviors they expect of their employees. Taking the previously identified job-related social behaviors, you may wish to devise a survey to distribute to local employers of your secondary students. Such a survey leads to social validation of the job-related skills necessary for your students to be successful in the workplace. Next, you may want to compare the information from the surveys to the school curriculum and adapt the social curriculum to better match the skills required. Table 11.2 portrays how job-related social skills taught during high school are generalized into the work environment.

---

**COMPREHENSION MONITORING OF KEY CONCEPTS**

### Work-Related Social Skills

*Rationale for Teaching Work-Related Social Skills*

1. Research studies and surveys of employers and employees show that work-related social skills are important to successful employment.

2. Many experts feel that jobs in the future will require more social skills as industries promote an increase in the use of production teams in the workplace.

*Identification of Work-Related Social Skills*

3. There is no consensus on specific work-related social skills, as some definitions rely on social competence and others on social skills.

*(continued on next page)*

**TABLE 11.2**   Generalization of School/Work-Related Social Skills

| School | Work |
| --- | --- |
| Going to class every day | Going to work every day |
| Arriving at school on time | Arriving at work on time |
| Bringing pencils, paper, and books to class | Bringing required materials and/or clothing to work |
| Turning in work on time | Completing work tasks in a timely manner |
| Talking to teachers without using "back talk" | Talking to supervisors with respect |
| Getting along with fellow students | Getting along with co-workers |
| Asking for help with school tasks | Asking for help with work tasks |
| Giving and receiving praise and criticism from teachers and fellow students | Giving and receiving praise and criticism from supervisors and co-workers |
| Engaging in appropriate conversation with teachers and fellow students | Engaging in appropriate conversation with supervisors and co-workers |
| Prioritizing school tasks | Prioritizing work tasks |
| Managing daily, weekly, monthly, and yearly schedules at school | Managing daily, weekly, monthly, and yearly schedules at work |
| Reading and following directions | Reading and following directions |

*Source:* From *Vocational Assessment: The Evolving Role* by C. A. Veir, in *Handbook of Vocational Special Needs Education* (2nd ed., p. 245) by G. D. Meers. Copyright © 1987 Aspen Publishers, Inc. Reprinted by permission.

4. Social competence is the overall demonstration of social behaviors as judged by others.

5. Social skills are strategies individuals use to negotiate daily social tasks.

6. The following social skills tend to be supported in research studies: a) understanding and following directions and instructions, (b) asking questions and requesting assistance, (c) accepting criticism from supervisors and co-workers, and (d) getting along and conversing with co-workers and supervisors.

## Instructional Strategies

Results of research studies suggest that it is possible to teach work-related social skills to students with mild disabilities (Clement-Heist, Siegel, & Gaylord-Ross, 1992; Foss et al., 1989; Montague, 1988; Park & Gaylord-Ross, 1989; Roessler & Johnson, 1987; Shapiro, 1989a; Warrenfeltz et al.,

1983; Whang et al., 1984). There are essentially two approaches for teaching social skills: the behavioral or cognitive/behavior skill approach, with its structured format, and the problem-solving approach, with its less structured format (Walker, Schwarz, Nippold, Irvin, & Noell, 1994). The cognitive/behavior skill approach aligns more with the reductionist paradigm of learning, with emphasis on teacher direction and lock-step procedures found in the teacher effectiveness research literature. The problem-solving approach aligns more with the social constructivist model, with more student direction and less structured procedures. However, these approaches are not mutually exclusive. For example, modeling and feedback can be used in either. Both approaches produce social changes (Dorwick, 1986), although the problem-solving procedure appears to teach students to generalize or transfer social skills more to work situations (Clement-Heist et al., 1992; Foss et al., 1989; Park & Gaylord-Ross, 1989).

### *The Cognitive/Behavior Skill Approach*

Combining techniques from both Direct Instruction (Engelmann & Carnine, 1982b) and the learning strategies model (Alley & Deshler, 1979; Schumaker, Nolan, & Deshler, 1985), procedures in the cognitive/behavior skill approach include instruction and sharing of rationales, modeling, role playing or behavioral rehearsal, coaching with prompts and feedback, and reinforcing. A final step involves generalizing the skill to the work site. Instruction proceeds in the following manner:

1. *Share the definition, the steps, and the rationale for the work-related social skill.* For example, if you are teaching the work-related social skill of requesting assistance, you may begin by stating "Requesting assistance means that you ask for information that you need in order to complete a task." The steps might be as follows: (1) Move closer to the supervisor and wait until the supervisor is unoccupied. (2) Make eye contact with the supervisor and state in a polite manner that you are having a problem ("Hi, I'm sorry, but I forgot what I was supposed to do after I . . ."). (3) Ask the supervisor a specific question in a polite manner ("What was the last thing I was supposed to do?"). (4) Listen (pay close attention to what is said). (5) Repeat the supervisor's answer ("So the last thing I need to do is . . ."). (6) Thank the supervisor ("Thank you for your help"). Next, you tell students the rationale or ask why the skill is important in the work site—(for example, "It is important to request assistance if you are stuck on a task, because you might do it wrong.") Continue by asking students to discuss how they will use the skill of requesting assistance on the work site.

2. *Model the social skill.* You should model the skill in an appropriate manner and in an inappropriate manner, and ask students to discriminate

between the two performances. When teaching work-related social skills to adolescents with learning disabilities, Clement-Heist et al. (1992) prepared a rating form and had the students rate the two performances. Students then discussed their ratings and their reasons for the ratings. Foss et al. (1989) found that students with mental disabilities performed better with videotape presentations of the problematic situation than with teacher presentations. The models were older students who assumed the role of the workers in entry-level positions similar to those held by the high school students in their work placement program.

3. *Provide opportunities for role playing and behavioral rehearsal of the skill.* Now, you bring in role-playing simulations for students to participate in. You may also wish to have students create their own role-playing situations. Clement-Heist et al. (1992) had students develop sample situations from the students' actual on-the-job experiences and describe their feelings after the role-play activity. Lund, Montague, and Reinholtz (1987) use job support groups for role-playing or simulation training exercises, with students observing and learning from watching one another.

4. *Prompt and give feedback.* During the role playing, the teacher gives feedback on the correct aspects of the response. Again, students may give feedback to their peers and even decide when a student has accurately demonstrated the skill. Lund et al. (1987) provide cues and prompts until students discover the socially appropriate responses.

5. *Provide contingent reinforcement.* Reinforcement may just be in the form of positive comments. Shapiro (1989b) taught secondary students with learning disabilities to self-reinforce as part of a self-management plan devised to solve work problems.

6. *Provide opportunities for students to transfer the skill.* Cartledge (1989) suggests training job coaches to help students generalize the skill to their work site. Montague and Lund (1991) teach students to self-monitor using job reports (see Figure 11.5). You may wish to assign homework that involves practicing the skill and then writing or telling about the practice. Before assigning homework, you should discuss how, when, and where the student will use the skill on the work site (Clement-Heist et al., 1992).

### The Problem-Solving Approach

The problem-solving approach to teaching work-related social skills tends to follow adaptations of McFall's (1982) process model of decoding, decision, performance, and evaluation. Students decode the meaning of a social situation, describe possible solutions, select one, try it, and then evaluate.

**FIGURE 11.5** Student Job Report

No. <u>24</u>

**Student Job Report**

Name <u>Sam Solo</u>          Job Site <u>Pilot Bottling</u>
Date <u>4/22</u>          Job Title <u>Warehouse helper</u>
          Supervisor <u>Mr. Johnson</u>

This report is an evaluation of your work behavior for the week of <u>4/18</u>.
Circle the rating for:

|  | Poor | Fair | Good | Excellent |
|---|---|---|---|---|
| 1. Your attitude at work | 1 | 2 | ③ | 4 |
| 2. Your completion of duties | 1 | 2 | ③ | 4 |
| 3. Your interaction with co-workers | 1 | 2 | ③ | 4 |
| 4. Your interaction with your supervisor | 1 | 2 | ③ | 4 |
| 5. Your work behaviors (on time, breaks, dress, etc.) | 1 | 2 | ③ | 4 |

Check the social skills you used at work this past week.

| | |
|---|---|
| ____ Ordering job responsibilities | ____ Taking messages |
| ✓ Understanding instructions | ✓ Engaging in coversation |
| ____ Making introductions | ____ Giving directions |
| ____ Asking questions | ____ Responding to compliments |
| ✓ Asking permission | ____ Giving compliments |
| ____ Asking of help | ____ Convincing others |
| ____ Accepting help | ____ Apologizing |
| ✓ Offering help | ____ Accepting criticism |
| ____ Requesting information | ____ Responding to a complaint |

Describe one of the times when you *successfully* used one of the social skills that you learned.
I talked to Bob at break.

Describe a time (if there was one) when you were *unsuccessful* using one of the social skills.
I offered to help the guys unload the truck.

Why do you think you were unsuccessful? They didn't need me.

Describe any problems that came up at work. Bill doesn't like me.

Describe one thing you did at work that you're proud of. Asked to leave early and

my boss said okay.

*Source:* Adapted from "Monitoring Students on the Job" by K. A. Lund, M. Montague, and M. Reinholtz, 1987, *Teaching Exceptional Children, 19*(3) pp. 58–60. Reprinted by permission.

The model relies on the student's understanding and acting upon the rules of a social situation (Trower, 1984). Roessler and Johnson (1987) provided their students with learning disabilities the mnemonic of SOAR to help them remember problem-solving steps used to improve their job-related social skills. The *S* in SOAR stands for interpret the *Situation*; *O*, enumerate the *Options*; *A*, consider outcomes *Anticipated*; and *R*, *Respond*. We adapt steps for problem-solving strategies from the recommendations of Elias and Clabby (1988) and Park and Gaylord-Ross (1989). You will probably notice similarities between these steps and those found in the discussion of problem solving for academic tasks in Chapter 9.

1. *Identify what is happening.* In this first step, the teacher or student presents or describes a situation. The teacher then facilitates the student's examination of the situation to help determine an appropriate behavior. For example, the teacher leads Jim to determine that his customer is very upset about the exchange policy of the store where he works.

2. *Identify feelings.* Often omitted from problem-solving programs, this step can act as a signal for students to begin problem solving, rather than attempting to resolve the conflict with flight-or-fight reactions (Elias & Clabby, 1988). For example, the teacher helps Jim to verbalize: "When a customer becomes upset, I feel nervous and get sick to my stomach and know it is time for me to think about what I can do."

3. *Decide on a goal.* Elias and Clabby (1988) describe the goal as the guide for effective behavior and problem resolution. Now, Jim may say "I need to calm the customer and explain our policy without becoming upset."

4. *Identify alternative responses.* Students can brainstorm possible solutions. For example, Jim supplied the following alternatives: (a) listen to the customer calmly and provide support by nodding until the customer calms down, (b) ignore the customer, (c) suggest that the customer may wish to see the manager, or (d) explain the return policy to the customer with an apology.

5. *Test alternatives.* Students now brainstorm about the consequences of the possible solutions by asking questions. For example, Jim asks what will happen if he tells the customer to go to the manager. Will the manager be angry with Jim for not taking care of the problem on his own? Each alternative is analyzed in the same manner.

6. *Decide on one alternative.* After examining all the consequences, the student decides on the most appropriate solution; the teacher may have to prompt here, or even select one for the student. For example, Jim decides to combine the two alternatives of apologizing while informing the customer of the policy and asking if the customer would like to see the manager.

7. *Emit the behavior and rethink it.* Students try the behavior first in the role-play setting and ask questions about its effectiveness. For example, Jim tries the behavior during the role play and asks if it worked.

8. *Evaluate feelings.* Students now evaluate how they felt and how others reacted to the behavior. For example, Jim tells how he felt and how the angry customer and the supervisor reacted to his behavior during the role-play situation.

9. *Transfer to the work setting.* Enlisting the aid of co-workers to help students transfer their new skills to the work environment is effective (Clement-Heist et al., 1992; Park & Gaylord-Ross, 1989). For example, the teacher decides to ask one of Jim's co-workers, who is also a student in the class, to remind Jim of the alternative behavior he selected.

## Curriculum Packages

If you do not wish to create your own materials, there are curriculum packages available that teach job-related social skills to adolescents. Carter and Sugai (1989) have developed a list of six programming questions that may help in your selection of a job-related social skills program:

1. Are assessment procedures/instruments included?

2. Is the curriculum adaptable to individual needs?

3. Can the curriculum be used with small groups?

4. Can personnel implement the curriculum without specialized training beyond that described in the curriculum?

5. Is the cost of implementation reasonable and manageable?

6. Are strategies included that will promote maintenance and generalization of skills? (p. 38)

To this list we add

7. Does the program have a cognitive/behavior skill or a problem-solving approach?

We discuss four curriculum packages, identifying the content, the materials, and the instructional strategies used.

### Life Centered Career Education: A Competency-Based Approach

In this section, we specifically examine the personal/social skills curriculum area of the Life Centered Career Education Curriculum (Brolin, 1993); the approach in its entirety is discussed earlier in the chapter. The idea behind the personal/social skills area is that "an individual's potential for successful, independent living cannot be judged merely on the basis of academic performance or competency assessments" (Brolin, 1995, p. 315).

*Content.* The program covers seven personal-skills competencies and their 28 subcompetencies. The seven competencies are (1) achieving self-awareness, (2) acquiring self-confidence, (3) achieving socially responsible behavior–community, (4) maintaining good interpersonal skills, (5) achieving independence, (6) making adequate decisions, and (7) communicating with others. A few of the subcompetencies under maintaining good interpersonal skills are (a) demonstrate listening and responding skills, (b) establish and maintain close relationships, and (c) make and maintain friendships.

*Materials.* Materials include a curriculum guide, assessment batteries, lesson plans, and staff training materials. The curriculum guide provides teachers with a framework for infusing the competencies into academic subjects. The two current assessment batteries are: the LCCE Knowledge Battery (Brolin, 1992a) and the LCCE Performance Battery (Brolin, 1992b). The LCCE Knowledge Battery serves as a screening instrument to assess the career-education knowledge of seventh- through twelfth-grade students, including personal/social skills, while the LCCE Performance Battery assesses the students' application of each subcompetency area, including those found in the personal/social skills competencies. The LCCE Self-Determination Scale (Brolin, in press) measures students' perceptions and beliefs relating to self-awareness, self-confidence, independence, and making adequate decisions—all personal/social skills competencies. The program provides consumers with worksheets, score sheets, procedures, and specific guidelines for administering the assessment batteries.

Additionally, the LCCE curriculum provides 370 lesson plans in the personal/social area. Most lesson plans include objectives, activities with procedures outlined, evaluation procedures and criteria, and identification of the career role and stage. The staff training materials allow school districts to train their own personnel and include handouts, transparencies, ten videotapes, activity sheets, resource materials, and assignments.

*Instructional strategies.* The teacher directs the lesson, leading the class in discussions, modeling role-play situations, and involving the students in role-play situations. Some cooperative group instruction is used, as students work in groups to complete activities or worksheets. Brolin (1995) also advances the idea that learning styles are important. He recommends that teachers analyze whether the mode of presentation involves auditory, visual, tactile, kinesthetic, and multisensory modalities and consideration of logical and analogical styles (also referred to as left- or right-brain functions).

### Job-Related Social Skills Training for Adolescents with Special Needs

According to the authors, Montague and Lund (1991), this program is designed for a semester course in vocational special education. The program is appropriate for 15- to 22-year-old low achievers and individuals with mild to moderate learning disabilities, emotional disabilities, and mental disabilities.

*Content.* The skills taught in the curriculum are ordered from simple to complex as identified through a literature review and conferences with employment experts. The 18 job-related skills are:

1. Ordering job responsibilities. Related behaviors in this area include "showing up for work on time, organizing one's duties, taking breaks at appropriate times, and knowing the rules and regulations for the job" (Montague, 1988, p. 28).
2. Understanding directions.
3. Giving instructions.
4. Asking questions.
5. Asking permission.
6. Asking for help.
7. Accepting help.
8. Offering help.
9. Requesting information.
10. Taking messages.
11. Engaging in a conversation.
12. Giving directions.
13. Receiving compliments.
14. Giving compliments.
15. Convincing others.
16. Apologizing.
17. Accepting criticism.
18. Responding to a complaint.

Students are also instructed in strategies of self-instruction, self-questioning, self-monitoring, and self-reinforcement. These strategies assist students in managing and evaluating their own behaviors.

*Materials.* Materials include 20 scripted lessons, master class charts, student cue cards, simulation activities, videotape activities, an instructional guide, and evaluation instruments. Each scripted lesson contains a goal, behavioral objectives, materials, and instructional and evaluation procedures. Three master class charts accompany each lesson. One chart lists the behaviors associated with the job-related social skill, a second chart lists the skill steps, and a third chart presents a nonsense word that stands for the various skill steps. Student cue cards contain the skill steps and the nonsense word (acronym) for students to memorize. Simulation activities, which consist of role-play activities or simulations of job situations, are described in detail. The lesson scripts suggest ways to incorporate videotape activities into the instructional plan. The Instructional Guide details directions for organizing and teaching, along with suggestions and recommendations for skill maintenance and generalization.

Two evaluation instruments, Job-Related Social Skills Assessment and Job-Related Social Skills Surveys, accompany the program. The Job-Related Social Skills Assessment is a criterion-referenced series of checklists designed to measure level of skill attainment for the 18 job-related social skills. The Job-Related Social Skills Surveys include student, parent, and teacher surveys. Each survey contains 36 questions and measures perceptions of skill performance levels and transfer of these skills to the school, home, and community environments.

*Instructional strategies.* The instructional strategies are found in the teacher effectiveness literature. The program includes task analysis of targeted skills, highly structured and organized lessons, small-group instruction, immediate feedback, reinforcement, and mastery learning (Montague & Lund, 1991). Students are actively involved as they participate in verbal rehearsal, visualization of the acronym and skill steps, role playing, and simulation activities. Teachers lead the discussion following a script, model the job-related social skills, and give positive and corrective feedback.

### Social Skills for Daily Living

Social Skills for Daily Living (Schumaker, Hazel, & Pederson, 1988) includes most of the skills that have been identified in the literature as necessary for vocational success. The program was designed for low-achieving adolescents and students with learning disabilities, mental disabilities, and emotional disabilities (VanNooten, 1991).

*Content.* The body basics, conversation and friendship skills, getting along with others, and problem-solving skills are broken down as follows:

*Body basics*

1. Facing the other person, maintaining eye contact, and using an appropriate voice tone, facial expression, and body posture

*Conversation and friendship skills*

2. Active listening—listening carefully and asking questions to check understanding

3. Greeting—saying hello and asking a question

4. Saying goodbye—ending the conversation in a friendly way

5. Answering questions—responding appropriately when asked a question

6. Asking questions when needed

7. Introducing oneself—saying one's name and shaking hands when meeting others

8. Interrupting—breaking into or joining a conversation appropriately

9. Carrying on a conversation with all nuances

10. Making friends—instigating a series of relationship-building encounters

*Getting along with others*

11. Accepting thanks—listening to thanks and showing appreciation

12. Thanking others with sincerity

13. Accepting compliments—listening to compliments and showing sincerity

14. Giving compliments at appropriate times

15. Apologizing—facing up to mistakes and offering amends

16. Accepting "no" from authority figures without argument

17. Resisting peer pressure—saying no and suggesting alternative appropriate activities

18. Responding to teasing appropriately without fighting

19. Accepting criticism—listening to and trying to understand criticism without anger

20. Giving criticism—explaining to others in a calm way why their behavior is upsetting

*Problem-solving skills*

21. Following instructions—listening to and carrying out instructions without argument

22. Getting help from appropriate people when needed

23. Asking for feedback—asking an appropriate person to analyze and suggest improvements in quality of work

24. Giving rationales—giving good reasons and the benefits for doing something

25. Solving problems—analyzing a problem, developing possible solutions, choosing the best solution, and developing an implementation plan

26. Persuasion—using good rationales to convince others to agree with something or to do what one wants

27. Negotiation—engaging in a series of interactions to reach an agreement and resolve a conflict

28. Joining group activities—appropriately asking group members to join an ongoing group activity

29. Starting activities with others by making the necessary arrangements

30. Giving help—assisting others, without taking over the task, and teaching others new skills.

*Materials.* The program contains skill books, workbooks, comic books, practice cards, rating scales, placement checklists, applications materials, management forms, and teaching manuals. All student materials are written at a fourth-grade reading level. Each skill is presented using an awareness, practice, and application teaching model. Teachers use skills books, workbooks, and comic books for student awareness of the skill, practice cards with role-play scenes for student practice, and surprise missions and bonus missions for student application. The program is individualized so that students may study as many skills as they need. Placement checklists and rating scales completed by the teacher and the student determine the skills each student needs. Management forms such as the "Class Plan" and the "Progress Chart" assist in tracking students' progress. The kit contains four teacher manuals for the four areas. Excerpts from the student's skill book, examples of when to use the skill, discussion topics, special difficulties, mastery role-play situations, generalization activities, and answer keys are provided for each of the 30 skills.

*Instructional strategies.* Once the program is introduced, the major role of the teacher is to supervise use of the materials and monitor students' progress. Suggestions for teaching are based on the Strategies Intervention Model developed at the University of Kansas Center for Research on Learning. Chapter 9 contains a detailed description of the intervention strategies, which we will not repeat here. Four major components are descriptive procedures, modeling, practice, and feedback (VanNooten, 1991). Descriptive procedures explain what the skill is, why it is important (rationale), where it can be used, and what the specific steps are. In modeling, the teacher presents the skill while students observe and evaluate. During practice, students may verbally rehearse the steps, model the skill, and generalize the skill with homework activities. In feedback, the teacher or other students evaluate the student performance during role-play situations.

### WORKING II: Interpersonal Skills Assessment and Training for Employment

The goal of the Working II program (Foss & Vilhauer, 1986) is to develop social competence for vocational success in adolescents and adults with mild and moderate disabilities. The program is built on a problem-solving model researched at the University of Oregon's Rehabilitation Research and Training Center in Mental Retardation.

*Content.* Job-related social skills are divided into the two categories of interactions with supervisors and interactions with workers:

*Interactions with supervisors*

1. Following instructions
2. Requesting assistance
3. Handling criticism and correction
4. Difficulty in understanding instructions
5. Disagreement with instructions
6. Handling serious work problems
7. Trouble getting help
8. Doing the job wrong
9. Breaking work rules

*Interactions with workers*

10. Cooperative work behavior
11. Distractions from co-workers
12. Disagreement over work tasks
13. Conflicts with co-workers
14. Handling teasing
15. Verbal teasing and provocation
16. Physical teasing and provocation
17. Resolving personal concerns
18. Making requests

*Materials.* The program contains 24 video lessons and an assessment scale. The videotapes present vignettes of job-related social skill situations to begin the problem-solving process. The Test of Interpersonal Competence for Employment (TICE) measures an individual's knowledge of critically important social skills required in work settings. The standardized test was developed for adolescents and adults with mild retardation (Foss et al., 1989).

*Instructional strategies.* The teacher models, then guides the students through problem solving and behavior rehearsal, and, last, requires students to demonstrate the skills in an actual job situation. The sequence is as follows:

Step 1: Review of Previous Lesson and Homework

Step 2: Problem Area Description

Step 3: Problem Presentation

Step 4: Understanding the Problem

Step 5: Problem Solving Discussion

Step 6: Problem Resolution

Step 7: Behavior Rehearsal

Step 8: Summary

Step 9: Homework Assignment (Patton, in press)

All four of these programs are summarized in Table 11. 3 which compares and contrasts the content, materials, and instructional strategies of each.

---

**COMPREHENSION MONITORING OF KEY CONCEPTS**

**Work-Related Social Skills**

*Instructional Strategies*

1. Most job-related social skills programs fall into either the cognitive/behavior skill model or the problem-solving model.

2. The cognitive/behavior skill approach has a structured format and is aligned more to the reductionist paradigm of learning, with emphasis on teacher direction and lock-step procedures found in the teacher effectiveness literature.

3. The problem-solving approach aligns itself more with the social constructivist literature, with more student direction and less structured procedures.

4. Some procedures, such as coaching, feedback, and modeling, are used in both models.

5. Both approaches produce social changes, although the problem-solving procedure appears to teach students to generalize or transfer social skills more to work situations.

6. The steps of the cognitive/behavior skill approach are (a) share the definition, the steps, and rationale for the job-related social skill; (b) model the social skill; (c) provide role-playing and behavioral rehearsal of the skill; (d) prompt and give feedback; (e) provide contingent reinforcement; and (f) provide opportunities for skill transfer.

7. The steps of the problem-solving approach are (a) identify what is happening; (b) identify feelings; (c) decide on a goal; (d) identify alternative responses; (e) test alternatives; (f) decide on one alternative; (g) emit the behavior and rethink it; (h) evaluate feelings; and (i) transfer to the work setting.

*Curriculum Packages*

8. Carter and Sugai (1989, p. 38) developed the following list of six programming questions that may help in your selection of a job-related social skills program: (a) Are assessment procedures/instruments included? (b) Is the curriculum adaptable to individual needs? (c) Can the curriculum be used with small groups? (d) Can personnel implement the curriculum without specialized training beyond that described in the curriculum? (e) Is the cost of implementation reasonable and manageable? (f) Are strategies included that will promote maintenance and generalization of skills?

**TABLE 11.3**     **A Comparison of Curriculum Packages**

|  | *Life Centered Career Education: Personal/ Social Skills Area (Brolin, 1993)* | *Job-Related Social Skills Training for Adolescents with Special Needs (Montague & Lund, 1991)* | *Social Skills for Daily Living (Schumaker, Hazel, & Pederson, 1988)* | *Working II: Interpersonal Skills Assessment and Training for Employment (Foss & Vilhauer, 1986).* |
|---|---|---|---|---|
| *Source* | The Council for Exceptional Children, P.O. Box 79026, Dept. K 5012, Baltimore, MD 21279-0026 | Exceptional Innovations, Inc., P.O. Box 6085, Ann Arbor, MI 48106 (tel. 419-536-8560) | AGS Publishers Bldg., P.O. Box 99, Circle Pines, MN 55014-1796 | James Stanfield & Co., P.O. Box 1983, Santa Monica, CA 90406 |
| *Content* |  |  |  |  |
| Number of job-related social skills | 7 competencies and 28 subcompetencies | 18 sequenced simple to complex with related behaviors; self-management skills of self-instruction, self-questioning, self-monitoring, and self-reinforcement | 30 skills in the categories of body basics, conversation and friendship skills, getting along with others, and problem solving skills | 18 skills in two categories of interactions with supervisors and interactions with workers |
| *Materials* |  |  |  |  |
| Assessment devices | Batteries to assess knowledge, application, and students' perceptions | Checklists to measure skill attainment and surveys for students, parents, and teachers to complete concerning performance levels | Rating scales for initial placements, completed by students and teachers; checklists to monitor mastery and student progress | Standardized test that measures knowledge of critically important job-related social skills |
| Lesson plans | 370 with objectives, activities, procedures, evaluation, and identification of career role and stage | 20 scripted lessons with goals, behavioral objectives, materials, procedures, and evaluations | Examples of when to use the skill, discussion topics, special difficulties, mastery role-play situations, generalization activities, and answer keys | 24 video lessons, problem-solving steps |
| Teacher guides | Yes | Yes | Yes | Yes |
| Videotapes | Yes | No | No | Yes |
| Charts and cue cards | No | Yes | Yes | No |

**TABLE 11.3** *(continued)*

| | *Life Centered Career Education: Personal/ Social Skills Area (Brolin, 1993)* | *Job-Related Social Skills Training for Adolescents with Special Needs (Montague & Lund, 1991)* | *Social Skills for Daily Living (Schumaker, Hazel, & Pederson, 1988)* | *Working II: Interpersonal Skills Assessment and Training for Employment (Foss & Vilhauer, 1986).* |
|---|---|---|---|---|
| *Instructional strategies* | | | | |
| Role play/simulations | Yes | Yes | Yes | Yes |
| Modeling | Yes | Yes | Yes | Yes |
| Behavioral rehearsal | Yes | Yes | Yes | Yes |
| Problem solving | No | No | No | Yes |
| Coaching | Yes | Yes | Yes | Yes |
| Feedback | Yes | Yes | Yes | Yes |
| Active student involvement | Yes | Yes | Yes | Yes |
| Learning styles considered | Yes | No | No | No |
| Small-group instruction | Yes | Yes | Yes, but may also be used independently | Yes |
| Generalization techniques | Yes | Yes | Yes | Yes |
| Scripted lessons | No | Yes | No | No |

 Now that you have read Chapter 11, reflect on your earlier predictions and compete this post organizer.

1. In your own words, explain what career education is and in what grades it should be taught. What would you include, and how would you infuse it into content classes?

2. If you were assessing an adolescent's vocational skills, what would you look for and how would you assess them? Compare your responses to what you listed before you read the chapter.

3. Identify five work-related social skills that you feel are needed for an adolescent to be successful in work and life. Share your thoughts with someone else who has read the chapter, and justify your responses.

# The Transition Planning Process

© Elizabeth Crews

**CHAPTER HIGHLIGHTS**

*Overview of Research, Legislation, and Current Perspectives*
*Transition Planning Domains and Strategies*
*Team Development of the Individualized Transition Plan (ITP)*
*Family Involvement*

---

 Before you read Chapter 12, use your prior knowledge to complete this advance organizer.

1. Working with three or four of your peers, list the challenges you experienced as an adolescent when you were close to graduating from high school.

2. Working with the same group, describe how teachers, family, and friends could have helped you better prepare for this important life transition.

3. Using what you already know about writing Individualized Transition Plans, write a plan for yourself when you were approaching graduation from high school.

4. Finally, write an Individualized Transition Plan for an adolescent with special needs as he/she nears graduation from high school.

---

One of the most critical turning points in the lives of adolescents is the transition from public school to the world of postsecondary education, employment, and life in the general community as an adult. Developing independence, examining one's talents and interests, deciding upon a career path, and pursuing either employment or additional schooling are just some of the challenges that youth in transition face. Unfortunately, the literature suggests that students with mild disabilities are faced with serious challenges as this period of transition approaches (Kranstover, Thurlow, & Bruininks, 1989; Wagner, 1993). They are unemployed at a higher rate than their nondisabled peers, they tend to drop out of school before graduation, they are involved with the criminal justice system to a higher degree, and they tend to be living in a dependent situation for a longer period of time (Edgar, 1988; Wagner, 1993).

The purpose of this chapter is to provide you with information and strategies for helping adolescents with mild disabilities systematically plan for their successful transition from school to the adult community. First, we present an overview of the background and current perspectives regarding transition planning, along with a definition of the transition planning process. Next, you will learn how to implement practical strategies for helping adolescents and their families plan for the future as college students, employees, homemakers, and other adult roles. Then, we discuss the role and function of the transition team, including practical suggestions for conducting transition planning meetings and completing an Individualized Transition Plan. Finally we discuss the role of the family in the transition process.

## Overview of Research, Legislation, and Current Perspectives

Every year thousands of students with mild disabilities exit high school and face the demands of independent living settings, postsecondary education programs, and ultimately, employment. In Chapter 2, we highlighted the legislation enacted over the years that has impacted secondary and employment programs for adolescents with mild disabilities. Please take time to review this information.

Public Law 101-476 (the 1990 amendments to the Individuals with Disabilities Education Act, or IDEA) mandated that the transition needs of students in high school special education programs be addressed in the IEP planning process to help them plan for life after high school (Sec. 20 U.S.C. 1401e,l,D). Postschool-outcome studies show that students with mild disabilities exiting high school become unemployed, unengaged (not working or not in school), and living in dependence to a greater degree than their nondisabled peers (Edgar, 1987, 1988; ERIC, 1987; Frank et al., 1991;

Gerber & Brown, 1991; Haring & Lovett, 1990; Haring et al., 1990; Heal, Copher, DeStefano, & Rusch, 1989; Kranstover et al., 1989; Roessler et al., 1990; Rusch & Phelps, 1987; Schalock, 1986; Siegel & Gaylord-Ross, 1991; Zetlin & Hossenini, 1989). Employment follow-up studies of students with mental retardation or learning disabilities (Roessler et al., 1990) indicate that individuals with disabilities have low rates of employment within the first year after exiting school.

Edgar (1987, 1988) examined the postschool outcomes of 1067 special education students from 1983 to 1986 and found that of those students who were working, 70% earned less than minimum wage, less than 50% were living independently, and more than 50% were unengaged—not working or not in school. More recent studies have validated these findings, revealing a trend of unsuccessful postschool outcomes (Wagner, 1993; Wehman, 1993).

The wealth of data generated by the transition literature suggests that students with mild disabilities need self-advocacy training, intensive employability skills training, systematic referral to adult agencies, family involvement, and immediate and ongoing job support in order to obtain and maintain employment over time (Clark, 1994; Edgar, 1988; Meers, 1992; Wagner, 1993; Wehman, 1993). Professionals and students alike perceive a significant need for instruction during high school in job placement, job maintenance skills, self-advocacy, job-related social skills, transportation skills, and other transition services (Karge, Patton, & De la Garza, 1992). Under Public Law 101-476, these needs must now be addressed in an Individualized Transition Plan (ITP), which is part of the Individualized Education Program for adolescents with disabilities.

The term *transition* refers to a more comprehensive set of services than career education (defined and discussed in Chapter 11). Transition services were first conceptualized in 1983 in Public Law 98-199, more commonly referred to as the Transition Initiative. This piece of legislation set forth the school-to-work model and provided funding for training personnel in supported employment practices. In 1990, Public Law 101-476 provided a specific definition of transition services and mandated that all IEPs for students with disabilities contain transition objectives by the student's 16th birthday. By statute, transition planning and services are now defined as follows:

> Transition services are a coordinated set of activities for a student, designed within an outcome-oriented process, which promotes movement from school to post-school activities, including post-secondary education, vocational training, integrated employment (including supported employment), continuing and adult education, adult services, independent living, or community participation. The coordinated

set of activities shall be based upon the individual student's needs, taking into account the student's preferences and interests, and shall include instruction, community experiences, the development of employment and other post-school adult living objectives, and, when appropriate, acquisition of daily living skills and functional vocational evaluation. (34 CFR 300.18)

The IEP for each student, beginning no later than age 16 (and at a younger age, if determined appropriate), must include a statement of the needed transition services. [34 CFR 300.346 (b)]

This contemporary definition sets the framework for the information that now must be included in the IEP. Note that transition services are *coordinated, outcome-oriented,* include *postsecondary services,* and are based upon *individual needs, preferences, and interests.* Objectives and activities for each student include instruction in school and in community-based settings that strategically address adult outcomes.

---

**COMPREHENSION MONITORING OF KEY CONCEPTS**

*Overview of Research, Legislation, and Current Perspectives*

1. When compared to their nondisabled peers, students with disabilities are more likely to drop out of school, to be unengaged (not working, not in school), and to be unemployed.

2. Federal legislation mandates that transition services be included in the students' Individualized Transition Plan (ITP) by their 16th birthday as part of the IEP.

3. The wealth of data generated by the transition literature suggests that students with mild disabilities need self-advocacy training, intensive employability skills training, systematic referral to adult agencies, family involvement, and immediate and ongoing job support in order to obtain and maintain employment over time.

4. The definition of *transition* includes such concepts as outcome-oriented, coordinated set of activities, movement from school to postschool activities, student-centered, and comprehensive services.

5. Transition planning includes not only school personnel and family, but also community representatives and active involvement on the part of the student.

## Transition Planning Domains and Strategies

The literature and demonstration programs over the past two decades have consistently revealed specific variables and domains critical to planning for the transition from school to the adult community. In this section, we describe 11 transition domains that should be included in the transition planning process for adolescents with mild disabilities. In addition, we offer some practical strategies for ensuring that these domains are addressed.

### Domain 1: Job Search Skills

A critical element in transition programs for high school students with mild disabilities is a job search curriculum (Cobb & Hasazi, 1987; Gerber & Brown, 1991; Polloway, Patton, Epstein, & Smith, 1989). Research has shown most former special education students rely on the self/family/ friend network to find jobs (Frank et al., 1991; Hasazi, Gordon, Roe, Hall, Finck, & Salembier, 1985). Adolescents with mild disabilities need instruction in skills such as conducting a personal job search, filling out job applications correctly, and preparing a résumé (Patton, 1991). Alternatives to traditional high school programs such as school-based vocational development and placement are also needed (Hasazi, Gordon & Roe, 1985; Roessler et al., 1990).

Critical job search skills must be incorporated into existing programs of academic study. We know that workers with disabilities are hired at a higher rate when they know how to apply for and interview for a job appropriately. It is also important that students know how to obtain necessary documentation for becoming a worker. We cannot assume that students know how to do this. These critical skills must be systematically taught during the high school years.

Many high school programs offer job search skills training courses as electives. As a teacher of adolescents with special needs, it is important that you build a job search curriculum into your students' programs. Because of the several job search curriculum packages available, you will not have to develop your own. Two exemplary packages are Life Centered Career Education (LCCE): Occupational Guidance and Preparation Domain (Brolin, 1995), described thoroughly in Chapter 11, and Employability Skills for Students with Mild Disabilities (Patton, De la Garza, & Harmon, in press). Both packages contain objectives, activities, worksheets, and scripted lessons for teaching job search skills.

The LCCE Occupational Domain includes lesson formats for teaching competencies and subcompetencies in (1) knowing and exploring occupational possibilities, (2) selecting and planning occupational choices, (3) exhibiting appropriate work habits and behavior, (4) seeking, securing, and maintaining employment, (5) exhibiting sufficient physical/manual skills, and (6) obtaining specific occupational skills.

The Employability Skills Curriculum contains 13 units of three to seven lessons each for teaching job search skills. An outline of this curriculum appears in Table 12.1. Figure 12.1 presents an example of a job preparation worksheet from Unit 1, Preparing to Look for a Job. The worksheet lists the documents necessary for employment.

## Domain 2: Job Maintenance Skills

Job success depends more on effective job maintenance skills such as communication skills, interpersonal skills, and good work habits, than upon actual job competence (Chamberlain, 1988; Montague, 1988). Employers consider worker behaviors and attitudes to be important or essential to job performance (Campbell, Hensel, Hudson, Schwartz, & Sealander, 1987; Hazler & Latto, 1987). When employers were asked to rank factors judged critical to job success for workers with disabilities, the five highest ranking factors were getting along well with others, interest in the job, efficiency, dependability, and being able to adapt to new work situations (Chamberlain, 1988).

Students with mild disabilities are jeopardized by their "hidden" disability, which manifests in the workplace as inappropriate socialization, lack of initiative, poor attitude, defiance, and other behaviors that cause loss of jobs early on. Transition programs should emphasize work-related social skills instruction and ongoing, systematic support once students are placed on the job. Students with mild disabilities need systematic instruction in order to learn and practice the critical skills of keeping a job. They also need on-the-job support to assure that appropriate job maintenance skills have been generalized in the workplace over time. Work-related social skills were discussed extensively in Chapter 11.

## Domain 3: Job-Related Functional Academics

Reading and writing on the job, figuring computations, estimating, making change, and managing time skills are functional academic skills that can be taught in the classroom to help students succeed on the job. Functional academics are also critical for independent living skills required in the home and community. However, many students with mild disabilities are not being exposed to functional curricula that prepare them for employment and transition to the adult community (California Education Transition Center, 1990). Parents of these students report a 45% utilization of vocational preparation programs, a 27% utilization of community living skills curricula, a 17% utilization of in-school work sites, a 10% utilization of

**TABLE 12.1** **Employability Skills Course Instructional Units**

*Unit 1* *Preparing to Look for a Job*
Lesson 1: Orientation to the Course
Lesson 2: Obtaining Documentation
Lesson 3: Key Parts of a Résumé
Lesson 4: References
Lesson 5: Preparing a Résumé
Lesson 6: Learning about Job Applications
Lesson 7: Completing a Job Application

*Unit 2* *What Kind of Work Would I Like?*
Lesson 1: Why Should I Work?
Lesson 2: Finding Out about Different Kinds of Work
Lesson 3: What Am I Interested In?
Lesson 4: What Conditions Would I Like to Work In?

*Unit 3* *Finding Out about Job Openings*
Lesson 1: Job Leads
Lesson 2: Organizing Job Lead Information
Lesson 3: Locating and Using Classified Want Ads
Lesson 4: Reading Classified Want Ads
Lesson 5: Using the Yellow Pages as a Resource
Lesson 6: Using the White Pages as a Resource

*Unit 4* *Contacting Employers*
Lesson 1: Making a Good First Impression
Lesson 2: Practicing Telephone Skills
Lesson 3: Telephoning Employers
Lesson 4: Visiting an Employer

*Unit 5* *How Do I Interview for a Job?*
Lesson 1: Preparing for a Job Interview
Lesson 2: Dressing for a Job Interview
Lesson 3: Preparing for Interview Questions
Lesson 4: Practicing Job Interviews
Lesson 5: Following Up a Job Interview

*Unit 6* *Handling Paperwork*
Lesson 1: Understanding Key Parts of Your Paycheck Stub
Lesson 2: Understanding Deductions from Your Pay
Lesson 3: Reading a Work Schedule
Lesson 4: Reading and Completing a Timecard
Lesson 5: Becoming Familiar with Tax Return Forms

*Unit 7* *What Makes a Good Employee?*
Lesson 1: Positive Worker Traits
Lesson 2: Starting a Job
Lesson 3: Dressing and Grooming Appropriately on the Job
Lesson 4: Taking Initiative on the Job

*Unit 8* *Getting Along with Others*
Lesson 1: Understanding the Role of a Supervisor
Lesson 2: Accepting Criticism from a Supervisor
Lesson 3: What Makes a Good Co-worker?
Lesson 4: Social Skill, "Greeting Your Co-Workers"
Lesson 5: Dealing with Customers

*Unit 9* *What If I Can't Make It to Work?*
Lesson 1: The Four Rules of Good Attendance
Lesson 2: Who to Notify and When
Lesson 3: Notifying Your Supervisor When You Must Be Absent
Lesson 4: Being on Time

*Unit 10* *How Will I Get to Work?*
Lesson 1: Telephoning for Bus Route Information
Lesson 2: Reading Maps and Schedules (Location Routes)
Lesson 3: Reading Maps and Schedules (Time Schedules)
Lesson 4: Selecting a Bus or Trolley Route
Lesson 5: Planning to Transfer
Lesson 6: Safe and Appropriate Behavior on Public Transit
Lesson 7: Problem-Solving Transportation Problems

*Unit 11* *Managing Your Personal Finances*
Lesson 1: Banking Services
Lesson 2: Choosing a Bank
Lesson 3: Opening a Savings Account
Lesson 4: Making a Deposit
Lesson 5: Withdrawing Money from Your Savings Account
Lesson 6: Reading Your Bank Statement
Lesson 7: Using Your Automated Teller Machine (ATM)

*Unit 12* *Making Positive Job Changes*
Lesson 1: Positive Ways to Handle Stress at Work
Lesson 2: Ending a Job in a Positive Way
Lesson 3: Giving Written Notice of Your Resignation

*Unit 13* *What Are My Goals for the Future?*
Lesson 1: Thinking about Your Future
Lesson 2: Guidelines for Setting Goals and Making a Plan
Lesson 3: The Individualized Transition Planning Meeting
Lesson 4: How to Be an Effective Self-Advocate

*Source:* "Employability Skills + Family Involvement + Adult Agency Support + On-the-Job Support = Employment Success" by P. Patton, D. De la Garza, and C. Harmon, in press, *Teaching Exceptional Children.* The Employability Skills Curriculum is available for the cost of duplicating from the ERIC Clearinghouse (1-703-264-9474).

**FIGURE 12.1** **Documentation Checklist**

You will need the following documents in order to become employed. You may already have some of these documents. If so, bring them in to show your teacher. Your teacher and family support specialist will help you obtain the other documents. When you have shown the document to your teacher, place a checkmark in the appropriate column and write the date in the appropriate column.

|  | Shown to Teacher | Date |
|---|---|---|
| BIRTH CERTIFICATE |  |  |
| SOCIAL SECURITY CARD |  |  |
| STATE-ISSUED IDENTIFICATION CARD |  |  |
| WORK PERMIT (if you are under age 18) |  |  |
| BUS IDENTIFICATION CARD |  |  |
| RÉSUMÉ |  |  |
| INTERVIEW CHECKLIST |  |  |

*Source:* "Employability Skills + Family Involvement + Adult Agency Support + On-the-Job Support = Employment Success" by P. Patton, D. De la Garza, and C. Harmon, in press, *Teaching Exceptional Children.* The Employability Skills Curriculum is available for the cost of duplicating from the ERIC Clearinghouse (1-703-264-9474).

community work sites, a 6% utilization of community-based instruction, but a 93% utilization of traditional academics (Halpern & Benz, 1987). Students with mild disabilities are unable to generalize traditional academics to the real world of employment and adult living (Polloway, Patton, Epstein, & Smith, 1989). You learned some strategies for teaching functional academics to adolescents with mild disabilities in Chapters 7 and 8. Table 12.2 contains a listing of functional curricula published by Science Research Associates. The sequence includes strategies for teaching writing, math, and reading skills applicable to independent living and employment. This is just one of several functional academic curricula available to assist your students in mastering functional academic skills.

**TABLE 12.2  Functional Academic Curricula**

*Writing for Independence*

How to Write Letters and Messages

How to Manage Your Personal Affairs

How to Complete Job Applications and Résumés

*Math for Independence*

How to Use Bank Accounts

How to Understand and Manage Your Time

How to Manage Your Money

How to Use Measurements

*Reading for Independence*

How to Follow Directions

How to Use Maps and Directions

How to Use Schedules

How to Use the Telephone Book

How to Use the Classified Ads

How to Use the Newspaper

*Source: Math for Independence, Reading for Independence,* and *Writing for Independence,* three sets of curricula by K. Jungjohann and B. R. Schenck, 1985, Chicago: Science Research Associates. All curriculum packages can be ordered from Science Research Associates, Inc.; 155 N. Wacker Dr.; Chicago, IL 60606.

## Domain 4: Mobility and Transportation Skills

Using public transit is a complex set of skills that is challenging to any inexperienced user. This is especially true if the individual has learning difficulties. Yet for many adolescents today, obtaining and keeping a job is virtually impossible without using public transit. The need for mobility skills has long been recognized by educators of individuals with severe disabilities (Laus, 1977), but overlooked by educators of students with mild disabilities.

Students cannot be successful on the job if they cannot first get to and from their jobs. A majority of students with disabilities depend on public transit for transportation. Most urban transit systems are extremely complex. Students with mild disabilities may have difficulty understanding bus routes, trolley routes, transfer points, and directionality. In addition, they may be naive about safety practices and appropriate social interactions when using public transit.

They need to learn, practice, and generalize the skills of knowing how to (1) apply for bus and subway passes, (2) call for and/or read and interpret bus route information, (3) use public transit safely, including emergency strategies, (4) use actual routes from home and school to places of work, whether driving or taking public transportation, and (5) travel independently from home to school to a work site, making at least one transfer.

Strategies for teaching transportation skills are the same as those for teaching any other skill. First, you model, or demonstrate, the skill. Next, you practice the skill with your students until they have reached mastery. Then, you ask them to demonstrate knowledge of the skill on their own. And finally, you build in generalization procedures to assure use and practice of the skill in the natural environment. For example, when teaching students how to use the bus, you may do the following:

1. Take a bus trip with your students, demonstrating all of the steps involved (waiting appropriately at the bus stop, presenting your coin or token, sitting on the bus appropriately, exiting the bus at the desired destination).

2. Take a bus trip with your students, requiring them to practice the above steps with you until they have mastered all the steps.

3. Require students to take a bus trip on their own, demonstrating mastering of bus-riding skills. Many teachers follow behind the bus in their own car during the first few independent bus rides by students.

4. Communicate to persons in the natural environment—bus driver, parents, persons at the beginning and end of the bus trip—to enhance generalization.

Many transportation skills can be taught very effectively using a teacher-directed instruction format. Box 12.1 presents an example of a scripted lesson on how to call for bus route information.

### Domain 5: Planning and Accessing Recreation Activities

Although the literature is rich with studies reporting the importance of recreation activities for youth with severe disabilities (Kennedy, Austin, & Smith, 1987), relatively little research has been done to examine appropriate recreation activities for students with mild disabilities. It is known that students with mild disabilities drop out of school at a high rate, have sporadic in-school attendance, and experience a high incidence of involvement with the criminal justice system (Nelson, Rutherford, Center, & Walker, 1991). Such behaviors and lifestyles suggest that these students are not involved in healthy recreational lifestyles, and preclude successful employment and adult living.

**BOX 12.1**

## Scripted Lesson: Asking for Bus Route Information

*Gain the ATTENTION of the learners*

T    We are going to begin, now.
(followed by silence until all students are attending)

*REVIEW relevant past learning*

T    Yesterday, Ms. Sweet talked to us about the importance of being able to use public transportation such as the city bus and the trolley. Why is it important to know how to ride the bus?

S    To get to work and home again.
To get to ball games, the zoo, or anywhere you might want to go.
So you don't have to count on someone else for a ride.
(Any other appropriate answer)

T    Good. It seems that you all know why it is important to know how to use public transportation.

*Communicate the GOAL of today's lesson*

T    Today we are going to learn how to call the Transit Authority (the people in charge of the buses) to find out how to get from one place to another. It is important to know how to call for specific bus routes because there are many bus routes. Calling for the route before you go to the bus stop can save you a lot of time, and possibly save you some money. Also, when you know bus routes and how to take the bus, you don't have to depend on someone else to go places. Why is it important to call for bus routes?

S    Save time.
Save money.
Don't have to depend on someone else for rides.

*Describe the STRATEGY*

T    Good. Now I am going to tell you what to do when calling for bus routes. There are six very important steps. *First,* you need to have a pen and paper ready so that you can write down the bus route information as it is told to you. What is the first step?

S    Have pen and paper ready.

T    *Second,* you need to call the San Diego Transit Authority. They are the people in charge of all the buses and trolleys in San Diego. They know everything there is to know about riding the buses and trolleys. The telephone number is *233-3004.* What is the telephone number for the Transit Authority?

S    233-3004.

*(continued on next page)*

**BOX 12.1**
*(continued)*

| | |
|---|---|
| T | Write down the telephone number now. |
| S | (Writes down 233-3004) |
| T | *The next step* is to tell them *three* things: (1) where you are; (2) where you want to go; and (3) what time of day you want to go. It is *very* important to be ready to tell them these three things when you call. If you tell them these three things quickly, they can tell you exactly what bus to take. What are the *three* things you need to tell the Transit Authority? |
| S | Where I am, where I want to go, and what time I want to go. |
| T | *Next,* you need to listen carefully to the directions that they will give you and write them down with the pen and paper you have ready. What is the next thing to do? |
| S | Listen carefully to the directions and write them down. |
| T | *Then,* read the directions back to the person you are talking to, to make sure that you understood correctly. What is the next thing to do? |
| S | Read the directions back. |
| T | The *last* thing to do is to thank them for giving you the bus route information. What is the last thing to do? |
| S | Thank them. |
| T | Very good. Now, I am going to show you how to call for bus routes. But first, let's review the six steps. (Teacher reviews the above six steps.) |

*MODEL the skill (I do it)*

T     OK, listen and watch as I follow the six steps to call for bus routes. The teacher:

1. Has pen and paper ready.
2. Dials 233-3004. (The Transit Authority answers, "How may I help you?")
3. Says, "I want to go from San Diego State University to the San Diego Zoo. I want to leave SDSU at 12:00 noon. Could you please tell me which bus to take?"
4. Listens carefully and writes down information. ("From SDSU, you take bus #115 which takes you downtown. This bus leaves from SDSU every 20 minutes, so you can get it at noon or at 12:20. Get off this bus at 10th and C Street. Go east to 11th and B Street and get on the #7 or #7b bus. This bus also runs every 20 minutes. Bus #7 or 7B will take you right to the zoo.")
5. Reads back directions that have been written down. ("From SDSU . . . Did I get that right?" "You got it, have a nice trip and enjoy the zoo!")
6. Thanks the informer. ("Thank you very much." Hangs up phone.)

BOX 12.1
(continued)

T    As you can see, calling for bus schedules can sometimes be confusing and complicated. So, it is important that you do each step correctly and in the right order. It is also important to listen carefully and write down everything they tell you. If you do that, you will be able to get information on how to get anywhere in San Diego. Now, let's do it together.

### Provide PROMPTED PRACTICE (We do it)

T    Let's pretend that you are at Horton Plaza and you want to go to Sea World. You want to go at 10:00 A.M. What materials should we have ready before we call? Get them out now.

S    Pen and paper ready.

T    What number do we call? Pretend to dial the number.

S    (Students dial 233-3004.) ("Transit Authority, may I help you?")

T    What do we say? Let's say it together. (Supply visual cue.)

S&T  I am at Horton Plaza and I want to go to Sea World. I want to go at 10:00 A.M. Could you tell me what bus to take?

T    Listen carefully and be ready to write down directions. (Plays tape of directions.) "Take bus #110 right from Horton Plaza to Sea World. It leaves every 20 minutes, so you can leave Horton Plaza at 10:20."

S    (Listen and write down directions as teacher monitors.)

T    After you have written down directions, what do you do next?

S    Repeat them back.

T    Good. Let's do that now.

S&T  I take bus #110 right from Horton Plaza to Sea World. I can leave Horton Plaza at 10:20. Is that right? ("Yes, it is.")

T    What is the last thing to do before hanging up?

S    Thank them for the information.

T&S  Thank you very much.

### CLOSE the lesson

T    We have learned how to call for bus route information. There are six steps for doing this. Let's review the six steps:
     1. Have pen and paper ready.
     2. Call 233-3004.
     3. Tell them where you are, where you want to go, and when.
     4. Listen carefully and write down instructions.
     5. Repeat instructions back after writing them down.
     6. Thank them.
     Tomorrow, I would like you to bring in two places that you would like to go and we will practice calling for bus routes to get there.

THE PROMPTED PRACTICE FOR THIS SKILL MAY TAKE SEVERAL DAYS BEFORE STUDENTS BECOME PROFICIENT. PROVIDE PROMPTED

(continued on next page)

**BOX 12.1**
*(continued)*

PRACTICE FOR *AS LONG AS IT TAKES TO MASTER THE SKILL.* THEN GO ON TO UNPROMPTED PRACTICE.

*Provide UNPROMPTED PRACTICE (You do it)*
If possible, the teacher should teach this skill in a room where telephones are available. The students should first practice on phones that are not plugged in. The teacher can give mock bus route information, or have an audiotape of instructions, so that students can practice writing down the information.

Monitor performance to provide immediate feedback, to correct errors, and to recognize success. Continue unprompted practice on unplugged phones until students are consistently proficient.

When students have mastered the skill on unplugged phones, have them make the actual phone call to the Transit Authority. Monitor performance closely and provide immediate feedback.

*Source:* "Employability Skills + Family Involvement + Adult Agency Support + On-the-Job Support = Employment Success" by P. Patton, B. De la Garza, and C. Harmon, in press, *Teaching Exceptional Children.* The Employability Skills Curriculum is available for the cost of duplicating from the ERIC Clearinghouse (1-703-264-9474).

Transition programs need to include structured planning for recreation activities. Students with mild disabilities need to be taught alternatives to "hanging out," being involved in gangs, and other counterproductive activities. Community collaboration is essential in this area of transition services. Community programs such as Big Brothers, Upward Bound, and YMCAs are just a few of the community programs that strive to guide youth toward healthy recreational pursuits. Appropriate recreational activities need to be included as goals in each student's IEP and ITP.

Schloss et al. (1995) describe how to guide a student in pursuing healthy leisure activities, using the following steps:

1. Recognize free time.
2. Know the leisure options that are appropriate and available during that free time.
3. Have attitudes or preferences about the leisure options.
4. Know how to manage and budget necessary resources to participate in a chosen leisure activity.
5. Have the skills to access and participate in the leisure activity.
6. Engage in appropriate social behavior related to that activity. (p. 314)

## Domain 6: Paid Jobs in the Community before Graduation

Students with disabilities who are gainfully employed before high school completion are more likely to (1) stay in school, (2) remain employed after school completion, (3) seek postsecondary education opportunities, and (4) become self-supporting adults (Edgar, 1987). Despite documentation that community-based instruction is effective in promoting future employment success (Edgar, 1987; Falvey, 1986), only 6% of parents of secondary students with mild disabilities report that their children receive community-based instruction (Halpern & Benz, 1987).

Since the early 1980s, millions of retail and service entry-level jobs have been made available in the general workforce (William T. Grant Foundation, 1988). Because of labor shortages, employers are willing to offer flexible hours and to spend more time training young workers in food service, cashiering, and other entry-level positions (Rudolph, 1988). Most students with mild disabilities are very capable of performing these jobs. Employers are becoming more aware of the benefits of hiring workers with disabilities and are more willing to hire them. The Marriott Corporation, Sea World, IBM, Hewlett Packard, Dupont, and KOA Campgrounds are some of the many large corporations throughout the country who have corporate commitments to hire workers with disabilities (DiLeo, 1991; Greenwood, 1990; Marriott Foundation, 1990).

As a teacher of adolescents with special needs, you will want to provide an instructional program that assures your students the necessary support to apply for and engage in paid, part-time employment during their high school years. You will be teaching them the responsibility of getting to work on time, completing designated work tasks, dressing and grooming appropriately, and other critical work-related demands. Paid job experiences should be closely integrated with your school-based instruction in job search and job maintenance skills. Ideally, each of your students enrolled in job search and job maintenance skills instruction will, simultaneously, be placed in a part-time job in the community. Skills learned in the classroom can then be practiced and generalized in the real world for permanency. You will be working closely with local employers to develop job sites for your students. Box 12.2 contains a six-step employer contact script that you can use as a model when conducting job development activities in your local community for your adolescents with mild disabilities.

You will also develop monitoring and evaluation procedures to assure success, and not failure, once the students are working. Many high school programs employ a job support specialist, or "job coach," to do this. However, as a teacher of adolescents with special needs, you will be very closely involved in job development, job placement, and job maintenance

**BOX 12.2**

### Scripted Employer Contact for Job Development

*STEP 1: Describe to the employer your knowledge of the company and its products and/or services.*

Good morning, Mr. Jones. My name is Tim Smith and I am a job support specialist from Awesome High School. I know that Grocery Link is one of the state's largest grocery store chains. At your site alone you employ 83 employees, seven of whom are stock clerks. You are known to have a training program which helps employees to be more success-ful at their particular job and also helps stimulate internal career ad-vancement. We are here to discuss with you the possibility of placing qualified students with disabilities in one or more of your stores.

*STEP 2: Describe your school-based vocational development program.*

At present, we have a student, Spencer White, who is enrolled in a program which is providing him with training in employability skills. For example, he has learned daily living skills wherein he has learned how to manage and use money appropriately, how to manage personal needs properly, how to purchase and prepare food, and how to select and care for clothing. His training in job-related social skills has helped him learn how to get along with others, co-workers and supervisors alike. He has learned how to practice punctuality on the job, how to follow directions, how to complete job tasks in a timely manner, and how to accept criticism and praise. Also, he has acquired employability skills including how to fill out a job application, how to interview for a job, how to maintain a positive attitude on the job, and how to stay on a work task until finished. Finally, through vocational counseling, he has identified his unique abilities, needs, and interests as they relate to employment and has discovered that he would like his first paid job to be in the area of groceries and food service. We believe Spencer has acquired the entry level skills to succeed as a stock clerk in your company.

*STEP 3: Describe the benefits of hiring workers with disabilities.*

Mr. Jones, I would like to briefly explain some of the benefits to you if you hire a worker with a disability. The Targeted Job Tax Credit (TJTC) offers tax credits of up to $3,000, depending on the wages paid to the worker. The TJTC form is a simple one page form that I can quickly and easily help you fill out. It is important that the form is postmarked prior to the date you hire your worker. Also, the Job Training Partnership Act (JTPA) can provide up to 50% wage subsidies for paying your worker. We will help you access these funds through your worker's vocational rehabilitation counselor. Further, research has proven that 90% of workers with disabilities receive "good" or "excellent" job performance ratings once they are hired. Employees with disabilities have also been found to maintain a 96% standard of safety compared to a 92% rate for regular employees.

In short, with tax benefits and wage subsidies, the average cost of hiring workers with disabilities is less than or equal to other workers. I

**BOX 12.2**

**(continued)**

might add that the cost of any job accommodations have been found to be of little or no cost to most employers. We will assist you with any necessary job accommodations if you decide to hire Spencer. If you do hire Spencer, you will get the added benefit of hiring a person who will perform his job with high performance and safety ratings. A job opportunity in your company can be invaluable in helping Spencer make the challenging transition from school to work.

*STEP 4: Describe your student's strengths as a worker.*
Spencer is well suited for the job of Stock Clerk. There are a number of qualities that indicate his potential for success. First, his vocational assessment results show he has a true interest in this area. He has the interpersonal skills to demonstrate responsibility, dependability, flexibility, self-control, punctuality, and appropriate co-worker and supervisor interactions. He is strong and healthy. He is seldom absent from school due to illness. He has excellent fine and gross motor abilities. He is able to easily lift 40 to 50 pounds. He is able to climb, stoop, kneel, and bend with ease. Finally, during his vocational assessment, Spencer demonstrated the ability to manage time and money which will help him in record-keeping duties.

*STEP 5: Describe how you will provide support services for your student.*
I will do whatever it takes to ensure Spencer's success as your employee. For example, I will come to the store during his initial training and help in this process. I can even train him at the store if you desire. After he has been trained, I will visit Spencer on the job two or three times a week to follow up on any questions or concerns that he has or that you have. During these visits, I will touch base with his supervisor to be alerted to any impending problems. I am committed to "nipping any problems in the bud" so that Spencer does not fail. I will conduct these visits promptly and leave quickly unless I am asked to stay for any reason. I can also be present during Spencer's job evaluation meetings if you wish. Finally, Spencer's supervisor will be able to contact me by phone whenever necessary.

*STEP 6: Describe specifically what your next steps will be.*
Mr. Jones, thank you for the time and consideration you have given me, our high school program, and Spencer. I would like to meet with you at your earliest convenience so you can interview Spencer yourself and see that he has the necessary qualifications and skills to do an outstanding job. He will bring his job application, his résumé, and his employment portfolio with him to the interview. I will be in your area next Monday. Is that a good time for you? Thank you again. It has been a pleasure. Spencer and I will see you next Monday at 10:00 A.M. in your office.

*Source:* "Employability Skills + Family Involvement + Adult Agency Support + On-the-Job Support = Employment Success" by P. Patton, B. De la Garza, and C. Harmon, in press, *Teaching Exceptional Children.* The Employability Skills Curriculum is available for the cost of duplicating from the ERIC Clearinghouse (1-703-264-9474.).

for your students. Following Telepak's (1995) model for engaging students in community-based job opportunities, you can develop job sites for your students using the following strategies:

1. *The initial student visit—application and interview.* You have already taught your students how to fill out a job application and how to conduct a job interview. You have also guided them in developing an employment portfolio containing a résumé, a short autobiography, and possibly samples of work done in class or on other jobs. The student, then, is ready for this initial visit with the employer.

2. *Observation and hands-on learning.* Students spend several days observing workers perform necessary job tasks. They then attempt the job tasks with prompting from you, the teacher, or the job support specialist. Once a student becomes proficient at the job tasks, you can fade the prompts. You can teach your students the following four-word strategy to focus on learning the skills of a specific job task. You can teach students to cue the strategy on their own, or you can verbally cue the strategy yourself.

   WATCH  Cue the student's attention to observing an employer, employee, or student trainer performing the steps of the work task.

   TELL  Request the student to communicate the responsibilities involved in successfully accomplishing the work task that has been observed.

   SHOW  Request the student to demonstrate the work task, either independently or with assistance.

   WORK  Indicate that the process of demonstrating and teaching the task is complete and that independent performance of the work task is expected. (p. 62)

3. *Student reporting.* This is a form of self-reporting that can be used during job training. A 5 × 7 index card contains a listing of the required job tasks with a place for the student to check each one as completed and sign and date at the bottom. A job report card will list such tasks as (1) punch in time clock, (2) say hello to my supervisor, (3) put on my apron and company shirt, (4) fill grocery bag holder, (5) bag groceries appropriately as taught, (6) continue to bag groceries as taught for two hours, (7) return company attire, (8) punch out time clock, (9) say good-bye to my supervisor. You can develop your own student self-report forms based upon the specific job tasks or use forms suggested by Telepak (1995) or Montague (1987b).

4. *Evaluation.* This is an evaluation of your student's work performance that you, the job support specialist, and/or the job supervisor completes.

It is best to conduct such an evaluation at about four- to six-week intervals. Upon completion of the evaluation, you sit down with the student and provide constructive feedback based on the job performance evaluation results. Telepak (1995) suggests an evaluation format that you can modify to meet the needs of your own students. Also, check with your local transition specialist for available job performance evaluation formats.

5. *Follow-up.* Work skills and behaviors that your student has acquired in the community-based job site can be generalized to other work settings. The purpose of the follow-up phase is to continue to help your students improve their employment capabilities. You will now begin to assist your students in finding higher-level jobs, summer jobs, or additional training for advancement.

## Domain 7: Counseling for Postsecondary Options

According to the Division on Career Development of the Council for Exceptional Children (1987), school counselors should take a more active role in career planning for students with disabilities and initiate early career planning with parents and students. Students need to become aware of the many programs that can help them beyond high school, including community college programs, services for students with disabilities, occupational preparation programs, vocational training programs, and adult agency services.

Remember to involve your school counselor as an integral part of the transition team so that he/she will be informed and knowledgeable about the multitude of postschool program options for your group of students. Often school counselors are in the position of advising all students but have little training or background about special education programs or about disabilities in general. High school special education teachers, job coaches, and other special education support personnel can play a vital role in collaborating with school counselors and soliciting their support on behalf of students with mild disabilities in their quest for successful employment and adult living. Of special value is the counselor's expertise in providing guidance relative to personal, financial, and independent living issues.

## Domain 8: Referral to Adult Agencies before Graduation

Unfortunately, students with disabilities have little contact with social and rehabilitation agencies during their high school years (Hasazi, Gordon, & Roe, 1985; Roessler et al., 1990). Most students rely on contacts with family and friends to obtain jobs and do not access agencies that could assist in job placement. Students with mild disabilities are even less likely than students with severe disabilities to be referred to appropriate adult agencies prior to graduation. Wehman (1993) outlines many effective strategies for assuring early referral and interagency collaboration, including how to develop an interagency agreement among schools, adult agencies, and local businesses. If you follow such strategies, you are more likely to effect early referral for your student with a mild disability. Additionally, most adult agencies provide assistance in planning for postsecondary training and education. Such assistance may include career counseling, transportation costs for traveling to and from school, reimbursement for tuition and books, and other services necessary to complete a postsecondary training program.

It is important that you begin the referral process to adult agencies early so that school personnel can assist with the application process and assure active client status with the appropriate adult agency *before* graduation. Once a student with mild disabilities graduates, there are a multitude of adult agencies to access. However, most of the agencies are burdened with large caseloads, bureaucratic complexities, discrepant eligibility criteria, and voluminous paperwork. Most adult agencies, such as state vocational rehabilitation agencies, require a formal application, medical exam, psychological exam, permission to access existing assessment information, interviews with the agency representative, eligibility determination, vocational evaluation, and/or extended vocational evaluation. This process can take anywhere from 12 to 24 months.

A planned and systematic process of adult agency referral should be included in a student's IEP and ITP during the tenth-grade year. The ultimate goal for your students is that they are in active client status with the adult agency before graduation. The best way to do this is to invite the adult agency representative to your students' IEP/ITP meetings beginning in the tenth or eleventh grade. Some adult agency personnel are reluctant to become involved before a student's senior year, but if you persist and establish a relationship with them early, your students will be better served.

Table 12.3 contains a brief description of some of the more commonly used adult agencies and services. See National Information Center for Children and Youth with Disabilities (1991) for an in-depth analysis of postsecondary options for adolescents with disabilities. The Center (P.O. Box 1492, Washington, DC 20013-1492) can also become an invaluable resource to you as a teacher when you have any questions about transition planning for your students.

### Domain 9: Self-Advocacy Skills for Job and Community

The ability to advocate for oneself on the job and in the community is essential. During their high school years, students need to learn how to advocate for themselves. Michaels (1989) delineates the following strategies that

**TABLE 12.3**     **Adult Agencies and Options for Adolescents with Disabilities**

| Agency | Description |
|---|---|
| Vocational Rehabilitation (VR) | VR is the nationwide federal/state program for assisting eligible persons with disabilities to define a suitable employment goal and become employed. VR provides medical exams, vocational assessment, job counseling, job placement, financial assistance to support employment, and other services. To contact VR, look under the state government listings in your telephone directory for Rehabilitation Services or Vocational Rehabilitation. |
| Developmental Disabilities Services | A state-operated agency designed to provide services and support to persons with mental retardation and other developmental disabilities. This agency can provide vocational assessment, supported employment programs, financial assistance, and other services. To contact your state's agency for persons with developmental disabilities, look under the state government listings in your telephone directory. |
| Social Security Administration: SSI and SSDI | SSI provides financial assistance to individuals under the age of 18 based on their disability. The disability is determined by the Social Security Administration. SSDI benefits are paid to persons who become disabled before the age of 22 if at least one of their parents has worked a certain amount of time under Social Security. Work incentives are included. To find out more about SSI and SSDI, look under the federal government listings in your telephone directory. |
| Plan for Achieving Self-Support (PASS) | PASS is a work incentive program that enables a person with a disability to receive earned and unearned income and to set some or all of these funds aside for up to 48 months. Work incentives are included. Your student's VR counselor or Social Security representative can write a PASS for your student. |
| Postsecondary Training and Employment Options | After graduation from high school, students can benefit from (1) community colleges with special programs for students with disabilities, (2) JTPA programs for disadvantaged youth, (3) adult education certificate programs, and (4) trade and technical schools. You can find out about these postsecondary options from your student's VR counselor. |
| Disability-Specific Organizations | Organizations such as the Association for Retarded Citizens (ARC), the United Cerebral Palsy Foundation (UCP), the Epilepsy Foundation, and others provide vocational assessment and training for youth and adults with disabilities. To find out more about disability-specific organizations operating in your state or local area, contact the National Information Center for Children and Youth with Disabilities, P.O. Box 1492, Washington, DC 20013-1492, for a state resource sheet. |

you can use to teach self-advocacy skills to your students: (1) accepting criticism and subsequently changing behavior to reflect input; (2) dealing with supervisors/managers, including discussing the disability and requesting appropriate accommodations; (3) evaluating one's own performance, monitoring task completion, and providing self-feedback; (4) setting goals, developing short- and long-term goals, and monitoring progress; (5) developing a vocational plan that includes goals for career advancement and job upgrading and ways to protect one's interests; and (6) developing social skills and appropriate behavior/interactions for the job setting.

## Domain 10: Family Involvement

Katz (1983) found that training parents to become career educators and advocates for their youth with disabilities results in improved services and opportunities, both during school and after graduation. Therefore, you should include parent involvement as an integral part of transition planning for adolescents with mild disabilities. However, as students progress through the special education system, there is a tendency for parents to become less involved in and informed about the programs in which their youth are participating (Halpern & Benz, 1987). Schools should set target goals for parent participation in transition planning and monitor frequently the extent and quality of parent participation (Cobb & Hasazi, 1987). Methods and techniques that you can use to increase family participation during the transition process will be discussed in more detail later in this chapter. Some basic techniques for communicating with parents were presented in Chapter 5.

## Domain 11: Student Participation in ITP Meetings

The Division on Career Development (Council for Exceptional Children, 1987) views transition as the phase of career development that involves the preparation of the student for success in employment and other work roles, including that of student, consumer, citizen, family member, and employee. Students should be encouraged to participate in the preparation of their ITP and to participate in their ITP meeting. However, it is estimated that only 50% of students with mild disabilities actually attend their own ITP meetings (Clark & Kolstoe, 1990).

Students with mild disabilities need to be the prime decision makers in their own transition planning. Many students do not see themselves as an integral part of the transition planning process. Conversely, some professionals do not see students as active participants in ITP development. It is an inherent right to be involved in one's own life planning. Frequently, these rights of students with mild disabilities are violated. All members of school-based transition teams must assure that each student is actively involved in his or her ITP development.

Van Reusen et al. (1994) have created a self-advocacy strategy that can be taught to students to enhance their interpersonal skills and participation in ITP meetings. To teach the strategy, the authors recommend the following techniques:

1. Give the student ample time to respond.
2. Use good eye communication with the student.
3. Ask the student to share information relevant to planning.
4. Take notes and integrate the student's input.
5. Ask for the student's opinion.

Figure 12.2 contains a worksheet that can be used in your classroom to facilitate student problem solving and participation relative to transition planning. After completing, discussing, and role-playing in class, the student can then take the worksheet to his/her IEP/ITP meeting to share with team members.

---

**COMPREHENSION MONITORING OF KEY CONCEPTS**

*Transition Planning Domains and Strategies*

1. Transition planning requires planning in a set of domains that prepare the student for employment, postsecondary training options, and independent living.

2. The transition domains that must be addressed are: (a) job search skills, (b) job maintenance skills, (c) job-related functional academics, (d) mobility and transportation skills, (e) planning and accessing recreation activities, (f) paid jobs in the community before graduation, (g) counseling for postsecondary options, (h) referral to adult agencies before graduation, (i) self-advocacy skills for job and community, (j) family involvement, and (k) student participation in ITP meetings.

3. Job search skills are frequently taught in elective courses, but special educators can use curriculum packages such as Life Centered Career Education (LCCE): Occupational Guidance and Preparation Domain (Roessler & Brolin, 1992) and Employability Skills for Students with Mild Disabilities (Patton et al., in press) to build a job search curriculum into the student's program.

*(continued on next page)*

4. Job success depends on such job maintenance skills as communication, interpersonal skills, and good work habits.

5. Job-related functional academics include reading and writing skills that are necessary for students to succeed on the job; special educators can choose from various curriculum programs to teach functional academics.

6. Mobility and leisure skills are just being explored for students with mild disabilities.

7. Students with disabilities who are gainfully employed before high school completion are more likely to (a) stay in school, (b) remain employed after school completion, (c) seek post-secondary education opportunities, and (d) become self-supporting adults.

8. School counselors should take a more active role in career planning for students with disabilities and initiate early career planning with parents and students.

9. A planned and systematic process of adult agency referral should be included in the student's IEP and ITP during the tenth-grade year.

10. Training parents to become career educators and advocates for their youth with disabilities results in improved services and opportunities, both during school and after graduation.

11. Even though students should be encouraged to participate in their ITP meeting, it is estimated that only 50% actually attend the meetings.

## Team Development of the Individualized Transition Plan (ITP)

As a teacher of adolescents with special needs, you will be involved in helping your students develop an Individualized Transition Plan (ITP). As we have seen, Public Law 101-476 mandated in 1990 that goals and objectives for providing transition services for students with disabilities be included in their IEPs by their 16th birthday. Most local school districts are choosing to develop separate Individualized Transition Plans (ITPs) for these students. To reiterate the federal definition of transition services, each student's ITP will include

a coordinated set of activities . . . which promotes movement from school to post-school activities. . . . The coordinated set of activities shall be based upon the individual student's needs, taking into account

**FIGURE 12.2** **Preparing for the Individualized Transition Plan**

---

### GOALS FOR MY FUTURE

DIRECTIONS: Read each question and fill in the blanks.

I want to be employed as a _____ by _____ .
(e.g., a clerk at Sears by July 1996)

In order to become qualified for this position, I will need to do the following:
1. _____
2. _____

My educational goal is to _____ by _____ .
(e.g., complete electronic technician program by January 1994)

In order to be accepted into this program or school, I need to do the following:
1. _____
2. _____

Upon being accepted into this program, I will need approximately
_____ to pay for tuition/fees.

One year after high school, I plan to live:
1. In an apartment _____
2. With my family _____
3. Other              _____

In order to do this, I will need to do the following:
1. _____
2. _____
   _____

---

*Source:* "Employability Skills + Family Involvement + Adult Agency Support + On-the-Job Support = Employment Success" by P. Patton, B. De la Garza, and C. Harmon, in press, *Teaching Exceptional Children.* The Employability Skills Curriculum is available for the cost of duplicating from the ERIC Clearinghouse (1-703-264-9474).

the student's preferences and interests, and shall include instruction, community experiences, the development of employment and other post-school adult living objectives, and, when appropriate, acquisition of daily living skills and functional vocational evaluation. (34 CFR 300:18)

## The Role and Function of the Transition Team

Although you may not be responsible for the entire transition planning process, you will be a key player in that process. This section outlines strategies for facilitating an effective ITP meeting, which results in a written ITP. The strategies are adapted from the Florida Department of Education (1993) statewide transition training manual and the Council for Exceptional Children transition planning guide (West et al., 1992). We discuss effective strategies to use before, during, and after the ITP meeting. We also explain how the written ITP emerges as the final product of the transition planning process. Remember, the ITP is not just a piece of paper. It is the reflection of a very comprehensive planning process by a team of professionals, family members, and students.

### Planning the Transition (ITP) Meeting

The time before the ITP meeting is a critical period. Careful planning and organization will help contribute to a smooth, productive meeting. If you practice good preplanning, it will help reduce the total time team members spend at the meeting itself. Following are the suggested steps in preplanning your ITP meeting.

***Step 1: Become familiar with adult agency services.*** If you are designated as the facilitator of the ITP meeting, it is important that you familiarize yourself with agencies and community providers of services that will assist administrators, teachers, and family members to meet your student's needs and interests. This may include such services as vocational rehabilitation, community college services for students with disabilities, and so on. The best way to do this is by inviting your local vocational rehabilitation representative to meet with you. The vocational rehabilitation counselor usually has vast knowledge of the available services and options available for adolescents with disabilities. You can contact your local vocational rehabilitation counselor by contacting the district vocational rehabilitation agency listed in the state government section of your telephone directory. Also review the information covered earlier in this chapter under Domain 8: Referral to Adult Agencies before Graduation.

***Step 2: Obtain releases of information.*** A release of information needs to be obtained from the student's family before any personally identifiable information can be sent to agencies. Therefore, you need to send a release of information form to the family well in advance of the ITP meeting. Check with your local school district to obtain a copy of the form used in your area.

© Kathy Sloane/Jeroboam

*A team of school professionals discusses transition planning.*

***Step 3: Assemble important information.*** Gathering background information on your student helps ensure that the ITP is based on the student's needs, preferences, and interests. This information typically includes (1) a vocational assessment report based on community-based vocational evaluation, work samples, situational assessment, standardized career interest tests, aptitude tests, rating scales, and others; (2) your student's work history; (3) your student's residential history; (4) vocational and career education courses taken and/or services used; (5) academic achievement information and graduation eligibility; (6) independent living goals; and (7) any other relevant information. You will also need to assemble the ITP form, all required releases of information, and any additional feedback from the student, family, and/or additional ITP team members.

***Step 4: Schedule the ITP meeting.*** As a teacher of adolescents with special needs, you will probably be the person responsible for scheduling the ITP meeting. Planning for the ITP meeting requires creativity and flexibility on your part to ensure the attendance and active participation of family members and other team members. Be sure to consult with your student, family members, and appropriate agency representatives to determine the best time for all to attend.

***Step 5: Invite all appropriate ITP team members.*** The ITP team will likely include school district personnel and representatives of community agencies who would not necessarily attend a traditional IEP meeting. Team members may change from meeting to meeting, depending on the individual student's needs. In addition to the student, family members, administrator, and teachers, other potential team members might include the following: (1) vocational education teacher, (2) job support specialist, (3) work/study coordinator, (4) guidance counselor, (5) vocational rehabilitation counselor, (6) community college representative, (7) community mental health service provider, and (8) other adult agency representatives.

### Conducting the ITP Meeting

As the special education teacher, you will be in charge of the ITP planning process, which means asking the right questions, listening, clarifying team members' responses, translating team input into usable concepts, and helping to translate ideas into action with the assignment of responsibility. Following are the suggested steps to follow during the ITP meeting.

***Step 1: Set the tone for the meeting.*** First, introduce the team members. If some members were unable to attend, explain why and assure those members present that absent members will receive feedback. Then, state the purpose of the meeting. For example:

> The purpose of this meeting is to plan for Mary's future. We hope to establish goals that will help her prepare for employment and/or college, independent living, access to community services, and friendships in the adult community.

***Step 2: Develop an outcome statement.*** The first task of the ITP team is to develop an outcome statement with the student. An outcome statement is a vision for the student, projecting one to five years after graduation. The outcome statement is very important because it establishes the direction for the rest of the ITP meeting. Relevant annual goals and meaningful objectives are generated from a clear vision of how the student wants to live, work, and participate in the community (Wehman, 1993). It is critical that your student is very actively involved in creating this vision statement. Strategies for student self-advocacy and student participation were discussed earlier in this chapter under Domain 9, Self-Advocacy Skills for Job and Community, and Domain 11, Student Participation in ITP Meetings.

Outcome statements vary by student preference, need, interest, age, and ability. Initially, postschool outcome statements may be very broad (such as employment versus college), becoming more focused in later meetings.

Your ITP team members should consider outcomes in (1) postschool education, (2) vocational training, (3) integrated employment, (4) adult services, (5) independent living, (6) community participation, and (7) others as expressed by your student. The following are examples of student outcome statements:

1. John desires to work independently as a food service worker, share an apartment with a friend, use community recreational facilities, and have a network of friends.

2. Mary wants to work full-time in retail or modeling, live in an apartment on her own, and attend the local community college to further her education.

**Step 3: Review student's present situation.** Once a general direction has been established through the outcome statement, the ITP team summarizes the student's present level of performance in areas relevant to the student's long-term postschool outcome. As a member of the ITP team, you can obtain this information from the student's records as well as from the student, family, and/or agency members. The following are examples of present situation statements:

1. John has received community-based job training at Morrison's Cafeteria and has worked in the school cafeteria preparing salads and sandwiches. He has no paid work experience. He has his Social Security card, a bus ID, and his official birth certificate. His high school program of study leads to a Certificate of Completion. He has been referred to ARC for adult services.

2. Mary has completed typing, art, modeling, and commercial art vocational education courses. She has received community-based job training at WonderCare Child Care and has done some baby-sitting. She has no other paid work experience. She has her Social Security card, state ID card, and her official birth certificate. Her high school program leads to a Special Diploma. She has been referred to Vocational Rehabilitation for adult services.

**Step 4: Develop transition goals, responsible persons, and timelines.** Throughout the meeting process, the ITP members begin to select priority goals for the coming year. The following transition service areas should be addressed: (1) instruction, (2) community experience, (3) training and/or employment, (4) postschool adult living, (5) daily living and domestic skills, (6) functional vocational evaluation, and (7) other related services. It is impossible to address all areas during a single ITP meeting. Thus, you and the ITP team will prioritize three or four areas to be addressed at one meeting. At the end of the meeting, you will then prioritize which areas will be addressed at the next meeting. The entire team develops the transition goals, which are customized to suit the student's specific outcome statement and identified needs. The following are examples of transition goal statements:

1. John will attend all meetings related to his future.
2. John will demonstrate the ability to communicate with adult agency representatives in his behalf.
3. John will sign up for swimming lessons at the park and recreation program.
4. Mary will explore a part-time job by meeting with a Career Tech and Vocational Rehabilitation counselor to discuss options for employment.
5. Mary will identify the most cost-effective housing options, rental costs, utility costs, deposit, furnished versus unfurnished, rules and regulations.
6. Mary will meet with the Vocational Rehabilitation counselor to discuss tuition reimbursement for community college modeling programs.

The ITP team determines how to help the student plan for getting from his/her present situation to his/her transition goal, and ultimately to accomplish the outcome statement (Step 2). The focus becomes the identification of transition services that will help achieve the vision expressed in the outcome statement. The transition goals must contain (1) specified transition services, (2) specified responsible persons, and (3) procedures, schedule, and criteria for evaluation.

The ITP is different from the IEP in that it is more of a service plan than an instructional plan. Instructional objectives appear in a student's IEP. (Review Chapter 3 for a discussion and description of how to develop instructional objectives in an IEP for adolescents with disabilities.) Transition service goals appear in the ITP. The focus is on planning for services that will result in the student's realizing his or her outcome statement.

***Step 5: Assign follow-up responsibilities.*** Responsibility for tracking the progress of a student's transition process rests with specified ITP team members. Transition services are a shared responsibility among school personnel, service providers, family, and student. It is especially important to include the student in this process. By giving your students the responsibility to accomplish specific transition service goals, you are helping to empower them so they can develop into adults capable of taking responsibility for their own future.

### Conducting Follow-up to the ITP Meeting

**Step 1: Complete ITP follow-up.** Follow-up activities may need to occur after the ITP meeting. A team member should be assigned the responsibility of coordinating the necessary follow-up activities to ensure that they occur. For example, follow-up is needed when services are specified in the ITP from a particular agency representative who was unable to attend the ITP meeting. This communication may occur through a telephone conference or correspondence. If the agency cannot provide the specified service, the ITP must be revised, which means that another ITP meeting must be held. This is why it is important to preplan so that all members can be present if at all possible.

**Step 2: Reconvene the ITP team, if necessary.** The ITP team may reconvene at any time prior to the annual review if revisions to the ITP are needed. If it is determined that the needed transition services are not being provided as planned, the team is responsible for reconvening a meeting to identify alternative strategies. These strategies may include inviting a representative from another agency, finding a low- or no-cost way of providing the service, or determining if the service is still needed.

**Step 3: Reconvene the ITP team for the annual review.** The ITP team is required to meet annually to review a student's ITP and revise it as appropriate. The annual ITP meeting allows the team to update the student's desired postschool outcome statement, revise the transition goals as needed, and determine the needed transition services for the upcoming year.

## The Individualized Transition Plan (ITP)

You have learned the steps for facilitating the transition planning process, which is comprehensive and outcome-oriented. The final product resulting from the process is the ITP document. Remember, the ITP is different from the IEP in that it is designed to focus on long-term future outcomes for students, not necessarily on academic achievement. Academic achievement is only one of several domains addressed. When developing an ITP, you will be writing transition service goals for your students that include the domains of postsecondary education, residential living, health and medical services, self-advocacy, employment and training, community recreation and leisure activities, financial and income management, adult agency linkages, personal management, family life and social activities, and transportation and mobility services. Contact your local school district for copies of ITP forms, formats, and guidelines that you will be required to use as a teacher of adolescents with mild disabilities.

Refer to Figures 12.3 and 12.4 for two examples of completed ITPs for adolescents with mild disabilities. Figure 12.3 contains an ITP for John, a student with a mild mental disability. Figure 12.4 contains an ITP for Mary, a student with a learning disability. Notice that the ITPs contain sections for postschool outcomes, work experience completed, documentation and referrals necessary for adult living, prioritized transition issues, transition goals, timelines, responsible persons, evaluation criteria, transition issues to be discussed at the next meeting, participants at the next meeting, and required signatures.

---

**COMPREHENSION MONITORING OF KEY CONCEPTS**

*Team Development of the Individualized Transition Plan (ITP)*

1. The transition planning process is a comprehensive process that moves from a planning stage to a follow-up stage.

2. The steps to follow before the ITP meeting are to become familiar with adult agency services, obtain releases of information, assemble important information, schedule the meeting, and invite the members of the team.

3. The steps to follow during the ITP meeting are to set the tone; develop an outcome statement; review the student's present situation; develop transition goals, personnel responsible, and timelines; and assign follow-up responsibilities.

4. The steps after the ITP meeting include completing follow-up, reconvening the team if necessary, and planning for the annual review.

5. The ITP document is focused on planning services and activities that help the student realize his/her outcome statement.

6. When developing an ITP, you will be writing transition service goals for your student that include the domains of postsecondary education, residential living, health and medical services, self-advocacy, employment and training, community recreation and leisure activities, financial and income management, adult agency linkages, personal management, family life and social activities, and transportation and mobility services.

7. The ITP must contain the outcome statement, prioritized transition issues, transition goals, personnel responsible, timelines, evaluation criteria, and required signatures.

**FIGURE 12.3  Completed Individualized Transition Plan: John Doe**

ITP for Student with Mild Mental Retardation Enrolled in a Ninth-Grade Functional Curriculum Program

*Student Profile.* John is a 15-year-old young man who is enrolled in a functional life skills program for students with mild mental retardation. He has worked in food preparation for the school cafeteria during the past school year. To date, this has been his only work experience. He works independently and is competent in all aspects of his job. John is a loner. He eats lunch alone and spends most of his time alone. He is not involved in any activities at home, at school, or in the community.

## Individualized Transition Plan

Name ___John Doe___  Birth Date ___01/31/80___  Age ___15___  Social Security # ___222-99-4545___

Graduation Status: ___ Diploma  ___ Special Diploma  _X_ Certificate of Completion  Expects to Graduate: ___1998___

Describe Postschool Outcomes:  Employment: _Full-time independent_  Residential: _Independent living_

Education: _N/A due to employment_  Other: _Friendship/health club_

Work Experience Completed:  Vocational Classes: _____

Community-Based Instruction: __3 hrs/day training at Morrison's Cafeteria__

Work Experience: __school cafeteria—food preparation (salad & sandwich prep)__

Other: _____

Preparation for Adulthood:

| Does Student Have? | Yes | No | When? | In Process |
|---|---|---|---|---|
| Social Security Card | X | | | |
| Driver's Education | | X | Spr 98 | |
| Driver's License | | X | Spr 98 | |
| State Identification Card | | X | ASAP | |
| Bus Identification Card | X | | | |
| Birth Certificate | X | | | |
| Résumé Completed | | X | Spr 97 | X |
| Other | | | | |

| Adult Agency Referral: | Date to be Referred | A-Active I-Inactive |
|---|---|---|
| Vocational Rehabilitation | 3/96 | I |
| Health & Human Services | 3/98 | I |
| Community College District (Dis Stu Svcs) | 2/98 | I |
| Social Security (SSI) | N/A | |
| Employment Development Department | N/A | |
| County Mental Health Services | 3/97 | I |
| Department of Social Services (Dev Dis) | 3/98 | I |
| Other (ARC) | 3/94 | A |

(continued on next page)

# FIGURE 12.3 (continued)

John Doe: Page 2

Prioritize Issues to Be Addressed for This ITP:

| | Postsecondary | | 3 | Employment/Training | | Adult Agency Linkages |
|---|---|---|---|---|---|---|
| | Residential | | 2 | Community Recreation/Leisure | | Personal/Domestic Management |
| | Health and Medical | | | Financial and Income | | Family Life and Social |
| 1 | Self-Advocacy | | | Mobility/Transportation | | Other |

| TRANSITION DOMAIN | TRANSITION GOALS | TIMELINE | AGENCY/PERSON RESPONSIBLE | EVALUATION |
|---|---|---|---|---|
| Self-Advocacy | John will attend all meetings related to his future: ITP, IEP, etc. | 6/98 | John, parents, teacher | ___ Met<br>___ Modify<br>___ Continue |
| Self-Advocacy | John will demonstrate the ability to communicate with adult agency representatives in his behalf. | 6/98 | John, parents, teachers | ___ Met<br>___ Modify<br>___ Continue |
| Recreation/Leisure | John will sign up for swimming lessons at the park and recreation program. | 6/95 | John, parent, social worker | ___ Met<br>___ Modify<br>___ Continue |
| Recreation/Leisure | John will meet with guidance counselor to discuss extracurricular activities and how to become involved. | 9/94 | John, counselor | ___ Met<br>___ Modify<br>___ Continue |
| Employment/Training | John will continue enrollment in the Functional Life Skills Program to receive community-based instruction in employment skills and job-related social skills. | 9/94–6/98 | John, parent, teacher | ___ Met<br>___ Modify<br>___ Continue |
| Employment/Training | John will participate in other employment possibilities within and outside of the school campus, such as library, hotel/motel, and so on. | 9/94–6/98 | John, parent, teacher | ___ Met<br>___ Modify<br>___ Continue |

Prioritize Issues to Be Addressed at Next ITP Meeting:

| | Postsecondary | | 3 | Employment/Training | | 2 | Adult Agency Linkages |
|---|---|---|---|---|---|---|---|
| | Residential | | | Community Recreation/Leisure | | | Personal/Domestic Management |
| | Health and Medical | | | Financial and Income | | | Family Life and Social |
| | Self-Advocacy | | 1 | Mobility/Transportation | | | Other |

Additional Participants at Next ITP Meeting:

Name ___ Mr. Rehab ___    Agency ___ State Department of Vocational Rehabilitation ___

Signatures:

| Student _____ | Parent(s) _____ |
|---|---|
| Teacher _____ | Adult Agency _____ |
| Transition Specialist _____ | Principal _____ |
| Counselor _____ | Other _____ |

# FIGURE 12.4 Completed Individualized Transition Plan: Mary Kingston

ITP for Student with a Learning Disability Enrolled in a Twelfth-Grade Functional Curriculum Program

*Student Profile.* Mary is a very tall, attractive young woman who dresses stylishly. Her academic skills are at about the fourth-grade level. Her disability was never discussed with her except in the context of educational goals, and Mary has never questioned what effect it might have on her future. Mary lives at home and has a close relationship with her parents. Her parents are very supportive and have encouraged her to pursue a modeling career.

## Individualized Transition Plan

Name  Mary Kingston  Birth Date  09/31/78  Age  17  Social Security #  232-91-4645

Graduation Status:  ___ Diploma  _X_ Special Diploma  ___ Certificate of Completion  Expects to Graduate:  1996

Describe Postschool Outcomes:  Employment:  Full-time retail or modeling  Residential: Independent living

Education:  Part-time community college  Other: _____

Work Experience Completed:  Vocational Classes:  Typing, art, modeling program, commercial art

Community-Based Instruction:  2 hrs/day training at WonderCare Child Care

Work Experience:  Baby-sitting/no other paid work experience

Other: _____

Preparation for Adulthood:

| Does Student Have? | Yes | No | When? | In Process |
|---|---|---|---|---|
| Social Security Card | X | | | |
| Driver's Education | | X | Spr 98 | |
| Driver's License | | X | Spr 98 | |
| State Identification Card | X | | | |
| Bus Identification Card | | X | ASAP | |
| Birth Certificate | X | | | |
| Résumé Completed | | X | Spr 97 | X |
| Other | | | | |

| Adult Agency Referral: | Date to be Referred | A-Active I-Inactive |
|---|---|---|
| Vocational Rehabilitation | 3/95 | A |
| Health & Human Services | N/A | |
| Community College District (Dis Stu Svcs) | 2/98 | I |
| Social Security (SSI) | N/A | |
| Employment Development Department | N/A | |
| County Mental Health Services | N/A | |
| Department of Social Services (Dev Dis) | N/A | |
| Other (ARC) | N/A | |

(continued on next page)

**FIGURE 12.4** *(continued)*  Mary Kingston:  Page 2

Prioritize Issues to Be Addressed for This ITP:

| 3 | Postsecondary | 1 | Employment/Training | 4 | Adult Agency Linkages |
|---|---|---|---|---|---|
| 2 | Residential | | Community Recreation/Leisure | | Personal/Domestic Management |
| | Health and Medical | | Financial and Income | | Family Life and Social |
| | Self-Advocacy | | Mobility/Transportation | | Other |

| TRANSITION DOMAIN | TRANSITION GOALS | TIMELINE | AGENCY/PERSON RESPONSIBLE | EVALUATION |
|---|---|---|---|---|
| Employment/Training | Mary will explore part-time job by meeting with the Career Tech and Voc Rehab Counselor to discuss options for employment. | 6/96 | Mary and counselor | ___ Met<br>___ Modify<br>___ Continue |
| Residential | Mary will identify the most cost-effective housing options, rental costs, utility costs, deposit, furnished versus unfurnished, rules and regulations. | 6/96 | Mary, parents, teachers | ___ Met<br>___ Modify<br>___ Continue |
| Postsecondary Options | Mary will meet with the vocational rehabilitation counselor to discuss tuition reimbursement for community college modeling programs. | 6/96 | Mary and counselor | ___ Met<br>___ Modify<br>___ Continue |
| Postsecondary Options | Mary will schedule a tour of the community college and talk to an adviser. | 6/96 | Mary and CC adviser | ___ Met<br>___ Modify<br>___ Continue |
| Adult Agency Linkages | Mary will ask her vocational rehabilitation counselor to attend her next ITP meeting to plan for postgraduation activities. | 11/95 | Mary, parent, teacher | ___ Met<br>___ Modify<br>___ Continue |
| Adult Agency Linkages | Mary will read the State Department of Vocational Rehabilitation Client Handbook to understand her rights and responsibilities pertaining to this agency | 9/95–6/96 | Mary, parent, teacher | ___ Met<br>___ Modify<br>___ Continue |

Prioritize Issues to Be Addressed at Next ITP Meeting:

| 1 | Postsecondary | 3 | Employment/Training | 4 | Adult Agency Linkages |
|---|---|---|---|---|---|
| | Residential | | Community Recreation/Leisure | | Personal/Domestic Management |
| | Health and Medical | | Financial and Income | | Family Life and Social |
| | Self-Advocacy | 2 | Mobility/Transportation | | Other |

Additional Participants at Next ITP Meeting:

Name   Mr. Rehab          Agency   State Department of Vocational Rehabilitation

Signatures:   Student _____          Parent(s) _____

Teacher _____          Adult Agency  Ms. Read, Comm. College Counselor

Transition Specialist _____          Principal _____

Counselor _____          Other _____

## Family Involvement

Parents of students in special education programs seem to decrease their level of involvement during the high school years. However, teachers and other professionals need and want active involvement from parents and families. It is important that you communicate with the parents of your students about (1) the concept of transition, (2) when school services end, (3) what adult services are available and how they differ from school services, (4) the issues they will address as the student becomes an adult, and (5) their roles as parents of students in transition.

Once parents have gathered information about transition, they can participate actively in the transition process. It is important that you are aware of the cultural diversity and economic status of your parents when discussing the transition process. Many parents are reluctant to "let go" of their sons and daughters. This reluctance may vary from culture to culture. If approached with sensitivity to cultural values, parent participation in the transition process can be an invaluable asset. Kelker and Hagan (1986) describe several roles parents can assume during the transition planning process:

1. *Members of the team.* Parents are required by law to be included as members of the IEP team. Since transition planning becomes a regular part of the business of the IEP team during high school, parents become members of the team and are actively involved in the transition planning process. It is important to recruit interpreters for students with parents who are non-English-speaking. These parents are more likely to involve themselves if communication gaps are not an issue.

2. *Providers of information.* Parents and students frequently can provide information about the student's daily functioning and past history that would otherwise be unavailable to the professionals working with the student. Parents and students have personal information about the student's medical history and needs, family history, independent living skills, work experience, and social/emotional development. Parents can also provide insights into the cultural background of the student and the family work ethic that may influence the student in his/her transition planning.

3. *Sources of values.* Parents have goals and values for the student that should be understood and supported by the professionals working with that student. Transition sometimes involves making decisions about important issues such as whether to mainstream a student or begin community-based training. The "right" decision in these matters is not always clear. Cultural differences may also come into play. Some family members may want a daughter only to get married and raise a family. Others may want their sons or daughters involved only in the family

business. Be sure to encourage family members to provide as much information as possible about their family values. Family values can have a strong influence on what options are eventually chosen.

4. *Determiners of priorities.* The sequence of skills that should be taught to a special education student is not always carefully laid out, especially if those skills involve community-based training. During the planning process, it is important to set priorities on how the student will spend his/her time. Sometimes conflicts arise between scheduling academic instruction, mainstreaming opportunities, and community-based instruction. Cultural beliefs may lead parents to insist on academic programs only. Other cultural beliefs may lead parents to value work readiness as a planning priority. Parents can help professionals decide how to resolve those conflicts by establishing which items should come first.

5. *Case managers.* Because of their ongoing commitment and interest, parents can be effective monitors of their child's program over time. They can draw the attention of professionals to areas that are not being covered or to services that are not being provided. They can point out inconsistencies in the student's program and areas in which better coordination between programs could be accomplished.

6. *Advocates.* Probably the most important role that parents can serve is as an advocate for the student. Parents can advocate in the school system and community for those service options that are not now available but that should be developed to meet their student's needs and the needs of others. Parents from different cultural backgrounds can provide invaluable insights regarding how to advocate best for their sons and daughters. As their student moves through the school system and into the adult community, parents can continue to be the most consistent and knowledgeable advocates in the service system for their student's unique needs.

7. *Role models.* Parents can be effective adult role models for their adolescents with disabilities, especially if they include the student in doing some of the daily tasks that adults normally do. Many parents are able to model appropriate adult behaviors that are critical for succeeding in the adult mainstream. It is important to encourage parents to serve as good role models. As a teacher of students with special needs, you can ask a panel of parents from different cultural backgrounds to speak to your students about cultural issues that abound in the workplace and community.

8. *Risk takers.* It is sometimes difficult for parents to let go of their children and allow them to grow up. This process of "letting go" can be particularly difficult when an adolescent with a disability is the focus of con-

cern for the parent. It may be even more difficult for parents from cultures that embrace tight family ties. There is, however, danger in restricting and protecting adolescents with disabilities unnecessarily. Adolescents with disabilities need experience just as other children do. Parents have to be willing to take some risks and allow their adolescents with disabilities to experience frustration and failure so that they also have the chance to learn from their mistakes.

For parents to be effective in the roles they assume in transition planning, they must be knowledgeable about their adolescent's needs, the service options that are or could be available, the processes within the school system, and the service agencies for accessing services. You can help inform parents when transition plans are being made. You need to give parents detailed information about the options for future placements and the requirements for accessing and being successful in those environments. The more that parents know, the more they can be helpful members of the ITP team throughout the transition planning process.

Once students reach the age of 18, they have the right to sign their own ITP. However, if the student is still a minor, the final planning decisions are made by parents. Specific ways of involving parents can include the use of questionnaires and home inventories (Florida Department of Education, 1993). You can provide parents with inventories at the first ITP meeting, or send them home prior to the meeting to be filled out and brought with them to the meeting. A home visit can also provide you with a chance to establish a working relationship with parents and gather important information about their desires, concerns, and home support for the adolescent's transition. You should begin informing parents about the transition planning process approximately three to four years before graduation.

There are a number of ways in which parents can help with the preparation for transition from school to work. Following is a partial list of what you can suggest to parents to ensure an effective transition process for their adolescent.

1. Initiate financial planning, including making a will, getting a Social Security number for the student, applying for SSI, and assisting with an application to vocational rehabilitation. Most of these adult services provide assistance for non-English-speaking persons. It is important that parents know this so they will not be intimidated by such services.

2. Make a determination about guardianship, if appropriate.

3. Encourage self-reliance and independence at home.

4. Reinforce good work habits.

5. Model and monitor good grooming habits.

6. Provide sex education.

7. Encourage and facilitate social activities with peers.

8. Help the adolescent to set realistic goals.

9. Encourage the adolescent to work at a community job or a job in the home or neighborhood.

10. Teach daily living skills such as cooking, laundering, cleaning, and home maintenance.

11. Encourage money management, budgeting, and saving.

12. Develop leisure-time skills in areas such as sports, daily exercise, hobbies, computer or table games.

13. Help the adolescent to develop advocacy and self- management skills, or assist the adolescent with these skills.

It is important to include structured parent training activities in your high school transition programs for students with mild disabilities. Family members, as well as the students themselves, need to be taught the process of adult agency referral, the mechanics of developing an ITP, effective strategies for supporting the efforts of a working student, strategies for accessing adult community services, and other information specific to the student's transition from school to the adult community. You can increase family involvement in your high school program by using the following strategies:

1. Designate someone on the transition team as the "family coordinator specialist." This person should make as many home visits as possible for the purpose of informing family members about the transition program in general and the adult living and employment goals for the students. If possible, recruit family coordinators who represent a variety of cultural backgrounds.

2. Provide incentives for parent participation, such as transportation assistance, child-care relief, positive and ongoing communication with parents, interpreters if necessary, and considerate scheduling practices.

3. Handle family involvement in a very sensitive, appreciative manner. Solicit parent involvement as a positive team player role, rather than as an obligation.

---

**COMPREHENSION MONITORING OF KEY CONCEPTS**

*Family Involvement*

1. Family members tend to become less involved in the school environment during the high school years.

2. Family members need to be educated about the transition planning process and informed about the process approximately three to four years before graduation.

3. Family members can assume the following roles: transition team member, information provider, source of values, determiner of priorities, case manager, advocate, role model, and risk taker.

4. Family members can assist by teaching and reinforcing transition skills at home.

5. You can involve parents by using questionnaires to be completed prior to the ITP meeting and through home visits.

6. You can assure more family participation in your high school program by (a) designating someone as the family support specialist, (b) providing incentives for parent participation, and (c) treating parents with sensitivity and compassion.

Now that you have read Chapter 12, reflect on your list of transition challenges and services and complete this post organizer.

1. Working with your group of three or four peers, compare the list of challenges developed in your advance organizer with the transition domains described in this chapter.

2. Working with your group again, compare your statements of how teachers and family could have helped you during transition from school to the adult community. Are any of these similar to those discussed in the chapter?

3. Using the format in Figures 12.3 and 12.4, write a transition plan for yourself.

4. Using the format in Figures 12.3 and 12.4, write a transition plan for an adolescent with special needs.

Adamson, D. R., Mathews, P., & Schuller, J. (1990). Promising programs to bridge the resource room to regular classroom gap. *Teaching Exceptional Children, 22*(2), 74–78.

Adelman, H. S., & Taylor, L. (1983). Enhancing motivation for overcoming learning and behavior problems. *Journal of Learning Disabilities, 16,* 384–392.

Adelman, H. S., & Taylor, L. (1986). *An introduction to learning disabilities.* Glenview, IL: Scott, Foresman.

Adelman, H. S., & Taylor, L. (1990). Intrinsic motivation and school misbehavior: Some intervention, implications. *Journal of Learning Disabilities, 23,* 587–594.

Adgar, C., Wolfram, W., & Detwyler, J. (1993). Language differences: A new approach for special educators. *Teaching Exceptional Children, 26*(1), 44–47.

Affleck, J. Q., Lowenbraun, S., & Archer, A. (1980). *Teaching the mildly handicapped in the regular classroom* (2nd ed.). Columbus, OH: Merrill.

Alberto, P. A., & Troutman, A. C. (1995). *Applied behavior analysis for teachers* (4th ed). Englewood Cliffs, NJ: Prentice-Hall.

Alexander, W., & McEwin, C. K. (1989). *Schools in the middle: Status and programs.* Columbus, OH: National Middle School Association.

Alley G. R., & Deshler, D. D. (1979). *Teaching the learning disabled adolescent: Strategies and methods* (3rd ed.). Denver: Love.

Altwerger, B., Edelsky, C., & Flores, B. M. (1987) Whole Language: What's new. *The Reading Teacher, 41*(2), 144–152.

Ambert, A., & Dew, N. (1982). *Special education for exceptional bilingual students: A handbook for educators.* Milwaukee: Midwest National Origin Desegregation Assistance Center.

American Psychiatric Association. (1994). *Diagnostic and statistical manual of mental disorders—Revised* (DSM-IV-R). Washington, DC: Author.

American Society for Training and Development. (1989). *Training America: Learning to work for the 21st century.* Alexandria, VA: Author.

American Vocational Association. (1968). Definitions of terms in vocational, technical, practical art education. Washington, DC: Author.

Anderson, J. (1988). Cognitive styles and multicultural populations. *Journal of Teacher Education, 39* (1), 2–9.

Archbald, D. A., (1992). Authentic assessment: Principles, practices, and issues. *School Psychology Quarterly, 6*(4), 279–293.

Archer, A. L., & Gleason, M. M. (1992). *Advanced skills for school success.* North Billerica, MA: Curriculum Associates.

Archer, A. L., & Gleason, M. M. (1994). *Skills for school success.* North Billerica, MA: Curriculum Associates.

Archer, A. L., & Gleason, M. M. (1995). Skills for school success. In P. T. Cegelka & W. H. Berdine (Eds.), *Effective instruction for students with learning difficulties* (pp. 227–263). Boston: Allyn & Bacon.

Ariel, A. (1992). Education of children and adolescents with learning disabilities. New York: Macmillan.

Arkin, E. B., & Funkhouser, J. E. (1991). *Communicating about alcohol and other drugs: Strategies for reaching populations at risk* (OSAP prevention monograph 5). Rockville, MD: Office for Substance Abuse Prevention. (ERIC Document Reproductive Service No. ED 334 291)

Armbruster, B. B., & Anderson, T. H. (1988). On selecting "considerate" content area textbooks. *RASE, 9*(1), 47–52.

Arter, J. A., & Jenkins, J. R. (1977). Examining the benefits and prevalence of modality considerations in special education. *Journal of Special Education, 11,* 281–298.

Arth, A. (1990). Moving into middle school: Concerns of transescent students. *Educational Horizons, 68,* 105–106.

Ascher, C. (1987). *Trends and issues in urban and minority education, 1987.* New York: ERIC Clearinghouse on Urban Education.

Ashlock, R. B. (1990). *Error patterns in computation: A semi-programmed approach* (5th ed.). Columbus, OH: Merrill/Macmillan.

Ashman, A. F., & Conway, R. N. F. (1989). *Cognitive strategies for special education.* New York: Routledge.

Associated Press. (1995, September 22). Birth rate among teens drops for 2nd consecutive year. *Orlando Sentinel,* p. A–3.

Austin, G. A. (Ed.). (1988). *Prevention research update number 2* (Report No. RCO 17181). Portland, OR: Northwest Regional Lab. (ERIC Document Reproduction Service No. ED 309 900)

Austin, K. (1990). *Incorporating the multicultural, non-sexist guidelines into the language arts curriculum, grades 9–12.* Cedar Falls, IA: Area Education Agency 7. (ERIC Document Reproduction Service No. ED 241 926)

Azrin, N. H., & Besalel, V. B. (1980). *Job club counselor's manual: A behavioral approach to vocational counseling.* Austin, TX: PRO-ED.

Bagai, E., & Bagai, J. (Eds.). (1979). *System FORE handbook.* North Hollywood, CA: Foreworks Publications.

Baker, A. (1990). *Educating at-risk youth: Practical tips for teachers.* Washington, DC: Office of Educational Research and Improvement. (ERIC Document Reproduction Service No. ED 319 876)

Baker, L., & Brown, A. L. (1980). *Metacognitive skills and reading* (Technical report no. 188). Urbana: University of Illinois, Center for the Study of Reading.

Banks, J. A. (1989). Integrating the curriculum with ethnic content: Approaches and guidelines. In J. A. Banks & C. A. McGee Banks (Eds.), *Multicultural education: Issues and perspectives* (pp. 189–207). Boston: Allyn & Bacon.

Banks, J. A. (1991). *Teaching strategies for ethnic studies* (5th ed.). Boston: Allyn & Bacon.

Banks, J. A. (1992, Fall). It's up to us. *Teaching Tolerance,* pp. 20–23.

Barker, L. L. (1971). *Listening behavior.* Englewood Cliffs, NJ: Prentice-Hall.

Baruth, L. G., & Manning, M. L. (1992). *Multicultural education of children and adolescents.* Boston: Allyn & Bacon.

Baughman, M. D. (1974). *Baughman's handbook of humor in education.* West Nyack, NY: Parker.

Baush, J. P. (1989). The transParent school model: New technology for parent involvement. *Educational Leadership, 47*(2), 32–35.

Bauwens, J., & Hourcade, J. (1991). Making co-teaching a mainstreaming strategy. *Preventing School Failure, 35*(4), 19–24.

Bauwens, J., Hourcade, J., & Friend, M. (1989). Cooperative teaching: A model for general and special education integration. *Remedial and Special Education, 10*(2), 17–22.

Beattie, J., & Algozzine, B. (1982). Improving basic academic skills of educable mentally retarded adolescents. *Education and Training of the Mentally Retarded, 17,* 255–258.

Bell, D., Feraios, A. J., & Bryan, T. (1991). Learning disabled adolescents' knowledge and attitudes about AIDS. *Learning Disabilities Research & Practice, 6*(2), 104–111.

Bender, M., & Valletutti, P. J. (1982). *Teaching functional academics: A curriculum guide for adolescents and adults with learning problems.* Baltimore: University Park Press.

Bender, W. N. (1985). Differences between learning disabled and non-learning disabled children in temperament and behavior. *Learning Disabilities Quarterly, 8,* 11–18.

Benz, M. R., & Halpern, A. S. (1987). Vocational and transition services needed and received by students with disabilities during their last year of high school. *Career Development for Exceptional Individuals, 16,* 197–211.

Berkell, D. E., & Brown, J. M. (1989). *Transition from school to work for persons with disabilities.* New York: Longman.

Berliner, D. C. (1984). The half-full glass: A review of research on teaching. In P. L. Hosford (Ed.), *Using what we know about teaching* (pp. 51–77). Alexandria, VA: Association for Supervision and Curriculum Development.

Berliner, D. C. (1986). In pursuit of the expert pedagogue. *Educational Research, 15,* 5–14.

Bigge, J. (1988). *Curriculum-based instruction for special education students.* Mountain View, CA: Mayfield.

Billingsley, B. S., & Wildman, T. W. (1990). Facilitating reading comprehension in learning disabled students: Metacognitive goals and instructional strategies, *Remedial and Special Education, 11*(2), 18–31.

Blackhurst, A. E., & Berdine, W. H. (1993). *An introduction to special education* (3rd ed.). New York: Harper Collins.

Blackman, S., & Goldstein, K. M. (1982). Cognitive styles and learning disabilities. *Journal of Learning Disabilities, 15,* 106–115.

Blackorby, J. (1993). Participation in vocational education by students with disabilities. In M. Wagner (Ed.), *The secondary school programs of students with disabilities: A report from the national longitudinal transition study of special education students* (pp. 122–169). Menlo Park, CA: SRI International. (ERIC Document Reproduction Service No. ED 365 084)

Blackorby, J., Edgar, E., & Kortering, L. J. (1991). A third of our youth: A look at the problem of high school dropout among students with mild handicaps. *Journal of Special Education, 25* 102–113.

Blackwood, R. O. (1970). The operant conditioning of verbally mediated self-control in the classroom. *Journal of School Psychology, 8,* 251–258.

Blalock, G., Polloway, E., & Patton, J. (1989). Strategies for working with significant others. In E.

Polloway, J. R. Patton, J. S. Payne, & R. A. Payne (Eds.), *Strategies for teaching learners with special needs* (pp. 125–147). Columbus, OH: Merrill.

Blankenship, C. S. (1985). Using curriculum-based assessment data to make instructional decisions. *Exceptional Children, 52,* 233–238.

Blankenship, C. S., & Lilly, M. S. (1981). *Mainstreaming students with learning and behavior problems.* New York: Holt, Rinehart & Winston.

Bloom, B. M., Englehart, E., Furst, W., & Krathwohl, D. (1956). *Taxonomy of educational objectives: Handbook 1. Cognitive domain.* New York: David McKay.

Blumberg, T. L. (1986). Transforming low achieving and disruptive adolescents into model students. *The School Counselor, 34,* 67–72.

Bodner, J. R., Clark, G. M., & Mellard, D. F. (1987). *State graduation policies and program practices related to high school special education programs: A national study.* Lawrence: University of Kansas, Department of Special Education. (ERIC Document Reproduction Service No. ED 294 347)

Borich, G. D. (1988). *Effective teaching methods.* Columbus, OH: Merrill.

Bos, C. S., & Vaughn, S. (1994). *Strategies for teaching students with learning and behavior problems* (3rd ed.). Boston: Allyn & Bacon.

Bostic, M. (1994, May). *Juvenile crime prevention strategies: A law enforcement perspective.* Paper presented at the Council of State Governments Conference on School Violence, Westlake Village, CA.

Bottge, B. A., & Hasselbring, T. S. (1993). A comparison of two approaches for teaching complex, authentic mathematics problems to adolescents in remedial math classes. *Exceptional Children, 59,* 556–566.

Boyer, E. L. (1983). *High school.* New York: Harper & Row.

Braddock, J. H., III (1990). Tracking the middle grades: National patterns of grouping for instruction. *Phi Delta Kappan, 71,* 445–449.

Bragman, R., & Cole, J. C. (1984). *Job–match: A process for interviewing and hiring qualified handicapped individuals.* Alexandria, VA: American Society for Personnel Administration.

Brigance, A. (1981). *Brigance diagnostic inventory of essential skills.* North Billerica, MA: Curriculum Associates.

Brigance, A. (1983). *Brigance diagnostic comprehensive inventory of basic skills.* North Billerica, MA: Curriculum Associates.

Brigance, A. (1995). *Brigance inventory of life skills.* North Billerica, MA: Curriculum Associates.

Briganti, M. (1989). *An ESE teacher's guide for working with the limited English proficient student.* Orlando, FL: Orange County Public Schools.

Briggs, S. J. (1991). The multilingual/multicultural classroom. *Kappa Delta Pi Record, 28*(1), 11–15.

Brolin, D. E. (1989). *Life centered career education: A competency-based approach.* Reston, VA: Council for Exceptional Children.

Brolin, D. E. (1992a). *Life centered career education: Competency assessment knowledge battery.* Reston, VA: Council for Exceptional Children.

Brolin, D. E. (1992b). *Life centered career education: Competency assessment performance battery.* Reston, VA: Council for Exceptional Children.

Brolin, D. E. (1992c). *Life centered career education (LCCE) curriculum program.* Reston, VA: Council for Exceptional Children.

Brolin, D. E. (1993). *Life centered career education: A competency-based approach* (4th ed.). Reston, VA: Council for Exceptional Children.

Brolin, D. E. (1995). *Career education: A functional life skills approach* (3rd ed.). Englewood Cliffs, NJ: Prentice-Hall.

Brolin, D. E. (in press). *Life centered career education: Self-determination scale.* Reston, VA: Council for Exceptional Children.

Brookins, G. K. (1991). Socialization of African-American adolescents. In R. M. Lerner, A. C. Petersen, & J. Brooks-Gunn (Eds.), *Encyclopedia of adolescence* (Vol. 11, pp. 1072–1076). New York: Garland.

Brophy, J. E. (1979). Teacher behavior and its effects. *Journal of Educational Psychology, 71,* 733–750.

Brophy, J. E. (1987). Synthesis of research on strategies for motivating students to learn. *Educational Leadership, 45,* 40–48.

Brophy, J. E., & Good, T. L. (1986). Teacher behavior and student achievement. In M. C. Wittrock (Ed.), *Handbook of research on teaching* (3rd ed.). New York: Macmillan.

Brough, J. A. (1995). Middle level education: An historical perspective. In M. J. Wavering (Ed.), *Educating young adolescents: Life in the middle* (pp. 27–52). New York: Garland.

Brown, A. L., & Palincsar, A. S. (1982). Inducing strategic learning from texts by means of informed, self-control training. *Topics in Learning and Learning Disabilities, 2*(1), 1–17.

Brown, B. B. (1990). Peer groups and peer cultures. In S. S. Felman & G. R. Elliot (Eds.), *At the threshold: The developing adolescent* (pp. 30–35). Cambridge: Harvard University Press.

Brown, G. L. (1991). *Reading and language arts curricula in elementary and secondary education for*

*American Indians and Alaska Natives.* Washington, DC: U.S. Department of Education. (ERIC Document Reproduction Service No. ED 343 766)

Brown, G. M., Kerr, M. M., Zigmond, N., & Harris, A. L. (1984). What's important for student success in high school? "Successful" and "unsuccessful" students discuss school survival skills. *High School Journal, 68*(1), 10–17.

Brown, J., & Retish, P. (1987). Postsecondary institutions and support systems for special needs learners. In G. D. Meers (Ed.), *Handbook of special vocational needs education* (2nd ed.). Rockville, MD: Aspen Systems.

Brown, J. S., Collins, A., & Dugrud, P. (1989). Situated cognition and culture of learning. *Educational Researcher, 18*(1), 32–41.

Bruininks, R. H., Thurlow, M. L., Lewis, D. R., & Larson, N. W. (1988). Post school outcomes for students in special education and other students one to eight years after high school. In R. H. Bruininks, D. R. Lewis, & M. L. Thurlow (Eds.), *Assessing outcomes, costs and benefits of special education programs* (pp. 9–111). Minneapolis: University of Minnesota, University Affiliated Program.

Bryan, T., Donahue, M., & Pearl, R. (1981). Learning disabled children's peer interactions during a small group problem-solving task. *Learning Disabilities Quarterly, 4*, 13–22.

Bryan, T., Werner, M., & Pearl, R. (1982). Learning disabled students' conformity responses to prosocial and antisocial situations. *Learning Disabilities Quarterly, 5*, 344–352.

Buchanan, C. M. (1991). Assessment of pubertal development. In R. M. Lerner, A. C. Petersen, & J. Brooks-Gunn (Eds.), *Encyclopedia of adolescence* (Vol. 11, pp. 875–883). New York: Garland.

Buis, J. M., & Thompson, D. N. (1989). Imaginary audience and personal fable: A brief review. *Adolescence, 24*, 773–782.

Bulgren, J. A., Deshler, D. D., & Schumaker, J. B. (1993). *The content enhancement series: The concept mastery routine.* Lawrence, KS: Edge Enterprises.

Bullis, M., & Gaylord–Ross, R. (1991). Moving on: *Transitions for youth with behavioral disorders.* Reston, VA: Council for Exceptional Children.

Burbach, H. (1995). *Violence and the public schools.* VA: Curry School of Education.

Burnette, J. (1987). *Adapting instructional materials for mainstreamed students.* Washington, DC: U.S. Department of Education, Office of Special Education Programs.

Burnham, S. C., & Housley, W. F. (1992). Pride in work: Perceptions of employers, service providers and students who are mentally retarded and learning disabled. *Career Development for Exceptional Individuals, 15*(1), 101–108.

Burns, N., & Shipstead, J. (1989). *Community referenced life skills curriculum for elementary school children with special needs.* Unpublished manuscript. Lawrence: University of Kansas, Department of Special Education.

Bursuck, B., Kinder, D., & Epstein, M. H. (1989). Teacher ratings of school survival skills and setting demands in junior high school settings. In S. L. Braaten, R. B. Rutherford, Jr., T. F. Reilly, & S. A. DiGangi (Eds.), *Programming for adolescents with behavioral disorders* (Vol. 4, pp. 19). Reston, VA: Council for Children with Behavioral Disorders.

Burton, L., & Bero, F. (1984). Is career education really being taught? A second look. *Academic Therapy, 19*, 389–395.

Butler, J. A. (1987). *Homework* (School improvement research series: Research you can use). Portland, OR: Northwest Regional Educational Laboratory. (ERIC Document Reproduction Service No. ED 291 145)

Byrom, E. (1990). Hypermedia (multimedia). *Teaching Exceptional Children, 22*(4), 47–48.

Byrom, E., & Katz, G. (1991). *HIV prevention and AIDS education: Resources for special educators.* Reston VA: Council for Exceptional Children.

Califano, J. (1994). *Cigarette, alcohol, marijuana: Gateways to illicit drug use.* New York: Columbia University Center on Addiction and Substance Abuse.

California Education Transition Center. (1990). *Synthesis of individual transition plans: Format and process.* Sacramento: Author.

Cameto, R. (1993). Support services provided by secondary schools. In M. Wagner (Ed.), *The secondary school programs of students with disabilities: A report from the national longitudinal transition study of special education students* (pp. 170–211). Menlo Park, CA: SRI International. (ERIC Document Reproduction Service No. ED 365 084)

Campbell, P., Hensel, J. W., Hudson, P., Schwartz, S. E., & Sealander, K. (1987). The successfully employed worker with a handicap: Employee/employer perceptions of job performance. *Career Development for Exceptional Individuals, 10*(2), 85–94.

Canter, L. (1986). *Assertive discipline.* Los Angeles: Canter & Associates.

Capuzzi, D. (1988). *Counseling and intervention strategies for adolescent suicide prevention* (Report No. 48109–1259). Washington, DC: Office of Educational Research and Improvement. (ERIC Document Reproduction ED290 119)

Carmen, R. A., & Adams, W. R. (1972). *Study skills: A student's guide for survival.* New York: Wiley.

Carnegie Council. (1989). *Turning points: Preparing American youth for the 21st century.* Washington, DC: Carnegie Council on Adolescent Development.

Carnevale, A. P., Gainer, L. J., & Meltzer, A. S. (1988). *Workplace basics: The skills employers want.* Alexandria, VA: American Society for Training and Development and the U.S. Department of Labor Employment and Training Administration.

Carr, E. M. (1985). Vocabulary overview guide: A metacognitive strategy to improve vocabulary comprehension and retention. *Journal of Reading, 8* (May), 684–689.

Carr, S. C., & Punzo, R. P. (1993). The effects of self-monitoring of academic accuracy and productivity on the performance of students with behavioral disorders. *Behavioral Disorders, 18*(4), 241–250.

Carter, J. F. (1993). Self-management: Education's ultimate goal. *Teaching Exceptional Children, 25*(3), 28–32.

Carter, J. F., & Sugai, G. (1989). Social skills curriculum analysis. *Teaching Exceptional Children, 22*(1), 36–39.

Cartledge, G. (1989). Social skills and vocational success for workers with learning disabilities. *Rehabilitation Counseling Bulletin, 33*(1), 74–79.

Cartledge, G., Stupay, D., & Kaczala, C. (1986). Social skills and social perception of LD and nonhandicapped elementary-school students. *Learning Disabilities Quarterly, 9,* 226–234.

Case, R. (1985). *Intellectual development: Birth to adulthood.* Orlando, FL: Academic Press.

Cawley, J. F., Miller, J. H., & School B. A. (1987). A brief inquiry of arithmetic word-problem-solving among learning disabled secondary students. *Learning Disabilities Focus, 2*(2), 87–93.

Cegelka, P. T., & Berdine, W. H. (1995). *Effective instruction for students with learning disabilities.* Needham Heights, MA: Allyn & Bacon.

Cegelka, P. T., & Greene, G. (1993). Transition to adulthood. In A. E. Blackhurst & W. H. Berdine (Eds.), *An introduction to special education* (3rd ed.) (pp. 137–176). New York: Harper Collins.

Centers for Disease Control and Prevention. (1992a, September). Facts about adolescents and HIV/AIDS. In *HIV/AIDS Prevention.* Rockville, MD: CDC National AIDS Clearinghouse.

Centers for Disease Control and Prevention. (1992b, Vol. 41—No. SS-5). Surveillance summaries: Abortion surveillance and influenza surveillance. In *Morbidity and Mortality Weekly Report.* Atlanta, GA: U.S. Department of Health and Human Services.

Centers for Disease Control and Prevention. (1995). *HIV/AIDS surveillance report* (Vol. 7, mid-year edition). Atlanta: U.S. Department of Health and Human Services.

Chadsey-Rusch, J. (1986). Identifying and teaching valued social behaviors. In F. R. Rusch (Ed.), *Competitive employment issues and strategies* (pp. 273–287). Baltimore: Paul H. Brookes.

Chalfant, J. C., Pysh, M. V., & Moultrie, R. (1979). Teacher assistance teams: A model for within-building based problem solving. *Learning Disabilities Quarterly, 2,* 85–96.

Chamberlain, M. (1988). Employer's rankings of factors judged critical to job success for individuals with severe disabilities. *Career Development for Exceptional Individuals, 11,* 141–147.

Chan, D. M. (1987). Curriculum development for limited-English-proficient exceptional Chinese children. In M. K. Kitano & P. C. Chin (Eds.), *Exceptional Asian children and youth* (pp. 61–69). Reston, VA: Council for Exceptional Children.

Chapman, J. E., & Heward, W. L. (1982). Improving parent-teacher communication through recorded phone messages. *Exceptional Children, 49,* 79–81.

Chase, J., & Parth, L. (1979). *Multicultural spoken here: Discovering America's people through language arts and library skills.* Santa Monica, CA: Goodyear.

Cheek, E. H., Jr., & Cheek, M. C. (1983). *Reading instruction through content teaching.* Columbus, OH: Merrill.

Cheney, D., & Foss, G. (1984). An examination of the social behavior of mentally retarded workers. *Education and Training of the Mentally Retarded, 19*(3), 216–221.

Chiang, B., Thorpe, H. W., & Darch, C. B. (1980). Effects of cross-age tutoring on word-recognition performance of learning disabled students. *Learning Disabilities Quarterly, 3*(4), 11–17.

Chinn, P. C., & Plata, M. (1987). Perspectives and educational implications of Southeastern Asian students. In M. K. Kitano & P. C. Chin (Eds.), *Exceptional Asian children and youth* (pp. 12–28). Reston, VA: Council for Exceptional Children.

Choate, J. S. (1995). Understanding curriculum. In J. S. Choate, B. E. Enright, L. J. Miller, J. A. Poteet, & T. A. Rakes (Eds.), *Curriculum-based assessment and programming* (3rd ed.) (pp. 22–42). Boston: Allyn & Bacon.

Choate, J. S., Enright, B. E., Miller, L. J., Poteet, J. A., & Rakes, T. A. (Eds.). (1995). *Curriculum-based assessment and programming* (3rd ed.). Boston: Allyn & Bacon.

Choate, J. S., & Miller, L. J. (1995). Curricular assessment and programming. In J. S. Choate, B. E. Enright, L. J. Miller, J. A. Poteet, & T. A. Rakes (Eds.),

*Curriculum-based assessment and programming* (3rd ed.). (pp. 43–77). Boston: Allyn & Bacon.

Christensen, J. W. (1991). *Global science* (3rd. ed.). Dubuque, IA: Kendall/Hunt.

Christenson, S. L., & Cleary, M. (1990). Consultation and the parent-educator partnership: A perspective. *Journal of Educational and Psychological Consultation, 1,* 219–241.

Christenson, S. L., Thurlow, M. L., & Ysseldyke, J. E. (1987). *Instructional effectiveness: Implications for effective instruction of handicapped students* (Monograph No. 4). Minneapolis: University of Minnesota, Instructional Alternatives Project.

Christenson, S. L., Ysseldyke, J. E., & Thurlow, M. L. (1989). Critical instructional factors for students with mild handicaps: An integrative review. *Remedial and Special Education, 10*(5), 21–29.

Church, G., & Bender, M. (1989). *Teaching with computers: A curriculum for special education.* Boston: College-Hill Press.

Clark, F. L., Deshler, D. D., Schumaker, J. B., Alley, G. R., & Warner, M. M. (1984). Visual imagery and self-questioning: Strategies to improve comprehension of written materials. *Journal of Learning Disabilities, 17,* 145–149.

Clark, G. M. (1991). *Functional curriculum and its place in the regular education initiative.* Paper presented at the Seventh International Conference of the Division on Career Development, Council for Exceptional Children, Kansas City, MO.

Clark, G. M. (1994). Is a functional curriculum approach compatible with an inclusive model? *Teaching Exceptional Children, 26*(2), 36–39.

Clark, G. M., Carlson, B. C., Fisher, S., Cook, I. D., & D'Alonzo, B. J. (1991). Career development for students with disabilities in elementary schools: A position statement of the Division on Career Development. *Career Development for Exceptional Individuals, 14*(2), 109–120.

Clark, G. M., & Kolstoe, O. P. (1990). *Career development and transition education for adolescents with disabilities.* Boston: Allyn & Bacon.

Clark, S. N., & Clark, D. C. (1994). *Restructuring the middle level school: Implications for school leaders.* New York: State University of New York Press.

Clement-Heist, K., Siegel, S., & Gaylord-Ross, R. (1992). Simulated and *in situ* vocational social skills training for youths with learning disabilities. *Exceptional Children, 58,* 336–345.

Click, T. (1990, January). Handout to school principals.

Cloud, N. (1991). Educational assessment. In E. V. Hamayan & J. S. Damico (Eds.), *Limiting bias in the assessment of bilingual students.* Austin, TX: PRO-ED.

Cobb, B., & Hasazi, S. (1987). School-aged transition services: Options for adolescents with mild handicaps. *Career Development for Exceptional Individuals, 10,* 15–23.

Cobb, R. B., & Larkin, D. (1985). Assessment and placement of handicapped pupils into secondary vocational education programs. *Focus on Exceptional Children, 17*(7), 1–14.

Cohen, M. W. (1986). Intrinsic motivation in the special education classroom. *Journal of Learning Disabilities, 19,* 258–261.

Cohen, P., Brook, J. S., & Kandel, D. B. (1991). Drug use, predictors and correlates of adolescent. In R. M. Lerner, A. C. Petersen, & J. Brooks-Gunn (Eds.), *Encyclopedia of adolescence* (Vol. 1, pp. 268–270). New York: Garland.

Cohen, S. A. (1987). Instructional alignment: Searching for the magic bullet. *Exceptional Researcher, 16*(8), 16–20.

Cole, C. L. (1987). Self-management. In C. R. Reynolds & L. Mann (Eds.), *Encyclopedia of special education* (pp. 1404–1405). New York: Wiley.

Cole, D. E., Protinsky, H. O., & Cross, L. H. (1992). An empirical investigation of adolescent suicidal ideation. *Adolescence, 27,* 813–818.

Coleman, M. C. (1986). *Behavior disorders: Theory and practice* (3rd ed.). Englewood Cliffs, NJ: Prentice-Hall.

Coleman, W. L., Levine, M. D., & Sandler, A. D. (1987). Learning disabilities in adolescents: Description, assessment, and management. In R. M. Lerner, A. C. Peterson, & J. Brooks-Gunn (Eds.), *Encyclopedia of adolescence, 1* (pp. 580–590). New York: Garland.

Collins, M., Carnine, D., & Gersten, R. (1987). Elaborated corrective feedback and the acquisition of reasoning skills: A study of computer-assisted instruction. *Exceptional Children, 54,* 254–262.

Comer, J. (1989). Children can: An address on school improvement. In R. Webb & F. Parkay (Eds.), *Children can: An address on school improvement by Dr. James Comer with responses from Florida's educational community* (pp. 4–17). Gainsville: University of Florida, College of Education Research and Development Center, in collaboration with the Alachua County Mental Health Association.

Conger, J. C., & Keane, S. P. (1981). Social skills intervention in the treatment of isolated or withdrawn children. *Psychological Bulletin, 90,* 478–495.

Conlin, J. R. (1985). *A history of the United States: Our land, our time.* Chicago: Coronado.

Cook, L., & Friend, M. (1990). Pragmatic issues in the development of special education consultation programs. *Preventing School Failure, 35*(1), 43–46.

Cooley, E. J., & Ayres, R. R. (1988). Self-concept and success-failure attributions of nonhandicapped students and students with learning disabilities. *Journal of Learning Disabilities 21,* 174–178.

Cooper, J. D. (1986). *Improving reading comprehension.* Boston: Houghton Mifflin.

Correa, V. I. (1989). Involving culturally diverse families in the education of their limited English proficient handicapped and at risk children. In S. Fradd & M. J. Weismantel (Eds.), *Meeting the needs of culturally and linguistically different students: A handbook for educators* (pp. 130–144). San Diego: College-Hill.

Costa, A. L., & Garmston, R. (1985). Supervision for intelligent teaching. *Educational Leadership, 42,* 70–80.

Cotton, K. (1988). *Monitoring student learning in the classroom* (School improvement research series close-up no. 4). Portland, OR: Northwest Regional Educational Lab, Assessment and Evaluation Program. (ERIC Document Reproduction Service No. ED 298 085)

Council for Exceptional Children. (1978). *Position paper on career education.* Reston, VA: Author.

Council for Exceptional Children. (1993, May). CEC policy on inclusive schools and community settings. *Teaching Exceptional Children, 25* (4, Suppl.), i–iv.

Council for Exceptional Children, Division on Career Development. (1987). *The transition of youth with disabilities to adult life.* Reston, VA: Author.

Crank, J. N., & Bulgren, J. A. (1993). Visual depictions as information organizers for enhancing achievement of students with learning disabilities. *Learning Disabilities Research & Practice, 8*(3), 140–147.

Cronin, M. E., & Gerber, P. J. (1982, October). Preparing the learning disabled adolescent for adulthood. *Topics in Learning and Learning Disabilities,* 55–68.

Cross, T. (1988). Services to minority populations: What does it mean to be a culturally competent professional? *Focal Point, 2,* 1–3.

Cruickshank, W. M. (1967). The development of education for exceptional children. In W. M. Cruickshank & G. O. Johnson (Eds.), *Education of exceptional children and youth* (2nd ed.) (pp. 3–42). Englewood Cliffs, NJ: Prentice-Hall.

Cruickshank, W. M., & Paul, J. (1980). The psychological characteristics of children with learning disabilities. In W. M. Cruickshank (Ed.), *Psychology of exceptional children and youth* (4th ed.) (pp. 497–541). Englewood Cliffs, NJ: Prentice-Hall.

Cuban, L. (1992). What happens to reforms that last? The case of the junior high school. *American Educational Research Journal, 29,* 227–251.

Cullinan, D., Epstein, M. H., & Sabornie, E. J. (1992). Selected characteristics of a national sample of seriously emotionally disturbed adolescents. *Behavioral Disorders, 17,* 273–280.

Cullinan, D., Schloss, P. J., & Epstein, M. H. (1987). Relative prevalence and correlates among seriously emotionally disturbed and nonhandicapped students. *Behavioral Disorders, 12,* 90–98.

Cummins, J. (1984). *Bilingual special education: Issues in assessment and pedagogy.* San Diego: College-Hill.

Curtis, M. J., & Meyers, J. (1988). Consultation: A foundation for alternative services in the schools. In J. L. Graden, J. E. Zins, & M. J. Curtis (Eds.), *Alternative educational delivery systems: Enhancing instructional options for all students* (pp. 35–48). Washington, DC: National Association of School Psychologists.

D'Alonzo, B. J. (1983). *Educating adolescents with learning and behavior problems.* Rockville, MD: Aspen.

Darch, C., & Gersten, R. (1986). Direction-setting activities in reading comprehension: A comparison of two approaches. *Learning Disabilities Quarterly, 9,* 235–243.

Dean, A. V., Salend, S. J., & Taylor, L. (1993). Multicultural education: A challenge for special educators. *Teaching Exceptional Children, 26*(1), 40–43.

Deci, E. L., & Chandler, C. L. (1986). The importance of motivation for the future of the LD field. *Journal of Learning Disabilities, 19,* 587–594.

Deci, E. L., Hodges, R., Pierson, L., & Tomassone, J. (1992). Autonomy and competence as motivational factors in students with learning disabilities and emotional handicaps. *Journal of Learning Disabilities, 23,* 457–471.

Delgado, M., & Rodriguez-Andrew, S. (1990). *Alcohol and other drug use among Hispanic youth. OSAP technical report 4.* (Report No. DHHS-ADM-90–1726). Rockville, MD: Office for Substance Abuse Prevention. (ERIC Document Reproduction Service No. ED 342 869)

Delquadri, J. C., Greenwood, C. R., Stretton, K., & Hall, R. V. (1983). The peer tutoring program: A classroom procedure for increasing opportunity to respond and spelling performance. *Education and Treatment of Children, 6,* 225–239.

Denham, C., & Lieberman, A. (1980). *Time to learn.* Washington, DC: National Institute of Education.

Deno, S. L. (1987). Curriculum-based measurement. *Teaching Exceptional Children, 20*(1), 41–42.

Derman-Sparks, L. (1989). *Anti-bias curriculum.* Washington, DC: National Association for the Education of Young Children.

Derry, S. J., & Murphy, D. A. (1986). Designing systems that treat learning ability: From theory to practice. *Review of Educational Research, 56,* 1–39.

Deshler, D. D., Alley, G. R., Warner, M. M., & Schumaker, J. B. (1981). Instructional practices for promoting skill acquisition and generalization in severely learning disabled adolescents. *Learning Disabilities Quarterly, 4,* 415–421.

Deshler, D. D., & Schumaker, J. B. (1986). Learning strategies: An instructional alternative for low-achieving adolescents. *Exceptional Children, 52,* 483–490.

Deshler, D. D., & Schumaker, J. B. (1988). An instructional model for teaching students how to learn. In J. L. Graden, J. E. Zins, & M. L. Curtis (Eds.), *Alternative educational delivery systems: Enhancing instructional options for all students* (pp. 391–411). Washington, DC: National Association of School Psychologists.

Deshler, D. D., Schumaker, J. B., Alley, G. R., Warner, M. M., & Clark, F. L. (1982). Learning disabilities in adolescents and young adult populations: Research implications (Part 1). *Focus on Exceptional Children, 15*(1), 1–12.

Deshler, D. D., Warner, M. M., Schumaker, J. B., & Alley, G. R. (1983). Learning Strategies Intervention Model: Key components and current status. In J. D. McKinney & L. Feagans (Eds.), *Current topics in learning disabilities* (pp. 245–283). Norwood, NJ: Ablex.

Dettmer, P., Thurston, L. P., & Dyck, N. (1993). *Consultation, collaboration, and teamwork for students with special needs.* Needham Heights, MA: Allyn & Bacon.

Dever, R. B. (1988). *Community living skills: A taxonomy.* Washington, DC: American Association on Mental Retardation.

Devine, T. G. (1987). *Teaching study skills.* Boston: Allyn & Bacon.

Devlin, S. D., & Elliott, R., Jr. (1992). Drug use patterns of adolescents with behavioral disorders. *Behavioral Disorders, 17,* 264–272.

DiLeo, D. (1991). Corporate-sponsored supported employment increasing. *Supported Employment InfoLines, 2*(2), 1–3.

Dillard, J. M. (1983). *Multicultural counseling: Toward ethnic and cultural relevance in human encounters.* Chicago: Nelson-Hall.

Dixon, R., & Engelmann, S. (1980). *Corrective spelling through morphographs.* Chicago: Science Research Associates.

Dodge, K. A., & Murphy, R. R. (1984). The assessment of social competence in adolescence. In P. L. Karoly & J. J. Steffen (Eds.), *Advances in child behavioral analysis and therapy: Vol. 3. Adolescent behavior disorders: Foundations and contemporary concerns* (pp. 61–96). Lexington, MA: Lexington Books.

Dohm, E., & Bryan, T. (1994). Attribution instruction. *Teaching Exceptional Children, 26*(4), 61–63.

Dorwick, P. (1986). *Social survival for children.* New York: Brunner/Mazel.

Drayer, A. M. (1979). *Problems in middle and high school teaching.* Boston: Allyn & Bacon.

Dubas, J. S., Graber, J. A., & Petersen, A. C. (1991). The effects of pubertal development on achievement during adolescence. *American Journal of Education, 99,* 444–460.

Dunn, K., & Dunn, R. (1978). *Diagnosing learning styles.* St. John's University: Center for the Study of Learning and Teaching Styles.

Dunn, R. (1990). Bias over substance: A critical analysis of Kavale and Forness' report on modality-based instruction. *Exceptional Children, 56,* 352–356.

Duran, R. P. (1989). Assessment and instruction of at-risk Hispanic students. *Exceptional Children, 56,* 154–159.

Eccles, J. S. (1991). Academic achievement. In R. M. Lerner, A. C. Petersen, & J. Brooks-Gunn (Eds.), *Encyclopedia of adolescence* (Vol. 1, pp. 1–5). New York: Garland.

Eccles, J. S., & Midgley, C. (1989). Stage environment fit: Developmentally appropriate classrooms for young adolescents. In R. E. Ames & C. Ames (Eds.), *Research in motivation in education* (Vol. 3, pp. 139–186). New York: Academic Press.

Edelman, M. W. (1988). Preventing adolescent pregnancy: A role for social work services. *Urban Education, 22,* 496–509.

Edelman, M. W. (1993). Testimony prepared for the Joint Senate–House Hearing on Keeping Every Child Safe: Curbing the Epidemic of Violence, 103rd Cong., 1st sess., March 10.

Edgar, E. (1987). Secondary programs in special education: Are many of them justifiable? *Exceptional Children, 53,* 555–561.

Edgar, E. (1988). Employment as an outcome for mildly handicapped students: Current status and future directions. *Focus on Exceptional Children, 2*(1), 1–8.

Education Commission of the States. (1985). *Clearinghouse notes. State activity: Minimum competency testing as of November, 1985.* Washington, DC: Author.

Educational Communications, Inc. (1993). *Who's who among American high school students.* Los Angeles: Author.

Edwards, L. L. (1983). Curriculum modification as a strategy for helping regular classroom behavior disordered students. In E. L. Meyen, G. A. Vergason, & R. J. Whelan (Eds.), *Promising practices for exceptional children: Curriculum implications.* Denver: Love.

Eichhorn, D. (1991). Why middle schools? In J. Capelluti & D. Stokes (Eds.), *Middle level education:*

*Programs, policies, and practices* (pp. 1–5). Reston, VA: National Association of Secondary School Principals.

Elias, M., & Clabby, J. (1988). Teaching social decision making. *Educational Leadership, 45*(6), 52–55.

Elkind, D. (1978). Understanding the young adolescent. *Adolescence, 13,* 127–134.

Elksnin, N., & Elksnin, L. K. (1988). Improving job–seeking skills of adolescents with handicaps through job clubs. *Career Development for Exceptional Individuals, 11*(2), 118–125.

Ellis, E. S. (1983). *The effects of teaching learning disabled adolescents an executive strategy to facilitate self-generation of task-specific strategies.* Unpublished doctoral dissertation, University of Kansas, Lawrence.

Ellis, E. S. (1986). The role of motivation and pedagogy on the generalization of cognitive strategy training. *Journal of Learning Disabilities, 19,* 66–70.

Ellis, E. S. (1989). A metacognitive intervention for increasing class participation. *Learning Disabilities Focus, 5,* 36–46.

Ellis, E. S. (1993). Integrative strategy instruction: A potential model for teaching content area subjects to adolescents with learning disabilities. *Journal of Learning Disabilities, 26,* 358–383, 398.

Ellis, E. S., Deshler, D. D., Lenz, B. K., Schumaker, J. B., & Clark, F. L. (1989). An instructional model for teaching learning strategies. In *The strategies intervention model: Planning for a strategic environment* (pp. 1–32). Lawrence: University of Kansas Institute for Research in Learning Disabilities.

Ellis, E. S., Deshler, D. D., & Schumaker, J. B. (1989). Teaching adolescents with learning disabilities to generate and use task-specific strategies. *Journal of Learning Disabilities, 22,* 108–119.

Ellis, E. S., & Lenz, B. K. (1987). A component analysis of effective learning strategies for LD students. *Learning Disabilities Focus, 2,* 94–107.

Ellis, E. S., & Lenz, B. K. (1990). Techniques for mediating content-area learning: Issues and research. *Focus on Exceptional Children, 22*(9), 1–16.

Ellis, E. S., Lenz, B. K., & Sabornie, E. J. (1987). Generalization and adaptation of learning strategies to natural environments: Part 2. Research into practice. *Remedial and Special Education, 8*(2), 6–23.

Elrod, G. F., & Lyons, B. A. (1987). A nation at risk or a policy at risk? How about career education. *Career Development for Exceptional Individuals, 10*(1), 10–14.

Emmer, E. T., Evertson, C. M., Clements, B. S., & Worsham, M. E. (1994). *Classroom management for secondary teachers* (3rd ed.). Boston: Allyn & Bacon.

Engelmann, S., Becker, W., Hanner, S., & Johnson, G. (1988). *Corrective reading: Decoding.* Chicago: Science Research Associates.

Engelmann, S., Becker, W., Hanner, S., & Johnson, G. (1989). *Corrective reading: Comprehension.* Chicago: Science Research Associates.

Engelmann, S., & Carnine, D. (1982a). *Corrective mathematics program.* Chicago: Science Research Associates.

Engelmann, S., & Carnine, D. (1982b). *Theory of instruction: Principles and applications.* New York: Irvington.

Engelmann, S., Osborn, J., & Hanner, S. (1978). *Corrective reading.* Chicago: Science Research Associates.

Englert, C. S. (1984). Effective direct instruction practices in special education settings. *Remedial and Special Education, 5*(2), 38–47.

Englert, C. S., Tarrant, K. L., & Mariage, T. V. (1992). Defining and redefining instructional practice in special education: Perspectives on good teaching. *Teacher Education and Special Education, 15*(2), 62–86.

Enright, B. E. (1983). *Enright diagnostic inventory of basic arithmetic skills.* North Billerica, MA: Curriculum Associates.

Enright, B. E., Gable, R. A., & Hendrickson, J. (1988). How do students get answers like these? *Diagnostique, 13*(2–4), 55–63.

Ensminger, E. E., & Dangel, H. L. (1992). The Foxfire pedagogy: A confluence of best practices for special education. *Focus on Exceptional Children, 24*(7), 1–16.

Ensminger, G. (1991). Defragmenting fragmented learners. *Hands-On: A Journal for Teachers, 39,* 44–48.

Epstein, J., & MacIver, D. (1989). *Education in the middle grades: Overview of a national survey of practices and trends.* Baltimore: Johns Hopkins University Center for Research on Elementary and Middle Schools.

Epstein, J. L. (1989). Building parent-teacher partnerships in inner-city schools. *Family Resource Coalition Report, 8,* 7.

Epstein, M. H. (1982). Special education programs for the handicapped adolescent. *School Psychology Review, 11*(4), 384–390.

Epstein, M. H., & Cullinan, D. (1988). Selected research issues in the education of adolescents with behavioral disorders. In R. B. Rutherford, Jr., & J. W. Maag (Eds.), Severe behavior disorders of children and youth (pp. 106–119). Boston: Little, Brown.

Epstein, M. H., Cullinan, D., & Polloway, E. A. (1986). Patterns of maladjustment among mentally retarded children and youth. *American Journal of Mental Deficiency, 91,* 127–134.

Epstein, M. H., Kauffman, J. M., & Cullinan, D. (1985). Patterns of maladjustment among the behaviorally disordered: 2. Boys aged 6–11, boys aged 12–18, girls aged 6–11, and girls aged 12–18. *Behavioral Disorders, 10,* 125–135.

Epstein, M. H., Patton, J. R., Polloway, E. A., & Foley, R. (1989, March). Mild retardation: Student characteristics and services. *Education and Training of the Mentally Retarded,* pp. 7–16.

ERIC. (1987). Post-school status of learning disabled students. *Research & Resources on Special Education: Abstract VII,* 1–2.

Erikson, E. (1968). *Identity, youth, and crisis.* New York: W. W. Norton.

ESOL. (1991). *Strategies for content area teaching: Teaching test-taking strategies* [Videotape]. Boca Raton: Florida International University, WLRN-TV.

Evans, R. N., & Herr, E. L. (1978). *Foundations of vocational education* (2nd ed.). Columbus, OH: Merrill.

Evans, S., & Evans, W. (1986). A perspective on assessment for instruction. *Pointer, 30,* 9–12. .

Fairweather, J. S., & Shaver, D. M. (1991). Making the transition to postsecondary education and training. *Exceptional Children, 57,* 264–270.

Falvey, M. A. (1986). *Community-based curriculum: Instructional strategies for students with severe handicaps.* Baltimore: Paul H. Brookes.

Farrington, D. P. (1987). Early precursors of frequent offending. In J. Q. Wilson & G. C. Loury (Eds.), *From children to citizens: Vol. 3. Families, schools, and delinquency prevention* (pp. 27–51). New York: Springer-Verlag.

Farris, R. A. (1990). Meeting their needs: Motivating middle level learners. *Middle School Journal, 22*(2), 22–26.

FDLRS/TECH. (1991). *Instructional technology: Classroom applications to assist ESE teachers.* Merritt Island, FL: Author.

FDLRS/TECH (1994). *Florida Department of Education educational software project: 1993–1994 software catalogue.* Merritt Island, FL: Author.

Feagans, L. (1983). A current review of learning disabilities. *Journal of Pediatrics, 5,* 487–493.

Feather, N. (Ed.). (1982). *Expectations and actions.* Hillsdale, NJ: Erlbaum.

Feighan, M. (1991). *School violence.* Report given to the House of Representatives Subcommittee on Crime Series No. 144, House of Representatives, One Hundred First Congress, Second Session, on H. R. 3757. Washington, DC: U.S. Government Printing Office.

Fenzel, L. M. (1989). Role strains and the transition to middle school: Longitudinal trends and sex differences. *Adolescence, 9,* 211–226.

Fenzel, L. M., & Blyth, D. A. (1991). Schooling. In R. M. Lerner, A. C. Petersen, & J. Brooks-Gunn (Eds.), *Encyclopedia of adolescence* (Vol. 11, pp. 974–975). New York: Garland.

Fenzel, L. M., Blyth, D. A., & Simmons, R. G. (1991). Secondary school transitions. In R. M. Lerner, A. C. Petersen, & J. Brooks-Gunn (Eds.), *Encyclopedia of adolescence* (Vol. 11, pp. 970–973). New York: Garland.

Figueroa, R. A. (1989). Psychological testing of linguistic-minority students: Knowledge gaps and regulations. *Exceptional Children, 56,* 145–153.

Figueroa, R. A., Fradd, S. H., & Correa, V. I. (1989). Bilingual special education and this special issue. *Exceptional Children, 56*(2), 174–178.

Fisher, C. B., & Brone, R. J. (1991). Eating disorders in adolescence. In R. M. Lerner, A. C. Petersen, & J. Brooks-Gunn (Eds.), *Encyclopedia of adolescence* (Vol. 1, pp. 272–273). New York: Garland.

Fitzgerald, G. (1990). *Tech Use Guide: Using the computer with students with emotional and behavioral disorders.* Washington, DC: Office of Special Education and Rehabilitative Services. (ERIC Document Reproduction Service No. ED 339 155)

Flavell, J. (1976). Metacognitive aspects of problem solving. In L. B. Resnick (Ed.), *The nature of intelligence.* Hillsdale, NJ: Erlbaum.

Flavell, J. (1977). *Cognitive development.* Englewood Cliffs, NJ: Prentice-Hall.

Florida Department of Education. (1989). *Evaluating effectiveness, usefulness, practicality of cooperative consultation: 1987–1988 pilot study in Florida secondary schools* (Research Report 10). Tallahassee: Author.

Florida Department of Education. (1993). *Transition the IDEA way.* Tallahassee: Bureau of Education for Exceptional Students.

Florida Department of Education. (1994). *Specialized curriculum for exceptional students: Instructor's manual.* Tallahassee: Bureau of Education for Exceptional Students.

Florida Hospital. (1987). *Suicide.* Orlando: Author.

Florida Performance Measurement System. (1984). *Domains: Knowledge base of the Florida Performance Measurement System.* Tallahassee: Florida Coalition for the Development of a Performance Measurement System, Office of Teacher Education, Certification and Inservice Staff Development.

Foley, R. M., & Epstein, M. H. (1993). A structured instructional system for developing the school survival skills of adolescents with behavioral disorders. *Behavioral Disorders, 18*(2), 139–147.

Forman, S. G. (1993). *Coping skills interventions for children and adolescents.* San Francisco: Jossey-Bass.

Forness, S. R., & Polloway, E. A. (1987). Physical and psychiatric diagnoses of pupils with mild mental retardation currently being referred for related services. *Education and Training in Mental Retardation, 22,* 221–228.

Foss, G., Auty, W. P., & Irvin, L. K. (1989). A comparative evaluation of modeling, problem-solving, and behavior rehearsal for teaching employment-related interpersonal skills to secondary students with mental retardation. *Education and Training of the Mentally Retarded, 24*(1), 17–27.

Foss, G., & Vilhauer, D. (1986). *Working I & II: Interpersonal skills assessment and training for employment.* Santa Monica, CA: James Stanfield.

Foster, V., & Sprinthall, N. A. (1992). Developmental profiles of adolescents and young adults choosing abortion: Stage sequence, decalage, and implications for policy. *Adolescence, 27,* 655–673.

Foster-Clark, F. S., & Blyth, D. A. (1991). Peer relations and influences. In R. M. Lerner, A. C. Petersen, & J. Brooks-Gunn (Eds.), *Encyclopedia of adolescence* (Vol. 11, pp. 767–771). New York: Garland.

Foyle, H. C., & Bailey, G. D. (1986). Homework: Its real purpose. *Clearing House, 60,* 187–188.

Frank, A. R., Sitlington, P. L., & Carson, R. (1991). Transition of adolescents with behavioral disorders: Is it successful? *Behavioral Disorders, 16,* 180–191.

Franklin, M. E. (1992). Culturally sensitive instructional practices for African-American learners with disabilities. *Exceptional Children, 59,* 115–122.

Friedman, B. (1986). If only I had one more computer. *Classroom Computer Learning, 7*(2), 44–45.

Friend, M., & Bauwens, J. (1988). Managing resistance: An essential consulting skill for learning disabilities teachers. *Journal of Learning Disabilities, 21*(9), 556–561.

Friend, M., & Cook, L. (1990). Pragmatic issues in the development of special education consultation programs. *Preventing School Failure, 35*(1), 43–46.

Friend, M., & Cook, L. (1992a). *Interactions: Collaboration skills for school professionals.* New York: Longman.

Friend, M., & Cook, L. (1992b). The new mainstreaming: How it really works. *Instructor, 10*(7), 30–36.

Fuchs, L. S., Bahr, C. M., & Rieth, H. J. (1989). Effects of goal structures and performance contingencies on the math performance of adolescents with learning disabilities. *Journal of Learning Disabilities, 22,* 554–560.

Fukuyama, M., & Inoue-Cox, C. (1992). Cultural perspectives in communicating with Asian/Pacific Islanders. In J. Wittmer (Ed.), *Valuing diversity and similarity: Bridging the gap through interpersonal skills* (pp. 93–112). Minneapolis: Educational Media Corporations.

Fuld, J. J. (1966). *The book of world-famous music: Classical, popular, and folk.* New York: Crown.

Furstenberg, F. F. (1991). Assessment of pubertal development. In R. M. Lerner, A. C. Petersen, & J. Brooks-Gunn (Eds.), *Encyclopedia of adolescence* (Vol. 11, pp. 803–807). New York: Garland.

Gable, R. A., Young, C. C., & Hendrickson, M. J. (1987). Content of special education teacher preparation: Are we headed in the right direction? *Teacher Education and Special Education, 10*(3), 135–139.

Gajar, A., Goodman, L., & McAfee, J. (1993). *Secondary schools and beyond: Transition of individuals with mild disabilities.* New York: Macmillan.

Gallagher, P. A. (1988). *Teaching students with behavior disorders: Techniques and activities for classroom instruction.* Denver: Love.

Games, P. A. (1991). Educational achievement and tracking in high school. In R. M. Lerner, A. C. Petersen, & J. Brooks-Gunn (Eds.), *Encyclopedia of adolescence* (Vol. 1, pp. 291–294). New York: Garland.

Gamoran, A., & Behends, M. (1987). Effect of stratification in secondary schools: Synthesis of survey and ethnographic research. *Review of Educational Research, 57,* 415–435.

Gans, K. D. (1985). Regular and special educators. *Teacher Education and Special Education, 8,* 188–197.

Garcia, S. B., & Malkin, D. H. (1993). Toward defining programs and services for culturally and linguistically diverse learners in special education. *Teaching Exceptional Children, 26*(1), 52–58.

Gardner, H. (1983). *Frames of mind: The theory of multiple intelligences.* New York: Basic Books.

Garibaldi, A. (1989). Educating and motivating young black men. *In Barriers and opportunities for America's young black men* (pp. 45–52). Washington, DC: House of Representatives, Select Committee on Children, Youth, and Families.

Gartner, A., & Lipsky, D. R. (1987). Beyond special education: Toward a quality system for all students. *Harvard Educational Review, 57,* 367–395.

Gaskins, I., & Elliot, T. (1991). *Implementing cognitive strategy training across the school: The Benchmark manual for teachers.* Cambridge, MA: Brookline.

Gaustad, M. G., & Messenheimer-Young, T. (1991). Dialogue journals for students with learning disabilities. *Teaching Exceptional Children, 23*(3), 28–32.

Gay, G. (1989). Ethnic minorities and educational equality. In J. A. Banks & C. A. McGee Banks

(Eds.), *Multicultural education: Issues and perspectives* (pp. 167–188). Boston: Allyn & Bacon.

Gaylord-Ross, R., Forte, J., Storey, K., Gaylord-Ross, C., & Jameson, D. (1987). Community-referenced instruction in technological work settings. *Exceptional Children, 54,* 112–120.

Gearhart, B. R., & Weishahn, M. W. (1984). *The exceptional student in the regular classroom.* Columbus, OH: Merrill.

Genaux, M., Morgan, D. P., & Friedman, S. G. (1995). Substance use and its prevention: A survey of classroom practices. *Behavioral Disorders, 20,* 279–289.

Gerber, P. J., & Brown, D. (1991). Report of the Pathways to Employment Consensus Conference on employability of persons with learning disabilities. *Learning Disabilities Research and Practice, 6*(2), 99–103.

Gersten, R., & Maggs, A. (1982). Teaching the general case to moderately retarded children: Evaluation of a five-year project. *Analysis and Intervention in Developmental Disabilities, 2,* 329–343.

Gersten, R., & Woodward, J. (1994). The language-minority student and special education: Issues, trends, and paradoxes. *Exceptional Children, 60,* 310–322.

Gickling, E. E., & Thompson, V. (1985). A personal view of curriculum-based assessment. *Exceptional Children, 52,* 205–218.

Gilligan, C., Kohlberg, L., Lerner, M., & Belenky, M. (1987). Moral reasoning about sexual dilemmas. (In U.S. Commission on Obscenity and Pornography, *Technical report* (Vol. 4, pp. 141–174). Washington, DC: Government Printing Office.

Glatthorn, A. A. (1988). What schools should teach in the English language arts. *Educational Leadership, 46*(1), 44–51.

Glatthorn, A. A. (1990). Cooperative professional development: Facilitating the growth of the special education teacher and the classroom teacher. *Remedial and Special Education, 11*(3), 29–35.

Gleason, M. M. (1988). Teaching study strategies. *Teaching Exceptional Children, 20*(3), 52–53.

Glomb, N., & West, R. P. (1990). Teaching behaviorally disordered adolescents to use self-management skills for improving the completeness, accuracy, and neatness of creative writing homework assignments. *Behavioral Disorders, 15,* 233–242.

GOALS 2000: Educate America Act. (1994). Washington, DC.

Goldsberry, L. F. (1986). *Colleague consultation: Another case of fools rush in.* Paper presented at the annual meeting of the American Educational Research Association, San Francisco.

Goldstein, A. P., Sprafkin, R. P., Gershaw, N. J., & Klein, P. (1980). *Skill-streaming the adolescent: A structured learning approach to teaching prosocial skills.* Champaign, IL: Research Press.

Gollnick, D. M., & Chin, P. C. (1990). *Multicultural education in a pluralistic society* (3rd ed.). Columbus, OH: Merrill.

Goodman, G. (1978). *SASHAtape user's manual.* Unpublished manuscript, Department of Psychology, University of California at Los Angeles.

Goplerud, E. N. (Ed.).(1990). *Breaking new ground for youth at risk: Program summaries* (Report No. DHHS-ADM-89–1658). Rockville, MD: Office for Substance Abuse Prevention. (ERIC Document Reproduction Service No. ED 336 489)

Gordon, T. (1974). *T. E. T.: Teacher effectiveness training.* New York: Wyden.

Gottesman, I. I. (1991). *Schizophrenia genesis: The origins of madness.* New York: W. H. Freeman.

Graden, J. L., Casey, A., & Christenson, S. L. (1985). Implementing a prereferral intervention system: Part I. The model. *Exceptional Children, 51,* 377–384.

Graham, S. (1985). Teaching basic academic skills to learning-disabled students: A model for the teaching–learning process. *Journal of Learning Disabilities, 18,* 528–534.

Graham, S., Harris, K. R., & Sawyer R. (1987). Composition instruction with learning disabled students: Self-instructional strategy training. *Focus on Exceptional Children, 20*(4), 1–11.

Graham, S., & Johnson, L. A. (1989). Research-supported teacher activities that influence the text reading of students with learning disabilities. *LD Forum, 15*(1), 27–30.

Grant, R. (1993). Strategic training for using text headings to improve students' processing of content. *Journal of Reading, 36,* 482–488.

Greenan, J. P. (1989). Curriculum and assessment in generalizable skills instruction. *Journal for Vocational Special Needs Education, 9*(1), 3–10.

Greenbaum, S., Turner, B., & Stephens, R. D. (1989). *Set straight on bullies* (Report No. ISBN-0-932612–23-7). Malibu, CA: National School Safety Center. (ERIC Document Reproduction Service No. ED 312 744)

Greenspan, S., & Shoultz, B. (1981). Why mentally retarded adults lost their jobs: Social competence as a factor in work adjustment. *Applied Research in Mental Retardation, 2,* 23–28.

Greenwood, C. R., & Rieth, H. J. (1994). Current dimensions of technology-based assessment in special education. *Exceptional Children, 61,* 105–113.

Greenwood, R. (1990). Employment and workers with disabilities. *OSERS News in Print, 3*(3), 25–28.

Gregory, R. P., Hackney, C., & Gregory, N. M. (1982). Corrective reading programs: An evaluation. *British Journal of Educational Psychology, 52,* 33–50.

Gresham, F. M. (1983). Social skills assessment as a component of mainstreaming placement decisions. *Exceptional Children, 48,* 331–336.

Griffin, R. S. (1988). *Underachievers in secondary schools: Education off the mark.* Hillsdale, NJ: Erlbaum.

Grosenick, J. K., George, N. L., & George, M. L. (1987). A profile of school programs for the behaviorally disordered: Twenty years after Morse, Cutler, and Fink. *Behavioral Disorders, 12,* 159–168.

Grossman, D. C. (1991). Risk factors for suicide attempts among Navajo adolescents. *American Journal of Public Health, 81,* 870–874.

Grossman, H. (1990). *Trouble-free teaching: Solutions to behavior problems in the classroom.* Mountain View, CA: Mayfield.

Guernsey, M. A. (1990). Curriculum based assessment and the regular classroom teacher. *Illinois Schools Journal, 69*(2), 15–19.

Guetzloe, E. C. (1991). *Suicide and the exceptional child: ERIC Digest #E508* (Report No. RI88062007). Washington, DC: Office of Educational Research and Improvement. (ERIC Document Reproduction Service No. ED 340 152)

Guiler, W. S. (1946). Difficulties in decimals encountered in ninth-grade pupils. *Elementary School Journal, 46,* 384–393.

Gutkin, T. B., & Curtis, M. J. (1982). School-based consultation: Theory and techniques. In C. R. Reynolds & T. B. Gutkin (Eds.), *The handbook of school psychology.* New York: Wiley.

Hale, J. E. (1982). *Black children: Their roots, culture, and learning styles.* Provo, UT: Brigham Young University Press.

Hale-Benson, J. E. (1986). *Black children: Their roots and their culture* (rev. ed.). Baltimore: Johns Hopkins University Press.

Hall, G. E., & Hord, S. M. (1984). *Change in schools: Facilitating the process.* Albany: State University of New York Press.

Hall, J., & Gerber, P. (1985). The awarding of Carnegie units to learning disabled school students: A policy study. *Educational Evaluation and Policy Analysis, 7,* 229–235.

Hallahan, D. P. & Kauffman, J. M. (1994). *Exceptional children: Introduction to special education* (6th ed.). Boston: Allyn & Bacon.

Hallahan, D. P., Kauffman, J. M., & Lloyd, J. W. (1985). *Introduction to learning disabilities* (2nd ed.). Englewood Cliffs, NJ: Prentice-Hall.

Hallahan, D. P., Keller, C. E., McKinney, J. D., Lloyd, J. W., & Bryan, T. (1988). Examining the research base of the Regular Education Initiative: Efficacy studies and the adaptive learning environments model. *Journal of Learning Disabilities, 21,* 29–35.

Halpern, A. S. (1992). Transition: Old wine in new bottles. *Exceptional Children, 58,* 202–211.

Halpern, A. S., & Benz, M. R. (1987). A statewide examination of secondary special education for students with mild disabilities: Implications for the high school curriculum. *Exceptional Children, 54,* 122–129.

Halpern, A. S., & Irvin, L. K. (1986). *Social and prevocational information battery.* Monterey, CA: CTB/McGraw-Hill.

Hare, B. R., & Castenell, L. A. (1985). No place to run, no place to hide: Comparative status and future prospects of black boys. In M. B. Spencer, G. K. Brookins, & W. R. Allen (Eds.), *Beginnings: The social and effective development of black children* (pp. 100–120). Hillsdale, NJ: Erlbaum.

Hargrove, L. J., & Poteet, J. A. (1984). *Assessment in special education: The educational evaluation.* Englewood Cliffs, NJ: Prentice-Hall.

Haring, K. A., & Lovett, D. L. (1990). A follow-up study of special education graduates. *Journal of Special Education, 23,* 463–477.

Haring, K. A., Lovett, D. L., & Smith D. D. (1990). A follow-up study of recent special education graduates of learning disabilities programs. *Journal of Learning Disabilities, 23,* 108–113.

Haring, N., & Eaton, M. (1978). Systematic instructional procedures: An instructional hierarchy. In N. Haring, T. Lovitt, M. Eaton, & C. Hansen (Eds.), *The fourth R: Research in the classroom* (pp. 23–40). Columbus, OH: Merrill/Macmillan.

Harrington, T., & O'Shea, A. (Eds.). (1984). *Guide to occupational exploration* (2nd ed.). Circle Pines, MN: American Guidance Service.

Harris, K. (1991). *A descriptive study of collaboration between bilingual and special educators* (USOE research grant award). Phoenix: Arizona State University West.

Harris, K. R., & Pressley, M. (1991). The nature of cognitive strategy instruction: Interactive strategy construction. *Exceptional Children* (March/April), 392–404.

Hartwell, L. K., Kroth, R. L., & Wiseman, D. E. (1983). Communicating with parents of LBP adolescents. In B. J. D'Alonzo (Ed.), *Educating adolescents with learning and behavior problems* (pp. 91–120). Austin, TX: PRO-ED.

Harvill, R. (1992). Eating disorders. In L. M. Bullock

(Ed.), *Exceptionalities in children and youth* (pp. 450–454). Boston: Allyn & Bacon.

Hasazi, S., & Cobb, R. B. (1988). Vocational education of persons with mild disabilities. In R. Gaylord–Ross (Ed.), *Vocational education for persons with handicaps* (pp. 331–354). Mountain View, CA: Mayfield.

Hasazi, S., Gordon, L., & Roe, C. (1985). Factors associated with the employment status of handicapped youth exiting high school from 1979 to 1983. *Exceptional Children, 51,* 455–569.

Hasazi, S., Gordon, L., Roe, C., Hall, M., Finck, K., & Salembier, G. (1985). A statewide follow-up on post high school employment and residential status of students labeled "mentally retarded." *Education and Training of the Mentally Retarded, 20,* 222–234.

Hasazi, S., Johnson, R., Hasazi, J., Gordon, L., & Hall, M. (1989). Employment of youth with and without handicaps following high school: Outcomes and correlates. *Journal of Special Education, 23,* 243–255.

Hasselbring, T. S., & Goin, L. I. (1993). Integrated technology and media. In E. A. Polloway & J. R. Patton, *Strategies for teaching learners with special needs* (pp. 145–162). New York: Macmillan.

*Hawaii transition project.* (1987). Honolulu: University of Hawaii, Department of Special Education.

Hawkins, J. (1988). Antecedent pausing as a direct instruction tactic for adolescents with severe behavioral disorders. *Behavioral Disorders, 13,* 263–272.

Hawley, W. D., & Rosenholtz, S. J. (1984). Effective teaching. *Peabody Journal of Education, 61*(4), 15–52.

Hayes, C. D. (Ed.). (1987). *Risking the future: Adolescent sexuality, pregnancy, and childbearing.* Washington, DC: National Academy Press.

Hayward, B. J., Thorne, J., & Ha, P. (1989). *The educational programs of high school special education students.* Washington, DC: Office of Special Education Programs.

Hazler, R. J., & Latto, L. D. (1987). Employers' opinions on the attitudes and skills of high school graduates. *Journal of Employment Counseling, 24,* 130–136.

Heal, L. W., Copher, J. I., DeStefano, L., & Rusch, F. (1989). A comparison of successful and unsuccessful placement of secondary students with mental handicaps into competitive employment. *Career Development for Exceptional Individuals, 12,* 167–177.

Hebbeler, K. (1993a). Secondary schools: The times they are a changin'. In M. Wagner (Ed.), *The secondary school programs of students with disabilities: A report from the national longitudinal transition study of special education students* (pp. 27–41).

Menlo Park, CA: SRI International. (ERIC Document Reproduction Service No. ED 365 084)

Hebbeler, K. (1993b). *Traversing the mainstream: Regular education and students with disabilities in secondary school: A special topic report from the national longitudinal transition study of special education students.* Menlo Park, CA: SRI International. (ERIC Document Reproduction Service No. ED 370 276)

Hebbeler, K. (1993c). Overview of the high school experience of students with disabilities. In M. Wagner (Ed.), *The secondary school programs of students with disabilities: A report from the national longitudinal transition study of special education students* (pp. 56–82). Menlo Park, CA: SRI International. (ERIC Document Reproduction Service No. ED 365 084)

Heflin, L. J. (1992). Pregnancy in young people. In L. M. Bullock (Ed.), *Exceptionalities in children and youth* (pp. 476–481). Boston: Allyn & Bacon.

Helmke, L. M., Havekost, D. M., Patton, J. R., & Polloway, E. A. (1994). Life skills programming: Development of a high school science course. *Teaching Exceptional Children, 26*(2), 49–53.

Henderson, A. T. (1987). *The evidence continues to grow: Parent involvement improves student achievement.* Silver Springs, MD: National Citizens Committee in Education.

Hernandez, C. A., & Estrada, D. (1992). Cultural perspectives in communicating with Cuban Americans, Puerto Ricans, and various other Hispanic Americans. In J. Wittmer (Ed.), *Valuing diversity and similarity: Bridging the gap through interpersonal skills* (pp. 113–142). Minneapolis: Educational Media Corporations.

Heron, T. E., & Harris, K. C. (1993). *The educational consultant: Helping professionals, parents, and mainstreamed students* (3rd ed.). Austin, TX: PRO-ED.

Herrera-Escobedo, T. (1983). Parent and community involvement: A blueprint for a successful program. In O. N. Saracho & B. Spodek (Eds.), *Understanding the multicultural experience in early childhood education* (pp. 107–122). Washington, DC: National Association for the Education of Young Children.

Heward, W. L. (1996). Exceptional children: An introduction to special education (5th ed.). Englewood Cliffs, NJ: Prentice-Hall.

Heward, W. L., & Orlansky, M. D. (1992). *Exceptional children* (4th ed.). Columbus, OH: Merrill.

Hiebert, B., Wong, B., & Hunter, M. (1982). Affective influences on learning disabled adolescents. *Learning Disabilities Quarterly, 5,* 334–343.

Higgins, A. T., & Turnure, J. E. (1984). Distractibility and concentration of attention in children's development. *Child Development, 44,* 1799–1810.

Hilke, E. V. (1990). *Cooperative learning* (Fastback 299). Bloomington, IN: Phi Delta Kappa Educational Foundation.

Hill, H. D. (1989). *Effective strategies for teaching minority students.* Bloomington, IA: National Educational Service.

Hill, J. P. (1987). Research on adolescents and their families: Past and prospect. In C. E. Irwin (Ed.), *Adolescent social behavior and health* (pp. 13–31). San Francisco: Jossey-Bass.

Hill, J. W., Wehman, P., Hill, M., & Goodall, P. (1986). Differential reasons for job separation of previously employed persons with mental retardation. *Mental Retardation, 24,* 347–351.

Hillerman, A. G. (1990). *Three Jim Chee mysteries: People of darkness, The darkwind, The ghostway.* New York: Wings Books, Random House.

Hilliard, A. G., III. (1989). Teachers and cultural styles in a pluralistic society. *Today, 7*(6), 65–59.

*HIV prevention education for exceptional youth: Why HIV prevention education is important: ERIC Digest #FE507* (Report No. EDO-EC-91–12). (1991) Washington, DC: Office of Educational Research and Improvement. (ERIC Document Reproduction Service No. ED 340 151)

Hock, M. (1988). Use with executive statement on SIM G1. In B. K. Lenz, F. L. Clark, D. D. Deshler, & J. B. Schumaker (Eds.), *The strategies intervention model: Planning for a strategic environment.* Lawrence: University of Kansas Institute for Research in Learning Disabilities.

Hoffer, A. R., Johnson, M. R., Leinwald, S. J., Lodholz, R. D., Musser, G. R., & Thoburn, T. (1991). *Mathematics in action.* New York: Macmillan.

Hoffman, F. J., Sheldon, K. L., Minskoff, E. H., Sautter, S. W., Steidle, E. E., Baker, D. P., Bailey, M. B., & Echols, L. D. (1987). Needs of learning disabled adults. *Journal of Learning Disabilities, 20,* 43–52.

Hoffman, L. (1994). *Eating disorders: Decade of the brain* (NIH Publication No. 94–3477). Washington, DC: National Institute of Mental Health.

Hofmeister, A. M., & Preston, C. N. (1981). *Curriculum-based assessment and evaluation procedures.* Unpublished monograph, University of Minnesota, Minneapolis.

Holcomb, N. (1989). Recharge! How to boost your computer resources (without breaking your budget). *Teaching and Computers, 6*(5), 12–20.

Holden, C. (1986). Youth suicide: New research focuses on a growing social problem. *Science, 223,* 839–841.

Hoover, J. J. (1988). *Teaching handicapped students study skills.* Lindale, TX: Hamilton.

Hoover, J. J. (1989). Study skills and the education of students with learning disabilities. *Journal of Learning Disabilities, 22,* 452–455.

Hopke, W. E. (1984). *Encyclopedia of career and vocational guidance.* Chicago: Doubleday.

Hops, H. (1976). *Systematic analysis of social interactions: Assessment and intervention.* Paper presented at the 84th annual meeting of the American Psychological Association, Washington, DC.

Horton, S. V., Lovitt, T. C., & Christensen, C. C. (1991). Notetaking from textbooks: Effects of a columnar format on three categories of secondary students. *Journal of Special Education, 22,* 447–462.

Houck, C. K. (1993). Ellis' "potential" integrative strategy instruction model: An appealing extension of previous efforts. *Journal of Learning Disabilities, 26,* 399–403, 416.

Houston, W. R., Clift, R. T., Freiberg, H. J., & Warner, A. R. (1988). *Touch the future: Teach!* New York: West.

Howell, K. W., Zucker, S. H., & Morehead, M. K. (1982). *Multilevel academic skills inventory.* Columbus, OH: Merrill.

Hoyt, K. B. (1993). Reaction to the three solutions for transition from school to employment. *Youth Policy, 15*(6/7), 36.

Hudson, P., Lignugaris-Kraft, B., & Miller, T. (1993). Using content enhancements to improve the performance of adolescents with learning disabilities in content classes. *Learning Disabilities Research and Practice, 8,* 106–126.

Hudson, P. J., Schwartz, S. E., Sealander, K. A., Campbell, P., & Hensel, J. W. (1988). Successfully employed adults with handicaps: Characteristics and transition strategies. *Career Development for Exceptional Individuals, 11*(1), 7–14.

Huefner, D. S. (1988). The consulting teacher model: Risks and opportunities. *Exceptional Children, 54,* 403–414.

Hughes, C. A., Schumaker, J. B., Deshler, D. D., & Mercer, C. (1987). *The test-taking strategy.* Lawrence, KS: Excel Enterprises.

Hughes, C. A., Schumaker, J. B., Deshler, D. D., & Mercer, C. D. (1988). *The test-taking strategy.* Lawrence, KS: Edge Enterprises.

Hughes, C. C., Ruhl, K. L., & Misra, A. (1989). Self-management with behaviorally disordered students in school settings: A promise unfulfilled. *Behavior Disorders, 14,* 250–262.

Hunt-Riegel, R. (1988). *Student Inventory (secondary level).* Novi, MI: RHR Consultation Services.

Hursh, N. C. (1989). Vocational evaluation with learning disabled students: Utilization guidelines for teachers. *Academic Therapy, 25,* 201–215.

Hybels, S., & Weaver, R. L. (1986). *Communicating effectively.* New York: Random House.

Hyde, J. S., Fennema, E., & Lamon, S. J. (1990). Gender differences in mathematics performance. *Psychological Bulletin, 107,* 139–155.

Hyun, J. K., & Fowler, S. A. (1995). Respect, cultural sensitivity, and communications: Promoting participation by Asian families in the individualized family service plan. *Teaching Exceptional Children, 28*(1), 25–28.

Idol, L. (1986). *Collaborative school consultation* (Report of the National Task Force on School Consultation). Reston, VA: Council for Exceptional Children, Teacher Education Division.

Idol, L. (1988). A rationale and guidelines for establishing a special education consultation program. *Remedial and Special Education Program, 9*(6), 48–62.

Idol, L., Nevin, A., & Paolucci-Whitcomb, P. (1994). *Collaboration consultation* (2nd ed.). Austin, TX: PRO-ED.

Idol, L., & West, J. F. (1987). Consultation in special education: Part 2. Training and practice. *Journal of Learning Disabilities, 20,* 474–494.

Idol-Maestas, L. (1983). *Special educator's consultation handbook.* Rockville, MD: Aspen.

Idol-Maestas, L. (1993). *Special educator's consultation handbook* (2nd ed.). Austin, TX: PRO-ED.

Idol-Maestas, L., & Ritter, S. (1985). A follow-up study of resource/consulting teachers. *Teacher Education and Special Education, 8,* 121–131.

International Reading Association. (1992). *Teens' favorite books: Young adults' choices 1987–1992.* Newark, DE: International Reading Association.

Isaacson, S. (1989). Confused dichotomies: A response to DuCharme, Earl, & Poplin. *Learning Disabilities Quarterly, 12,* 243–247.

Jackson, P. (1968). *Life in classrooms.* New York: Holt, Rinehart & Winston.

Jacobs, H. E., Kardashian, S., Kreinbring, R. K., Ponder, R., & Simpson, A. R. (1984). A skills-oriented model for facilitating employment among psychiatrically disabled persons. *Rehabilitation Counseling Bulletin, 78,* 87–96.

Jacobs, W. W. (1937). *The monkey's paw: A story in three scenes.* New York: Samuel French.

Johnson, C., & Connors, M. E. (1987). *The etiology and treatment of bulimia nervosa: A biopsychosocial perspective.* New York: Basic Books.

Johnson, D. (1985, March 27). Warning signals for teen suicides. *Orlando Sentinel,* p. E–5.

Johnson, J. H., & Markle, G. C. (1986). *What research says to the middle level practitioner.* Columbus, OH: National Middle School Association.

Johnson, L. J., Pugach, M. C., & Hammitte, D. J. (1988). Barriers to effective special education consultation. *Remedial and Special Education, 9*(6), 41–47.

Johnson, M. J. (1991). *American Indians and Alaska natives with disabilities.* Washington, DC: U.S. Department of Education. (ERIC Document Reproduction Service No. ED 343 706)

Johnson, R. T., & Johnson, D. W. (1983). Effects of cooperative, competitive, and individualistic learning experiences on social development. *Exceptional Children, 49,* 323–329.

Johnson, R. T., & Johnson, D. W. (1986). Mainstreaming and cooperative learning strategies. *Exceptional Children, 52,* 553–561.

Johnson, S. W., & Maile, L. J. (1987). *Suicide and the schools: A handbook for prevention, intervention, and rehabilitation.* Springfield, IL: Charles C Thomas.

Johnston, L. D. (1994, December). *Monitoring the future study: Drug use among 8th, 10th, and 12th graders* (Press Release). Washington, DC: U.S. Department of Health and Human Services.

Johnston, L. D., O'Malley, P. M., & Bachman, J. G. (1994). *National survey results on drug use from the Monitoring the Future study, 1975–1993: Vol. 1. Secondary school students.* Rockville, MD: U.S. Department of Health and Human Services.

Jones, B. F., Palincsar, A. S., Ogle, D. S., & Carr, E. G. (1987). *Strategic teaching and learning: Cognitive instruction in the content areas.* Alexandria, VA: Association for Supervision and Curriculum Development.

Jones, V. F., & Jones, L. S. (1990). *Comprehensive classroom management: Motivating and managing students* (3rd ed.). Boston: Allyn & Bacon.

Jongsma, E. (1985). Research views: Homework: Is it worthwhile? *Reading Teacher, 38,* 702–704.

Joyce, B. R., & Showers, B. (1983). *Power in staff development through research on training.* Alexandria, VA: Association for Supervision and Curriculum Development.

Jungjohann, K., & Schenck, B. R. (1985a). *Math for independence.* Chicago: Science Research Associates.

Jungjohann, K., & Schenck, B. R. (1985b). *Reading for independence.* Chicago: Science Research Associates.

Jungjohann, K., & Schenck, B. R. (1985c). *Writing for independence.* Chicago: Science Research Associates.

Jurgensen, R. C., Brown, R. G., & Jurgensen, J. W. (1992). *Geometry.* Boston: Houghton Mifflin.

Juvenile Justice Bulletin. (1990). Weapons in schools. *Beyond Behavior, 2*(1), 5–9.

Kandel, D. (1991). Drug use, epidemiology and developmental stages of involvement. In R. M. Lerner, A. C. Petersen, & J. Brooks-Gunn (Eds.), *Encyclopedia of adolescence* (Vol. 1 pp. 262–264). New York: Garland.

Kane, B. J., & Alley, G. R. (1980). A peer-tutored, instructional management program in computational mathematics for incarcerated, learning disabled juvenile delinquents. *Journal of Learning Disabilities, 13,* 39–42.

Karge, B., Patton, P., & De la Garza, B. (1992). Transition services for students with mild disabilities: Do they exist? Are they needed? *Career Development for Exceptional Individuals, 15*(1), 47–68.

Karp, H. (1984). Working with resistance. *Training and Development Journal, 38*(3), 69–73.

Kataoka, J. C., & Lock, R. (1995). Whales and hermit crabs: Integrated programming and science. *Teaching Exceptional Children, 27*(4), 17–21.

Katz, W. (1983). *Summary of three task force planning activities to provide recommendations to achieve effective parent/educator partnerships.* Washington, DC: National Association of State Directors of Special Education.

Katz, W. L. (1987). *The Black West.* Seattle: Open Hand.

Kauffman, J. M. (1993). *Characteristics of emotional and behavioral disorders of children and youth* (5th ed.). New York: Macmillan.

Kauffman, J. M., Gerber, M. M., & Semmel, M. I. (1988). Arguable assumptions underlying the Regular Education Initiative. *Journal of Learning Disabilities, 21,* 6–11.

Kauffman, J. M., & Hallahan, D. K. (1993). Toward a comprehensive delivery system for special education. In J. L. Goodlad & T. C. Lovitt (Eds.), *Integrating general and special education* (pp. 76–102). Columbus, OH: Merrill/Macmillan.

Kaufman, T., & Pullen, P. (1989). A historical look at perspective on our history of service to mildly handicapped and at-risk students. *Remedial and Special Education, 10,* 12–14.

Kavale, K. A., & Forness, S. R. (1990). Substance over style: A rejoinder to Dunn's animadversions. *Exceptional Children, 56,* 357–361.

Kaywell, J. E. (1992). *Adolescents at risk.* Westport, CT: Greenwood Press.

Kea, K., Schumaker, J., & Deshler, D. (1987). *Critical teaching behaviors handout.* Lawrence: University of Kansas Institute for Research in Learning Disabilities.

Kelker, K., & Hagan, M. (1986). *Parents and transition: A self-teaching workbook.* Billings: Montana Center for Handicapped Children.

Kelly, B. W., & Holmes, J. (1979). The guided lecture procedure. *Journal of Reading, 22,* 602–604.

Kennedy, D. W., Austin, D. R., & Smith, R. W. (1987). Special recreation: *Opportunities for persons with disabilities.* Philadelphia: Saunders College.

Kerka, S. (1992). *Bilingual vocational education: Trends and issues alerts.* Washington, DC: Office of Educational Research and Improvement. (ERIC Document Reproduction Service No. ED 349-396)

Kerns, A. F., & Neeley, R. E. (1987). *Dictionary of worker traits* (Vols. 1–2). Philadelphia Vocational Research Institute.

Kerr, M. M., & Nelson, C. M. (1989). *Strategies for managing behavior problems in the classroom* (2nd ed.). Columbus, OH: Merrill.

Kerr, M. M., Nelson, C. M., & Lambert, D. L. (1987). *Helping adolescents with learning and behavior problems.* Columbus, OH: Merrill/Macmillan.

Kerr, M. M., Zigmond, N., Schaeffer, A. L., & Brown G. M., (1986). An observational follow-up study of successful and unsuccessful high school students. *High School Journal, 71,* 20–32.

Kinder, D., Bursuck, B., & Epstein, M. (1992). An evaluation of American history textbooks. *Journal of Special Education, 25,* 472–491.

King-Sears, M. E., Mercer, C. D., & Sindelar, P. T. (1992). Toward independence with keyword mnemonics: A strategy for science vocabulary instruction. *RASE, 13*(5), 22–33.

Kirk, S. A., McCarthy, J. J., & Kirk, W. D. (1968). *Illinois test of psycholinguistic abilities* (rev. ed.). Urbana: University of Illinois Press.

Kitano, M. K. (1987). Gifted and talented Asian children. In M. K. Kitano & P. C. Chin (Eds.), *Exceptional Asian children and youth* (pp. 54–60). Reston, VA: Council for Exceptional Children.

Klein, G. (1985). *Reading into racism: Bias in children's literature and learning materials.* New York: Routledge & Kegan Paul.

Knackendoffel, E. A., Robinson, S. M., Deshler, D. D., & Schumaker, J. B. (1992). *Collaborative problem solving—teaming technique series.* Lawrence, KS: Edge.

Knight, M. F., Meyers, H. W., Paolucci-Whitcomb, P., Hasazi, S. E., & Nevin, A. (1981). A four-year evaluation of consulting teacher service. *Behavioral Disorders, 6,* 92–100.

Kokaska, C. J., & Brolin, D. E. (1985). *Career education for handicapped individuals* (2nd ed.). Columbus, OH: Merrill/Macmillan.

Kortering, L. J., & Blackorby, J. (1992). High school dropout and students identified with behavior disorder. *Behavioral Disorders, 18,* 24–32.

Kortering, L. J., & Elrod, G. F. (1991). Programs for adolescents with mild handicaps: Evaluating where we are and contemplating change. *Career Development for Exceptional Individuals, 14,* 145–157.

Kortering, L., Julnes, R., & Edgar, E. (1990). An instructive review of the law pertaining to the graduation of special education students. *Remedial and Special Education, 11*(4), 7–13.

Kotlowitz, A. (1992). *There are no children here: The story of two boys growing up in the other America.* New York: Doubleday.

Kranstover, L. L., Thurlow, M. L., & Bruininks, R. H. (1989). Special education graduates versus non-graduates: A longitudinal study of outcomes. *Career Development for Exceptional Individuals, 12,* 153–166.

Kroth, R. L. (1985). *Communication with parents of exceptional children: Improving parent–teacher relationships.* Denver: Love.

Kuykendall, C. (1992). *From rage to hope: Strategies for reclaiming Black and Hispanic students.* Bloomington, IA: National Educational Service.

LaChance, L. (1988). *Alcohol and drug use among adolescents.* Washington, DC: Office of Educational Research and Improvement. (ERIC Document Reproduction Service No. ED 304–628)

LaFromboise, T. (1982). *Assertion training with American Indians: Cultural/behavioral issues for trainers.* New York: ERIC Clearinghouse on Rural Education and Small Schools.

Lambie, R. A. (1983). A systematic approach for changing materials, instruction and assignments to meet individual needs. In E. L. Meyen, G. A. Vergason, & R. J. Whelan (Eds.), *Promising practices for exceptional children: Curriculum implications* (pp. 67–86). Denver: Love.

Lang, D. C., Quick, A. F., & Johnson, J. A. (1981). *A partnership for the supervision of student teachers.* DeKalb, IL: Creative Educational Materials.

Langan, J. (1982). *Reading and study skills* (2nd ed.). New York: McGraw-Hill.

Langer, J. A. (1981). From theory to practice: A pre-reading plan. *Journal of Reading, 25,* 152–156.

Lathrop, A. (1992, May/June). 1991 CD-ROM evaluation project completed. CUE Newsletter, pp. 19–20.

Laus, M. (1977). *Travel instruction for the handicapped.* Springfield, IL: Charles C Thomas.

Lazear, D. (1991). *Seven ways of knowing: Teaching from multiple intelligences.* Palatine, IL: Skylight.

Lee, W. W. (1987). Microcomputer courseware production and evaluation guidelines for students with learning disabilities. *Journal of Learning Disabilities, 20,* 436–438.

Leitch, M. L., & Tangri, S. S. (1988, Winter). Barriers to home–school collaboration. *Educational Horizons,* pp. 70–74.

Lenz, B. K. (1992). *Handout of the Unit Organizer.* Lawrence: Kansas Center for Research on Learning.

Lenz, B. K., Alley, G., & Schumaker, J. (1987). Activating the inactive learner: Advance organizers in the secondary content classroom. *Learning Disabilities Quarterly, 19,* 53–67.

Lenz, B. K., & Bulgren, J. A. (1995). Promoting learning in content classes. In P. T. Cegelka & W. H. Berdine (Eds.), *Effective instruction for students with learning difficulties.* Boston: Allyn & Bacon.

Lenz, B. K., with Bulgren, J. A., Schumaker, J. B., Deshler, D. D., & Boudah, D. A. (1994). *The unit organizer routine.* (Instructor's Manual). Lawrence, KS: Edge Enterprises.

Lenz, B. K., Clark, F. C., Deshler, D. D., & Schumaker, J. B. (1988). *The strategies instructional approach* (Preservice Training Package). Lawrence: University of Kansas Institute for Research in Learning Disabilities.

Lenz, B. K., Ehren, B. J., & Smiley, L. R. (1991). A goal attainment approach to improve completion of project-type assignments by adolescents with learning disabilities. *Learning Disabilities Research and Practice, 6,* 165–176.

Lenz, B. K., Marrs, R. W., Schumaker, J. B., & Deshler, D. D. (1993). *The lesson organizer routine.* Lawrence, KS: Edge Enterprises.

Leon, G. R. (1991). Bulimia nervosa in adolescence. In R. M. Lerner, A. C. Petersen, & J. Brooks-Gunn (Eds.), *Encyclopedia of adolescence* (Vol. 1, pp. 95–97). New York: Garland.

Leone, P. E., Greenberg, J. M., Trickett, E. J., & Spero, E. (1989). A study of the use of cigarettes, alcohol, and marijuana by students identified as "seriously emotionally disturbed." *Counterpoint, 9*(3), 6–7.

Lerner, J. W. (1985). *Learning disabilities: Theories, diagnosis, and teaching strategies* (4th ed.). Boston: Houghton Mifflin.

Lerro, M. (1994). Teaching adolescents about AIDS. *Teaching Exceptional Children, 26*(4), 49–51.

Leung, E. K. (1989). Cultural and acculturational commonalities and diversities among Asian Americans: Identification and programming considerations. In A. A. Ortiz & B. A. Ramirez (Eds.), *Schools and the culturally diverse exceptional student: Promising practices and future directions.* Reston, VA: Council for Exceptional Children.

Levine, M. D. (1987). *Developmental variation and learning disorders.* Cambridge, MA: Educators Publishers Service.

Levine, M. D., & Sandler, A. D. (1987). Learning disabilities in adolescents: Description, assessment, and management. In R. M. Lerner, A. C. Petersen, & J. Brooks-Gunn (Eds.), *Encyclopedia of adolescence.* New York: Garland.

Levy, T. (1991, Winter). Social studies instruction: Connecting students and their society. *Schools in the Middle,* pp. 7–9.

Lewis, R. B., & Doorlag, D. H. (1995). *Teaching special students in the mainstream* (pp. 53–62). Englewood Cliffs, NJ: Prentice-Hall.

Lewis, R. G., & Ho, M. K. (1989). Social work with

Native Americans. In D. R. Atkinson, G. Morten, & D. W. Sue (Eds.), *Counseling American minorities* (3rd ed.) (pp. 65–72). Dubuque, IA: Wm. C. Brown.

Lewis, T., Heflin, J., & DiGiani, S. (1991). *Teaching students with behavior disorders: Basic questions and answers.*

Licht, B. G., & Kistner, J. A. (1986). Motivational problems of learning-disabled children: Individual differences and their implications for treatment. In J. Torgesen & B. Wong (Eds.), *Psychological and educational perspectives on learning disabilities* (pp. 225–255). New York: Academic.

Lieberman, L. M. (1985). Special education and regular education: A merger made in heaven? *Exceptional Children, 51,* 513–516.

Lilly, S. M. (1988). The Regular Education Initiative: A force for change in general and special education. *Education and Training in Mental Retardation, 23,* 253–260.

Linkenhoker, D., & McCarron, L. (1985). *Adaptive behavior: The street survival skills questionnaire.* Dallas: Common Market Press.

Linn, M. C., & Songer, N. B. (1991). Cognitive and conceptual change in adolescence. *American Journal of Education, 99,* 379–417.

Litt, I. F. (1991). Medical complications of eating disorders. In R. M. Lerner, A. C. Petersen, & J. Brooks-Gunn (Eds.), *Encyclopedia of adolescence* (Vol. 1, pp. 278–280). New York: Garland.

Little, J. W. (1982). Norms of collegiality and experimentation: Workplace conditions of school success. American Education Research Journal, 19, 325–340.

Littlejohn, E. M., & Henderson, S. B. (1992). African American communication styles and their effect on intercultural communication. In J. Wittmer (Ed.), *Valuing diversity and similarity: Bridging the gap through interpersonal skills* (pp. 75–92). Minneapolis: Educational Media Corporations.

Lloyd, J. W. (1980). Academic instruction and cognitive behavior modification: The need for attack strategy training. *Exceptional Children Quarterly, 1(1),* 53–63, 75.

Locke, D. C. (1988). Teaching culturally-different students: Growing pine trees or bonsai trees. *Contemporary Education, 59,* 130–133.

Lombardi, T. P. (1995). Teachers develop their own learning strategies. *Teaching Exceptional Children, 27(3),* 52–55.

Lombardino, L., & Mangan, N. (1983). Parents as language trainers: Language programming with developmentally delayed children. *Exceptional Children, 49,* 358–361.

Lounsberry, J. H. (1991). The middle school curriculum—or is it curricula? In J. Capelluti & D. Stokes (Eds.), *Middle level education: Programs, policies, and practices* (pp. 12–18). Reston, VA: National Association of Secondary School Principals.

Lovett, D. L., & Harris, M. B. (1987). Important skills for adults with mental retardation: The client's point of view. *Mental Retardation, 25,* 351–356.

Lueder, D. C. (1989). Tennessee parents were invited to participate—and they did. *Educational Leadership, 47(2),* 15–17.

Lum, D. (1986). *Social work practice and people of color: A process-stage approach.* Pacific Grove, CA: Brooks/Cole.

Lund, K. A., Montague, M., & Reinholtz, M. (1987). Monitoring students on the job. *Teaching Exceptional Children, 19(3),* 58–60.

Maheady, L., Sacca, M. K., & Harper, G. F. (1987). Classwide student tutoring teams: The effects of peer-mediated instruction on the academic performance of secondary mainstreamed students. *The Journal of Special Education, 21,* 107–120.

Maheady, L., Sacca, M. K., & Harper, G. F. (1988). Classwide peer tutoring with mildly handicapped high school students. *Exceptional Children, 55,* 52–59.

Maher, C. (1984). Handicapped adolescents as cross-age tutors: Program description and evaluation. *Exceptional Children, 51,* 56–63.

Maher, C. (1987). Involving behaviorally disordered adolescents in instructional planning: Effectiveness of the GOAL procedures. *Journal of Child and Adolescent Psychotherapy, 4,* 204–210.

Maker, C. J., Nielson, A. B., & Rogers, J. A. (1994). Multiple intelligences: Giftedness, diversity, and problem-solving. *Teaching Exceptional Children, 27(1),* 4–19.

Male, M. (1988). *Technology for inclusion: Meeting the special needs of all students* (2nd ed.). Boston: Allyn & Bacon.

Males, M. (1990). Youth behavior: Subcultural effect or mirror of adult behavior? *Journal of School Health, 60,* 505–508.

Malone, L. D., & Mastropieri, M. A. (1992). Reading comprehension instruction: Summarization and self-monitoring training for students with learning disabilities. *Exceptional Children 58,* 270–279.

Mandlebaum, L. H., & Wilson, R. (1989). Teaching listening skills in the special education classroom. *Academic Therapy, 24,* 449–457.

Manning, B. (1993). Personal reflections. In J. M. Kauffman, *Characteristics of emotional and behavioral disorders of children and youth* (5th ed.) (pp. 276–278). New York: Macmillan.

Marder, C. (1992). Education after secondary school. In M. Wagner, R. D'Amico, C. Marder, L. Newman, & J. Blackorby, (Eds.), *What happens next? Trends in postschool outcomes of youth with disabilities: The second comprehensive report from the national longitudinal transition study of special education students* (pp. 58–97). Menlo Park, CA: SRI International. (ERIC Document Reproduction Service No. ED 356 603)

Marder, C., & Cox, R. (1991). More than a label: Characteristics of youth with disabilities. In M. Wagner (Ed.), *Youth with disabilities: How are they doing? The first comprehensive report from the national longitudinal transition study of special education students.* Menlo Park, CA: SRI International. (ERIC Document Reproduction Service No. ED 341 228)

Margolis, H., & McGettigan, J. (1988). Managing resistance to instructional modifications in mainstreamed environments. *Remedial and Special Education, 9*(4), 15–21.

Marland, S. P. (1971, January 23). *Career education now.* Speech presented at the annual Convention of the National Association of Secondary School Principals, Houston.

Marriott Foundation for People with Disabilities. (1990). Employment of people with disabilities: A sound business decision. *The Special Edge, 4*(9), 8–9.

Marshall, R. H., & Jacobs, D. H. (1987). *Physical science: Investigating matter and energy.* Baltimore: Media Materials.

Mason, D. A. (1995). Organization of the middle level school: Evolution and a vision for restructuring. In M. J. Wavering (Ed.), *Educating young adolescents: Life in the middle* (pp. 201–232). New York: Garland.

Masters, L. F., Mori, B. A., & Mori, A. A. (1993). *Teaching secondary students with mild learning and behavior problems: Methods, materials, and strategies* (2nd ed.). Austin, TX: PRO-ED.

Mastropieri, M. A. (1989). Using general education teacher effectiveness literature in the preparation of special education personnel. *TESE, 12,* 170–172.

Mastropieri, M. A., & Scruggs, T. E. (1989). Reconstructive elaborations: Strategies for adapting content area information. *Academic Therapy, 24,* 391–405.

Mayer, R. E. (1988). Learning strategies: An overview. In C. Weinstein, E. Goetz, & P. A. Alexander (Eds.), *Learning and study strategies* (pp. 11–22). New York: Academic Press.

Mboya, M. M. (1986). Black adolescents: A descriptive study of their self-concept and academic achievement. *Adolescence, 21,* 689–696.

McCarron, L., & Dial, J. (1976). McCarron–Dial work evaluation system: Evaluation of the mentally disabled—A systematic approach. Dallas: Common Market Press.

McCarthy, B. (1987). *The 4MAT system: Teaching to learning styles with right/left mode techniques.* Barrington, IL: EXCEL.

McCray, P. M. (1980). *Suggested guidelines for evaluating work samples.* Menomonie, WI: Stout Vocational Rehabilitation Institute, Materials Development Center.

McCutcheon, G. (1985). Curriculum theory/curriculum practice: A gap or the grand canyon? *Current thought on curriculum: 1985 ASCD yearbook* (pp. 45–52). Alexandria, VA: Association for Supervision and Curriculum Development.

McFall, R. M. (1982). A review and reformulation of the concept of social skills. *Behavioral Assessment, 4,* 1–33.

McKenry, P. C. (1991). Minority youth and drug use. In R. M. Lerner, A. C. Petersen, & J. Brooks-Gunn (Eds.), *Encyclopedia of adolescence* (Vol. 1, pp. 265–267). New York: Garland.

McKenzie, H. S. (1972). Special education and consulting teachers. In F. Clark, D. Evans, & L. Hammerlynk (Eds.), *Implementing behavioral programs for schools and clinics.* Champaign, IL: Research Press.

McKenzie, R. G. (1991). Content area instruction delivered by secondary learning disabilities teachers: A national survey. *Learning Disabilities Quarterly, 14,* 115–123.

McKenzie, R. G., & Houk, C. S. (1993). Across the great divide: Transition from elementary to secondary settings for students with mild disabilities. *Teaching Exceptional Children, 25*(2), 16–21.

McKissack, P., & McKissack, F. (1990). *Taking a stand against racism and racial discrimination.* New York: Franklin Watts.

McLeod, T. M., & Armstrong, S. W. (1982). Learning disabilities in mathematics: Skill deficits and remedial approaches at the intermediate and secondary level. *Learning Disabilities Quarterly, 5,* 305–311.

McLoughlin, J. A., & Kelly, D. (1982). Issues facing resource teachers. *Learning Disabilities Quarterly, 5,* 58–64.

McLoughlin, J. A., & Lewis, R. B. (1990). *Assessing special students.* Columbus, OH: Merrill/Macmillan.

McLoughlin, J. A., & Lewis, R. B. (1994). *Assessing special students* (4th ed.). Columbus, OH: Merrill/Prentice-Hall.

McNutt, G. (1984). A holistic approach to language arts instruction in the resource room. *Learning Disabilities Quarterly, 7,* 315–320.

McWhirter, J. J., McWhirter, B. T., McWhirter, A. M., & McWhirter, E. H. (1993). *At risk youth: A comprehensive response*. Pacific Grove, CA: Brooks/Cole.

Meek, M. (1992, Fall). The peacekeepers. *Teaching Tolerance,* pp. 46–52.

Meers, G. (1992). Getting ready for the next century: Vocational preparation of students with disabilities. *Teaching Exceptional Children, 26*(2), 36–39.

Meese, R. (1994). *Teaching learners with mild disabilities: Integrating research and practice*. Pacific Grove, CA: Brooks/Cole.

Mehrabian, A., & Ferris, S. R. (1967). Influence of attitudes from nonverbal communication in two channels. *Journal of Consulting Psychology, 32,* 248–252.

Meichenbaum, D. (1977). *Cognitive behavior modification: An integrative approach*. New York: Plenum Press.

Meichenbaum, D. (1983). Teaching thinking: A cognitive behavioral approach. In Carnine, D. (Ed.), *Interdisciplinary voices in learning disabilities and remedial education* (pp. 1–28). Austin, TX: PRO-ED.

Meichenbaum, D., & Goodman, J. (1971). Training impulsive children to talk to themselves: A means of developing self-control. *Journal of Abnormal Psychology, 77,* 115–126.

Meier, F. E. (1995). *Competency-based instruction for teachers of students with special learning needs*. (2nd ed.)Boston: Allyn & Bacon.

Melaville, A. I., & Blank, M. J. (1991). *What it takes: Structuring interagency partnerships to connect children and families with comprehensive services*. Washington, DC: Education and Human Resources Consortium.

Mercer, C. D. (1987). *Children and adolescents with learning disabilities* (3rd ed.). Columbus, OH: Merrill.

Mercer, C. D. (1992). *Students with learning disabilities* (4th ed.). Columbus, OH: Merrill.

Mercer, C. D., & Mercer, A. R. (1993). *Teaching students with learning problems* (4th ed.). New York: Merrill/Macmillan.

Mercer, J. R., & Rueda, R. (1991, November). *The impact of changing paradigms of disabilities in assessment for special education*. Paper presented at Council for Exceptional Children Topical Conference on At-Risk Children and Youth, New Orleans.

Messerer, J., & Learner, J. (1989). Word processing for learning disabled students. *Learning Disabilities Focus, 5*(1), 13–17.

Michaels, C. A. (1989). Employment: The final frontier: Issues and practices for persons with learning disabilities. *Rehabilitation Counseling Bulletin, 33*(1), 67–73.

Miller, D. (1994). Suicidal behavior of adolescents with behavior disorders and their peers without disabilities. *Behavioral Disorders, 20*(1), 61–68.

Miller, L. J. (1990). Tips for analyzing spelling errors. *Diagnostique, 16*(1), 38–40.

Miller, S. R., Osborne, S. S., & Burt, E. (1987). The use of mediation essays in modifying inappropriate behavior of three behaviorally disordered youth. *Teaching Behaviorally Disordered Youth, 3,* 18–27.

Minner, S., Beane, A., & Prater, G. (1986). Try telephone answering machines. *Teaching Exceptional Children, 19,* 62–63.

Minskoff, E. H., Sautter, S. W., Sheldon, K. L., Steidle, E. F., & Baker, D. P. (1988). A comparison of learning disabled adults and high school students. *Learning Disabilities Research, 3,* 115–123.

Mithaug, D. E., Mar, D. K., & Stewart, J. E. (1978). *Prevocational assessment and curriculum guide*. Seattle: J. E. Stewart.

Mizell, L. (1992). *Think about racism*. New York: Walker.

Mohr, P., Gerler, E., & Sprinthall, N. (1987). Moral reasoning in early adolescence: Implications for drug abuse. *The School Counselor, 35,* 120–127.

Moles, O. C. (1987, April). *Trends in student misconduct: The 70s and 80s*. Paper presented at the meeting of the American Educational Research Association, Washington, DC. (ERIC Document Reproduction Service No. 286 954)

Moll, L. C. (1988). Some key issues in teaching Latino students. *Language Arts, 65,* 465–472.

Montague, M. (1987a). Job-related socialization training for mildly to moderately handicapped adolescents. In R. B. Rutherford, C. M. Nelson, & S. R. Forness (Eds.), *Severe behavior disorders of children and youth* (pp. 173–185). Boston: Little, Brown.

Montague, M. (1987b). Self-management strategies for job success. *Teaching Exceptional Children, 19*(3), 74–76.

Montague, M. (1988). Job-related social skills training for adolescents with handicaps. *Career Development for Exceptional Individuals, 11,* 26–41.

Montague, M., & Leavell, A. G. (1994). Improving the narrative writing of students with learning disabilities. *RASE, 15*(1), 21–33.

Montague, M., & Lund, K. A. (1991). *Job-related social skills: A curriculum for adolescents with special needs*. Ann Arbor, MI: Exceptional Innovations.

Montemayor, R. (1986). Family variation in parent–adolescent storm and stress. *Journal of Adolescent Research, 1,* 15–31.

Moon, S., Goodall, P., Barcus, M., & Brooke, V. (1986). *The supported work model of competitive employment for citizens with severe handicaps: A guide for job trainers* (rev.). Richmond: Virginia Commonwealth

University, Rehabilitation Research and Training Center.

Morsink, C. V. (1984). *Teaching special needs students in regular classrooms*. Boston: Little, Brown.

Morsink, C. V., Thomas, C. C., & Correa, V. I. (1991). *Interactive teaming consultation and collaboration in special programs*. New York: Macmillan.

Mueller, H., Wilgosh, L., & Dennis, S. (1989). Employment survival skills for entry-level occupations. *Canadian Journal of Rehabilitation, 2*, 203–221.

Murphy, D. M. (1986). The prevalence of handicapping conditions among juvenile delinquents. *Remedial and Special Education, 7*, 7–17.

Murray, C. B., & Clark, R. M. (1990). Targets of racism. *American School Board Journal, 177*(6), 22–24.

Murtaugh, M., & Zetlin, A. G. (1989). How serious is the motivation problem in secondary special education? *High School Teacher, 72*, 151–159.

Muth, K. D., & Alvermann, D. E. (1992). *Teaching and learning in the middle grades*. Boston: Allyn & Bacon.

Nacson, J. (1982). *Prepared statement at the Hearings on the Reauthorization of the Vocational Education Act of 1963 before the House Joint Hearing of the Subcommittee on Elementary, Secondary, and Vocational Education and the Subcommittee on Select Education of the Committee on Education and Labor*. Washington, DC: U.S. Government Printing Office.

National Association of State Directors of Special Education. (1990). *Reference notes for speechmaking for understanding the forces at work which are driving social policy*. Washington, DC: Author.

National Center for Education Statistics. (1994). *Latest report on dropout rates in the United States, released 1993* (Report No. 065–000–00684–7). Washington, DC: Office of Educational Research and Improvement.

National Council of Teachers of Mathematics. (1989). *Curriculum and evaluation standards for school mathematics*. Reston, VA: Author.

National Council on Disability. (1989). *The education of students with disabilities: Where do we stand?* Washington, DC: Author.

*National drug control strategy: Strengthening communities' response to drugs and crime*. (1995). Washington, DC: U.S. Government Printing Office.

National Information Center for Children and Youth with Disabilities. (1991). Options after high school for youth with disabilities. *Transition Summary, 7*, 1–28.

National Institute of Mental Health (1995). *Completed suicides, U.S., 1992*. Washington, DC: Author.

National Public Radio (1993, February 17). Report on teen violence.

National School Safety Center. (1995). *The school safety checkbook*. Westlake Village, CA: Author.

Nauman, A. K. (1987). School librarians and cultural pluralism. *The Reading Teacher, 41*, 201–205.

Neal, R., Meadows, N., Levine, P., & Edgar, E. (1988). What happens after special education: A statewide follow-up study of secondary students who have behavioral disorders. *Behavioral Disorders, 13*, 209–216.

Nelson, C. M., Rutherford, R. B., Center, D. B., & Walker, H. M. (1991). Do public schools have an obligation to serve troubled children and youth? *Exceptional Children, 57*, 406–414.

Nelson, C. M., & Stevens, K. B. (1981). An accountable model for mainstreaming behaviorally disordered children. *Behavioral Disorders, 6*(2), 82–91.

Netherton, L., Wickham, C., Gipson, R., Platt, J., & Corrales, J. (1992). *Creating visual displays for a strategic learning environment*. FDLRS/EAST, Brevard County, Florida.

Neubert, D. A., Tilson, G. P., & Ianacone, R. N. (1989). Postsecondary transition needs and employment patterns of individuals with mild disabilities. *Exceptional Children, 55*, 494–500.

Newcomb, M. D., & Bentler, P. M. (1988). *Consequences of adolescent drug use*. Newbury Park, CA: Sage.

Newcomb, M. D., & Bentler, P. M. (1991). Antecedents/predictors of cocaine use among adolescents and young adults. In R. M. Lerner, A. C. Petersen, & J. Brooks-Gunn (Eds.), *Encyclopedia of adolescence* (Vol. 1, pp. 114–118). New York: Garland.

Newman, J. M. (Ed.). (1985). *Whole language: Theory in use*. Portsmouth, NH: Heinemann Educational Books.

Newman, J. M., & Church, S. M. (1990). Commentary: Myths of whole language. *The Reading Teacher, 44*, 20–27.

Newman, L. (1992). *Hispanic secondary school students with disabilities: How are they doing?* Washington, DC: Special Education Programs (ED/OSERS). (ERIC Document Reproduction Service No. ED 346 667)

Newman, L. (1993). Academic course-taking. In M. Wagner (Ed.), *The secondary school programs of students with disabilities: A report from the national longitudinal transition study of special education students* (pp. 83–121). Menlo Park, CA: SRI International. (ERIC Document Reproduction Service No. ED 365 084)

Nichols, R. G., & Stevens, L. A. (1957). *Are you listening?* New York: McGraw-Hill.

Nihira, K., Foster, R., Shellhaas, M., & Leland, H. (1981). *AAMD adaptive behavior scale* (school edition). Monterey, CA: CTB/McGraw–Hill.

Niles, S. G., & Tiffany, S. A. (1990). Strategies for an effective vocational assessment program. *Academic Therapy, 25,* 547–559.

Northwest Regional Educational Laboratory. (1990). *Effective schooling practices: A research synthesis 1990 update.* Portland, OR: Author.

Nuckolls, C. W. (1991). Culture and causal thinking: Diagnosis and prediction in a South Indian fishing village. *Ethos, 19*(1), 3–51.

Nuttall, E. V., Landurand, P. M., & Goldman, P. (1984). A critical look at testing and evaluation from a cross-cultural perspective. In P. C. Chinn (Ed.), Education of culturally and linguistically different exceptional children (pp. 42–62). Reston, VA: Council for Exceptional Children.

Oakes, J. (1990). *Multiplying inequities: The effects of race, socioeconomic status and tracking on opportunities to learn mathematics and science.* Santa Monica, CA: Rand Corporation.

OCPS/FDLRS. (1988). *Recipe for success.* Orlando, FL: Author.

Offer, D. (1985). A portrait of normal adolescents. *American Educator, 9*(2), 34–37.

Offer, D., & Church, R. B. (1991). Adolescent turmoil. In R. M. Lerner, A. C. Petersen, & J. Brooks-Gunn (Eds.), *Encyclopedia of adolescence* (Vol. 11, pp. 1148–1152). New York: Garland.

Ogbu, J. U. (1987). Variability in minority school performance: A problem in search of an explanation. *Anthropology and Education Quarterly, 18,* 312–334.

Ogbu, J. U., & Matute-Bianchi, M. E. (1986). Understanding sociocultural factors: Knowledge, identity, and school adjustment. In Bilingual Education Office Staff, *Beyond language: Social and cultural factors in schooling language minority students* (pp. 73–143). Los Angeles: California State University, Evaluation, Dissemination, and Assessment Center.

Ogle, D. M. (1986). K-W-L: A teaching model that develops active reading of expository text. *The Reading Teacher, 39,* 564–570.

Olson, J., & Platt, J. (1996). *Teaching children and adolescents with special needs* (2nd ed.). Columbus, OH: Merrill/Prentice-Hall.

O'Melia, M. C., & Rosenberg, M. S. (1994). Effects of cooperative homework teams on the acquisition of mathematics skills by secondary students with mild disabilities. *Exceptional Children, 60,* 538–548.

Orange County Public Schools. (1986). *Orange County curriculum guide.* Orlando, FL: Author.

Orange County Public Schools (1995). *Block scheduling.* Orlando, FL: Author.

Ortiz, A. A. (1984). Language and curriculum development for exceptional bilingual children. In P.

C. Chinn (Ed.), *Education of culturally and linguistically different exceptional children* (pp. 77–100). Reston, VA: Council for Exceptional Children.

Ortiz, A. A. (1993). Personal reflections. In J. M. Kauffman, *Characteristics of emotional and behavioral disorders of children and youth* (5th ed.) (pp. 281–283). New York: Macmillan.

Ortiz, A. A., & Garcia, S. B. (1988). A prereferral process for preventing inappropriate referrals of Hispanic students to special education. In A. A. Ortiz & B. A. Ramirez (Eds.), *Schools and the culturally diverse exceptional student: Promising practices and future directions* (pp. 6–18). Reston, VA: Council for Exceptional Children.

Ortiz, A. A., & Yates, J. (1982). Teacher training associated with serving bilingual exceptional students. *Teacher Education and Special Education, 5*(3), 61–68.

Osborne, S. S., Kiburz, C. S., & Miller, S. (1986). Treatment of self-injurious behavior using self-control techniques with a severely behaviorally disordered adolescent. *Behavioral Disorders, 12,* 60–67.

Overton, T. (1992). *Assessment in special education: An applied approach.* Columbus, OH: Merrill/Macmillan.

Owings, J., & Stocking, C. (1986). *High school and beyond, a national longitudinal study for the 1980's: Characteristics of high school students who identify themselves as handicapped.* Washington, DC: National Center for Education Statistics. (ERIC Document Reproduction Service No. ED 294 885).

Packer, J. (1990 September 6,). *Remarks made to the House of Representatives Subcommittee on Crime.* 101 Cong. 2nd sess., Series 144.

Palincsar, A. S. (1986). Metacognitive strategy instruction. *Exceptional Children, 53,* 118–124.

Palincsar, A. S., & Brown, A. L. (1984). The reciprocal teaching of comprehension fostering and comprehension monitoring activities. *Cognition and Instruction, 1,* 117–175.

Palincsar, A. S., & Brown, A. L. (1986). Interactive teaching to promote independent learning from text. *The Reading Teacher, 39,* 771–777.

Palincsar, A. S, & Brown, A. L. (1987). Enhancing instructional time through attention to metacognition. *Journal of Learning Disabilities, 20,* 66–75.

Palincsar, A. S., & Brown, A. L. (1988). Teaching and practicing thinking skills to promote comprehension in the context of group problem solving. *Remedial and Special Education, 9*(1), 53–59.

Parent Advocacy Coalition for Educational Rights. (1988). *Students in transition using planning.* Minneapolis: Author.

Paris, S. G. (1988). Models and metaphors of learning strategies. In C. E. Weinstein, E. T. Goetz, & P. A.

Alexander (Eds.), *Learning and study strategies: Issues in assessment, instruction, and evaluation* (pp. 299–321). San Diego: Academic Press.

Paris, S. G., & Byrnes, J. P. (1989). The constructivist approach to self-regulation and learning in the classroom. In B. Zimmerman & D. Schunk (Eds.), *Self-regulated learning and academic achievement: Theory, research, and practice* (pp. 169–200). New York: Springer-Verlag.

Paris, S. G., & Cross, D. R. (1983). Ordinary learning: Pragmatic connections among children's beliefs, motives, and actions. In J. Disanz, G. L. Disanz, & R. Kail (Eds.), *Learning in children* (pp. 137–169). New York: Springer-Verlag.

Paris, S. G., Lipson, M. Y., Jacobs, J., Oka, E., Debritto, A. M., & Cross, D. (1982). *Metacognition and reading comprehension.* Symposium conducted at the annual meeting of the International Reading Association, Chicago.

Paris, S. G., & Oka, E. R. (1986). Self-regulated learning among exceptional children. *Exceptional Children, 53,* 103–108.

Park, H., & Gaylord-Ross, R. (1989). A problem-solving approach to social skills training in employment settings with mentally retarded youth. *Journal of Applied Behavior Analysis, 22,* 373–380.

Parker, R. (1991a). *The OASIS-2 aptitude survey—2.* Austin, TX: Pro–Ed.

Parker, R. (1991b). *The OASIS-2 interest schedule—2.* Austin, TX: Pro–Ed.

Pascoe, E. (1985). *Issues in American history: Racial prejudice.* New York: Franklin Watts.

Paterson, M. (1981). *Curriculum-based assessment: Metric measurement.* Unpublished manuscript, University of Illinois, Department of Special Education, Champaign-Urbana.

Patriarca, L. A., & Lamb, M. A. (1990). Preparing secondary special education teachers to be collaborative decision makers and reflective practitioners: A promising practicum model. *Teacher Education and Special Education, 13,* 228–232.

Patton, J. M. (1992). Assessment and identification of African-American learners with gifts and talents. *Exceptional Children, 59,* 150–159.

Patton, P. L. (1991). *A survey of employers of students with mild disabilities.* Unpublished manuscript, San Diego.

Patton, P. L. (1996). Transition skills: Career education and related social skills. In J. Olson & J. Platt, *Teaching children and adolescents with special needs* (2nd ed.) (pp. 367–383). Columbus, OH: Merrill/Prentice-Hall.

Patton, P. L., De la Garza, B., & Harmon, C. (in press). Employability skills + family involvement + adult agency support + on-the-job support = employment success. *Teaching Exceptional Children.*

Pauk, W. (1978). A notetaking format: Magical but not automatic. *Reading World, 18,* 96–97.

Pauk, W. (1989). *How to study in college.* Boston: Houghton Mifflin.

Paulson, F. L., Paulson, P. R., & Meyer, C. A. (1991). What makes a portfolio a portfolio? *Educational Leadership, 48*(5), 60–63.

Pearl, R., Bryan, T., & Donahue, M. (1980). Learning disabled children's attributions for success and failure. *Learning Disabilities Quarterly, 3,* 3–9.

Pearson, P. D. (1985). Changing the face of reading comprehension instruction. *The Reading Teacher, 38,* 724–738.

Pennsylvania State University Institute for the Study of Adult Literacy. (1993). *A day in the life.* North Billerica, MA: Curriculum Associates.

Petersen, A. C. (1988). Adolescent development. *Annual Review of Psychology, 39,* 583–607.

Petersen, A. C., & Epstein, J. L. (1991). Development and education across adolescence: An introduction. *American Journal of Education, 99,* 373–378.

Peterson, M. R., & Bircher, J. (1988). Trends in human immunodeficiency virus infections among civilian applicants for military service—U.S., Oct. 1985–March 1988. *Journal of the American Medical Association, 260,* 3113–3114.

Peterson, N. L. (1987). *Early intervention for handicapped and at-risk children: An introduction to early childhood special education.* Denver: Love.

Phillips, V., & McCullough, L. (1990). Consultation-based programming: Instituting the collaborative ethic in schools. *Exceptional Children, 56,* 291–304.

Polirstok, S. R. (1989). Parents and teachers as self-evaluation trainers for adolescents with behavior disorders. In S. L. Braten, R. B. Rutherford, Jr., T. F. Reilly, & S. A. DiGamgi (Eds.), *Programming for adolescents with behavior disorders* (Vol. 4). Reston, VA: Council for Children with Behavior Disorders.

Polloway, E. A., Epstein, M. H., & Cullinan, D. (1985). Prevalence of behavior problems among educable mentally retarded students. *Education and Training of the Mentally Retarded, 20,* 3–13.

Polloway, E. A., Epstein, M. H., Polloway, C. H., Patton, J. R., & Ball, D. W. (1986). Corrective reading program: An analysis of effectiveness with learning disabled and mentally retarded students. *Remedial and Special Education, 7*(4), 41–47.

Polloway, E. A., & Patton, J. R. (1993). *Strategies for teaching learners with special needs* (5th ed.). New York: Merrill/Macmillan.

Polloway, E. A., Patton, J. R., Epstein, M. H., & Smith, T. E. (1989). Comprehensive curriculum for students with mild handicaps. *Focus on Exceptional Children, 21,* 1–12.

Polloway, E. A., Patton, J. R., Payne, J. S., & Payne, R. A. (1989). *Strategies for teaching learners with special needs* (4th ed.). Columbus, OH: Merrill.

Polloway, E. A., & Smith, T. E. C. (1989). *Language instruction for students with disabilities.* Denver: Love.

Poplin, M. S. (1983). The science of curriculum development applied to special education and the IEP. In E. L. Meyen, G. A. Vergason, & R. J. Whelan (Eds.), *Promising practices for exceptional children: Curriculum implications* (pp. 37–65). Denver: Love.

Poplin, M. S. (1988). Holistic/constructivist principles of the teaching/learning process: Implications for the field of learning disabilities. *Journal of Learning Disabilities, 21,* 401–416.

Posner, G. J. (1996). *Field experience: A guide to reflective teaching* (4th ed.). White Plains, NY: Longman.

Poteet, J. A. (1995a). Educational assessment. In J. S. Choate, B. E. Enright, L. J. Miller, J. A. Poteet, & T. A. Rakes (Eds.), *Curriculum-based assessment and programming* (3rd ed.) (pp. 1–25). Boston: Allyn & Bacon.

Poteet, J. A. (1995b). Written expression. In J. S. Choate, B. E. Enright, L. J. Miller, J. A. Poteet, & T. A. Rakes (Eds.), *Curriculum-based assessment and programming* (3rd ed.) (pp. 204–238). Boston: Allyn & Bacon.

Prentice, L., & Cousin, P. T. (1993). Moving beyond the textbook to teach students with learning disabilities. *Teaching Exceptional Children, 26*(1), 14–17.

Pressley, M., Borkowski, J. G., & O'Sullivan, J. T. (1984). Memory strategy instruction is made of this: Metamemory and durable strategy use. *Educational Psychologist, 1,* 94–107.

Pressley, M., Burkell, J., Cariglia-Bull, T., Lysynchuk, L., Snyder, B. L., Symons, S., & Woloshyn, V. E. (1990). *Cognitive strategy instruction that really improves children's academic performance.* Cambridge, MA: Brookline Books.

Pritchard, D. G. (1963). *Education and the handicapped: 1760–1960.* London: Routledge and Kegan Paul.

Project WORK. (1994). *An employability skills program for students with learning handicaps: Final report* (Grant # HO 95–6042721). San Diego: San Diego State University Foundation.

Psychiatry Star Team. (1995). *Facts for families: Teen suicide* (Report No. 10). Washington, DC: American Academy of Child and Adolescent Psychiatry.

Public Law 93–112. (1973). *Rehabilitation Act of 1973* (504, 29 U.S.C. 794). Washington, DC: U.S. Congress.

Public Law 94–142. (1975). *The Education for All Handicapped Children Act.* Washington, DC: U.S. Congress.

Public Law 98–199. (1983). *Amendments to PL 94–142: School to work transition initiative.* Washington, DC: U.S. Congress.

Public Law 98–524. (1990). *Carl D. Perkins Vocational and Applied Technology Education Act* (20 U.S.C 2335). Washington, DC: U.S. Congress.

Public Law 99–506. (1986). *Rehabilitation Act Amendments of 1986.* Washington, DC: U.S. Congress.

Public Law 101–336. (1990). *Americans with Disabilities Act.* Washington, DC: U.S. Congress.

Public Law 101–476. (1990). *Amendments to PL 94–142: Individuals with disabilities education act.* Washington, DC: 101st Congress.

Public Law 103–239. (1993). *School to Work Opportunities Act.* 20 U.S.C. 6103. Washington, DC: U.S. Congress.

Pugach, M. C., & Johnson, L. J. (1988). Rethinking the relationship between consultation and collaborative problem-solving. *Focus on Exceptional Children, 21*(4), 1–8.

Pugach, M. C., & Johnson, L. J. (1989). The challenge of implementing collaboration between general and special education. *Exceptional Children, 56*(3), 232–235.

Putnam, M. L. (1992). The testing practices of mainstream secondary classroom teachers. *Remedial and Special Education, 13,* 11–21.

Putnam, M. L., & Wesson, C. L. (1990). The teacher's role in teaching content-area information. *LD Forum, 16*(1), 55–60.

Quality Education for Minorities Project. (1990). *Education that works: An action plan for the education of minorities.* Cambridge: Massachusetts Institute of Technology.

Rafoth, M. A., & Leal, L. (1993). Improving the study skills of middle school students. *Middle School Journal, 25*(1), 51–54.

Rakes, T. A. (1992). Content and study strategies. In J. S. Choate, B. E. Enright, L. J. Miller, J. A. Poteet, & T. A. Rakes (Eds.), *Curriculum-based assessment and programming* (2nd ed.) (pp. 314–355). Boston: Allyn & Bacon.

Rakes, T. A. (1995). Content and study strategies. In J. S. Choate, B. E. Enright, L. J. Miller, J. A. Poteet, & T. A. Rakes (Eds.), *Curriculum-based assessment and programming* (3rd ed., pp. 320–361). Boston: Allyn & Bacon.

Ramirez, B. A. (1993). Personal reflections. In J. M. Kauffman, *Characteristics of emotional and behavioral disorders of children and youth* (5th ed.) (pp. 280–281). New York: Macmillan.

Ramirez, M., & Castaneda, A. (1974). *Cultural democracy, bicognitive development, and education.* New York: Academic Press.

Randall-David, E. (1989). *Strategies for working with culturally diverse communities and clients.* Rockville, MD: Association for the Care of Children's Health.

Rauch, J. M., & Huba, G. J. (1991). Adolescent drug use. In R. M. Lerner, A. C. Petersen, & J. Brooks-Gunn (Eds.), *Encyclopedia of adolescence* (Vol. 1, pp. 256–261). New York: Garland.

Ray, J., & Warden, M. K. (1995). *Technology, computers and the special needs learner.* Albany, NY: Delmar.

Redditt, S. (1991, Fall). Two teachers working as one: Co-teaching for special/regular education integration. *Equity and Choice,* pp. 49–56.

Reetz, L. J., & Hoover, J. H. (1992). The acceptability and utility of five reading approaches as judged by middle school LD students. *Learning Disabilities Research and Practice, 7*(1), 11–15.

Reeve, R. A., & Brown, A. L. (1985). Metacognition reconsidered: Implications for intervention research. *Journal of Abnormal Child Psychology, 13,* 343–356.

Reid, D. K., & Hresko, W. P. (1982). Life span instruction for the learning disabled. *Topics in Learning and Learning Disabilities, 2*(3), 40–55.

Reid, D. K., & Stone, C. A. (1991). Why is cognitive instruction effective? Underlying learning mechanisms. *Remedial and Special Education, 12,* 8–19.

Reifel, P. S. (1992). Cultural and historical perspectives in communicating with Native Americans. In J. Wittmer (Ed.), *Valuing diversity and similarity: Bridging the gap through interpersonal skills* (pp. 143–163). Minneapolis: Educational Media.

Repetto, J. B., White, W. J., & Snauwaert, D. T. (1990). Individualized transition plans (ITP): A national perspective. *Career Development for Exceptional Individuals, 13,* 110–119.

Report: America remains separate and unequal. (1993, March 1). *Orlando Sentinel,* p. A-3.

Resnick, L., & Resnick, D. (1985). Standards, curriculum and performance: An historical and comparative perspective. *Educational Researcher, 14,* 5–29.

Resource Center on Substance Abuse Prevention and Disability. (1995). *A look at alcohol and other drug abuse prevention and mental retardation.* Washington, DC: Author.

Reynolds, A. (1992). What is competent beginning teaching? A review of the literature. *Review of Educational Research, 62,* 1–35.

Reynolds, M. C., Wang, M. C., & Walberg, H. J. (1987). The necessary restructuring of special and regular education. *Exceptional Children, 53,* 391–398.

Rhodes, L. K., & Dudley-Marling, C. (1988). *Readers and writers make a difference: A holistic approach to teaching learning disabled and remedial students.* Portsmouth, NH: Heinemann Educational Books.

Rice, F. P. (1990). *The adolescent* (6th ed.). Boston: Allyn & Bacon.

Rich, D. (1987). *School and families: Issues and actions.* Washington, DC: National Education Association.

Riegel, R. H., Mayle, J. A., & McCarthy-Henkel, J. (1988). *Beyond maladies and remedies: Suggestions and guidelines for adapting materials for students with special needs in the regular class.* Novi, MI: RHR Consultation Services.

Rieth, H., Bahr, C., Polsgrove, L., Okolo, C., & Eckert, R. (1987). The effects of microcomputers on the secondary special education classroom ecology. *Journal of Special Education Technology, 8*(4), 36–43.

Rieth, H., Polsgrove, L., Okolo, C., Bahr, C., & Eckert, R. (1987). An analysis of the secondary special education classroom ecology with implications for teacher training. *TESE, 10*(3), 113–119.

Rieth, H., Polsgrove, L., & Semmel, M. I. (1981). Instructional variables that make a difference: Attention to task and beyond. *Exceptional Education Quarterly, 2,* 61–82.

Ritter, S., & Idol-Maestas, L. (1986). Teaching middle school students to use a test-taking strategy. *Journal of Educational Research, 79,* 357.

Roberts, G. H. (1968). The failure strategies of third grade arithmetic pupils. *The Arithmetic Teacher, 15,* 442–446.

Robinson, S. M., Braxdale, C. T., & Colson, S. E. (1985). Preparing dysfunctional learners to enter junior high school: A transitional curriculum. *Focus on Exceptional Children, 18*(4), 1–12.

Roblyer, M. D. (1989). *Making the most of computers in the classroom: Effective models for integrating computer courseware into school instructional programs.* Tallahassee: Florida Department of Education.

Roehler, L. R., & Duffy, G. G. (1984). Direct explanation of comprehension processes. In G. G. Duffy, L. R. Roehler, & J. Mason (Eds.), *Comprehension instruction: Perspectives and suggestions* (pp. 265–280). New York: Longman.

Roessler, R. T., & Brolin, D. E. (1992). *Life centered career education: A competency based approach.* Reston, VA: Council for Exceptional Children.

Roessler, R. T., Brolin, D. E., & Johnson, J. M. (1990). Factors affecting employment success and quality of life: A one year follow-up of students in special education. *Career Development for Exceptional Individuals, 13,* 95–107.

Roessler, R. T., & Johnson, V. A. (1987). Developing job maintenance skills in learning disabled youth. *Journal of Learning Disabilities, 20,* 428–432.

Rooney, K. J., & Hallahan, D. P. (1988). The effects of self-monitoring on adult behavior and student independence. *Learning Disabilities Research, 3*(2), 88–93.

Rosenberg, M. S. (1989). The effects of daily homework assignments on the acquisition of basic skills by students with learning disabilities. *Journal of Learning Disabilities, 22,* 314–323.

Rosenshine, B. (1990). *Scaffolds for teaching content-specific higher-level skills.* Unpublished manuscript, University of Illinois, Urbana.

Rosenshine, B., & Stevens, R. (1986). Teaching functions. In M. C. Wittrock (Ed.), *Handbook of research on teaching* (3rd ed.).New York: Macmillan.

Roth, L. (1991). Middle level transition. In J. Capelluti & D. Stokes (Eds.), *Middle level education: Programs, policies, and practices* (pp. 42–48). Reston, VA: National Association of Secondary School Principals.

Rotheram-Borus, M. J., & Koopman, C. (1991). AIDS and adolescents. In R. M. Lerner, A. C. Petersen, & J. Brooks-Gunn (Eds.), *Encyclopedia of adolescence* (Vol. 1, pp. 29–36). New York: Garland.

Rudolph, B. (1988, July 18). All hands on deck! *Time,* 42–44.

Ruiz, N. T. (1989). An optimal learning environment for Rosemary. *Exceptional Children, 56,* 130–144.

Rusch, F. R. (1990). *Supported employment: Models, methods, and issues.* Sycamore, IL: Sycamore.

Rusch, F. R., & Phelps, L. A. (1987). Secondary special education and transition from school to work: A national priority. *Exceptional Children, 53,* 487–492.

Rusch, F. R., Schutz, R. P., Mithaug, D. E., Stewart, J. E., & Mar, D. K. (1982). *Vocational assessment and curriculum guide.* Seattle: J. E. Stewart.

Ryan, E. B., Short, E. J., & Weed, K. A. (1986). The role of cognitive strategy training in improving the academic performance of learning disabled children. *Journal of Learning Disabilities, 19,* 521–529.

Rydell, L. (1990). *The least biased assessment: Implications for special education* (Crosscultural Special Education Series, Vol. 1). Sacramento, CA: Resources in Special Education. (ERIC Document Reproduction Service No. ED 337 945)

Sabornie, E. J. (1985). Social mainstreaming of handicapped students: Facing an unpleasant reality. *Remedial and Special Education, 6,* 12–16.

Sailor, W. (1991). Special education in the restructured school. *Remedial and Special Education, 12*(6), 8–22.

Salend, S. J. (1990). *Effective mainstreaming.* New York: Macmillan.

Salpeter, J. (1990). (Almost) 101 ways to access a videodisc. *Classroom Computer Learning, 10*(4), 6–8.

Salvia, J., & Hughes, C. (1990). *Curriculum-based assessment: Testing what is taught.* New York: Macmillan.

Salvia, J., & Ysseldyke, J. E. (1991). *Assessment* (5th ed.). Boston: Houghton Mifflin.

Salzberg, C. L., Lignugaris-Kraft, B., & McCuller, G. L. (1988). Reasons for job loss: A review of employment termination studies of mentally retarded workers. *Research in Developmental Disabilities, 9,* 153–170.

Sanders, D. (1987). Cultural conflicts: An important factor in the academic failures of American Indian students. *Journal of Multicultural Counseling and Development, 15,* 81–90.

Sands, D. J., Adams, L., & Stout, D. M. (1995). A statewide exploration of the nature and use of curriculum in special education. *Exceptional Children, 62,* 68–83.

Santrock, J. W. (1987). *Adolescence: An introduction* (3rd ed.). Dubuque, IA: Wm. C. Brown.

Sarkees, M. D., & Scott, J. L. (1985). *Vocational special needs* (2nd ed.). Chicago: American Technical Publishers.

Sarzynski, E. J. (1988). Disciplining a handicapped student. *West's Education Law Reporter, 46,* 17–26.

Saski, J., Swicegood, P., & Carter, J. (1983). Notetaking formats for learning disabled adolescents. *Learning Disabilities Quarterly, 6,* 265–272.

Scales, P. C. (1991). *A portrait of young adolescents in the 1990s: Implications for promoting healthy growth and development.* Carrboro, NC: Center for Early Adolescence. (ERIC Document Reproduction Service No. ED 346 990).

Scales, P. C. (1992). From risks to resources: Disadvantaged learners and middle grades teaching. *Middle School Journal, 23*(5), 3–9.

Scanlon, D. J., Duran, G. Z., Reyes, E. I., & Gallego, M. A. (1992). Interactive semantic mapping: An interactive approach to enhancing LD students' content area comprehension. *Learning Disabilities Research and Practice, 7,* 142–146.

Scardamalia, M., & Bereiter, C. (1985). Helping students become better writers. *School Administrator, 42*(4), 16–26.

Schaeffer A. L., Zigmond, N., Kerr, M. M., & Farra, H. E. (1990). Helping teenagers develop school survival skills. *Teaching Exceptional Children, 23*(1), 6–9.

Schalock, R. L. (1986). Employment outcomes from secondary school programs. *Remedial and Special Education, 7*(6), 37–39.

Schiff, A. R., & Knopf, I. J. (1985). The effects of task demands on attention allocation in children of different ages. *Child Development, 56,* 621–630.

Schiff-Myers, N. B., Djukic, J., McGovern-Lawler, J., & Perez, D. (1994). Assessment considerations in the evaluation of second-language learners: A case study. *Exceptional Children, 60,* 237–248.

Schloss, P. J. (1987). Self-management strategies for adolescents entering the work force. *Teaching Exceptional Children, 19*(4), 40–43.

Schloss, P. J., & Schloss, C. N. (1987). A critical review of social skills research in mental retardation. In R. P. Barrett & J. L. Matson (Eds.), *Advances in developmental disorders.* Greenwich, CT: JAI Press.

Schloss, P. J., Schloss, C. N., Wood, C. E., & Kiehl, W. S. (1986). A critical review of social skills research with behaviorally disordered students. *Behavioral Disorders, 12,* 1–14.

Schloss, P. J., & Smith, M. A. (1994). *Applied behavior analysis in the classroom.* Boston: Allyn & Bacon.

Schloss, P. J., Smith, M. A., & Schloss, C. N. (1995). *Instructional methods for adolescents with learning and behavior problems* (2nd ed.). Boston: Allyn & Bacon.

Schmidt, J. L. (1983). *The effects of four generalization conditions on learning disabled adolescents' written language performance in the regular classroom.* Unpublished doctoral dissertation, University of Kansas, Lawrence.

Schmidt, J. L., Deshler, D. D., Schumaker, J. B., & Alley, G. R. (1989). Effects of generalization instruction on the written language performance of adolescents with learning disabilities in the mainstream classroom. *Journal of Reading, Writing, and Learning Disabilities, 4,* 291–311.

Schniedewind, N., & Salend, S. J. (1987). Cooperative learning works. *Teaching Exceptional Children, 19*(2), 22–25.

*School violence alert: Practical strategies for maintaining safe schools.* (1995). *1*(3), 1–9.

Schulte, A., Osborne, S., & McKinney, J. (1990). Academic outcomes for students with learning disability in consultation and resource programs. *Exceptional Children, 57,* 162–171.

Schumaker, J. B., Denton, P. H., & Deshler, D. D. (1984). *Learning strategies curriculum: The paraphrasing strategy.* Lawrence: University of Kansas.

Schumaker, J. B., Deshler, D. D., Alley, G. R., & Warner, M. M. (1983). Toward the development of an intervention model for learning disabled adolescents. *Exceptional Education Quarterly, 4*(1), 45–74.

Schumaker, J. B., Deshler, D. D., Alley, G. R., Warner, M. M., & Denton, P. H. (1982). Multipass: A learning strategy for improving reading comprehension. *Learning Disabilities Quarterly, 5,* 295–304.

Schumaker, J. B., Deshler, D. D., Nolan, S., & Alley, G. R. (1994). *The self-questioning strategy.* Lawrence: University of Kansas.

Schumaker, J. B., Hazel, J. S., & Pederson, C. S. (1988). *Social skills for daily living.* Circle Pines, MN: American Guidance Service.

Schumaker, J. B., Nolan, S., & Deshler, D. (1985). *The error monitoring strategy.* Lawrence: University of Kansas.

Schumaker, J. B., & Sheldon, J. (1985). *Learning strategies curriculum: The sentence writing strategy.* Lawrence: University of Kansas.

Scott, C. M. (1991). Problem writers: Nature, assessment, and intervention. In A. G. Kamhi & H. W. Catts (Eds.), *Reading disabilities: A developmental language perspective* (pp. 303–344). Boston: Allyn & Bacon.

Scott, M. L., Ebbert, A., & Price, D. (1986). Assessing and teaching employability skills with prevocational work samples. *The Directive Teacher, 8*(1), 3–7.

Scott-Jones, D. (1991). Educational levels of adolescent childbearers at first and second births. *American Journal of Education, 99,* 461–480.

Scott-Jones, D. (1993, November). Adolescent childbearing: Whose problem? What can we do? *Kappan Special Report,* pp. 1–12.

Scott-Jones, D., Roland, E. J., & White, A. B. (1989). Antecedents and outcomes of pregnancy in Black adolescents. In R. J. Jones (Ed.), *Black adolescents* (pp. 341–372). Berkeley, CA: Cobb & Henry.

Scruggs, T. E., & Marsing, L. (1987). Teaching test-taking skills to behaviorally disordered students. *Behavioral Disorders, 13*(4), 240–244.

Scruggs, T. E., Mastropieri, M. A., & Richter, L. (1985). Peer tutoring with behaviorally disordered students: Social and academic benefits. *Behavioral Disorders, 10*(4), 283–294.

Seidenberg, P. L. (1988). Cognitive and academic instructional intervention for learning disabled adolescents. *Topics in Language Disorders, 8*(3), 56–71.

Seman, M. (1995). Homework. In T. P. Lombardi (Ed.), Teachers develop their own learning strategies. *Teaching Exceptional Children, 27*(3), 52–55.

Shafi, M. (1988). *Suicidal children. Medical aspects of human sexuality, 22,* 63–65.

Shan, S. J., & Bailey, P. (1991). Education for equality and justice: Part 2: Appropriate learning context for raising issues of culture equality and justice. *Mathematics Teaching, 133,* 58–59.

Shapiro, E. S. (1989a). *Academic skills problems: Direct assessment and intervention.* New York: Guilford Press.

Shapiro, E. S. (1989b). Teaching self-management skills to learning disabled adolescents. *Learning Disabilities Quarterly, 12,* 275–287.

Shimabukuro, K. W. (1993). Personal reflections. In J. M. Kauffman, *Characteristics of emotional and behavioral disorders of children and youth* (5th ed.) (pp. 278–280). New York: Macmillan.

Shinn, M. R., Rosenfield, S., & Knutson, N. (1989). Curriculum-based assessment: A comparison of models. *School Psychology Review, 18,* 297–370.

Shrieves, L. (1993, April 3). Romance regroups. *Orlando Sentinel,* p. E-1.

Siegel, S. (1988). The career leader program: Implementing RE-ED principles in vocational settings. *Behavior Disorders, 14,* 16–26.

Siegel, S., & Gaylord-Ross, R. (1991). Factors associated with employment success among youths with learning disabilities. *Journal of Learning Disabilities, 24,* 40–47.

Sigmon, S. B. (1987). *Radical analysis of special education: Focus on historical development and learning disabilities.* New York: Falmer Press.

Silbert, J., Carnine, D., & Stein, M. (1990). *Direct instruction mathematics* (2nd ed.). Columbus, OH: Merrill/Macmillan.

Sileo, T., Rude, H., & Luckner, J. (1988). Collaborative consultation: A model for transition planning for handicapped youth. *Education and Training in Mental Retardation, 23,* 333–339.

Silverman, R., Zigmond, N., & Sansone, J. (1981). Teaching coping skills to adolescents with learning problems. *Focus on Exceptional Children, 13*(6), 1–19.

Silverman, R., Zigmond, N., & Sansone, J. (1983). Teaching coping skills to adolescents with learning problems. In E. L. Meyen, G. A. Vergason, & R. J. Whelan (Eds.), *Promising practices for exceptional children: Curriculum implications* (pp. 167–198). Denver: Love.

Simmonds, E. P. M., Luchow, J. P., Kaminsky, S., & Cottone, V. (1989). Applying cognitive learning strategies in the classroom: A collaborative training institute. *Learning Disabilities Focus, 4,* 96–105.

Simmons, R. G., Black, A., & Zhou, Y. (1991). African-American versus White child and the transition into junior high school. *American Journal of Education, 99,* 481–520.

Simmons, R. G., & Blyth, D. A. (1987). *Moving into adolescence: The impact of pubertal change and school context.* New York: Aldine.

Siskin, L. S. (1991). Departments as different worlds: Subject subcultures in secondary schools. *Educational Administration Quarterly, 27,* 134–169.

Sitlington, P. L. (1979). Vocational assessment and training of the handicapped. *Focus on Exceptional Children, 12*(4), 1–11.

Sitlington, P. L., Frank, A. R., & Carson R. (1992). Adult adjustment among high school graduates with mild disabilities. *Exceptional Children, 59,* 221–233.

Sitlington, P. L., & Wimmer, D. (1978). Vocational assessment techniques for the handicapped adolescent. *Career Development for Exceptional Individuals, 1,* 74–87.

Slavin, R. E. (1988a). Cooperative learning and student achievement. *Educational Leadership, 46*(2), 31–33.

Slavin, R. E. (1988b). *Student team learning: An overview and practical guide* (2nd ed.). Washington, DC: National Education Association.

Sleeter, C. E., & Grant, C. A. (1988). *Making choices for multicultural education: Five approaches to race, class, and gender.* Columbus, OH: Merrill.

Smith, D. (1991). *Caught in the crossfire: A report on gun violence in our nation's schools, September, 1990.* Submitted to the Subcommittee on Crime of the House of Representatives. Sponsored by The Center to Prevent Handgun Violence. Appendix A, 1–8.

Smith, D. D., & Luckasson, R. (1992). *Introduction to special education.* Boston: Allyn & Bacon.

Smith, M. A., & Schloss, C. N. (1990). *Instructional methods for adolescents with learning and behavior problems.* Boston: Allyn & Bacon.

Smith, M. A., & Schloss, P. J. (1988). Teaching to transition. In P. J. Schloss, C. A. Hughes, & M. A. Smith (Eds.), *Community intergration for persons with mental retardation* (pp. 1–16). Austin, TX: PRO-ED.

Smith, P. L., & Tompkins, G. E. (1988). Structured notetaking: A new strategy for content area readers. *Journal of Reading, 32,* 46–53.

Smith, T. E. C., Finn, D., & Dowdy, C. A. (1993). *Teaching students with mild disabilities.* Ft. Worth, TX: Harcourt Brace Jovanovich.

Smith, T. E. C., Polloway, E. A., Patton, J. R., & Dowdy, C. A. (1995). *Teaching students with special needs in inclusive settings.* Boston: Allyn & Bacon.

Snider, V. E. (1992). Learning styles and learning to read: A critique. *Remedial and Special Education, 13*(1), 6–18.

Sparrow, S. S., Balla, D. A., & Cicchetti, D. V. (1985). *Vineland adaptive behavior scales.* Circle Pines, MN: American Guidance Service.

Spencer, M. B. (1991). Development of minority identity. In R. M. Lerner, A. C. Petersen, & J. Brooks-Gunn (Eds.), *Encyclopedia of adolescence* (Vol. 1, pp. 525–527). New York: Garland.

Spencer, M. B., & Dornbush, S. M. (1990). Challenges in studying minority youth. In S. Feldman &

G. Elliott (Eds.), *At the threshold: The developing adolescent* (pp. 123–146). Cambridge, MA: Harvard University Press.

Speziale, M. J., & LaFrance, L. M. (1992, November). Multimedia and students with learning disabilities: The road to success. *The Computing Teacher,* pp. 31–34.

Spires, H. A., & Stone, P. D. (1989). The directed notetaking activity: A self-questioning approach. *Journal of Reading, 33,* 36–39.

Sprick, R. S. (1985). *Discipline in the secondary classroom: A problem-by-problem survival guide.* East Nyack, NY: Center for Applied Research in Education.

Spruill, J. A. (1993). Secondary assessment: Structuring the assessment process. *Learning Disabilities Research and Practice, 18,* 127–132.

Stainback, W., & Stainback, S. (1984). A rationale for the merger of special and regular education. *Exceptional Children, 51,* 102–111.

Stallin, H., & Magnusson, D. (1990). *Paths through life: Pubertal maturation in female development* (Vol. 2). Hillsdale, NJ: Erlbaum.

Stallings, J., Needels, M., & Staybrook, N. (1979). *The teaching of basic reading skills in secondary schools: Phase II & Phase III.* Menlo Park, CA: SRI International.

Stefanko, M. (1988, August). *Trends and comparisons in secondary schools vandalism and assault.* Paper presented at the annual meeting of the American Psychological Association, Atlanta. (ERIC Document Reproduction Service No. ED 303 709)

Stein, R. C. (1983). Hispanic parents' perspectives and participation in their children's special education program: Comparisons by program and race. *Learning Disabilities Quarterly, 6,* 432–439.

Steinberg, L. (1989). *Adolescence* (2nd ed.). New York: Knopf.

Stevens, R., & Rosenshine, B. (1981). Advances in research on teaching. *Exceptional Education Quarterly, 2*(1), 1–9.

Stevens, R. J., & Slavin, R. E. (1991). When cooperative learning improves the achievement of students with mild disabilities: A response to Tateyama-Sniezek. *Exceptional Children, 57,* 276–280.

Stewart, D. B. (1990). *A curriculum framework for secondary-aged handicapped students.* Washington, DC: Special Education Programs (ED/OSERS). (ERIC Document Reproduction Service No. ED 328 039)

Stocking, C. (1986). *High school and beyond, a national longitudinal study for the 1980's: Characteristics of high school students who identify themselves as handicapped.* Washington, DC: National Center for Education Statistics.

Stodden, R. A., & Browder, P. M. (1986). Community based competitive employment preparation of developmentally disabled persons: A program description and evaluation. *Education and Training of the Mentally Retarded, 21,* 43–53.

Stodden, R. A., Ianacone, R. N., Boone, R. M., & Bisconer, S. W. (1987). *Curriculum-based vocational assessment: A guide for addressing youth with special needs.* Honolulu: TRI.

Stowitschek, J. J., Gable, R. A., & Hendrickson, J. M. (1980). *Instructional materials for exceptional children.* Rockville, MD: Aspen.

Strober, M., & Humphrey, L. L. (1987). Familial contributions to the etiology and course of anorexia nervosa and bulimia. *Journal of Consulting and Clinical Psychology, 55,* 654–659.

Sue, S., & Padilla, A. (1986). Ethnic minority issues in the United States: Challenges for the educational system. In Bilingual Education Office Staff, *Beyond language: Social and cultural factors in schooling language minority students* (pp. 35–72). Los Angeles: California State University, Evaluation, Dissemination, and Assessment Center.

Sugai, G. M., & Tindal, G. A. (1993). *Effective school consultation: An interactive approach.* Pacific Grove, CA: Brooks/Cole.

Suritsky, S. K., & Hughes, C. A. (1991). Benefits of notetaking: Implications for secondary and postsecondary students with learning disabilities. *Learning Disabilities Quarterly, 14,* 7–18.

Swicegood, P. R., & Parsons, J. L. (1991). The thematic unit approach: Content and process instruction for secondary learning disabled students. *Learning Disabilities Research and Practice, 6,* 117–128.

Swisher, J., & Clark, G. M. (1991). *Practical arts evaluation system (PAES).* Jacksonville, FL: Talent Assessment.

Szulanczyk, J. (1992, January). *Practical applications for the multimedia classroom.* Paper presented at the meeting of the Florida Educational Technology Conference, Tampa.

Takayama, C. (1992). Chemical dependency. In L. M. Bullock (Ed.), *Exceptionalities in children and youth* (pp. 455–459). Boston: Allyn & Bacon.

Tateyama-Sniezek, K. M. (1990). Cooperative learning: Does it improve the academic achievement of students with handicaps? *Exceptional Children, 56,* 426–437.

Taylor, A., & Valentine, B. (1985). *Effective schools: What research says about Series No. 1, data-search reports.* Washington, DC: National Education Association. (ERIC Document Reproduction Service No. ED 274 073)

Taylor, R. L., Sternberg, L., & Richards, S. B. (1995). *Exceptional children: Integrating research and teaching* (2nd ed.). San Diego: Singular Publishing Group.

Taylor, S. E. (1964). *Listening.* Washington, DC: National Education Association.

Telepak, T. A. (1995). The local business community: A natural resource for transition from school to work. *Teaching Exceptional Children, 27*(3), 60–64.

Test, D. W., Farebrother, C., & Spooner, F. (1988). A comparison of the social interactions of workers with and without disabilities. *Journal of Employment Counseling, 25,* 123–131.

Thomas, D. W., Williams, P., & Zonana, V. (1994). *Federal agencies focus on youth violence: Convene national conference* (Press Release). Washington, DC: U.S. Government.

Thousand, J., & Villa, R. (1990). Sharing expertise and responsibilities through teaching teams. In W. Stainback & S. Stainback (Eds.), *Support networks for inclusive schooling: Interdependent integrated education* (pp. 151–166). Baltimore: Brookes.

Thurston, L. P. (1987). *Survival skills for women: Facilitator manual.* Manhattan, KS: Survival Skills and Development.

Tiedt, P. L., & Tiedt, I. M. (1986). *Multicultural teaching.* Boston: Allyn & Bacon.

Tindal, G. A., & Marston, D. B. (1990). *Classroom-based assessment: Evaluating instructional outcomes.* Columbus, OH: Merrill/Macmillan.

Tindal, G., Shinn, M., Walz, L., & Germann, G. (1987). Mainstream consultation in secondary settings. *Journal of Special Education, 21,* 94–106.

Tindal, G. A., & Taylor-Pendergast, S. J. (1989). A taxonomy for objectively analyzing the consultation process. *Remedial and Special Education, 10*(2), 6–16.

Tindall, L. (1985). *Utilizing job training partnership act programs for handicapped individuals.* Paper presented at the School to Work Transition for Handicapped Youth Forum, University of Illinois, Urbana.

Tobias, R. (1992). *Nurturing at-risk youth in math and science: Curriculum and teaching considerations.* Bloomington, IA: National Educational Service.

Tobin, K. (1987). The role of wait time in higher cognitive level learning. *Review of Educational Research, 57,* 69–95.

Toch, T., with Gest, T., & Guttman, M. (1993, November 8). When killers come to class: Violence in schools. *U.S. News & World Report,* pp. 30–36.

Tonjes, M. J., & Zintz, M. V. (1981). *Teaching reading/thinking/study skills in content classrooms.* Dubuque, IA: Wm. C. Brown.

Torgesen, J. K., (1982). The learning disabled child as an inactive learner: Educational implications. *Topics in Learning and Learning Disabilities, 2,* 45–52.

Trower, P. (1984). A radical critique and reformulation: From organism to agent. In P. Trower (Ed.), *Radical approaches to social skills training* (pp. 47–88). New York: Croom Helm.

Tuchscherer, P. (1988). *TV interactive toys: The new high tech threat to children.* Bend, OR: Pinnaroo Publishing.

Tucker, M. B. (1985). U.S. ethnic minorities and drug abuse: An assessment of the science and practice. *International Journal of the Addictions, 20,* 1021–1047.

Turnbull, A. P., Strickland, B. B., & Brantley J. C. (1982). *Developing and implementing individualized education programs.* Columbus, OH: Merrill/Macmillan.

Turnbull, A. P., & Turnbull, H. R. (1986). *Families, professionals, and exceptionality: A special partnership.* Columbus, OH: Merrill.

Upchurch, D., & McCarthy, J. (1990). The timing of a first birth and high school completion. *American Sociological Review, 55,* 224–234.

U.S. Bureau of the Census. (1991). *Resident population distribution for the U.S. by race and Hispanic origin.* Washington, DC: Cendata Data Base.

U.S. Bureau of the Census. (1992). *Current population survey.* Washington, DC: U.S. Department of Commerce.

U.S. Commission on Civil Rights. (1983). *Teachers and students: Differences in teacher interaction with Mexican American and Anglo students.* Washington, DC: U.S. Government Printing Office.

U.S. Department of Education. (1986). *Report to the U.S. Senate: President's Committee on Employment of the Handicapped.* Washington, DC: Author.

U.S. Department of Education. (1991). *To insure the free appropriate public education of all handicapped children: Thirteenth annual report to Congress.* Washington, DC: Division of Innovation and Development. (U.S. Documents, ED 1. 32. 991)

U.S. Department of Education. (1993). *To assure the free appropriate education of children with disabilities: Fifteenth annual report to Congress on the implementation of the Education of Individuals with Disabilities Act.* Washington, DC: Author. (U.S. Documents, ED 1. 32. 993)

U.S. Department of Education, Office of Civil Rights. (1994). *The 1992 elementary and secondary school civil rights compliance report.* Washington, DC: Author.

U.S. Department of Justice, Office of Justice Programs, Bureau of Justice Statistics. (1989). *National Crime Survey.* Washington, DC: U.S. Government Printing Office.

U.S. Department of Labor. (1977). *Dictionary of occupational titles.* Washington, DC: U.S. Government Printing Office.

U.S. Department of Labor. Secretary's Commission on Achieving Necessary Skills (SCANS). (1993). *What work requires of schools: A SCANS report for American 2000.* Washington, DC: Author.

Valentine, J., Clark, D. C., Irvin, J. L., Keefe, J. W., & Melton, G. (1993). *Leadership in middle level education: A national survey of middle level leaders and schools* (Vol. 1). Reston, VA: National Association of Secondary School Principals.

Valpar International. (1982). *Prevocational readiness battery—Valpar 17.* Tucson, AZ: Author.

VanNooten, N. (1991). *A social skills curriculum.* (ERIC Document Reproduction Service No. 349 719)

Van Reusen, A. K., & Bos, C. S. (1994). Facilitating student participation in individualized education programs through motivation strategy instruction. *Exceptional Children, 60,* 466–475.

Van Reusen, A. K., Bos, C. S., Schumaker, J. B., & Deshler, D. D. (1994). *The self-advocacy strategy for education and transition planning.* Lawrence: Edge Enterprises.

Van Reusen, A. K., Deshler, D. D., & Schumaker, J. B. (1989). Effects of a student participation strategy in facilitating the involvement of adolescents with learning disabilities in the individualized educational program planning process. *Learning Disabilities, 1*(2), 23–34.

Van Til, W. (1978). *Secondary education: School and community.* Boston: Houghton Mifflin.

Veir, C. A. (1987). Vocational assessment: The evolving role. In G. D. Meers (Ed.), *Handbook of vocational special needs education* (pp. 213–255). Rockville, MD: Aspen.

Ventura, S. J., Taffel, S. M., Mosher, W. D., Wilson, B., & Henshaw, S. (1995). *Trends in pregnancies and pregnancy rates: Estimates for the United States, 1980–1993.* Hyattsville, MD: National Center for Health Statistics.

Villegas, A. M. (1991). *Culturally responsive pedagogy for the 1990s and beyond.* Washington, DC: ERIC Clearinghouse on Teacher Education.

Virginia Department of Education. (1991). *Family life education: Effective instruction for students in special education.* Richmond: Virginia Department of Education, Division of Special Education Programs.

Vitello, S. J. (1988). Handicapped students and competency testing. *Remedial and Special Education, 9*(5), 22–27.

Vocational Research Institute. (1989). *Apticom.* Philadelphia: Jewish Employment and Vocational Service.

Vockell, E. L., & Mihail, T. (1993). Behind computerized instruction for students with exceptionalities. *Teaching Exceptional Children, 25*(3), 39–43.

*Voices from the inside: A report on schooling from inside the classroom.* (1992). Claremont, CA: Clarement Graduate School, Institute for Education in Transformation.

Wagner, M. (1991a). *The benefits of secondary vocational education for young people with disabilities: Findings from the national longitudinal transition study of special education students.* Paper presented at the meeting of the American Educational Research Association, Chicago.

Wagner, M. (1991b). Secondary school programs. In M. Wagner, L. Newman, R. D'Amico, E. D. Jay, P. Butler, C. Marcher, & R. Cox, *Youth with disabilities: How are they doing? The first comprehensive report from the national longitudinal transition study of special education students.* Menlo Park, CA: SRI International. (ERIC Document Reproduction Service No. ED 341 228)

Wagner, M. (1992). "A little help from my friends": The social involvement of young people with disabilities. In M. Wagner, R. D'Amico, C. Marder, L. Newman, & J. Blackorby, *What happens next? Trends in postschool outcomes of youth with disabilities: The second comprehensive report from the national longitudinal transition study of special education students, postschool outcomes.* Menlo Park, CA: SRI International.

Wagner, M. (1993). What have we learned about the secondary school programs of students with disabilities? In M. Wagner (Ed.), *The secondary school programs of students with disabilities: A report from the national longitudinal transition study of special education students* (pp. 212–224). Menlo Park, CA: SRI International. (ERIC Document Reproduction Service No. ED 365 084)

Wagner, M., Blackorby, J., Cameto, R., Hebbeler, K., & Newman, L. (1993). *The transition experience of young people with disabilities: A summary of findings from the national longitudinal transition study of special education students, postschool outcomes.* Menlo Park, CA: SRI International. (ERIC Document Reproduction Service No. ED 365 086)

Wagner, M., Blackorby, J., & Hebbeler, K. (1993). *Beyond the report card: The multiple dimensions of secondary school performance of students with disabilities. A special topic report from the national longitudinal transition study of special education students.* Menlo Park, CA: SRI International. (ERIC Document Reproduction Service No. ED 365 088)

Wagner, M., & Shaver, D. M. (1989). *Educational programs and achievements of secondary special education students: Findings from the national longitudinal transition study.* Menlo Park, CA: SRI International. (ERIC Document Reproduction Service No. ED 306 292)

Walker, D. M., Colvin, G., & Ramsey, E. (1995). *Antisocial behavior in school: Strategies and best practices.* Pacific Grove, CA: Brooks/Cole.

Walker, D. M., & Lirgg, C. D. (1995). Early adolescent social and emotional development: A constructivist perspective. In M. J. Wavering (Ed.), *Educating young adolescents: Life in the middle* (pp. 53–83). New York: Garland.

Walker, D. M., Schwarz, I. E., Nippold, M. S., Irvin, L. K., & Noell, J. W. (1994). Social skills in school-age children and youth: Issues and best practices in assessment and intervention. *Topics in Language Disorders, 14*(3), 70–82.

Wallace, G., Cohen, S. B., & Polloway, E. A. (1987). *Language arts: Teaching exceptional students.* Austin, TX: PRO-ED.

Walsh, J. M. (1991). *Student, teacher, and parent preference for less restrictive special education models—cooperative teaching.* (ERIC Document Reproduction Service No. ED 333 664)

Wang, M. C., Reynolds, M. C., & Walberg, H. J. (1986). Rethinking special education. *Educational Leadership, 44*(1), 26–31.

Ward, T. (1995). Personal communication (Director, Florida Inclusion Network)

Warner, M. M., Schumaker, J. B., Alley, G. R., & Deshler, D. D. (1980). Learning disabled adolescents in public schools: Are they different from low achievers? *Exceptional Education Quarterly, 1*(2), 27–36.

Warrenfeltz, R. B., Kelly W. J., Salzberg, C. L., Beegle, C. P., Levy S. M., Adams, T. A., & Crouse, T. R. (1983). Social skills training of behaviorally disordered adolescents with self-monitoring to promote generalization to a vocational setting. *Behavioral Disorders, 7*, 18–27.

Wehman, P. (1993). *Life beyond the classroom: Transition services for youth with disabilities.* Boston: Paul H. Brookes.

Weinstein, E., & Rosen, E. (1991). The development of adolescent sexual intimacy: Implications for counseling. *Adolescence, 102*, 331–339.

West, J. F., & Cannon, G. S. (1988). Essential collaborative consultation competencies for regular and special educators. *Journal of Learning Disabilities, 21*, 56–63.

West, J. F., & Idol, L. (1990). Collaborative consultation in the education of mildly handicapped and at-risk students. *Remedial and Special Education, 11*(1), 22–31.

West, J. F., Idol, L., & Cannon, G. (1989). *Collaboration in the schools: An inservice and preservice curriculum for teachers, support staff, and administrators.* Austin, TX: PRO-ED.

West, L., Corbey, S., Boyer-Stephens, A., Jones, B., Miller, R. J., Sarkees-Wircenski, M. (1992). *Integrating transition planning into the IEP process.* Reston, VA: Council for Exceptional Children.

Whang, P. L., Fawcett, S. B., & Mathews, R. M. (1984). Teaching job-related social skills to learning disabled adolescents. *Analysis and Intervention in Developmental Disabilities, 4*, 29–38.

Wheeler, R. (1988). Attribution processing: The way in which students react to success and failure has a substantial effect on subsequent efforts to learn. *Middle School Journal, 19*(4), 26–27.

Whisler, J. S. (1990). *Young adolescents and middle level education: A review of current issues, concerns, and recommendations.* Washington, DC: Office of Educational Research and Improvement. (ERIC Document Reproduction Service No. ED 346 960)

White, O. R., & Haring, N. G. (1976). *Exceptional teaching.* Columbus, OH: Merrill/Macmillan.

White, W. J. (1992). The postschool adjustment of persons with learning disabilities: Current status and future projections. *Journal of Learning Disabilities, 25*, 448–456.

White, W. J., & Thurston, L. P. (1992). Transition skills: Career education and related social skills. In J. Olson & J. Platt (Eds.), *Teaching children and adolescents with special needs* (pp. 355–374). New York: Merrill/Macmillan.

White House. (1990). *National goals for education* (Press Release). Washington, DC: Author.

White House. (1991, February 4). *The national education goals: A second report to the nation's governors.* Washington, DC: Author.

Whiting, B. B. (1950). *Paiute sorcery.* New York: Viking Fund.

Whiting, B. B., & Whiting, J. W. (1991). Adolescence in the preindustrial world. In R. M. Lerner, A. C. Petersen, & J. Brooks-Gunn (Eds.), *Encyclopedia of adolescence* (Vol. 11, pp. 814–829). New York: Garland.

Wiederholt, J. L., & Chamberlain, S. P. (1989). A critical analysis of resource programs. *Remedial and Special Education, 10*(6), 15–27.

Wiig, E., & Semel, E. (1984). *Language assessment and intervention for the learning disabled* (2nd ed.). Columbus, OH: Merrill/Macmillan.

Wilber, M. M. (1992). *Three is a crowd? No way—three is a team! Collaborative consultation techniques for educators.* Paper presented at the Midwest Symposium for Leadership in Behavior Disorders, Kansas City, MO.

Wiles, J., & Bondi, J. (1986). *Making middle schools work.* Alexandria, VA: ASCD.

Wilgosh, L., & Mueller, H. H. (1993). Work skills for disadvantaged and unprepared youth and adults. *International Journal for the Advancement of Counseling, 16*(2), 99–105.

Will, M. (1984). *OSERS program for the transition of youth with disabilities: Bridges from school to working life.* Washington, DC: U.S. Department of Education, Office of Special Education and Rehabilitative Services.

Will, M. (1986). Educating children with learning problems: A shared responsibility. *Exceptional Children, 52,* 411–415.

William T. Grant Foundation Commission on Work, Family, and Citizenship. (1988, February). The forgotten half: Non-college bound youth in America. *Phi Delta Kappan,* pp. 409–414.

Williams, R. M., & Rooney, K. J. (1986). *A handbook of cognitive behavior modification procedures for teachers.* Charlottesville: University of Virginia Learning Disabilities Research Institute.

Williamson, P. (1994). Tech prep . . . the win/win program. *Missouri Schools, 60*(2), 11–14.

Wilson, A. B. (1989). Theory into practice: An effective program for urban youth. *Educational Horizons, l67,* 136–144.

Winograd, P., & Hare, V. C. (1988). Direct instruction of reading comprehension strategies: The nature of teacher explanation. In E. T. Goetz, P. Alexander, & C. Weinstein (Eds.), *Learning and study strategies: Assessment, instruction, and evaluation* (pp. 25–56). New York: Academic Press.

Winzer, M. A. (1993). *The history of special education from isolation to integration.* Washington, DC: Gallaudet University Press.

Wiseman, D. E., & Hartwell, L. K. (1979). *Parallel alternate curriculum: A planning model for secondary level instructors.* Tempe: Arizona State University.

Witt, J. C., Elliott, S. N., Gresham, F. M., & Kramer, J. J. (1988). *Assessment of special children: Tests and the problem-solving process.* Glenview, IL: Scott, Foresman.

Wolvin, A. D., & Coakley, C. G. (1985). *Listening instruction.* Falls Church, VA: Speech Communications Association.

Wong, B. Y. L. (1986). Metacognition and special education: A review of a view. *Journal of Special Education, 20,* 9–29.

Woodward, J., & Gersten, R. (1993). Innovative technology for secondary students with learning disabilities. In E. L. Meyen, G. A. Vergason, & R. J. Whelan (Eds.), *Challenges facing special education* (pp. 141–161). Denver: Love.

Wyche, K. F., & Rotheram-Borus, M. J. (1990). Suicidal behavior among minority youth in the United States. In A. R. Stiffman & L. E. Davis (Eds.), *Ethnic issues in adolescent mental health* (pp. 323–338). Newbury Park, CA: Sage.

Yee, L. Y. (1988). Asian children. *Teaching Exceptional Children, 20*(4), 49–50.

Yee, M. L. (1989). *Honig v. Doe:* The suspension and expulsion of handicapped students. *Exceptional Children, 56,* 60–69.

Young, T. J. (1987). Inhalant use among American Indian youth. *Child Psychiatry and Human Development, 18*(10), 36–46.

Youniss, J., & Smollar, J. (1985). *Adolescent relations with mothers, fathers, and friends.* Chicago: University of Chicago Press.

Ysseldyke, J E., & Algozzine, B. (1984). *Introduction to special education.* Boston: Houghton-Mifflin.

Ysseldyke, J. E., & Algozzine, B. (1990). *Introduction to special education* (2nd ed.). Boston: Houghton Mifflin.

Ysseldyke, J. E., & Algozzine, B. (1992). *Critical issues* (2nd ed.). Boston: Houghton Mifflin.

Ysseldyke, J. E., Thurlow, M. L., & Christenson, S. L. (1987). *Teacher effectiveness and teacher decision making: Implications for effective instruction of handicapped students* (Monograph No. 5). Minneapolis: University of Minnesota, Instructional Alternatives Project.

Zanger, V. V. (1990). Monolingual teachers of bilingual students: Strategies for success. In V. V. Zanger (Ed.), *Drawing on diversity: A handbook of effective teaching techniques for the multicultural classroom* (pp. 32–34). Boston: Boston University/Boston Public Schools Collaborative.

Zetlin, A. G., & Hossenini, A. (1989). Six postschool case studies of mildly learning handicapped young adults. *Exceptional Children, 55,* 405–411.

Zigmond, N. (1990). Rethinking secondary school programs for students with learning disabilities. *Focus on Exceptional Children, 23*(1), 1–21.

Zigmond, N. (1993). Rethinking secondary school programs for students with learning disabilities.

In E. L. Meyen, G. A. Vergason, & R. J. Whelan (Eds.), *Challenges facing special education* (pp. 105–140). Denver: Love.

Zigmond N., Kerr, M. M., Schaeffer, A., Brown, G. M., & Farra, H. E. (1986). *School survival skills curriculum*. Pittsburgh, PA: University of Pittsburgh.

Zigmond, N., & Sansone, J. (1986). Designing a program for the learning disabled adolescent. *Remedial and Special Education, 7*(5), 13–17.

Zigmond, N., Sansone, J., Miller, S. E., Donahue, K. R., & Kohnke, R. (1986). *Teaching learning disabled students at the secondary school level*. Reston, VA: Council for Exceptional Children.

Zigmond, N., & Thornton, H. S. (1989). Learning disabilities in adolescents and adults. In S. Vaughn & C. S. Bos (Eds.), *Research in learning disabilities: Issues and future directions* (pp. 180–205). Boston: Little Brown/College Hill.

Zins, J. E., Curtis, M. J., Graden, J. L., & Ponti, C. R. (1988). *Helping students succeed in the regular classroom*. San Francisco: Jossey-Bass.

Zirpoli, T. J., & Melloy, K. J. (1993). *Behavior management: Applications for teachers and parents*. New York: Macmillan.